OpenGL Insights

OpenGL Insights

Edited by
Patrick Cozzi and Christophe Riccio

CRC Press
Taylor & Francis Group
Boca Raton London New York

CRC Press is an imprint of the
Taylor & Francis Group, an **informa** business

AN A K PETERS BOOK

CRC Press
Taylor & Francis Group
6000 Broken Sound Parkway NW, Suite 300
Boca Raton, FL 33487-2742

First issued in paperback 2020

© 2012 by Taylor & Francis Group, LLC
CRC Press is an imprint of Taylor & Francis Group, an Informa business

No claim to original U.S. Government works

ISBN-13: 978-1-4398-9376-0 (hbk)
ISBN-13: 978-0-367-65921-9 (pbk)

Contents

30 WebGL Models: End-to-End   431   WebGL
Won Chun

31 In-Game Video Capture with Real-Time Texture Compression   455   OpenGL
Brano Kemen

32 An OpenGL-Friendly Geometry File Format and Its Maya
    Exporter   467   OpenGL
Adrien Herubel and Venceslas Biri   OpenGL ES

VI   Debugging and Profiling   481

VII   Software Design   541

Foreword

Barthold Lichtenbelt

OpenGL is not a single API anymore. OpenGL has involved into a family of APIs, with OpenGL, OpenGL ES, and WebGL being closely related siblings that enable application developers to write and deploy graphics applications on a wide variety of platforms and operating systems. OpenGL has become an ecosystem; 3D graphics is truly everywhere now. OpenGL is the cross platform 3D API for desktop machines and work stations. OpenGL ES is the 3D API for mobile devices, like tablets and cell phones, and embedded platforms from settop boxes to cars. WebGL ties this all together by providing a pervasive 3D API in browsers, based on OpenGL ES, that run on any platform. It doesn't stop with graphics. Combining the use of OpenGL with a compute API like OpenCL or CUDA enables the creation of amazing visual computing applications on the desktop.

It is Khronos' job to provide APIs that serve their targeted developers, their markets, and their platforms, while encouraging silicon vendors to innovate underneath the API. Because the power consumption budget, hardware gate budget, and cost budget is larger for desktop GPUs than it is for mobile GPUs, the 3D API reflects this. Hence, OpenGL will generally be the first to expose leading edge functionality, on desktop platforms. The focus for OpenGL ES is to provide maximum functionality with the most optimal hardware and power budget for mobile and embedded devices. WebGL has a unifying focus; the goal for WebGL is to provide the same functionality everywhere, regardless of whether the underlying platform is capable of OpenGL 4.2 or OpenGL ES 2.0. This is fundamental to achieving the browser vision of "write once, deploy everywhere." It is exciting to see WebGL provide access to the GPU, and therefore hardware accelerated 3D rendering, everywhere. The HTML5 standard provides a rich set of APIs to develop web applications. WebGL is leading the way to do so in a hardware accelerated way within HTML5. This will truly transform the type of web applications that will be available to us to enjoy, precisely because WebGL integrates into the HTML5 standard.

Given the widespread adoption of OpenGL and OpenGL ES across all flavors of Linux and Windows, as well as iOS and Android, these APIs are serving a real need. The adoption of WebGL by almost all browser vendors underscores its importance as a web API for 3D graphics. Exquisite graphics applications have been developed using the OpenGL family of APIs. Of course there is much more to developing a great graphics application than the API. The ability to debug GPU code, to measure and optimize performance of graphics code to push the GPU to its limits, to use the right rendering technique given the underlying GPU, and to deploy that code to a wide variety of devices, are all critical factors to success.

This book explores the OpenGL ecosystem in depth. It provides debugging and performance tips, rendering techniques, clever tricks, software development, and porting advice, as well as best practices written by experts in various areas of the OpenGL ecosystem, to help you build the perfect graphics application. These experts have put in effort and time to share their OpenGL insights with us because they passionately believe in the OpenGL ecosystem and want to share that passion with us. This includes Patrick Cozzi and Christophe Riccio, who have done an amazing job editing and putting *OpenGL Insights* together. Thank you for sharing!

—Barthold Lichtenbelt
Khronos OpenGL ARB working group chair
Director of Tegra graphics software for NVIDIA

Preface

Sometimes I wish I had been involved in computer graphics 40 years ago when the field was unfolding with early research in visible surfaces and shading. There were many fundamental problems to solve, and the forthcoming solutions would have a great impact.

However, I'm grateful for the time we live in; the foundations of modeling, rendering, and animation are well established. Hardware-accelerated rendering is available on practically all devices. As developers, we are now capable of reaching an immense number of users with captivating, real-time graphics.

In part, we have the swiftness and availability of rendering APIs, including OpenGL, OpenGL ES, and WebGL, to thank. Frequent OpenGL specification updates coupled with drivers exposing these new features make OpenGL the API of choice for cross-platform desktop developers seeking access to recent GPU capabilities. With the explosion of smartphones and tablets, OpenGL ES is *the* API for hardware-accelerated rendering on iOS and Android. Even more recently, WebGL has rapidly emerged to provide truly zero-footprint hardware-accelerated 3D graphics on web pages.

With the widespread use of OpenGL, OpenGL ES, and WebGL, we recognize the need for developers using these APIs to learn from each other and go well beyond the basics. To this end, we have created the *OpenGL Insights* series, with this first volume containing contributions from developers, vendors, researchers, and educators. It is both a celebration of the breadth of the OpenGL family of APIs and a collection of deep, experienced-backed articles on practical and future-looking techniques.

Breadth is demonstrated through the diversity of topics—from using OpenGL in the classroom to recent extensions, optimizing for mobile devices, and designing WebGL libraries. Depth is realized by the deep corners into which many chapters take us, for example, asynchronous buffer and texture transfers, performance state tracking, and programmable vertex pulling.

It is our passion for these APIs and the passionate surrounding developer community that motivated us to start this series. In our day, there may be fewer fundamental problems to solve, but the breadth and complexity of the problems we solve is astonishing. It is an outstanding time to be an OpenGL developer.

—Patrick Cozzi
February 2012

First of all, I would like to thank Patrick, who asked me to join him on this project. I still remember that night when, after seeing a great movie at the cinema, *Somewhere*, I received his email. There was really only one answer I could possibly give, but I certainly tried to fool myself that it could be otherwise: "Oh, let's think this through." That hesitation lasted no longer than five seconds. The rest was just a lot of work and a lot of learning in the process.

Despite our differences in culture and background, Patrick and I were connected by a shared vision: we wanted to make a good book revealing, without preconception, the views of the entire OpenGL community, embracing everyone who shares our passion for the graphics variety that the OpenGL ecosystem can provide.

The OpenGL specifications are the foundation of OpenGL, but they are far from enough to understand its potential and limitations. With a dictionary and a grammar manual we can know a lot about a language, but it is still not enough for us to write poetry. I hope *OpenGL Insights* will bring a little bit of the secret ingredient—experience—so that we can improve the everyday life of the OpenGL programmer and lead to the creation of more efficient development and graphics software.

If you enjoy this book and share the belief that it takes the contribution of everyone to build real-time graphics, don't hesitate to contact us. We look forward to hearing from you and learning from your experiences in a future volume.

—Christophe Riccio
February 2012

Acknowledgments. Significant effort is required to get a community-based book like this off the ground. We are grateful to have had a lot of help on everything from our book proposal to getting the word out to authors. For these tasks, we thank Quarup Barreirinhas (Google), Henrik Bennetsen (Katalabs), Eric Haines (Autodesk), Jon Leech (Khronos Group), Barthold Lichtenbelt (NVIDIA), Jon McCaffrey (NVIDIA), Tom Olson (ARM), Kevin Ring (AGI), Ken Russell (Google), and Giles Thomas (Resolver Systems).

This book benefited from an open culture of reviews. As editors, we reviewed chapters, but this was only the beginning. Fellow contributors took initiative to do peer reviews, and many external reviewers volunteered their time. For this, we thank Guillaume Chevelereau (Intersec), Mikkel Gjoel (Splash Damage), Dimitri Kudelski (Aix-Marseille University), Eric Haines (Autodesk), Andreas Heumann (NVIDIA), Randall Hopper (L-3 Communications), Steve Nash (NVIDIA), Deron Ohlarik (AGI), Emil Persson (Avalanche Studios), Aras Pranckevičius (Unity Technologies), Swaroop Rayudu (Autodesk), Kevin Ring (AGI), Mathieu Roumillac (e-on software), Kenneth Russell (Google), Graham Sellers (AMD), Giles Thomas (Resolver Systems), and Marco Weber (Imagination Technologies).

The value of this book is made possible by the many authors that contributed to it. We thank every author for their contribution, peer reviews, and enthusiasm. We also thank Alice Peters, Sarah Chow, and Kara Ebrahim for their hard work in publishing this book.

The time requirements for preparing this book were often intense. We owe a great deal of our success to the flexibility provided by our employers. At Analytical Graphics, Inc., we thank Paul Graziani, Frank Linsalata, Jimmy Tucholski, and Shashank Narayan. At the University of Pennsylvania, we thank Norm Badler, Steve Lane, and Joe Kider.

Creating a book on top of our full-time jobs was not just hard on us, it was hard on our friends and families who saw less of us during nights, weekends, and even holidays. For their understanding and support, we thank Anthony Cozzi, Margie Cozzi, Peg Cozzi, and Jilda Stowe.

Website

The companion *OpenGL Insights* website contains source code and other supplements:

www.openglinsights.com

Please email us with your comments or corrections:

editors@openglinsights.com

Tips

OpenGL `glCreateShaderProgram` may provide faster build performance than a sequence of `glCompilerShader` and `glLinkProgram`. However, it only creates a single shader stage program.

OpenGL
WebGL
OpenGL ES Not all shader objects need a `main()` function. Multiple shader objects can be linked together in the same program to allow sharing the same code between different programs.

OpenGL
WebGL
OpenGL ES Build all GLSL shaders and programs first, and then query the results to hide build and query latency.

OpenGL
WebGL
OpenGL ES Call `glDeleteShader` after attaching a shader to a program to simplify cleanup later.

OpenGL Five OpenGL 4.2 functions generate info logs:

- `glCompileShader`
- `glCreateShaderProgram`
- `glLinkProgram`
- `glValidateProgram`
- `glValidateProgramPipeline`

OpenGL
OpenGL ES Functions like `glGenTextures` do not create an object, they return a name for use with a new object. Objects are typically created with `glBind*` unless they are based on direct state access, in which case any other function may actually create the object.

OpenGL
WebGL
OpenGL ES

`glGenerateMipmap` may execute on the CPU, and therefore may be especially slow. Generate mipmaps offline or profile this function.

OpenGL
WebGL
OpenGL ES

When using the default texture scanline alignment, `GL_PACK_ALIGNMENT`, of four bytes, with `glTexImage2D` or `glTexSubImage2D`, the end of each row of pixel data may need to be padded to the next multiple of the alignment.

OpenGL

Texture rectangle, texture multisample, and buffer textures can't have mipmaps.

OpenGL

Integer textures, `GL_EXT_texture_integer`, do not support filtering.

OpenGL

A buffer texture is a 1D texture with a buffer object as storage which can only be fetched, not sampled.

OpenGL
WebGL
OpenGL ES

Unmap buffers as soon as possible to allow the driver to start the transfer or to schedule the transfer.

OpenGL
WebGL
OpenGL ES

Use buffer usage flags appropriately: `COPY`, GL to GL; `DRAW`, APP to GL; `READ`, GL to APP; `STREAM`, update always, `DYNAMIC`, update often, `STATIC`, update rarely.

OpenGL
WebGL
OpenGL ES

Set a GLSL sampler uniform to the texture unit number, not the OpenGL texture ID.

OpenGL
WebGL
OpenGL ES

`glGetUniformLocation` returns −1 but doesn't generate an error if the uniform name does not correspond to an active uniform. All declared uniforms are not active; uniforms that do not contribute to the shader's output can be optimized out by the compiler.

OpenGL

An OpenGL context must always be current for the duration of OpenGL/compute interoperability.

OpenGL

An OpenGL object should not be accessed by OpenGL while it is mapped for usage within the compute portion.

OpenGL
WebGL
OpenGL ES

Avoid extraneous `glBindFramebuffer` calls. Use multiple attachments to a FBO rather than managing multiple FBOs.

OpenGL
WebGL
OpenGL ES

FBOs must always be validated before use to ensure that the selected format is renderable.

OpenGL

Only one OpenGL query per query type, e.g., timer or occlusion, can be active at a time.

OpenGL

For occlusion queries, using GL_ANY_SAMPLES_PASSED may be more effective than GL_SAMPLES_PASSED, as a rendering doesn't have to continue as soon as one fragment passed.

OpenGL
WebGL
OpenGL ES

For image-space rendering on GPUs with a large clipping guard band clipping, e.g., GeForce, Radeon, and PowerVR series 6 use a large clipped triangle instead of a quad. Measure both if in doubt.

OpenGL
WebGL
OpenGL ES

To test vertex throughput, do not render to a 1×1 viewport because parallelism is lost; instead, render outside of the view frustum.

OpenGL
WebGL
OpenGL ES

glGetError is particularly slow, especially in multi-process WebGL architectures. Only use it in debug builds or instead use GL_ARB_debug_output when available.

OpenGL

Geometry shaders are usually output bound so spending ALU time to reduce the amount of data output is a performance win.

WebGL

In addition to #defining GL_OES_standard_derivatives before using dFdx, dFdy, and fwidth, also remember to call context.getExtension("OES_standard_derivatives") in JavaScript.

OpenGL
WebGL
OpenGL ES

To accurately compute the length of a gradient, avoid fwidth(v); instead use sqrt(dFdx(v) * dFdx(v) + dFdy(v) * dFdy(v)).

WebGL
OpenGL ES

highp is only available in fragment shaders if GL_FRAGMENT_PRECISION_HIGH is #defined. Beware of the performance implications of using highp in vertex or fragment shaders.

OpenGL

In OpenGL, precision qualifiers were reserved in GLSL 1.20 and OpenGL 2.1 but actually introduced with GLSL 1.30 and OpenGL 3.0. From GLSL 1.40 and OpenGL 3.1, and for the purpose of convergence with OpenGL ES 2.0, `GL_FRAGMENT_PRECISION_HIGH` is defined as 1 in a fragment shader.

OpenGL

By default, precision for vertex, tessellation, and geometry shader stages is `highp` for `int` types, and `mediump` for the fragment shader stage `int` types. This may lead to warnings on some implementations. `float` is always `highp` by default.

WebGL

Given a WebGL context `gl`, `gl.TRUE` is undefined. When porting OpenGL or OpenGL ES code, do not change `GL_TRUE` to `gl.TRUE` because it will silently evaluate to false.

OpenGL
WebGL
OpenGL ES

Depth writes only occur if `GL_DEPTH_TEST` is enabled.

OpenGL
WebGL
OpenGL ES

The noise functions are still unimplemented in GLSL. Chapter 7 fixes this.

OpenGL

`gl_VertexID` get values in [`first, first+count-1`] when generated from a `DrawArray*` command, and not in [`0, count-1`]. Especially useful when using a zero input attributes vertex shader.

OpenGL

There are two ways to work with point size: `glPointSize` in the client-side code or `gl_PointSize` in the GLSL code if `PROGRAM_POINT_SIZE` is enabled.

GLSL compatibility

GLSL es

GLSL core

The GLSL core profile and GLSL ES are different subsets of keywords of the GLSL compatibility profile. The GLSL core profile allows us to write GLSL code with a fully programmable pipeline approach. GLSL ES takes advantage of the precision qualifiers, but GLSL doesn't.

 Discovering

In this section, we discover many facets of OpenGL: teaching modern OpenGL in academia; using OpenGL on the web with WebGL; tessellation shaders in OpenGL 4.0; procedural textures; the safety critical variant, OpenGL SC; and multi-GPU OpenGL and CUDA interop.

OpenGL enjoys widespread use in computer graphics courses around the world. Now-depreciated OpenGL features such as fixed-function lighting, immediate mode, and built-in transforms made the barrier to entry low. However, modern OpenGL has removed many of these features, resulting in a lean API that exposes the functionality of the underlying hardware. Academia has taken these changes in stride, updating their graphics courses to modern OpenGL. In Chapter 1, "Teaching Computer Graphics Starting With Shader-Based OpenGL," Edward Angel discusses how an introductory computer graphics course can be taught using modern OpenGL. In Chapter 2, "Transitioning Students to Post-Deprecation OpenGL," Mike Bailey presents C++ abstractions and GLSL naming conventions to bridge the gap between depreciated and modern OpenGL for use in course assignments.

When we announced our call for authors for *OpenGL Insights* in May 2011, we included WebGL as a desired topic. Since then, WebGL has gained such traction that an entire book could easily be justified. In Chapter 3, "WebGL for OpenGL Developers," Patrick Cozzi and Scott Hunter present WebGL for those who already know OpenGL. In the following chapter, "Porting Mobile Apps to WebGL," Ashraf Samy Hegab shows the benefits, differences, and trade-offs of using WebGL for mobile applications. Several chapters in later sections continue our WebGL exploration.

Christophe Riccio takes a rigorous look at communication between the OpenGL API and GLSL and different shader stages in Chapter 5, "The GLSL Shader Interfaces." He carefully examines using varying blocks; attribute, varying, and fragment output variable locations; linked and separated programs; using semantics in our designs; and more.

Today, one of the differences between movie-quality rendering and real-time rendering is geometric complexity; movies generally have much higher geometric detail. To improve geometric detail in real-time rendering, tessellation can be done in hardware. Although this has been available on ATI cards since the ATI Radeon 8500 in 2001, tessellation shaders were recently standardized and made part of OpenGL 4.0. In Chapter 6, "An Introduction to Tessellation Shaders," Philip Rideout and Dirk Van Gelder introduce the new fixed and programmable tessellation stages.

As the gap between compute power and memory bandwidth continues to widen, procedural techniques become increasingly important. Small size is speed. Procedural textures not only have trivial memory requirements, but can also have excellent visual quality, allowing for analytic derivatives and anisotropic antialiasing. Stefan Gustavson introduces procedural textures, including antialiasing and using Perlin and Worley noise in Chapter 7, "Procedural Textures in GLSL." Best of all, he provides GLSL noise functions for OpenGL, OpenGL ES, and WebGL.

OpenGL SC, for safety critical, may be one of the lesser-known OpenGL variants. In Chapter 8, "OpenGL SC Emulation Based on OpenGL and OpenGL ES," Hwanyong Lee and Nakhoon Baek explain the motivation for OpenGL SC and describe the benefits of implementing it based on other OpenGL variants, instead of creating custom drivers or a software implementation.

In the past 15 years, consumer GPUs have transformed from dedicated fixed-function graphics processors to general-purpose massively-parallel processors. Technologies like CUDA and OpenCL have emerged for developing general data-parallel algorithms on the GPU. There is, of course, a need for these general algorithms, like particle systems and physical simulation, to interop efficiently with OpenGL for rendering. In the final chapter of this section, "Mixing Graphics and Compute with Multiple GPUs," Alina Alt reviews interoperability between CUDA and OpenGL and presents interoperability between multiple GPUs where one GPU is used for CUDA and another for OpenGL.

Teaching Computer Graphics Starting with Shader-Based OpenGL

1

Edward Angel

1.1 Introduction

For at least ten years, OpenGL has been used in the first computer graphics course taught to students in computer science and engineering, other branches of engineering, mathematics, and the sciences. Whether the course stresses basic graphics principles or takes a programming approach, OpenGL provides students with an API to support their learning. One of the many features of the OpenGL API that makes it popular for teaching is its stability and backward compatibility. Hence, instructors needed to make only minor changes in their courses as OpenGL evolved. At least that used to be true: over the last few years, OpenGL has changed rapidly and dramatically.

Starting with version 3.1, the fixed function pipeline was eliminated, an action that deprecated immediate mode and many of the familiar OpenGL functions and state variables. Every application must provide at least a vertex shader and a fragment shader. For those of us who use OpenGL to teach our graphics courses, these changes and the introduction of three additional shader stages in subsequent releases of OpenGL have led to a reexamination of how we can best teach computer graphics. As the authors of a popular textbook [Angel 09] used for the first course, we realized that this reexamination was both urgent and deep, requiring input from instructors at a variety of institutions. In the end, we wrote a new edition [Angel and Shreiner 12] that was entirely shader-based. Some of the key issues were addressed briefly in [Angel and Shreiner 11] but this chapter will not only discuss the reasons for the change but will also include practical observations and issues based on the actual teaching of a fully shader-based course.

I start with a historical overview, stressing how the software used in the first computer graphics course has changed over the years while the concepts we teach have remained largely unchanged. I review the key elements of a first course in computer graphics. Then I present a typical first *Hello World* program using the fixed-function pipeline. Next, the reader will see how we have to change that first program when moving to a shader-based course. Finally, I examine how each of the major topics in our standard course is affected by use of a shader-based OpenGL.

1.2   A Basic Course

Computer graphics has been taught in most colleges and universities since the 1970s. A comparison between what was taught then and what is taught now leads to some interesting observations. The first textbook that took the modern approach to graphics was Newman and Sproull's [Newman and Sproull 79]. Subsequently, Foley, van Dam, et al. [Foley et al. 96] became the standard. Not only do these two classic works agree as to the key topics, but so do all the recent textbooks [Angel and Shreiner 12, Hearn et al. 11]. These topics include

- modeling,

- geometry,

- transformations,

- lighting and shading,

- texture mapping and pixel processing.

A major theme of this chapter is that using a shader-based OpenGL in the introductory course not only is possible but actually reinforces these key concepts. I will examine each area individually, but first one of the major worries confronting instructors needs to be addressed, namely, the perception that it is much harder to get started with a version of OpenGL that not only requires the application to provide its own shaders but also forces the programmer to use new constructs, such as vertex buffer objects, that were not required previously.

1.3   Hello World in OpenGL: Old Style

Let's start with a simple example (shown in Listing 1.1) that we might teach in the first week of a typical class using pre-3.1 OpenGL: drawing a white rectangle on a black background using default values for most variables and, to delay any discussion of coordinate systems and transformations, giving vertex positions in clip coordinates.

```
#include <GL/glut.h>

void display(void)
{
  glClear(GL_COLOR_BUFFER_BIT);
  glBegin(GL_POLYGON);
    glVertex2f(-0.5, -0.5);
    glVertex2f(-0.5, 0.5);
    glVertex2f(0.5, 0.5);
    glVertex2f(0.5, -0.5);
  glEnd();
  glutSwapBuffers();
}

int main(int argc, char **argv)
{
  glutInit(&argc, argv);
  glutInitDisplayMode(GLUT_RGBA | GLUT_DOUBLE);
  glutCreateWindow("Hello World");
  glutDisplayFunc(display);
  glutMainLoop();
}
```

Listing 1.1. Hello World.

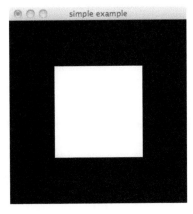

Figure 1.1. Hello World output.

As trivial as this program is, it possesses many of the features that instructors have built on.[1] For example, it is easy to add colors, normals, and texture coordinates between the **glBegin** and **glEnd**. Adding transformations and viewing is straightforward. Note that although we use GLUT in this example to interface with the window system and input devices and will use it in our other examples, its use is not crucial to the discussion. The output is shown in Figure 1.1.

There are three major issues with this code and all its extensions:

1. Use of immediate mode.

2. Reliance on the fixed-function pipeline.

3. Use of default values for state variables.

First, with a shader-based OpenGL, all the OpenGL functions in this example except **glClear** have been deprecated. Understanding why these functions have been deprecated is key to understanding why we have switched to a more recent OpenGL. The pipeline model (see a simplified version in Figure 1.2), that underlies OpenGL stresses immediate-mode graphics. As soon as each vertex is generated, it triggers an execution of the vertex shader. Because this geometry processing is carried out on the GPU by the vertex shader, this simple program requires four separate vertex positions to be sent to the GPU each time we want to display the rectangle.

---

[1] We could eliminate the double buffering to make the example even simpler. However, some systems would then require a **glFlush** instead of **glutSwapBuffers** to reliably display the output.

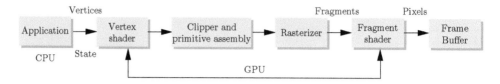

Figure 1.2. Simplified pipeline.

Such a program masks the bottleneck between the CPU and GPU and hides the parallelism available on the GPU. Hence, although it is not the kind of program we want our students to write, the reasons are not apparent from the code.

Second, although it seems nice to be able to rely on the fact that our data will be processed in a known way, students tend to think the use of the immediate mode is the only way to display their geometric models. Later, when they process more complex geometry, they wonder why their applications run so slowly.

Third, this type of program leads to a somewhat outdated view of OpenGL as a state machine. Although state is important, the use of the fixed-function pipeline and default values hides a multitude of state variables within OpenGL that control how the geometry is rendered. As the simple program is expanded, students tend to get lost in the multitude of state variables and have great difficulty with unintended side effects of state variable changes. With recent versions of OpenGL, most state variables have been deprecated, and the application creates its own state variables.

1.4   Starting with Programmable Pipelines

Now, let's review some of the issues with programmable pipelines starting with OpenGL 3.0. Although programmable pipelines have been in OpenGL since version 2.0, not only was their use optional, but an application programmer still had access to all the functions that are now deprecated. An application could have its own shaders and also use immediate mode. The shaders had access to most OpenGL state variables, which simplified writing applications with shaders. Hence, an instructor could start with our trivial application and introduce shaders later. However, in a first course that starts with immediate mode and the fixed-function pipeline, very few instructors actually get to programmable shaders. At best, shaders are given a short introduction at the end of the course.

OpenGL 3.0 announced that starting with OpenGL 3.1, backward compatibility would no longer be required of an implementation. OpenGL 3.1 has a core that is shader-based and a compatibility extension that supports the deprecated functions. Later versions introduced core and compatibility profiles. Implementors could supply either or both profiles. The option we took was to design a first course that was totally shader based, consistent with the OpenGL 3.1 core.[2] To develop a first program, we had to examine what was absolutely required.

A shader-based program requires at least a vertex shader and a fragment shader. Hence, the instructor must introduce a minimal amount of the OpenGL Shading Language (GLSL). Because GLSL is semantically close to C with a few C++-style enhancements, we can present the almost trivial shaders required for a Hello World program without going into an in-depth discussion of GLSL. The instructor must introduce some concepts such as program objects and, of course, what the shaders do. Although these concepts take some time to present, they are core to understanding how modern graphics systems work, and introducing them early in the course should be viewed as a benefit of our approach.

The biggest problem in introducing shaders is that the application must read, compile, and link the shaders with the application. These operations require a set of OpenGL functions that contribute little to the student's understanding of basic graphics concepts. Consequently, we decided to give the students a function, `InitShaders`, that reads in the shader files, compiles them, links them, and, if successful, returns a program object, as in the code fragment

```
GLuint program = InitShaders("vertex_shader_file", "fragment_shader_file");
```

The source code was made available, and the individual functions used in it were discussed later or assigned as a reading exercise. As seemingly trivial as this decision appears, it was a departure from previous courses in which we never gave the students any code without a detailed presentation of its contents.

A second, perhaps more controversial, decision along these lines was to give the students a small C++ package with two-, three-, and four-dimensional matrix and vector classes. Although an OpenGL application can be written in C and use programmable shaders, GLSL relies on some additional matrix and vector types, uses C++-style constructors, and employs operator overloading. Consequently, if we're going to teach a shader-based course, our students have to know a little bit of C++. In practice, this is not a problem as most students have already used an object-oriented programming language, and even for those who haven't, the required parts of C++ are simple and take little time to introduce.

Although we could just use the C++ features required by GLSL in shader code only, there are two major advantages to having a C++ matrix/vector package that mirrors the types and operations in GLSL. One advantage is that the application code is a lot cleaner and clearer, eliminating most `for` loops. The second is that many algorithms that are studied in a typical class, such as lighting, can be applied either in the application or in one of the shaders. By using application code with similar types and operations, such algorithms can be applied in any of the possible

---

[2]Most OpenGL 2.0 implementations support all the functionality needed for our course, either directly or with a few OpenGL extensions. Hence, OpenGL 3.1 or any later version is not a requirement for using our approach.

ways with almost identical code. We have found this feature to be extremely helpful in teaching some of the more difficult parts of a course. These advantages override the potential objections that, once again, we are giving students code instead of having them write their own and also acknowledge that we really are using some C++ to teach the introductory course.

1.5   Hello World: New Style

Even the simplest application program can be divided into three parts: an initialization that sets up the shaders and the interface with the window system, a stage that forms the data and sends the data to the GPU, and a stage that renders the data on the GPU. In the shader-based approach, the first stage is no more difficult than with the traditional approach if we use `InitShaders`. For beginning examples, the third stage requires only a clearing of some buffers and a call to `glDrawArrays`. The middle stage is fundamentally different from immediate-mode programming. We have to introduce vertex buffer objects and perhaps vertex array objects for even the simplest program. Let's examine all of these issues with a new Hello World program. A program that produces the same output as our first Hello World program is shown in Listing 1.2. The corresponding vertex shader is in Listing 1.3, and the fragment shader is in Listing 1.4.

The include file `Angel.h` brings in the `InitShaders` code and the matrix and vector classes. The next thing we notice about the program is that the data are for two triangles with shared vertices rather than for a single quadrilateral. Starting with OpenGL 3.1, triangles are the only filled type that is supported. This single initialization of an array, which uses our `vec2` data type, leads to a good discussion of why we are restricted to triangles. We can also discuss the alternative of using either a triangle strip or a triangle fan.

Next comes the most difficult part to explain (although it's only five lines of code). We allocate a vertex array object (VAO) and a vertex buffer object (VBO). The three lines of code for setting up the vertex array data should follow from the discussion of VBOs. The basic idea that we are setting up storage is clear but why we need a VBO and a VAO in such a simple program is a tough one since we probably don't want to spend a lot of time on that issue early in a course.[3]

The rest of the program is almost identical to the immediate-mode version with the exception of the use of `glDrawArrays`, but that function presents no problems to students, and the display callback is almost trivial to explain.

Not much time is necessary to discuss the shaders; they don't require much knowledge of GLSL. One nice aspect of the use of shaders is that even these simple shaders can be changed in interesting ways without going any deeper into GLSL.

---

[3]Alternately, some instructors may choose to leave out any discussion of VAOs by removing these two lines of code. The program will still run and at this point in the course, the potential efficiency of using a VAO is not of crucial importance.

```
#include "Angel.h"

void init( void )
{
  vec2 points[6] =
  {
    vec2( -0.5, -0.5 ), vec2( 0.5, -0.5 ),
    vec2( 0.5, 0.5 ), vec2( 0.5, 0.5 ),
    vec2( -0.5, 0.5 ), vec2( -0.5, -0.5 )
  };
  GLuint vao, buffer;
  GLuint glGenVertexArrays(1, &vao);
  glBindVertexArray(vao);

  GLuint glGenBuffers(1, &buffer);
  glBindBuffer(GL_ARRAY_BUFFER, buffer);
  glBufferData(GL_ARRAY_BUFFER, sizeof(points), points, GL_STATIC_DRAW);

  GLuint program = InitShader("vsimple.glsl", "fsimple.glsl");
  glUseProgram(program);

  GLuint loc = glGetAttribLocation(program, "vPosition");
  glEnableVertexAttribArray(loc);
  glVertexAttribPointer(loc, 2, GL_FLOAT, GL_FALSE, 0, 0);

  glClearColor(0.0, 0.0, 0.0, 1.0);
}

void display(void)
{
  glClear(GL_COLOR_BUFFER_BIT);
  glDrawArrays(GL_TRIANGLES, 0, 6);
  gutSwapBuffers();
}

int main(int argc, char **argv)
{
  glutInit(&argc, argv);
  glutInitDisplayMode(GLUT_RGBA | GLUT_DOUBLE);
  glutCreateWindow("Hello World");
  init();
  glutDisplayFunc(display);
  glutMainLoop();
}
```

Listing 1.2. Hello World redux.

```
in vec4 vPosition;

void main()
{
  gl_Position = vPosition;
}
```

Listing 1.3. Hello World vertex shader.

```
out vec4 FragColor;

void main()
{
  FragColor = vec4(1.0, 1.0, 1.0, 1.0);
}
```

Listing 1.4. Hello World fragment shader.

1.5.1   OpenGL ES and WebGL

In my classes, students have always been free to choose to use Macs, PCs, or Linux computers. With OpenGL, that flexibility has never been a problem. The advent of OpenGL ES 2.0 and WebGL opens up even more possibilities. OpenGL ES 2.0 is totally shader-based and is supported on a variety of devices, including iPhones. WebGL is a JavaScript implementation of OpenGL ES 2.0 that runs on the latest browsers. Last semester, students in our class used all five options. Although JavaScript is usually not part of the standard CS curriculum at most schools, it's pretty easy for upper-class and graduate students to pick up the basics. The ability to share their work via a URL was an enormous benefit to students.

1.5.2   The First Assignment

Once we get past the Hello World example, students are ready for their first programming assignment. We like to give a three-dimensional project to start. Because one of the goals of the first assignment is to check whether students have the programming skills to handle later projects, it's important to assign this type of project early. One possibility is to base the assignment on modeling and rendering a cube. Although without transformations, the axis-aligned cube will look like a square, students can change the vertex data, either to show more than one face of the cube or to create more interesting objects. Another possibility is an extension of some simple fractal to three dimensions. Other possibilities are morphing one simple object into another, twists, and two- or three-dimensional maze generation. You can also focus on shader code by starting with either a simple model or giving the class the data for a more complex model and having the students manipulate the model in the vertex shader. At this point in a typical course, it is better to focus on an assignment using vertex shaders rather than fragment shaders since the major topics an instructor will likely be covering in class at that time are geometry and transformations.

1.6   The Rest of the Course

In most courses that have a programming component, instructors want to get their students programming as soon as possible so they can move on to the core topics. Comparing our experience with the two Hello World examples, it takes about an extra week to get students to write their first assignment using the shader-based approach. This extra time comes back to the instructor because the details of using shader-based code that we needed to explain for the Hello World example would have been introduced later in a traditional course. Let's look at each part of what we claim is core to all senior-level graphics courses and discuss how a shader-based OpenGL fits into each one.

1.6.1 Geometry

Computer graphics is built on some basic geometric concepts. Every introductory computer graphics class introduces the basic types (scalars, points, vectors), simple objects (triangles, planes, polylines), and methods of representation (coordinate systems, frames). Our approach has been to spend some time on building geometric models through vertex buffers. This section of most courses need not change with a shader-based OpenGL. Nevertheless, there are some interesting ways in which shaders can be used.

Consider modeling a cube. It's a very useful object to have available as we develop transformations, viewing, lighting, and texture mapping. Because we can only render triangles, we have multiple ways we can build a model for the cube. Since we have already introduced vertex buffers for the Hello World program, an extension to using simple data structures and `glDrawElements` is a nice topic. Color is usually added at this point in the course. Since the old built-in state variables, including the current color and the vertex position, are no longer part of the OpenGL state, these and other state variables must be defined in the application and their values sent to the GPU. Courses that are programming-oriented can use the flexibility of how data are organized and transferred to the GPU to experiment with various strategies, such as using uniform variables versus vertex attributes or various ways to mix geometric and color data in the application and on the GPU.

More generally, the issue of efficiency is often a neglected topic. With the standard immediate-mode approach, when students are asked to see how close their programs come to the advertised ratings of their graphics card, they are amazed and perplexed with how poorly their programs perform. With the flexibility of newer versions of OpenGL, students can try various strategies and achieve performances close to spec. In addition, if they use a compatibility profile, they can compare immediate-mode and retained-mode performance.

1.6.2 Transformations and Viewing

This part of the course is fairly standard and takes the most time. We introduce the standard affine transformations—translation, rotation, scaling, shear—and how to build them. We then move on to projective transformations and derive from them the standard orthographic and perspective transformations. Courses differ in how an instructor divides between theory and application. Before OpenGL 3.1, the API provided support through some simple matrix functions (`glMatrixMode`, `glLoadMatrix`, `glLoadIdentity`, `glMultMatrix`), the standard transformation functions (`glTranslate`, `glRotate`, `glScale`), matrix stacks (`glPush Matrix`, `glPopMatrix`), and the projection functions (`glOrtho`, `glFrustum`). All these functions have been deprecated. Moreover, because most state variables have been eliminated, the notion of a current matrix is gone, and thus the concept of a matrix function that alters a current matrix by post multiplication is also gone. All these changes have major consequences.

At this point in a typical class, the instructor develops the standard affine transformations in homogeneous coordinates. Although the basic translation, rotation about a coordinate axis, and scaling functions are simple for the students to write themselves, rotation about an arbitrary axis is more difficult and can be done in a number of ways. One of the advantages of not having these functions available in the API is that students pay more attention to the instructor and the textbook since they can no longer rely on the functionality being part of the API. Nevertheless, we have added functions to our matrix/vector classes that form the basic matrices, including the standard viewing matrices. One reason for this is that we often want to make comparisons between carrying out a transformation in the application and carrying it out in the shader. By providing these matrices, students can carry out these comparisons with almost identical code.

One of the exercises that has proved helpful has been to use the same model we used in the geometric section (the cube) and look at different methods of rotating it in an idle callback. One extreme, in terms of efficiency, is to rotate the vertices in the application and resend the data. Students can then compare this immediate-mode strategy with the strategies of sending rotation matrices to the vertex shader or just sending the angles to a shader.

If the instructor covers hierarchical models, it is simple to add matrix push and pop functions to implement matrix stacks. Some instructors are interested in teaching about quaternions as part of a discussion on rotation. Quaternions can be implemented with just a few lines of code in a shader and thus fit well into a shader-based course.

1.6.3 Lighting and Shading

This section, more than any other, shows the benefits of the shader-based approach. In the past, students were able to use only the Blinn-Phong lighting because it was the only model supported by the fixed-function pipeline. Other models could be discussed but could only be implemented in an offline manner. Equally problematic was that only vertex lighting was available. Thus, while students could study Phong and Gouraud shading, they could not implement Phong shading within the pipeline. Consequently, students focussed on a single lighting and shading model. With programmable shaders, both per-vertex and per-fragment lighting can be accomplished with almost identical code. Students can even use our matrix and vector types to implement per-vertex lighting in the application. Once students have covered texture mapping, it is fairly easy to add bump mapping as an additional shading method.

The deprecation of most state variables and immediate-mode functions does cause some problems. Applications must provide their own normals, usually as a vertex attribute. The larger problem occurs with transforming normals. When students implement a lighting shader, they must provide a normal matrix because the state variable `gl_NormalMatrix` has been deprecated. Students can either implement this matrix themselves, either in the application or the shader, or a normal matrix function can be added to the `mat.h` file.

1.6.4 Texturing and Discrete Processing

Most of the pre-3.1 texture functions have not changed with recent versions of OpenGL. The application sets up a texture object. Texture coordinates can be produced in either the application as a vertex attribute or in the vertex shader and then interpolated by the rasterizer. Finally, a sampler is used in the fragment shader that applies the shader to coloring each fragment.

Starting with OpenGL 3.1, pixel processing is dramatically different. Both the bitmap- and pixel-writing functions have been deprecated, as have some of the related functions, such as those for using an accumulation buffer. Although these functions were easy to use, they were extremely inefficient. Here is a case where ease of programming leads to poor use of the GPU and a bottleneck due to large amounts of data that go back and forth between the CPU and the GPU. The alternative is to take an approach based on using fragment shaders to manipulate textures. For example, the simple fragment shader in Listing 1.5 is sufficient to illustrate image smoothing and can be altered easily to do other imaging operations.

```
in vec2 texCoord;
out vec4 FragColor;
uniform float d;

uniform sampler2D image;

void main()
{
  FragColor =
    (texture( image, vec2(texCoord.x + d, texCoord.y))
    + texture( image, vec2(texCoord.x,     texCoord.y + d))
    + texture( image, vec2(texCoord.x - d, texCoord.y))
    + texture( image, vec2(texCoord.x,     texCoord.y - d))) / 4.0;
}
```

Listing 1.5. Image-smoothing shader.

1.6.5 Advanced Topics

The topics we discussed above are central to most first courses in computer graphics. Depending on the instructor and the focus (programming vs. theory, survey vs. depth), three additional topics fit in well at this level. The first is curves and surfaces. Although evaluators have been deprecated, they are easy to create on the application side. If we use a more recent version of OpenGL, a much more interesting approach is to introduce geometry shaders for generating parametric cubic curves. Geometry shaders do not add a significant amount of programming complexity, and they can also be used for an introduction to subdivision curves and surfaces. Tessellation shaders may be better for parametric polynomial surfaces but are most likely much too complex for a first course.

The second topic that an instructor might consider introducing is framebuffer objects (FBOs). Although FBOs require the introduction of more OpenGL detail, they open up many new areas that lead to excellent student projects. Consider rendering to a texture. Because textures are shared by all instances of shaders, they provide shared memory. Doing a single pass through a texture as in the previous section is simple, but dynamic imaging operations are much more interesting. Such examples are usually best done by rendering to an off-screen buffer and then using this buffer as a texture for the next iteration. This type of double buffering (or buffer ping-ponging) is not only the basis for nongraphical uses of GPUs, as with CUDA or OpenCL, but is also used for games, particle systems, and agent-based simulations.

Lacking the necessary hardware and software, the early courses in computer graphics spent a lot of time on algorithms for rasterization, clipping, and hidden-surface removal. As better hardware and APIs such as OpenGL became available, much of that emphasis has been lost. Instructors can rely on the graphics system to do these tasks, and the discussion of such algorithms tends to be short and at the end of a typical introductory course. Programmable shaders allow the student to study and implement a wide range of graphics algorithms as possible class projects.

1.6.6   Issues

As exciting as we find the shader-based approach, there are some issues. Some instructors may find that the extra time needed to get to the first programming assignment is a problem. We have not found that to be the case, nor did we find that we had less time to teach the core topics. What is more significant is that there is a real change in emphasis from a focus on interactions between the CPU and GPU to the capabilities of the GPU itself. With a shader-based OpenGL, some of the standard interactive operations involve much more application overhead than they did with immediate-mode graphics. The main reason is that interactive techniques, such as the use of menus or rubber-banding of objects as they are moved across the display, can be done very easily with immediate-mode graphics. With a fully shader-based OpenGL, data must first be moved to the GPU. Most techniques are doable with a shader-based OpenGL, but they're not as simple or elegant as with immediate mode. Our view is that the time is better spent on other topics that more accurately reflect what is possible with recent GPUs.

The problem of how to interface with the window system has become more problematic. The OpenGL Utility Toolkit (GLUT) provided an interface to all the standard windowing systems. It allowed an application to open and manipulate one or more windows, use a mouse and keyboard with OpenGL, provided some nice extras such as the teapot (with normals), and system independent text. GLUT has been unchanged for 10 years. Consequently, many of its features, including text rendering and some of its objects, should not work with a shader-based OpenGL using only a core profile, because many GLUT functions rely on deprecated OpenGL functions. The freeglut project (freeglut.sourceforge.net) addresses some of these issues, but it too uses deprecated functions. Surprisingly, many applications work correctly with GLUT or freeglut, depending on the graphics card and driver that is used. This situation is of dubious benefit for many instructors. For example, many implementations support GLUT or freeglut menus even though the source for these toolkits use the deprecated `glRasterPos` function to implement menus, and the situation may not hold for long. For example, Mac OS X Lion supports OpenGL 3.2, but the 3.2 profile is incompatible with the GLUT framework.

There are a few possible approaches to fixing this problem, although the better ones may take a while to develop. Most instructors do not want to go back to using the native windowing functions on their architectures. Such an approach would be in conflict with the ability to teach a course in which students can use Windows, Mac OS X, Linux, OpenGL ES, or WebGL. There are a few cross-platform alternatives to GLUT out there, but it remains to be seen if any of them will become established. Perhaps a more desirable path would be for some group to update freeglut so it is fully compatible with a shader-based OpenGL.

An interesting alternative would be to use WebGL for beginning classes. Although academic CS departments have an aversion to JavaScript, there is a lot to be said for such an approach. WebGL is supported by almost all the latest browsers on Windows, Mac OS X, and Linux. Hence, there is no need to worry about differences among systems. In addition, there is a wide range of tools available for interaction with WebGL.

Finally, there are issues with the various versions of OpenGL and GLSL and with the associated drivers. Although OpenGL 3.1 was the first version to require the application to provide shaders and deprecated many functions from earlier versions, it was plagued by many ambiguities and some features that were reexamined in later versions. Starting with OpenGL 3.2, OpenGL introduced multiple profiles that allow the programmer to request a core profile or a compatibility profile that includes the deprecated functions. However, with the rapid release of new versions and the simultaneous evolution of GLSL, OpenGL drivers vary dramatically in which versions and profiles they support and in how they interpret the standards. In practice, with the variety of versions, drivers, profiles, and GPUs available, getting students started can take some effort. However, once students get the Hello World program running, they have little trouble with the mechanics of their assignments.

1.7 Conclusion

Overall, we are convinced that starting with a shader-based OpenGL is not only possible but makes for a much better first course in computer graphics. The feedback from the students has been overwhelmingly positive. Students who used WebGL or

OpenGL ES were especially happy with the course. We attribute a large part of their enthusiasm to the ease with which they could demo their assignments to their cohorts, friends, and families.

The code for our class is available at www.cs.unm.edu/~angel, and many other examples can be found starting at www.opengl.org.

Acknowledgments. Dave Shreiner (ARM, Inc.) has been an enormous help over many years, both as a coauthor of our textbook and copresentor of many SIGGRAPH courses. My students were the first to get me interested in OpenGL over 15 years ago. More recently, my students at the University of New Mexico and colleagues at the Santa Fe Complex pushed me toward teaching a fully shader-based introductory course.

Bibliography

[Angel and Shreiner 11] Edward Angel and Dave Shreiner. "Teaching a Shader-Based Introduction to Computer Graphics." *IEEE Computer Graphics and Applications* 31:2 (2011), 9–13.

[Angel and Shreiner 12] Edward Angel and Dave Shreiner. *Interactive Computer Graphics, Sixth Edition.* Boston: Addison-Wesley, 2012.

[Angel 09] Edward Angel. *Interactive Computer Graphics, Fifth Edition.* Boston: Addison-Wesley, 2009.

[Foley et al. 96] James D. Foley, Andries van Dam, Steven K. Feiner, and John F. Hughes. *Computer Graphics, Second Edition.* Reading: Addison-Wesley, 1996.

[Hearn et al. 11] Donald Hearn, M. Pauline Baker, and Warren R. Carithers. *Computer Graphics, Fourth Edition.* Boston: Prentice Hall, 2011.

[Newman and Sproull 79] William M. Newman and Robert F. Sproull. *Principles of Interactive Computer Graphics, Second Edition.* New York: McGraw Hill, 1979.

Transitioning Students to Post-Deprecation OpenGL

2

Mike Bailey

2.1   Introduction

From an educator's perspective, teaching OpenGL in the past has been a snap. The separation of geometry from topology in the **glBegin-glEnd**, the simplicity of **glVertex3f**, and the classic organization of the postmultiplied transformation matrices has been fast and easy to explain. This has considerably excited the students because going from zero knowledge to "cool 3D program you can smugly show your friends" was the task of a single lesson. This made motivation easy.

The Great OpenGL Deprecation has changed that. Creating and using vertex buffer objects is a lot more time consuming to explain than **glBegin-glEnd** [Angel 11]. It's also much more error-prone. Creating and maintaining matrices and matrix stacks now requires deft handling of matrix components and multiplication order [GLM 11]. In short, while postdeprecation OpenGL might be more streamlined and efficient, it has wreaked havoc on those who need to teach it and even more on those who need to learn it.

So the "old way" is not current, but the "new way" takes a long time to learn before one can see a single pixel. How can we keep students enthusiastic and motivated but still move them along the road to learning things the new way?[1] This chapter

---

[1] One option, of course, is not to transition at all, where the current penalty is simply falling behind the OpenGL curve. However, in some instances, most notably, OpenGL ES 2.0 [Munshi 08], failing to transition is not even an option.

discusses intermediate solutions to this problem by presenting C++ classes that ease the transition to postdeprecation OpenGL. These C++ classes are

1. Create vertex buffers with methods that look suspiciously like `glBegin`-`glEnd`.

2. Load, compile, link, and use shaders.

This chapter also suggests a naming convention that can be instrumental in keeping shader variables untangled from each other.

2.2 Naming Shader Variables: Introduction

This isn't exactly a transition issue. It's more of a confusion-prevention issue.

With seven different places that GLSL variables can be set, it is convenient to adopt a naming convention to help recognize what variables came from what sources. This works very well, as shown in Table 2.1.

Beginning letter(s)	Means that the Variable
a	Is a per-vertex attribute from the application
u	Is a uniform variable from the application
v	Came from a vertex shader
tc	Came from a tessellation control shader
te	Came from a tessellation evaluation shader
g	Came from a geometry shader
f	Came from a fragment shader

Table 2.1. Variable name prefix convention.

2.3 Naming Shader Variables: Details

Variables like `gl_Vertex` and `gl_ModelViewMatrix` have been built-in to the GLSL language from the start. They are used like this:

```
vec4 ModelCoords = gl_Vertex;
vec4 EyeCoords   = gl_ModelViewMatrix * gl_Vertex;
vec4 ClipCoords  = gl_ModelViewProjectionMatrix * gl_Vertex;
vec3 TransfNorm  = gl_NormalMatrix * gl_Normal;
```

However, starting with OpenGL 3.0, they have been deprecated in favor of user-defined variables that we pass in from the application. The built-ins still work if compatibility mode is enabled, but we should all be prepared for them to go away some day. Also, OpenGL ES has already completely eliminated the built-ins.

We have chosen to pretend that we have created variables in an application and have passed them in. So, the previous lines of code would be changed to look like this:

```
vec4 ModelCoords = aVertex;
vec4 EyeCoords   = uModelViewMatrix * aVertex;
vec4 ClipCoords  = uModelViewProjectionMatrix * aVertex;
vec3 TransfNorm  = uNormalMatrix * aNormal;
```

If they really are being passed in from the application, we can go ahead and use these names. But, if we haven't made that transition yet, the new names can still be used (thus preparing for an eventual transition) by including a set of **#defines** at the top of their shader code, as shown in Listing 2.1.

If the graphics driver supports the **ARB_shading_language_include** extension,[2] then these lines can be **#included** right into the shader code. If it is not supported, an **#include** can be "faked" by copying these lines into the first of the multiple strings that are used to load shader source code before compiling.

The **#line** statement is there so that compiler error messages give the correct line numbers and do not include these lines in the count.

Later on in this chapter, this set of **#include** lines will be referred to as gstap.h.[3]

```
// uniform variables:

#define uModelViewMatrix              gl_ModelViewMatrix
#define uProjectionMatrix             gl_ProjectionMatrix
#define uModelViewProjectionMatrix    gl_ModelViewProjectionMatrix
#define uNormalMatrix                 gl_NormalMatrix
#define uModelViewMatrixInverse       gl_ModelViewMatrixInverse

// per-vertex attribute variables:

#define aColor                        gl_Color
#define aNormal                       gl_Normal
#define aVertex                       gl_Vertex
#define aTexCoord0                    gl_MultiTexCoord0
#define aTexCoord1                    gl_MultiTexCoord1
#define aTexCoord2                    gl_MultiTexCoord2
#define aTexCoord3                    gl_MultiTexCoord3
#define aTexCoord4                    gl_MultiTexCoord4
#define aTexCoord5                    gl_MultiTexCoord5
#define aTexCoord6                    gl_MultiTexCoord6
#define aTexCoord7                    gl_MultiTexCoord7

#line 1
```

Listing 2.1. #include file to translate new names to old names.

---

[2] ...and if this line is placed at the top of the shader code: **#extension GL_ARB_shading_language_include : enable.**

[3] ...which stands for *Graphics Shaders: Theory and Practice*, the book in which this file originally appeared (Second Edition, A K Peters, 2011).

2.4   Indexed Vertex Buffer Object C++ Class

There is no question that using `glBegin-glEnd` is convenient, especially when beginning to learn OpenGL. With this in mind, here is a C++ class that looks like the application is using `glBegin-glEnd`, but inside, its data structures are preparing to use indexed vertex buffer objects (VBOs) [Shreiner 09] when the class's `Draw( )` method is called. The `Print( )` method's print format shows the data in VBO-table form so the students can see what they would have created if they had used VBOs in the first place. The following methods are supported by the class, as shown in Listing 2.2.

```
void CollapseCommonVertices( bool collapse );
void Draw( );
void Begin( GLenum type );
void Color3f( GLfloat red, GLfloat green, GLfloat blue );
void Color3fv( GLfloat *rgb );
void End( );
void Normal3f( GLfloat nx, GLfloat ny, GLfloat nz );
void Normal3fv( GLfloat *nxyz );
void TexCoord2f( GLfloat s, GLfloat t );
void TexCoord2fv( GLfloat *st );
void Vertex2f( GLfloat x, GLfloat y );
void Vertex2fv( GLfloat *xy );
void Vertex3f( GLfloat x, GLfloat y, GLfloat z );
void Vertex3fv( GLfloat *xyz );
void Print( char *str = '', FILE *out = stderr );
void RestartPrimitive( );
void SetTol( float tol );
```

Listing 2.2. `VertexBufferObject` class methods.

2.4.1   Usage Notes

- This implements an indexed VBO; that is, it keeps track of the vertices' index in the VBO and then uses `glDrawElements( )` to display the object.

- Passing a TRUE to the `CollapseCommonVertices( )` method's Boolean argument says that any vertices *close enough* to each other should be collapsed to be treated as a single vertex. "Close enough" is defined by the distance specified in `SetTol( )`. The advantage to this is that the single vertex gets transformed only once per display update. The disadvantage is that the collapsing process takes time, especially for large lists of vertices.

- The `RestartPrimitive( )` method invokes an OpenGL-ism that restarts the current primitive topology without starting a new VBO. It is especially handy for triangle strips and line strips. For example, if the topology is triangle strip, then `RestartPrimitive( )` allows the application to end one strip and start another and have all the vertices end up in a single VBO. This saves overhead.

- The first call to the **Draw( )** method sends the VBO data to the graphics card and draws it. Subsequent calls to **Draw( )** just do the drawing.

2.4.2 Example Code

Listing 2.3 and Figure 2.1 show an example of using the **VertexBufferObject** class to draw a colored cube.

```
#include "VertexBufferObject.h"

VertexBufferObject VB;
. . .

// this goes in the part of the program where graphics things
// get initialized once:

VB.CollapseCommonVertices( true );
VB.SetTol( .001f );                  // how close need to be to collapse

VB.Begin( GL_QUADS );
for( int i = 0; i < 6; i++ )
{
        for( int j = 0; j < 4; j++ )
        {
                VB.Color3fv( . . . );
                VB.Vertex3fv( . . . );
        }
}
VB.End( );
VB.Print( "VB:" );      // verify that vertices were really collapsed

. . .


// this goes in the display-callback part of the program:

VB.Draw( );
```

Listing 2.3. VertexBufferObject class used to draw a colored cube.

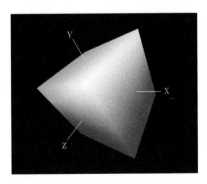

Figure 2.1. Colored cube created with the VertexBufferObject class.

```
// create an instance of the class:
// (the real constructor'' is in the Begin method)
VertexBufferObject VB;
VB.CollapseCommonVertices( true );
VB.SetTol( .001f );
. . .


// this goes in the part of the program where graphics things
// get initialized once:

int x, y;          // loop indices
float ux, uy;      // utm coordinates

VB.Begin( GL_LINE_STRIP );

for( y = 0, uy = meteryMin; y < NumLats;  y++, uy += meteryStep )
{
      VB.RestartPrimitive(  );
      for( x = 0, ux = meterxMin; x < NumLngs   x++, ux += meterxStep )
      {
                float uz = Heights[ y*NumLngs + x ];
                VB.Color3f( 1., 1., 0. );       // single color = yellow
                VB.Vertex3f( ux, uy, uz );
      }
}

for( x = 0, ux = meterxMin; x < NumLngs; x++, ux += meterxStep )
{
      VB.RestartPrimitive(  );
      for( y = 0, uy = meteryMin; y < NumLats; y++, uy += meteryStep )
      {
            float uz = Heights[  y*NumLngs + x  ];
            VB.Color3f( 1., 1., 0. );
            VB.Vertex3f( ux, uy, uz );
      }
}

VB.End(  );
VB.Print( "Terrain VBO:" );
. . .


// this goes in the display-callback part of the program:

VB.Draw(  );
```

Listing 2.4. `VertexBufferObject` class used to draw a wireframe terrain.

This next example, shown in Listing 2.4 and Figure 2.2, shows drawing gridlines on a terrain map. The already-defined `Heights[ ]` array holds the terrain heights. This is a good example of using the `RestartPrimitive( )` method so that the next grid line doesn't have to be in a new line strip. The entire grid is saved as a single line strip and is drawn by blasting a single VBO into the graphics pipeline.

Figure 2.2. Wireframe terrain created with the `VertexBufferObject` class.

2.4.3 Implementation Notes

- This class uses the C++ standard template library (STL) *vector* function to maintain the ever-expanding array of vertices.

- It also uses the C++ STL *map* function to speed the collapsing of common vertices.

2.5 GLSLProgram C++ Class

The act of creating, compiling, linking, using, and passing parameters to shaders is very repetitive [Rost 09, Bailey 11]. When teaching students, we have found it helpful

```
bool   Create( char *, char * = NULL, char * = NULL, char * = NULL, char * = NULL );
bool   IsValid( );
void   SetAttribute( char *name, int val );
void   SetAttribute( char *name, float val );
void   SetAttribute( char *name, float val0, float val1, float val2 );
void   SetAttribute( char *name, float *valp );
void   SetAttribute( char *name, Vec3& vec3 );
void   SetAttribute( char *name, VertexBufferObject& vb, GLenum which );
void   SetGstap( bool set );
void   SetUniform( char *name, int );
void   SetUniform( char *name, float );
void   SetUniform( char *name, float, float, float );
void   SetUniform( char *name, float[3] );
void   SetUniform( char *name, Vec3& );
void   SetUniform( char *name, Matrix4& );
void   Use( );
void   UseFixedFunction( );
```

Listing 2.5. GLSLProgram class methods.

to create a C++ class called *GLSLProgram* that implements this process. This class has the tools to manage all the steps of shader program development and use, including source-file opening, loading, and compilation. It also has methods that implement setting attribute and uniform variables. The following methods are supported by the class, as shown in Listing 2.5.

2.5.1 Usage Notes

- The `Create( )` method takes up to five shader file names as arguments. From the filename extensions shown in Table 2.2, it figures out what type of shaders these are, loads them, compiles them, and links them all together. All errors are written to `stderr`.[4] It returns true if the resulting shader binary program is valid, or false if it is not. The `IsValid( )` method can be called later if the application wants to know if everything succeeded or not. The files listed in the `Create( )` call can be in any order. The filename extensions that the `Create( )` method is looking for are shown in Table 2.2.

Extension	Shader Type
.vert	GL_VERTEX_SHADER
.vs	GL_VERTEX_SHADER
.frag	GL_FRAGMENT_SHADER
.fs	GL_FRAGMENT_SHADER
.geom	GL_GEOMETRY_SHADER
.gs	GL_GEOMETRY_SHADER
.tcs	GL_TESS_CONTROL_SHADER
.tes	GL_TESS_EVALUATION_SHADER

Table 2.2. Shader type filename extensions.

- The `SetAttribute( )` methods set attribute variables to be passed to the vertex shader. The vertex buffer version of the `SetAttribute( )` method lets a `VertexBufferObject` be specified along with which data inside it is to be assigned to this attribute name. For example, one might say:

```
GLSLProgram  Ovals;
VertexBufferObject VB;
      . . .
Ovals.SetAttribute ( "aNormal", VB, GL_NORMAL_ARRAY );
```

- The `SetUniform( )` methods set uniform variables destined for any of the shaders.

---

[4]Standard error is used for these messages because it is unbuffered. If a program crashes, the helpful messages sent to standard output might still be trapped in a buffer and will not be seen. Those messages sent to standard error were seen right away.

- The `Use( )` method makes this shader program active so that it affects any subsequent drawing. If someone insists on using the fixed functionality, the `UseFixedFunction( )` method returns the state of the pipeline to doing so.

- The `SetGstap( )` method is there to give the option to have the gstap.h code included automatically. Just pass TRUE as the argument. Call this before the call to the `Create( )` method.

2.5.2 Example Code

Listing 2.6 shows an example `GLSLProgram` class application.

```
#include "GLSLProgram.h"

float        Ad, Bd, NoiseAmp, NoiseFreq, Tol;
GLSLProgram Ovals;
VertexBufferObject VB;

. . .

// set everything up once:

Ovals.SetVerbose( true );
Ovals.SetGstap( true );
bool good = Ovals.Create( "ovalnoise.vert", "ovalnoise.frag" );
if( ! good )
{
        fprintf( stderr, "GLSL Program Ovals wasn't created.\n" );
        . . .
}


. . .



// do this in the display callback:

Ovals.Use( );
Ovals.SetUniform( "uAd", Ad );
Ovals.SetUniform( "uBd", Bd );
Ovals.SetUniform( "uNoiseAmp", NoiseAmp );
Ovals.SetUniform( "NoiseFreq", NoiseFreq );
Ovals.SetUniform( "uTol", Tol );
Ovals.SetAttribute( "aVertex", VB, GL_VERTEX_ARRAY );
Ovals.SetAttribute( "aColor",  VB, GL_COLOR_ARRAY );
Ovals.SetAttribute( "aNormal", VB, GL_NORMAL_ARRAY );

VB.Draw( );
```

Listing 2.6. GLSLProgram class application example.

2.5.3 Implementation Notes

The `SetAttribute( )` and `SetUniform( )` methods use the C++ STL *map* function to relate variable names to variable locations in the shader program symbol table. It only ever really looks them up once.

2.6   Conclusion

From a teaching perspective, the simplicity of explanation and the speed to develop an application have long been advantages of using OpenGL in its fixed-function, predeprecation state. Students of OpenGL do need to learn how to use OpenGL in the postdeprecation world. However, they don't need to learn it right from the start.

This chapter has presented a way of starting students out in a way that is easier for them to learn but that still uses the recommended methods underneath. As they get comfortable with graphics programming, the "underneath" can be revealed to them. This sets the students up for using shaders and VBOs.

This chapter has also suggested a shader-variable naming convention. As shaders become more complex, and as more variables are being passed between the shaders, we have found that this is useful to keep shader-variable names untangled from each other. This naming convention, along with the gstap.h file, sets students up for passing their own quantities into their shaders.

Bibliography

[Angel 11] Edward Angel and Dave Shreiner, *Interactive Computer Graphics: A Top-down Approach with OpenGL,* 6th edition, Reading, MA: Addison-Wesley, 2011.

[Bailey 11] Mike Bailey and Steve Cunningham, *Computer Graphics Shaders: Theory and Practice,* Second Edition, Natick, MA: A K Peters, 2011.

[GLM 11] GLM. "OpenGL Mathematics." http://glm.g-truc.net/, 2011.

[Munshi 08] Aaftab Munshi, Dan Ginsburg, and Dave Shreiner, *OpenGL ES 2.0,* Reading, MA: Addison-Wesley, 2008.

[Rost 09] Randi Rost, Bill Licea-Kane, Dan Ginsburg, John Kessenich, Barthold Lichtenbelt, Hugh Malan, and Mike Weiblen, *OpenGL Shading Language,* 3rd edition. Reading, MA: Addison-Wesley, 2009.

[Shreiner 09] Dave Shreiner, *OpenGL 3.0 Programming Guide,* 7th edition. Reading, MA: Addison-Wesley, 2009.

WebGL for OpenGL Developers   3

Patrick Cozzi and Scott Hunter

3.1 Introduction

Don't get us wrong—we are C++ developers at heart. We've battled triple-pointers, partial template specialization, and vtable layouts under multiple inheritance. Yet, through a strange series of events, we are now full-time JavaScript developers. This is our story.

At the SIGGRAPH 2009 OpenGL BOF, we first heard about WebGL, an upcoming web standard for a graphics API based on OpenGL ES 2.0 available to JavaScript through the HTML5 canvas element, basically OpenGL for JavaScript. We had mixed feelings. On the one hand, WebGL brought the promise of developing zero-footprint, cross-platform, cross-device, hardware-accelerated 3D applications. On the other, it requires us to develop in JavaScript. Could we do large-scale software development in JavaScript? Could we write high-performance graphics code in JavaScript?

After nearly a year of development resulting in over 50,000 lines of JavaScript and WebGL code, we have answered our own questions: properly written JavaScript scales well, and WebGL is a very capable API with tremendous momentum. This chapter shares our experience moving from developing with C++ and OpenGL for the desktop to developing with JavaScript and WebGL for the web. We focus on the unique aspects of moving OpenGL to the web, not on porting OpenGL code to OpenGL ES.

3.2   The Benefits of WebGL

Loosely speaking, WebGL brings OpenGL ES 2.0 to JavaScript and, therefore, to the web. From a web developer's point of view, this is a natural progression for web-deliverable media types: first there was text, then images, then video, and now interactive 3D. From an OpenGL developer's point of view (our point of view), we have a new way to deliver applications: the web. Compared to traditional desktop applications, the web has several advantages.

3.2.1   Zero-Footprint

Plugins aside, browsing to a web page does not require an install, nor does it require the user to have administrator privileges. Users simply browse to a URL and expect their content. As application developers, having such a low barrier to entry enables us to reach the widest possible market. In our work at Analytical Graphics, Inc. (AGI), many of our users do not have administrator privileges and have to go through long processes to have new software installed. WebGL helps us overcome these barriers.

3.2.2   Cross-Platform

The web provides a convenient way to reach all the major desktop operating systems: Windows, Linux, and OS X. In fact, part of our motivation for using WebGL at AGI was to support multiple platforms. We have found very few differences across plat-forms, with the biggest difference being the presence of ANGLE on Windows, which translates WebGL (OpenGL ES 2.0) to Direct3D 9, as discussed in Chapter 39.

As of this writing, which comes less than a year after the release of the WebGL 1.0 specification, desktop browsers supporting WebGL include Chrome, Firefox, Safari, and the Opera 12 alpha. Internet Explorer (IE) does not support WebGL; however, several workarounds exist, with our preferred option being Google Chrome Frame.[1] Chrome Frame is an IE plugin that does not require administrator privileges to install and that brings Chrome's JavaScript engine and open web technologies, including WebGL, to IE. IE's networking layer is still used, but pages that include a meta tag requesting Chrome Frame are presented using Chrome Frame and are able to use WebGL.

Even with multiple developers actively working in the same code base using dif-ferent operating systems and browsers, we have found very few differences across browsers, especially Chrome and Firefox.

3.2.3   Cross-Device

Another advantage of WebGL is that web browsers supporting WebGL are start-ing to become available on tablets and phones. See Figure 3.1. Currently, Firefox

---

[1] developers.google.com/chrome/chrome-frame/

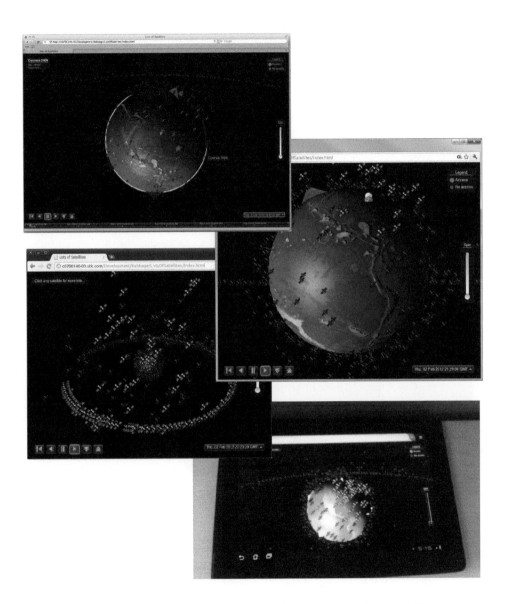

Figure 3.1. From top to bottom, WebGL running in Safari on OS X, in Chrome on Windows, in Chromium on Linux, and in Firefox Mobile on Android. Over 800 satellites are propagated server-side, streamed, and interpolated client-side and rendered as billboards. The globe is rendering with day and night textures; a specular map; a bump map; and a cloud map with shadows.

Mobile supports WebGL on Android; wide support for the stock browser is expected soon. Given that Sony recently released their WebGL implementation in the Android 4 browser for their Xperia phones as open source [Edenbrandt 12], we expect Android support to continue to improve. On iOS, WebGL is officially available to iAd developers.

As mobile platforms mature, WebGL developers will be able to write code that targets both desktops and mobile devices. However, some areas will still need special consideration. For example, code to handle mouse and keyboard events on the desktop will be different than code to handle touch events on mobile. Likewise, desktop and mobile versions may use different shaders and textures and perhaps different optimizations, as discussed in Chapter 24. Although web apps currently do not deliver the same experience as native apps on mobile, they are becoming very close with recent HTML5 standards such as geolocation, device orientation, and acceleration [Mahemoff 11, Meier and Mahemoff 11].

Supporting multiple platforms and devices can be done with more traditional means, as discussed in Chapter 44, but we feel that JavaScript and WebGL is the most straightforward way to do so. See Chapter 4 for more on using WebGL with mobile.

3.2.4 It's Easy

For OpenGL developers, WebGL is easy. Listing 3.1 is a JavaScript/WebGL port of the C++/OpenGL code in Listing 1.2 that draws a white rectangle on a black background using clip coordinates. A WebGL context is created by requesting a WebGL context from an HTML canvas element. Positions for two triangles are stored in an array, which is then copied to an array buffer using a familiar call to `bufferData`. All WebGL calls are part of the context object and are not global functions as in OpenGL. A shader program is created using a helper function that is not part of WebGL, but uses the familiar sequence of calls to `createShader`, `shaderSource`, `compileShader`, `attachShader`, `createProgram`, and `linkProgram`. Finally, the position vertex attribute is defined and the screen is cleared, before entering the draw loop.

The `draw` function executes once to draw the scene. The call to `window.``requestAnimFrame` at the end of the function requests that the browser call `draw` again when it thinks the next frame should be drawn. This creates a draw loop controlled by the browser, which allows the browser to perform optimizations such as not animating hidden tabs [Irish 11].

For OpenGL developers, the challenge of moving to WebGL is not in learning WebGL itself. It is in moving to the web in general and developing in JavaScript, as explained in Section 3.5.

```
var canvas = document.getElementById("canvas");
var context = canvas.getContext("webgl") || canvas.getContext("experimental-webgl");

var points = new Float32Array([
  -0.5, -0.5,   0.5, -0.5,
   0.5,  0.5,   0.5,  0.5,
  -0.5,  0.5,  -0.5, -0.5
]);

var buffer = context.createBuffer();
context.bindBuffer(context.ARRAY_BUFFER, buffer);
context.bufferData(context.ARRAY_BUFFER, points, context.STATIC_DRAW);

var vs = "attribute vec4 vPosition;" +
  "void main(void) { gl_Position = vPosition; }";
var fs = "void main(void) { gl_FragColor = vec4(1.0); }";
var program = createProgram(context, vs, fs, message);  // Helper; not part of WebGL
context.useProgram(program);

var loc = context.getAttribLocation(program, "vPosition");
context.enableVertexAttribArray(loc);
context.vertexAttribPointer(loc, 2, context.FLOAT, false, 0, 0);

context.clearColor(0.0, 0.0, 0.0, 1.0);

function draw() {
  context.clear(context.COLOR_BUFFER_BIT);
  context.drawArrays(context.TRIANGLES, 0, 6);
  window.requestAnimFrame(animate);
}
draw();
```

Listing 3.1. Hello WebGL. Drawing a white rectangle on a black background.

3.2.5   Strong Tool Support

When we first started investigating WebGL, we were not sure what kind of tool support to expect. Both Chrome and Firefox with Firebug have excellent JavaScript debuggers with the features we expect: breakpoints, variable watches, call stacks, etc. They also provide built-in tools for profiling. Currently, both browsers have six-week release cycles for stable, beta, and developer releases. For developers, this means we get new features and bug fixes quickly. Both browsers have public bug trackers that allow us to submit and follow requests.

For WebGL, the WebGL Inspector provides gDEBugger-like capabilities, such as stepping through draw call by draw call and viewing the contents and history of vertex buffers and textures. See Chapter 36 for more on WebGL profiling and tools.

3.2.6   Performance

As C++ developers, our gut reaction to JavaScript is that it is slow. Given the nature of the JavaScript language, with its loose type system, functional features, and garbage collection, we don't expect it to run as fast as our C++ code.

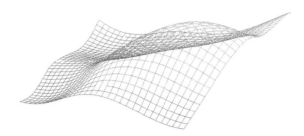

Figure 3.2. A 32 × 32 grid evenly spaced in the *xy* plane; each point's *z* component is determined by a 3D noise function given the *xy* position and the current time.

To get a feel for the performance difference, we ported the 3D simplex noise function discussed in Chapter 7 from GLSL to both C++ and JavaScript for use in a CPU-intensive application. We then wrote code that perturbs a 2D grid originally in the *xy* plane over time. At each time step, the *z* component for each grid point is computed as `z = snoise(x, y, time)` on the CPU. To render a wireframe like that shown in Figure 3.2, we use trivial shaders, store *x* and *y* in a static vertex buffer, and stream *z* into a separate vertex buffer every frame with `glBufferSubData`. See Chapter 28 for additional ways to improve streaming performance.

Given that each noise function call involves a fair amount of computation, this test simulates a CPU-intensive application that is constantly streaming vertex data to the GPU—a common use case in our work at AGI, where we simulate and visualize dynamic objects like satellites and aircrafts. Table 3.1 shows the results in milliseconds per frame for various grid sizes for C++ and JavaScript. The C++ version is a default release build using Visual C++ 2010 Express and GLM with SIMD optimizations. The test laptop has an Intel Core 2 Duo at 2.13 GHz with an NVIDIA GeForce 260M with driver version 285.62.

As grid size increases, all implementations slow down. For all grid sizes, C++ is much faster than JavaScript. Given that this is a CPU-intensive application, we expect C++ to be faster. JavaScript supports only double-precision floating-point, not single-precision; this plays a role since the noise function uses `float` in C++ and is not able to do so in JavaScript.[2]

Mesh resolution	32 × 32	64 × 64	128 × 128
C++	1.9 ms	6.25 ms	58.82 ms
JavaScript—Chrome 18	27.77 ms	111.11 ms	454.54 ms
Relative slowdown	14.62	17.78	7.73

Table 3.1. C++ vs. JavaScript performance for our CPU-intensive example.

---

[2]However, in JavaScript, the noise function's return value is put into a `Float32Array` for streaming to WebGL.

Mesh resolution	32×32	64×64	128×128
C++	3.33 ms	9.43 ms	37.03 ms
JavaScript—Chrome 18	12.82 ms	22.72 ms	41.66 ms
Relative slowdown	3.85	2.41	1.13

Table 3.2. C++ vs. JavaScript performance for our GPU-intensive example. The mesh is drawn 256 times per frame.

Seeing JavaScript take 7.73–17.78 times longer than C++ is initially disheartening. However, let's consider performance for a GPU-intensive application. To do so, we no longer execute the noise function on the CPU, nor do we stream a vertex buffer for the z components. Instead, we call the original GLSL noise function from the vertex shader as shown in Listing 3.2 and simply draw a static mesh. To increase the GPU workload, we draw the mesh 256 times per frame with sequential calls to `glDrawElements`.

The GPU-intensive performance numbers, shown in Table 3.2, are more favorable for WebGL. In the most GPU-intense case where a 128×128 mesh is drawn 256 times per frame, JavaScript in Chrome takes only 1.13 times longer than C++. Of course, we should expect such performance; the heavy computation is offloaded to the GPU, and JavaScript is no longer the bottleneck.

The CPU- and GPU-intensive examples are not the norm for most applications, but they illustrate an important point: to maximize WebGL performance, we must utilize the GPU as much as possible. Tavares applies this principle to render 40,000 dynamic objects at 30–40 fps in WebGL [Tavares 11].

Besides pushing work onto the GPU, we can offload JavaScript by pushing other work to the server. At AGI, we use numerically intense algorithms to simulate the dynamics of satellites and other objects. We perform these computations server-side and periodically transfer keyframes, which are interpolated client-side. Balancing the

```
attribute vec2 position;

uniform float u_time;
uniform mat4 u_modelViewPerspective;

varying vec3 v_color;

float snoise(vec3 v) { /* ... */ }

void main(void)
{
    float height = snoise(vec3(position.x, position.y, u_time));
    gl_Position = u_modelViewPerspective * vec4(vec3(position, height), 1.0);
    v_color = mix(vec3(1.0, 0.2, 0.0), vec3(0.0, 0.8, 1.0), (height + 1.0) * 0.5);
}
```

Listing 3.2. Vertex shader used for the GPU-intensive example.

amount of work done on the client and the server and the amount of data transfered requires care. Chapter 30 discusses efficient techniques for transferring models.

Heavy client-side computation can also be moved off the rendering thread using web workers and transferable objects [Bidelman 11].

We don't argue that JavaScript and WebGL will perform better than C++ and OpenGL; however, given that raw JavaScript performance continues to improve and that WebGL, server-side computation, and web workers allow us to minimize the JavaScript bottleneck, we feel that lack of performance is not a reason to dismiss WebGL.

3.3   Security

When moving from OpenGL to WebGL, a new topic familiar to web developers but perhaps unfamiliar to desktop developers emerges: security. OpenGL allows undefined values in certain areas. For example, reading outside of the framebuffer using `glReadPixels` is undefined, as are the contents of a buffer created by `glBufferData` with a `NULL` data pointer. Uninitialized and undefined values can lead to security holes, so WebGL defines values for cases like theses; `readPixels` returns an RGBA of $[0, 0, 0, 0]$ for pixels outside of the framebuffer, and `bufferData` initializes the contents to zero if no data are provided. These API changes usually do not affect us as developers. However, other security considerations do.

3.3.1   Cross-Origin Requests

In OpenGL, image data provided to a texture with, for example, `glTexImage2D` or `glTexSubImage2D`, can come from anywhere. Image data may be procedurally generated in code, read from a file, or received from a server. In WebGL, if the image comes from a server, it must be from the same domain that sent the web page. For example, a WebGL page hosted at myDomain.com cannot download images from anotherDomain.com, and this results in an `SECURITY_ERR` exception, as shown in Figure 3.3. This restriction is in place to prevent sites from using a user's browser as a proxy to access images that are meant to be private or are behind a firewall. However, accessing image data from another site is actually a common use case. Consider all the sites that embed Google Maps; the images for map tiles come from Google servers, regardless of the server hosting the web page embedding the map.

There are two ways to work around this restriction. The first is the use of crossorigin resource sharing (CORS). A server enables CORS by explicitly allowing it in its HTTP response headers.[3] Many servers, such as Google Maps, are starting to provide images intended for public access this way. As shown in Figure 3.4, in JavaScript, the image is requested using CORS with the line `img.crossOrigin`

---

[3]Setting this up on the server is straightforward; see enable-cors.org.

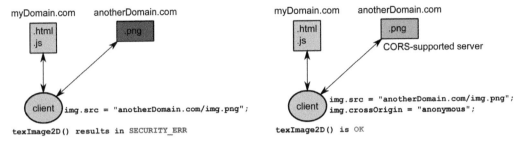

Figure 3.3. Attempting to create a texture from an image from another domain without CORS or a proxy.

Figure 3.4. Creating a texture from an image from another domain using CORS.

= "anonymous";. We expect that servers of public image data will enable these headers over time.

If a server does not support CORS, the image request can be made through a proxy server hosted on the web page's domain, as shown in Figure 3.5. Instead of sending the image request directly to anotherDomain.com, the image url is sent as an HTTP argument to a proxy server hosted on myDomain.com, which then requests the image from anotherDomain.com and sends it back to the client. The image can be used to create a texture because, from the client's perspective, it comes from the same domain.

Set up a proxy server with care. Do not let it forward arbitrary requests, which would open up a security hole. Also, some services require a direct browser connection and, therefore, do not work with proxies.

Cross-origin restrictions can also prevent local file access for images used as textures. Instead of testing html files using the filesystem, they should be hosted by a local web server. When testing on Linux and Mac, this can be as simple as

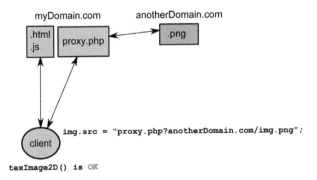

Figure 3.5. Creating a texture from an image from another domain by transferring it through a proxy.

running `python -m SimpleHTTPServer` in the same directory as the index.html file, and then browsing to http://localhost:8000/. Alternatively, these restrictions can be relaxed by starting Chrome with the `--allow-file-access-from-files` command line argument or changing `security.fileuri.strict_origin_policy` to false in Firefox. This should be done for testing only.

Although we discuss cross-origin requests in the context of images, the same restrictions are also true of videos. For more information on CORS, see "Using CORS" [Hossain 11].

3.3.2   Context Loss

Windows Vista introduced a new driver model that reset the graphics driver if a draw call or other operation took too long, e.g., more than two seconds. This surprised the GPGPU community, whose draw calls intentionally took a long time due to expensive computations done in vertex and fragment shaders to execute general computations like physical simulations. In WebGL, a similar watchdog model is used to protect against denial of service attacks, where malicious scripts with complex shaders or large batches or both could cause a machine to become unresponsive.

When a long running operation is detected and the graphics driver is reset, all contexts, including innocent ones, are *lost*. Using the `GL_ARB_robustness` WebGL extension, the WebGL implementation is notified, which can warn the user that WebGL content might have caused the reset, and the user can decide if they want to continue. As WebGL developers, we need to be prepared to restore our context when it is lost due to a reset [Sherk 11], similarly to how Direct3D 9 developers handle a *lost device*, in which GPU resources are lost due to a user changing the window to or from full screen, a laptop's cover opening/closing, etc.

For more on WebGL security, see the Khronos Group's WebGL Security white paper [Khronos 11].

3.4   Deploying Shaders

JavaScript is served to clients via .js files. With WebGL, the source for vertex and fragment shaders also needs to be sent to clients. There are several options:

- Store the shader source as JavaScript strings, as done in Listing 3.1. Only a single HTTP request needs to be made to request the JavaScript and shaders. However, it is painful to author shaders as JavaScript strings.

- Store the shader source in an HTML `script` tag, as shown in Listing 3.3. In JavaScript, the text content of the script can be extracted [Vukićević 10]. Shaders can be shared among multiple HTML files by dynamically generating the page. This cleanly separates JavaScript and GLSL, and does not require additional HTTP requests for shaders. Although it is not as painful to author

```
<script id="fs" type="x-shader/x-fragment">
void main(void)
{
  gl_FragColor = vec4(1.0);
}
</script>
```

Listing 3.3. Storing a fragment shader in an HTML `script` tag.

a shader this way as compared to using JavaScript strings, it is not as productive as having separate files for each shader.

- Store each shader in a separate file, creating the best scenario for shader authoring. Shaders can be transferred to the client individually on an as-needed basis using `XMLHttpRequest` [Salga 11]. This has the downside of requiring an HTTP request per shader; however, this is unlikely to be significant compared to other HTTP requests for vertex and texture data.

At AGI, we use a hybrid: shaders are authored individually in separate files, but deployed as strings in a single JavaScript file. The build converts each GLSL file to a JavaScript string and concatenates the strings with the existing JavaScript code.

In addition to determining how to organize shaders, shader deployment in WebGL can also include minifying the GLSL code to reduce the amount of data transfered. Minification tools such as glsl-unit's GLSL compiler[4] and GLSL Minifier[5] perform a series of transforms that do not change the behavior of the code but reduce its size, such as removing white space, comments, and dead functions and renaming variables and functions. This makes the code less readable but is only done for deployment, not development.

Now that we've seen what WebGL has to offer and some of the differences from OpenGL, let's look at the biggest bridge to cross when moving from OpenGL to WebGL: JavaScript.

3.5   The JavaScript Language

In many ways, JavaScript is a very different language than other commonly used languages such as C++, Java, or C#. Despite the name, JavaScript is not related to Java; the names are similar for historical reasons. Attempting to write substantial programs in JavaScript without understanding their important differences from C-like languages can easily lead to confusing and frustrating results.

The core JavaScript language is standardized under the name ECMAScript, with Version 5.1 being the latest version at the time of writing. Confusingly, there are

---

[4]http://code.google.com/p/glsl-unit/wiki/UsingTheCompiler

[5]http://www.ctrl-alt-test.fr/?p=171

```
<!doctype html>
<html>
<head>
  <meta charset="utf-8">
  <script src="script.js" type="text/javascript">
  </script>
</head>
<body>
</body>
</html>
```

Listing 3.4. A skeleton HTML file.

also versions of JavaScript providing new language features that are only supported in Firefox. We only discuss ECMAScript features that work in all modern browsers.

Since JavaScript is primarily a browser-based programming language, we need a web browser to run programs. Unlike C++, there is no compilation step for JavaScript programs, so all that is necessary to execute JavaScript on a web page is to add a **script** tag to an HTML page for each JavaScript file we want to include. Listing 3.4 contains a simple HTML skeleton showing how to include a JavaScript file named script.js in the same directory as the HTML file.

JavaScript does not currently have a standard way to include files, except by adding script tags for each JavaScript file, which will execute sequentially in a single context. In Section 3.5.7, we discuss some techniques for code organization.

Because JavaScript has some unusual features that can easily cause mistakes, a tool named JSLint is available online[6] to analyze our source code to detect potential errors. Section 3.5.8 describes several common errors.

Despite similar syntax, expecting JavaScript to behave the same way as C++ can lead an unsuspecting developer into a number of traps. We will highlight some important ways in which JavaScript is unlike C++.

3.5.1   JavaScript Types

Unlike C++, there are very few built-in types in the JavaScript language:

Object. An unordered set of name-value pairs, called the properties of the object. Property names can be strings, or, as long as the name is a valid identifier, the quotes can be omitted. Property values can be of any type, including another object. Object literals are declared as a comma-separated list of colon-separated name-value pairs, surrounded by curly brackets:

```
{
  a : "value",
  "long property" : 1.2
}
```

---

[6]www.jslint.com

Number. A signed, double-precision 64-bit IEEE 754 floating-point number. There are no integer types or smaller types, though some bitwise operators treat their inputs as 32-bit signed integers. *NaN* is a special value meaning "not a number."

String. An immutable Unicode character sequence. There is no type representing a single character, and string literals are declared using matching pairs of either " or '.

null and undefined. These are both present in JavaScript. A variable or property's value is *undefined* before it has been assigned. *null* values can be explicitly assigned.

Boolean: true or false. In addition, any value can be treated as a boolean, commonly using the terms "truthy" and "falsy," with the following values being considered "falsy": false, 0, "", null, undefined, and NaN. All other values are considered "truthy."

JavaScript also provides several built-in kinds of objects, all of type `Object`, though they differ in how they are constructed and the properties present. Some of the more commonly used objects are

Array. A random-access sequence of values. Arrays are mutable, resizable, and can contain values of any type. Array literals are declared as a comma-separated list of items, surrounded by square brackets:

```
[1, "two", false]
```

Function. In JavaScript, all functions are also `Objects`. They are typically declared using the function keyword, and neither return types nor argument types are declared:

```
function foo(bar, baz) {
  return bar + baz;
}
```

There are also built-in **Date** and **RegExp** objects, and web browsers also provide additional kinds of objects to represent the structure of web pages and allow changes from JavaScript, called the document object model, or DOM. The standardization of the browser DOM is not as complete as ECMAScript, but modern generations of web browsers are very close.

3.5.2 Dynamic Typing

Unlike most compiled languages like C++, which are usually statically typed, JavaScript is a dynamically typed language, like many other scripting languages, such as Ruby, Perl, or PHP. In dynamically typed languages, variables are not declared to be of any particular type, but instead are always simply declared as `var`. One variable can hold values of different types over time, though this can become confusing to read. Similarly, arguments to functions do not have declared types. As a result, functions cannot be overloaded by argument type as in C++. A commonly used replacement technique in JavaScript libraries is to accept multiple kinds of data for a given argument, and interpret them differently, as a convenience to callers. For example, if a function accepts a web browser DOM object, it might also accept a string identifier, which is then looked up to find and use the corresponding DOM object.

Because there are very few distinct types—most values are of type `Object`, variables don't declare types, and properties can be added to objects after their construction—determining the type of an object can be difficult. As a result, most JavaScript programs rarely concern themselves with the types of values and simply expect that the values passed to functions have the right properties. A commonly used term for this approach is *duck typing* from a metaphor suggesting that "if it walks and talks like a duck, it must be a duck." For example, if a function takes a set of coordinates, it could be designed to accept an object with *x* and *y* properties, regardless of what kind of object it is.

3.5.3 Functional Scoping

Another important difference in JavaScript, as compared to C++, is that the scope of variables is only limited by function and not by any other kind of block, e.g., if or for blocks. For example, Listing 3.5 shows how a variable persists outside the block where it is declared.

A good mental model is to envision that all variables declared throughout a function are instead declared once at the top and nowhere else. We can write code this way to help avoid confusion, and JSLint has rules we can use to enforce this.

```
function f() {
  var x = 1;  // x will be declared throughout the function.

  if (x === 1) {
    var a = "a string";
    // a will also be declared throughout the function,
    // not just within this if block!
  }

  // a will also retain its value, after leaving the if block.
  while (a === "a string") {
    var a = 0;  // This still affects the same a! Redeclaring a
    // variable with "var" has no effect, but can be confusing.
  }
}
```

Listing 3.5. An example of scopes differing from blocks.

3.5.4 Functional Programming

Because JavaScript functions are first-class objects, functions can be stored in variables or property values, passed as arguments to other functions, and returned as results of functions. In this way, JavaScript functions are closer to C++ function objects (functors), or the new lambda functions in C++11. Listing 3.6 shows some ways we can make use of this.

When functions are declared in JavaScript, they can refer to variables declared outside the function itself, forming a *closure*. In Listing 3.6, the anonymous function returned by `logAndCall` refers to `func` and `name`, both declared outside the anonymous function, and can access their values at a later time, even after `logAndCall` itself has returned. Any variables can be closed over in this way simply by accessing them, so no special syntax is necessary.

```
// Functions can be declared using this syntax:
function f(a) {
  return a + 1;
}

// or this syntax.
var g = function(a) {
  return a + 1;
};

// Both produce a function that can be invoked the same way.
var x = f(1), y = g(1); // => x == y == 2

// Objects can contain functions as property values:
var obj = {
  v: "Some value",
  m: function(x, y) {
    return x + y;
  }
};

var result = obj.m(x, y); // => result == 4

// Functions can be passed and returned from functions:
function logAndCall(func, name) {
  return function() {
    // (assume log is defined elsewhere)
    log("calling function " + name);
    return func();
  }
}

var originalFunc = function() {
  return "some value";
};
var newFunc = logAndCall(originalFunc, "originalFunc");

var result2 = newFunc(); // => result2 == "some value",
// and log is called with "calling function originalFunc"
```

Listing 3.6. Examples of using functions as objects.

3.5.5   Prototypal Objects

JavaScript is an object-oriented language, but does not use classes for inheritance. Instead, every object has a *prototype* object, and if a particular requested property is not defined on an object, the prototype is checked next, then the prototype's prototype, and so on. The benefit is that data or functions can be declared on a prototype and shared by many object instances that share that same prototype.

The easiest mechanism for creating objects that share a prototype is the use of constructor functions. A constructor function is no different from any other function, except that it is invoked using the *new* keyword, which has the following effects:

1. A new object is created, with its prototype set to the `prototype` property of the constructor function itself.

2. The constructor function is executed with the `this` keyword set to the newly created object. This allows the constructor to set properties on the new object.

3. The new object is implicitly returned as the result of the constructor call.

Listing 3.7 provides an example of defining values on the prototype of a constructor function and using it to create an object.

```
// A constructor function. To distinguish them from other functions,
// by convention their names start with capital letters.
function Rectangle(width, height) {
  // 'this' will refer to the new instance being constructed.
  this.width = width;
  this.height = height;
}

// By declaring 'area' on the prototype, it will be available
// on any object constructed using the Rectangle constructor.
Rectangle.prototype.area = function() {
  return this.width * this.height;
}

var r = new Rectangle(10, 20);

// Accessing properties directly on the object:
var w = r.width; // => w == 10

// Accessing properties on the object's prototype:
var a = r.area(); // => a == 200
```

Listing 3.7. An example of object construction.

3.5.6   The this Keyword

In Listing 3.7, we made use of the `this` keyword inside the `area` function to access properties of the object. One confusing aspect of JavaScript is that the `this` keyword is bound when a function is called, not when it is defined. This is somewhat

```
var obj = {
  f: function (){
    return this;
  }
};

// When invoking a function normally, 'this' is set as expected.
obj.f() === obj; // => true

// Even though f points to the same function, invoking it directly
// results in a different value of 'this'.
var f = obj.f;
f() === obj; // => false

// Functions have a call function that allows you to explicitly
// provide a value for 'this'.
f.call(obj) === obj // => true
```

Listing 3.8. The this keyword depends on how a function is invoked.

analogous to problems in C++ when attempting to pass the address of a member function as a regular function pointer: the **this** reference is lost. In normal usage, as in Listing 3.7, **this** works as expected because **area** was invoked in the context of **r**. Listing 3.8 shows a different case where **this** behaves unexpectedly.

One common problematic situation with **this** is in creating callback functions, where we may not have control over how our callback function is invoked. In cases like this, it may be easier to avoid using **this**. Instead, we can use closures for

```
var obj = {
  x: 10,
  getX: function () {
    return this.x * 2;
  },
  createCallbackIncorrect: function () {
    // Here we use 'this' from a context where it may be incorrect.
    return function () {
      return this.getX();
    }
  },
  createCallbackClosure: function () {
    // By storing 'this' in a variable, we always use the right one.
    var that = this;
    return function () {
      return that.getX();
    }
  },
  createCallbackBind: function () {
    // 'bind' returns a function that always uses the right 'this'.
    return this.getX.bind(this);
  }
};
```

Listing 3.9. Two ways to preserve a value of this.

a similar effect by assigning `this` to a local variable at a point where we know it will be correct and referring to that local variable from inside our callback instead. Alternatively, ECMAScript 5 defines a `bind` function on all `Functions`, which returns an adapter function that executes the original function with a given `this` specified, similar to a combination of the `mem_fun` and `bind1st` functions from the STL functional library. Listing 3.9 shows these two approaches.

3.5.7 Code Organization

Unlike C++, JavaScript does not have namespaces, so all global variables and functions exist in the same context, across all scripts included in a web page. Because of this, it is best to minimize the number of global variables our code creates to avoid conflicts with our own code or third-party libraries. One technique is the use of *self-executing functions* to limit the scope of variables by default and create a single global variable containing all of our functions and constructors. Listing 3.10 shows how this works.

```
// This variable will be our only global variable.
var MyLib = {};

(function() {
  // This syntax declares, then immediately invokes, an anonymous
  // function. The parentheses surrounding the function are necessary
  // for syntactic reasons.

  var constantValue = 5; // This variable is local to this function.

  // So is this constructor function...
  function MyData(x) {
    this.x = x + constantValue;
  }

  // ...but we can 'export' it for use elsewhere.
  MyLib.MyData = MyData;
})();

// Elsewhere, perhaps in a later script file:

(function() {
  // This has the appearance of a function in a namespace, but is
  // merely accessing a property on our global container object.
  var d = new MyLib.MyData(10);
})();
```

Listing 3.10. An example of how to hide variables in self-executing functions.

3.5.8 Common Errors

Besides the larger differences already discussed, there are also several smaller differences that can lead to accidental errors.

In JavaScript, global variables can be declared at any time by simply assigning a value to each, usually as a result of accidentally forgetting a `var` keyword when trying to create a local variable. This can lead to confusing problems in entirely unrelated areas of the code. To help with this, ECMAScript 5 defines a *strict mode* which makes it an error to assign an undeclared variable and also fixes other, more esoteric parts of the language. To use strict mode, write `"use strict"`; at the top of a function to enable it for that function and any nested functions. This syntax was chosen because older browsers will simply ignore it. If we are using self-executing functions, described in Section 3.5.7, we can enable it for all the contained code at once.

Another confusing JavaScript language feature is the standard equality operators `==` and `!=`. Unfortunately, in JavaScript these operators will attempt to coerce the types of the values being compared, resulting in the string "1" being equal to the number 1 and white-space strings being equal to the number 0, for example. Since this is almost never desirable, we should use the noncoercing operators `===` and `!==` instead. We can use JSLint to detect any use of the coercing equality operators.

3.6 Resources

Although we miss developing in C++ and using the latest features of desktop OpenGL, we found that the benefits of JavaScript and WebGL make the transition well worth it. For getting up to speed with WebGL, the best resources are the "Learning WebGL blog," learningwebgl.com/blog/, and "WebGL Camp," www.webglcamp.com. For JavaScript, we recommend *JavaScript: The Good Parts* [Crockford 08], and for general modern web development, check out "HTML5 Rocks," www.html5rocks.com.

Bibliography

[Bidelman 11] Eric Bidelman. "Transferable Objects: Lightning Fast!" http://updates. html5rocks.com/2011/12/Transferable-Objects-Lightning-Fast, 2011.

[Crockford 08] Douglas Crockford. *JavaScript: The Good Parts*. San Jose, CA: Yahoo Press, 2008.

[Edenbrandt 12] Anders Edenbrandt. "WebGL Implementation for XPeria Phones Released as Open Source." http://developer.sonyericsson.com/wp/2012/01/25/ webgl-implementation-for-xperia-phones-released-as-open-source/, 2012.

[Hossain 11] Monsur Hossain. "Using CORS." http://www.html5rocks.com/en/tutorials/ cors/, 2011.

[Irish 11] Paul Irish. "RequestAnimationFrame for Smart Animating." http://paulirish.com/ 2011/requestanimationframe-for-smart-animating/, 2011.

[Khronos 11] Khronos. "WebGL Security White Paper." http://www.khronos.org/webgl/ security/, 2011.

[Mahemoff 11] Michael Mahemoff. "HTML5 vs. Native: The Mobile App Debate." http://www.html5rocks.com/en/mobile/nativedebate.html, 2011.

[Meier and Mahemoff 11] Reto Meier and Michael Mahemoff. "HTML5 versus Android: Apps or Web for Mobile Development?" *Google I/O 2011.*

[Salga 11] Andor Salga. "Defenestrating WebGL Shader Concatenation." http://asalga.wordpress.com/2011/06/23/defenestrating-webgl-shader-concatenation/, 2011.

[Sherk 11] Doug Sherk. "Context Loss: The Forgotten Scripts." *WebGL Camp 4.*

[Tavares 11] Gregg Tavares. "WebGL Techniques and Performance." *Google I/O 2011.*

[Vukićević 10] Vladimir Vukićević. "Loading Shaders from HTML Script Tags." http://learningwebgl.com/cookbook/index.php/Loading_shaders_from_HTML_script_tags, 2010.

Porting Mobile Apps to WebGL 4

Ashraf Samy Hegab

4.1 Introduction

WebGL provides direct graphics hardware acceleration hooks into web browsers, allowing for a richer application experience. This experience is now becoming comparable with native applications. However, the development environment for creating these new types of rich web apps using WebGL is different.

This chapter walks us through the aspects of porting a typical OpenGL mobile app from Android and iOS to the web, covering steps from setting up your GL context to drawing a textured button or handling the camera and controls to finally debugging and maintaining your application.

This chapter includes accompanying source code that demonstrates the concepts introduced in iOS, Android, Qt, and WebGL to help developers get up to speed on web development using WebGL.

4.2 OpenGL across Platforms

Mobile apps have exploded into the scene since the arrival of smartphones. The new app model introduced by Apple drove the development for interface and style, which meant a higher utilization of graphics hardware to power animations and graphics in mobile games and apps. In order for this model to successfully move over to the web, Microsoft lead the way in providing a hardware-accelerated HTML5 canvas component. Next to come was the standardization of a 3D hardware-accelerated API named WebGL, built as a standard component of a modern web browser. WebGL is based on the OpenGL ES spec and used in the context of a web browser and JavaScript. And now, with companies like Facebook and Google leading the way with web app stores, the app market on the web is projected to grow [Gartner 11b].

As application developers, the more platforms we can retail our app on, the more potential revenue we can earn. One way of architecting our app's user interface is to utilize the native drawing components provided per platform, which means Objective C's UIKit on iOS, Java's native Android views and Canvas for Android, and C# and Silverlight for Windows Phone 7. While our application will benefit from the platform's natural look and feel, most of the specific UI code will be required to be rewritten per platform. However, with the emergence of gamification [Gartner 11b], which suggests the use of game mechanics to provide for a more enticing user experience, the design trends of breaking a platform's standard UI for something more game-like is now practiced among newer mobile apps. This practice requires us to develop our UI using OpenGL ES in order to do more than what the native components offer and, as a design task, tone down the experience to respect the natural interface of the platform.

With web apps moving to WebGL and mobile apps moving to OpenGL ES, porting between them can be made much easier because they share a common API. But that's not the end of the story: as the implementation of WebGL becomes more robust and optimized, we see a future where the norm may be to develop our application completely for the web and deploy a native shell application that launches the native web view component directed to the web source as used in Phone-Gap [Adobe 11]. This further reduces the cost involved in porting.

4.3   Getting Started

This section covers how to go from drawing things on an iOS and Android NDK app to drawing things on a WebGL app. This requires us to initialize the OpenGL ES context, load basic shaders, initialize draw buffers, and finally draw.

4.3.1   Initializing an OpenGL ES context

iOS. In order to initialize OpenGL ES on iOS, we need to allocate and set an EAGLContext. To generate and bind render buffers, `CAEAGLLayer` is provided to allow us to allocate storage on native views (see Listing 4.1).

iOS typically sets the render buffer's size to the device's screen resolution. We can request different sizes by modifying the properties of the `EAGLLayer`:

```
// Set the back buffer to be twice the density in resolution.
glView.contentScaleFactor = 2.0f;
eaglLayer.contentsScale = 2.0;
```

```
EAGLContext *context = [[EAGLContextalloc] initWithAPI:kEAGLRenderingAPIOpenGLES2];
[EAGLContextsetCurrentContext:context];
glGenFramebuffers( 1, &frameBuffer );
glBindFramebuffer( GL_FRAMEBUFFER, frameBuffer );
glGenRenderbuffers( 1, &renderBuffer );
glBindRenderbuffer( GL_RENDERBUFFER, renderBuffer );
[context renderbufferStorage:GL_RENDERBUFFERfromDrawable:(CAEAGLLayer*)gView.layer];
glFramebufferRenderbuffer( GL_FRAMEBUFFER, GL_COLOR_ATTACHMENT0, GL_RENDERBUFFER, ←
    renderBuffer );
```

Listing 4.1. iOS OpenGL initialization.

Android NDK. Android provides a `GLSurfaceView` class to handle creating a
framebuffer and compositing it into the view system for us. This view requires us to
override the `GLSurfaceView.Renderer`'s provided `onDrawFrame`, `onSurface`
`Changed`, and `onSurfaceCreated` functions, which are called on a separate thread.

WebGL. WebGL's approach is much simpler. We create an HTML5 canvas object
either in JavaScript or in the HTML, then request a `webgl` context:

```
var canvas = document.createElement( 'canvas' );
document.body.appendChild( canvas );
var gl =canvas.getContext( 'webgl' ) || canvas.getContext( 'experimental-webgl' );
```

For WebGL, the size of the canvas determines the resolution of the back buffer.
The best practices recommend we specify a fixed `width` and `height` for the canvas
and instead modify the style properties `width` and `height` when resizing the context, as internally modifying the canvas size requires the back buffers to be recreated,
which can be slow when resizing the window:

```
// Keep the back buffer size as 720x480, but stretch it to be the browser window ←
    size
canvas.width         = 720;
canvas.height        = 480;
canvas.style.width   = document.body.clientWidth;
canvas.style.height  = document.body.clientHeight;
```

4.3.2 Loading Shaders

While creating a context is different for most platforms, loading shaders is an OpenGL
specified operation, so platform implementations follow the same convention.

In iOS and Android, we create a shader by calling `glCreateShader`, then
setting the source with `glShaderSource`, and finally compiling the shader with
`glCompileShader`. Using WebGL, we create a shader by calling the function of the
WebGL context `createShader`, then set the `shaderSource` to point to a string
of the shader we wish to load, before finally calling `compileShader`. The only

```
GLuint *shader = glCreateShader( GL_VERTEX_SHADER );
glShaderSource( *shader, 1, &source, NULL );
glCompileShader( *shader );
```

Listing 4.2. iOS/Android compiling shaders.

difference is that in OpenGL on iOS, we use C-style functions, and WebGL uses the WebGL context for function calls. See Listings 4.2 and 4.3.

```
var shader = gl.createShader( gl.VERTEX_SHADER );
gl.shaderSource( shader, source );
gl.compileShader( shader );
```

Listing 4.3. WebGL compiling shaders.

4.3.3 Drawing Vertices

Let's now compare drawing a basic square using client-side arrays in iOS to using vertex buffer objects (VBOs) in WebGL. In iOS or Android NDK, we can simply specify an array of floats and then pass it to the **VertexArributePointer** function (see Listing 4.4).

```
const float vertices[] = {
        start.x,      start.y,      start.z,      // Top left
        end.x,        start.y,      start.z,      // Top right
        start.x,      end.y,        end.z,        // Bottom left
        end.x,        end.y,        end.z,        // Bottom right
};
glVertexAttribPointer( ATTRIB_VERTEX, 3, GL_FLOAT, 0, 0, vertices );
glDrawArrays( GL_TRIANGLE_STRIP, 0, 4 ); // Draw the square
```

Listing 4.4. iOS/Android NDK drawing vertices.

In contrast, in WebGL we first create a vertex buffer object, bind it, copy in our data, and then proceed with rendering (see Listing 4.5).

Once we have our VBO, we can render by calling **vertexAttribPointer** and **drawArrays** just as in the example shown in Listing 4.4:

```
gl.vertexAttribPointer( shaderProgram.vertexPositionAttribute,
bufferObject.itemSize, gl.FLOAT, false, 0, 0 );
gl.drawArrays( gl.TRIANGLE_STRIP, 0, bufferObject.numItems );
```

The **Float32Array** object is an array of 32-bit floats. Regular arrays in JavaScript are dynamically typed; this provides flexibility from a coding standpoint at the cost of performance. Typed arrays that can't be resized and have their values converted to the array's storage type are an attempt [Alexander 11] to help the JavaScript virtual machine avoid unnecessary overhead.

```
varbufferObject = gl.createBuffer();
bufferObject.itemSize = 3;
var vertices = [
    start.x, start.y, start.z,      // Top left
    end.x,   start.y, start.z,      // Top right
    start.x, end.y,   end.z,        // Bottom left
    end.x,   end.y,   end.z,        // Bottom right
];
bufferObject.numItems = 4;
var data = new Float32Array( vertices );
gl.bindBuffer( gl.ELEMENT_ARRAY_BUFFER, bufferObject );
gl.bufferData( gl.ELEMENT_ARRAY_BUFFER, data, gl.STATIC_DRAW );
```

Listing 4.5. WebGL creating a VBO.

4.4 Loading Textures

Most apps need a way to draw textured squares to represent buttons. In this section, we compare the process of loading textures for such widgets.

Generally, mobile apps have their texture data packaged with the application. In order to load a texture, we must load in the raw binary data and unpack the data appropriately according to the encoded format.

4.4.1 Assigning a Texture

iOS and Android provide native texture loaders to load and unpack image data. We can always use other libraries to load any specific formats that aren't supported, but this will require more coding. Listing 4.6 shows the minimum necessary steps to get a square multiple-of-two PNG loaded on iOS, and Listing 4.7 shows an Android implementation. This operation is synchronous; if we want to avoid blocking, we have to manage creating a new thread ourselves.

```
CGDataProviderRefcgDataProviderRef = CGDataProviderCreateWithFilename( imageData );
CGImageRef image = CGImageCreateWithPNGDataProvider( cgDataProviderRef, NULL, false,↩
    kCGRenderingIntentDefault );
CGDataProviderRelease( cgDataProviderRef );
CFDataRef data = CGDataProviderCopyData( CGImageGetDataProvider( image ) );
GLubyte *pixels = (GLubyte*)CFDataGetBytePtr( data );
floatimageWidth = CGImageGetWidth( image );
floatimageHeight = CGImageGetHeight( image );
glGenTextures( 1, &glName );
glbindTexture( glName );
glTexImage2D( GL_TEXTURE_2D, 0, GL_RGBA, imageWidth, imageHeight, 0, format, ↩
    GL_UNSIGNED_BYTE, pixels );
```

Listing 4.6. iOS using CoreGraphics to load a texture.

```
Bitmap bitmap;
InputStream is = context.getResources().openRawResource( R.drawable.imageName );
try {
      bitmap = BitmapFactory.decodeStream( is );
      is.close();
} catch( Exception e ) {}
int[] glName = new int[];
gl.glGenTextures( 1, glName );
gl.glBindTexture( GL10.GL_TEXTURE_2D, glName[0] );
GLUtils.texImage2D( GL10.GL_TEXTURE_2D, 0, bitmap, 0 );
bitmap.recycle(); // Release the image data
```

Listing 4.7. Android using Bitmap to load a texture.

In WebGL, texture loading is almost as easy as specifying an `img` tag in HTML (see Listing 4.8). The main difference between OpenGL ES and WebGL is that instead of creating an ID using `glGenTextures`, in WebGL, we call `gl.create Texture()`, which returns a WebGLTexture object. This object is then supplied with a DOM image object, which handles supporting the loading and unpacking of all the native browser image formats. When the `image.onload` function is called, signaling that the image has been downloaded and loaded by the browser, we can hook in our call to `gl.TexImage2D` to bind the image data to the CanvasTexture.

```
var texture = gl.createTexture();
varimage = new Image();
image.onload = function() {
      gl.bindTexture( gl.TEXTURE_2D, texture );
      gl.texImage2D( gl.TEXTURE_2D, 0, gl.RGBA, gl.RGBA, gl.UNSIGNED_BYTE, image );
}
texture.src = src;        // URL of an image to download
```

Listing 4.8. WebGL loading in textures using DOM image objects.

4.4.2   Handling Asynchronous Loads

The big difference in loading textures between OpenGL ES and WebGL is porting over the logic of asynchronous texture loading. Sometimes, our application's loading may depend on the type and size of the texture being loaded. For example, if we're loading in a texture we would like to draw as a button, we might want to size the widget the same size as the texture. Because images load asynchronously in JavaScript, we don't know the image's width until it has been loaded. To get around this, we

```
var texture = loadTexture( src, function(image) {
      setSize( image.width, image.height );
} );
```

Listing 4.9. Using callbacks in JavaScipt.

can use callbacks. In Listing 4.9, we define a callback function that is passed to the `loadTexture` function.

In `loadTexture`, once the texture is loaded, the callback function is called, and the widget is sized appropriately:

```
function loadTexture(src, callback){
    var texture = gl.createTexture();
    var image = new Image();
    image.onload = function() {
        callback( image );
        gl.bindTexture( gl.TEXTURE_2D, texture );
        gl.texImage2D( gl.TEXTURE_2D, 0, gl.RGBA, gl.RGBA, gl.UNSIGNED_BYTE, ←
            tihs.image );
    }
    image.src = src;
    return texture;
}
```

4.5 Camera and Matrices

In order to set up the camera, we need to specify the size of the viewport. Doing so across platforms is the same, with the only difference being accessing the size of the back buffer. In OpenGL ES, the backbuffer size is known from when the buffer is bound:

```
glGetRenderbufferParameteriv( GL_RENDERBUFFER, GL_RENDERBUFFER_WIDTH, &←
    backBufferWidth );
glGetRenderbufferParameteriv( GL_RENDERBUFFER, GL_RENDERBUFFER_HEIGHT, &←
    backBufferHeight );
glViewport( 0, 0,backBufferWidth, backBufferHeight );
```

In WebGL, the width and height properties of the canvas object are used to scale how much of the view we're rendering to:

```
gl.viewport( 0, 0, canvas.width, canvas.height );
```

4.5.1 float vs. Float32Array

Previously, in Section 4.3.3, we introduced the **Float32Array** object in JavaScript, which is heavily used for efficient matrix implementations. In the sample code, we used an open source library called glMatrix,[1] which wraps the **Float32Array** object and provides matrix and vertex helper functions, to avoid having to port our C++ code.

---

[1] https://github.com/toji/gl-matrix

4.5.2   Passing a Matrix to a Shader

The final piece of the puzzle is passing a matrix, which uses `UniformMatrix4fv` on all platforms—with OpenGL ES:

```
GLUniformMatrix4fv( uniform, 1, GL_FALSE, pMatrix );
```

or with WebGL:

```
gl.uniformMatrix4fv( uniform, false, pMatrix );
```

4.6   Controls

Now comes the fun part: making what we're drawing react to touch and mouse inputs. To do so, we need to handle touch event callbacks, get the position of the touch, project the touch into the view, collide with objects along the path, and handle the collisions accordingly.

4.6.1   Getting Touch Events

```
-(void)touchesBegan:(NSSet*)touches withEvent:(UIEvent*)event {
    NSArray *touchesArray = [touches allObjects];
    for( uint i=0; i<[touchesArray count]; ++i ){
        UITouch *touch = [touchesArrayobjectAtIndex:i];
        CGPoint position = [touch locationInView:view];
    }
}
```

Listing 4.10. iOS demonstrating how to get the position of a touch.

In iOS, a `UIView` object that provides the `EAGLLayer` also provides `touches Began`, `touchesMoved`, `touchesEnded`, and `touchesCancelled` events, which provide the touches' position and state (see Listing 4.10).

```
public Boolean onTouchEvent(final MotionEvent event) {
    int action = event.getAction() &MotionEvent.ACTION_MASK;
    int index = ( event.getAction() &MotionEvent.ACTION_POINTER_INDEX_MASK ) >>↵
        MotionEvent.ACTION_POINTER_INDEX_SHIFT;
    intpointerId = event.getPointerId( index );
    float x = event.getX();
    float y = event.getY();
    return true;
}
```

Listing 4.11. Android demonstrating how to get the position and action of a touch.

```
canvas.addEventListener( 'touchstart', function(event) {
                    var touch = event.touches[0];
                    if( touch )
                    {
                            this.x = touch.clientX;
                            this.y = touch.clientY;
                    }
            }, false );
```

Listing 4.12. JavaScript demonstrating how to get the position of a touch.

In Android, we override the **onTouchEvent** function of an activity, which is the callback for all touch events (see Listing 4.11).

In WebGL, we can add event listeners to react to **touchstart**, **touchmove**, **touchend**, and **touchcancel** events as well as overriding the **onmouseup**, **onmousedown**, and **onmousemove** events (see Listing 4.12).

4.6.2   Using Touch Events with the Camera and Collision

In the **CCSceneAppUI** files in the example code, the **handleTilesTouch** function projects the control's position into 3D via the camera's project3D function. The resulting **projectionNear** and **projectionFar** vectors are then queried by the collision system in order to return an object that's colliding (see Listing 4.13).

```
CCSceneAppUI.prototype.handleTilesTouch = function(touch, touchAction){
    var camera = this.camera;
    if( camera.project3D( touch.x, touch.y ) ){
        var objects = this.objects;
        var length = objects.length;

        // Scan to see if we're blocked by a collision
        varhitPosition = vec3.create();
        varhitObject = this.basicLineCollisionCheck( objects, length, camera.↵
            projectionNear, camera.projectionFar, hitPosition, true );

        for( var i=0; i<length; ++i ){
            var tile = objects[i];
            if( tile.handleProjectedTouch( hitObject, hitPosition, touch, ↵
                touchAction ) == 2 )
            {
                return true;
            }
        }
    }
    return false;
}
```

Listing 4.13. JavaScript demonstrating how to detect touch collisions.

4.7 Other Considerations

Now that we can render buttons and control them, we are close to understanding how to port between mobile apps and WebGL apps. However, there are a few other things to consider while porting.

4.7.1 Animation

In order to animate the view, many mobile apps create another thread to run the 3D rendering loop. Android provides an encapsulated version of this with GLSurface-View; on iOS, we can hook into the applications run loop; however, it's always best to create another thread for the 3D rendering loop to avoid UI thread stalls.

For the web, there's a nifty function called **requestAnimationFrame**, which requests the browser to call our update function at the next best available time. This allows browsers to not call our update function when, say, the user is looking at a different tab and not our app. If we call this function continuously, we can create an upload loop for our animations:

```
function update(){
    window.requestAnimationFrame( Update );
    gEngine.updateEngine();
}
```

4.7.2 Inheritance

JavaScript uses prototypal inheritance instead of classical inheritance. This pattern can be counterintuitive when porting apps that are based off classical inheritance.

```
functioncopyPrototype(descendant, parent, parentName) {
    var aMatch = parent.toString().match( /\s*function (.*)\(/ );
    if( aMatch != null )
    {
        descendant.prototype[aMatch[1]] = parent;

    }
    // Make a copy all the functions in our parent
    for( var parentMethod in parent.prototype ) {
        if( parentName ){
            // Make a copy with our parent's name as a prefix to allow the
                child to override the parent's function
            var combined = parentName + '_' + parentMethod;
            descendant.prototype[combined] = parent.prototype[parentMethod];
        }
        descendant.prototype[parentMethod] = parent.prototype[parentMethod];
    }
};
```

Listing 4.14. JavaScript demonstrating inheritance through copying parent prototype.

Since JavaScript is a dynamic language, there are various ways to simulate classical inheritance; the way presented in the samples is by copying the parent object's function prototypes and renaming them with a prefix, allowing us to call the parent object's function implementation when overriding a function (see Listing 4.14).

Now, when declaring a "class" in JavaScript, we call the `copyPrototype` function to assign its parent:

```
function Parent() {}
Parent.prototype.doSomething = function() {
    alert( 'Hello Parent' );
}
function Child() {}
copyPrototype( Child, Parent, 'Parent' );
```

When overriding the parent's `doSomething` function, we have the option of calling the parent's implementation:

```
Child.prototype.doSomething = function() {
    this.Parent_doSomething();
    alert( 'Hello Child' );
}
```

4.8   Maintenance

Debugging a WebGL app is a fun experience. In the world of native apps, our debugger lives in the IDE, and our app runs on a device or in a simulator/emulator. In the world of web apps, the debugger lives in the web browser, and our app also runs in the web browser.

4.8.1   Debugging

Web browsers provide many tools for debugging JavaScript apps on desktop operating systems. In the native world, our application code is pretty much static. In JavaScript, we can continually chop and change our JavaScript code while our application is running. For Google Chrome, we can use the built-in JavaScript debugger; for Firefox, we can use the renowned Firebug[2] extension for debugging capabilities.

When debugging a WebGL app, it is wise to call `requestAnimationFrame` after the update and render functions, as calling it before will trigger another frame to be rendered even if the program has hit a breakpoint.

There are a few drawbacks. Firstly, as of this writing, the current generation of mobile web browsers do not support debugging. If we plan on deploying our WebGL app to a mobile device, we must prepare for lots of manual debug logging. Secondly, the debugger lives inside the web browser, and our app runs inside the web browser.

---

[2] getfirebug.com

In the case of a serious crash, our means to debug our application crashes along with our app.

4.8.2 Profiling

Profiling is supported as part of our debugger. In the console view, we generally find a profile tab, which allows us to profile certain portions of the app. Native mobile apps, in comparison, aren't as intuitive. iOS requires recompiling for profiling in another application; Android supports profiling Java code, but not NDK; but both solutions are very ad hoc, while profiling a web app is part of the web browser debugging package. Please refer to Chapter 36 for more on profiling.

4.8.3 Performance and Adoption

As of this writing, WebGL is increasingly being supported on mobile devices. Android's version of Firefox supports most of the WebGL spec; however, its performance is currently lacking compared to its desktop counterpart. This will be improved, but currently, to help alleviate these performance issues on mobile devices, lowering the resolution of the canvas and ensuring we batch draw calls is recommended.

Apple officially supports WebGL in their iAd framework for iOS. Currently, you can also enable WebGL on a UIWebViewby using the private API function `_setWebGLEnabled`, as explained by Nathan de Vries [Vries 11]; however, this should be used for experimentation only, as use of private APIs are forbidden by Apple's App Store. It is expected to be supported in the standard mobile Safari once the security and performance issues over WebGL have passed.

Microsoft has yet to support WebGL in their desktop browser, but it seems like only a matter of time until they have to because WebGL applications will soon go mainstream.

Given the current state of WebGL's maturity, if porting over an application, it's best to continue to maintain both a native and web port but move toward a data-driven scene management system if the application does not already do so.

4.9 Conclusion

As of this writing, there are still some features, such as gyroscope, compass, and camera integration, that the web doesn't support. There are still some features that are in flux, such as local storage, WebSQL, and WebSockets. But there are some features that are natural to the web apps, which native applications try to emulate with a more convoluted implementation, such as JSON/XML parsing, accessing, and caching web content.

Hopefully this chapter showed that porting apps from native mobile languages to the web isn't hard once we get our heads around the differences between the ecosystems. Google Web Toolkit already provides a Java to JavaScript cross compiler, and while there isn't an equivalently mainstream C++ to JavaScript cross compiler, porting basic parts of C++ to JavaScript is very possible, especially if we consider that most rendering implementations avoid the complexities of C++ and are data driven.

With porting, the next challenge of performances: efficiency. Of course, JavaScript is getting faster; however, language concepts such as Garbage Collection will limit the amount of memory consumption an application can utilize before the garbage collection cycle becomes too taxing. But it's not a dead end, as mobile platforms such as Android and Windows Phone 7 have proven that it is possible to utilize hardware acceleration in a garbage collected environment.

The web's promise of "write once, run everywhere" is powerful. As hardware becomes more standardized, it's very easy to imagine a future where WebGL and WebCL [Khronos 11] enable us to bypass the current in-vogue, closed ecosystems with performance-sensitive code where it is required. We already have the promise of Google's Native Client [Google 11], which allows native code to utilize OpenGL directly within a web browser. And with the emergence of cloud computing, the apps can already run in the cloud and stream the client a video of what's going on directly, as OnLive [OnLive 11], a cloud-based gaming service, does.

Whatever ends up being the case, it is a very exciting and emerging world. New standards are emerging that will challenge the status quo of the last ten years of application development.

For more tutorials on WebGL, we recommend Giles Thomas' "Learning WebGL" website [Thomas 11].

Bibliography

[Adobe 11] Adobe. "PhoneGap." Available at www.phonegap.com, October 31, 2011.

[Alexander 11] Ryan Alexander. "Using Float32Array Slower than var." github.com/empaempa/GLOW/issues/3, July 10, 2011.

[Gartner 11a] Gartner. "Gartner Says Companies Will Generate 50 Percent of Web Sales Via Their Social Presence and Mobile Applications by 2015." gartner.com/it/page.jsp?id=1826814, October 19, 2011.

[Gartner 11b] Gartner. "Gartner Predicts Over 70 Percent of Global 2000 Organisations Will Have at Least One Gamified Application by 2014." gartner.com/it/page.jsp?id=1844115, November 9, 2011.

[Google 11] Google. "nativeclient." code.google.com/p/nativeclient/, October 31, 2011.

[Khronos 11] Khronos. "WebCL." www.khronos.org/webcl/, October 31, 2011.

[OnLive 11] OnLive. "OnLive." www.onlive.com/, October 31, 2011.

[Thomas 11] Giles Thomas. "Learning WebGL." www.learningwebgl.com, October 31, 2011.

[Vries 11] Nathan de Vries. "Amazing Response to My iOS WebGL Hack." atnan.com/blog/2011/11/07/amazing-response-to-my-ios-webgl-hack/, November 7, 2011.

The GLSL Shader Interfaces 5

Christophe Riccio

5.1 Introduction

The shader system is a central module of a graphics engine, providing flexibility, performance, and reliability to an application. In this chapter we explore various aspects of the GLSL shader interfaces to improve its quality.

These interfaces are the elements of the language that expose buffers and textures within a shader stage. They allow communication between shader stages and between the application and the shader stages. This includes input interfaces, output interfaces, interface blocks, atomic counters, samplers, and image units [Kessenich 12].

On the *OpenGL Insights* website, www.openglinsights.com, code samples are provided to illustrate each section. A direct output from this chapter is a series of functions that can be directly used in any OpenGL program for detecting *silent errors*, errors that OpenGL doesn't catch by design, but eventually result in an unexpected rendering.

I target three main goals:

- Performance. Description of some effects of the shader interface on memory consumption, bandwidth, and reduction of the CPU overhead.

- Flexibility. Exploration of cases to ensure the reuse of a maximum number of objects.

- Reliability. Options in debug mode for detecting silent errors.

5.2   Variables and Blocks

5.2.1   User-Defined Variables and Blocks

The GLSL shader interfaces are the elements of the OpenGL API and GLSL that allow communication. On the application side, we can create various kinds of buffers and textures that are used in a shader pipeline. In GLSL, these resources need to be exposed through variables and blocks. It's the duty of the OpenGL programmer to make sure that the required resources are bound and that these resources are actually compatible with the variables and blocks that expose them. It is called *shader interface matching* [Leech 12].

A GLSL variable may be a scalar, a vector, a matrix, an array, a structure, or an opaque type according to which interface it is declared for. See Table 5.1.

	vertex input	varying	fragment output	uniform
scalar	yes	yes	yes	yes
vector	yes	yes	yes	yes
matrix	yes	yes	no	yes
array	yes	yes	ycs	yes
structure	no	yes	no	yes
opaque type	no	no	no	yes
block	no	yes	no	yes

Table 5.1. Elements of languages and interfaces where they can be used.

An opaque type is a type that abstracts and exposes an element of the GPU fixed functions. GLSL 4.20 has three different opaque types: samplers, images, and atomic counters.

Blocks (Listing 5.1) were introduced in OpenGL 3.1 and GLSL 1.40 to expose uniform buffers in shaders. With OpenGL 3.2 and the introduction of the geometry-shader stage, the use of blocks has been extended to varying variables in GLSL 1.50 to cope with a namespace issue, which *block-name* and *instance-name* solve.

Blocks are containers of variables, called block members, which can be anything but opaque types or blocks. A block looks like a structure at first, but it has at least two differences: a block can't be declared and defined at two different spots in the shader; a block decouples its name into two parts: the block name and the instance

```
[layout-qualifier] interface-qualifier block-name
{
  member-list
} [instance-name];
```

Listing 5.1. Block syntax.

```
[Vertex Shader Stage]
in vec4 AttribColor;
out vec4 VertColor;




[Geometry Shader Stage]
in vec4 VertColor;
out vec4 GeomColor;




[Fragment Shader Stage]
in vec4 GeomColor;
out vec4 FragColor;
```

```
[Vertex Shader Stage]
in vec4 Color;

out block{
   vec4 Color;
} Out;

[Geometry Shader Stage]
in block{
   vec4 Color;
} In;

out block{
   vec4 Color;
} Out;

[Fragment Shader Stage]
in block{
   vec4 Color;
} In;

out vec4 Color;
```

Listing 5.2. A trivial shading pipeline using variables. What if a program wants to add or remove the geometry shader stage in this pipeline? The variable names won't match.

Listing 5.3. A trivial shading pipeline using blocks. Blocks resolve the issue with Listing 5.2.

name. A block name is used to identify a block for a shader interface; the instance name is used to identify a block within a shader stage. Listings 5.2 and 5.3 present some differences between variables and blocks when used for the communication between stages.

Tips   – Use varying blocks instead of varying variables to simplify the naming convention.
        – Use varying blocks instead of varying variables to bring more flexibility to the rendering pipeline.

5.2.2   Built-in Variables and Blocks

GLSL exposes a large collection of constants for various limits defined by the specifications. Along with the user-defined variables and blocks, GLSL provides built-in variables and blocks to connect the programmable part of the rendering pipeline with the fixed-function part of the pipeline. As we stand with the OpenGL 4.2 core profile, only a few built-in variables remain useful; gl_PerVertex is the only one that requires our attention, as it might be required in the vertex, tessellation control, tessellation evaluation, and geometry shader stages (see Listing 5.4).

Built-in variables are assumed to be declared and don't have to be re-declared unless the application is using them within a separate program [Kilgard 12], in which case a built-in block is required.

```
out gl_PerVertex {
  vec4  gl_Position;
  float gl_PointSize;
  float gl_ClipDistance[];
};
```

Listing 5.4. Vertex shader built-in output block: gl_PointSize and gl_ClipDistance are optional.

5.3   Locations

5.3.1   Definitions

Location is an abstract representation of memory that reflects the vectorized nature of GLSL and a key OpenGL concept. Unfortunately, it isn't globally defined but sparsely applied all over the OpenGL or GLSL specifications. This concept is essential because it defines how different elements may or may not match, and it also defines the sizes that may be allocated or used.

As an example, any vertex array object can't be used with a vertex shader stage. The vertex array object must match the *vertex shader input interface*—the list of all the vertex shader stage input variables. For this matching to be successful, at least all the active input variables (see Section 5.3.2) need to be backed by an array buffer to expect a relevant result. Also, the maximum number of locations defines the maximum number of variables that may be declared by a vertex shader input interface.

We acknowledge three kinds of locations:

- Attribute locations. Communication between array buffers and vertex shader inputs.

- Varying locations. Communication of output and input variables used across shader stages.

- Fragment output variable locations. Communication of fragment shader outputs and the glDrawBuffers indirection table.

5.3.2   Counting Locations

It is essential for an OpenGL programmer to know how to count locations for three main reasons. First, the number of locations taken by a variable defines the size of a shader interface. Second, matching may rely on explicit locations, and third, there is no GLSL operator to count the number of locations for us. In practice, understanding this aspect allows us to write more advanced design and prevents GLSL compiler, linker, and silent errors, which may be time consuming to fix.

Attribute locations and fragment shader output locations are very similar, as they behave like indexes. One attribute location corresponds to one vertex array attribute; likewise, one fragment shader output location corresponds to one entry in the `glDrawBuffers` indirection table with the framebuffer attachments. A vertex array attribute and a framebuffer attachment can hold up to four components, which shows the vectorized nature of the locations.

Neither a single vertex array attribute nor a single framebuffer attachment can store a matrix or an array of vectors. However, vertex shader inputs and fragment shader outputs may be arrays, and vertex shader inputs can even be matrices. To make this possible, each element of an array is assigned its own locations. Similarly, matrices are considered as arrays of column vectors, which leads us to the interesting fact that a `mat2x4` requires two locations but a `mat4x2`—with the same number of components—requires four locations. This model for assigning locations to matrices and arrays also applies to varying and uniform locations.

Double-precision floating-point types, e.g., `dvec3`, `dmat4`, etc., are slightly more complex beasts. For attribute locations, they are indexes, like single-precision ones. A `dvec4` takes one location just like a `vec4`. However, double types are not allowed for fragment shader outputs, and varying variables may double the required number of locations. Because of GPU design constraints, instead of being an index, we can consider that a varying location is an abstract representation for the memory of a `vec4`. A GPU relies on a number of registers used as binding points to feed the pipeline with buffers and textures. However, to communicate between stages, a GPU relies on caches that are eventually limited in size. A `dvec4` takes twice the memory of a `vec4`; thus, it requires twice the number of locations. A double or a `dvec2` fits within the memory space of a `vec4`, so only one location is required for those. The specification explicitly says that the number of varying locations may be either one or two for `dvec3` and `dvec4`, depending on the implementation. Unfortunately, there is no convenient way to figure out the actual size, so an application needs to assume that it takes two locations to maximize portability, which will underutilize some hardware not bound by this limitation.

Some varying variables may be arrayed if the shader stage is accessing *multiple input primitives* or if it is generating *multiple output primitives*. This is the case for the tessellation control, tessellation evaluation, and geometry shader stages. Contrary to arrays, the number of locations is computed for a single primitive—a single element of an arrayed variable—as it is only a feature to expose fixed-function parts of the pipeline.

For locations and components to be consumed, a variable must be *active*, that is to say that the variable must contribute to the result of the shader execution; otherwise, the implementation will typically eliminate these variables at compile or link times. For the case of separated programs, `GL_ARB_separate_shader_objects`, all the input and output variables and blocks are considered active by the GLSL linker.

Table 5.2 summarizes this discussion by applying the rules we just discussed to examples.

Variable	Vertex attribute locations	Varying locations	Fragment output locations
vec4 v;	1	1	1
uvec3 v;	1	1	1
float s;	1	1	1
dvec2 v;	1	1	N/A
dvec4 v;	1	1 or 2	N/A
vec2 a[2];	2	2	2
uint a[3];	3	3	3
vec4 a[];	N/A	1	N/A
mat4x3 m;	4	4	4
dmat3x2 m;	3	3	N/A
dmat2x3 m;	2	2 or 4	N/A

struct S{
  vec3 A;
  float B;
  ivec2 C;
} s;
	N/A	3	N/A

struct S{
  mat3x4 A;
  double B[2];
  ivec2 C;
} a[3];
	N/A	18	N/A

Table 5.2. Examples of variable types and their count of locations.

Tips – An application may assume for portability that dvec3 and dvec4 each take two
locations, as there is no convenient way to know the actual requirement by a
specific implementation.

– Consider packing the components when locations are used as indexes (e.g., ivec4
instead of int [4]).

5.3.3 Location Limits

Locations are an abstraction of memory and because memory is limited, the number of locations is limited too. OpenGL defines various minimum maximums and provides queries for actual limits.

Since attribute locations should be considered like indices, both vertex array attributes and vertex shader input variables share the same limit given by GL_MAX_VERTEX_ATTRIBS. Both OpenGL 3.x and 4.x specifications require a minimum of 16 attribute locations. However, Direct3D 11 requires 32 attribute locations so that, in theory, GeForce GTX 400 series, Radeon HD 5000 series, and newer GPUs should support at least 32 attribute locations. In practice, a GeForce GTX 470 supports 16 attribute locations, and a Radeon HD 5850 supports 29 attribute locations.

Similarly, the number of fragment shader output variables is bound by the maximum number of draw buffers given by GL_MAX_DRAW_BUFFERS. This value must be at least 8, which matches the maximum number of framebuffer color attachments given by GL_MAX_COLOR_ATTACHMENTS. This is what GeForce GTX 470 and Radeon HD 5850 currently expose.

The limit for varying locations is relative to the number of components declared by a shader interface. A single location is used to identify a float, int, uint, [i|u]vec2, [i|u]vec3, and [i|u]vec4. However, a component is used to identify a single float, int, or uint. Hence, a vec4 takes four components. This definition implies that the number of varying locations isn't a constant; it depends on how many components we use per location. Because double-precision floating-point variables consume twice the internal storage of single-float variables, they consume twice the number of components as well.

OpenGL used to have the values GL_MAX_VARYING_COMPONENTS and GL_MAX_VARYING_VECTORS to query the number of component limits, but these are deprecated, so we ignore them here. Instead, OpenGL provides a dedicated value for each output and input interface (Table 5.3) of each shader stage.

Looking at this table, we notice that the OpenGL requirements don't necessarily make the most sense, but actual available implementations streamline these numbers.

If a shader interface exceeds these limits, the GLSL compiler will return an error. Following these results, an application may assume that an implementation supports a minimum of 32 varying locations for any shader stage. Unfortunately, the OpenGL 4.2 specification doesn't provide any feature to query either the number of varying locations consumed or a varying variable query API. This prevents any kind of application-side validation of the shader-varying interfaces and implies that if such feature is required by the application, then this management needs to be taken care of up front by the application, which would need to generate the shader interface's code.

Values	OpenGL 4.2 requirement	Radeon HD 5850	GeForce GTX 470
MAX_VERTEX_OUTPUT_COMPONENTS	64	128	128
MAX_TESS_CONTROL_INPUT_COMPONENTS	128	128	128
MAX_TESS_CONTROL_OUTPUT_COMPONENTS	128	128	128
MAX_TESS_EVALUATION_INPUT_COMPONENTS	128	128	128
MAX_TESS_EVALUATION_OUTPUT_COMPONENTS	128	128	128
MAX_GEOMETRY_INPUT_COMPONENTS	64	128	128
MAX_GEOMETRY_OUTPUT_COMPONENTS	128	128	128
MAX_FRAGMENT_INPUT_COMPONENTS	128	128	128

Table 5.3. Number of components requirement and actual support.

5.4   Matching Interfaces

For a successful rendering, a minimum requirement is to have interfaces that match. Each interface must provide the necessary information with an appropriate layout to the subsequent interface. If such conditions aren't fulfilled, then rendering is likely to result either with an OpenGL error or, worse, a silent error.

5.4.1   Partial and Full Match

OpenGL and GLSL support two types of interface matching: full matching and partial matching. A full match is a matching where each element on each side of the interface has a corresponding element on the other side of the interface (Figure 5.1). A partial match is a matching where at least all the elements on the subsequent interface have a matching element on the precedent interface (Figure 5.2). In some cases, built-in blocks or variables may not have corresponding blocks or variables because they are only present for the interaction with the fixed pipeline. For example, a pipeline with only a vertex and a fragment stage requires exposing the gl_Position in the vertex shader stage but doesn't allow declaring it in the fragment shader stage.

This definition applies on many levels:

- The vertex array object matching with the vertex shader input interface.

- Any shader stage with its subsequent shader stage.

- The fragment shader output interface with the draw buffers table.

- The draw buffers indirection table with the framebuffer color attachments.

- An uniform buffer range with its associated uniform block.

Choosing between a software design approach based on partial or full matching is actually making a choice between flexibility and performance: generating more inputs that we need may have an absolute performance cost but may also support a higher variety of combinations for the subsequent elements.

Regarding the performance issue, by making a difference between variables and active variables, the specification allows unused-variable elimination. Using linked programs, this optimization can even be extended to previous shader stages.

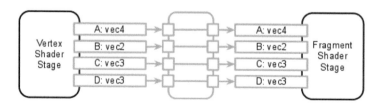

Figure 5.1. Full match.

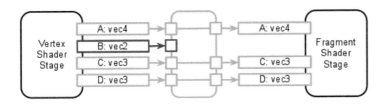

Figure 5.2. Partial match.

Figure 5.3 is when everything works perfectly, but some cases are more troubling like partial matching between the vertex array object and the vertex shader input interface. It's tricky for the implementation not to emit vertex array attributes that are not exposed in the vertex shader stage. Even if it might automatically disable unused vertex arrays, if vertex attributes are interleaved, the implementation might fetch unused data, consuming the bandwidth and polluting the cache due to the minimum memory burst size [Kime and Kaminski 08].

Tip – Be careful with partial matching, especially with the vertex array object when performance matters.

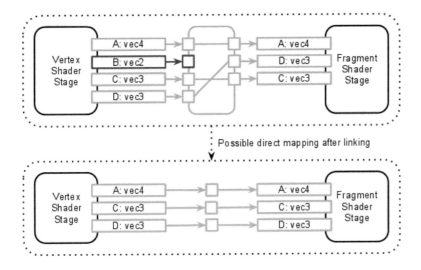

Figure 5.3. Linked program with partial matching. On top, resolve with an indirection table. On bottom with previous shader stage unused variables elimination and resolve with direct mapping.

5.4.2   Type Matching

From the very first GLSL specification release, the language provides some flexibility on the type matching. For two types to match, these types don't necessarily need to be the same. OpenGL requires a strict type matching between shader stages but not for assets connected to a program pipeline.

The matching between vertex array attributes and vertex shader input variables is very flexible due to the nature of attribute locations: They are vec4 based. Hence, even if some vector components are missing on any side of the interface, they will match, as illustrated in Figure 5.4. If the vertex shader input exposes more components that the vertex array attribute provides, the extra component will be filled with the default vector vec4(0, 0, 0, 1). Similarly, OpenGL is very flexible regarding the data types of the vertex array attributes, as traditionally all types are cast by the hardware to floating-point values when using glVertexAttribPointer. For example, if an array buffer stores RGB8 colors, the color will be exposed as a vec3 by the corresponding vertex shader input variable: the buffer actually stores unsigned byte data, but at vertex attribute fetching, the values are converted on the fly.

To escape from this flexibility, we can use glVertexAttribIPointer, which can only expose vertex arrays that store integers, GL_BYTE, GL_UNSIGNED_BYTE, GL_SHORT, GL_UNSIGNED_SHORT, GL_INT, and GL_UNSIGNED_INT, with integer-based vertex input variables. We can also use glVertexAttribLPointer for double-float storage (GL_DOUBLE), exposed as double-based shader input variables.

Double-based vectors are more restricted because a double-based vector may or may not take two varying locations. If the subsequent stage declares a dvec2 variable

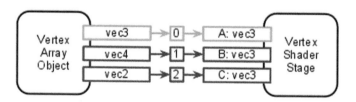

Figure 5.4. Example of vertex array attributes and vertex shader inputs based on float.

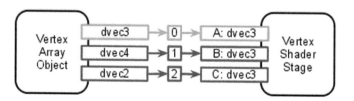

Figure 5.5. Example of vertex array attributes and vertex shader inputs based on double.

Vertex array attribute type	Vertex shader input type	Match?
3 x float	vec3	yes
4 x float	vec3	yes
2 x float	vec3	yes
2 x int	int	yes
2 x int	float	yes
2 x double	vec2	yes
2 x double	dvec2	yes
3 x double	dvec2	no
2 x float	ivec2	no
2 x float	dvec2	no

Table 5.4. Example of type-matching vertex input variable types and vertex array attribute types.

while the previous stage provides a dvec3, for example, then the two variables are not using the same number of locations. Thus, the interfaces can't possibly match. Consequently, OpenGL requires double variables to be exactly the same type either when assigning to attribute locations (Figure 5.5).

Table 5.4 gives a list of examples and indicates whether the vertex array attribute types and the vertex shader input types match or not.

NVIDIA also supports 64-bit integers through GL_NV_vertex_attrib_integer_64bit, in which case, GL_INT64_NV and GL_UNSIGNED_INT64_NV may also be used with glVertexAttribLPointer and exposed as int64_t, i64vec2, i64vec3, i64vec4, uint64_t, u64vec2, u64vec3, u64vec4 in the vertex shader input interface.

Tips – Avoid submitting more vertex attribute components than the shader interface will use.
      – OpenGL 4.2 doesn't provide an API to validate that double shader input has been submitted with glVertexAttribLPointer or not. This may lead to a silent error and is an OpenGL specification bug.

5.4.3   Matching by Name, Matching by Location

From the first version of GLSL, it has been possible to match varying variables by name: on both sides of the shader interface, the variables must match by name, type, and have compatible qualification. For vertex input variables and fragment output variables, matching with resources has always relied on locations.

With OpenGL 4.1 and the introduction of separate programs, matching by name is no longer able to resolve partial matches between shader stages because the GLSL linker doesn't necessarily know both sides of the shader interface anymore. Typically,

```
[Vertex Shader Stage]
in vec4 AttribColor;
out vec4 VertColor;

[Geometry Shader Stage]
in vec4 VertColor;
out vec4 GeomColor;

[Fragment Shader Stage]
in vec4 GeomColor;
out vec4 FragColor;
```

Listing 5.5. Matching-by-name declarations.

```
[Vertex Shader Stage]
layout (location = 0) in vec4 Color;
layout (location = 0) out vec4 VertColor;

[Geometry Shader Stage]
layout (location = 0) in vec4 Color;
layout (location = 0) out vec4 GeomColor;

[Fragment Shader Stage]
layout (location = 0) in vec4 Color;
layout (location = 0) out vec4 FragColor;
```

Listing 5.6. Matching-by-location declarations.

with separate programs, the implementation packs input and output active variables one after the other and expects to retrieve them the same way on the subsequent shader stage. If a variable is unused, all the following variables will be in a different memory location than the expected one.

The solution adopted was to introduce matching by location to varying variables (compare Listings 5.5 and 5.6). A variable is qualified with an explicit location and this location defines a position in memory. This is where the subsequent shader stage should expect to find the value of this variable, relieving the GLSL compiler of part of its duty that it can't perform anymore.

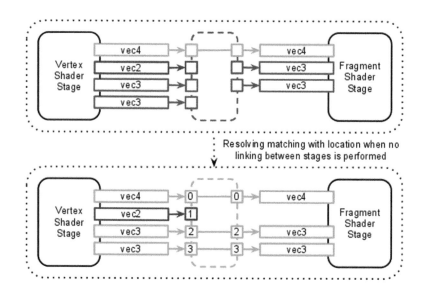

Figure 5.6. Resolution of partial matching on separate programs with matching by location.

Comparing Figure 5.6 with Figure 5.3, we notice that, by design, linked programs may generate more compact shader interfaces than separate programs. In practice, with the drivers of AMD Catalyst 11.12, this is a limitation that we encounter through an effective reduction in the number of components available, but this is not the case with NVIDIA Forceware 290.53, which lets us suppose that the drivers do an implicit linking between stages through the pipeline program object.

An apparent side effect of using matching by location is the freedom for naming variables, which doesn't have to be the same across shader stages; however, OpenGL provides something better with blocks.

5.4.4 Matching with Blocks

Blocks can't have locations, so the only possible matching is by block-name (Listing 5.7). Thus, when using separated programs with OpenGL, partial matching of block-based shader interfaces will result in a silent error.

```
block-qualifier block-name
{
  variable-qualifier type block-member;
} block-instance;
```

Listing 5.7. Block syntax.

An interface may contain both blocks and variables, in which case, partial matching is possible on the variables, but the blocks must fully match, as illustrated in Figure 5.7. This is actually a typical scenario of a partial matching interface.

Blocks allow the GLSL compiler to perfectly pack the components of the block members, leading to maximum use of the hardware capabilities.

Using blocks also guarantees that a vertex shader output will always have a possible matching tessellation or geometry shader input (compare the matching arrays in Listings 5.8 and 5.9). GLSL 4.20 only supports 1D arrays, but the corresponding

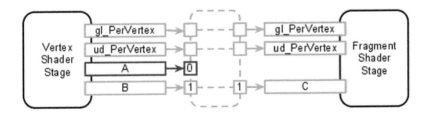

Figure 5.7. Typical scenario of partial matching with separated programs. A, B, C are variables with explicit location. gl_PerVertex the built-in block and ud_PerVertex a user-defined block.

```
[Vertex Shader Stage]
out gl_PerVertex {
  vec4 gl_Position;
};

out block {
  vec4 Color[2];
} Out;

[Geometry Shader Stage]
in gl_PerVertex{
  vec4 gl_Position;
} gl_in[];

in block {
  vec4 Color[2];
} In[];
```

```
[Vertex Shader Stage]
out vec4 gl_Position;
out vec4 Color[2]; // OK




[Geometry Shader Stage]
in vec4 gl_Position[];
in vec4 Color[][2]; // Error with GLSL 420!
```

Listing 5.8. Matching block member array.

Listing 5.9. Matching variable array, valid with GL_EXT_geometry_shader.

geometry shader input variable of a vertex shader output array variable is an arrayed array; in others words, a 2D array. A possible solution to this specification issue is to clearly state the difference between arrayed variables and arrays in the specification, but so far, an arrayed variable is simply an array.

With blocks, arrayed varying blocks are allowed, but varying block arrays are forbidden, allowing the programmer to avoid this issue by generating a GLSL compiler error instead of a possible silent error.

Tips   – Favor blocks rather than variables for program robustness in time.
   – Uniform blocks may be declared as arrays with each element backed by a different uniform buffer range.
   – Varying blocks can't be declared as arrays but can be arrayed to reflect fixed-function multiple input or output primitives.
   – Separate programs with partial match blocks is an undefined state in the OpenGL specification.

5.4.5   Matching with Structures

Blocks are great, and we should enjoy using them. However, due to the role of the block-name for the shader matching, this name must be uniquely used, and the declaration of the block must be done where the `block-instance` is defined. Structures don't share this language property, making them more attractive at first sight.

For many scenarios, we would like to reuse a maximum of programs to reduce the number of objects created and the number of state changes at program execution to reduce CPU overhead. To do this, we need to be sure that the subsequent shader stage will have the same shader interface. One solution is to declare a structure in a separated shader source and use this declaration in any shader we want to mix and match. Making this structure declaration unique and shared implies that any change is applied to any shaders using it. This will most likely generate a lot of GLSL compiler errors in all the noncompliant shaders with the updated structure. However, this provides direct input about where we should update the code instead of causing us to a lot of mismatches and silent errors later on, which are very difficult and time consuming to catch.

Unfortunately, using structures for varying variables shares the same drawbacks as using typical varying variables and magnifies the location counting issue. With a structure, each member takes a certain number of locations; adding or removing a member will eventually change the number of locations taken by this structure. If a scenario is using multiple structures for a shader interface and explicit locations for matching, then it becomes our responsibility to assign the locations to each structure and to make sure that they remain perfectly packed one after the other.

During development, we will add and remove from time to time members of our structures that would lead us to have to count again the number of locations

```
[Shared shader code]
struct vertex {
  vec4 Color;
  vec2 Texcoord;
};

[Vertex Shader Stage]
out gl_PerVertex {
  vec4 gl_Position;
};

out blockA {
  vertex Vertex;
} OutA;

out blockB {
  vertex Vertex;
} OutB;

[Geometry Shader Stage]
in gl_PerVertex{
  vec4 gl_Position;
} gl_in[];

in blockA {
  vertex Vertex;
} InA;

in blockB {
  vertex Vertex;
} InB;
```

Listing 5.10. Matching block member array.

```
[Shared shader code]
struct vertex {
  vec4 Color;
  vec2 Texcoord;
};

[Vertex Shader Stage]
out vec4 gl_Position;

layout(location = 0)
  out vec4 vertex OutA;

layout(location = ???)
  out vec4 vertex OutB;




[Geometry Shader Stage]
in vec4 gl_Position[];

layout(location = 0)
  in vec4 vertex InA[];

layout(location = ???)
  in vec4 vertex InB[];
```

Listing 5.11. Matching variable array. The ideal location for OutB and InB is dependent on the number of locations taken by the structure vertex. Here, and in Listing 5.10, this value is 2, the number we can use in the present case. However, in a classic development phase, the structure will evolve, which requires that we manually change the locations each time we update vertex.

taken by the structure and update the explicit locations of the others structures accordingly. This works, but it is not an effective way to code. Listings 5.10 and 5.11 illustrate that GLSL doesn't provide any operator to help us in counting the number of locations of a structure.

Tip   – Use structures...but only within blocks!

5.4.6   Linked and Separated Programs

From the beginning, GLSL has had a very different programming model than HLSL, Cg, or even the old assembly-like OpenGL programs [Brown 02, Lipchak 2002]. In those environments, each shader stage is independent This approach follows very well the way a graphics programmer designs his software, where, for example, the vertex program may define how objects are transformed and the fragment programs may define materials. Many objects can share the same transformation method (the same vertex shader) but have different fragment shaders. This strategy models how we can sort the objects for rendering to minimize shader stage changes and how we can batch multiple objects into a lower number of draw calls to maximize performance. We call it the *separate shader* program approach.

However, GLSL previously followed a different approach where all the shader stages were linked into a single program object. On a rendering pipeline composed of two shader stages, both vertex and fragment shader stage were bound at the same time. This approach has some performance advantages because the linker is able to perform cross-stage optimizations. For example, if a vertex output variable is never used by the fragment shader, then not only does the fragment shader discard it, but the vertex shader may not need to compute it either. Another even more important advantage is that the GLSL linker can detect errors of matching interface between stages. The OpenGL specification refers to this approach as linked programs or monolithic programs.

These two approaches raise a dilemma: software design flexibility and performance against compiler performance and error detection. Fortunately, with OpenGL 4.1 and GL_ARB_separate_program_objects, not only can we finally take advantage of separate programs, but OpenGL gives us the opportunity to take advantage of both linked programs and separate programs on a single *program pipeline object*, a container for all the shader program stages. For example, thanks to the program pipeline, an application may choose to link all the prerasterization shader stages together and keep the fragment shader stage separately.

An application may find it interesting to use both linked programs and separate programs to validate whether the shader interfaces match in debug and to take advantage of the flexibility of separate programs in release builds. In such a case, an application may consider always declaring the built-in blocks, as they are required for separate programs.

Tips   – Always declare built-in blocks to be able to switch between linked and separate programs.
        – In debug mode only, link all stages to get shader interface errors.
        – Always use program pipeline objects, which handle both linked and separate programs.

5.5 Working with Semantics

With OpenGL, a semantic is a software design concept that gives a meaning to a slot, associating a variable and a resource. For example, a semantic may guarantee for the code or a part of the code that a specific location will be used for the semantic "color." The vertex array that stores the color data will be bound to this attribute location, and the vertex shader will know that it can access this specific buffer with the variable using this dedicated location.

SAS [Bjork 08] was an attempt to define a common list of semantics. However, semantics are software-specific associations, so a set of them may only be valid for a single application or only a subset of its code if we don't want to waste resources.

5.5.1 Varying Compiler-Generated Locations and Explicit Locations

GLSL typically provides two methods to allocate locations. Either the GLSL compiler does it, or the OpenGL programmer does it.

When the GLSL compiler generates locations, there is no specification rule that lets us know what locations are reserved for a specific variable. Consequently, these locations need to be queried on the application side, which requires us to deal with building an association between the variable and the resource.

Alternatively, the application can manually assign the locations, in which case, we can use the "semantic" scheme and always assume that the resources are where we expect to find them. This second approach can provide significantly better performance because, thanks to sorting and semantics, an application can reuse bound objects, reducing the overall number of bindings [Collins 11].

5.5.2 Vertex Array Attributes and Vertex Shader Inputs

The location of a vertex input can either be generated by the implementation, or we can assign it with either `glBindAttribLocation` (OpenGL 2.0) or the location layout qualifier (OpenGL 3.3).

When we let the compiler set the attribute locations to the vertex input variables, we must query these values using `glGetAttribLocation` and use these values to assign a vertex array attribute to the corresponding vertex input variable. In most cases, this approach defeats the strength of OpenGL because it results in a

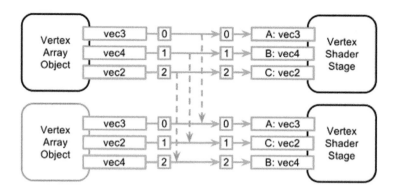

Figure 5.8. With implicit attribute locations, each vertex program requires a dedicated vertex array object.

dependency between the vertex arrays and the GLSL programs. This choice introduces software design complexity but also a performance hit due to the necessity to duplicate similar programs and similar vertex array objects. This forces us to bind a vertex array object each time we bind a new program object and vice versa.

When the GLSL compiler assigns attribute locations, even if two programs share the same vertex input variables, the interfaces may be different. An example of this is different orders of declarations (Figures 5.8 and 5.9).

In practice, some GLSL compilers always order the variable locations the same way, a fact we may think we can rely on, but we can't. Different implementations or newer drivers may generate different orders.

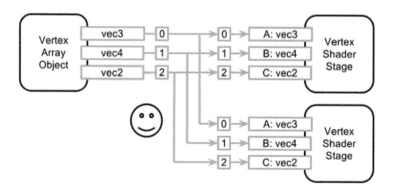

Figure 5.9. With explicit attribute locations, a vertex array object is shared by multiple vertex programs and vice versa.

From an application-design point of view, `glBindAttribLocation` may be used to set the default attribute location to a vertex input variable, and the layout location qualifier may be used to overload these default values. An issue with user-defined location is that the application may potentially set attribute locations that are already used by another variable, generating a link error.

OpenGL vertex array attributes are typically specified with the command `glVertexArrayAttrib*Pointer`. These commands define the vertex format, the vertex binding, and the vertex array buffers in a per-attribute fashion. Since the OpenGL 3.2 core profile, applications require the use of a vertex array object as a container of the vertex array attributes.

Working with semantics implies that within a certain frame (e.g., a rendering pass, an effect, or the entire software), a vertex input can assume that the buffer range that backed it contains the semantically expected data. Positions, colors, texture coordinates, normals, tangents are all classic examples of semantics associated with attribute locations.

Tip   – Do not let the compiler automatically generate vertex input locations.

5.5.3 Fragment Shader Outputs and Framebuffer Color Attachments

We might expect that the fragment shader output interface works with framebuffer color attachments in a similar way to the way the vertex shader input interface works with the vertex array attributes, but there are major differences. The fragment shader output locations don't refer to framebuffer color attachments but to an indirection table exposed by `glDrawBuffers`. This table is not a framebuffer state, but it requires that a framebuffer object is bound (see Figure 5.10).

Each output has a location that should be considered an index in the indirection table.   Using `glDrawBuffers`, we control this table to specify which

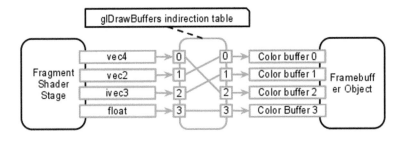

Figure 5.10. Example of fragment shader output variables and framebuffer attachments matching.

fragment output is going to feed which colorbuffer. In practice, we will typically assign a location corresponding directly to the framebuffer attachment number so that the `glDrawBuffers` table only does a direct mapping. This is so typical that OpenGL ES 2 doesn't support this table.

A fragment shader output that isn't backed by a framebuffer attachment will be silently ignored, but a framebuffer attachment that isn't fed by a fragment output will have undefined values. A workaround for this is to disable writes for each attachment concerned using `glColorMaski`. In some special cases like rendering to images [Bolz 12], we actually want to render without framebuffer, in which case, we can disable it with `glDrawBuffer(GL_NONE)`.

Once again, we can use semantics to handle this association. We need to assign the framebuffer color attachments to the indexes identifying the semantics and use the same semantics for the framebuffer output. Using a direct mapping for the `glDrawBuffers` table simplifies the design so that the application only needs to call this function each time a framebuffer is bound. Some typical names for fragment ouputs and framebuffer attachments semantics include diffuse, specular, position, normal, tangent.

> Tip   – Using `glDrawBuffers` as an indirection table may increase the complexity of a
>   software design unnecessarily. Consider using direct mapping at first.

5.5.4   Varying Outputs and Varying Inputs

When we use linked programs, we don't need to consider semantics for the varying outputs and inputs because the GLSL linker will resolve the interface. Thus, we should not use the location qualifier and semantics, because we can't do component packing as well as the compiler can.

However, if we step back a little, we notice that separate programs actually fit well in a software design based on semantics. Chances are that a vertex shader may be reused with multiple fragment shaders. In such a case, using semantics for the variable locations can ensure the matching. Sharing a vertex shader with multiple fragment shaders has the advantage that when we change the fragment program, we only need to bind the resources used by the new fragment program, and we don't even need to validate on the application side whether the vertex array object, the texture buffer, and the uniform buffer associated with the vertex shader stage are correct. If they were, they still are. Indeed, such an example of update strategy can be extended to any shader stage and for any update rate of any stage, bringing a lot of flexibility to the rendering optimizations.

Ultimately, varying locations are only required for partial matching. Semantics are typically attached to locations, but we can use block names to carry the semantics. Examples of block names for semantics include texture mapping, normal mapping, vertex lighting, two-face colors; a strategy for defining semantics of blocks is to name the blocks based on the feature capabilities that output the interface. With varying variables, we need to cope with a finer level of granularity and assign variables with locations having semantics of position, light direction, normal, tangent, texture coordinates, etc.

Tip – Using separated programs, sorting, and semantics reduces the amount of binding.

5.5.5 Uniform Buffers and Uniform Blocks

Uniform buffers and uniform blocks were introduced in OpenGL 3.1. They offer a great replacement to uniform variables, especially for semantics-based software design. Using uniform variables, we have no other choice than letting the compiler assigning the location to the variables. A uniform variable is a state of a program that implies that this variable can't be reused for any other program. With uniform blocks, the storage is a buffer that can be reused with other programs.

The OpenGL specification requires at least 12 uniform blocks per shader stage (Table 5.5).

OpenGL requires as many buffer bindings (GL_MAX_UNIFORM_BUFFER_BINDING) as combined uniform blocks so that each single uniform block may be backed by a different uniform buffer. An application is also free to back multiple uniform blocks with the same uniform buffer binding. Each of these binding point is an opportunity for us to define a dedicated semantic to change a shader stage without changing the uniform buffer bindings.

With the rest of the uniform buffer API, glUniformBlockBinding was introduced to associate a uniform block index with a uniform buffer binding. GLSL 4.20 introduced the binding layout qualifier that allows us to directly set a default binding to a uniform block. Both approaches can work for semantics, but used directly, the default binding avoids carrying around the uniform block index. Semantics for uniform buffers are assigned by update rates: per-camera transform, per-object transform, per-material, etc.

Values	OpenGL 4.2 requirement	Radeon HD 5850	GeForce GTX 470	HD Graphics 3000
MAX_VERTEX_UNIFORM_BLOCKS	12	15	12	12
MAX_TESS_CONTROL_UNIFORM_BLOCKS	12	15	12	N/A
MAX_TESS_EVALUATION_UNIFORM_BLOCKS	12	15	12	N/A
MAX_GEOMETRY_UNIFORM_BLOCKS	12	15	12	N/A
MAX_FRAGMENT_UNIFORM_BLOCKS	12	15	12	12
MAX_COMBINED_UNIFORM_BLOCKS	60	75	12	24

Table 5.5. Uniform block limitations.

Tips   – Use the binding qualifier to avoid unnecessary complexity on the application side.

– Organize uniform buffer and uniform block by update rates.

– Uniform buffer range must be aligned on GL_UNIFORM_BUFFER_OFFSET_ALIGNMENT.

5.6   Application-Side Validations for Debug Build Only

Bugs are not a problem, because they are part of the DNA of programming. The problem is to detect them as soon as we encounter them, which will be the purpose of this section, a tricky aspect of OpenGL.

If interfaces don't match, OpenGL will either generate an error at draw call—if we are lucky—or we will have to deal with a silent error. In both cases, fixing the problem is time consuming. OpenGL provides the functions glValidateProgram and glValidateProgramPipeline, which, according to the specification, "...will check for all the conditions that could lead to a GL_INVALID_OPERATION error when rendering commands are issued, and may check for other conditions as well" [Segal and Akeley 10, p. 104].

Unfortunately, as it stands with Catalyst 12.1a preview and Forceware 290.53, the other conditions seem to be reduced to none even with a debug context. We could imagine using glValidateProgram and glValidateProgramPipeline for the following reasons:

- To validate whether the bound vertex array object and a program object vertex shader input interface match.

- To validate whether the framebuffer attachments are fed by fragment outputs.

- To validate whether varying output variables match with varying input variables.

- To validate that uniform blocks are backed by bound uniform buffers.

- To validate that uniform samplers are backed by a completed texture object.

- To validate that the uniform sampler is declared accordingly to the texture object.

- To validate that the texture sampler is appropriate to the texture image.

Fortunately, understanding all the details of the GLSL Shader Interfaces allows us to do some application-side validations to detect OpenGL errors and even silent errors as early as possible. For this purpose, OpenGL provides many shader query functions to allow the application to catch these issues. Unfortunately, OpenGL 4.2 is missing some queries to iterate over varying variables and fragment shader outputs.

Because of the page-count limit, the briefly described validation capabilities are only illustrated by the companion source code of this chapter.

Tip   – Picture validation as assert-based validation. Encapsulate the validation in a
          function, and call this function only within an asset to ensure doing this valida-
          tion only in debug builds. Such validation introduces a lot of CPU overhead.

5.6.1   Vertex Inputs Validation

For the vertex array object, we may assume that we already know the attribute parameter, as we actually created this object on the application side. However, using
`glGetVertexArray*` might be a more convenient solution because it allows us to
validate the actual states. We need to use `glGetActiveAttrib*` to query information about the vertex shader inputs, including its name, which we will use to query
separately the attribute locations with `glGetAttribLocation` that aren't given by
`glGetActiveAttrib`.

  To ensure the validity of the matching, it is also necessary to check if the requested format conversion is valid, that is to say, if the user calls the appropriate
functions between `glVertexAttribPointer`, `glVertexAttribIPointer`, and
`glVertexAttribLPointer`. Unfortunately, there is a specification bug here, as
the value `GL_VERTEX_ATTRIB_ARRAY_LONG` is missing in the OpenGL 4.2 specification.

5.6.2   Varying Interfaces Validation

With OpenGL 4.2, there is only one main validation that we can't really do. We can't
query varying outputs and varying inputs from separated programs; hence we can't
validate these interfaces. The only possible workaround is to link separated programs
together and query the status of this operation. Such an approach is possible but may
hurt software designs that rely on separate programs.

  Here, we are reaching a limitation of the OpenGL API that we can only hope to
see fixed for the benefit of our programming experience.

Tips   – Be extra careful when writing the varying shader interface. There is no API to
          detect mismatching between shader stages with separate programs. We may hope
          that `glValidateProgramPipeline` will give us meaningful feedback.
        – Consider using structures declared in a shared shader sources across shader stages.

5.6.3   Fragment Outputs Validation

To avoid writing undefined pixels into framebuffer attachments, it is necessary that
each active attachment is backed by a fragment shader output, which implies that
each element of the `glDrawBuffers` indirection table must be backed by a fragment
shader ouput. If a fragment shader output doesn't reach the framebuffer attachments,
the fragment program is doing more work than it could.

This analysis builds the strategy for validating the fragment shader output interface; however, OpenGL doesn't provide APIs to query the list of the fragment shader outputs. The best we can do is to ensure that the glDrawBuffers table doesn't redirect output to nonexisting framebuffer attachments. To iterate on glDrawBuffers table elements, use glGetIntegerv with GL_DRAW_BUFFERi until GL_MAX_DRAW_BUFFER. To iterate on framebuffer attachments, we use glGetFramebufferAttachmentParameter with GL_COLOR_ATTACHMENTi until GL_MAX_COLOR_ATTACHMENTS.

> Tip   – Be extra careful when writing the fragment shader output interface. There is no
>   API to enumerate fragment shader stage output variables.

5.6.4   Variables Validation

We can query all the information about uniform variables by iterating over glGetActiveUniform until GL_ACTIVE_UNIFORMS, which we obtain through glGetProgram. By doing this, we are querying all the uniform variables, including opaque type uniforms: samplers, images, and atomics.

Rich with all this information, we can go further and validate the texture used with a specific sampler. If the sampler is a usampler* or a isampler* then the texture should have been created with the GL_*_INTEGER format. We can check this by querying the value for GL_RGBA_INTEGER_MODE with glGetIntergerv on the currently bound texture.

Going further, we can even validate whether the sampler applied on a texture is appropriate. It is very unlikely that a texture with no mipmaps should be associated with a GL_LINEAR_MIPMAPS_LINEAR sampler, but this could be a classic production pipeline issue.

We can query the GL_TEXTURE_MIN_FILTER parameter of a filter with glGetSamplerParameteriv, but it's surprisingly more complex to handle the number of mipmaps. One approach is to compute the difference between GL_TEXTURE_MAX_LEVEL and GL_TEXTURE_BASE_LEVEL, but too many applications don't pay any attention to GL_TEXTURE_MAX_LEVEL. With OpenGL 4.2, the only way around this is to carry around the texture levels from the texture creation.

5.6.5   Uniform Blocks Validation

OpenGL provides an API for validating uniform blocks by iterating over them using glGetActiveUniformBlockiv until GL_ACTIVE_UNIFORM_BLOCKS, a value we can get from glGetProgram. At this point, we are only iterating over blocks, but we need to iterate as well on block members. We are using GL_UNIFORM_BLOCK_ACTIVE_UNIFORMS to query the number of block members and GL_UNIFORM_BLOCK_ACTIVE_UNIFORM_INDICES to query the list of the active uniform indices.

By using the indices of this list, we can now use `glGetActiveUniform` on each of them to retrieve the information we need.

We can also validate that a block is effectively backed by a uniform buffer by using `GL_UNIFORM_BLOCK_BINDING` with `glGetActiveUniformBlockiv` to retrieve the binding of a uniform buffer binding. Finally, using `GL_UNIFORM_BUFFER_BINDING` with `glGetIntegeri_v`, we can retrieve the actual buffer bound, if any.

5.7 Conclusion

I hope this chapter clarifies that a shader interface is not just declaring a bunch of variables. I would love to give some clearer guidelines in the conclusion, but those mostly depend on the development scenario, and many more pages could be written on this complex topic. However, I can identify some good starting recommendations that could be extended according to the specific nature of each application. For example, simply considering OpenGL ES 2 will largely challenge these rules.

Initial recommendations for reliability and effectiveness of the shader interfaces:

- Always declare the built-in `gl_PerVertex` blocks.

- Use only blocks for varying interfaces.

- Declare the content of the block in external structures shared across shader sources.

- Don't let the compiler set the locations to vertex inputs and fragment outputs.

- Give program-based semantics to attributes and fragment output locations.

- Give program-based semantics to uniform buffer, texture, and image binding points.

- Rely on full matching, including the number of components.

- Avoid matching by location.

- Match the fragment output interface with the framebuffer attachment through the `glDrawBuffes` indirection table. Don't rely on the implementation for this.

- Match separate programs varying interfaces with care, as we can't rely on the implementation for that. Consider using validation by linking all stages together.

- Use assert-based validation in debug to detect issues as soon and as often as we can.

For more information on this discussion, have a look at the companion code samples of this chapter.

Acknowledgments. I am taking advantage of these last few words to thank Pat Brown for the very insightful, in-depth discussions on this topic and the ongoing work to improve OpenGL on this topic. Finally, I am very grateful for the support from Arnaud Masserann, Daniel Rákos, Dimitri Kudelski, and Patrick Cozzi who reviewed this chapter.

Bibliography

[Bjork 08] Kevin Bjork. "Using SAS with CgFX and FX File Formats," OpenGL Extension Specifications, 2008.

[Bolz 12] Jeff Bolz and Pat Brown. "GL_ARB_shader_image_load_store," OpenGL Extension Specifications, 2012.

[Brown 02] Pat Brown. "GL_ARB_vertex_program," OpenGL Extension Specifications, 2002.

[Collins 11] Matt Collins. "Advances in OpenGL for MacOS X Lion," OpenGL Extension Specifications, 2011.

[Kessenich 12] John Kessenich. "Interface Blocks, Input Variables, Output Variables, Uniform, Opaque Type." GLSL 4.20 specification, 2012. Sections 4.3.8, 4.3.4, 4.3.6, 4.3.5, and 4.1.7.

[Kilgard 12] Mark Kilgard, Greg Roth, and Pat Brown. "GL_ARB_separate_shader_objects," OpenGL Extension Specifications, 2012.

[Kime and Kaminski 08] Charles Kime and Thomas Kaminski. "Memory Basics." *Logic and Computer Design Fundamentals*. Upper Saddle River, NJ: Pearson Education, 2008.

[Leech 12] Jon Leech. "Shader Interface Matching." *OpenGL 4.2 Core Profile Specification*, 2012.

[Lipchak 2002] Benj Lipchak. "GL_ARB_fragment_program," OpenGL Extension Specifications, 2002.

[Segal and Akeley 10] Mark Segal and Kurt Akeley. *The OpenGL Graphics System: A Specification, Version 4.1 (Core Profile)*. www.scribd.com/jhoni_vieceli/d/69474584-gl-spec41-core-20100725, July 25, 2010.

An Introduction to Tessellation Shaders   6

Philip Rideout and Dirk Van Gelder

6.1   Introduction

Tessellation shaders open new doors for real-time graphics programming. GPU-based tessellation was possible in the past only through trickery, relying on multiple passes and misappropriation of existing shader units.

OpenGL 4.0 finally provides first-class support for GPU tessellation, but the new shading stages can seem nonintuitive at first. This chapter explains the distinct roles of those stages in the new pipeline and gives an overview of some common rendering techniques that leverage them.

GPUs tend to be better at "streamable" amplification; rather than storing an entire post-subdivided mesh in memory, tessellation shaders allow vertex data to be amplified on the fly, discarding the data when they reach the rasterizer. The system never bothers to store a highly-refined vertex buffer, which would have an impractical memory footprint for a GPU.

Pretessellation graphics hardware was already quite good at rendering huge meshes, and CPU-side refinement was often perfectly acceptable for static meshes. So why move tessellation to the GPU?

The gains are obvious for animation. On a per-frame basis, only the control points get sent to the GPU, greatly alleviating bandwidth requirements for high-density surfaces.

Animation isn't the only killer application of subdivision surfaces. *Displacement mapping* allows for staggering geometric level-of-detail. Previous GPU techniques required multiple passes over the geometry shader, proving awkward and slow. Tessellation shaders allow displacement mapping to occur in a single pass [Castaño 08].

Tessellation shaders can also compute geometric level-of-detail on the fly, which we'll explore later in the chapter. Previous techniques required the CPU to resubmit new vertex buffers when changing the level-of-detail.

6.1.1 Subdivision Surfaces

One of the most compelling uses of GPU tessellation is efficiently rendering Catmull-Clark subdivision surfaces. Most of these techniques use tessellation shaders to evaluate a parametric approximation of the limit surface rather than performing iterative subdivision. Iterative subdivision can still be done on the GPU but is often better suited for CUDA or OpenCL.

Parametric approximation of Catmull-Clark surfaces (ACC) arose from Charles Loop's research at Microsoft in 2008 [Loop and Schaefer 08], and was subsequently enhanced to support creases [Kovacs et al. 09]. An excellent overview of the state of the art can be found in [Ni et al. 09]. This includes a report from Valve, the first major game developer to use tessellation shaders in this way.

6.1.2 Smoothing Polygonal Data

Catmull-Clark surfaces are not the only way to make good use of tessellation shaders; game developers may find other surface definitions more attractive. For example, tessellation can be used to simply "smooth out" traditional polygonal mesh data. PN triangles are a popular example of this. An even simpler application is *Phong tessellation*, the geometric analogue of a Phong lighting.

6.1.3 GPU Compute

OpenCL or CUDA can be used in conjunction with tessellation shaders for various techniques. The compute API can be used for simulation, e.g., hair physics, [Yuksel and Tariq 10], or it can be used to perform a small number of iterative subdivisions to "clean up" the input mesh, removing extraordinary vertices before submitting the data to the OpenGL pipeline [Loop 10].

6.1.4 Curves, Hair, and Grass

Tessellation shaders can also be applied to lines with isoline tessellation, which opens up several possibilities for data amplification. One is tessellating a series of line segments into a smooth cubic curve. In this way, application code works only with a small number of points. Smooth curves are generated entirely on the GPU, either for 3D applications like hair or rope or for 2D applications such as Bézier curves from a drafting tool. Isoline tessellation can also be used to generate multiple curves from a single curve.

Figure 6.1. Hairy teapot; lines grown from patches.

Geometry shaders can be used in conjunction with isoline tessellation, which can be useful for applications such as grass and hair. Figure 6.1 is a screenshot from the accompanying sample code in which a surface is tessellated into many small polygons, then extruded into hairs using a geometry shader.

6.1.5 Other Uses

There are also many less obvious uses for tessellation. If a post-tessellated mesh is sufficiently refined, its geometry can be deformed to simulate lens distortion. These effects include pincushion warping and panoramic projection. Because GPU rasterizers can only perform linear interpolation, traditional techniques relying on post-processing often result in poor sampling.

Figure 6.2 depicts an example of cylindrical warping using tessellation shaders applied to a cubescape. The vertex buffer sent to the GPU is extremely light because each cube face is a 4-vertex patch.

Figure 6.2. Cylindrical distortion using tessellation shaders.

6.2   The New Shading Pipeline

Figure 6.3 depicts a simplified view of the OpenGL shading pipeline, highlighting the new OpenGL 4.0 stages. The pipeline has two new shader stages and one new fixed-function stage.

Those who come across Direct3D literature should be aware that the control shader is there known as the *hull shader*; the evaluation shader is known as the *domain shader*.

To start off, OpenGL 4.0 introduces a new primitive type, `GL_PATCHES`, that must be used to leverage tessellation functionality. Unlike every other OpenGL primitive, patches have a user-defined number of vertices per primitive, configured like so:

```
glPatchParameteri(GL_PATCH_VERTICES, 16);
```

The tessellator can be configured in one of three domains: `isolines`, `quads`, and `triangles`. Later in the chapter, we'll examine each of these modes in detail.

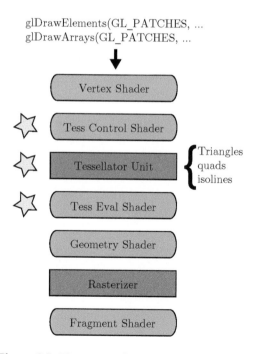

Figure 6.3. The new tessellation stages in OpenGL 4.0.

6.2.1   Life of a Patch

Although vertex data always starts off arranged into patch primitives, it gets transformed as it progresses through the pipe, as
depicted in Figure 6.4.

If desired, the tessellation control shader
can perform some of the same transformations that were traditionally done in the
vertex shader. However, unlike the vertex
shader, the tessellation control shader has
access to all data within the local patch as
well as a patch-relative *invocation identifier*.
It also acts as a configurator for the fixed-
function tessellator stage, telling it how to
split up the patch into triangles or lines. The
tessellation control shader can be thought of
as a "control point shader" because it operates on the original, pretessellated vertices.

Next, the tessellator stage inserts new
vertices into the vertex stream according to
tessellation levels stipulated by the control
shader and the tessellation mode stipulated
by the evaluation shader.

The evaluation shader then transforms
vertices in the expanded stream, making
them able to read data from any vertex
within the local patch.

After this point in the OpenGL pipeline,
vertices are finally arranged into triangles or
lines, and the patch concept is effectively discarded.

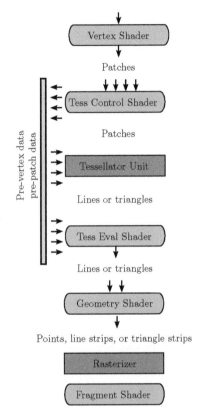

Figure 6.4.   Tessellation data flow;
GLSL arrays are depicted by multiple in-
cident arrows.

6.2.2   Threading Model

Table 6.1 shows how the new programable stages are invoked, relative to the number of elements in the vertex buffer.

The threading model of the control shader is unique in that the relative order of
multiple invocations is somewhat controllable, and it can access a shared read/write
area for each patch.

Control shaders allow developers to specify a synchronization point where all
invocations for a patch must wait for other threads to reach the same point. Such a
synchronization point can be defined using the built-in `barrier()` function.

Unit	Invocation Scheme
Vertex Shader	one invocation per input vertex
Tess Control Shader	one invocation per output vertex
Tess Eval Shader	one invocation per post-tessellated vertex

Table 6.1. Threading in the new OpenGL shading pipeline.

The function `barrier()` is different from `memoryBarrier()`; the latter was introduced in OpenGL 4.2 and can be used from *any* shader unit.

Control shaders can access per-patch shared memory by qualifying a set of **out** variables with the new `patch` keyword. If multiple invocations within a patch write different values into the same `patch` variable, the results are undefined.

6.2.3 Inputs and Outputs

Table 6.2 enumerates all the built-in variables available to the two tessellation shader stages.

The built-in arrays of struct, `gl_in` and `gl_out`, provide access to vertex position, point size, and clipping distance. These are the same variables that can be output from the vertex shader and processed by the geometry shader.

In addition to the built-ins in Table 6.2, tessellation shaders can declare a set of custom **in** and **out** variables as usual. Per-vertex data must always be declared as

Identifier	Shader Unit(s)	Access
`gl_PatchVerticesIn`	Control and Eval	in
`gl_PrimitiveID`	Control and Eval	in
`gl_InvocationID`	Control Shader	in
`gl_TessLevelOuter[4]`	Control Shader	out
`gl_TessLevelInner[2]`	Control Shader	out
`gl_TessLevelOuter[4]`	Evaluation Shader	in
`gl_TessLevelInner[2]`	Evaluation Shader	in
`gl_in[n].gl_Position`	Control and Eval	in
`gl_in[n].gl_PointSize`	Control and Eval	in
`gl_in[n].gl_ClipDistance[m]`	Control and Eval	in
`gl_out[n].gl_Position`	Control and Eval	out
`gl_out[n].gl_PointSize`	Control and Eval	out
`gl_out[n].gl_ClipDistance[m]`	Control and Eval	out
`gl_TessCoord`	Evaluation	in

Table 6.2. Built-in GLSL variables for tessellation.

an array, where each element of the array corresponds to a single element within the patch. Per-patch data, qualified with `patch`, is not arrayed over the patch.

Tessellation shaders have read-only access to `gl_PatchVerticesIn`, which represents the number of vertices in a patch. In the evaluation shader, this number can vary between patches.

The read-only `gl_PrimitiveID` variable is also available to both tessellation shaders. This describes the index of the patch within the current draw call.

As with any other shader stage in OpenGL, tessellation shaders can also read from uniforms, uniform buffers, and textures.

6.2.4 Tessellation Control Shaders

This stage is well suited for change-of-basis transformations and deciding on level-of-detail. Control shaders can also be used to achieve early rejection by culling patches when all corners are outside the viewing frustum, although this gets tricky if the evaluation shader performs displacement.

Listing 6.1 presents a template for a tessellation control shader.

```
layout(vertices = output_patch_size) out;

// Declare inputs from vertex shader
in float vFoo[];

// Declare per-vertex outputs
out float tcFoo[];

// Declare per-patch outputs
patch out float tcSharedFoo;

void main()
{
  bool cull = ...;
  if (cull)
  {
    gl_TessLevelOuter[0] = 0.0;
    gl_TessLevelOuter[1] = 0.0;
    gl_TessLevelOuter[2] = 0.0;
    gl_TessLevelOuter[3] = 0.0;
  }
  else
  {
    // Compute gl_TessLevelInner...
    // Compute gl_TessLevelOuter...
  }
  // Write per-patch data...
  // Write per-vertex data...
}
```

Listing 6.1. Tessellation control shader template.

The layout declaration at the top of the shader defines not only the size of the output patch but also the number of invocations of the control shader for a given input patch. All custom out variables must be declared as arrays that are either explicitly sized to match this count or implicitly using empty square brackets.

The size of the input patch is defined at the API level using glPatch Parameteri, but the size of the output patch is defined at the shader level. In many cases, we want these two sizes to be the same. Heavy insertion of new elements into the vertex stream is best done by the fixed-function tessellator unit and not by the control shader. The implementation-defined maximum for both sizes can be queried at the API level using GL_MAX_PATCH_VERTICES. At the time of this writing, 32 is the common maximum.

The application code can determine the output patch size defined by the active shader:

```
GLuint patchSize;
glGetIntegerv(GL_TESS_CONTROL_OUTPUT_VERTICES, &patchSize);
```

Tessellation modes. The tessellation mode (known as *domain* in Direct3D parlance) is configured using a layout declaration in the evaluation shader. There are three modes available in OpenGL 4.0:

- triangles. Subdivides a triangle into triangles.

- quads. Subdivides a quadrilateral into triangles.

- isolines. Subdivides a quadrilateral into a collection of line strips.

The array gl_OuterTessLevel[] always has four elements, and gl_Inner TessLevel always has two elements, but only a subset of each array is used depending on the tessellation mode. Similarly, gl_TessCoord is always a vec3, but its z component is ignored for isolines and quads. Table 6.3 summarizes how domain affects built-in variables.

Domain	Outer	Inner	TessCoord
triangles	3	1	3D (Barycentric)
quads	4	2	2D (Cartesian)
isolines	2	0	2D (Cartesian)

Table 6.3. The effective sizes of the tess level arrays and the gl_TessCoord vector.

Fractional tessellation levels. The inner and outer tessellation levels control the number of subdivisions along various edges. All tessellation levels are floating points, not integers. The fractional part can have a different meaning depending on the *spacing* (known as *partitioning* in Direct3D parlance). Spacing is configured in the evaluation shader using a `layout` declaration. For example,

```
layout(quads , equal_spacing) in;
```

The three spacing schemes are

- `equal_spacing`. Clamp the tess level to [1,*max*]; then round up to the nearest integer. Every new segment has equal length.

- `fractional_even_spacing`. Clamp the tess level to [2,*max*]; then round up to the nearest even integer. Every new segment has equal length, except for the two segments at either end, whose size is proportional to the fractional part of the clamped tess level.

- `fractional_odd_spacing`. Clamp the tess level to [1,*max*-1]; then round up to the nearest odd integer. Every new segment has equal length, except for the two segments at either end, whose size is proportional to the fractional part of the clamped tess level.

In the above descriptions, *max* refers to the value returned by

```
GLuint maxLevel;
glGetIntegerv(GL_MAX_TESS_GEN_LEVEL, &maxLevel);
```

If we're computing tessellation levels on the fly, the two fractional spacing modes can be used to create a smooth transition between levels, resulting in a diminished popping effect. See Figure 6.5 for how fractional tessellation levels can affect edge subdivision.

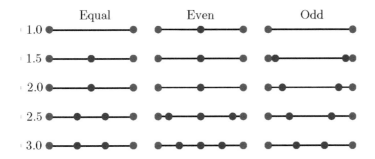

Figure 6.5. Fractional tessellation levels.

Computing the tessellation levels. Writing to `gl_TessLevelInner` and `gl_TessLevelOuter` is optional; if they are not set by the control shader, OpenGL falls back to the API-defined defaults. Initially, these defaults are filled with 1.0, but they can be changed like so:

```
GLfloat inner[2] = { ... };
GLfloat outer[4] = { ... };
glPatchParameterfv(GL_PATCH_DEFAULT_INNER_LEVEL, inner);
glPatchParameterfv(GL_PATCH_DEFAULT_OUTER_LEVEL, outer);
```

At the time of this writing, the latest drivers do not always honor the defaults, so the tessellation levels should always be set from the shader. In practical applications, we often need to compute this dynamically anyway, which is known as *adaptive tessellation*. One approach for computing the level-of-detail is based on screen-space edge lengths:

```
uniform float GlobalQuality;

float ComputeTessFactor(vec2 ssPosition0, vec2 ssPosition1)
{
  float d = distance(ssPosition0, ssPosition1);
  return clamp(d * GlobalQuality, 0.0, 1.0);
}
```

The `GlobalQuality` constant may be computed in application code using the following heuristic:

$$GlobalQuality = 1.0/(TargetEdgeSize * MaxTessFactor).$$

Another adaptive scheme uses the orientation of the patch relative to the viewing angle, leading to higher tessellation along silhouettes. This technique requires an edge normal, which can be obtained by averaging the normals at the two endpoints:

```
uniform vec3 ViewVector;
uniform float Epsilon;

float ComputeTessFactor(vec3 osNormal0, vec3 osNormal1)
{
  float n = normalize(mix(0.5, osNormal0, osNormal1));
  float s = 1.0 - abs(dot(n, ViewVector));
  s = (s - Epsilon) / (1.0 - Epsilon);
  return clamp(s, 0.0, 1.0);
}
```

For more on dynamic level-of-detail, see Chapter 10.

6.2.5   Tessellation Evaluation Shaders

The evaluation stage is well suited for parametric evaluation of patches and computation of smooth normal vectors.

```
layout(quads , fractional_even_spacing, cw) out;

// Declare inputs from tess control shader
in float tcFoo[];

// Declare per-patch inputs
patch in float tcSharedFoo;

// Declare per-vertex outputs
out float teFoo;

void main()
{
  vec3 tc = gl_TessCoord;
  teFoo = ... ;
  gl_Position = ... ;
}
```

Listing 6.2. Tessellation evaluation shader template.

Listing 6.2 presents a template for a tessellation evaluation shader. Unlike the control shader, the outputs are not arrayed over the patch.

For a visualization of **gl_TessCoord** in **quads** mode, see Figure 6.6. The meaning of **gl_TessCoord** varies according to the tessellation mode. For example, in **triangles** mode, it's a Barycentric coordinate; see Table 6.3.

By default, the progression of **gl_TessCoord** is counter-clockwise for every triangle. This is consistent with OpenGL's default definition of front-facing polygons. If desired, the **layout** declaration can flip this behavior using the **cw** token.

By default, the evaluation shader generates triangles for **quads** and **triangles** domains and lines for the **isolines** domain. However, any domain can be overridden to generate point primitives by adding the **point_mode** token to the layout declaration.

Figure 6.6. Gumbo's bicubic patches and their **gl_TessCoord** parameterizations.

6.2.6   Primitive Generation Using quads

The procedure for tessellation in the **quads** domain is described next (follow along with Figure 6.7):

1. The edges of a rectangular input patch are fed into the tessellator.

2. The patch is first divided into quads according to the two inner tessellation levels.

3. All of the quads produced by Step 1 except the bordering quads are decomposed into triangle pairs.

4. The outer edges of the patch are then subdivided according to the four outer tessellation levels.

5. The outer ring is then filled with triangles by connecting the points from Step 2 with the points from Step 4. The algorithm for this step is implementation-dependent.

Figure 6.7 illustrates this procedure using the following tessellation levels:

```
gl_TessLevelInner = { 4, 5 };
gl_TessLevelOuter = { 2, 3, 2, 4 };
```

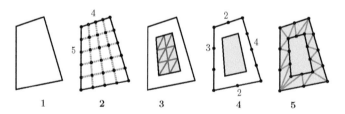

Figure 6.7. Primitive generation in the quads domain.

6.2.7   Primitive Generation Using triangles

Next, we'll describe the procedure for tessellation in the **triangles** domain, following along with Figure 6.8:

1. The edges of a triangular patch are fed into the tessellator.

2. The patch is first divided into concentric triangles according to the inner tessellation level.

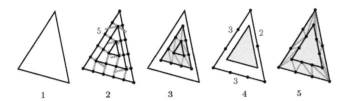

Figure 6.8. Primitive generation in the `triangles` domain.

3. The spaces between the concentric triangles, except the outer ring, are decomposed into triangles.

4. The outer edges of the triangles are then subdivided according to the three outer tessellation levels.

5. The outer ring is then filled with triangles by connecting the points from Step 2 with the points from Step 4.

The concentric triangles in Step 2 are formed from the intersections of perpendicular lines extending from the original edges.

Figure 6.8 illustrates this procedure using the following tessellation levels:

```
gl_TessLevelInner = { 5 };
gl_TessLevelOuter = { 3, 3, 2 };
```

6.3 Tessellating a Teapot

This section illustrates tessellation in the **quads** domain using simple bicubic patches. Conveniently, the famous Utah Teapot was originally modelled using bicubic patches. Tessellation levels for this demo are depicted in Figure 6.9.

Since we are not performing skinning or other deformations, we defer model-view-projection transformation until the evaluation shader; this makes our vertex shader trivial. See Listing 6.3.

Figure 6.9. From left to right: inner and outer tess levels of 1, 2, 3, 4, and 7.

```
in vec3 Position;
out vec3 vPosition;

void main()
{
   vPosition = Position;
}
```

Listing 6.3. Teapot vertex shader.

Before diving into the control shader, a brief review of bicubic patches is in order. In its most general form, the parametric formulation of a bicubic surface uses a total of 48 coefficients:

$$
\begin{aligned}
x(u, v) &= a_x u^3 v^3 + b_x u^3 v^2 + c_x u^3 v + d_x u^3 + e_x u^2 v^3 + \ldots p_x, \\
y(u, v) &= a_y u^3 v^3 + b_y u^3 v^2 + c_y u^3 v + d_y u^3 + e_y u^2 v^3 + \ldots p_y, \\
z(u, v) &= a_z u^3 v^3 + b_z u^3 v^2 + c_z u^3 v + d_z u^3 + e_z u^2 v^3 + \ldots p_z.
\end{aligned}
\tag{6.1}
$$

The (u, v) coordinates in the above formulation correspond to `gl_TessCoord` in the evaluation shader.

The 48 coefficients can be neatly arranged into 4×4 matrices. We can denote a_x through p_x with the matrix $\mathbf{C}_x$:

$$
x(u, v) = (u^3 \ u^2 \ u \ 1) \ \mathbf{C}_x
\begin{pmatrix}
v^3 \\
v^2 \\
v \\
1
\end{pmatrix}.
$$

Given a set of knot points, we need to generate a set of coefficient matrices ($\mathbf{C}_x$, $\mathbf{C}_y$, $\mathbf{C}_z$). First, we select a basis matrix from a list of popular choices (e.g., Bézier, B-spline, Catmull-Rom, and Hermite) and represent it with $\mathbf{B}$. Next, we arrange the knot points into matrices ($\mathbf{P}_x$, $\mathbf{P}_y$, $\mathbf{P}_z$). The coefficient matrices can then be derived as follows:

$$
\begin{aligned}
\mathbf{C}_x &= \mathbf{B} * \mathbf{P}_x * \mathbf{B}^T, \\
\mathbf{C}_y &= \mathbf{B} * \mathbf{P}_y * \mathbf{B}^T, \\
\mathbf{C}_z &= \mathbf{B} * \mathbf{P}_z * \mathbf{B}^T.
\end{aligned}
$$

Because the coefficient matrices are constant over the patch, computing them should be done in the control shader rather than the evaluation shader. See Listing 6.4.

Listing 6.4 does not make the best use of the threading model. Listing 6.5 makes a 3 times improvement by performing the computations for each dimension (x, y, z) across separate invocations.

In some cases, the first return statement in Listing 6.5 will not improve performance due to the SIMD nature of shader execution.

```
layout(vertices = 16) out;
in vec3 vPosition[];
out vec3 tcPosition[];
patch out mat4 cx, cy, cz;
uniform mat4 B, BT;

#define ID gl_InvocationID

void main()
{
  tcPosition[ID] = vPosition[ID];

  mat4 Px, Py, Pz;
  for (int idx = 0; idx < 16; ++idx)
  {
    Px[idx / 4][idx % 4] = vPosition[idx].x;
    Py[idx / 4][idx % 4] = vPosition[idx].y;
    Pz[idx / 4][idx % 4] = vPosition[idx].z;
  }

  // Perform the change of basis:
  cx = B * Px * BT;
  cy = B * Py * BT;
  cz = B * Pz * BT;
}
```

Listing 6.4. Teapot control shader.

```
layout(vertices = 16) out;
in vec3 vPosition[];
out vec3 tcPosition[];
patch out mat4 c[3];
uniform mat4 B, BT;

#define ID gl_InvocationID

void main()
{
  tcPosition[ID] = vPosition[ID];
  tcNormal[ID] = vNormal[ID];
  if (ID > 2)
  {
    return;
  }

  mat4 P;
  for (int idx = 0; idx < 16; ++idx)
  {
    P[idx / 4][idx % 4] = vPosition[idx][ID];
  }

  // Perform the change of basis:
  c[ID] = B * P * BT;
}
```

Listing 6.5. Improved control shader.

```
layout(quads) in;
in vec3 tcPosition[];
patch in mat4 cx, cy, cz;
uniform mat4 Projection;
uniform mat4 Modelview;

void main()
{
  float u = gl_TessCoord.x, v = gl_TessCoord.y;
  vec4 U = vec4(u * u * u, u * u, u, 1);
  vec4 V = vec4(v * v * v, v * v, v, 1);
  float x = dot(cx * V, U);
  float y = dot(cy * V, U);
  float z = dot(cz * V, U);
  gl_Position = Projection * Modelview * vec4(x, y, z, 1);
}
```

Listing 6.6. Evaluation shader.

Current drivers have trouble with varying arrays of matrices; we had to replace the c[] array with three separate matrices.

Further gains could be achieved by removing the for loop and using the barrier instruction, but current drivers do not support the barrier instruction robustly.

Next, we come to the evaluation shader, which is best suited for performing the computations in Equation 6.1 and performing the model-view-projection transform. See Listing 6.6.

6.4   Isolines and Spirals

So far, we've examined the triangles and quads domains, which both decompose input patches into many tiny polygons. The remaining tessellation mode, isolines, changes each input patch into a series of line segments. Listing 6.7 is an excerpt from an evaluation shader that generates multiple smooth curves from a single coarse curve.

This shader requests that the tessellator unit generates evenly spaced isolines. The control shader needs to specify values for only two of the outer tessellation levels, and all inner levels are ignored. Specifically, gl_TessLevelOuter[0] describes how many curves to generate, and gl_TessLevelOuter[1] describes how many samples generate for each of those curves. For example, if our application needs to turn a coarsely specified curve into a single smooth curve, set gl_TessLevelOuter[0] to 1.0 and set gl_TessLevelOuter[1] to 64.0 to finely sample the output curve. Conversely, setting gl_TessLevelOuter[0] to 64.0 and gl_TessLevelOuter[1] to 4.0 causes the tessellator to generate 64 coarse curves.

Listing 6.7 performs B-spline interpolation between the four vertices of each patch, using gl_TessCoord.x to indicate the parametric position along the curve,

```
layout(isolines, equal_spacing, cw) in;

void main()
{
  float u = gl_TessCoord.x, v = gl_TessCoord.y;

  float B[4];
  EvalCubicBSpline(u, B); // See accompanying sample for definition

  vec4 pos = B[0] * gl_in[0].gl_Position +
             B[1] * gl_in[1].gl_Position +
             B[2] * gl_in[2].gl_Position +
             B[3] * gl_in[3].gl_Position;

  // Offset in the y coordinate using v so multiple
  // curves aren't drawn on top of each other.
  pos += vec4(0.0, v * 5.0, 0.0, 0.0);

  gl_Position = Projection * Modelview * pos;
}
```

Listing 6.7. Spirals shader.

and `gl_TessCoord.y` here is used to offset different curves generated by the tessellator unit.

In this example, a series of five "patches" are created in a spiral with four vertices each. In the first image, both outer tessellation levels are set to one, so we get a single curve. See Figure 6.10.

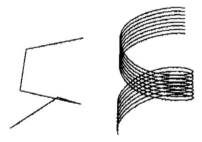

Figure 6.10. Isoline control points (left). Post-tessellated curves (right).

6.5   Incorporating Other OpenGL Features

Many types of animation and deformation are well suited to the current vertex shader. For example, skinning is still optimally done in a vertex shader; NVIDIA's Gregory patch demo is one example of this.

OpenGL's *transform feedback* functionality can be used to turn off the rasterizer and send post-tessellated data back to the CPU, possibly for verification or debugging, further processing, or to be leveraged by a CPU-side production-quality renderer.

Transform feedback could also be used to perform iterative refinement, although this is rarely done in practice due to the large memory requirements of the resulting vertex buffers. For more on transform feedback, see Chapter 17.

Bibliography

[Castaño 08] Ignacio Castaño. "Displaced Subdivision Surfaces." Presented at Gamefest: http://developer.download.nvidia.com/presentations/2008/Gamefest/Gamefest2008-DisplacedSubdivisionSurfaceTessellation-Slides.PDF, 2008.

[Kovacs et al. 09] Denis Kovacs, Jason Mitchell, Shanon Drone, and Denis Zorin. "Real-Time Creased Approximate Subdivision Surfaces." In *Proceedings of the 2009 symposium on Interactive 3D graphics and games, I3D '09*, pp. 155–160. New York: ACM, 2009.

[Loop and Schaefer 08] Charles Loop and Scott Schaefer. "Approximating Catmull-Clark subdivision surfaces with bicubic patches." *ACM Trans. Graph.* 27 (2008), 8:1–8:11. Available online (http://doi.acm.org/10.1145/1330511.1330519).

[Loop 10] Charles Loop. "Hardware Subdivision and Tessellation of Catmull-Clark Surfaces." Presented at GTC. http://www.nvidia.com/content/GTC-2010/pdfs/2129_GTC2010.pdf, 2010.

[Ni et al. 09] Tianyun Ni, Ignacio Castaño, Jörg Peters, Jason Mitchell, Philip Schneider, and Vivek Verma. "Efficient Substitutes for Subdivision Surfaces." In *ACM SIGGRAPH 2009 Courses, SIGGRAPH '09*, pp. 13:1–13:107. New York: ACM, 2009.

[Yuksel and Tariq 10] Cem Yuksel and Sarah Tariq. "Advanced Techniques in Real-Time Hair Rendering and Simulation." In *ACM SIGGRAPH 2010 Courses, SIGGRAPH '10*, pp. 1:1–1:168. New York: ACM, 2010. Available online (http://doi.acm.org/10.1145/1837101.1837102).

Procedural Textures in GLSL   7

Stefan Gustavson

7.1 Introduction

Procedural textures are textures that are computed on the fly during rendering as opposed to precomputed image-based textures. At first glance, computing a texture from scratch for each frame may seem like a stupid idea, but procedural textures have been a staple of software rendering for decades, for good reason. With the ever-increasing levels of performance for programmable shading in GPU architectures, hardware-accelerated procedural texturing in GLSL is now becoming quite useful and deserves more consideration. An example of what can be done is shown in Figure 7.1.

Figure 7.1. Examples of procedural textures. A modern GPU renders this image at full screen resolution in a few milliseconds.

Writing a good procedural shader is more complicated than using image editing software to paint a texture or edit a photographic image to suit our needs, but with procedural shaders, the pattern and the colors can be varied with a simple change of parameters. This allows extensive reuse of data for many different purposes, as well as fine-tuning or even complete overhauls of surface appearance very late in a production process. A procedural pattern allows for analytic derivatives, which makes it less complicated to generate the corresponding surface normals, as compared to traditional bump mapping or normal mapping, and enables analytic anisotropic anti-aliasing. Procedural patterns require very little storage, and they can be rendered at an arbitrary resolution without jagged edges or blurring, which is particularly useful when rendering close-up details in real-time applications where the viewpoint is often unrestricted. A procedural texture can be designed to avoid problems with seams and periodic artifacts when applied to a large area, and random-looking detail patterns can be generated automatically instead of having artists paint them. Procedural shading also removes the memory restrictions for 3D textures and animated patterns. 3D procedural textures, *solid textures*, can be applied to objects of any shape without requiring 2D texture coordinates.

While all these advantages have made procedural shading popular for offline rendering, real-time applications have been slow to adopt the practice. One obvious reason is that the GPU is a limited resource, and quality often has to be sacrificed for performance. However, recent developments have given us lots of computing power even on typical consumer-level GPUs, and given their massively parallel architectures, memory access is becoming a major bottleneck. A modern GPU has an abundance of texture units and uses caching strategies to reduce the number of accesses to global memory, but many real-time applications now have an imbalance between texture bandwidth and processing bandwidth. ALU instructions can essentially be "free" and cause no slowdown at all when executed in parallel to memory reads, and image-based textures can be augmented with procedural elements. Somewhat surprisingly, procedural texturing is also useful at the opposite end of the performance scale. GPU hardware for mobile devices can incur a considerable penalty for texture download and texture access, and this can sometimes be alleviated by procedural texturing. A procedural shader does not necessarily have to be complex, as demonstrated by some of the examples in this chapter.

Procedural methods are not limited to fragment shading. With the ever-increasing complexity of real-time geometry and the recent introduction of GPU-hosted tessellation as discussed in Chapter 6, tasks like surface displacements and secondary animations are best performed on the GPU. The tight interaction between procedural displacement shaders and procedural surface shaders has proven very fruitful for creating complex and impressive visuals in offline shading environments, and there is no reason to assume that real-time shading would be fundamentally different in that respect.

This chapter is meant as an introduction to procedural shader programming in GLSL. First, I present some fundamentals of procedural patterns, including antialiasing. A significant portion of the chapter presents recently developed, efficient methods for generating Perlin noise and other noise-like patterns entirely on the GPU, along with some benchmarks to demonstrate their performance. The code repository on the *OpenGL Insights* website, www.openglinsights.com, contains a cross-platform demo program and a library of useful GLSL functions for procedural texturing.

7.2 Simple Functions

Procedural textures are a different animal than image-based textures. The concept of designing a function to efficiently compute a value at an arbitrary point without knowledge of any surrounding points takes some getting used to. A good book on the subject, in fact, *the* book on the subject, is *Texturing and Modeling: A Procedural Approach* [Ebert et al. 03]. Its sections on hardware acceleration have become outdated, but the rest is good. Another classic text on software procedural shaders well worth reading is *Advanced Renderman: Creating CGI for Motion Pictures* [Apodaca and Gritz 99].

Figure 7.2 presents a varied selection of regular procedural patterns and the GLSL expression that generates them. The examples are monochrome, but, of course, black and white can be substituted with any color or texture by using the resulting pattern as the last parameter to the mix() function.

For antialiasing purposes, a good design choice is to first create a continuous distance function of some sort, and then threshold it to get the features we want. The last three of the patterns in Figure 7.2 follow this advice. None of the examples implement proper antialiasing, but I will cover this in a moment.

As an example, consider the circular spots pattern. First, we create a periodic repeat of the texture coordinates by scaling st by 5.0 and taking the fractional part of the result. Subtracting 0.5 from this creates cells with 2D coordinates in the range −0.5 to 0.5. The distance to the cell-local origin as computed by length() is a continuous function everywhere in the plane, and thresholding it by smoothstep() yields circular spots of any desired size.

There is a knack to designing patterns like this from scratch, and it takes practice to do it well, but experimenting is a fun learning experience. However, take warning from the last example in Figure 7.2: writing these kinds of functions as one-liners will quickly make them unreadable even to their author. Use intermediate variables with relevant names and comment all code. One of the advantages of procedural textures is that they can be reused for different purposes, but that point is largely moot if the shader code is impossible to understand. GLSL compilers are reasonably good at simple optimizations like removing temporary variables. Some spoon-feeding of GLSL compilers is still necessary to create optimal shader code, but readability does not have to be sacrificed for compactness.

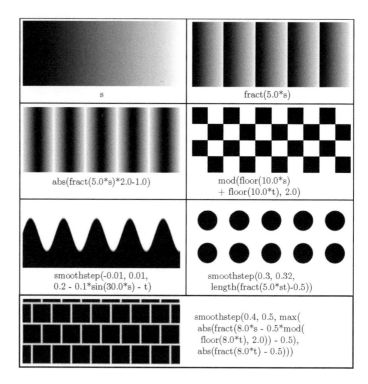

Figure 7.2. Examples of regular procedural patterns. Texture coordinates are either `float` `s,t` or `vec2 st`; $0 \leq s \leq 1$ and $0 \leq t \leq 0.4$.

7.3   Antialiasing

Beginners' experiments with procedural patterns often result in patterns that alias terribly, but that problem can be solved. The field of software shader programming has methods of eliminating or reducing aliasing, and those methods translate directly to hardware shading. Antialiasing is even more important for real-time content because the camera view is often unrestricted and unpredictable. Supersampling can always reduce aliasing, but it is not a suitable routine remedy, because a well written procedural shader can perform its own antialiasing with considerably less work than what a brute force supersampling would require.

Many useful patterns can be generated by thresholding a smoothly varying function. For such thresholding, using conditionals (`if-else`), or the all-or-nothing `step()` function will alias badly and should be avoided. Instead, use the `mix()` and `smoothstep()` functions to create a blend region between the two extremes, and take care to make the width of the blend region as close as possible to the size of one fragment. To relate shader space (texture coordinates or object coordinates) to fragment space in GLSL, we use the automatic derivative functions `dFdx()` and `dFdy()`.

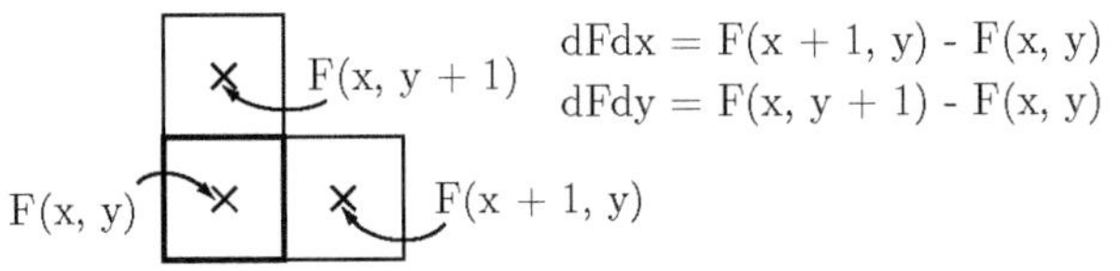

$$dFdx = F(x + 1, y) - F(x, y)$$
$$dFdy = F(x, y + 1) - F(x, y)$$

Figure 7.3. "Automatic derivatives" `dFdx()` and `dFdy()` in a fragment shader are simply differences between arbitrary computed values of two neighboring fragments. Derivatives in x and y in one fragment (bold square) are computed using one neighbor each (thin squares). If the right or top neighbors are not part of the same primitive or for reasons of efficiency, the left or bottom neighbors may be used instead.

There have been some teething problems with these functions, but now they can be expected to be implemented correctly and efficiently on all GLSL-capable platforms. The local partial derivatives are approximated by differences between neighboring fragments, and they require very little extra effort to compute (see Figure 7.3). The partial derivative functions break the rule that a fragment shader has no access to information from other fragments in the same rendering pass, but it is a very local special case handled behind the scenes by the OpenGL implementation. Mipmapping and anisotropic filtering of image-based textures use this feature as well, and proper antialiasing of textures would be near impossible without it.

For smooth, anisotropic antialiasing of a thresholding operation on a smoothly varying function F, we need to compute the length of the gradient vector in fragment space and make the step width of the `smoothstep()` function dependent on it. The gradient in fragment space (x, y) of F is simply $(\partial F / \partial x, \partial F / \partial y)$. The built-in function `fwidth()` computes the length of that vector as $|\partial F / \partial x| + |\partial F / \partial y|$ in a somewhat misguided attempt to be fast on older hardware. A better choice in most cases nowadays is to compute the true length of the gradient,

$$\sqrt{\left(\frac{\partial F}{\partial x}\right)^2 + \left(\frac{\partial F}{\partial y}\right)^2},$$

according to Listing 7.1. Using ± 0.7 instead of ± 0.5 for the step width compensates for the fact that `smoothstep()` is smooth at its endpoints and has a steeper maximum slope than a linear ramp.

```
// 'threshold' is constant, 'value' is smoothly varying
float aastep(float threshold, float value)
{
  float afwidth = 0.7 * length(vec2(dFdx(value), dFdy(value)));
  // GLSL's fwidth(value) is abs(dFdx(value)) + abs(dFdy(value))
  return smoothstep(threshold - afwidth, threshold + afwidth, value);
}
```

Listing 7.1. Anisotropic antialiased step function.

```
// st is a vec2 of texcoords, G2_st is a vec2 in texcoord space
mat2 Jacobian2 = mat2(dFdx(st), dFdy(st));
// G2_xy is G2_st transformed to fragment space
vec2 G2_xy = Jacobian2 * G2_st;
// stp is a vec3 of texcoords, G3_stp is a vec3 in texcoord space
mat2x3 Jacobian3 = mat2x3(dFdx(stp), dFdy(stp));
// G3_xy is G3_stp projected to fragment space
vec2 G3_xy = Jacobian3 * G3_stp;
}
```

Listing 7.2. Transforming a vector in (s, t) or (s, t, p) texture space to fragment (x, y) space.

In some cases, the analytical derivative of a function is simple to compute, and it may be inefficient or inaccurate to approximate it using finite differences. The analytical derivative is expressed in 2D or 3D texture coordinate space, but antialiasing requires knowledge of the length of the gradient vector in 2D screen space. Listing 7.2 shows how to transform or project vectors in texture coordinate space to fragment coordinate space. Note that we need two to three times as many values from `dFdx()` and `dFdy()` to project an analytical gradient to fragment space compared to computing an approximate gradient directly in fragment space, but automatic derivatives come fairly cheap.

7.4   Perlin Noise

Perlin noise, introduced by Ken Perlin, is a very useful building block of procedural texturing [Perlin 85]. In fact, it revolutionized software rendering of natural-looking surfaces. Some patterns generated using Perlin noise are shown in Figure 7.4, along with the shader code that generates them. By itself, it is not a terribly exciting-looking function—it is just a blurry pattern of blotches within a certain range of sizes. However, noise can be manipulated in many ways to create impressive visual effects. It can be thresholded and summed to mimic fractal patterns, and it has great potential also for introducing some randomness in an otherwise regular pattern. The natural world is largely built on or from stochastic processes, and manipulations of noise allows a large variety of natural materials and environments to be modeled procedurally.

The examples in Figure 7.4 are static 2D patterns, but some of the more striking uses of noise use 3D texture coordinates and/or time as an extra dimension for the noise function. The code repository for this chapter contains an animated demo displaying the scene in Figure 7.1. The left two spheres and the ground plane are examples of patterns generated by one or more instances of Perlin noise.

When GLSL was designed, a set of noise functions was included among the built-in functions. Sadly, though, those functions have been left unimplemented in almost every OpenGL implementation to date, except for some obsolete GPUs by

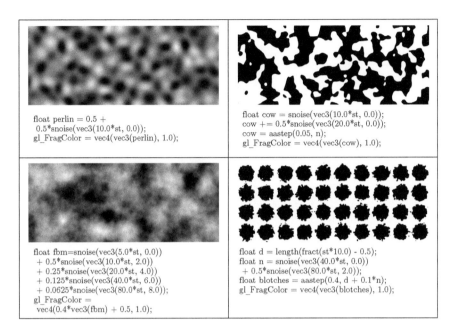

Figure 7.4. Examples of procedural patterns using Perlin noise. Texture coordinates are either `float s,t` or `vec2 st`.

3DLabs. Native hardware support for noise on mainstream GPUs may not appear for a good while yet, or indeed ever, but there are software workarounds. Recent research [McEwan et al. 12] has provided fast GLSL implementations of all common variants of Perlin noise which are easy to use and compatible with all current GLSL implementations, including OpenGL ES and WebGL. Implementation details are in the article, and a short general presentation of Perlin noise in its classic and modern variants can be found in [Gustavson 05]. Here, we will just present a listing of 2D *simplex noise*, a modern variant of Perlin noise, to show how short it is. Listing 7.3 is a stand-alone implementation of 2D simplex noise ready to cut and paste into a shader: no setup or external resources are needed. The function can be used in vertex shaders and fragment shaders alike. Other variants of Perlin noise are in the code repository for this book.

The different incarnations of Perlin noise are not exactly simple functions, but they can still be evaluated at speeds of several billion fragments per second on a modern GPU. Hardware and software development have now reached a point where Perlin noise is very useful for real-time shading, and everyone is encouraged to use it.

```
// Description : Array- and textureless GLSL 2D simplex noise.
// Author : Ian McEwan, Ashima Arts. Version: 20110822
// Copyright (C) 2011 Ashima Arts. All rights reserved.
// Distributed under the MIT License. See LICENSE file.
// https://github.com/ashima/webgl-noise

vec3 mod289(vec3 x)
{
  return x - floor(x * (1.0 / 289.0)) * 289.0;
}
vec2 mod289(vec2 x)
{
  return x - floor(x * (1.0 / 289.0)) * 289.0;
}
vec3 permute(vec3 x)
{
  return mod289(((x*34.0)+1.0)*x);
}

float snoise(vec2 v)
{
  const vec4 C = vec4(0.211324865405187,  // (3.0-sqrt(3.0))/6.0
                      0.366025403784439,  // 0.5*(sqrt(3.0)-1.0)
                     -0.577350269189626,  // -1.0 + 2.0 * C.x
                      0.024390243902439); // 1.0 / 41.0
  // First corner
  vec2 i = floor(v + dot(v, C.yy));
  vec2 x0 = v - i + dot(i, C.xx);
  // Other corners
  vec2 i1 = (x0.x > x0.y) ? vec2(1.0, 0.0) : vec2(0.0, 1.0);
  vec4 x12 = x0.xyxy + C.xxzz;
  x12.xy -= i1;
  // Permutations
  i = mod289(i); // Avoid truncation effects in permutation
  vec3 p = permute( permute( i.y + vec3(0.0, i1.y, 1.0 ))
          + i.x + vec3(0.0, i1.x, 1.0 ));
  vec3 m = max(0.5 - vec3(dot(x0,x0), dot(x12.xy,x12.xy),
                          dot(x12.zw,x12.zw)), 0.0);
  m = m * m;
  m = m * m;
  // Gradients
  vec3 x = 2.0 * fract(p * C.www) - 1.0;
  vec3 h = abs(x) - 0.5;
  vec3 a0 = x - floor(x + 0.5);
  // Normalize gradients implicitly by scaling m
  m *= 1.79284291400159 - 0.85373472095314 * ( a0*a0 + h*h );
  // Compute final noise value at P
  vec3 g;
  g.x = a0.x * x0.x + h.x * x0.y;
  g.yz = a0.yz * x12.xz + h.yz * x12.yw;
  return 130.0 * dot(m, g);
}
```

Listing 7.3. Complete, self-contained GLSL implementation of Perlin simplex noise in 2D.

7.5 Worley Noise

Another useful function is the *cellular basis function* or *cellular noise* introduced by Steven Worley [Worley 96]. Often referred to as *Worley noise*, this function can be used to generate a different class of patterns than Perlin noise. The function is based on a set of irregularly positioned, but reasonably evenly spaced *feature points*. The basic version of the function returns the distance to the closest one of these feature points from a specified point in 2D or 3D. A more popular version returns the distances to the two closest points, which allows more variation in the pattern design. Worley's original implementation makes commendable efforts to be correct, isotropic, and statistically well-behaved, but simplified variants have been proposed over the years to cut some corners and make the function less cumbersome to compute in a shader. It is still more complicated to compute than Perlin

```
// Cellular noise ("Worley noise") in 2D in GLSL, simplified version.
// Copyright (c) Stefan Gustavson 2011-04-19. All rights reserved.
// This code is released under the conditions of the MIT license.
// See LICENSE file for details.

vec4 permute(vec4 x)
{
  return mod((34.0 * x + 1.0) * x, 289.0);
}

vec2 cellular2x2(vec2 P)
{
  const float K  = 1.0/7.0;
  const float K2 = 0.5/7.0;
  const float jitter = 0.8; // jitter 1.0 makes F1 wrong more often
  vec2 Pi = mod(floor(P), 289.0);
  vec2 Pf = fract(P);
  vec4 Pfx = Pf.x + vec4(-0.5, -1.5, -0.5, -1.5);
  vec4 Pfy = Pf.y + vec4(-0.5, -0.5, -1.5, -1.5);
  vec4 p = permute(Pi.x + vec4(0.0, 1.0, 0.0, 1.0));
  p = permute(p + Pi.y + vec4(0.0, 0.0, 1.0, 1.0));
  vec4 ox = mod(p, 7.0) * K + K2;
  vec4 oy = mod(floor(p * K),7.0) * K + K2;
  vec4 dx = Pfx + jitter * ox;
  vec4 dy = Pfy + jitter * oy;
  vec4 d = dx * dx + dy * dy; // distances squared
  // Cheat and pick only F1 for the return value
  d.xy = min(d.xy, d.zw);
  d.x = min(d.x, d.y);
  return d.xx; // F1 duplicated, F2 not computed
}
varying vec2 st; // Texture coordinates
void main(void) {
  vec2 F = cellular2x2(st);
  float n = 1.0 - 1.5 * F.x;
  gl_FragColor = vec4(n.xxx, 1.0);
}
```

Listing 7.4. Complete, self-contained GLSL implementation of our simplified version of Worley noise in 2D.

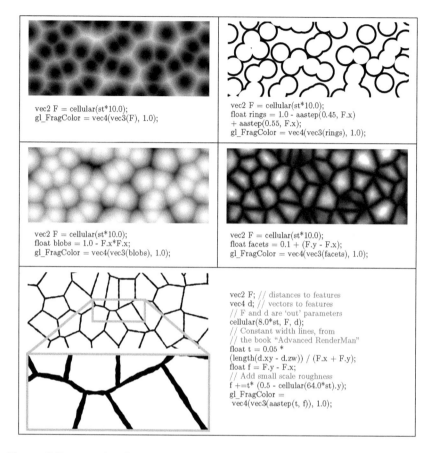

Figure 7.5. Examples of procedural patterns using Worley noise. Texture coordinates are `vec2 st`. For implementations of the `cellular()` functions, see the code repository.

noise because it requires sorting of a number of candidates to determine which feature point is closest, but while Perlin noise often requires several evaluations to generate an interesting pattern, a single evaluation of Worley noise can be enough. Generally speaking, Worley noise can be just as useful as Perlin noise, but for a different class of problems. Perlin noise is blurry and smooth by default, while Worley noise is inherently spotty and jagged with distinct features.

There have not been any recent publications of Worley noise algorithms for real-time use, but using concepts from my recent Perlin noise work and ideas from previous software implementations, I created original implementations of a few simplified variants and put them in the code repository for this chapter. Detailed notes on the implementation are presented in [Gustavson 11]. Here, I just point to their existence and provide them for use. The simplest version is presented in Listing 7.4.

Some patterns generated using Worley noise are shown in Figure 7.5, along with the GLSL expressions that generate them. The right two spheres in Figure 7.1 are examples of patterns generated by a single invocation of Worley noise.

7.6 Animation

For procedural patterns, all properties of a fragment are computed anew for each frame, which means that animation comes more or less for free. It is only a matter of supplying the shader with a concept of time through a uniform variable and making the pattern dependent on that variable in some manner. Animation speed is independent of frame rate, and animations do not need to loop but can extend for arbitrary long periods of time without repeating (within the constraints of numerical precision if a floating-point value is used for timing). Animation literally adds a new dimension to patterns, and the unrestricted animation that is possible with procedural textures is a strong argument for using them. Perlin noise is available in a 4D version, and its main use is to create textures where 3D spatial coordinates and time together provide the texture coordinates for an animated solid texture. The demo code that renders the scene in Figure 7.1 animates the shaders simply by supplying the current time as a uniform variable to GLSL and computing patterns that depend on it.

Unlike prerendered image sequences, procedural shader animation is not restricted to simple, linear time dependencies. View-dependent changes to a procedural texture can be used to affect the level-of-detail for the rendering so that, for example, bump maps or small-scale features are computed only in close-up views to save GPU resources. Procedural shading allows arbitrary interactive and dynamic changes to a surface, including extremely complex computations like smoke and fluid simulations performed on the GPU. Animated shaders have been used in software rendering for a long time, but interactivity is unique to real-time shading, and a modern GPU has considerably more computing power than a CPU, paving the way to many fun and wonderful avenues to explore.

7.7 Texture Images

Procedural texturing is all about removing the dependency on image-based textures, but there are applications where a hybrid approach is useful. A texture image can be used for coarse detail to allow better artistic control, and a procedural pattern can fill in the details in close-up views. This includes not only surface properties in fragment shaders, but also displacement maps in vertex shaders. Texture images can also be used as data for further processing into a procedural pattern, as in the manner presented in Chapter 12 or in the halftoning example in Figure 7.6, rendered by the shader in Listing 7.5. The bilinear texture interpolation is performed explicitly in

Figure 7.6. A halftone shader using a texture image as input. The shader is listed in Listing 7.5. Small random details become visible in close-up views (inset, lower right). For distance views, the shader avoids aliasing by gradually blending out the halftone pattern and
blending in the plain RGB image (inset, lower left).

shader code. Hardware texture interpolation often has a limited fixed-point precision
that is unsuitable for this kind of thresholding under extreme magnifications.

Of course, some procedural patterns that are too cumbersome to compute for
each frame can be rendered to a texture and reused between frames. This approach
maintains several of the advantages from using procedural patterns (flexibility, compactness, dynamic resolution), and it can be a good compromise while we are waiting
for complex procedural texturing to be easily manageable in true real time. Some of
the advantages are lost (memory bandwidth, analytic anisotropic antialiasing, rapid
animations), but it does solve the problem of extreme minification. Minification can
be tricky to handle analytically but is solved well by mipmapping an image-based
texture.

```
uniform sampler2D teximage;
uniform vec2 dims; // Texture dimensions (width and height)
varying vec2 one;  // 1.0/dims from vertex shader
varying vec2 st;   // 2D texture coordinates

// Explicit bilinear lookup to circumvent imprecise interpolation.
// In GLSL 1.30 and above, 'dims' can be fetched by textureSize().
vec4 texture2D_bilinear(sampler2D tex, vec2 st, vec2 dims, vec2 one)
{
  vec2 uv = st * dims;
  vec2 uv00 = floor(uv - vec2(0.5)); // Lower left of lower left texel
  vec2 uvlerp = uv - uv00 - vec2(0.5); // Texel-local blends [0,1]
  vec2 st00 = (uv00 + vec2(0.5)) * one;
  vec4 texel00 = texture2D(tex, st00);
  vec4 texel10 = texture2D(tex, st00 + vec2(one.x, 0.0));
  vec4 texel01 = texture2D(tex, st00 + vec2(0.0, one.y));
  vec4 texel11 = texture2D(tex, st00 + one);
  vec4 texel0 = mix(texel00, texel01, uvlerp.y);
  vec4 texel1 = mix(texel10, texel11, uvlerp.y);
  return mix(texel0, texel1, uvlerp.x);
}

void main(void)
{
  vec3 rgb = texture2D_bilinear(teximage, st, dims, one).rgb;
  float n = 0.1 * snoise(st * 200.0);
  n += 0.05 * snoise(st * 400.0);
  n += 0.025 * snoise(st * 800.0); // Fractal noise, 3 octaves
  vec4 cmyk;
  cmyk.xyz = 1.0 - rgb; // Rough CMY conversion
  cmyk.w = min(cmyk.x, min(cmyk.y, cmyk.z)); // Create K
  cmyk.xyz -= cmyk.w; // Subtract K amount from CMY

  // CMYK halftone screens, in angles 15/-15/0/45 degrees
  vec2 Cuv = 50.0 * mat2(0.966, -0.259, 0.259, 0.966) * st;
  Cuv = fract(Cuv) - 0.5;
  float c = aastep(0.0, sqrt(cmyk.x) - 2.0 * length(Cuv) + n);
  vec2 Muv = 50.0 * mat2(0.966, 0.259, -0.259, 0.966)*st;
  Muv = fract(Muv) - 0.5;
  float m = aastep(0.0, sqrt(cmyk.y) - 2.0 * length(Muv) + n);
  vec2 Yuv = 50.0 * st; // 0 deg
  Yuv = fract(Yuv) - 0.5;
  float y = aastep(0.0, sqrt(cmyk.z) - 2.0 * length(Yuv) + n);
  vec2 Kuv = 50.0 * mat2(0.707, -0.707, 0.707, 0.707) * st;
  Kuv = fract(Kuv) - 0.5;
  float k = aastep(0.0, sqrt(cmyk.w) - 2.0 * length(Kuv) + n);

  vec3 rgbscreen = 1.0 - vec3(c, m, y);
  rgbscreen = mix(rgbscreen, vec3(0.0), 0.7 * k + 0.5 * n);
  vec2 fw = fwidth(st);
  float blend = smoothstep(0.7, 1.4, 200.0 * max(fw.s, fw.t));
  gl_FragColor = vec4(mix(rgbscreen, rgb, blend), 1.0);
}
```

Listing 7.5. The fragment shader to generate the halftone pattern in Figure 7.6.

7.8 Performance

Shader-capable hardware comes in many variations. An older laptop GPU or a low-cost, low-power mobile GPU can typically run the same shader as a brand new high-end GPU for gaming enthusiasts, but the raw performance might differ by as much as 100 times. The usefulness of a certain procedural approach is therefore highly dependent on the application. GPUs get faster all the time, and their internal architectures change between releases, sometimes radically so. For this reason, absolute benchmarking is a rather futile exercise in a general presentation like this one. Instead, I have measured the performance of a few of the example shaders from this chapter on a selection of hardware. The results are summarized in Table 7.1.

The list should not be considered a representative or carefully picked selection—it is just a few random GPUs of different models, neither top performing nor particularly new, as well as some of the shaders we have presented in this chapter. The program to run this benchmark is included in the code repository. The absolute figures depend on operating system and driver version and should only be taken as a general indication of performance. The most useful information in the table is the relative performance within one column: it is instructive to compare a constant color shader or a single texture lookup with various procedural shaders on the same GPU. As is apparent from the benchmarks, it is very hard to beat a single texture lookup for raw speed, not least because most current GPUs are specifically designed to have a high texture bandwidth. However, reasonably complex procedural textures can run at perfectly useful speeds, and they become more competitive when the limiting factor for GPU performance is memory bandwidth. Procedural methods can execute in parallel to memory reads and add to the visual complexity of a textured surface without necessarily slowing things down. For the foreseeable future, GPUs will continue to have a problem with memory bandwidth, and

Shader	NVIDIA 9600M	AMD HD6310	AMD HD4850	NVIDIA GTX260
Constant color	422	430	2,721	3,610
Single texture	412	414	2,718	3,610
Dots (Fig 7.2, lower right)	360	355	2,720	3,420
Perlin noise (Fig 7.4, top left)	63	97	1,042	697
5x Perlin (Fig 7.4, bottom left)	11	23	271	146
Worley noise (Fig 7.5, top left)	82	116	1,192	787
Worley tiles (Fig 7.5, bottom)	26	51	580	345
Halftone (Fig 7.6)	34	52	597	373

Table 7.1. Benchmarks for a few example shaders. Numbers are in millions of fragments per second. NVIDIA 9600M is an old laptop GPU, AMD HD6310 is a budget laptop GPU. AMD HD4850 and NVIDIA GTX260 were mid-range desktop GPUs in 2011. High-end GPUs of 2011 perform several times better.

their computational power will keep increasing. There is certainly lots of room to experiment here.

7.9 Conclusion

The aim of this chapter was to demonstrate that modern shader-capable GPUs are mature enough to render procedural patterns at fully interactive speeds, and that GLSL is a good language for writing procedural shaders very similar to the ones that have become standard tools in offline rendering over the past two decades. In a content production process that includes procedural textures, some of the visuals need to be created using math and a programming language as tools for creative visual expression, and this requires a different kind of talent than what it takes to be a good visual artist with traditional image editing tools. Also, the GPU is still a limited resource, and care needs to be taken not to overwhelm it with overly complex shaders. Procedural texturing is not yet a wise choice in every situation. However, there are situations where a procedural pattern simply does the job better than a traditional, image-based texture, and the tools and the required processing power are now available to do it in real-time. Now is a good time to start writing procedural shaders in GLSL.

Bibliography

[Apodaca and Gritz 99] Anthony Apodaca and Larry Gritz. *Advanced RenderMan: Creating GCI for Motion Pictures*. San Francisco: Morgan Kaufmann, 1999.

[Ebert et al. 03] David Ebert, Kenton Musgrave, Darwyn Peachey, Ken Perlin, and Steve Worley. *Texturing and Modeling: A Procedural Approach*. San Francisco: Morgan Kaufmann, 2003.

[Gustavson 05] Stefan Gustavson. "Simplex Noise Demystified." http://www.itn.liu.se/~stegu/simplexnoise/simplexnoise.pdf, March 22, 2005.

[Gustavson 11] Stefan Gustavson. "Cellular Noise in GLSL: Implementation Notes." http://www.itn.liu.se/~stegu/GLSL-cellular/GLSL-cellular-notes.pdf, April 19, 2011.

[McEwan et al. 12] Ian McEwan, David Sheets, Stefan Gustavson, and Mark Richardson. "Efficient Computational Noise in GLSL." *Journal of Graphics Tools* 16:2 (2012), to appear.

[Perlin 85] Ken Perlin. "An Image Synthesizer." *Proceedings of ACM Siggraph 85* 19:3 (1985), 287–296.

[Worley 96] Steven Worley. "A Cellular Texture Basis Function." In *SIGGRAPH '96, Proceedings of the 23rd Annual Conference on Computer Graphics and Interactive Techniques*, pp. 291–293. New York: ACM, 1996.

OpenGL SC Emulation Based on OpenGL and OpenGL ES

8

Hwanyong Lee and Nakhoon Baek

8.1   Introduction

OpenGL is one of the most widely used 3D graphics APIs. It originated from IRIS GL in the 1980s and is now available on various platforms. Currently, Khronos Group, the open standard consortium, consistently manages all the standard specifications for the OpenGL family, including OpenGL, OpenGL ES (for embedded systems), OpenGL SC (safety critical profile), and WebGL.

At this time, the latest version for desktops and workstations is OpenGL 4.2, which was released in August 2011. On embedded systems and handheld devices, OpenGL ES 1.1 and 2.0 are widely used. These embedded versions are smashingly successful, especially for smart phones and tablet PCs.

Another sibling in the OpenGL family is OpenGL SC, the safety-critical profile [Stockwell 09] derived from OpenGL ES. Historically, this safety-critical profile was started as a subset of OpenGL ES to minimize implementation and safety certification costs, mainly for the DO-178B requirements [RTCA/DO-178B 92]. However, due to the different targets and requirements, OpenGL SC became another independent specification. Currently, OpenGL SC and OpenGL ES are not compatible with each other despite some common features. Figure 8.1 shows OpenGL SC-based cockpit displays.

In safety-critical markets for avionics, industrial, military, medical, and automotive applications, OpenGL SC plays a major role for the graphical interfaces and applications. The need for this 3D graphics API is rapidly increasing with the growth of the safety-critical market. For medical and automotive applications, consumer electronics markets are starting to strongly ask for this standard.

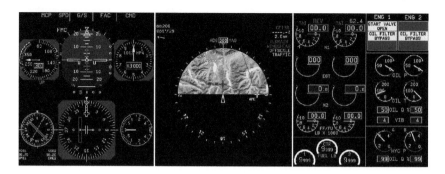

Figure 8.1. OpenGL SC-based cockpit displays. *Image courtesy of ESTEREL Technology Inc.*

We naturally need a cost-effective way of implementing OpenGL SC, based on commercial off-the-shelf items [Cole 05, Snyder 05, Beeby 02]. We have a few OpenGL SC implementations at this time, some of which provide fully dedicated OpenGL SC semiconductor chips or exclusive device drivers on existing OpenGL chips. These solutions require a large amount of development cost. Though some full software solutions are also available, their performance is not satisfying for many applications.

Implementation of a graphics library over another existing graphics pipeline has advantages such as cost-effectiveness and portability. For OpenGL ES, we have an example of OpenGL ES 1.1 implementation over OpenGL ES 2.0, where the ES 2.0 pipeline was modified to fully support ES 1.1 features [Hill et al. 08]. OpenGL ES 1.1 emulation over desktop OpenGL is also available [Lee and Baek 09, Baek and Lee 12]. To support WebGL features on Windows PCs, an OpenGL ES 2.0 emulation on the top of Direct3D 9 was developed as discussed in Chapter 39.

In this chapter, an OpenGL SC emulation library is implemented based on the OpenGL 1.1 fixed rendering pipeline and the `ARB_multitexture` extension [Leech 99], which may be one of the lowest-end hardware profiles for embedded 3D graphics systems. We also demonstrate emulating OpenGL SC on OpenGL ES hardware. Finally, our OpenGL SC emulation can be used for desktop-based OpenGL SC development. One of the most widely used graphics devices on low-end embedded systems is OpenGL ES 1.1, which is based on OpenGL 1.3, and is mainly used because of its stability, cost-effectiveness, and small footprint.

This kind of implementation is strongly required for the following reasons:

- Cost-effectiveness. Although we could develop the whole OpenGL SC facilities from scratch, there are already hardware devices and their corresponding drivers with OpenGL or OpenGL ES support. Our goal is to provide additional OpenGL SC support at a relatively low cost by utilizing these existing hardware devices.

- **Efficient development environment.** Most embedded systems are typically developed on desktop PCs and then downloaded on the target devices
  since the target embedded systems do not often have sufficient computing
  power for development tools. Thus, for these cross-compiling environments,
  emulation libraries for the PCs are required.

- **Rapid and stable implementation.** Before the delivery of the whole independent OpenGL SC hardware or full software implementations, we rapidly
  created a stable product with a low-level emulation library based on the desktop OpenGL.

In the next section, we first show the previous OpenGL SC implementations
and other related cases of emulation library implementations for the 3D graphics
API's. Our overall design and implementation details are presented in Section 8.3.
Implementation results and conclusions follow in Sections 8.4 and 8.5, respectively.

8.2   OpenGL SC Implementations

OpenGL SC simplifies safety-critical certification, guarantees repeatability, allows
compliance with real-time requirements, and facilitates porting of legacy safety-critical
applications [Pulli et al. 07].

OpenGL SC 1.0.1 targets various application areas, including

- **Avionics applications.** The Federal Aviation Administration (FAA) mandated DO-178B certification for software airplane cockpits, demanding 100%
  reliable graphics drivers for instrumentation, navigation, and controls [Khronos
  Group 11].

- **Automotive applications.** Integrated dashboard applications will need
  OpenGL SC safety-critical reliability.

- **Military applications.** Primarily avionics and also increasingly embedded
  training and visualization on handheld devices use OpenGL SC.

- **Industrial applications.** Equipment for power plant instrumentation,
  transportation monitoring and control, networking, surveillance, etc., will all
  eventually be updated with commercial off-the-shelf graphics that meet safety-
  critical certification.

- **Medical applications.** Real-time display of medical data requires 100%
  reliability for surgery.

Currently, it is more cost-effective to develop separate OpenGL SC device drivers
over the commercially available OpenGL semiconductor chips, as shown in Figure 8.2, rather than to build up fully-dedicated OpenGL SC chips and device drivers

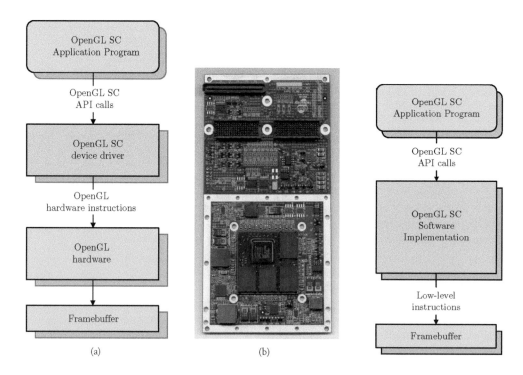

Figure 8.2. An OpenGL SC implementation based on the OpenGL-family semiconductor chip. (a) API call flow (b) XMC G1 Graphic Board *Image courtesy of COTS Technology Inc.*

Figure 8.3. A full software OpenGL SC implementation.

from scratch using register-level instructions. Even with the limitations, developers can accomplish high execution speeds due to hardware support. There are two examples in this implementation category: ALT Software Inc. uses AMD OpenGL chips, and Presagis Inc. developed their OpenGL SC drivers over NVIDIA OpenGL chips.

There are also a few full software OpenGL SC implementations, such as IGL178 from Quantum3D Inc. and Vincent SC from Vincent3D Inc. In these cases, as shown in Figure 8.3, it was relatively easy to adopt new hardware. In contrast, slow execution speeds are unavoidable. However, software implementations provide stable systems with easy modification at reasonably low costs.

The third implementation method is building up an OpenGL SC emulation library based on an OpenGL device driver and hardware. More precisely, we developed an OpenGL SC emulator on the OpenGL device driver, as shown in Figure 8.4. These emulators can be implemented with minimal cost if we choose a suitable underlying library. However, generally, it is not simple to bridge the gap between the target API and the underlying library.

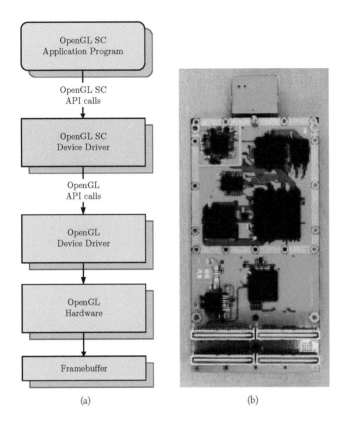

Figure 8.4. OpenGL SC emulator library on the OpenGL device driver. (a) API call flow (b) PMC OpenGL ES Graphic Board. *Image courtesy of HUONE Inc.*

8.3 Design and Implementation

8.3.1 Overall Pipeline

The OpenGL SC specification has 101 functions based on the OpenGL 1.3 specification [Leech 01]. These API functions can be classified into the core API functions and several extensions: a core extension of OES_single_precision, a mandatory extension of EXT_paletted_texture, and an optional extension of EXT_shared_texture_palette [Leech 99]. These two texture-related extensions are critical to most avionics 2D mapping applications. They separate color tables from texture data to allow rapid color table change and permit palettes to be shared between multiple textures [Stockwell 09]. Our implementation supports all OpenGL SC extensions. Figure 8.5 shows the block diagram of the entire OpenGL SC rendering pipeline.

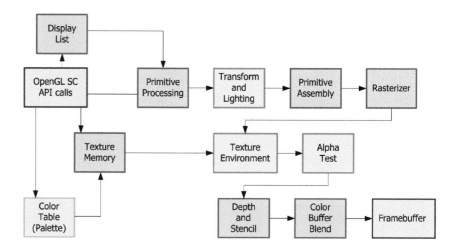

Figure 8.5. The OpenGL SC rendering pipeline.

Although the same function names are defined in OpenGL SC and its ancestor OpenGL specifications, they do not provide the same functionality. Customized to safety-critical devices, the features and acceptable parameter values for the OpenGL SC functions are different from the original OpenGL specifications. Thus, to fulfill OpenGL SC requirements, we perform strict error checking and proper numerical conversions prior to OpenGL hardware execution. This extra work is performed on a case-by-case basis, similar to the implementation of OpenGL ES 1.1 over desktop OpenGL [Baek and Lee 12].

OpenGL SC functions and extensions	Requirements for OpenGL hardware	Implementation Strategy
most of core functions	OpenGL 1.1 core	error checking and function emulation
ARB_multitexture extension	more than two texture units	use ARB functions (instead of 1.3 core)
OES_single_precision extension	none	numerical conversion and error checking codes
EXT_paletted_texture extension	none	use paletted texture processing pipeline
EXT_shared_texture_palette extension	none	use paletted texture processing pipeline

Table 8.1. Summary of our implementation strategy.

Our implementation strategy for OpenGL SC features is summarized in Table 8.1:

- Core functions from OpenGL 1.1. These functions are basically provided by the underlying OpenGL hardware pipeline. Some of them additionally require numerical conversions before calling the underlying OpenGL functions.

- Core functions from OpenGL 1.3. Excluding OpenGL 1.1 functions from OpenGL SC specification, the remaining pure OpenGL 1.3 core functions are all related to the ARB_multitexture extension.

- OES_single_precision extension. The single precision extension is a mandatory extension. Fortunately, these functions are single-precision floating point type variations of the original double-precision floating point based API functions in the original OpenGL specification. Thus, from the viewpoint of OpenGL SC implementers, these functions can be used to convert the user-provided single-precision floating point values into double-precision floating point values; they then call the underlying OpenGL functions. In the case of OpenGL SC specifications, the following four functions are effective:

```
void glDepthRangef(GLclampf near, GLclampf far);
void glFrustumf(GLfloat left, GLfloat right,
                GLfloat bottom, GLfloat top,
                GLfloat near, GLfloat far);
void glOrthof(GLfloat left, GLfloat right,
              GLfloat bottom, GLfloat top,
              GLfloat near, GLfloat far);
void glClearDepthf(GLclampf depth);
```

- EXT_paletted_texture extension. This mandatory extension is used to support legacy avionics applications, and currently available OpenGL-related devices do not support it. With this extension, a texture can be defined as an index-based texture and its corresponding *color table* or *color palette*. Currently, most graphics devices use the direct color system and do not support indexed color features. To fully support this extension, we introduced a full software implementation of a new texture processing pipeline.

- EXT_shared_texture_palette extension. This optional extension allows multiple textures to share a single color palette. Thus, it can be applied only when the above EXT_paletted_texture extension is already supported, and meets the same problem. Our newly designed texture processing pipeline also supports this optional extension.

8.3.2 Texture Pipeline

To support the EXT_paletted_texture and EXT_shared_texture_palette extensions, we made a large amount of modifications to the texture handling functions,

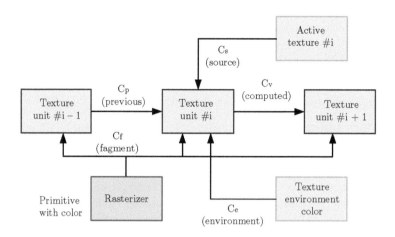

Figure 8.6. Texture color calculation for a texture unit.

including `glTexImage2D` and others. Figure 8.6 shows the multiple texture units and their relationships: a texture unit gets the previous color, active texture color, and texture environment color and then calculates its computed color and passes it to the next texture unit.

For each texture unit, as shown in Figure 8.7, we need a dedicated color table to support paletted texture extensions. An extra color table in the global context is also required to support the **EXT_shared_texture_palette** extension. We can

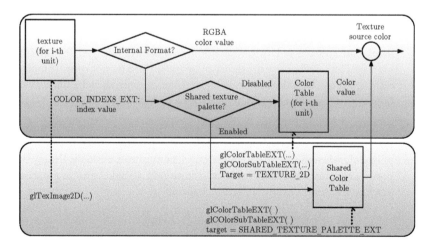

Figure 8.7. Our implementation of a texture unit with paletted texture support.

use `glColorTableEXT` and `glColorSubTableEXT` functions to store color values of the quadruple (red, green, blue, alpha) for each index.

When defining a texture with the internal format of RGBA, each pixel in the texture is stored in a 4-byte quadruple color. These quadruple colors are directly used as the texture source colors, as specified in the typical texture processing pipelines.

For palette textures, pixels are expressed as 1-byte color index values. Later, our texture processing pipeline uses these indices to pick up the actual quadruple color values from the color tables in the texture unit or the global context, according to the user-specified flag values. Conceptually, these color restoration procedures would be repeatedly performed whenever those textures are needed. In our implementation, we naturally introduce a texture cache for each texture unit. Thus, the system may repeatedly use the corresponding cached texture instead of the original paletted texture. When the user provides a new texture or when updates the corresponding color table, the cached texture is discarded, and we perform a new restoration process.

8.4 Results

Our first-stage implementation was done on a Linux-based system with a hardware-accelerated OpenGL device driver. Most of the optimization and debugging were performed on this Linux-based implementation with a set of OpenGL chips from different vendors. The OpenGL SC conformance test suite from the Khronos group was used to verify the correctness of our implementation.

In the second stage, our target was low-powered embedded systems, which are equipped with OpenGL 1.2–based graphics chips with the multitexture extension. We verified the execution of all the OpenGL SC test applications on these systems, as shown in Figure 8.8.

(a) (b)

Figure 8.8. Developing on an embedded system: (a) development environment; (b) screen output.

	(a) OpenGL 1.1 (frames per second)	(b) OpenGL SC emulation (frames per second)	ratio (b/a)	delays
gears	1325.5	1301.8	98.21%	1.79%
clock	1178.6	1159.0	98.34%	1.66%
spin	1261.3	1239.0	98.23%	1.77%
angles	339.4	332.6	97.99%	2.01%
average			98.27%	1.73%

Table 8.2. Execution speeds from the test programs.

Table 8.2 shows the overall cost of our OpenGL SC emulation library. We first executed the original OpenGL sample programs, converted them into OpenGL SC programs, and then compared their performance. OpenGL SC programs cannot use OpenGL-specific GL_QUAD or GL_POLYGON primitives and additionally perform extra software emulations for the paletted textures. Despite these handicaps, our implementation shows less than 2% delay time. All the experiments were performed

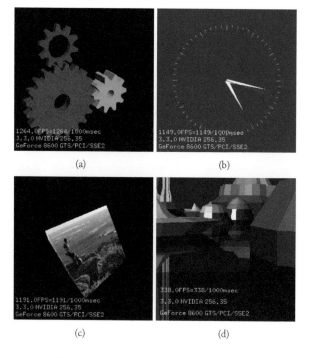

Figure 8.9. Screenshots from the test programs: (a) gears, (b) clock, (c) spin, and (d) angles.

on an Intel Core2 Duo–based system with 4GB of RAM and NVIDIA GeForce 8600 graphics card. Figure 8.9 shows some screenshots from the test programs.

8.5   Conclusion

According to our tests, all the core and extension features of OpenGL SC can be achieved as an emulation layer over OpenGL 1.1 hardware equipped with the multi-texture extension. The results demonstrate the effectiveness of our approach. Our implementation is able to run various OpenGL SC applications and conformance tests correctly with less than 2% performance overhead. Our next step is to imple-ment OpenGL SC over lower-powered chips such as multimedia processors or DSP chips.

When the OpenGL working group released OpenGL 3.0, the working group announced that later OpenGL versions will not support the "begin-end" scheme any more. OpenGL ES is designed without "begin-end" scheme at the beginning of de-sign stage. Paletted textures are not supported by the current OpenGL hardware. Therefore, to implement OpenGL SC on OpenGL or OpenGL ES hardware, we should use a chipset released quite a long time ago, or we should make software emu-lation that can increase performance overhead and cost. Furthermore, current safety critical applications also request high performance rendering with various visual ef-fects, image processing, and blending.

Khronos held a face-to-face meeting in Phoenix, Arizona, in September 2011 that included discussions on the future roadmap for OpenGL SC. There was agree-ment that OpenGL SC should evolve to meet the needs of the safety critical market and that Khronos should consider basing that evolution on OpenGL ES 2.0, which is itself a streamlined API. However, more discussion is required to find the right combination of OpenGL SC 1.0 and OpenGL ES 2.0 to effectively develop the OpenGL SC roadmap.

Bibliography

[Baek and Lee 12] N. Baek and H. Lee. "OpenGL ES 1.1 Implementation Based on OpenGL." *Multimedia Tools and Applications* 57:3 (2012), 669–685.

[Beeby 02] M. Beeby. "Aviation Quality COTS Software: Reality or Folly." In *21st Digital Avionics Systems Conference,* 2002.

[Cole 05] P. Cole. "OpenGL ES SC: Open Standard Embedded Graphics API for Safety Critical Applications." In *24th Digital Avionics Systems Conference,* 2005.

[Hill et al. 08] S. Hill, M. Robart, and E. Tanguy. "Implementing OpenGL ES 1.1 over OpenGL ES 2.0." In *Digest of Technical Papers, IEEE International Conference on Con-sumer Electronics,* pp. 1–2, 2008.

[Khronos Group 11] Khronos Group. "The Khronos Group Inc." http://www.khronos.org/, 2011.

[Lee and Baek 09] H. Lee and N. Baek. "Implementing OpenGL ES on OpenGL." In *Proc. of the 13th IEEE International Symposium on Consumer Electronics*, pp. 999–1003, 2009.

[Leech 99] J. Leech. *Appendix F. ARB Extensions, The OpenGL Graphics System: A Specification, Version 1.2.1*. OpenGL ARB, 1999.

[Leech 01] J. Leech. *The OpenGL Graphics System: A Specification, Version 1.3*. OpenGL ARB, 2001.

[Pulli et al. 07] K. Pulli, J. Vaarala, V. Miettinen, T. Aarnio, and K. Roimela. *Mobile 3D Graphics: With OpenGL ES and M3G*. San Francisco: Morgan Kaufmann, 2007.

[RTCA/DO-178B 92] RTCA/DO-178B. *Software Considerations in Airborne Systems and Equipment Certification*. RTCA Inc., 1992.

[Snyder 05] M. Snyder. "Solving the Embedded OpenGL Puzzle: Making Standards, Tools, and APIs Work Together in Highly Embedded and Safety Critical Environments." In *24th Digital Avionics Systems Conference*, 2005.

[Stockwell 09] B. Stockwell. *OpenGL SC: Safety-Critical Profile Specification, Version 1.0.1 (Difference Specification)*. Khronos Group, 2009.

Mixing Graphics and Compute with Multiple GPUs 9

Alina Alt

9.1   Introduction

In recent years, GPU computing has evolved to deliver teraflops of floating point compute power to desktop systems. This trend has necessitated that scientific and visualization applications require a mix of compute and graphics capabilities in addition to efficiently processing large amounts of data. Examples of such applications include physically based simulations (e.g., particle systems) and image/video processing (e.g., special effects, image recognition, augmented reality, etc.).

To maximize this compute and graphics capability, the applications need to be designed with interoperability in mind, which allows data passing between compute and graphics contexts.

Current compute APIs include functions dedicated to interoperability with OpenGL. To illustrate the concept of graphics and compute API interoperability, the first section of this chapter uses the CUDA C API. The second part of the chapter focuses on interoperability on a system scale. In particular, what are the challenges and benefits of dedicating one GPU for compute and another for graphics? And how does this translate to application design decisions helping to enable efficient, cross-GPU, compute and graphics interoperability?

9.2 Graphics and Compute Interoperability on an API Level

Since they were developed many years after the development of the graphics APIs, GPU computing languages and APIs, such as the CUDA C API, which is NVIDIA's platform computing interface, and OpenCL, which is a cross-platform computing interface, were tasked with providing a way to interact with graphics API objects to avoid unnecessary data movement through both the GPU and system memory. As of OpenGL Version 4.2, there is no OpenGL mechanism for interaction with any of the compute APIs; therefore, it is exclusively up to each of the compute APIs to provide such a mechanism. The mechanism of interaction with OpenGL is very similar for each of the compute APIs, and we will illustrate this mechanism with the usage of the CUDA C Runtime API [NVIDIA 11]. This section of the chapter will only deal with interoperability on an API level.

9.2.1 Interoperability Preparation

CUDA and OpenGL interoperability requires a current OpenGL context. Also, the context must remain current in the interoperability execution thread for the duration of the interoperability.

Before CUDA can begin working with an OpenGL object, a correspondence between the object and a CUDA graphics resource must be established. Each OpenGL object must first be registered with the CUDA context as a CUDA graphics resource. This is a costly operation, as it can allocate resources in the CUDA context and must be done only once per object after its creation and before CUDA starts working with the object.

There are two registering CUDA API calls: one for buffer objects and another for texture and renderbuffer objects. Listing 9.1 illustrates registering an OpenGL Pixel Buffer Object (PBO) with CUDA using `cudaGraphicsGLRegisterBuffer`.

```
GLuint imagePBO;
cudaGraphicsResource_t     cudaResource;
//OpenGL buffer creation
glGenBuffers(1, &imagePBO);
glBindBuffer(GL_PIXEL_UNPACK_BUFFER_ARB, imagePBO);
glBufferData(GL_PIXEL_UNPACK_BUFFER_ARB, size, NULL, GL_DYNAMIC_DRAW);
glBindBuffer(GL_PIXEL_UNPACK_BUFFER_ARB,0);
//Registration with CUDA
cudaGraphicsGLRegisterBuffer(&cudaResource, imagePBO,
cudaGraphicsRegisterFlagsNone);
```

Listing 9.1. Registering on OpenGL PBO with CUDA.

```
GLuint imageTex;
cudaGraphicsResource_t    cudaResource;
//OpenGL texture creation
glGenTextures(1, &imageTex);
glBindTexture(GL_TEXTURE_2D , imageTex);
//set texture parameters here
glTexImage2D(GL_TEXTURE_2D ,0, GL_RGBA8UI_EXT , width , height , 0,
GL_RGBA_INTEGER_EXT, GL_UNSIGNED_BYTE , NULL);
glBindTexture(GL_TEXTURE_2D , 0);
//Registration with CUDA
cudaGraphicsGLRegisterImage (&cudaResource , imageTex , GL_TEXTURE_2D ,
cudaGraphicsMapFlagsNone);
```

Listing 9.2. Registering an OpenGL Texture with CUDA.

OpenGL texture and renderbuffer objects are registered using `cudaGraphics GLRegisterImage`, which currently supports the following image formats:

- GL_RED, GL_RG, GL_RGBA, GL_LUMINANCE, GL_ALPHA, GL_LUMINANCE_ALPHA, GL_INTENSITY.

- {GL_R, GL_RG, GL_RGBA} X {8, 16, 16F, 32F, 8UI, 16UI, 32UI, 8I, 16I, 32I}.

- {GL_LUMINANCE, GL_ALPHA, GL_LUMINANCE_ALPHA, GL_INTENSITY} X {8, 16, 16F_ARB, 32F_ARB, 8UI_EXT, 16UI_EXT, 32UI_EXT, 8I_EXT, 16I_EXT, 32I_EXT}.

Note that for brevity's sake, the list is abbreviated. For example, {GL_R, GL_RG} x{8x16} would expand into {GL_R8, GL_R16, GL_RG8, GL_RG16}. The most up-to-date list can be found in [NVIDIA 01].

Applications that require the usage of textures of unsupported formats have two options: either perform format conversion to and from the supported format before and after CUDA-GL interoperability, or have CUDA interact with a PBO and then copy pixels from the PBO to the texture object.

Listing 9.2 illustrates registering an unnormalized integer texture with CUDA.

After the application is done with the resource, it should unregister it from the CUDA context using `cudaGraphicsUnregisterResource`.

9.2.2 OpenGL Object Interaction

Both OpenGL and CUDA logically partition device memory into two kinds of memory: texture memory and linear memory (Figure 9.1). An OpenGL buffer object, which is unformatted device memory, will map to a CUDA linear memory object, which is a CUDA buffer in device memory that can be referenced via pointer. Similarly, OpenGL texture and renderbuffer objects will map to a CUDA array, which is an opaque memory layout optimized for texture hardware access, and which will be

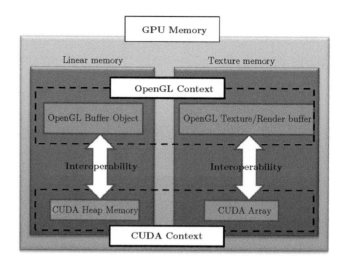

Figure 9.1. Device memory map for interoperability.

setup by the driver to take advantage of the available texture hardware features such as caching, filtering, etc.

Typically, the driver will try to share the graphics resource with OpenGL instead of creating a copy in the CUDA context, but there are times where the driver will choose to create a separate copy, for example, when the OpenGL and CUDA contexts reside on separate GPUs or when OpenGL allocates the resource in system memory instead of device memory. The latter can happen when the application frequently needs to upload or download data to or from the GPU, or when the OpenGL context spans multiple GPUs, as is in the case for scalable, multi-GPU visualization solutions.

Every time CUDA interacts with an OpenGL object, the object must be mapped and subsequently unmapped from the CUDA context. This is done with `cuda GraphicsMapResources` and `cudaGraphicsUnmapResources`. These calls have dual responsibility: (1) gating object access to ensure that all outstanding work on the object is complete (map ensures that all prior OpenGL operations that use the resource have completed before CUDA accesses the resource, and unmap does the same for CUDA operations) and (2) synchronizing between the contents of the resource copies if there is more than one copy. The driver will attempt to perform all synchronization on the GPU as much as possible, but in some cases, it cannot guarantee that the CPU thread will not stall as well, e.g., on Mac OS or on Linux with indirect rendering.

The last parameter of `cudaGraphicsGLRegister*` is a flag that tells CUDA how the resource will be used. Currently, possible options include

- `cudaGraphicsRegisterFlagsNone,`

```
unsigned char *memPtr;
cudaGraphicsMapResources(1, &cudaResource, 0);
cudaGraphicsResourceGetMappedPointer((void **)&memPtr, &size,←
    cudaResource);
//call CUDA kernel on memPtr
cudaGraphicsUnmapResources(1, &cudaResource,0);
```

Listing 9.3. CUDA operating on an OpenGL buffer.

- `cudaGraphicsRegisterFlagsReadOnly`,

- `cudaGraphicsRegisterFlagsWriteDiscard`, and

- `cudaGraphicsRegisterFlagsSurfaceLoadStore`.

Choosing the right value for this flag can eliminate unnecessary data movement between CUDA and OpenGL during map/unmap time when synchronizing between the contents of the resource copies (if a copy was created by CUDA). The map/unmap behavior can also be specified anytime using `cudaGraphicsResourceSet` `MapFlags`.

Applications where CUDA is the producer and OpenGL is the consumer should register the objects with a write-discard flag: then, the content synchronization will be skipped at map time, and the map operation becomes a hardware wait operation. Conversely, applications, where OpenGL is the producer and CUDA is the consumer should register the objects with a read-only flag: then, the content synchronization step will be skipped at unmap time, and the unmap operation becomes a hardware wait operation. Once the graphics resource is mapped into CUDA, the application can obtain a pointer to an object in the CUDA address space using one of the `cudaGraphicsResourceGetMapped*` calls to start interacting with the object. An OpenGL object should not be accessed by OpenGL within the application while it is mapped in CUDA, as it can cause data corruption. Listings 9.3 and 9.4 illustrate the preparation needed for interacting with a buffer object and a texture object, respectively.

```
cudaArray *arrayPtr;
cudaGraphicsMapResources(1, &cudaResource, 0);
cudaGraphicsResourceGetMappedArray((void **) &arrayPtr, cudaResource, ←
    0, 0);
//call CUDA kernel on arrayPtr
cudaGraphicsUnmapResources(1, &cudaResource,0);
```

Listing 9.4. CUDA operating on an OpenGL texture.

9.3° Graphics and Compute Interoperability on a System Level

There are many situations when the application requires distributing graphics and compute portions across two or more GPUs. In other words, one GPU will be dedicated to the computation, while another is dedicated to rendering the scene. In these situations, communication between the compute and graphics contexts turns into communication between devices in a system (Figure 9.2).

Motivations for multi-GPU system architectures:

- Increase in system processing power. Offloading intensive computation from the main-display GPU will always result in overall system interactivity improvement. Also, an additional GPU can often allow applications to overlap graphics and compute tasks (this is possible when one of the APIs is a producer and the other is a consumer).

- More FLOPS per dollar. A combination of a dedicated compute GPU and a low-end graphics GPU can often have the same or better performance for a lower cost than a single, high-end GPU.

- Increase in system functionality. System configuration can happen without the required graphics capabilities on the compute GPU, for example, a simulation application, previously running on the nondisplay GPU, such as the NVIDIA Tesla GPU, now adding advanced visualization features.

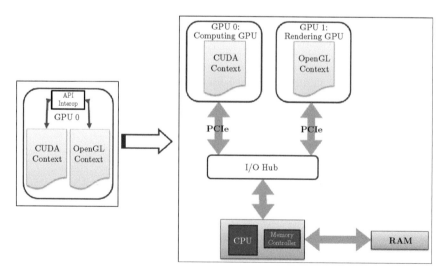

Figure 9.2. Single-GPU ecosystem (left) versus multi-GPU ecosystem (right).

- **Increased determinism.** A Windows application can minimize compute kernel launch overhead by bypassing the Windows Driver Display Model (WDDM) if a nondisplay device is used for the simulation portion. For example, the NVIDIA Tesla GPU can be configured as a nondisplay device by using the TCC driver mode.

Developers must keep in mind that cross-GPU interoperability will inevitably involve data transfers as part of the content synchronization between the contexts, which, depending on the data size, can impact the application performance. This is an important point to consider in addition to the potential benefits of multi-GPU configurations, such as improvement in system interactivity, task overlap, etc.

An example of task overlap achieved by dedicating one GPU for compute and another for graphics is illustrated in Figure 9.3. Both parts of the figure show a timeline of GPU commands in an application that uses API interoperability where CUDA is the producer and OpenGL is the consumer. In this example, CUDA and OpenGL have similar workloads. Figure 9.3(a) shows the timeline of commands as they are executed on a single GPU. Figure 9.3(b) shows the timeline where compute and graphics commands are executed on two different GPUs. In this case, the application will incur an overhead from contents synchronization occurring during the unmap operation.

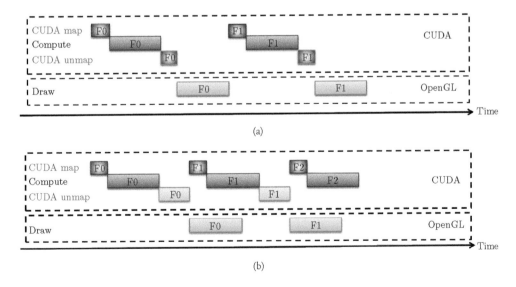

Figure 9.3. GPU timeline. (a) CUDA and OpenGL reside on a single GPU. (b) CUDA and OpenGL reside on separate GPUs.

When implementing multi-GPU compute-graphics interoperability, developers are faced with multiple design options:

1. API interoperability. Context interaction as it was described in Section 9.3. In other words, letting the driver handle the communication between the contexts. This option requires practically no code changes in the existing, single-GPU applications.

2. CUDA memory copy + API interoperability. This approach gives the application fine-grained control over the data movement. It leaves it up to the driver to decide whether the data transfer will happen as a direct peer-to-peer transfer or as a staged transfer through system memory. It requires creating an auxiliary CUDA context setup with OpenGL interoperability on the rendering GPU and then having the application initiate the transfer between the CUDA contexts using CUDA memcpy. This approach can allow applications to implement double buffering for overlapping transfers with compute/draw or transfer only a portion of the object, etc.

3. Naïve interoperability. This is a completely manual implementation of CUDA and OpenGL interoperability. It requires mapping of the CUDA and OpenGL objects to system memory, copying data between the mapped objects, and then unmapping the objects. This is the slowest implementation because the data transfer involves an additional CPU memcpy. This implementation should be used where manual data movement is preferred/required but option (2) is not applicable, for example, applications that have separate code bases for the simulation and the visualization portions, i.e., a simulation plugin for a modeling application that requires simulated results to reside in system memory.

Aside from the options above, one can also set up an auxiliary OpenGL context on the computing GPU, perform the API interoperability on that GPU, and then use OpenGL copy extension [NVIDIA 09] to copy the objects to the rendering GPU. This implementation will not be considered as an option as it has no real benefits over the presented options, in addition to being limited to texture objects and applications that support graphics context creation on the compute GPU (for example, TCC driver mode on Windows disables graphics support on the GPU).

Figures 9.4(a)–(c) depict all possible design combinations. For any particular application, one combination will be more suitable than others. Table 9.1 summarizes properties of each combination in Figures 9.4(a)–(c) based on the following aspects:

• Implementation overhead. In comparison to a single GPU architecture.

• Synchronization overhead. Characterization of content synchronization overhead.

• Compatibility. Application use-cases classification.

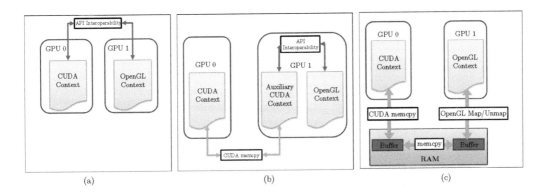

Figure 9.4. Various ways for cross-GPU compute and graphics context interaction: (a) API interoperability, (b) CUDA `memcpy` + API interoperability, (c) naïve interoperability.

Combination	Implementation Overhead	Synchronization Overhead	Compatibility
(a) API interoperability	Code written for a single GPU works well on multi-GPU configurations with almost no code changes.	Similar to option (b)	Best suited for applications that require quick development turnaround and don't mind the driver controlling of cross-GPU communication.
(b) CUDA `memcpy`+API interoperability	Auxiliary CUDA context management, CUDA `memcpy`.	Involves a direct GPU-to-GPU data transfer.	Best suited for applications that can benefit from fine-grain control over the data transfers.
(c) Naïve interoperability	Management of multiple in-flight buffer copies in system memory.	Involves GPU-to-host memory data transfer, a CPU memory copy, and a host memory-to-GPU data transfer.	Best suited for applications that can benefit from fine-grain control over the data transfers but cannot implement option (b).

Table 9.1. Summary of cross-GPU compute and graphics contexts interaction.

9.4   Conclusion

We have covered interoperability between CUDA and OpenGL at two different levels: at an API level and at a system level. Often times, CUDA and OpenGL contexts can reside on two different GPUs, and even though multi-GPU configurations promise a significant increase in functionality and productivity, they also introduce some complexity when it comes to context communication across multiple GPUs. The analysis presented in this chapter can provide developers with some background and tools to navigate through compute-graphics interoperability complexities introduced by multi-GPU configurations.

Bibliography

[NVIDIA 01] NVIDIA.   "CUDA   Reference   Manual."   http://developer.nvidia.com/cuda-toolkit, 2001.

[NVIDIA 11] NVIDIA. "CUDA C Programming guide." http://developer.download.nvidia.com/compute/cuda/4_0/toolkit/docs/CUDA_C_Programming_Guide.pdf, pp. 37–39 and pp. 48–50. May 6, 2011.

[NVIDIA 09] NVIDIA. "NV_Copy_Image OpenGL Specification" http://www.opengl.org/registry/specs/NV/copy_image.txt, July 29, 2009.

II

Rendering Techniques

We can't possibly imagine a book about OpenGL without rendering, and neither could the authors of this book.

António Ramires Fernandes and Bruno Oliveira provide a use case for the new OpenGL 4 tessellation pipeline through terrain rendering in their chapter "GPU Tessellation: We Still Have a LOD of Terrain to Cover," providing an entirely GPU-based method for continuous level of detail maintaining a high level of fidelity to the original mesh.

Sébastien Hillaire brings us to a parallel universe where rendering is defined by lines in his chapter "Antialiased Volumetric Lines Using Shader-Based Extrusion." He comes back on the line primitives exposed by OpenGL and their issues before bringing perspective to line rendering thanks to two approaches: one based on the vertex shader stage and one based on the geometry shader stage for perspective correct and antialiased lines.

Stefan Gustavson leads us close to new borders through his chapter "2D Shape Rendering by Distance Fields," allowing perfectly antialiased contours. He is pushing his concept to font rendering and distance field-based effects.

Benjamin Encz analyses WebGL font rendering in his chapter "Efficient Text Rendering in WebGL" by describing canvas- and bitmap-based methods. He concludes his chapter with a performance analysis with both the frame rate and the memory footprint in mind.

Dzmitry Malyshau discusses an approach inspired by Blender in his chapter "Layered Textures Rendering Pipeline." He aims at providing more flexibility to the rendering pipeline to handle complex object materials so that artists may express their creativity during the producing while maintaining real-time performance.

Charles de Rousiers and Matt Pettineo present a method for "Depth of Field with Bokeh Rendering." Their method, developed around OpenGL 4 hardware atomic counter, image load and store, and indirect draw, provides a level of performance for real-time application.

Finally, Jochem van der Spek introduces a technique he calls "Shadow Proxies," which provides, for appropriate scenarios, real-time soft shadows with color bleeding.

GPU Tessellation: We Still Have a LOD of Terrain to Cover 10

António Ramires Fernandes and Bruno Oliveira

10.1   Introduction

Terrain rendering has come a long way from the days where all data fit in the graphics memory to algorithms that deal with massive amounts of information that do not fit in the system's RAM. Nowadays, a full-blown terrain engine has to deal with out-of-core issues: a first step of the level of detail (LOD) might happen in the CPU to determine which data goes to the GPU, and a second step of LOD may be required to draw all those triangles at interactive rates.

In this chapter we are going to explore how OpenGL 4.x can boost performance in this last step. The algorithms presented will use GPU tessellation for shader-based LOD and view-frustum culling.

Although LOD can substantially reduce the amount of geometry rendered, it may also cripple the fidelity of the representation. An approach will be introduced to render heightmap-based terrains, which can be included in most of the available terrain-rendering engines, that captures in a simple process the irregularities of a terrain, maintaining a very high level of visual fidelity to the original data.

Previous knowledge on the subject of GPU tessellation is assumed. See Chapter 6 or "Programming for Real-Time Tessellation on GPU" [Tatarchuk et al. 09], for an introduction to the subject.

10.2 Rendering Terrains with OpenGL GPU Tessellation

The goal of this section is to present a heightmap-based, fully tessellated terrain rendering implementation, upon which the LOD solutions will grow (see Figure 10.1).

We assume that the heightmap is a regular grid, represented by a greyscale image loaded as a texture. However, the terrain size is not limited by the texture's size, as height values between *texels* can be sampled. The GPU has dedicated hardware for sampling, such as GLSL `texture*` functions, according to the sampler or texture sampler state. The terrain size, in terms of grid points, is, therefore, theoretically unlimited. To avoid the almost flatness of the regions represented by the sampled points, noise-based approaches can be used to provide high-frequency detail.

The terrain size, in terms of physical units, can be further parameterized by defining a grid spacing; in other words, the number of units between two consecutive points in the final grid.

To render the terrain, we use the new primitive introduced with tessellation, the `patch`. A patch can cover as many grid points as the maximum tessellation levels permitted by hardware, a square grid of 64 quads in the current OpenGL 4.0 hardware. This defines a patch as 65×65 vertices, as the edges of patches are shared between adjacent patches. To render a terrain, we define a grid of such patches. As an example, to render a terrain of $8K \times 8K$ points, a grid of 128×128 patches is required. Other patch sizes are possible, but the reported tests (shown later in Figure 10.9), show a performance penalty when using smaller patches.

Since the terrain grid is a highly regular structure, only one vertex to define a patch is needed (e.g., the lower left corner). The regular nature of the terrain's grid allows the developer to compute all other patch elements based solely on this vertex. The final vertex positions, texture coordinates, and normals will be computed in the shaders.

The patch positions are defined as if the terrain were to be drawn in a normalized square, ranging from 0 to 1. A translation and scale operation will be applied in the tessellation evaluation shader to place the terrain where needed.

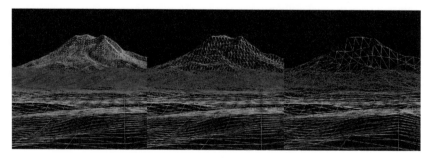

Figure 10.1. Full tessellation (left); high LOD (middle); low LOD (right).

10.2.1   GPU Tessellation Shaders

The vertex shader is a simple pass-through, as vertex transformations will be performed later in the pipeline. It receives the vertex *xz* position, and outputs it to a

```
// one vertex per patch
layout(vertices = 1) out;
// XZ position from the vertex shader
in vec2 posV[];
// XZ position for the tessellation evaluator shader
out vec2 posTC[];

void main()
{
  // Pass through the position
  posTC[gl_InvocationID] = posV[gl_InvocationID];
  // Define tessellation levels
  gl_TessLevelOuter = ivec4(64);
  gl_TessLevelInner = ivec2(64);
}
```

Listing 10.1. Tessellation control shader (full tessellation).

```
layout(quads , fractional_even_spacing, cw) in;

// The heightmap texture sampler
uniform sampler2D heightMap;
// Scale factor for heights
uniform float heightStep;
// Units between two consecutive grid points
uniform float gridSpacing;
// Number of height samples between two consecutive texture texels
uniform int scaleFactor;
// The Projection * View * Model matrix
uniform mat4 pvm;

// Vertices XZ position from the tessellation control shader
in vec2 posTC[];
// Output texture coordinates for the fragment shader
out vec2 uvTE;

void main()
{
  ivec2 tSize = textureSize(heightMap, 0) * scaleFactor;
  vec2 div = tSize * 1.0/64.0;
  // Compute texture coordinates
  uvTE = posTC[0].xy + gl_TessCoord.st/div;
  // Compute pos (scale x and z) [0..1] -> [0..tSize * gridSpacing]
  vec4 res;
  res.xz = uvTE.st * tSize * gridSpacing;
  // Get height for the Y coordinate
  res.y = texture(heightMap, uvTE).r * heightStep;
  res.w = 1.0;
  // Transform the vertices as usual
  gl_Position = pvm * res;
}
```

Listing 10.2. Tessellation evaluator shader.

```
// the normal matrix
uniform mat3 normalMatrix;
// texUnit is the color texture sampler
uniform sampler2D texUnit, heightMap;
uniform float heightStep, gridSpacing, scaleFactor;

// Texture coordinates from the tessellation evaluator shader
in vec2 uvTE;
// Color output
out vec4 outputF;

// Function to retrieve heights
float height(float u, float v)
{
  return (texture(heightMap, vec2(u, v)).r * heightStep);
}

void main()
{
  // compute the normal for the fragment
  float delta =  1.0 / (textureSize(heightMap, 0).x * scaleFactor);
  vec3 deltaX = vec3(
    2.0 * gridSpacing,
    height(uvTE.s + delta, uvTE.t) - height(uvTE.s - delta, uvTE.t),
    0.0);

  vec3 deltaZ = vec3(
    0.0,
    height(uvTE.s, uvTE.t + delta) - height(uvTE.s, uvTE.t - delta),
    2.0 * gridSpacing);

  normalF = normalize(normalMatrix * cross(deltaZ, deltaX));
  // The light direction is hardcoded. Replace with a uniform
  float intensity = max(dot(vec3(0.577, 0.577, 0.577), normalF), 0.0);
  // Diffuse and ambient intensities - replace by uniforms
  vec4 color = texture2D(texUnit, uvTE) * vec4(0.8, 0.8, 0.8, 1.0);

  outputF =  color * intensitiy + color * vec4(0.2, 0.2, 0.2, 1.0);
}
```

Listing 10.3. Fragment shader.

vec2 named posV.[1] The heights, or y coordinates, will be sampled in the tessellation evaluator shader.

The tessellation control shader for a fully tessellated terrain (Listing 10.1) sets all tessellation levels to maximum, as defined by the patch size, configuring the next step, the nonprogrammable tessellation primitive generator. The position from the vertex shader is passed through to the tessellation evaluator shader.

After the execution of this shader, the tessellation primitive generator has all the data it needs, in other words, the tessellation control levels. The output will be a grid of uv coordinates, 65×65, which will be the input of the next programmable stage, the tessellation evaluator (Listing 10.2).

---

[1]As a rule of thumb, in the code displayed in this chapter, all **out** variables are defined with a suffix, which represents the shader that outputs the variable, so **pos** is the input of the vertex shader, and **posV** is the output. In the tessellation control shader, **posV** will be the input, and **posTC** the output and so on.

The tessellation evaluator is responsible for the transformation of the vertex positions and computation of the texture coordinates (uvTE). Although normals could also be computed here, when using LOD it is advisable to compute them in the fragment shader (see Section 10.5.2).

The fragment shader (Listing 10.3) has as input the vertex position through gl_Position, and the texture coordinates through uvTE. The shader is pretty standard apart from the normal computation, which is based on the approach suggested by [Shandkel 02].

And...that's it! A full tessellated terrain can be obtained with these four simple shaders.

10.3 A Simple Approach to Dynamic Level of Detail

When using GPU tessellation, LOD naturally becomes a synonym for tessellation levels. Hence, a simple approach for LOD can be implemented by computing a tessellation level for each patch edge, the outer tessellation levels, while the inner tessellation levels can be computed as the maximum of the respective outer tessellation levels.

A criteria that has been commonly used in previous CPU LOD implementations is the projected screen size of an object's bounding box. Using this approach for the tessellation outer levels, the tessellation level of an edge becomes a function of its projected size. Therefore, adjoining patches will share the same tessellation level for the common edge, thus ensuring a crack-free geometry.

Dynamic LOD requires smooth geometry transitions as the LOD varies. OpenGL offers a tessellation approach that resembles geomorphing, using either fractional_even_spacing or fractional_odd_spacing as the output layout qualifier in the tessellation evaluator shader.

Tessellation levels are defined in the tessellation control shader, so this is where the changes happen. All other shaders remain the same. As in the previous section, the only data available to this shader is a corner of the patch.

Picking the two points that constitute an edge of the patch, one can compute its projected length [Boesch 10]. The projected length is then used to define a level of tessellation based on a single parameter: pixels per edge. For instance, if a segment has a projected size of 32 pixels and we want 4 pixels per triangle edge, then we should compute 32/4, or 8, as the respective outer tessellation level.

The main issue with this approach is that patch edges that are almost collinear with the view direction tend to have very low tessellation levels, as the projected size will be very small; however, this can be fixed with some extra parameterization or over-tessellation. Another solution, provided by [Cantlay 11], is to consider the projected size of a sphere with diameter equal to the length of the edge of the patch. This solution deals effectively with the collinearity issue.

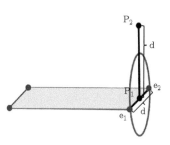

To compute the projected size of the sphere (Figure 10.2) we pick two corners sharing the same edge, e_1 and e_2, and compute the edge's length in world space, d. Then, we compute the midpoint of the edge, P_1, and a new point above the centre, P_2, displaced by the edge's length, d. Points P_1 and P_2 are then transformed to screen space. The distance between the transformed points provides the screen-space diameter of the enclosing sphere.

Figure 10.2. Diagram to compute the projected sphere screen size.

Function `screenSphereSize` (Listing 10.4) performs these computations and determines the tessellation level for the edge, based on the computed diameter divided by the parameter `pixelsPerEdge`, clamped to ensure a valid tessellation level.

Patches outside the view frustum should be discarded by setting their edge tessellation levels to zero. In order to test if a patch is inside the view frustum, we must consider the available information, the four corners of the patch, and, hence, its edges. The heights for points inside the patch are unknown at this stage, so we cannot afford to perform culling based on the y-axis information. However, it is safe

```
// Viewport dimension in pixels
uniform ivec2 viewportDim;
// LOD parameter
uniform int pixelsPerEdge;

// Sphere screen size based on segment e1-e2
float screenSphereSize(vec4 e1, vec4 e2)
{
  vec4 p1 = (e1 + e2) * 0.5;
  vec4 p2 = viewCenter;
  p2.y += distance(e1, e2);
  p1 = p1 / p1.w;
  p2 = p2 / p2.w;
  float l = length((p1.xy - p2.xy) * viewportDim * 0.5);
  return(clamp(l / pixelsPerEdge, 1.0, 64.0));
}


// determining if an edge of a patch is inside the XZ frustum
bool edgeInFrustum(vec4 p, vec4 q)
{
  return !((p.x < -p.w && q.x < -q.w) || (p.x > p.w && q.x > q.w) ||
           (p.z < -p.w && q.z < -q.w) || (p.z > p.w && q.z > q.w));
}
```

Listing 10.4. Auxiliary functions for the tessellation evaluator shader.

to perform conservative culling in clip space based on the *xz* coordinates of the transformed corners of the patch. The function **edgeInFrustum** (Listing 10.4) performs this computation. See [Ramires 07] for more details on how to perform view frustum culling in clip space.

Listing 10.5 shows the tessellation control shader. Functions in Listing 10.4 are also part of the shader's code. Initially, the remaining three corners of the patch are computed. All four corners are then transformed into clip space. Then, for each edge, we check whether it is at least partially inside the view frustum using function

```
layout(vertices = 1) out;
// ...
void main() {
  vec4 posTransV[4];
  vec2 pAux, posAux[4];

  vec2 tSize = textureSize(heightMap, 0) * scaleFactor;
  float div = 64.0 / tSize.x;
  posTC[ID] = posV[ID];
  // Compute the fours corners of the patch
  posAux[0] = posV[0];
  posAux[1] = posV[0] + vec2(0.0, div);
  posAux[2] = posV[0] + vec2(div, 0.0);
  posAux[3] = posV[0] + vec2(div, div);
  // Transform the four corners of the patch
  for (int i = 0; i < 4; ++i )
  {
    pAux = posAux[i] * tSize * gridSpacing;
    posTransV[i] = pvm * vec4(pAux[0], height(posAux[i].x,posAux[i].y), pAux[1], ↩
      1.0);
  }
  // check if a patch is inside the view frustum
  if (edgeInFrustum(posTransV[ID], posTransV[ID + 1]) ||
      edgeInFrustum(posTransV[ID], posTransV[ID + 2]) ||
      edgeInFrustum(posTransV[ID + 2], posTransV[ID + 3]) ||
      edgeInFrustum(posTransV[ID + 3], posTransV[ID + 1])))
  {
    // Compute the tess levels as function of the patch's edges
    gl_TessLevelOuter = vec4(
      screenSphereSize(posTransV[ID], posTransV[ID + 1]),
      screenSphereSize(posTransV[ID], posTransV[ID + 2]),
      screenSphereSize(posTransV[ID + 2], posTransV[ID + 3]),
      screenSphereSize(posTransV[ID + 3], posTransV[ID + 1]));
    gl_TessLevelInner = vec2(
      max(gl_TessLevelOuter[1], gl_TessLevelOuter[3]),
      max(gl_TessLevelOuter[0], gl_TessLevelOuter[2]));
  }
  else
  {
    // Discard patches by setting tessellation levels to zero
    gl_TessLevelOuter = vec4(0);
    gl_TessLevelInner = vec2(0);
  }
}
```

Listing 10.5. Tessellation control shader for simple LOD.

`edgeInFrustum`. If all edges are outside the view frustum, the tessellation levels are set to zero, and the patch is culled. Otherwise, the outer tessellation level is computed for each edge using the function `screenSphereSize`. The inner levels are set to the maximum of the respective outers to ensure a sound subdivision.

10.4 Roughness: When Detail Matters

The LOD solution presented in the previous section does a great job in reducing the number of triangles, and creating a terrain that can be rendered with a high frame rate. However, there is an implicit assumption that all patches are born equal. A terrain may be considered homogeneous, when the roughness of its surface is similar at every point, or heterogeneous, where both very smooth and very rough areas can be found. An approach based on the projected size of the patch edges does not take into account the variation of the heights inside a patch or its roughness, and it will either over-tessellate flat distant patches or under-tessellate rougher patches. Hence, the previous method is more suitable for homogeneous terrains.

The goal of this section is to present an LOD solution to the aforementioned problem, considering heterogeneous terrains, by taking into account the roughness of a patch to compute its tessellation levels. To achieve this, a roughness factor for each patch is calculated to be used as a scale factor. These factors are precomputed on the CPU and submitted to the GPU along with the patch's coordinates. This information can be precalculated outside the rendering application, speeding up bootstrapping.

Due to the preprocessing stage, this approach is unsuitable for terrains with dynamic geometry. However, if only a small part of the terrain is affected, this approach can still be used for the static part of the terrain, and over-tessellation can be used for the dynamic areas.

10.4.1 Adding the Roughness Factor

To compute the roughness factor, the average patch normal is determined considering the four corners of the patch. The maximum difference between the normals of each individual vertex of the fully tessellated patch and the average normal is the value stored as the patch's roughness.

For each outer tessellation level, the roughness applied will be the maximum between the two patches that share the edge, hence ensuring crack-free geometry.

Once again, the only shader affected is the tessellation control shader. Listing 10.6 shows the changes to this shader. The function `getRoughness` fetches the roughness value for a patch, stretching it to create a wider range of values. This stresses irregularities in the terrain, which may otherwise be ignored. The function's constants are experimental, and it can be an interesting exercise to find the best scaling factor for roughness.

```
uniform sampler2D roughFactor;

float getRoughness(vec2 disp)
{
  return (pow((1.8 - texture(roughFactor, posV[0] + disp / textureSize(roughFactor ↩
      ,0)).x ),  4)));
}

// Place this code in the main function presented before
// replacing the outer tessellation level computation
//(...)
  vec4 rough;
  float roughForCentralP = getRoughness(vec2(0.5));
  rough[0] = max(roughForCentralP, getRoughness(vec2(-0.5, 0.5)));
  rough[1] = max(roughForCentralP, getRoughness(vec2(0.5, -0.5)));
  rough[2] = max(roughForCentralP, getRoughness(vec2(1.5, 0.5)));
  rough[3] = max(roughForCentralP, getRoughness(vec2(0.5, 1.5)));
  gl_TessLevelOuter = vec4(
    screenSphereSize(posTransV[ID], posTransV[ID + 1]) * rough[0],
    screenSphereSize(posTransV[ID + 0], posTransV[ID + 2]) * roughs[1],
    screenSphereSize(posTransV[ID + 2], posTransV[ID + 3]) * rough[2],
    screenSphereSize(posTransV[ID + 3], posTransV[ID + 1]) * roughn[3]);
//(...)
```

Listing 10.6. Snippet of the tessellation control shader for LOD with a roughness factor.

10.5 Crunching Numbers, or Is This All That Matters?

Now that the different techniques for rendering terrains with tessellation and LOD have been introduced, it is time to look at the numbers. These tests are not, however, entirely related to how many triangles, or frames-per-second, the application can score. The visual quality of what is being rendered is also important, and so image comparison tests were also conducted.

10.5.1 Test Setup

The data used for the tests is a 16-bit heightmap and its corresponding color texture (Figure 10.3), are used, for instance, in [Lindstrom and Pascucci 01]. These files report geographical data from the Puget Sound area in the USA.

In all tests, the color texture was $2K \times 2K$, whereas the resolution of the terrain grids tested ranged from $1K \times 1K$ to $64K \times 64K$. The height data are based on a heightmap of up to $8K \times 8K$, with greater resolutions resorting to in-shader height sampling.

This terrain was chosen particularly for this LOD study since it is highly heterogeneous. It contains areas that are almost flat, green and blue, and areas that are very irregular, most of the red and white.

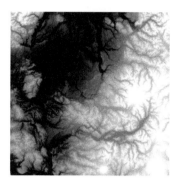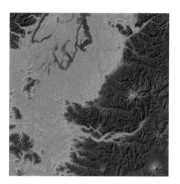

Figure 10.3. Terrain height and color maps.

10.5.2 Evaluating the Quality of the LOD Solutions

To evaluate an LOD solution, we must take several factors into account, as LOD is not only about performance. Using LOD causes the geometry to change as the

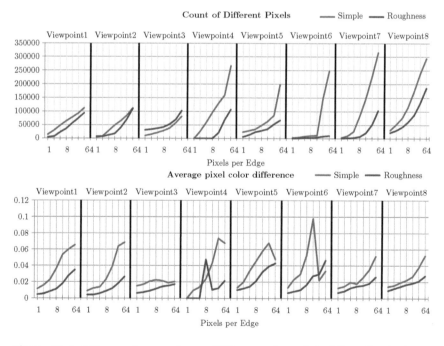

Figure 10.4. Differences between the two LOD approaches and the full tessellated solution computed from eight viewpoints. The total number of different pixels (top); the average color difference per pixel (bottom).

Figure 10.5. Close-ups for full tessellation (left), roughness approach (center), and simple method (right), with 16 pixels per edge.

camera moves in the scene, triggering variations in tessellation, and this may lead to visual artifacts. Another issue is related to the similarity to the original model. An LOD solution can be high performing without significant visual artifacts; still there may exist meaningful differences when compared to the original model.

The first test relates to the visual quality of the LOD solutions. The method used was to take the framebuffer from a fully tessellated terrain and compare it to the results of both LOD solutions, as presented in Sections 10.3 and 10.4. In both cases, there is only one parameter to control the LOD, the number of pixels per edge. For each comparison, two differences were computed: the number of different pixels and a pixelwise color difference. This test was performed from eight different viewpoints. The chart in Figure 10.4 provides the results.

Regarding the LOD parameter, pixels per edge ($\{1, 2, 4, 8, 16, 32, 64\}$), the methods behave as expected. As the number of pixels per edge increases, so does the amount of different pixels. In general, both the count of different pixels and the average color difference are lower for the roughness approach.

A clearer perspective can be obtained by looking at the actual images. Figure 10.5 shows close-ups of snapshots taken from viewpoint 1 for both the LOD methods and the fully tessellated geometry. The figure shows that the simple method tends to oversimplify patches that are further away, and it does alter the shape of the distant mountains. The LOD with a roughness factor, on the other hand, provides a nearly perfect contour.

Figure 10.6 was also built looking from the first viewpoint. The top row shows that the simple method clearly is more prone to misrepresenting the contour of the distant irregular geometry. The bottom row shows that, although the number of pixel differences is relatively the same for both methods, these correspond to very small color differences when using the roughness factor. For instance, considering the roughness factor with 16 pixels per edge, the differences are barely noticeable.

Concluding this test, one can state that, even when considering higher values for the parameter pixels per edge, the results are perceptually better when using the

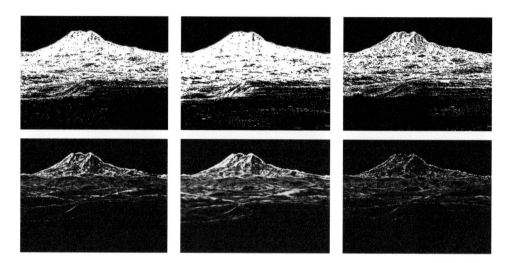

Figure 10.6. Differences between both LOD approaches and the full tessellation result. Top row: pixel difference; bottom row: five times enhanced color difference. Left column: simple method, 8 pixels per edge. Middle column: simple method, 16 pixels per edge. Right column: roughness approach, 16 pixels per edge.

roughness factor, as the shape of distant geometry seems to be significantly affected if patch roughness is not considered.

The second test relates to the expected differences when the camera moves from viewpoint $P(d)$ to viewpoint $P(d + \text{step})$, where step is the distance traveled in two consecutive frames. These differences occur during the course of camera navigation. At point $P(d)$, a feature of the terrain being observed may look differently when the camera moves a single step, due to dynamic tessellation.

Using LOD, it is to be expected that the tessellation levels vary when the camera moves, and this can cause visual artifacts that reveal the dynamic nature of the algorithm. To have zero visual artifacts, the result using tessellation computed at point $P(d)$ should be indistinguishable from the result using tessellation computed at point $P(d + \text{step})$, both being observed at point $P(d + \text{step})$.

This test calculates the differences between images generated at point $P(d+\text{step})$, using tessellation levels computed for point $P(d)$ and point $P(d + \text{step})$, for values of step in the set $\{1, 2, 4, 8, 16, 32, 64\}$ units. The chart in Figure 10.7 presents the average number of different pixels considering eight test viewpoints and using values of pixels per edge from 1 to 64. As expected, the errors reported for both LOD methods increase as the step increases. The error also grows as pixels per edge gets bigger.

The chart in Figure 10.7 clearly shows that, for the same value of pixels per edge, the differences that can be expected using the simplest method are always significantly higher than using a roughness factor.

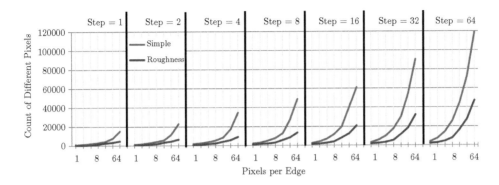

Figure 10.7. Differences in the step forward test, using both LOD methods.

10.5.3 Performance

Now it is time to see if the suggested LOD implementation using hardware tessellation pays off. It has already been shown that LOD introduces errors. These may be controlled by the number of pixels per edge, or some other more sophisticated approach, but there will be errors. So, the performance reports must be conclusive; otherwise, what is the point?

The hardware used for testing was a desktop system with a GeForce 460 GTX with 1GB of RAM and a laptop system with a Radeon 6990M with 2GB of RAM.

The results are presented for the terrain described previously, where the camera completed a full circle, advancing one degree per step, performing a total of 360 frames. The total time and the number of primitives generated, found using OpenGL queries, were recorded for each trial.

The test was performed with terrain grids ranging from 1K × 1K to 64K × 64K, varying the value of pixels per edge for both LOD methods. As a comparison, full tessellation, traditional submission of geometry (up to 4K × 4K) and instancing (up to 8K × 8K) are also presented.

The first chart, Figure 10.8, compares the performance obtained for full tessellation (with and without culling) with both full triangle grid submission and instancing with a patch of 64 × 64 vertices, which is replicated to cover the full terrain. The terrain grid size varies from 1K up to 8K.

Full tessellation is only beaten by the full triangle grid submission. The instancing approach does not match the performance of either in this case. Culling, as expected, boosts the tessellation approach, making it worthwhile to include the extra bit of code in the shaders.

Considering the largest terrains, and comparing to the full tessellation with culling approach, the frame rates of the other approaches are simply to low for any practical use. Notice that to show the data, the chart was created with a logarithmic FPS scale (base 2); otherwise, some of the data would not show up meaningfully.

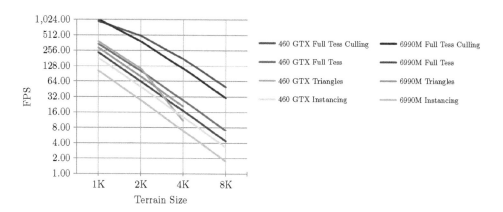

Figure 10.8. Frames-per-second performance on rendering a terrain without LOD.

The chart in Figure 10.9 reports on the performance of the roughness approach and full tessellation (with and without culling), considering three possible patch sizes on a Radeon 6990M.

In all cases, LOD introduces a very significant performance boost. In fact, the boost is so significant that, again, a logarithmic scale was used to show visible curves for every method. The patch size does influence performance, with larger sizes performing better overall; in particular, culling with larger patches is clearly more efficient. The other feature that is highlighted from the chart is the relevance of the LOD factor, pixels per edge, performancewise. The parameter works as expected, with performance increasing with the number of pixels per edge.

Now that the benefits of culling have been shown and the patch size impact on performance has been observed, all the remaining tests make use of culling and a

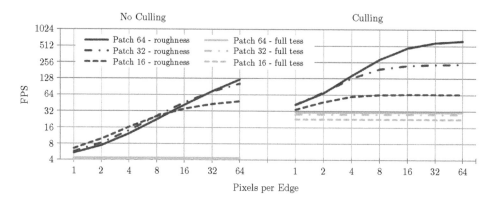

Figure 10.9. Comparison on the effect of culling in full tessellation and roughness methods.

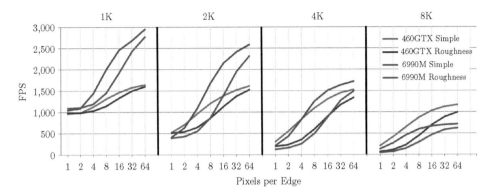

Figure 10.10. Frames per second for both LOD methods, with terrain sizes up to 8K.

patch size of 65 × 65. The goal is to test how the variation of the terrain's grid size affects performance and also to see how far one can push GPU LOD based on tessellation with OpenGL.

The chart in Figure 10.10 reports the tests in terrains up to 8K × 8K. Performancewise, both LOD methods achieve very high frame rates. As expected, the simple method performs better than the roughness approach. However, as seen before, the errors obtained with the latter approach are lower than the errors obtained with the former method, and a global comparison should take this into consideration.

Pushing further, we have tested both LOD methods using terrains up to 64K × 64K (Figure 10.11). Such a grid has over four billion vertices, so its a huge challenge for any technique. Since, presently, there is no hardware that is even remotely capable of handling this massive requirement, optimization techniques such as culling and LOD are mandatory.

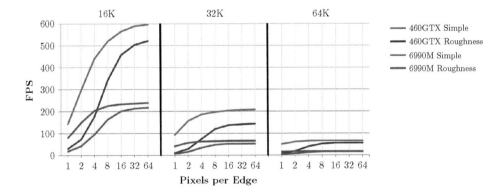

Figure 10.11. Frames per second for both LOD methods, with terrain sizes up to 64K.

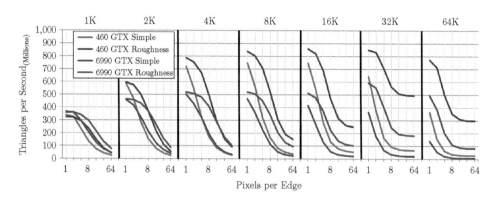

Figure 10.12. Triangles per second on both LOD methods, with terrain sizes up to 64K.

The throughput of primitives created by the tessellation primitive generator stage has much higher values when using the roughness approach, particularly as the terrain grows larger. This is the price to pay for having higher fidelity to the original model, but it also suggests that our implementation might be too conservative.

Regarding the number of triangles processed per second (Figure 10.12), the results show the GeForce 460 GTX achieving over 800 million, and the Radeon 6990M topping out at 500 million.

10.6   Conclusion

Taking advantage of the new tessellation engine and corresponding shaders, a GPU-based LOD algorithm was presented. The algorithm takes into account the roughness of the terrain to preserve a high level of fidelity to the original data, which is specially required in highly irregular, distant patches. It can be either used as a standalone method for terrains that fit in graphics memory, or, when considering larger terrains, as the final rendering stage of full-blown terrain-rendering engines, enhancing the fidelity of the rendered terrain while not compromising the frame rate.

Bibliography

[Boesch 10] Florian Boesch. "OpenGL 4 Tessellation." http://codeflow.org/entries/2010/nov/07/opengl-4-tessellation/, 2010.

[Cantlay 11] Iain Cantlay. "DirectX 11 Terrain Tessellation." Technical report, NVIDIA, 2011.

[Lindstrom and Pascucci 01] P. Lindstrom and V. Pascucci. "Visualization of Large Terrains Made Easy." In *Proceedings of the Conference on Visualization'01*, pp. 363–371. IEEE Computer Society, 2001.

[Ramires 07] António Ramires. "Clip Space Approach: Extracting the Planes." http://www.lighthouse3d.com/tutorials/view-frustum-culling/clip-space-approach-extracting-the-planes, 2007.

[Shandkel 02] Jason Shandkel. "Fast Heightfield Normal Calculation." In *Game Programming Gems 3*. Hingham, MA: Charles River Media, 2002.

[Tatarchuk et al. 09] Natalya Tatarchuk, Joshua Barczak, and Bill Bilodeau. "Programming for Real-Time Tessellation on GPU." Technical report, AMD, Inc., 2009.

Antialiased Volumetric Lines Using Shader-Based Extrusion   11

Sébastien Hillaire

11.1   Introduction

The ability to render lines has always been an important feature in computer graphics. Lines are useful for several purposes. They can be used as a debugging tool to display vertex normals or to visualize triangles in order to evaluate the complexity of a scene. Line rendering is also an important feature of CAD applications to help users to better perceive silhouettes and shapes by emphasizing object edges, or for GUI information like a wireframe cube around a selected object, gizmos, etc. Lines are also used in several games such as *PewPew* [Geyelin 09] or remakes of old games like *Battlezone* [Coy 09] where line rendering is part of the retro visual style. Finally, they are also used in GIS and simulation applications for roads, country borders, and vehicles path.

Nowadays, rendering high-quality antialiased lines is still not a trivial task. Graphics APIs like Direct3D or OpenGL allow the programmer to render basic 2D/3D lines with a limited width. However, those lines are not properly antialiased on all hardware [Lorach 05], and there is no perspective effect, i.e., a line always has the same size on the screen whatever its distance to the viewer. Furthermore, they lack of an overall *volumetric look*. McNanmara [McNamara et al. 00] and Chan [Chan and Durand 05] have proposed methods to render antialiased lines, but they do not feature any perspective effect. Cozzi [Cozzi and Ring 11] proposed a geometry shader extruding quads from 3D lines in screen space for high-quality antialiased lines without any perspective effect. Lorach [Lorach 05] has proposed to render volumetric antialiased lines by using an extended quad in screen space using a vertex shader. Line appearance is represented by 16 texture tiles that were interpolated based on the camera position as compared to the line direction. However, the trick used is still noticeable when viewing a line along its direction.

This chapter presents three methods to render high-quality antialiased lines. The first method relies on the fixed-width line-rendering possibility of the OpenGL API. The last two methods exploit shaders in order to extrude geometry around the line that will be shaded to achieve a volumetric appearance without aliasing.

11.2   Antialiased Lines Using Postprocess Antialiasing

One existing solution to rendering antialiased lines is to use the OpenGL line primitives with hardware multisampling activated. The selected multisampling quality, 4, 8, or 16 times, will directly influence the required memory and bandwidth. As an example, 8 times multisampling will require eight samples per pixel instead of one, eight times more memory, and the execution of a *resolve step* computing final pixel color from samples.

Over the last year, researchers have proposed a new way to achieve real-time antialiasing as a postprocess without requiring huge memory and with a low computational cost: postprocess antialiasing. A complete overview is presented in [Jimenez et al. 11]. Basically, these methods use screen-space information such as color, depth, normals, and geometry to detect edges in the rendered picture and apply a smart blur filter, taking advantage of the hardware linear filtering to reduce aliasing. Of all the algorithms, FXAA [Lottes 11] is a good choice as it only relies on the color buffer, and it only needs the luminance information. Another advantage is that the full shader file provided can be used either in OpenGL, Direct3D, or on consoles,

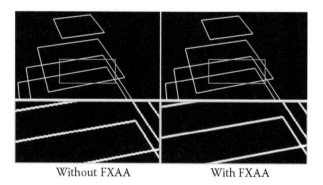

Without FXAA   With FXAA

Figure 11.1. OpenGL line primitives without and with postprocess antialiasing (FXAA). The green rectangles represent the zoomed-in areas.

and it can be easily tweaked using preprocessor directives. It is one of the fastest post-process antialiasing algorithm available [Jimenez et al. 11]. As visible in Figure 11.1, FXAA makes it possible to render high-quality antialiased lines using the standard line-rendering features of OpenGL. No matter how many lines we need to render, FXAA always has a constant cost. This approach not only improves the quality of lines, it improves the quality of the entire scene.

11.3 Antialiased Volumetric Lines Using Geometry Extrusion

This section presents two methods that take advantage of the shaders to render antialiased volumetric lines. The volumetric look is achieved via geometry extrusion using either a vertex shader or geometry shader. Antialiasing is achieved using a texture that controls the appearance of the lines [Chan and Durand 05].

11.3.1 Geometry Extrusion Using a Vertex Shader

This method renders three quads modeled by triangle strips extruded from the line segment (in Figure 11.2). The middle quad is a billboard that can only rotate around the line direction. The two others are "caps," or *half-billboard*, that are always facing the camera.

This method can be used on older hardware as it only relies on a vertex shader. To generate the extruded geometry, we need to submit the same vertex several times to form the triangle strip. The extrusion of each vertex by the vertex shader requires several inputs:

- `currentVertex`. The vertex of the line currently processed,

- `otherVertex`. The other vertex of the line, e.g., it will be B if `currentVertex` is A (Figure 11.2),

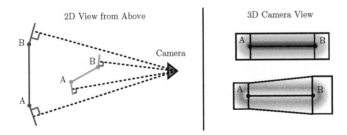

Figure 11.2. 2D and 3D views showing how quads are extruded and oriented as a function of the line segment and camera position.

- offset. A **vec2** specifying the vertex displacement length along and perpendicular to the line direction in clip space,

- UV. A **vec2** representing a texture coordinate from the texture controlling the appearance of the line.

For each line, height vertices are required to draw the triangle strip. The data are sent to the vertex shader according to a repetitive template that is visible in Figure 11.3. These data are submitted to the GPU by modifying the content of vertex buffer objects. However, **offset** and UV are constant data. They are packed in a single static vertex buffer object created and filled once during initialization. The size of these two static buffers corresponds to the maximum number of lines that can be rendered per batch. The element array is also filled once during initialization because its content does not need to be modified. Multiple lines are drawn in a single draw call using a *primitive restart* element as specified by the GL_NV_primitive_restart extension, which was promoted to core in OpenGL 3.0.

The extrusion vertex shader is shown in Listing 11.1. Geometry extrusion is done in clip space. The direction of the line on the screen is first computed. Then, a comparison is used to avoid the line direction being wrong when one of the line vertices is not on the same side of the near clip plane. Finally, that direction is used to displace the current vertex along and perpendicular to the line direction according to its offset vector. Visually, the final triangle strip is extruded along the line, thus giving the illusion of a volumetric line (Figure 11.4). Using a mipmapped appearance texture is recommended in order to get nice filtering when line widths decrease [Chan and Durand 05]. For very thin lines, multisampling, or postprocess antialiasing, will help to hide jaggies.

This simple method allows the rendering of volumetric lines using only six triangles per line and few additional ALU operations in the vertex shader. Furthermore, it has the advantage of being usable on hardware that only supports programmable vertex shading.

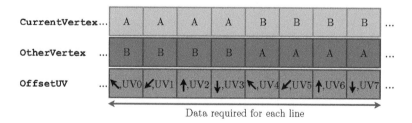

Figure 11.3. Buffer arrays layout required to render volumetric lines using vertex shader–based extrusion.

```
// [GLSL version, varying values and vertex attributes...]
uniform mat4 MVP;
uniform float radius;
uniform float invScrRatio;
uniform sampler2D lineTexture;
void main()
{
  Out.Texcoord = OffsetUV.zw;

  // Compute vertex position in clip space
  vec4 vMVP = MVP * vec4(Position,1.0);
  vec4 otherMVP = MVP * vec4(PositionOther,1.0);

  // (1) line direction on the (XY) plane of clip space (perspective division ↩
      required)
  vec2 lineDirProj = radius * normalize((vMVP.xy / vMVP.ww) - (otherMVP.xy / ↩
      otherMVP.ww));

    // (2) trick to avoid inversed condition when points are not on the same side of↩
        near plane (sign(otherMVP.w)!=sign(vMVP.w))
  if(otherMVP.w * vMVP.w < 0)
  {
    lineDirProj = -lineDirProj;
  }

  // (3) offset along and orthogonal to line direction (takes into account screen ↩
      aspect ratio)
  vec2 iscrRatio = vec2(1.0,invScrRatio);
  vMVP.xy += lineDirProj.xy * OffsetUV.xx * iscrRatio;
  vMVP.xy += lineDirProj.yx * OffsetUV.yy * vec2(1.0,-1.0) * iscrRatio;

  gl_Position = vMVP;
}
```

Listing 11.1. Geometry extrusion vertex shader.

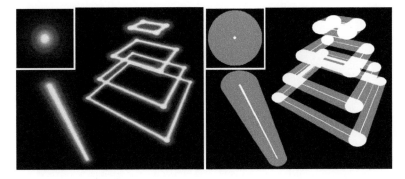

Figure 11.4. Volumetric lines rendered using a vertex shader–based geometry extrusion. Two different appearance textures are shown here (small icon on the top-left of pictures).

11.3.2 Geometry Extrusion Using a Geometry Shader

The vertex shader–based extrusion method has the drawback of not being able to render correct volumetric lines when they are viewed along their own direction: the triangle strip becomes visible at the grazing angle (Figure 11.5). The method using a geometry shader–based extrusion does not suffer from this problem.

Figure 11.5. The visual error resulting from using the vertex shader–based extrusion while viewing a line along its direction (left). Corrected version using geometry shader–based extrusion (right).

Given the two input vertices, the geometry shader extrudes an object-oriented bounding box (OOBB). An orthonormal basis is first computed with its x-axis set parallel to the line direction. The y- and z-axes are then generated according to basic geometry relations, but we do not care about their direction. However, it is important that the line is tightly contained inside the OOBB according to its width. The OOBB is generated using two triangle strips. Each of its vertices is associated with a view-ray direction expressed in view-space that is interpolated and passed to be used in the fragment shader.

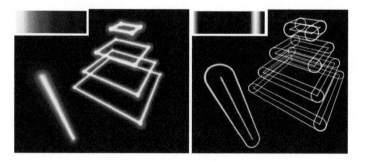

Figure 11.6. Volumetric lines rendered using a geometry shader–based geometry extrusion. Two different appearance gradients are shown here (small icon on the top-left of pictures).

Figure 11.7. Advanced effect possible when using the geometry-shader based extrusion: fog-like effect with smooth intersections with the virtual environment (left) and with the virtual camera when it is inside the volume (right).

The task of the fragment shader is simple. It computes the distance between the two closest points on the line segment and on the view direction corresponding to the currently rasterized fragment. This distance is finally scaled by the inverse radius of the line and is used as a coordinate to sample a 1D gradient texture that will define the appearance of the volumetric line (Figure 11.6). The drawback of this method is that a lot of geometry is output from the geometry shader for each line: sixteen vertices and two triangle strips. This is usually not recommended for a geometry shader and is a huge cost to render a single line. A solution would be to implement culling in the geometry shader [AMD 11].

This geometry shader–based volumetric line-rendering method results in higher-quality volumetric lines than the vertex-based one. Moreover, it does not require changing the way we send line vertices to the GPU. This method only requires us to enable the shader before the line rendering section of the code. More visual effects using the fragment shader can be achieved with this approach, such as volumetric participating media, taking into account intersections with the camera [Hillaire 10] (Figure 11.7) or meshless tubes [Rideout 11].

11.4 Performance

The performance of the previously discussed methods are shown in Figure 11.8 when rendering 1024 lines with equal width and using additive blending. Performance was recorded on an `Intel Core i5` and a `GeForce GTX 275`. On such hardware, FXAA (PC version) takes only 0.2 milliseconds to complete the rendering on a 720p RGB8 buffer when using the green channel as luminance. Performance is given for the 720p and 1080p resolutions as well as with lines rendered out of the frustum. This last condition is used to ignore most of the rasterization cost and to focus on

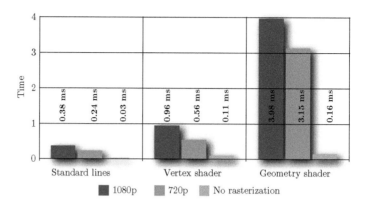

Figure 11.8. Performance in milliseconds when rendering 1024 lines without FXAA according to three conditions. Additive blending was used, and each line had the same width.

the draw-call setup and vertex processing costs. In this case, lines were rendered out of the view frustum.

Results show that the vertex extrusion method is twice as costly as the standard line-rendering method. This is the cost of higher quality antialiasing together with an overall volumetric and perspective look achieved using texture sampling. It is important to note that this methods could be faster if data were interleaved, and that, on recent hardware, the repetitive `offsetUV` could be read from a uniform array using the `gl_VertexID%8` as an index (OpenGL 2.0 required).

It is important to note that the cost overhead due to the use of the heavy-extrusion geometry shader is not the problematic part of the geometry-shader method. As measured under the no rasterization condition, the overall computational cost is 50% higher than that of the vertex shader–based geometry extrusion. However, in the 720p condition, it appears to be almost six times more costly. This suggests that the more complex fragment shader may be the bottleneck in this case. This is the cost of having consistent volumetric and antialiased lines whatever the line direction is as compared to the camera relative position.

11.5   Conclusion

We have explored three methods for rendering high-quality antialiased lines of variable width. The first method uses the standard line-drawing feature of OpenGL and relies on a postprocess antialiasing method to achieve antialiasing. The last two methods take advantage of the programmable pipeline for the purpose of geometry extrusion in order to achieve additional volumetric and perspective effects. Antialiasing is achieved using texture sampling and mipmapping. Furthermore, these methods can also be combined with postprocess antialiasing to reduce the jaggy effect resulting from thin lines.

The source code, available on the OpenGL Insights website, www.openglinsights. com, contains implementation of each method. Each method has specific advantages and drawbacks that resume our choice as a tradeoff between quality and computational cost.

Bibliography

[AMD 11] AMD. "ATI Radeon HD 2000 Programming Guide." http://developer.amd.com/media/gpu_assets/ATI_Radeon_HD_2000_programming_guide.pdf, 2011.

[Chan and Durand 05] Eric Chan and Frédo Durand. "Fast Prefiltered Lines." In *GPU Gems 2*, pp. 15–30. Reading, MA: Addison-Wesley, 2005.

[Coy 09] Stephen Coy. "Simplified High Quality Anti-aliased Lines." In *ShaderX7: Advanced REndering Techniques*, pp. 15–30. Hingham, MA: Charles Rriver Media, 2009.

[Cozzi and Ring 11] Patrick Cozzi and Kevin Ring. *3D Engine Design for Virtual Globes*. Natick, MA: A K Peters, 2011.

[Geyelin 09] Jean-Francois Geyelin. "PewPew." http://pewpewgame.blogspot.com, 2009.

[Hillaire 10] Sebastien Hillaire. "Volumetric Lines 2." http://tinyurl.com/5wt8nmx, 2010.

[Jimenez et al. 11] Jorge Jimenez, Diego Gutierrez, Jason Yang, Alexander Reshetov, Pete Demoreuille, Tobias Berghoff, Cedric Perthuis, Henry Yu, Morgan McGuire, Timothy Lottes, Hugh Malan, Emil Persson, Dmitry Andreev, and Tiago Sousa. "Filtering Approaches for Real-Time Anti-Aliasing." In *ACM SIGGRAPH 2011 Courses, SIGGRAPH '11*, pp. 6:1–6:329. New York: ACM, 2011.

[Lorach 05] Tristan Lorach. "CG Volume Lines, NVIDIA SDK 9.52 Code Samples." http://tinyurl.com/6jbe2bo, 2005.

[Lottes 11] Timothy Lottes. "FXAA." http://tinyurl.com/5va6ssb, 2011.

[McNamara et al. 00] Robert McNamara, Joel McCormack, and Norman P. Jouppi. "Prefiltered Antialiased Lines Using Half-Plane Distance Functions." In *The ACM SIGGRAPH/EUROGRAPHICS Workshop on Graphics Hardware*. S.N. Spencer, 2000.

[Rideout 11] Philip Rideout. "Tron, Volumetric Lines, and Meshless Tubes." http://prideout.net/blog/?p=61, 2011.

2D Shape Rendering by Distance Fields   12

Stefan Gustavson

12.1   Introduction

Every now and then, an idea comes along that seems destined to change the way certain things are done in computer graphics, but for some reason it's very slow to catch on with would-be users. This is the case with an idea presented in 2007 by Chris Green of Valve Software in a SIGGRAPH course chapter entitled "Improved Alpha-Tested Magnification for Vector Textures and Special Effects" [Green 07]. Whether the slow and sparse adoption is due to an obscure title, the choice of publication venue, a lack of understanding from readers, lack of source code, or the shortcomings of Green's original implementation, this chapter is an attempt to fix that.

The term *vector textures* refers to 2D surface patterns built from distinct shapes with crisp, generally curved boundaries between two regions: foreground and background. Many surface patterns in the real world look like this, for example printed and painted text, logos, and decals. Alpha masks for blending between two more complex surface appearances may also have crisp boundaries: bricks and mortar, water puddles on asphalt, cracks in paint or plaster, mud splatter on a car. For decades, real-time computer graphics has been long plagued by an inability to accurately render sharp surface features up close, as demonstrated in Figure 12.1. Magnification without interpolation creates jaggy, pixelated edges, and bilinear interpolation gives a blurry appearance. A common method for alpha masks is to perform thresholding after interpolation. This maintains a crisp edge, but it is wobbly and distorted, and the pixelated nature of the underlying data is apparent.

Jaggy Blurry Wobbly

Figure 12.1. Up close, high-contrast edges in texture images become jaggy, blurry, or wobbly.

Shape rendering by the method described here solves the problem in an elegant and GPU-friendly way, and it does not require rethinking the production pipeline for texture creation. All it takes is some insight into what can be done. First, I present the principles of the method and explain what it is good for. Following that, I provide a summary of recent research on how to make better distance fields from regular artwork, removing Green's original requirement for special high-resolution 1-bit alpha images. Last, I present concrete shader code in GLSL to perform this kind of rendering, comment on its performance and shortcomings, and point to trade-offs between speed and quality.

12.2 Method Overview

Generally speaking, a crisp boundary cannot be sampled and reconstructed properly using standard texture images. Texel sampling inherently assumes that the pattern is *band limited*, i.e., that it does not vary too rapidly and does not have too-small details, because the pattern is going to be rendered by a smooth interpolation of the texel samples. If we keep one of these constraints, that the pattern must not contain too-small details, but want the transitions between background and foreground to be crisp, formally representing an infinite gradient, we can let a shader program perform thresholding by a *step function* and let the texels represent a smoothly varying function on which to apply the step. A suitable smooth function for this purpose is a *distance field*.

A typical distance field is shown in Figure 12.2. Here, texels do not represent a color, but the distance to the nearest contour, with positive values on one side of the contour and negative values on the other. An unsigned distance field, having distance values only outside the contour, is useful, but for flexibility and proper antialiasing, it is highly preferable to have a signed distance field with distance values both inside and outside the contour. The contour is then a *level set* of the distance field: all points with distance value equal to zero. Thresholding the distance function at zero will generate the crisp 2D shape. Details smaller than a single texel cannot be represented, but the boundary between background and foreground can be made infinitely sharp, and because the texture data is smoothly varying and can be closely approximated as a linear ramp at most points, it will behave nicely under both magnification and minification using ordinary bilinear interpolation.

Figure 12.2. A 2D shape (left), its smoothly varying distance field shown in a rainbow-color map (middle), and three level sets (right) showing the original outline (thick line) and inward and outward displaced outlines (thin lines).

Thresholding by a step function will alias badly, so it is desirable to use instead a linear ramp or a `smoothstep` function with the transition region extending across approximately one fragment (one pixel sample) in the rendered output. Proper antialiasing is often overlooked, so Listing 12.1 gives the source code for an anisotropic antialiasing step function. Using the built-in GLSL function `fwidth()` may be faster, but it computes the length of the gradient slightly wrong as $|\partial F/\partial x|+|\partial F/\partial y|$ instead of

$$\sqrt{\left(\frac{\partial F}{\partial x}\right)^2 + \left(\frac{\partial F}{\partial y}\right)^2}.$$

Using ± 0.7 instead of ± 0.5 for the thresholds compensates for the fact that `smoothstep()` is smooth at its endpoints and has a steeper maximum slope than a linear ramp.

Because the gradient of a distance field has a constant magnitude except at localized discontinuities, the *skeleton points*, gradient computation is straightforward and robust. The gradient can be stored with the distance field using a multichannel (RGB) texture format, but it can also be accurately and efficiently estimated by the automatic derivatives `dFdx()` and `dFdy()` in the fragment shader. Thus, it is not necessary to sample the texture at several points. By carefully computing the gradient

```
// 'threshold' is constant, 'distance' is smoothly varying
float aastep(float threshold, float dist.)
{
   float afwidth = 0.7 * length(vec2(dFdx(dist.), dFdy(dist.)));
   return smoothstep(threshold - afwidth, threshold + afwidth, dist.);
}
```

Listing 12.1. Anisotropic antialiased step function.

projection to screen space, an accurate, anisotropic analytical antialiasing of the edge can be performed with little extra effort.

12.3   Better Distance Fields

In digital image processing, distance fields have been a recurring theme since the 1970s. Various *distance transform* methods have been proposed, whereby a binary (1-bit) image is transformed into an image where each pixel represents the distance to the nearest transition between foreground and background. Two problems with previously published methods are that they operate on binary images and that they compute distance as a vector from the center of each foreground or background pixel to the center of the closest pixel of the opposite type. This only allows for distances that are of the form $\sqrt{i^2 + j^2}$, where i and j are both integers, and the measure of distance is not consistent with the distance to the *edge* between foreground and background. These two restrictions have recently been lifted [Gustavson and Strand 11]. The new *antialiased Euclidean distance transform* is a straightforward extension of traditional Euclidean distance transform algorithms, and for the purpose of 2D shape rendering, it is a much better fit than previous methods. It takes as its input an antialiased, area-sampled image of a shape, it computes the distance to the closest point on the underlying edge of the shape, and it allows fractional distances with arbitrary precision, limited only by the antialiasing accuracy of the input image. The article cited contains the full description of the algorithm, with source code for an example implementation. The demo code for this chapter contains a similar implementation, adapted for stand-alone use as a texture preprocessing tool.

12.4   Distance Textures

The fractional distance values from the antialiased distance transform need to be supplied as a texture image to OpenGL. An 8-bit format is not quite enough to represent both the range and the precision required for good-quality shapes, but if texture bandwidth is limited, it can be enough. More suitable formats are, of course, the single channel **float** or **half** texture formats, but a 16-bit integer format with a fixed-point interpretation to provide enough range and precision will also do the job nicely.

For maximum compatibility with less-capable platforms such as WebGL and OpenGL ES, I have chosen a slightly more cumbersome method for the demo code for this chapter: I store a 16-bit fixed-point value with 8 bits of signed integer range and 8 bits of fractional precision as the R and G channels of a traditional 8-bit RGB texture. This leaves room to also have the original antialiased image in the B channel, which is convenient for the demo and allows for an easy fallback shader in case the shape rendering turns out to be too taxing for some particularly weak GPU.

The disadvantage is that OpenGL's built-in bilinear texture interpolation incorrectly interpolates the integer and fractional 8-bit values separately, so we need to use nearest-neighbor sampling, look up four neighbors explicitly, reconstruct the distance values from the R and G channels, and perform bilinear interpolation by explicit shader code. This adds to the complexity of the shader program. Four nearest-neighbor texture lookups constitute the same memory reads as a single bilinear lookup, but most current hardware has built-in bilinear filtering that is faster than doing four explicit texture lookups and interpolation in shader code. (The OpenGL extension `GL_ARB_texture_gather`, where available, goes some way towards addressing this problem.)

A bonus advantage of the approach using dual 8-bit channels is that we work around a problem with reduced precision in the built-in bilinear texture interpolation. We are no longer interpolating colors to create a blurry image, but computing the location of a crisp edge, and that requires better precision than what current (2011) GPUs provide natively. Moving the interpolation to shader code guarantees an adequate accuracy for the interpolation.

12.5 Hardware Accelerated Distance Transform

In some situations where a distance field might be useful, it can be impractical or impossible to precompute it. In such cases, a distance transform can be performed on the fly using a multipass rendering and GLSL. An algorithm suitable for the kind of parallel processing that can be performed by a GPU was originally invented in 1979 and published as little more than a footnote in [Danielsson 80] under the name *parallel Euclidean distance transform*. It was recently independently reinvented under the name *jump flooding* and implemented on GPU hardware [Rong and Tan 06]. A variant that accepts antialiased input images and outputs fractional distances according to [Gustavson and Strand 11] is included in the accompanying demos and source code for this chapter. The jump flooding algorithm is a complicated image processing operation that requires several iterative passes over the image, but on a modern GPU, a reasonably sized distance field can be computed in a matter of milliseconds. The significant speedup compared to a pure CPU implementation could be useful even for offline computation of distance fields.

12.6 Fragment Rendering

The best way of explaining how to render the 2D shape is probably to show the GLSL fragment shader with proper comments. See Listing 12.2. The shader listed here assumes that the distance field is stored as a single-channel floating-point texture.

```
// Distance map 2D shape texturing, Stefan Gustavson 2011.
// A re-implementation of Green's method, using a single
// channel high precision distance map and explicit texel
// interpolation. This code is in the public domain.

#version 120
uniform sampler2D disttex; // Single-channel distance field
uniform float texw, texh;  // Texture width and height (texels)
varying float oneu, onev;  // 1/texw and 1/texh from vertex shader
varying vec2 st;           // Texture coords from vertex shader

void main(void)
{
  vec2 uv = st * vec2(texw, texh); // Scale to texture rect coords
  vec2 uv00 = floor(uv - vec2(0.5)); // Lower left of lower left texel
  vec2 uvlerp = uv - uv00 - vec2(0.5); // Texel-local blends [0,1]

  // Perform explicit texture interpolation of distance value D.
  // If hardware interpolation is OK, use D = texture2D(disttex, st).

  // Center st00 on lower left texel and rescale to [0,1] for lookup
  vec2 st00 = (uv00  + vec2(0.5)) * vec2(oneu, onev);
  // Sample distance D from the centers of the four closest texels
  float D00 = texture2D(disttex, st00).r;
  float D10 = texture2D(disttex, st00 + vec2(0.5 * oneu, 0.0)).r;
  float D01 = texture2D(disttex, st00 + vec2(0.0, 0.5 * onev)).r;
  float D11 = texture2D(disttex, st00 + vec2(0.5 * oneu,0.5 * onev)).r;
  vec2 D00_10 = vec2(D00, D10);
  vec2 D01_11 = vec2(D01, D11);
  vec2 D0_1 = mix(D00_10, D01_11, uvlerp.y);  // Interpolate along v
  float D = mix(D0_1.x, D0_1.y, uvlerp.x);    // Interpolate along u

  // Perform anisotropic analytic antialiasing
  float aastep = 0.7 * length(vec2(dFdx(D), dFdy(D)));
  // 'pattern' is 1 where D > 0, 0 where D < 0, with proper AA around D = 0.
  float pattern = smoothstep(-aastep, aastep, D);
  gl_FragColor = vec4(vec3(pattern), 1.0);
}
```

Listing 12.2. Fragment shader for shape rendering.

```
#version 120
uniform sampler2D disttex; // Single-channel distance field
varying vec2 st;           // Texture coords from vertex shader

void main( void )
{
  float  D = texture2D(disttex, st).
  float aastep = 0.5 * fwidth(D);
  float pattern = smoothstep(-aastep, aastep, D);
  gl_FragColor = vec4(vec3(pattern), 1.0);
}
```

Listing 12.3. Minimal shader, using built-in texture interpolation and antialiasing.

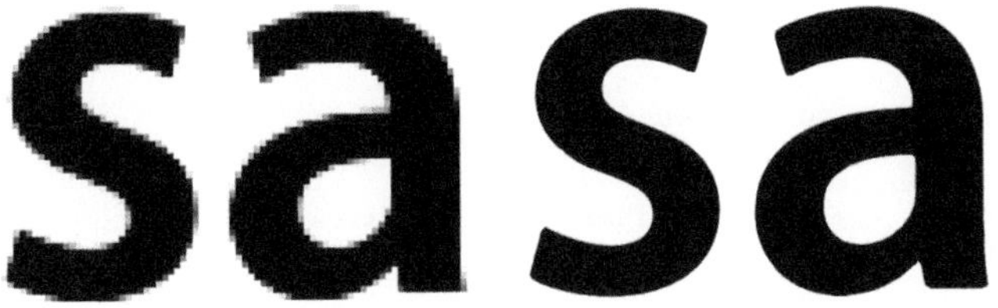

sasa

Figure 12.3. A low resolution, antialiased bitmap (left). Shapes rendered using a distance field generated from that bitmap (right).

As mentioned above, the interactive demo instead uses a slightly more cumbersome 8-bit RGB texture format for maximum compatibility. A minimal shader relying on the potentially problematic but faster built-in texture and antialiasing functionality in GLSL is presented in Listing 12.3. It is very simple and very fast, but on current GPUs, interpolation artifacts appear even at moderate magnification. A final shape rendering is demonstrated in Figure 12.3, along with the antialiased image used to generate the distance field.

12.7 Special Effects

The distance field representation allows for many kinds of operations to be performed on the shape, like thinning or fattening of features, bleed or glow effects and noise-like disturbances to add small-scale detail to the outline. These operations are readily performed in the fragment shader and can be animated both per-frame and per-fragment. The distance field representation is a versatile image-based component for more general procedural textures. Figure 12.4 presents a few examples of special effects, and their corresponding shader code is shown in Listing 12.4. For brevity, the example code does not perform proper antialiasing. Details on how to implement the `noise()` function can be found in Chapter 7.

Figure 12.4. Shader special effects using plain distance fields as input.

```
// Glow effect
  float inside = 1.0 - smoothstep(-2.0, 2.0, D);
  float glow = 1.0 - smoothstep(0.0, 20.0, D);
  vec3 insidecolor = vec3(1.0, 1.0, 0.0);
  vec3 glowcolor = vec3(1.0, 0.3, 0.0);
  vec3 fragcolor = mix(glow * glowcolor, insidecolor, inside);
  gl_FragColor = vec4(fragcolor, 1.0);

// Pulsate effect
  D = D - 2.0 + 2.0 * sin(st.s * 10.0);
  vec3 fragcolor = vec3(smoothstep(-0.5, 0.5, D));
  gl_FragColor = vec4(fragcolor, 1.0);

// Squiggle effect
  D = D + 2.0 * noise(20.0 * st);
  vec3 fragcolor = vec3(1.0 - smoothstep(-2.0, -1.0, D) + smoothstep(1.0, 2.0, D));
  gl_FragColor = vec4(fragcolor, 1.0);
```

Listing 12.4. Shader code for the special effects in Figure 12.4.

12.8   Performance

I benchmarked this shape-rendering method on a number of current and not-so-current GPUs, and instead of losing myself in details with a table, I summarize the results very briefly.

The speed of this method on a modern GPU with adequate texture bandwidth is almost on par with plain, bilinear interpolated texturing. Using the shader in Listing 12.3, it is just as fast, but the higher-quality interpolation of Listing 12.2 is slightly slower. Exactly how much slower depends strongly on the available texture bandwidth and ALU resources in the GPU. With some trade-off in quality under extreme magnifications, single channel 8-bit distance data can be used, but 16-bit data comes at a reasonable cost. Proper antialiasing requires local derivatives of the distance function, but on the hardware level this is implemented as simple interfragment differences with very little overhead.

In short, performance should not be a problem with this method. Where speed is of utmost importance, decals and alpha masks could in fact be made smaller with this method than with traditional alpha masking. This saves texture memory and bandwidth and can speed up rendering without sacrificing quality.

12.9   Shortcomings

Even though the shapes rendered by distance fields have crisp edges, a sampled and interpolated distance field is unable to perfectly represent the true distance to an arbitrary contour. Where the original underlying edge has strong curvature or a corner, the rendered edge will deviate slightly from the true edge position. The deviations are small, only fractions of a texel in size, but some detail may be lost or

Figure 12.5. Rendering defects in extreme magnification. The black and white shape is overlaid with the grayscale source image pixels in purple and green. For this particularly problematic italic lowercase "n," the left edge of the leftmost feature is slightly rounded off, and the narrow white region in the middle is distorted where two opposite edges cross a single texel.

distorted. Most notably, sharp corners will be shaved off somewhat, and the character of such distortions will depend on how each particular corner aligns with the texel grid.

Also, narrow shapes that are less than two texels wide cannot be accurately represented by a distance field, and if such features are present in the original artwork, they will be distorted in the rendering. To avoid this, some care needs to be taken when designing the artwork and when deciding on the resolution of the antialiased image from which to generate the distance field. Opposite edges of a thin feature should not pass through the same texel, nor through two adjacent texels. (This limitation is present also in traditional alpha interpolation.) Both these artifacts are demonstrated by Figure 12.5, which is a screenshot from the demo software for this chapter.

12.10   Conclusion

A complete cross-platform demo with full source code for texture creation and rendering is freely available on the OpenGL Insights website, www.openglinsights.com.

This chapter and its accompanying example code should contain enough information to get you started with distance field textures in OpenGL projects where appropriate. Compared to [Green 07], I provide a much improved distance transform method taken from recent research and give example implementations with full source code for both texture generation and rendering. I also present shader code for fast and accurate analytic antialiasing, which is important for the kind of high-frequency detail represented by a crisp edge.

While distance fields certainly do not solve every problem with rendering shapes with crisp edges, they do solve some problems very well, for example text, decals, and alpha-masked transparency for silhouettes and holes. Furthermore, the method does not require significantly more or fundamentally different operations than regular texture images, neither for shader programming nor for the creation of texture assets. It is my hope that this method will find more widespread use. It certainly deserves it.

Bibliography

[Danielsson 80] Per-Erik Danielsson. "Euclidean Distance Mapping." *Computer Graphics and Image Processing* 14 (1980), 227–248.

[Green 07] Chris Green. "Improved Alpha-Tested Magnification for Vector Textures and Special Effects." In *SIGGRAPH07 Course on Advanced Real-Time Rendering in 3D Graphics and Games, Course 28*, pp. 9–18. New York: ACM Press, 2007.

[Gustavson and Strand 11] Stefan Gustavson and Robin Strand. "Anti-Aliased Euclidean distance transform." *Pattern Recognition Letters* 32:2 (2011), 252–257.

[Rong and Tan 06] Guodong Rong and Tiow-Seng Tan. "Jump Flooding in GPU with Applications to Voronoi Diagram and Distance Transform." In *Proceedings of ACM Symposium on Interactive 3D Graphics and Games*, pp. 109–116, 2006.

Efficient Text Rendering in WebGL

13

Benjamin Encz

13.1 Introduction

As the first plugin-free 3D rendering API for browsers, WebGL is an interesting technology for the development of web applications. Since it is a low-level graphics API, the basic functionality is slim, and many features need to be implemented by the application developer. One of the missing functions is native support for text rendering. In many applications, especially on the web, text content is an important factor.

Being a young standard, only a few WebGL applications using text rendering exist. Furthermore, in contrast to OpenGL, to date, hardly any extensions or libraries for text rendering are available. Currently we need to implement it on our own. This chapter introduces and discusses two approaches.

One approach is *bitmap fonts*, a common technique where single characters are rendered as textured quads. For WebGL developers, a second approach exists: we can use the 2D capabilities of the HTML5 element canvas to create textures containing dynamically rendered text.

This chapter discusses both approaches. It describes each concept, provides implementation details, and compares the efficiency in different scenarios. Demos and documented source code are available on the OpenGL Insights website, www.openglinsights.com.

13.2   Canvas-Based Font Rendering

Canvas-based font rendering is a WebGL-specific technique. We can use the HTML5 element canvas to generate a texture font.

13.2.1   The HTML5 Canvas

The canvas element is part of the HTML5 standard. It provides two APIs for graphics. WebGL's functionality is provided by the canvas' 3D context. Canvas' 2D context, in turn, offers an API for drawing 2D raster and vector images, including text.

13.2.2   Concept

When the canvas' 2D context is used to draw characters or shapes, the result is presented on the canvas and stored as a bitmap. This bitmap can be be transformed into a WebGL texture. Using the 2D context, canvas-based text rendering is implemented in three steps:

1. Use 2D context to render text onto the canvas,

2. Capture the resulting bitmap as a WebGL texture,

3. Render viewport-aligned triangles shaded with the texture.

Canvas-based text rendering requires two canvas elements: one with a 2D context, to generate the texture, and another with a 3D context, to render the 3D scene, as shown in Figure 13.1.

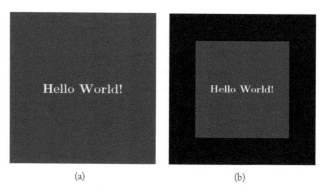

(a)   (b)

Figure 13.1. Canvas-based font rendering: (a) texture creation canvas, (b) rendered 3D scene.

13.2.3 Implementation

The first implementation step is to render text using the 2D context as shown in Listing 13.1. We begin with requesting `ctx`, the 2D context of the canvas, and setting up the parameters for our text. Several attributes can be used to vary the font appearance, including CSS syntax, which allows us to reuse styles from existing web applications. By calling `ctx.fillRect()`, we fill the canvas with a blue background. Then, we call `ctx.fillText()` to render white text on top. Now, the image is drawn, and we create a WebGL texture from it, as shown in Listing 13.2.

```
var dynamicImage = document.getElementById("text");
var ctx = dynamicImage.getContext("2d");
var text = "Hello World";
var leftOffset = ctx.canvas.width / 2;
var topOffset = ctx.canvas.height / 2;

ctx.fillStyle = "blue";
ctx.fillRect(0, 0, ctx.canvas.width, ctx.canvas.height);
ctx.fillStyle = "white";
ctx.lineWidth = 5;
ctx.font = "bold 44px Arial";
ctx.textAlign = "center";
ctx.textBaseline = "middle";
ctx.fillText(text, leftOffset, topOffset);
handleLoadedTexture(dynamicImage);
```

Listing 13.1. 2D context text rendering.

First, we initialize `dynamicTexture` with the call to `gl.createTexture()`. Then, we activate flipping for our image, which has an inverted *y*-axis and would be displayed upside down otherwise. Next, we copy the content of the 2D context to the WebGL texture, passing it as the last argument to `gl.texImage2D()`. We

```
function handleLoadedTexture(image) {
  var dynamicTexture =  gl.createTexture();
  gl.bindTexture(gl.TEXTURE_2D, dynamicTexture);
  gl.pixelStorei(gl.UNPACK_FLIP_Y_WEBGL, true);
  gl.texImage2D(gl.TEXTURE_2D, 0,gl.LUMINANCE_ALPHA, gl.LUMINANCE_ALPHA, gl.↩
      UNSIGNED_BYTE ,image);
  gl.texParameteri(gl.TEXTURE_2D, gl.TEXTURE_MIN_FILTER, gl.LINEAR_MIPMAP_LINEAR);
  gl.texParameteri(gl.TEXTURE_2D, gl.TEXTURE_MAG_FILTER, gl.LINEAR);
  // Generate the mipmap required for the minimization filter
  gl.generateMipmap(gl.TEXTURE_2D);
}
```

Listing 13.2. Texture creation.

```
var quadBuffer = gl.createBuffer();
gl.bindBuffer(gl.ARRAY_BUFFER, quadBuffer);
var vertices = [
  -5,  -5,  1,  0,  1  //P0
   5,  -5,  1,  0,  0  //P1
   5,   5,  1,  1,  0  //P2
  -5,  -5,  1,  0,  1  //P0
   5,  -5,  1,  0,  0  //P2
   5,   5,  1,  1,  0  //P3
];
gl.bufferData(gl.ARRAY_BUFFER, new Float32Array(vertices), gl.STATIC_DRAW);
```

Listing 13.3. Interleaved buffer for a quad.

choose Luminance-Alpha as the texture format since that saves us 2 bytes per pixel. The color information does not need to be stored characterwise; instead, we can store it globally or with each string. Finally, we set up bilinear texture filtering. This demo allows us to move and translate the rendered text from its initial viewport-aligned position so we use texture filtering to create a smooth font appearance at any world position.

In the third step, we create a surface using two triangles and shade them with our texture. To do so, we create an interleaved buffer with vertices and texture coordinates, as shown in Listing 13.3.

In each line, the first three floats describe the world position of each vertex, and the last two describe which point of the texture is mapped to it. Finally, we bind that buffer and call **gl.drawArrays()**. The vertex shader, shown in Listing 13.4, transforms our quad to clip coordinates, and passes the texture coordinates to the fragment shader.

Canvas-based text rendering is straightforward. We have access to several font attributes and can put the actual text rendering details, such as character placing, off to the canvas' 2D context.

```
attribute vec3 aVertexPosition;
uniform mat4 uMVPMatrix;
attribute vec2 aTextureCoord;
varying vec2 vTextureCoord;

void main(void) {
  gl_Position = uMVPMatrix * vec4(aVertexPosition, 1.0);
  vTextureCoord = aTextureCoord;
}
```

Listing 13.4. Vertex shader.

13.3 Bitmap Font Rendering

In contrast to canvas-based rendering, bitmap font rendering is a low-level approach. We need to render every character individually.

13.3.1 Concept

Every character in a string is drawn as a rectangular surface (*tile*) and shaded with a texture representing the corresponding character, as shown in Figure 13.2.

To create these tiles, we need texture and meta information for the characters in our fonts. Bitmap fonts are usually provided as a set of two components:

1. One or multiple textures containing the images for all characters in a charset.

2. A meta file, providing a descriptor for all characters.

The character descriptor defines the size of a character and is used to create a `TextureCoordBuffer`, which describes the part of a texture applied to a WebGL primitive. Figure 13.2 shows how a subimage is extracted from a bitmap font and applied to a character tile. To access the character descriptors and implement tile creation, we need the following components:

- bitmap font parser,

- bitmap font representation,

- character hub to provide character information, and

- character-creating and character-placing component (*text unit*).

Figure 13.3 shows how these components work together. Before rendering begins, the font texture is loaded, and the bitmap font descriptor is parsed. After the

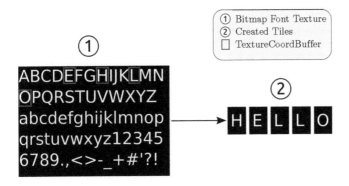

Figure 13.2. Bitmap font texture application.

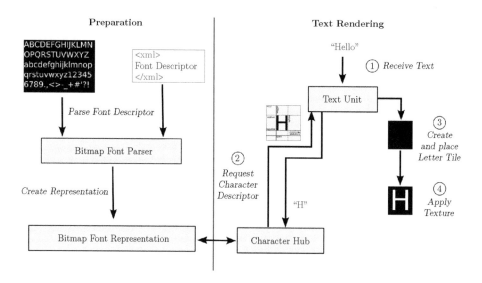

Figure 13.3. Bitmap font rendering structure.

preparation is complete, the text unit receives the strings to be rendered. It iterates through all characters in these strings and requests the character descriptor for each of them. It creates vertices and texture coordinates for each character tile and stores them in one buffer.

Before I discuss how this concept can be implemented, I will discuss a necessary preparation step: creating bitmap fonts.

13.3.2   Creating Bitmap Fonts

Creating a bitmap font requires the creation of textures and a font descriptor. The textures contain a complete charset, and the font descriptor provides the necessary meta information for the contained characters. We use a free tool, BMFont, to create a bitmap font [Angel 04]. The tool provides many settings, e.g., the resolution of the texture and the characters it should contain. It generates a set of textures and a XML font descriptor.

13.3.3   Implementation

In the first step, we load the bitmap font texture and parse the bitmap font descriptor. The bitmap font texture is initialized in the same manner as for canvas-based rendering, shown in Listing 13.2. The only change is that we load the texture from a file. The demo uses an XML font descriptor. We process the XML and store the parsed character descriptors in the *bitmap font representation*. Now, we have access

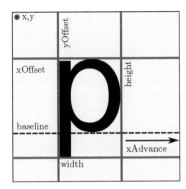

Figure 13.4. Bitmap font character descriptor.

to all character descriptors. Let's look at the information contained in a character descriptor:

```
<char id="47" x="127" y="235" width="26" height="66" xoffset="0"
 yoffset="15" xadvance="25" page="0" chnl="15" />
```

In this sample entry, x, y, `width`, and `height` define the character's subimage in the bitmap font texture file. The `page` parameter defines in which texture the character is stored; it is only necessary if a bitmap font is spread over several textures. Figure 13.4 visualizes the important attributes of this descriptor. They are necessary to create the vertices and texture coordinates of the character tiles.

Creating character tiles. Listing 13.5 shows the source code for the character tile creation. It contains two loops. We use the outer loop to iterate through all strings and the inner loop to iterate through all characters contained in the strings. In the outer loop, we store the origin of the currently selected string, which we need to initialize the position vertices.

In the inner loop, we create the vertices and texture coordinates for our character tiles. We load the character's descriptor and transform its properties using a font size factor. Next, we initialize the position vertices for our character tile. We calculate the positions of our vertices, using the string's origin and the information provided through the character descriptor. We complete the definition of our tile by adding the texture coordinates of the character to the buffer. Finally, we increase the xOffset, so that the next character is placed a correct distance from the current one.

After the loop terminates, the vertices and texture coordinates for all characters are contained in only one interleaved buffer. This means we can render all the scene's strings in a single draw call.

The actual rendering is the same as for canvas-based rendering. We bind the interleaved buffer and use the same shader program.

```
// Outer loop: is executed for every string
for ( i = 0; i < stringAmount; i++) {
  // set offsets to string's origin
  var yOffset = renderString[i].originY;
  var xOffset = renderString[i].originX;

  // Inner loop: is executed for every character
  for (n = 0; n < renderString[i].text.length; n++) {
    var charDescriptor = bmFontDescriptor.getCharacter(renderString[i].text[n]);
    var char_xOffset = charDescriptor.xoffset * fontSizeFactor;
    var char_yOffset = - (charDescriptor.yoffset * fontSizeFactor);
    var char_xAdvance = charDescriptor.xadvance * fontSizeFactor;
    var charHeight = charDescriptor.height * fontSizeFactor;
    var charWidth = charDescriptor.width * fontSizeFactor;

    // Get textureCoords for the current char
    textureCoords = (charDescriptor.textureBuffer);

    // Initialize P1
    vertices[vertices_i] = 0 + xOffset + char_xOffset;
    vertices[vertices_i+1] = -charHeight + yOffset + char_yOffset;
    vertices[vertices_i+2] = 1.0;
    vertices[vertices_i+3] = textureCoords[0];
    vertices[vertices_i+4] = textureCoords[1];
    // Initialize P2
    vertices[vertices_i+5] = charWidth + xOffset + char_xOffset;
    vertices[vertices_i+6] = -charHeight + yOffset  + char_yOffset;
    vertices[vertices_i+7] = 1.0;
    vertices[vertices_i+8] = textureCoords[2];
    vertices[vertices_i+9] = textureCoords[3];
    // Initialize P3
    // Initialize P4
    // [...]

    xOffset += char_xAdvance;
    // [...]
  }
}
```

Listing 13.5. Tile creation and initial placing.

13.4 Comparison

This section compares both text rendering approaches and determines when to use each. The following configuration was used for the performance tests:

- CPU. QuadCore AMD Phenom II, 2.80 GHz,

- System Memory. 4GB,

- GPU. ATI Radeon HD 4600 Series (1GB memory),

- Browser. Google Chrome 15,

- OS. Windows 7 (32bit).

13.4.1 Performance

To supply a reliable performance analysis, the different approaches were tested in the following scenarios:

- Static text (10,000 characters and 20,000 characters),

- Dynamic text (1,000 characters, 2,000 characters, and 10,000 characters).

The vertex shader we use for the demo is processed so fast that the GPU has to wait for the CPU to fill the buffers. This means that the performance of the text-rendering implementations mainly depends on the used CPU Time. To reach the maximum frame rate of 60 FPS, we have a time slot of about 16 ms per frame for our JavaScript code to execute. Table 13.1 shows the consumed CPU time for each benchmark.

In the first test, using static text, the CPU load is low. Both approaches reach 60 FPS for 10,000 and for 20,000 rendered characters using less than 0.2 ms of CPU time. Once the buffers are filled, the only expensive CPU operation is one draw call per frame. Using bitmap-font rendering, we can render about 130,000 characters before the frame rate drops below 60 FPS due to the GPU performance.

In the second test, we change all rendered characters every frame. This performance depends on the CPU load. The benchmark reveals enormous differences in the consumed CPU time for both approaches. The results are displayed in Figure 13.5. This figure shows that bitmap font rendering is a lot faster than canvas-based rendering for frequently changing text.

When the strings change for the bitmap font approach, we need to refill the buffers for the character tiles. In canvas-based rendering, we need to refresh the drawing on the canvas' 2D context and generate a new texture from it, a much more expensive operation.

The buffer recreation for 1,000 characters consumes 7 ms of CPU time and leaves our demo with enough time for buffer bindings. We reach the maximum frame rate of 60 FPS. In total, we only use 11 ms of our available CPU time.

Canvas-based rendering is much slower. To generate a texture of 1024 × 1024 pixels, we need 66 ms, 99% of the complete CPU time, and only reach a frame rate of 14.7 FPS.

	Bitmap Fonts	Canvas-Based
Static		
10,000 characters	0.2 ms	0.2 ms
20,000 characters	0.2 ms	0.2 ms
Dynamic		
1,000 characters	11.0 ms	66.0 ms
2,000 characters	11.2 ms	230.0 ms
10,000 characters	21.0 ms	1240.0 ms

Table 13.1. Consumed CPU time per frame.

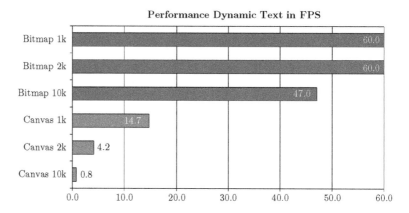

Figure 13.5. Performance comparison dynamic text.

In the second test, we render 2,000 characters. The differences between both approaches expand further. Using canvas-based rendering a texture size of 2048×2048 pixels[1] is required. The generation of this texture takes 230 ms and lets the frame rate drop to 4.2 FPS. The CPU time for bitmap font rendering increases marginally to 11.2 ms, and we still achieve 60 FPS.

In the last test, rendering 10,000 characters, bitmap font rendering's performance decreases to 47 FPS. Now, creating the vertices and filling the buffer consumes 15 ms CPU time. In total we need 21 ms on the CPU. The performance of canvas-based rendering decreases further to 0.8 FPS since the necessary texture size increases to 4096×4096 for 10,000 characters.

The following are the performance conclusions:

- The performance of our text rendering implementation depends on how much CPU time we use per frame.

- For static text, both rendering approaches are very efficient.

- For frequently changing text, bitmap font rendering is a lot faster than canvas-based rendering.

- The efficiency of canvas-based rendering depends on the size of the generated texture. Implementations can try to use as little texture space as possible by developing a placing strategy for the several strings.

---

[1]WebGL does not support mipmapping for non-power-of-two (NPOT) textures, and we are using mipmapping for our texture filters.

13.4.2 Memory Footprint

Next to the frame rate, the memory consumption is an important comparison factor. Figure 13.6 shows the memory usage of my approach in three different scenarios. The result of canvas-based rendering for 10,000 characters is not contained, because the graphic memory consumption of 32 MB would distort the graph. Further, mipmapping is not activated for the memory benchmark since it uses additional graphic memory.

Canvas-based rendering is able to beat bitmap font rendering for 200 characters since it only stores a small number of buffer entries. Using bitmap font rendering, the most memory per character is used by the vertices. We can describe a character using 26 float values. Together with the required data structures the process consumes about 300 Bytes per character. For the chosen font resolution, we additionally need a texture consuming 512 KB.

For canvas-based rendering, the characters are defined as textures, and one pixel consumes 2 bytes of graphic memory in luminance-alpha format. Our characters have a font size of 44 pixels, so a single character will use up to 3872 bytes![2] This explains the enormous differences in the memory usage. To render 2,000 characters using canvas-based rendering, we need a 2048×2048 pixel texture, which uses 8 MB graphic memory.

However, the number of characters is not the only factor that influences the memory consumption. What if we want to use several fonts? With the demo's font resolution, bitmap font rendering will require 512 KB graphic memory for every font, assuming we include the same charset for each. Canvas-based rendering, in contrast, uses system fonts and renders them dynamically, not requiring any

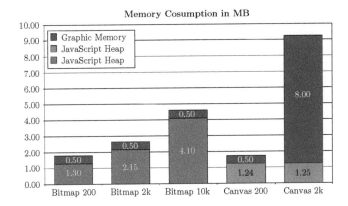

Figure 13.6. Memory consumption in MB.

---

[2]Maximum character size: $44 \times 44 = 1936$ pixels. Using 2 bytes per pixel: $1936 \times 2 = 3872$ bytes.

additional memory. I draw the following conclusions:

- The memory consumption of canvas-based rendering mainly grows with the number of rendered characters.

- Bitmap font rendering's memory usage mainly grows with the number of used fonts.

13.4.3 Ease of Development

Canvas-based font rendering has the advantage of access to the native font API of the canvas' 2D context. Further, the setup is lightweight; only one additional canvas element is necessary for its 2D context.

Bitmap font rendering, in contrast, requires a large initial development effort. We need to generate fonts; parse font descriptors; and create, shade, and place individual character tiles. However, user interaction is easier to handle using bitmap font rendering: we know the positions for each character and can use standard collision detection algorithms for our character tiles. This enables mouse-pointer–based interaction.

This is different for canvas-based rendering: the text is rendered as one single tile, and we need calculations to determine character-based interaction. The following conclusions can be made:

- Canvas-based rendering can be implemented simply and quickly.

- Bitmap font rendering can be used with collision detection, to allow user interaction.

13.5 Conclusion

In general, applications that don't focus on text content will tend to use canvas-based rendering due to its simple implementation. For noninteractive, static text, the canvas approach offers a reasonable performance. For applications mainly based on text presentation, bitmap font rendering is the better approach due to its performance and flexibility once all required components are implemented.

However, there are also special cases: applications using a large number of fonts will probably prefer canvas-based rendering since it is memory efficient in this scenario. Further, the two approaches can be combined, for example, by rendering large amounts of text with bitmap font rendering and using canvas-based rendering for smaller fragments with lots of different fonts.

Bibliography

[Angel 04] Angelcode.com. "Bitmap Font Generator." http://www.angelcode.com/products/bmfont/, 2004.

Layered Textures Rendering Pipeline 14

Dzmitry Malyshau

14.1   Introduction

Texture mapping is a fundamental part of the contemporary rendering pipeline. It provides various shading models with surface-varying properties, such as diffuse color, specular color and glossiness, normal direction and displacement offset. During rendering, these properties become parameters of the lighting equation producing the final pixel colors. There are many ways to define the coordinates used for texture sampling, such as prebaked UV, parametric projections, including the screen position, world position, normal vector, reflection vector, etc. When applied to an existing primitive, texture data can be mixed using various blending equations and coefficients: add, mix, alpha blend, replace. Table 14.1 shows many of the parameters of the texturing pipeline.

Texture Type	Semantics	Coordinates	Blending Mode
1D file	Diffuse	One of the UV channels	Mix
2D file	Opacity	Screen position	Add
3D file	Specular	World position	Subtract
Cube file	Glossiness	Normal vector	Multiply
Generated	Normal	Reflection vector	Overlay
Encoded	Displace	Tangent vector	Difference
...	...	...	...

Table 14.1. Texturing pipeline parameters.

Any combination of these parameters may be requested by an artist, hence the $6^4 = 1296$ variations already shown in this limited example. Unlike filtering and wrapping modes, these parameters are not encapsulated in the OpenGL texture sampling state. Supporting these parameters in the real-time pipeline requires different execution paths on both the CPU and the GPU.

Some 3D engines have a limited number of material profiles like Diffuse only, Diffuse + Normal, Diffuse + Environment. Source engine [Valve 11] gives an example: "The Phong mask is a greyscale image stored in the alpha channel of the model's normal map." There is always a workaround to write our own shader that implements any combination of the parameters in our table. However, an artist is not going to do it, and it is too time consuming to be used in the prototyping stage. These limitations basically leave no way for an artist to experiment with texturing pipeline in a full degree of freedom in real time.

This article presents an original rendering pipeline designed to support a flexible texture pipeline, allowing any combination of texture and blending options. It was inspired by the Blender texturing pipeline [KatsBits 00] and designed for it. Our pipeline allows artists to use Blender's texturing expressiveness during the early development stage, while retaining the advantage of 3D engines' real-time performance when visualizing the results of texturing experiments.

14.1.1   Terminology

Let's start by clearing up some terminology:

- **Phong lighting.** A commonly used lighting model with the following parameters: diffuse and specular colors, shininess, surface normal, camera, and light vectors.

- **G-buffer.** A storage of material properties baked in screen space. Can be represented by a number of textures or a single layered texture. The information is extracted from the G-buffer when the light contribution to the fragment is evaluated.

- **Deferred rendering.** A family of rendering pipelines that split material properties and lighting evaluation. Generally, it is implemented in two steps: G-buffer creation and light resolution.

14.1.2   Textures in Blender

A Blender material contains a list of textures. Material properties correspond to the uniform properties of a geometric primitive and define the initial parameter values. Textures are applied in a sequence, modifying some of these values in a high-frequency manner. Table 14.1 is constructed from a core set, but not all of the Blender texture parameters. After the primitive parameters are set by the material

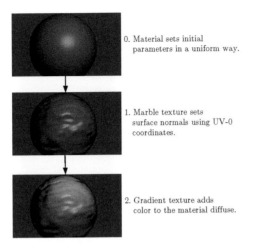

0. Material sets initial
   parameters in a uniform way.

1. Marble texture sets
   surface normals using UV-0
   coordinates.

2. Gradient texture adds
   color to the material diffuse.

Figure 14.1. Example Blender material.

and textures, the lighting equations produce the final sample color. An example material sequence of operations is presented in Figure 14.1.

14.2 Layered Pipeline

The most natural storage for surface properties is a 2D texture. We render an array of textures several times: one for the material parameters and one for each texture. Think of it as applying a sequence of layers onto the material.

An important choice that is easy to miss is the coordinate system of the surface parameters. Screen space is the straightforward solution that I followed, but it is not the only possibility. For example, we can choose the UV space defined by one of the UV coordinate layers. This alternative would produce aliasing and filtering issues for the camera projection but could be used for multiple cameras at once.

There is already a known screen-space surface baking technique in real-time 3D graphics. It is a part of the *deferred rendering* algorithm [Calver 03], referred to as "G-Buffer creation." The method proposed and the original G-buffer creation aim to produce the same result: primitive properties baked in the screen space. The difference is that we are applying layer after layer, while the classical approach is to fill the G-buffer in a single pass. Obviously, the latter is faster but less flexible; it also has higher requirements on the memory space and the number of FBO attachments used for rendering. As for the second stage, lighting evaluation, I will not propose any improvements and will describe just one variation of the known procedure. This procedure adds Phong-based lighting contributions in screen space by drawing light volumes on the final FBO and sampling the surface properties from the G-buffer.

14.2.1 G-buffer Creation

Our G-buffer has three RGBA textures in the format shown in Table 14.2. Note that the last vector is in range $[-1, 1]$, packed in a fixed-point format.

Format	RGB data	Alpha data
RGBA8	Diffuse color	Emissive amount
RGBA8	Specular color	Glossiness amount
RGBA12	World-space normal	Displacement

Table 14.2. G-buffer format.

The G-buffer does not include reflection color, which may be required for the environmental map. We can apply an environmental map later, if needed, over the final framebuffer instead of baking that into the G-buffer.

There is also a depth texture used in the pipeline for reconstructing the world position of the point and performing the depth test. We fill it during the material parameters pass, but the developer can decide to perform a separate *early-depth* pass in advance. These three textures plus the depth texture should be attached to a framebuffer object (FBO) in the same order they are listed. The algorithm is as follows:

1. Clear all color attachments with black. Clear depth with 1.0.

2. Set depth test and write enabled. Set draw buffers to 111b (binary) to affect all attachments.

3. Draw all objects with a dedicated shader program.

The vertex shader only computes the world-space normal and projects the vertex into camera space. The fragment shader is even more trivial, updating the G-buffer with the raw primitive parameters.

At this point, we have material information baked into the G-buffer. Theoretically, we could skip the rest and apply lighting right away, but the produced image would lack a lot of detail.

14.2.2 Layers Resolution

This stage is a core part of the pipeline. We apply textures one by one, setting the proper OpenGL state for each, including blending, draw buffers, color masking, and the shader. The procedure for applying a texture has separate code paths for color modifiers and normal maps.

Color maps.   See Listing 14.1 for a color layer fragment shader.

1. Set draw buffers to 011b to prevent normals from being affected.

2. Set color mask for each attachment separately to affect only the required set of parameters, which are a subset of Table 14.2. These are the parameters checked by the artist in the "Influence" tab of Blender texture properties.

3. Set blending equation and factors to correspond to the ones chosen in Blender. Our implementation supports "Multiply," "Add," and "Mix" at the moment, but this list can be extended by adding, at least, "Difference," "Lighten," and "Saturation."

4. Set depth mask to **GL_FALSE**. Draw the object with depth test.

5. The vertex shader transforms the position into clip coordinates. It may also provide the texture coordinates used for sampling. This is the case when these coordinates are dependent on the vertex input, like most of the coordinates: UV layers, world position, reflection, etc.

6. The fragment shader samples the texture and dispatches sampled parameters to the first two color attachments of the FBO. The shader may also need to generate the texture coordinates if they were impossible to obtain from the vertex shader, e.g., clip coordinates. Blender has an option to convert RGB values to intensity. If this option is used, the fragment shader needs to use the manual user color with an intensity derived from the original color.

```
// Obtain the texture coordinates
vec4 tc4 = tc_unit();
// Apply parallax offset
vec2 tc = make_offset(tc4.xy);
// Finally, sample
vec4 value = texture(unit_texture, tc);
// Alpha test (optional)
if (value.w < 0.01)
{
  discard;
}
// compute intensity
float single = dot(value.xyz, luminance);
// Compute alternative color
vec3 alt = single * user_color.xyz;
vec3 color = mix(value.xyz, alt, user_color.w);
// Output the same value into both attachments
c_diffuse = c_specular = vec4(color, value.w);
```

Listing 14.1. Color layer fragment shader.

Normal maps. See Listing 14.2 for a normal layer fragment shader.

1. Set draw buffers to 100b, making the rendering affect only the third texture.

2. Set the color mask to affect either normal only or the displacement.

3. Draw the object with the depth test and disabled depth mask.

4. The vertex shader transforms the position into clip coordinates and generates texture coordinates. It also has to compute the coordinate space in which the normal map is given: tangent or object space. This space, or its mapping to the world, is represented by a rotational transform in the form of a (quaternion,handedness) pair [Malyshau 10].

5. The fragment shader extracts the normal, transforms it into world space and encodes into the output [0, 1] range vector.

```
// Obtain the texture coordinates
vec4 tc = tc_unit();
// Sample from the normal map
vec4 value = texture(unit_texture, tc.xy);
// Re-normalize filtered normal
vec3 normal = normalize(value.xyz * 2.0 - vec3(1.0));
// Re-normalize interpolated map->world transformation
vec4 quat = normalize(n_space);
// Transform the normal into world space
vec3 n = qrot(quat, normal) * vec3(handedness, 1.0, 1.0);
// Encode the normal
c_normal = 0.5 * vec4(n, 0.0) + vec4(0.5);
```

Listing 14.2. Normal layer fragment shader.

14.2.3 Unified parallax offset

Parallax mapping [Welsh 04] is a natural improvement to normal mapping. It shifts texture coordinates according to the normal vector and viewer position. This, in turn, makes the surface look more bumpy and natural. We will not explain the particular equation used, but instead show the general routine required to implement any kind of texture offset (see Listing 14.3).

The resulting offset should be produced in the space of the coordinates used for sampling the texture. Hence, we developed an algorithm for universal parallax offsets in order to support arbitrary texture coordinates. This algorithm uses GLSL derivative instructions in order to get the world-to-texture transformation; then, it gets view and normal vectors into the texture space and finally computes the offset.

```
in  vec3  view, var_normal;
// World-space view vector and the vertex interpolated normal
vec2 make_offset(vec2 tc)
{
  vec2 tscreen = gl_FragCoord.xy / screen_size.xy;
  vec4 bump = 2.0 * texture(unit_bump, tscreen) - vec4(1.0);
  // Read the world space normal from the G-buffer
  vec3 bt = bump.xyz;
  vec3 vt = normalize(view); //world space view vector
  vec3 pdx = dFdx(-view);    //world space derivation
  vec3 pdy = dFdy(-view);
  vec2 tdx = dFdx(tc);  //texture space derivation
  vec2 tdy = dFdy(tc);
  // Construct the transition transform and orthogonalize it
  vec3 t = normalize(tdy.y * pdx - tdx.y * pdy);
  vec3 b = normalize(tdy.x * pdx - tdx.x * pdy);
  vec3 n = normalize(var_normal);
  t = cross(b, n); b = cross(n, t);
  // Texture -> world transform
  mat3 t2w = mat3(t,b,n);
  bt = bt * t2w;  // Reverse order multiplication
  vt = vt * t2w;  // To get into texture space
  // finally, compute parallax offset
  vec2 offset = parallax * bump.w * bt.z * vt.xy;
  return tc + offset;
}
```

Listing 14.3. Unified parallax offset code.

14.2.4 Lighting

Lighting is standard for a deferred rendering approach. Before adding the light contribution to the final rendered image, we fill it with emissive color read from the G-buffer. I will describe it step by step from the OpenGL state down to the pixel on the final FBO color attachment.

Initialization.

1. Select the final framebuffer with its color attachment for drawing.

2. A quad is drawn with a simple shader with no depth test. A large triangle will work as well.

3. The vertex shader scales the quad/triangle to cover the viewport.

4. The fragment shader generates the emissive color based on the first G-buffer texture:

```
// sample diffuse color and emissive amount
vec4 diff = texture(unit_g0, tex_coord);
rez_color = diff.w * diff;
```

Light shading.

1. Select the final framebuffer with its color attachment for drawing.

2. Set blending equation to `GL_ADD` with coefficients 1, 1.

3. Depth testing enabled in read-only mode with `GL_GEQUAL` function.

4. Cull front faces.

5. Draw light volume as a mesh with a dedicated shader.

6. The vertex shader scales and modifies the shape according to light ranges.

7. The fragment shader starts by extracting the depth value from the depth texture and transforming it into the world space.

8. Surface parameters are extracted from G-buffer and used to compute Phong-model lighting.

14.3   Results

14.3.1   Implementation

This pipeline is implemented as a module for the KRI engine [Malyshau 10]. The implementation consists of three parts.

The Blender-to-engine translation part starts with a Python exporter. It dumps material and texture properties unchanged in a format accepted by the engine. The scene loader checks that the selected set of parameters is supported. It also assigns a shader object for each texture-coordinate method used.

The core rendering part substitutes the G-buffer fill routine. It initializes the G-buffer and fills it with textures, layer after layer as described in Section 14.2. It can be swapped with an alternative G-buffer filling routine at any time. For example, once the artist is satisfied with the result, we can ask the programmer to combine all texture stages into one shader. This optimized shader may be used instead of our layered routine in the production phase.

Finally, the KRI Viewer is an engine client that supports our pipeline. We can switch to it at any point while viewing a scene and compare the result to alternative pipelines, such as flat shading, forward lighting, and classical deferred rendering.

14.3.2   Results

An experimental scene has a single sphere object lit by one omnidirectional light (see Figure 14.2). The material of the sphere has three textures:

1. Tangent-space normal map using UV coordinates.

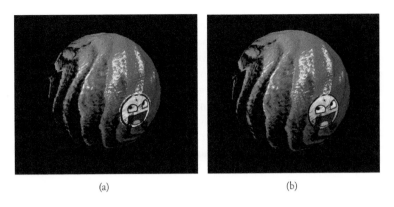

(a)   (b)

Figure 14.2. Rendered scene: (a) Blender image, (b) KRI image.

2. Diffuse gradient map using local object coordinates. It is mixed with an underlying material color.

3. Diffuse map with alpha testing. Uses dummy object world coordinates for sampling. It is also mixed with the previous color.

Blender was not able to produce a 100% match in the output picture. Blender samples the textures slightly differently, leaving a thin visible outline of the decal texture.

Performance numbers (see Table 14.3) were obtained using the KRI Viewer profiler in an 800×600 OpenGL area. The test machine had a Radeon 2400 HD video card, Core 2 Quad 2.4GHz CPU, and 3 GB RAM.

Stage	Layered pipeline	Deferred pipeline
Early-depth	77 μs	77 μs
G-buffer fill	2094 μs	839 μs
Deferred lighting	2036 μs	1997 μs
Total	4207 μs	2913 μs

Table 14.3. Performance comparison.

14.3.3   Conclusion

This chapter has presented a new rendering pipeline that replaces the G-buffer filling procedure of the deferred rendering pipeline. The filling method applies textures separately layer after layer. It supports various texture-coordinate-generating methods, blending equations, and normal map spaces. It also features the parallax offset algorithm that transforms world-space normal and view vectors into the space of target texture coordinates.

The actual implementation of the pipeline does not support all listed texture parameters at the moment. For example, environmental textures are not yet supported. However, this method provides a framework, which simplifies the process of adding support for these parameters as easy as possible.

The separation of layers gives better granularity of the rendering system. It provides more options for real-time texture mapping. This comes at the cost of reduced performance. The layered pipeline is compatible with regular deferred rendering and can be switched with a standard G-buffer fill procedure on the fly.

The presented rendering pipeline method allows artists to see the precise real-time interpretation of their work in Blender. This ability streamlines the preproduction and prototyping stages of development.

Future work. The biggest issue of the described pipeline is performance. This issue is being addressed by creating a shader composing system. This system will work in a way similar to the fixed GPU pipeline by creating a complete shader program for each material. This program will apply all textures with corresponding blending modes in a single pass, producing the same results.

I am also going to extend the texture parameter support. This includes making an additional rendering step for applying environmental textures on the final image.

Bibliography

[Calver 03] Dean Calver. "Photo-Realistic Deferred Lighting." http://www.beyond3d.com/content/articles/19, July 31, 2003.

[KatsBits 00] KatsBits. "Blender 2.5 Texturing Tutorial." http://www.katsbits.com/tutorials/blender/blender-basics-2.5-materials-textures-images.php, 2000.

[Malyshau 10] Dzmitry Malyshau. "KRI Engine Wiki." http://code.google.com/p/kri/w/list, 2010.

[Valve 11] Valve. "Source Engine Wiki." http://developer.valvesoftware.com/wiki/, June 30, 2011.

[Welsh 04] Terry Welsh. "Parallax Mapping with Offset Limiting." https://www8.cs.umu.se/kurser/5DV051/VT09/lab/parallax_mapping.pdf, January 18, 2004.

Depth of Field with Bokeh Rendering 15

Charles de Rousiers and Matt Pettineo

15.1 Introduction

In order to increase realism and immersion, current games make frequent use of depth of field to simulate lenticular phenomena. Typical implementations use screen-space filtering techniques to roughly approximate a camera's circle of confusion for out-of-focus portions of a scene. While such approaches can provide pleasing results with minimal performance impact, crucial features present in real-life photography are still missing. In particular, lens-based cameras produce a phenomenon known as *bokeh* (blur in Japanese). Bokeh manifests as distinctive geometric shapes that are most visible in out-of-focus portions of an image with high local contrast (see Figure 15.1). The actual shape itself depends on the shape of the camera's aperture, which is typically circular, octagonal, hexagonal, or pentagonal.

Current and upcoming Direct3D 11 engines, e.g., CryENGINE, Unreal Engine 3, Lost Planet 2 Engine, have recently demonstrated new techniques for simulating bokeh depth of field, which reflects a rising interest in reproducing such effects in real time. However, these techniques have performance requirements that can potentially relegate them to high-end GPUs. The precise implementation details of these techniques also aren't publicly available, making it difficult to integrate these techniques into existing engines. Consequently, it remains an active area of research, as there is still a need for implementations that are suitable for a wider range of hardware.

A naive approach would be to explicitly render a quad for each pixel, with each quad using a texture containing the aperture shape. While this can produce excellent

Figure 15.1. Comparison between a simple blur-based depth of field (left) and a depth of field with bokeh rendering (right).

results [Sousa 11, Furturemark 11, Mittring and Dudash 11], it is also extremely inefficient due to the heavy fill rate and bandwidth requirements. Instead, we propose a hybrid method that mixes previous filtering-based approaches with quad rendering. Our method selects pixels with high local contrast and renders a single textured quad for each such pixel. The texture used for the quad contains the camera's aperture shape, which allows the quads to approximate bokeh effects. In order to achieve high performance, we use atomic counters in conjunction with an image texture for random memory access. An indirect draw command is also used, which avoids the need for expensive CPU-GPU synchronization. This efficient OpenGL 4.2 implementation allows rendering of thousands of aperture-shaped quads at high frame rates, and also ensures the temporal coherency of the rendered bokeh.

15.2 Depth of Field Phenomemon

Depth of field is an important effect for conveying a realistic sense of depth and scale, particularly in open scenes with a large viewing distance. Traditional real-time applications use a pinhole camera model [Pharr and Humphreys 10] for rasterization, which results in an infinite depth of field. However, real cameras use a thin lens, which introduces a limited depth of field based on aperture size and focal distance. Objects outside this region appear blurred on the final image, while objects inside it remain sharp (see Figure 15.2).

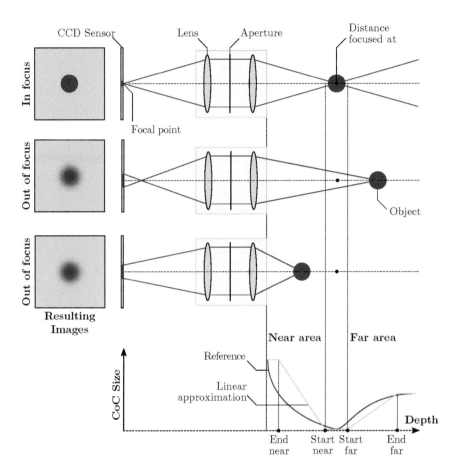

Figure 15.2. Depth of field phenomenon, where a thin lens introduces a limited depth of field. In-focus objects appear sharp, while out-of-focus objects appear blurred. The size of the circle of confusion depends on the distance between object and the point at which the camera is focused. We use a linear approximation in order to simplify parameters as well as run-time computations.

The "blurriness" of an object is defined by its *circle of confusion* (CoC). The size of this CoC depends on the distance between the object and the area on which the camera is focused. The further an object is from the focused area, the blurrier it appears. The size of the CoC does not increase linearly based on this distance. The size actually increases faster in the out-of-focus foreground area than it does in the out-of-focus background area (see Figure 15.2). Since the CoC size ultimately depends on focal distance, lens size, and aperture shape, setting up the simulation parameters may not be intuitive to someone inexperienced with photography. This

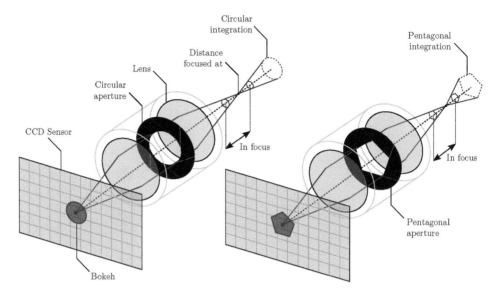

Figure 15.3. Aperture shape of a camera. Aperture blocks a portion of the incoming light. Its shape modifies the pixel integration and, hence, changes the bokeh shape.

is why we use a simple linear approximation as proposed by [Earl Hammon 07] (see Figure 15.2).

The *aperture* of a camera is responsible for allowing light to pass through the lens and strike the sensor (or film).[1] The shape of this aperture directly impacts the formation of the image since each out-of-focus point is convolved with the aperture shape (see Figure 15.3).

While it is often difficult to see distinct bokeh patterns in areas with low contrast, bokeh is clearly visible in areas that are significantly brighter than their surroundings. We use this observation as a heuristic to determine where bokeh quads need to be drawn in order to provide a plausible approximation.

15.3   Related Work

Several methods have been proposed during the last decade for efficiently approximating a depth-of-field effect. However, those methods use a Gaussian blur or heat diffusion to simulate out-of-focus areas [Earl Hammon 07, Lee et al. 09, Kosloff and Barsky 07] and are therefore unable to reproduce bokeh effects.

---

[1]If an object or the camera moves while the aperture is open, the objects will appear blurred. This is known as motion blur.

An earlier approach from Krivanek [Krivanek et al. 03] uses sprite splatting as a means for implementing depth of field rather than a filtering approach. While this brute-force method does produce bokeh shapes, it is quite inefficient due to excessive overdraw and bandwidth consumption.

The video game industry has shown a recent interest in bokeh effects [Capcom 07, Sousa 11, Furturemark 11, Mittring and Dudash 11]. While complete implementation details are not available, the methods used by video game developers largely take a similar approach to Krivanek where sprites are rendered for each pixel. Consequently, these techniques make use of complex optimizations, e.g., hierarchical rasterization, multiple downscaling passes, in order to improve performance.

A recent approach proposed by White [White and Brisebois 11] reproduces hexagonal bokeh using several directional blur passes. While efficient, this method does not support arbitrary aperture shapes.

15.4 Algorithm

We observe that only points with a high local contrast will produce distinct bokeh shapes. We use this heuristic to detect bokeh positions in screen space [Pettineo 11] and then splat textured quads at those locations. The remaining pixels use a blur-based approach to simulate a circle of confusion.

15.4.1 Overview

Our approach is divided into four passes (see Figure 15.4). The first pass computes the CoC size for each pixel based on its depth value, and then outputs a linear depth

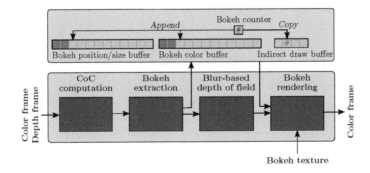

Figure 15.4. Overview of the pipeline. It is composed of four passes and takes as input the color and depth buffers of the current frame. It outputs a final color image with depth of field and bokeh effects.

value to a framebuffer attachment.[2] Then, the second pass computes the contrast of the current pixel by comparing the pixel's brightness with the brightness of the 5×5 neighboring pixels. If this contrast is above a predefined threshold, its position, CoC size, and average color are appended to a buffer. During the third pass, a blur-based depth of field is computed with one of the previous methods, e.g., Gaussian blur. Finally, a fourth pass splats textured quads at the bokeh positions that were appended to the buffer in the second pass.

In order to maintain high performance, it is crucial to avoid CPU/GPU synchronization. We ensure this by making use of an indirect draw command [Bolz et al. 09], which renders a number of quads based on the count stored in the append buffer. This way, the number of bokeh points detected by the GPU is never read back by the CPU.

15.4.2   Circle of Confusion Computation

Setting up depth of field using physical camera parameters, such as focal length and aperture size, can be nonintuitive for those not familiar with optics or photography. Instead, we define two areas where geometry is out of focus: a near/foreground area and a far/background area. Both areas are delimited with a near and far depth value (see Figure 15.2). In both regions, the blur amount is linearly interpolated between the two bounds. This allows a simple and intuitive means of describing the depth of field for a given scene.

$$\mathrm{CoC} = \frac{Z_{\mathrm{pixel}} - Z_{\mathrm{start}}}{Z_{\mathrm{end}} - Z_{\mathrm{start}}}.$$

The resulting CoC size from this equation is normalized to [0,1]. An extra parameter `MaxRadius` determines the final size of the blur in screen space a posteriori. This setting can be tweaked by artists in order to achieve the desired appearance and provides a means of balancing performance: smaller values of `MaxRadius` result in greater performance.

15.4.3   Bokeh Detection

The detection pass aims to detect pixels from which we will generate bokeh shapes. To detect such pixels, we use the following heuristic: *a pixel with high contrast in a given neighborhood will generate a bokeh shape.* We compare the current pixel luminance L_{pixel} to its neighborhood luminance L_{neigh}. If the difference $L_{\mathrm{pixel}} - L_{\mathrm{neigh}}$ is greater than the threshold, `LumThreshold`, then the current pixel is registered as a bokeh point.[3] Pixels detected as bokeh are sparse, which means writing them into a framebuffer attachment would be wasteful in terms of both memory usage

---

[2] If a linear depth buffer is available as an input, the first two passes can be merged together.
[3] We also use the threshold `CoCThreshold` to discard bokeh with a small radius.

and bandwidth.[4] To address this problem, we use the OpenGL `ImageBuffer` [Bolz et al. 11] in combination with an "atomic counter" [Licea-Kane et al. 11]. This allows us to build a vector in which we append parameters for detected bokeh points. `ImageBuffers` have to be preallocated with a given size, i.e., the maximum number of bokeh sprites that can be displayed on screen. The atomic counter `BokehCounter` stores the number of appended bokeh points. Its current value indicates the next free cell in the `ImageBuffer` vector. Two `ImageBuffer` variables, `BokehPosition` and `BokehColor`, are used to store the CoC size, position, and color of the detected bokeh points. See Listings 15.1 and 15.2 and Figure 15.5.

```
// Create indirect buffer
GLuint indirectBufferID;
glGenBuffers(1, &indirectBufferID);
glBindBuffer(GL_DRAW_INDIRECT_BUFFER, indirectBufferID);
DrawArraysIndirectCommand indirectCmd;
indirectCmd.count = 1;
indirectCmd.primCount = 0;
indirectCmd.first = 0;
indirectCmd.reservedMustBeZero = 0;
glBufferData(GL_DRAW_INDIRECT_BUFFER, sizeof(DrawArraysIndirectCommand), &←
    indirecCmd, GL_DYNAMIC_DRAW);

// Create a texture proxy for the indirect buffer
// (used during bokeh count synch.)
glGenTextures(1, &bokehCountTexID);
glBindTexture(GL_TEXTURE_BUFFER, bokehCountTexID);
glTexBuffer(GL_TEXTURE_BUFFER, GL_R32UI, indirectBufferID);

// Create an atomic counter
glGenBuffers(1, &bokehCounterID);
glBindBuffer(GL_ATOMIC_COUNTER_BUFFER, bokehCounterID);
glBufferData(GL_ATOMIC_COUNTER_BUFFER, sizeof(unsigned int), 0, GL_DYNAMIC_DRAW);

// Create position and color textures with a GL_RGBA32F inner format
...

// Bind atomic counter
glBindBufferBase(GL_ATOMIC_COUNTER_BUFFER, 0, bokehCounterID);

// Bind position image buffer
glActiveTexture(GL_TEXTURE0 + bokehPosionTexUnit);
glBindImageTexture(bokehPostionTexUnit, bokehPositionTexID, 0, false, 0, ←
    GL_WRITE_ONLY, GL_RGBA32F);

// Bind color image buffer
glActiveTexture(GL_TEXTURE0 + bokehColorTexUnit);
glBindImageTexture(bokehColorTexUnit, bokehColorTexID, 0, false, 0, GL_WRITE_ONLY,←
    GL_RGBA32F);

DrawSceenTriangle();
```

Listing 15.1. Host application for extracting bokehs *(Pass 2)*.

---

[4] During our tests, less than 1% of pixels are detected as bokeh at 720p.

```
#version 420
// Bokeh counter, position (x,y,z,size), and color
layout(binding = 0, offset = 0) uniform atomic_uint BokehCounter;
layout(size4x32) writeonly uniform image1D BokehPositionTex;
layout(size4x32) writeonly uniform image1D BokehColorTex;

// Constrast and CoC thresholds
uniform float LumThreshold;
uniform float CoCThreshold;
...

float cocCenter;   // Current CoC size
vec3 colorCenter;  // Current pixel color
vec3 colorNeighs;  // Average color of the neighborhood

// Append pixel whose constrast is greater than the user's threshold
float lumNeighs = dot(colorNeighs, vec3(0.299f, 0.587f, 0.114f));
float lumCenter = dot(colorCenter, vec3(0.299f, 0.587f, 0.114f));
if((lumCenter - lumNeighs) > LumThreshold && cocCenter > CoCThreshold)
{
  int current = int(atomicCounterIncrement(BokehCounter));
  imageStore(BokehPositionTex, current,vec4(gl_FragCoord.x, gl_FragCoord.y, depth, ←
      cocCenter));
  imageStore(BokehColorTex, current, vec4(colorCenter, 1));
}
```

Listing 15.2. Fragment shader for extracting bokehs *(Pass 2)*.

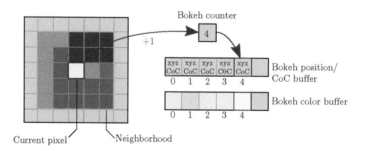

Figure 15.5. Bokeh detection. The luminance of the current pixel is compared to its neighborhood. If the difference is greater than LumThreshold, bokeh parameters, i.e., position, color, and CoC, are appended into BokehPosition and BokehColor image buffers. The atomic counter BokehCounter is also incremented.

15.4.4   Blur-Based Depth of Field

Several approaches are possible for this pass. We refer readers to previous work for this step. Nevertheless, here is a short summary of popular approaches:

- Perform a Gaussian blur with fixed kernel width at various resolutions, and apply a linear interpolation to blend them according to CoC size.

- Perform a Poisson disc sampling in screen space, with radius determined by pixel CoC size.[5]

- Apply a large-width bilateral filter where invalid pixels are rejected based on depth.[6]

The Hammon's approach [Earl Hammon 07] can be used for processing the foreground out-of-focused area. This approach is compatible with the bokeh rendering technique presented here.

15.4.5 Bokeh Rendering

In order to avoid CPU/GPU synchronization, we use the indirect drawing command `glDrawArraysIndirect`. This command draws instances where the count is read from a buffer located in GPU memory. This buffer can be updated from either the CPU or the GPU. In order to allow the GPU to operate independently of the CPU, we update this buffer from the GPU before the last pass. We bind this indirect buffer as an `ImageTexture` and copy the value of the atomic counter into it. Thus, the number of instances drawn is equal to the number of detected bokeh points (see Listing 15.3).

We use this command in combination with a vertex array object (VAO), describing a single vertex to render a point primitive. The instanced points are translated by the vertex shader so that they are located at the screen-space bokeh position. This position is read from the `BokehPosition` array buffer, which is indexed using

```
#version 420
layout(binding = 0, offset = 0) uniform atomic_uint BokehCounter;
layout(size1x32) writeonly uniform uimage1D IndirectBufferTex;
out vec4 FragColor;

void main()
{
  imageStore(IndirectBufferTex, 1, uvec4(atomicCounter(BokehCounter), 0, 0, 0));
  FragColor = vec4(0);
}
```

Listing 15.3. Synchronization of the indirect buffer with the atomic counter *(Pass 3/4)*. The function `glMemoryBarrier` has to be call before this shader in order to ensure that all bokeh data have been written.

---

[5]A random rotation can be applied to a Poisson sampling pattern for transforming aliasing into noise.

[6]For implementation details, we refer the reader to the code sample. This approach offers a good compromise between quality and performance. However, larger filter kernels require a large sampling radius. An OpenCL implementation would allow for better performance since shared memory can be used to cache texture fetches.

```
#version 420
uniform mat4 Transformation;
uniform vec2 PixelScale;
in float vRadius[1];
in vec4 vColor[1];
out vec4 gColor;
out vec2 gTexCoord;
layout(points) in;
layout(triangle_strip, max_vertices = 6) out;

void main()
{
  gl_Layer = 0;
  vec4 offsetx = vec4(PixelScale.x * Radius[0], 0, 0, 0);
  vec4 offsety = vec4(0, PixelScale.y * Radius[0], 0, 0);
  gColor = vColor[0];
  gl_Position  = Transformation * (gl_in[0].gl_Position - offsetx - offsety);
  gTexCoord = vec2(0,0);
  EmitVertex();
  gl_Position = Transformation * (gl_in[0].gl_Position + offsetx - offsety);
  gTexCoord = vec2(1,0);
  EmitVertex();
  gl_Position = Transformation * (gl_in[0].gl_Position - offsetx + offsety);
  gTexCoord = vec2(0,1);
  EmitVertex();
  gl_Position = Transformation * (gl_in[0].gl_Position + offsetx + offsety);
  gTexCoord = vec2(1,1);
  EmitVertex();
  EndPrimitive();
}
```

Listing 15.4. Geometry shader for rendering bokeh *(Pass 4)*.

the built-in gl_InstanceID input variable. After being transformed in the vertex shader, each point is expanded into a quad in the geometry shader. The size of this quad is determined by the bokeh size, which is also read from the BokehPosition array buffer. Finally, the fragment shader applies the alpha texture bokeh onto the quad and multiplies it by the bokeh color, which is read from the BokehColor array buffer (see Listing 15.4).

15.5   Results

Figures 15.1, 15.6, and 15.7 show the rendering of a tank using our method. Since the final bokeh shape is texture-driven, we can apply arbitrary shapes (see Figure 15.7).

Figure 15.8 details the rendering times of each pass as well as the number of detected bokeh points. We can see that the blur-based depth-of-field pass is the most expensive, indicating that a more optimal approach might be more suitable. Unlike the blur and detection passes, the rendering pass is strongly dependent on the number of detected bokeh points and is fill-rate bound. When the scene is entirely out of focus, our algorithm detects around 5,000 bokeh points in the tank scene. In this case, the cost of the rendering pass is less than 2 ms.

Figure 15.6. Rendering of a tank with a small depth of field. Bokeh shapes are clearly visible on the more reflective surfaces of the tank.

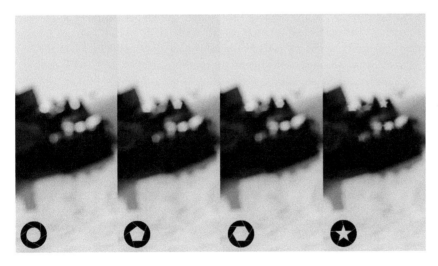

Figure 15.7. Rendering of the same scene with different aperture shapes. Bokeh textures are 32 × 32 pixel grayscale bitmap. From left to right: a circle aperture, a pentagonal aperture, an hexagonal aperture, and a star aperture.

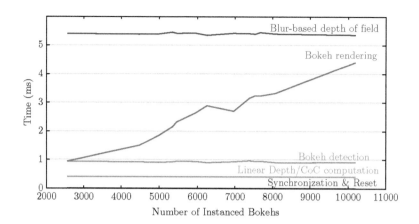

Figure 15.8. Timings of the different passes for varying numbers of detected bokeh points. Those timings have been recorded on an NVIDIA GeForce GTX 580 at 1280 × 720.

15.6 Discussion

Temporal coherence is a natural concern for this approach. Like other methods, we base our approach on the final color buffer. If subpixel aliasing is addressed by previous rendering steps, our approach is stable, and bokeh shapes are coherent from frame to frame. In the case of subpixel aliasing, our method exhibits the same limitations as all previous methods, and the resulting bokeh shapes may flicker.

Also, our method requires preallocated buffers for storing the bokeh position and color. Consequently, a maximum number of bokeh points has to be specified. If this number is too low, bokeh points may pop and flicker from frame to frame with little coherency. If this number is too large, then GPU memory is potentially wasted. Thus, the maximum number of sprites must be carefully chosen to suit the type of scene being displayed.

15.7 Conclusion

We have presented an efficient implementation for rendering a depth-of-field effect with bokeh. This method allows us to combine an efficient blur-based approach with plausible bokeh reproduction. We use a heuristic to identify pixels that produce distinct bokeh shapes and then render those shapes as textured quads. This implementation avoids costly CPU/GPU synchronization through the use of indirect draw commands. These commands allow the GPU to directly read the number of instances without the need for CPU readback.

While this approach provides good visual results, several optimizations can be made in order to improve performance. In particular, large CoC sizes require rasterization of quads that cover a significant portion of the screen. Using hierarchical rasterization,[7] as proposed in [Furturemark 11], could improve performance by reducing the number of pixels that need to be shaded and blended.

Bibliography

[Bolz et al. 09] Jeff Bolz, Pat Brown, Barthold Lichtenbelt, Bill Licea-Kane, Merry Bruce, Sellers Graham, Roth Greg, Haemel Nick, Boudier Pierre, and Piers Daniell. "ARB_draw_indirect." OpenGL extension, 2009.

[Bolz et al. 11] Jeff Bolz, Pat Brown, Barthold Lichtenbelt, Bill Licea-Kane, Eric Werness, Graham Sellers, Greg Roth, Nick Haemel, Pierre Boudier, and Piers Daniell. "ARB_shader_image_load_store." OpenGL extension, 2011.

[Capcom 07] Capcom. "Lost Planet 2 DX10 Engine." 2007.

[Earl Hammon 07] Earl Hammon Jr. "Blur Practical Post-Process Depth of Field." In *GPU Gems 3: Infinity Ward*. Reading, MA: Addison Wesley, 2007.

[Furturemark 11] Furturemark. "3DMark11 Whitepaper." 2011.

[Kosloff and Barsky 07] Todd Jerome Kosloff and Brian A. Barsky. "An Algorithm for Rendering Generalized Depth of Field Effects Based on Simulated Heat Diffusion." Technical report, University of California, Berkeley, 2007.

[Krivanek et al. 03] Jaroslav Krivanek, Jiri Zara, and Kadi Bouatouch. "Fast Depth of Field Rendering with Surface Splatting." *Proceedings of Computer Graphics International*. 2003.

[Lee et al. 09] Sungkil Lee, Elmar Eisemann, and Hans-Peter Seidel. "Depth-of-Field Rendering with Multiview Synthesis." *SIGGRAPH Asia '09*, pp. 134:1–134:6, 2009.

[Licea-Kane et al. 11] Bill Licea-Kane, Barthold Lichtenbelt, Chris Dodd, Eric Werness, Graham Sellers, Greg Roth, Jeff Bolz, Nick Haemel, Pat Brown, Pierre Boudier, and Piers Daniell. "ARB_shader_atomic_counters." OpenGL extension, 2011.

[Mittring and Dudash 11] Martin Mittring and Bryan Dudash. "The Technology Behind the DirectX 11 Unreal Engine "Samaritan" Demo." GDC. Epics Games, 2011.

[Pettineo 11] Matt Pettineo. "How to Fake Bokeh." Ready At Dawn Studios, 2011.

[Pharr and Humphreys 10] Matt Pharr and Greg Humphreys. *Physically Based Rendering, Second Edition: From Theory To Implementation*, Second edition. San Francisco, CA: Morgan Kaufmann Publishers Inc., 2010.

---

[7] Quads are rasterized into different viewports according to their size: full resolution, half resolution, quarter resolution, etc. The bigger a quad is, less the viewport resolution is.

[Sousa 11] Tiago Sousa. "Crysis 2 DX11 Ultra Upgrade." Crytek, 2011.

[White and Brisebois 11] John White and Colin Barre Brisebois. "More Performance Five
    Rendering Ideas from Battlefield 3 and Need for Speed: The Run." Siggraph talk. Black
    Box and Dice, 2011.

Shadow Proxies 16

Jochem van der Spek

16.1 Introduction

For real-time rendering of the virtual painting machines that I regularly show in exhibitions (see Figure 16.1), I needed a shadowing technique capable of rendering soft shadows without any rendering artifacts such as banding or edge jitter no matter how close the the camera came to the penumbra. I call such shadows *infinitely soft*. In addition, I wanted a method to render color bleeding so that the color and shadow of one object could reflect onto others (see Figure 16.2). Searching through the existing

Figure 16.1. Stills from a virtual painting machine.

Figure 16.2. Still from the demo movie.

real-time soft shadow techniques [Hasenfratz et al. 03], I found that most were either too complex to implement in the relatively short time available, or they were simply not accurate enough, especially when it came to getting the camera infinitely close to the penumbra. Most techniques for rendering the color bleeding required setting up some form of real-time radiosity rendering that would be prohibitively complex and expensive in terms of computing power.

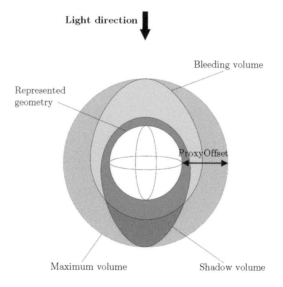

Figure 16.3. The volume regions of a shadow proxy.

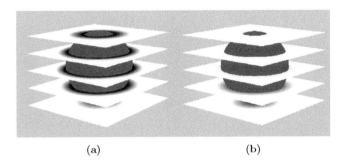

(a)   (b)

Figure 16.4. The shadow volume of a proxy. (a) The volume without modulation. (b) The volume multiplied by the dot product of the surface normal and light direction.

The solution came in the form of a reversed argument: if we cannot globally model the way the light influences the objects, why not locally model the way the objects influence the light? Given that in a diffusely lit environment, shadows and reflections have limited spatial influence, some sort of *halo* around the model could function as a *light subtraction* volume (see Figures 16.3 and 16.4). In order to model directional lighting, the shadow volume could be expanded in the direction away from the light source and contracted to zero in the opposite direction. The color-bleeding volume could be expanded toward the light in the same manner. We call these volumes *shadow proxies*,[1] because they serve as a stand-in for the actual geometry. The volume of a proxy covers the maximum spatial extent of the shadow and color bleeding of the geometry that the proxy represents. The technique is therefore limited to finite shadow volumes and is most useful for diffusely lit environments. This is similar to the Ambient Occlusion Fields technique by [Kontkanen and Laine 05], although with ShadowProxies, modeling and modulating the shadow volumes is done on the fly rather than precalculating the light accessibility of the geometry into a cubemap.

16.2   Anatomy of a Shadow Proxy

In the current implementation, each shadow proxy can only represent a simple geometrical shape like a sphere, box, or cylinder, allowing quick proximity calculations in the fragment shader that eventually renders the shadows.

An implementation that uses *super-ellipsoids* [Barr 81] has also been attempted. Even though the surface lookup is fast enough to be used in real time, the method

---

[1] The ShadowProxies technique is implemented in the OpenGL-based cross-platform scenegraph library called RenderTools, available under the GNU Public License (GPL) which ensures open source distribution. RenderTools is available on Sourceforge at http://sourceforge.net/projects/rendertools and through the OpenGL Insights website, www.openglinsights.com

```
vec3 closestPoint(int shape, mat4 proxy, vec3 fragment)
{
  vec3 local = (inverse(proxy) * fragment).xyz;
  vec3 localSgn = sign(local);
  vec3 localAbs = abs(local);

  if (shape == SPHERE)
  {
    localAbs = normalize(localAbs);
  }
  else if (shape == BOX)
  {
    localAbs = min(localAbs, 1.0);
  }
  else if(shape == CYLINDER)
  {
    if (length(localAbs.xy) > 1.0 )
    {
      localAbs.xy = normalize(localAbs.xy);
    }
    localAbs.z = min(localAbs.z, 1.0);
  }
  return(proxy * (localSgn * localAbs));
}
```

Listing 16.1. The nearest point on the surface of a shadow proxy from the worldposition of a fragment.

presents problems with the requirement of perfectly smooth penumbra. This is because the search for the boundary of an implicit surface typically results in an approximation and zooming in onto the penumbra area or a zooming in onto the error of the approximation, which quickly becomes visible in the form banding. An adaptive algorithm where accuracy is dependent on camera proximity has not been attempted. Furthermore, a version has been implemented where the sharp edges of the shapes are replaced by arcs. A parameter allows the dynamic modification of the radius of the arc, making possible quite a host of different shapes. In practice, this method has turned out to be ineffective for the relative high computational cost.

Surprisingly, the extremely simple, almost trivial surface-determination algorithm now implemented outperforms both previous approaches in terms of efficiency, simplicity, and quality (see Listing 16.1).

Aside from shape information, position, orientation and size, each shadow proxy holds information about the material it represents such as the diffuse and reflective colors of the geometry. Instead of specifying the exact extent of each proxy volume, a fixed offset distance is added to the size of the geometry as the maximum extent of the volume that the proxy represents. This single-valued **ProxyOffset** parameter is represented in the shader as a uniform float. Other global parameters include the falloff of the shadows as the exponent to the attenuation function, a cutoff value to allow for an offset between the surface and the start of the shadow falloff, the amount of shadow contribution, the amount of color bleeding, etc. The complete list can be found in the ShadowProxyTest example in the RenderTools library.

16.3   Setting Up the Pipeline

The flow of information from the scene to the screen is as follows:

1. Collect the objects that cast shadows or reflect their color, and collect their shadow proxy objects.

2. Clip the proxies against the viewing clip planes.

3. Pass the information about the shadow proxies, such as size, color, position, etc., that are in view to the uniforms in the `ShadowProxy`-enabled fragment shader.

4. Render the geometry that receives shadows using the `ShadowProxy`-enabled shader.

Because a scene could have hundreds of different shadow proxies inside the view frustum, the last step in the process is a bottleneck, as each fragment needs to be tested against each shadow proxy. In order to reduce the number of pairwise comparisons, a spatial subdivision scheme is needed so that each fragment is only tested against proxies that were nearby. This is done by subdividing the viewport into an orthogonal grid and then testing the overlap of the bounding box of each shadow proxy projected onto the near plane of the frustum with each cell in the grid (see Figure 16.5). This overlap calculation is quite straightforward: the corners of the non–axis-aligned bounding box of each proxy are projected onto the near plane of the frustum, and then the minima and maxima are calculated in terms of grid-indices. The index of that proxy is then added to the rectangle of cells within those minima and maxima. The proxy index is simply the index of the proxy in the list of proxies that are in view. Each grid's cell should be able to hold several shadow proxies, but not very many. In fact, in my experience, situations with more than three proxies overlapping the same cell are rare.

The information of each grid's cell is encoded in a texture called the IndexMap, using a fixed number of pixels to store the indices of the shadow proxies. For portability, we chose to use the `GLubyte` data type, limiting the number of unique proxy indices to 255, as each color component of a texel holds one single proxy index. This limitation can be overcome by using less portable floating point textures or by using more than one component for an index. Thus, in order to encode a grid of 64×64 cells with each cell capable of holding 16 indices, an RGBA texture of 128×128 pixels suffices. The information for each proxy neatly fits into a 4×4 floating-point matrix by using one float for the type, three for size, four for position and orientation, and one float each for the colors, packing the RGBA values into a single float. I wrote a simple packing function for this, only to find out later that GLSL 4.0 introduces some handy pack/unpack functions. Using this encoding scheme, the proxies can be sent to the shader as an array of uniform mat4. The array is ordered as indexed by

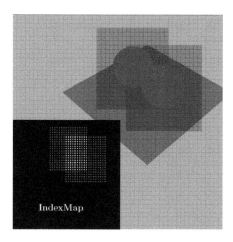

Figure 16.5. Index storage: a red pixel in the IndexMap means that the first index of that cell is set with the index of a proxy ranging from 0–255, yellow means the first two indices are set.

the clipping algorithm so that each index in the `IndexMap` corresponds directly to the index in the array.

16.4   The ShadowProxy-Enabled Fragment Shader

The algorithm (see Listing 16.2) for determining whether a fragment needs shadowing or additional coloring because of color bleeding is summarized as follows:

1. Calculate the index of the grid's cell that contains the current fragment.

2. Fetch the indices of the proxies that that grid's cell overlaps.

3. For each shadow proxy index, retrieve the corresponding mat4 uniform that contains all the positional, type, and color data, and construct a 4 × 4 transformation matrix for that proxy.

4. Using the proxies' transformation matrices, test if the fragment overlaps any of the proxies' influence volume.

First, we obtain a list of shadow proxies that are potentially influencing the color of the fragment. For each proxy in that list, we test if the fragment is contained within its influence volume. This containment test is performed by comparing the distance from the fragment to the closest point on the surface of the shadow proxy.

```
// Find the cell index for this fragment
vec2 index = floor((gl_FragCoord.xy / viewport) * proxyGridSize);
// Find out the uv- coordinate of the center of the pixel
vec2 uv = index * vec2(cellSizeX, cellSizeY) + vec2(0.5, 0.5);

// Loop over each pixel of the cell that this fragment is in
for (int j = 0; j < cellSizeX; j++)
{
  for(int i = 0; i < cellSizeY; i++)
  {
    // Get 4 proxy indices from this pixel (scaled to 255)
    vec4 proxies = texture2D(IndexMap, ((uv + vec2(i, j)) / IndexMapSize2));
    for(int k = 0; k < 4; k++)
    {
      // If this index == 0, the algorithm ends
      if (proxies[ k ] == 0.0)
      {
        return returnStruct;
      }
      // Retrieve the index of the proxy from the texel
      int currentIndex = int(proxies[k] * 255.0) - 1;
      if (currentIndex == (proxyIndex - 1))
      {
        // Ignore self -shadows
        continue;
      }
      // We have a valid index , so find the associated parameters
      mat4 params = proxyParams[currentIndex];

      //... calculate and accumulate shadow and bleed values
    }
  }
}
```

Listing 16.2. GLSL code to retrieve the proxy index and data.

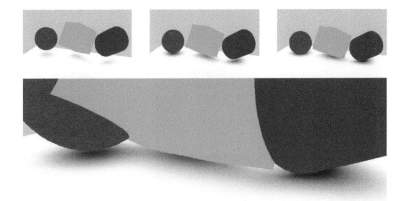

Figure 16.6. Shadow of the different shapes. Notice how the shadow is sharper where the distance to the geometrical surface is smaller.

If the distance is smaller than the `ProxyOffset` parameter, the fragment is deemed inside the volume. To calculate this closest point, we recognize that all three shapes under consideration are symmetrical in the three planes *xy*, *xz*, and *yz*. This allows us to take the absolute value of the local fragment coordinate relative to the shadow proxy's reference frame and clamp that vector to the positive boundaries for each axis so that we consider just the positive quadrant of the shape. Finally we obtain the true point on the surface by multiplying the result with the original sign of the local fragment coordinate and the shadow proxy's reference frame (see Listing 16.1 and Figure 16.6).

16.5   Modulating the Shadow Volume

When we want to model a directional light, the shadow and bleeding volumes need to be modulated to an egg-shaped volume that snugly fits the geometry (see Figure 16.7). This is done by multiplying the dot product of the normal at the proxy surface with the normalized vector from that point toward the light (see Listing 16.3). Exactly the same calculation but with reversed normal gives the volume of the color bleeding in the opposite direction. The direction in which the shadow or color bleeding is cast is taken to be the normalized directional vector from the fragment world coordinate to the closest point on the surface of the maximally extended volume.

Figure 16.7. The combined effect of shadow and color bleeding.

```
// modulate the shadow to an egg-shaped volume around the geometry
shadow *= clamp(dot(lightDirection, surface.normal), shadowCutoffValue, 1.0 );
```

Listing 16.3. Modulating the shadow volume. The surface normal is the normal at the closest point on the proxy surface.

16.6   Performance

Performance is mostly influenced by the `ProxyOffset` parameter that determines the size of the shadow volumes. When the parameter is small compared to the geometry, volume overlaps occur less often and shader performance scales with the number of overlaps. However, due to the limited size of the volumes, scaling is linear, as can be seen in Figure 16.8.

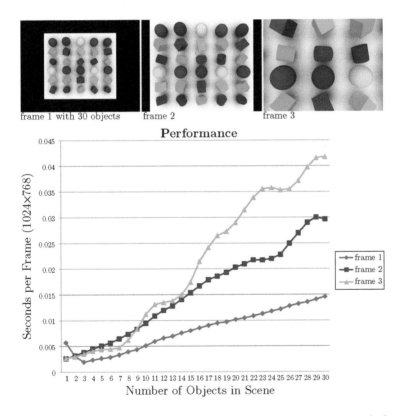

Figure 16.8. Duration of each frame was measured using `glQueryCounter` at the beginning and end of the render calls. The graph shows the performance of rendering a single frame at three distances from the camera with increasing numbers of objects in the scene. The test was run on a MacBook Pro 2.4GHz with an NVIDIA GeForce GT330M.

16.7   Conclusion and Future Work

The ShadowProxies technique was developed for a specific purpose, and the quality of the result is sufficient for the project at hand, but the technique is admittedly limited. However, the technique has proven to be very useful in small games and other projects like the painting machines and can be particularly effective in situations with relatively simple geometrical shapes and scenery. Because the technique is so easy to implement and provides an original rendering style, I believe many games that otherwise cannot afford soft shadows, much less color bleeding, could benefit a great deal by using it.

A simple but useful extension to the algorithm can introduce multiple colored light sources with similarly colored overlapping shadows. This can be achieved by iterating over the available light sources when doing the shadow calculations. Another feature that is almost trivial to add is light emission by the proxy or, a bit less trivial, modeling caustics like those caused by a semitransparent marble. A more sophisticated light transport model can be envisioned where the orientation of the receiving surface and the direction of the incoming shadow or color reflection plays a much greater role than is currently the case. Finally, representation of the geometrical shapes could be extended by implementing some form of constructive solid geometry, or could be replaced altogether by reconstructing the represented geometry from its spherical harmonics representation [Mousa et al. 07].

Bibliography

[Barr 81] A. Barr. "Superquadrics and Angle-Preserving Transformations." *IEEE Computer Graphics and Applications* 1:1 (1981), 11–23. http://vis.cs.brown.edu/results/bibtex/Barr-1981-SAP.bib(bibtex: Barr-1981-SAP).

[Hasenfratz et al. 03] J.-M. Hasenfratz, M. Lapierre, N. Holzschuch, and F.X. Sillion. "A Survey of Real-Time Soft Shadows Algorithms." *Computer Graphics Forum* 22:4 (2003), 753–774.

[Kontkanen and Laine 05] Janne Kontkanen and Samuli Laine. "Ambient Occlusion Fields." In *Proceedings of ACM SIGGRAPH 2005 Symposium on Interactive 3D Graphics and Games*, pp. 41–48. New York: ACM Press, 2005.

[Mousa et al. 07] Mohamed Mousa, Raphalle Chaine, Samir Akkouche, and Eric Galin. "Efficient Spherical Harmonics Representation of 3D Objects." In *15th Pacific Graphics*, pp. 248–257, 2007. Available online (http://liris.cnrs.fr/publis/?id=2972).

Bending the Pipeline

Today GPUs are masters of performance, considering either high-end desktop GPUs or even mobile GPUs, which deliver an unbelievable amount of graphics relative to the power consumption. The future of graphics raises a lot of question regarding how to scale performance, doing more with less. Based on research on petascale and exoscale supercomputers, we notice that such a scale of performance forces us to reconsider memory, bandwidth, and data movement. Challenges are ahead for GPU innovations. Under the name "bending the pipeline," we include all ideas that push the graphics pipeline to explore alternative ways to feed the rendering pipeline.

We start with two classic techniques. The first one, "Real-Time Physically-Based Deformation Using Transform Feedback," presented by Muhammad Mobeen Movania and Lin Feng, explores the OpenGL transform feedback for GPU-based physical simulation. The second technique, "Hierarchical Depth-Culling and Bounding-Box Management on GPU," presented by Dzmitry Malyshau, presents a method based on the depth buffer and bounding boxes to discard invisible objects before the actual rendering even starts.

Maybe shadow mapping is a way to bend the pipeline, but Daniel Rákos certainly pushes it further in his chapter "Massive Number of Shadows with Layered Rendering" with a rendering method allowing him to generate multiple shadow maps per draw call thanks to layered rendering.

In their chapter "Efficient Layered Fragment Buffer Techniques," Pyarelal Knowles, Geoff Leach, and Fabio Zambetta lead us to explore one of the most interesting innovations of OpenGL 4 hardware, image load store, and atomic operations, through an example of order-independent transparency with a special highlight of performance resulting from different approaches.

One step further into innovation, Daniel Rákos introduces "Programmable Vertex Pulling," a radical change of perspective, where we don't submit work to the GPU, but let the GPU query the work. No doubt this approach will evolve and gain a lot of importance in the years to come.

If pushing the boundaries of today's graphics requires a shift in paradigm, bringing new asset representations might be an answer. This is the direction of the work on Gigavoxels of Cyril Crassin and Simon Green. For their *OpenGL Insights* chapter "Octree-Based Sparse Voxelization Using the GPU," they explain how a GPU may be efficiently used to build voxel-based representation.

Real-Time Physically Based Deformation Using Transform Feedback

17

Muhammad Mobeen Movania and Lin Feng

17.1 Introduction

This chapter describes a method for implementing real-time deformation using the transform feedback mechanism of the modern GPU. We will begin with an introduction to the transform feedback mechanism and how it might be exploited to implement a deformation pipeline. Numerous physically based deformation models have been proposed in the literature [Nealen et al. 06]. To demonstrate the power of the proposed acceleration techniques, we implement a basic cloth simulation using the mass spring system (see Figure 17.1).

The vertex shader usually transforms input vertex positions from object space to clip space. This is carried out by multiplying the current object space vertex position with the combined modelview projection matrix. However, modern GPUs allow the vertex shader to circulate its result in a loop to perform iterative tasks on the input again and again. The advantage is that the data remains on the GPU and it is

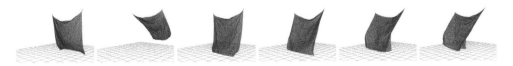

Figure 17.1. Real-time cloth simulation using transform feedback.

not transferred back to the CPU. This feature is called *transform feedback* [Richard et al. 10]. Using this feature, the output values from a vertex or geometry shader can be stored back into a buffer object. These buffer objects are called *transform feedback buffers*. The recorded data may be read back on the CPU using `glMapBuffer`, for instance, or it may be visualized directly as we see in a later section.

Our quest for real-time physically based deformation will commence with a look at the hardware support and evolution of the transform feedback. Following this, an introduction to the transform feedback mechanism will be given. Next, we describe the mathematical background needed to comprehend the mass spring system in general. The specifics related to the cloth simulation using the mass spring system will be presented after. Then, we look into how we map the cloth simulation to the transform feedback mechanism. Results and performance assessment will be given. Finally, we conclude with a look at the possible extensions to this approach.

17.2   Hardware Support and Evolution of Transform Feedback

The transform feedback mechanism was first proposed by NVIDIA as a vendor-specific extension, `GL_NV_transform_feedback`, in OpenGL 3.0. This extension introduced the general transform feedback mechanism. It was promoted to `GL_EXT_transform_feedback` and was finally included in OpenGL 3.0 specifications. This work was later extended by NVIDIA in the form of `GL_NV_transform_feedback2`, which gave way to four extensions in OpenGL 4.0, `GL_ARB_transform_feedback2`, `GL_ARB_transform_feedback3`, `GL_ARB_draw_indirect` (partially), and `GL_ARB_gpu_shader5` (partially).

`GL_ARB_transform_feedback2` defines a transform feedback object similar to other OpenGL objects. In addition, it includes two new features: first, it enables the capability of pausing and resuming transform feedback so that multiple transform feedback objects can record their attributes one after the other; second, it provides `glDrawTransformFeedback` to directly render the transform feedback object without querying the total primitives written. `GL_ARB_transform_feedback3` defines two features: first, it allows writing interleaved varyings in several buffers, and second, it allows attaching multiple vertex streams to transform feedback.

`GL_ARB_draw_indirect` provides new draw calls `glDrawArraysIndirect` and `glDrawElementsIndirect`. It also provides a new buffer binding point `GL_DRAW_INDIRECT_BUFFER`. The behavior of these is similar to `glDraw[Arrays/Elements]InstancedBasedVertex` except that the parameters are read from a buffer bound to `GL_DRAW_INDIRECT_BUFFER` binding. This buffer can be generated by transform feedback or using any other API like OpenCL or CUDA.

While all of these promising features were exposed, one key feature of the OpenGL 3.2 core `GL_ARB_draw_instanced` was ignored; thus, it was not possible to draw instances from a transform feedback buffer without querying the output primitive count. In OpenGL 4.2, this was fixed by GL_ARB_transform_feedback _instanced, which provided two functions, glDrawTransformFeedback Instanced and glDrawTransformFeedbackStreamInstanced.

The transform feedback mechanism is available on a wide range of hardware from both NVIDIA and ATI/AMD. The OpenGL 3.x transform feedback and OpenGL 4.x transform feedback has been supported on the Radeon 2000 series by ATI/AMD via ARB_transform_feedback2 and ARB_transform_feedback3. On NVIDIA hardware, OpenGL 3.x transform feedback is supported by the GeForce 8 series, whereas OpenGL 4.x ARB_transform_feedback2 is supported by the GeForce GTX 200 series, and OpenGL 4.x ARB_transform_feedback3 is supported by the GeForce 400 series.

17.3   The Mechanism of Transform Feedback

In OpenGL 4.0 and above, we can create a transform feedback object by calling glGenTransformFeedbacks. This object encapsulates the transform feedback state. Once we have used the object, we must delete it by calling glDelete TransformFeedbacks.

After the creation of the transform feedback object, the object should be bound to the current OpenGL context. This is done by issuing a call to glBindTransform Feedback. We must also register the vertex attributes that we need to record using transform feedback. This is done by issuing a call to glTransformFeedback Varyings. The first parameter is the name of the program object that will output the attributes. The second parameter is the number of output attributes that will be recorded using transform feedback. The third parameter is the array of C-style strings containing the names of the output attributes. The last parameter identifies the mode of recording. This mode can be either GL_INTERLEAVED_ATTRIBS if the attributes are recorded into a single buffer or GL_SEPARATE_ATTRIBS if the attributes are recorded into separate buffers. After specifying the transform feedback varyings, we need to link our program again.

Now that our output attributes have been linked to the transform feedback, we must also identify the buffer object where the attributes will be written to. This is done by issuing a call to glBindBufferBase. We must identify the index and the buffer object we need to bind to that index. We can bind as many buffer objects as we need depending on how many attributes we are outputting from our vertex or geometry shader. After this, we may issue a call to glBeginTransformFeedback. The only parameter is the type of primitive we are interested in. Next, we issue a call to glDraw* to draw the primitive we want. Finally, we terminate the transform feedback by issuing a call to glEndTransformFeedback.

In OpenGL 4.0, if we want to draw the transform feedback buffer directly, we can call glDrawTransformFeedback and pass it the type of primitive we want. This

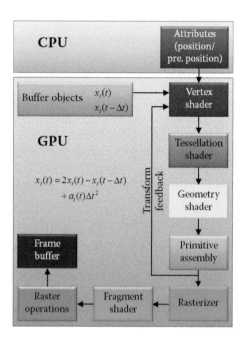

Figure 17.2. Real-time physically based deformation pipeline using transform feedback.

is very convenient since we no longer need to query the number of primitives output from transform feedback as was needed in the previous OpenGL versions. There are some more new features introduced in OpenGL 4.0 and above like pausing and resuming transform feedback, but we are limiting our discussion to the functionality used in this chapter. For interested readers, more information can be obtained from the references given at the end of this chapter.

The transform feedback mechanism can be exploited to implement a real-time deformation pipeline entirely on the GPU. Our real-time deformation pipeline highlighting the transform feedback stage is given in Figure 17.2. We will start by discussing the mathematical underpinnings required to understand the later sections.

17.4   Mathematical Model

There are numerous methods for cloth modeling. These range from more accurate continuum mechanics models, for example, the finite element (FEM), to less-accurate particle models like the mass spring model. A *mass spring system* is based on

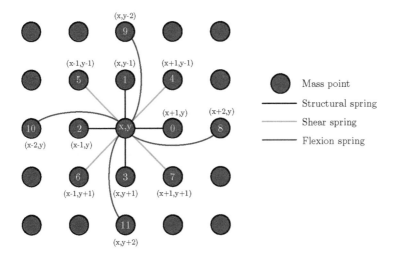

Figure 17.3. Different spring types used in a mass spring system.

a collection of virtual masses that are linked to their neighbors using massless springs (see Figure 17.3) [Yan Chen 98]. These springs include

1. structural springs that link the node to its immediate neighbor in x-, y-, and z-axis only,

2. shear springs that connect the remaining neighbors, including all of the diagonal links, and

3. flexion springs that are structural springs connected to the nodes one node away.

Each of these springs is constrained by a different force, i.e., under pure stress, shear springs are constrained, under pure compression/traction stress, or stretching, only structural springs are constrained, and under pure flexion stresses, or bending, only flexion springs are constrained. All of the connections act as linear springs which bring the mesh towards equilibrium. Each mass point is associated with a set of physical properties, including mass (m), position (x), velocity (v), and acceleration (a). At any point in time, the system is governed by the following second-order ordinary differential equation:

$$m\ddot{\mathbf{x}} = -c\dot{\mathbf{x}} + \sum(\mathbf{f}_{int} + \mathbf{f}_{ext}), \qquad (17.1)$$

where c is the damping coefficient, $\mathbf{f}_{int}$ is the internal (spring) force, and $\mathbf{f}_{ext}$ is the external force, which may be due to the user's intervention, wind, or a gravity or collision force due to collision of the object with other objects. The spring force $\mathbf{f}_{int}$ may be defined as

$$\mathbf{f}_{int}(t) = k_i(\|\mathbf{x}_i(t) - \mathbf{x}_j(t)\| - l_i)\frac{\mathbf{x}_i(t) - \mathbf{x}_j(t)}{\|\mathbf{x}_i(t) - \mathbf{x}_j(t)\|}, \qquad (17.2)$$

where k_i is the spring's stiffness, l_i is the resting length of the spring, x_i is the spring's position and x_j is the position of its neighbor.

The system in Equation (17.1) may be solved using any of the numerical integration schemes. We may either use the explicit integration schemes [Yan Chen 98, Georgii and Westermann 05] or the implicit integration schemes [Baraff and Witkin 98]. Some examples of the explicit integration schemes include Euler integration, the midpoint method (second-order Runge Kutta), Verlet integration, and fourth-order Runge Kutta integration. An example of the Implicit integration scheme is implicit Euler integration [Baraff and Witkin 98]. Whatever integration scheme we use, the acceleration (a) may be calculated using the Newton's second law of motion,

$$\mathbf{a}_i(t) = \frac{\mathbf{f}_i(t)}{m_i}.$$

In the case of the explicit integration schemes, the formulation is as follows. For the explicit Euler integration [Yan Chen 98], the velocity (v) and position (x) are updated separately using the following equations:

$$\mathbf{v}_i(t + \Delta t) = \mathbf{v}_i(t) + \Delta t \mathbf{a}_i(t),$$
$$\mathbf{x}_i(t + \Delta t) = \mathbf{x}_i(t) + \Delta t \mathbf{v}_i(t).$$

For the Verlet integration [Georgii and Westermann 05], there is no need to calculate and store velocity (v) since the new position (x) is obtained from the current and the previous position using the following numerical operations:

$$\mathbf{x}_i(t + \Delta t) = 2\mathbf{x}_i(t) - \mathbf{x}_i(t - \Delta t) + \mathbf{a}_i(t)\Delta t^2. \qquad (17.3)$$

For this to work, both the current and the previous positions are needed. In the case of the midpoint Euler method, the new velocity and the new position are given as

$$\mathbf{v}_i(t + \Delta t) = \mathbf{v}_i(t) + \Delta t \mathbf{a}_i(t + \frac{\Delta t}{2}),$$
$$\mathbf{x}_i(t + \Delta t) = \mathbf{x}_i(t) + \Delta t \mathbf{v}_i(t + \frac{\Delta t}{2}). \qquad (17.4)$$

In Equation (17.4), both the acceleration as well as the velocity are evaluated at the midpoint between t and $(t + \Delta t)$, i.e., $(t + \Delta t/2)$.

Finally, for the fourth-order Runge Kutta method, the new velocities are first obtained using the following set of operations:

$$\mathbf{v}_i(t + \Delta t) = \mathbf{v}_i(t) + \frac{1}{6}(\mathbf{F}_1 + 2(\mathbf{F}_2 + \mathbf{F}_3) + \mathbf{F}_4),$$

$$\mathbf{F}_1 = \frac{\Delta t}{2}\mathbf{a}_i(t),$$

$$\mathbf{F}_2 = \frac{\Delta t}{2}\frac{\mathbf{F}_1}{m_i},$$

$$\mathbf{F}_3 = \Delta t\frac{\mathbf{F}_2}{m_i},$$

$$\mathbf{F}_4 = \Delta t\frac{\mathbf{F}_3}{m_i}.$$

The new positions are then obtained by the following set of operations:

$$\mathbf{x}_i(t + \Delta t) = \mathbf{x}_i(t) + \frac{1}{6}(\mathbf{k}_1 + 2(\mathbf{k}_2 + \mathbf{k}_3) + \mathbf{k}_4),$$

$$\mathbf{k}_1 = \frac{\Delta t}{2}\mathbf{a}_i(t),$$

$$\mathbf{k}_2 = \frac{\Delta t}{2}\mathbf{k}_1,$$

$$\mathbf{k}_3 = \Delta t\mathbf{k}_2,$$

$$\mathbf{k}_4 = \Delta t\mathbf{k}_3.$$

All of the explicit integration schemes suffer from stability problems and require the time-step value to be very small. This is because the velocity and position evaluation is carried out explicitly without taking notice of the wildly changing derivatives. On the contrary, the implicit integration schemes are unconditionally stable because the system is solved as a couple unit. It starts backward in time to find a new position that has a given output state. The implicit Euler integration is given as [Baraff and Witkin 98],

$$\Delta\mathbf{x} = \Delta t(\mathbf{v}_0 + \Delta\mathbf{v}),$$

$$\Delta\mathbf{v} = \Delta t(\mathbf{M}^{-1}\mathbf{F}),$$

$$\mathbf{F} = \mathbf{f}_0 + \frac{\partial\mathbf{f}}{\partial x}\Delta\mathbf{x} + \frac{\partial\mathbf{f}}{\partial v}\Delta\mathbf{v}.$$

The implicit integration schemes can be solved using any iterative solvers like the Newton Raphson (Newton) method or the conjugate gradient (CG) method [Baraff and Witkin 98]. We can implement both implicit and explicit integration schemes with the proposed pipeline. For this chapter, we restrict our discussion to the Verlet integration scheme. This is because Verlet integration is second-order accurate.

Moreover, it does not require estimation of velocity since it represents velocity implicitly in the formulation using the current and previous position.

The new positions obtained through any of the integration schemes discussed earlier are then applied certain constraints like the positivity constraint to prevent the masses from falling under the ground plane. The positivity constraint is given as

$$\mathbf{x}_i.y = \begin{cases} \mathbf{x}_{i+1}.y & \text{if } \mathbf{x}_{i+1}.y > 0 \\ 0 & \text{else,} \end{cases} \tag{17.5}$$

where $\boldsymbol{x}_i.y$ is the y component of the position x, assuming that the y axis is the world up axis. Likewise, other constraints like collision of the mass with an arbitrary polygon may be implemented very easily in the vertex shader. For instance, we consider a constraint on collision of the masses with a sphere. Assuming we have a sphere having a center $(\mathbf{C})$ and a radius (r), we have a mass at position (x_i), and it is transformed to a new position (x_{i+1}). The collision constraint is given as

$$\mathbf{x}_{i+1} = \begin{cases} \mathbf{C} + \frac{(\mathbf{x}_i - C) \cdot r}{|\mathbf{x}_i - C|} & \text{if } |\mathbf{x}_i - C| < r \\ \mathbf{x}_i & \text{else.} \end{cases}$$

17.5   Implementation

Now that the mathematical foundation is laid out, we can begin looking into the implementation details. To understand how the different steps of the algorithm work, for the rest of this discussion, we discuss the steps needed to implement the Verlet integration as an example. To give a bird's-eye view, we do the integration calculation in the vertex shader. Then, using transform feedback, we direct the new and previous positions to a set of buffer objects held as the binding point of a set of vertex array objects. Exactly how all this is carried out is detailed in the next sections.

17.5.1   The Verlet Integration Vertex Shader

The most important piece in our implementation is the Verlet integration vertex shader. We will dissect the whole vertex shader to understand how it works. We first store the current and previous positions of the cloth mass points into a 2D grid. These are stored on the GPU into a pair of buffer objects. In order to efficiently obtain the neighborhood information, we attach the current and the previous position buffer objects to the texture buffer target. This allows us to fetch the neighbor's current and previous positions in the vertex shader using the corresponding `samplerBuffer`.

The vertex shader starts with extracting the current position, the previous position, and the current velocity:

```
void main()
{
  float m = position_mass.w;
  vec3 pos = position_mass.xyz;
  vec3 pos_old = prev_position.xyz;
  vec3 vel = (pos - pos_old) / dt;
  float ks = 0, kd = 0;
  // ...
```

Next, the index of the current vertex is determined using the built-in register (gl_
VertexID). Using this global index, the x, y index into the 2D grid is obtained. This
is used to extract the correct neighbor from the samplerBuffer:

```
int index = gl_VertexID;
int ix = index % texsize_x;
int iy = index / texsize_x;
```

Since we do not want the upper corner vertices to move, we assign them a mass
of 0. Next, the external force is calculated using the acceleration due to gravity and
the damping force due to the current velocity:

```
if(index ==0 || index == (texsize_x - 1))
{
  m = 0;
}
vec3 F = (gravity * m) + (DEFAULT_DAMPING * vel);
```

Next, we loop through the 12 neighbors of the current vertex. Each time, we
obtain the neighbor's coordinates using basic arithmetic as shown in Figure 17.3 and
check whether they are within the bounds of the texture. If they are, we determine
the appropriate index of the neighbor node and fetch its current and the previous
position from the samplerBuffer:

```
for(int k=0;k<12;k++)
{
  ivec2 coord = getNextNeighbor(k, ks, kd);
  int j = coord.x;
  int i = coord.y;
  if (((iy + i) < 0) || ((iy + i) > (texsize_y-1)))
  {
    continue;
  }
  if (((ix + j) < 0) || ((ix + j) > (texsize_x-1)))
  {
    continue;
  }
  int index_neigh = (iy + i) * texsize_x + ix + j;
  vec3 p2 = texelFetchBuffer(tex_position_mass, index_neigh).xyz;
  vec3 p2_last = texelFetchBuffer(tex_prev_position_mass, index_neigh).xyz;
  // ...
```

Next, we obtain the rest length of the spring and finally determine the spring force using Equation (17.2):

```
vec2 coord_neigh = vec2(ix + j, iy + i) * step;
float rest_length = length(coord * inv_cloth_size);

vec3 v2 = (p2 - p2_last) / dt;
vec3 deltaP = pos - p2;
vec3 deltaV = vel - v2;
float dist = length(deltaP);

float leftTerm = -ks * (dist - rest_length);
float rightTerm = kd * (dot(deltaV, deltaP) / dist);
vec3 springForce = (leftTerm + rightTerm) * normalize(deltaP);
F += springForce;
}
```

Once the total force is calculated, the acceleration is obtained. For mass points with 0 mass, the acceleration is set as 0, which prevents the mass from moving:

```
vec3 acc = vec3(0);
if (m != 0)
{
  acc = F / m;
}
```

Finally, the current position is obtained using Equation (17.3). In addition, the positivity constraint is also applied using Equation (17.5) to prevent the mass from falling under the floor, and then the output attributes are written:

```
vec3 tmp = pos;
pos = pos * 2.0 - pos_old + acc* dt * dt;
pos_old = tmp;
pos.y = max(0, pos.y);
out_position_mass = vec4(pos, m);
gl_Position = vec4(pos_old, m);
}
```

17.5.2   Registering Attributes to Transform Feedback

For the following, refer to Listing 17.1. First, we generate the transform feedback object using **glGenTransformFeedbacks** and then bind it to the current context using **glBindTransformFeedback**. Our Verlet integration vertex shader outputs two attributes, the current position, which gets written out to **out_position_mass**, and the previous position, which gets written to **gl_Position**. We must register our attributes to the transform feedback object. This is done by issuing a call to **glTransformFeedbackVaryings** and passing it the names of our attributes **out_position_mass** and **gl_Position**. After this call, we must relink our vertex shader.

```
// Setup transform feedback attributes
glGenTransformFeedbacks(1, &tfID);
glBindTransformFeedback(GL_TRANSFORM_FEEDBACK, tfID);
const char *varying_names[] = {"out_position_mass", "gl_Position"};
glTransformFeedbackVaryings(massSpringShader.GetProgram(), 2, varying_names, ←
    GL_SEPARATE_ATTRIBS);
glLinkProgram(massSpringShader.GetProgram());
```

Listing 17.1. Registering attributes with transform feedback object.

17.5.3 The Array Buffer and Buffer Object Setup

So far, we have only looked at half of the story. The other half is the actual buffer objects and array object setup. The application pushes a set of positions (current and previous positions) to the GPU. Each element is a vec4 with x, y, z in the first three components and mass in the fourth component. The reason we use a set of buffer objects for positions is so that we may use the ping-pong strategy to read from a set of positions while we write to another set using the transform feedback approach. We do this because we cannot write to a transform feedback attribute when we are reading from it. We have two array objects for updating the physics and two more array objects for rendering of the resulting positions. Referring to

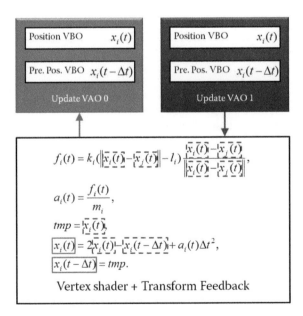

Figure 17.4. The array object and buffer object setup for transform feedback: the blue rectangles show the attributes written to an array object; the red rectangles show the attributes being read simultaneously from another array object.

```
// Set update vao
for (int i = 0; i < 2; i++)
{
  glBindVertexArray(vaoUpdateID[i]);
  glBindBuffer(GL_ARRAY_BUFFER, vboID_Pos[i]);
  glBufferData(GL_ARRAY_BUFFER, X.size() * sizeof(glm::vec4), &(X[0].x), ←
      GL_DYNAMIC_COPY);
  glEnableVertexAttribArray(0);
  glVertexAttribPointer(0,  4, GL_FLOAT, GL_FALSE, 0, 0);

  glBindBuffer(GL_ARRAY_BUFFER, vboID_PrePos[i]);
  glBufferData(GL_ARRAY_BUFFER, X_last.size() * sizeof(glm::vec4), &(X_last[0].x), ←
      GL_DYNAMIC_COPY);
  glEnableVertexAttribArray(1);
  glVertexAttribPointer(1,  4, GL_FLOAT, GL_FALSE, 0,0);
}

// Set render vao
for(int i = 0; i < 2; i++)
{
  glBindVertexArray(vaoRenderID[i]);
  glBindBuffer(GL_ARRAY_BUFFER, vboID_Pos[i]);
  glEnableVertexAttribArray(0);
  glVertexAttribPointer(0,  4, GL_FLOAT, GL_FALSE, 0, 0);

  glBindBuffer(GL_ELEMENT_ARRAY_BUFFER, vboIndices);
  if(i==0)
  {
    glBufferData(GL_ELEMENT_ARRAY_BUFFER, indices.size() * sizeof(GLushort), &←
        indices[0], GL_STATIC_DRAW);
  }
}
```

Listing 17.2. The array object/buffer object setup code.

Figure 17.4 for the following, each array object stores a set of buffer objects for current and previous positions. The usage flags for the position buffer objects are set as dynamic (GL_DYNAMIC_COPY in OpenGL) since the data will be dynamically modified using the shaders. This gives an additional hint to the GPU so that it may put the buffers in the fastest accessible memory. The setup code is given in Listing 17.2.

Referring to Figure 17.5, for each rendering cycle, we swap between the two buffers to alternate the read/write pathways. Before the transform feedback can proceed, we need to bind the update array object to the current render device so that the appropriate buffer objects can be set up for recording data. We bind the appropriate buffer object for reading the current and previous positions to the current transform feedback buffer base by issuing a call to **glBindBufferBase**. The rasterizer is disabled to prevent the execution of the rest of the programmable pipeline. The draw-point call is issued to allow us to write vertices to the buffer object. The transform feedback is then disabled. Following the transform feedback, the rasterizer is enabled, and then the points are drawn. This time, the render array object is bound. This renders the deformed points on screen.

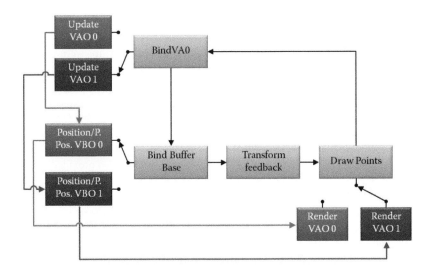

Figure 17.5. The transform feedback data flow for the update and render cycle.

17.5.4   On-the-Fly Modification of Data

Often, it is required to modify the data in the buffer object dynamically, for example, in the case of collision detection and response. In such a case, we need to obtain the pointer to data. We can do so in the current deformation pipeline by first binding the appropriate array object. Next, the appropriate buffer object is bound to the array object. Finally, the glMapBuffer call is made to obtain the data pointer. In the demo application, we execute the function calls listed in Listing 17.3 to modify the position based on the point picked by the user.

```
glBindVertexArray(vaoRenderID[readID]);
glBindBuffer(GL_ARRAY_BUFFER, vboID_Pos[writeID]);
GLfloat* pData = (GLfloat *)glMapBuffer(GL_ARRAY_BUFFER, GL_READ_WRITE);
pData[selected_index * 4] += Right[0] * valX;
float newValue = pData[selected_index * 4 + 1] + Up[1] * valY;
if (newValue > 0)
{
  pData[selected_index * 4 + 1] = newValue;
}
pData[selected_index * 4 + 2] += Right[2] * valX + Up[2] * valY;
glUnmapBuffer(GL_ARRAY_BUFFER);
glBindBuffer(GL_ARRAY_BUFFER, 0);
```

Listing 17.3. The code for dynamically modifying the data stored in the buffer object.

17.6   Experimental Results and Comparisons

We have looked at how the whole deformation pipeline is set up; we now look at some results from the demo application accompanying this chapter (see Figure 17.6). The full source code is on the OpenGL Insights website, www.openglinsights.com. This application implements a cloth simulation using the Verlet integration. In addition, it provides three modes that can be toggled using the space bar key. The first mode is the GPU mode using the transform feedback mechanism. The second mode is the unoptimized CPU mode, which implements the exact same cloth simulation; however, it uses CPU for deformation. An additional mode is also provided that uses the OpenMP-based optimized deformation on the CPU.

For performance analysis, we compare the performance of the cloth simulation with different cloth resolutions ranging from 64×64 mass points to 1024×1024 mass points on our test machine, a Dell Precision T7500 desktop with an Intel Xeon E5507 with a 2.27Mhz CPU. The machine is equipped with an NVIDIA Quadro FX 5800 graphics card. The operating system is Windows 7 64-bit. The performances were compared against the three modes, namely, the unoptimized CPU mode (column "Unoptimized CPU (a)" in Table 17.1), the optimized CPU mode (column "Optimized CPU (b)" in Table 17.1), and the GPU mode using transform feedback (column "GPU TF (c)" in Table 17.1).

As can be seen, the GPU mode clearly outperforms both of the CPU modes. The CPU code proceeds sequentially both for calculating the forces and for integration. It then transfers the updated positions to the GPU for rendering. On the contrary, the transform feedback–based code fetches the neighbor node positions efficiently and performs the calculation of forces and integration in parallel. In addition, the data are used directly for rendering without GPU transfer as was required for the CPU mode.

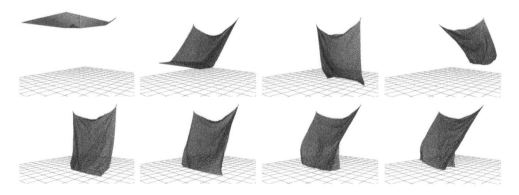

Figure 17.6. Several animation frames from the cloth simulation implemented using the transform feedback mechanism.

Grid Size	Frame Rate (in frames per second).		
	Unoptimized CPU (a)	Optimized CPU (b)	GPU TF (c)
64 × 64	224.12	503.40	941.71
128 × 128	64.11	177.81	650.35
256 × 256	18.13	57.84	220.75
512 × 512	4.11	14.02	45.49
1024 × 1024	0.98	2.74	34.55

Table 17.1. Performance comparison between unoptimized CPU code, optimized CPU code and GPU code using transform feedback.

This gives massive speedup as is evident in the statistics given in Table 17.1. Thanks to the efficiency of the transform feedback mechanism, real-time deformations can now be carried out entirely on the GPU.

17.7 Conclusion

We have presented a novel GPU pipeline for implementing real-time deformation. Our approach is based on the mechanism of transform feedback available in the new-generation GPUs. The data is pushed once to the GPU, and then, using the ping-pong approach with multiple vertex buffer objects, the read/write pathways are modified. As a proof-of-concept, we have implemented a basic cloth simulation; however, the ideas presented in this chapter can be extended quite easily to accommodate other physically based animation areas like particle systems, modeling of fire, water waves, realistic lighting, etc. We are in the process of expanding the algorithm to address specific applications such as biomedical modeling and simulation [Lin et al. 96, Lin et al. 07].

Bibliography

[Baraff and Witkin 98] David Baraff and Andrew Witkin. "Large Steps in Cloth Simulation." In *Proceedings of the 25th Annual Conference on Computer Graphics and Interactive Techniques, SIGGRAPH '98*, pp. 43–54. New York: ACM, 1998.

[Georgii and Westermann 05] Joachim Georgii and Rudiger Westermann. "Mass-Spring Systems on the GPU." *Simulation Practice and Theory* 13:8 (2005), 693–702.

[Lin et al. 96] Feng Lin, Hock Soon Seah, and Tsui Lee Yong. "Deformable Volumetric Model and Isosurface: Exploring a New Approach for Surface Construction." *Computers and Graphics* 20:1 (1996), 33–40.

[Lin et al. 07] Feng Lin, Hock Soon Seah, Zhongke Wu, and Di Ma. "Voxelisation and Fabrication of Freeform Models." *Virtual and Physical Prototyping* 2:2 (2007), 65–73.

[Nealen et al. 06] Andrew Nealen, Matthias Mueller, Richard Keiser, Eddy Boxerman, and Mark Carlson. "Physically Based Deformable Models in Computer Graphic." *STAR Report Eurographics 2005* 25:4 (2006), 809–836.

[Richard et al. 10] S. Wright Jr. Richard, Haemel Nicholas, Sellers Graham, and Lipchak Benjamin. *OpenGL Superbible, Fifth Edition.* Upper Saddle River, NJ: Addison Wesley, 2010.

[Yan Chen 98] Arie Kaufman Yan Chen, Qing-hong Zhu. "Physically-Based Animation of Volumetric Objects." In *Technical Report TR-CVC-980209*, 1998.

Hierarchical Depth Culling and Bounding-Box Management on the GPU

18

Dzmitry Malyshau

18.1 Introduction

Optimizing the data passed to the GPU is one of the keys to achieving high and stable frame rates. The fewer data that go into a GPU, the better the performance. This is what geometry-culling techniques are for: they reduce the number of fragments, polygons, or even whole objects processed by the GPU.

There are several common culling methods today [Fernando 04]:

- Frustum culling. On a high level, the graphics engine determines the objects outside the view frustum and leaves them out of drawing. It generally uses a bounding-volume approximation (e.g., box, sphere, etc.) to compute the intersection with the frustum. On a low level, the OpenGL rasterizer discards polygons and polygon parts outside of the clip space. This process is performed after the vertex processing stage. Thus, some GPU time may be wasted on the shading of vertices, which don't belong to visible triangles.

- Backface culling. GPU-accelerated and exposed by OpenGL, this method discards polygons facing away from the viewer. It may be implemented via one scalar product per face, but it is fully optimized by the hardware.

- Depth buffer. Exposed by OpenGL, this method stores the closest depth value per fragment in order to discard fragments lying beyond that depth. Immediate rendering implementation requires one read-modify-write operation on the GPU per fragment. Efficiency may be improved by preordering opaque objects, polygons, and fragments from the nearest to the farthest at drawing.

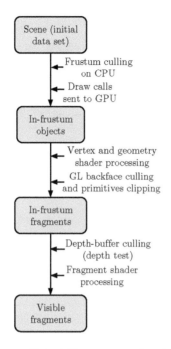

Figure 18.1. Culling stages combined.

Most of the time, a developer will apply all three categories simultaneously (see Figure 18.1).

Moving from stage to stage introduces additional computational cost. Culling unnecessary input as early as possible yields the highest efficiency. This chapter introduces one of the ways to use the depth buffer for culling whole objects while drawing. The method is known as *hierarchical depth culling* (alternatively, *occlusion culling*). It combines different levels of the rendering pipeline for the common goal of discarding invisible primitives. These levels include: framebuffer for the depth buffer, spatial level for bounding volumes, and the rendering sequence for the early depth pass. The chapter presents a core OpenGL 3.0 implementation of the hierarchical depth culling pipeline performed with minimal CPU-GPU synchronization.

18.2   Pipeline

The pipeline (see Figure 18.2) can be expressed in the following short steps:

- Obtain the depth buffer of occluders (may be the whole scene).

- Construct depth mipmaps.

- Update objects' bounding boxes.

- Perform depth culling of the bounding boxes.

- Draw the scene using culling results.

This sequence does not mention DMA memory transfers, such as retaining culling results in the system memory or debugging during the stage of drawing bounding boxes; nor does it specify the exact order of commands, e.g., we may use the depth buffer of the previous frame for culling. In the latter case, the culling results would have a one frame delay and therefore would not be exact.

In the following sections, I will describe each stage in detail. The source GLSL code of a working implementation can be found on the *OpenGL Insights* website, www.openglinsights.com.

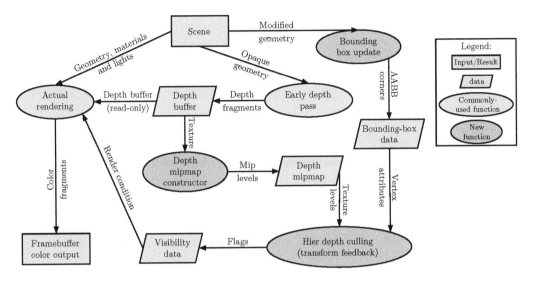

Figure 18.2. Hierarchical depth culling pipeline data flow.

18.2.1 Early Depth Pass

The early depth pass is a special rendering stage that draws an opaque part of a scene into the depth buffer without any color output. The pixel processing cost for this operation is minimal. It guarantees that only visible fragments will be processed by heavy pixel shaders when the actual drawing of a scene is performed, with the depth buffer attached in read-only mode. This pass utilizes the double-speed, depth-only function implemented in the hardware for many cards [Cozzi 09].

The implementation assumes that we have a user-controlled FBO, where the color attachment is supposed to store the rendered frame. The early depth pass is computed this way:

- Make sure the FBO has a texture as the depth attachment. We will need to sample from it later. Thus, the depth-stencil format is not allowed.

- Bind the FBO and set the draw buffer to GL_NONE, meaning that no color layers are affected.

- Enable depth test and write. Clear the depth with "1.0." Set the depth test function to GL_LEQUAL.

- Render opaque objects of the scene. The vertex shader does plain model-view-projection transformation. No fragment shader is attached.

Note that no polygon offset is needed since we assume that the same geometry and transformations in the same order will take place later in the frame. OpenGL invariance rules [Group 10, Appendix A] guarantee that the same polygons will cover the same fragments each time we draw them, as long as we use the same vertex-shader transformation code.

The depth buffer after this stage should not include transparent objects, because they are not occluders. They can still be culled by the hierarchical depth check described below.

18.2.2   Depth LOD Construction

In general, the hierarchical depth culling technique (see Figure 18.3) can operate on mipmaps of a noncomplete depth buffer. For example, one can draw only the biggest occluders into the depth buffer and start with a lower resolution than the original one. However, we prefer to build the whole depth mipmap set because we can use the depth buffer produced by the early depth pass for it. This approach is also better to discard primitives based on the mipmap level containing the bounding box in the pixel neighbors (see Section 18.2.4 for an example).

During the culling process we can only discard an object if its closest parts are occluded by the farthest approximated occluder in the area. Therefore, when producing the depth level of detail (LOD) chain, we are going to get the maximum depth from the pixel neighbors instead of an averaged one. Construction of each level i (ranges from 1 to the max LOD of the depth texture) takes the following steps:

- Set the depth function to GL_ALWAYS, enable depth test, and write.

- Set the GL_TEXTURE_BASE_LEVEL and GL_TEXTURE_MAX_LEVEL of the depth texture to $i - 1$.

- Activate the framebuffer object (FBO) with draw buffer set to GL_NONE. Attach depth texture level i.

- Draw a unit quad (or a large triangle) with a dedicated shader.

The vertex shader copies the position directly into gl_Position, and no transformation is required. The fragment shader (Listing 18.1) fetches the depth from the texture bound as sampler_depth. We are using texelFetch with LOD $= 0$ because the base level of the texture is set to $i - 1$.

Figure 18.3. Depth levels of detail: 0,2,4,6.

```
ivec2 tc = ivec2(gl_FragCoord.xy * 2.0);
vec4 d = vec4(
  texelFetch(sampler_depth, tc, 0).r,
  texelFetch(sampler_depth, tc+ivec2(1,0), 0).r,
  texelFetch(sampler_depth, tc+ivec2(0,1), 0).r,
  texelFetch(sampler_depth, tc+ivec2(1,1), 0).r);
gl_FragDepth = max( max(d.x,d.y), max(d.z,d.w) );
```

Listing 18.1. Depth buffer downsampling fragment shader.

18.2.3 Bounding-Boxes Update

An axis-aligned bounding box serves as an approximation of an object volume. It can be easily transformed into projection space for hierarchical depth culling. The traditional approach is to keep bounding box information updated on the client side (CPU), involving special tricks to deal with animated objects.

Our approach is to utilize the GPU to iterate over vertices (see Figure 18.4). It naturally supports real-time mesh animation modifiers like skinning and morphing. The stage can be implemented using color blending and geometry shaders. We are going to store the bounding-box corners of each object in two pixels inside a render-buffer. Given a set of objects with outdated bounding boxes A, the algorithm works as follows:

- Make an FBO with a color attachment only, which is a floating-point RGB renderbuffer of size $2n \times 1$, where n is the number of objects in the scene.

- Set the blending mode to **GL_MAX** and the blend weighting factors to **GL_ONE**, **GL_ONE**.

- For each object in A: Set the scissor test and the viewport to include only 2 pixels designated for the object. Clear the color buffer with $+\infty$ (floating point).

- For each object in A, draw the object using a dedicated shader program.

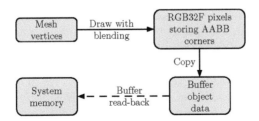

Figure 18.4. GPU-assisted AABB calculation data flow.

```
in   vec3   position [];
out   vec4   color;
void main ()   {
  gl_Position = vec4 (-0.5 ,0.0 ,0.0 ,1.0);
  color = vec4 (+position [0] ,1.0);
  EmitVertex ();
  gl_Position = vec4 (+0.5 ,0.0 ,0.0 ,1.0);
  color = vec4 (-position [0] ,1.0);
  EmitVertex ();
}
```

Listing 18.2. Bounding-box update geometry shader.

- Read back the bounding box texture in a buffer attached to the GL_PIXEL _PACK_BUFFER target.

The vertex shader just passes the local vertex position to the geometry stage. This position is set as a color of the first pixel by the geometry shader, while the negated position is written to the second pixel color (see Listing 18.2). We negate the position here in order to reverse the effect of **GL_MAX** blending: $\max(-x) = -\min(x)$.

The result of this step is a buffer containing two floating-point positions per object: the maximum of the local vertex coordinates and negated minimum of these same coordinates. These values define an axis-aligned bounding box of an object in local space.

Note that we cannot use the buffer for an FBO attachment right away as a texture buffer object, because it is forbidden by OpenGL specification (see [Group 10]). Also, the algorithm will behave inefficiently in the case of a small number of objects because the GPU will have a hard time parallelizing the computations going into such a small pixel area. In further research, this issue can be addressed by dividing the vertex stream of each object over several destination pixel pairs with a dedicated function that combines the result from these pairs.

18.2.4   Hierarchical Depth Cull

Now that we have the depth LOD chain and bounding boxes on the GPU, we can finally do the main step, which is culling. We reuse the same shader inputs declared in Section 18.2.5. In addition, we bind the depth buffer to a texture unit accessed by the shader as a uniform variable. It is important to set the border color to 0. This will cull objects outside the frustum side planes.

We are going to use OpenGL transform feedback (TF) in order to get a single visibility flag per scene object in a resulting buffer. Note that it is also possible to draw into a 1D texture for that, but TF was chosen due to its simplicity (no rasterizer/fragment processing/PBO involved). It is also better in terms of concurrency because each output primitive offset is known in advance by the driver.

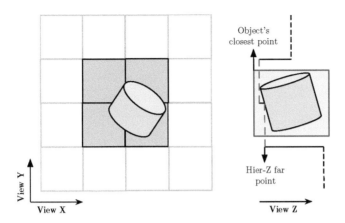

Figure 18.5. Hierarchical depth cull main stage.

Here are the steps to check each object visibility against the depth mipmap set performed in the vertex processing stage (see Figure 18.5):

- Compute the bounding box in the normalized device coordinates (NDC, range in $[0, 1]$) using the camera projection.

- Determine the LOD level of the depth mipmap set containing a tightest 2×2 pixel area covering the whole NDC box.

- Discard the primitive if the LOD level is less than some threshold. For example, setting this threshold to 2 will cull out all objects in the bounding boxes that fit inside a 4×4 pixel area.

- Find the maximum depth of the area by sampling from these pixels.

- Return true if the NDC minimum z-coordinate is less than the maximum sampled depth.

18.2.5 Bounding-Box Debug Draw

Rendering bounding volumes on top of the scene is a convenient way to debug a range of visibility issues. In a previous stage (Section 18.2.3), we gathered all bounding boxes in a scene into the OpenGL buffer object. It is possible, therefore, to draw all boxes at once by supplying correct vertex attributes together with model-to-world transformations (Figure 18.6). Here is the procedure:

- Declare two floating-point, four-component attributes interleaved in the given buffers containing the bounding box information.

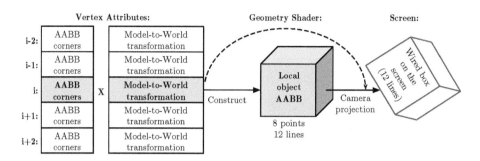

Figure 18.6. Bounding-box drawing pipeline.

- Upload an array of model-to-view transformations per object on the GPU. It can be a buffer object or a range of uniforms.

- Enable depth test. Disable depth write.

- Issue an *n*-points draw call with the special shader program.

The vertex shader is supposed to pass bounding box and transformation data to the geometry stage. The geometry shader generates twelve lines per input in the shape of a box and transforms them into the projection space.

18.3   Order of Operations

I have described all the stages of the culling pipeline. Now, I will talk about the way these bricks follow each other in the frame-processing sequence. The order is important because trying to perform an action that depends on the previous action when the previous action is not complete may stall the graphics pipeline.

There are dependencies among these stages. For example, generating a depth LOD chain requires the depth buffer to be initialized by the early depth pass. Bounding-box drawing and culling requires boxes to be updated first. Main scene rendering is supposed to happen after the culling in order to use the results. Culling is just an optimization task. Therefore, it does not require precise implementation as long as our visible objects do not disappear for a noticeable amount of time.

GPU time may be saved during the processing of our culling tasks by stretching the computations over one or more frames. For example, we have a graphics application running at 60 fps that will make the one-frame visibility delay barely noticeable. The rendering sequence designed to avoid stalls is shown in Figure 18.7.

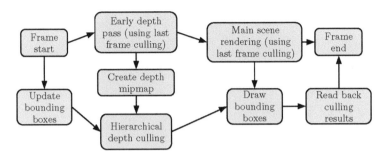

Figure 18.7. Example full pipeline.

18.4 Experimental Results

We have two untextured scenes (Figure 18.8) rendered with different pipelines in an 800×600 window. The City scene view from Blender is also shown in Figure 18.9. The results are shown in Table 18.1. Our measurements use OpenGL time queries to determine the time spent on each rendering stage. Both compared pipelines evaluated lighting according to the Phong model. The first pipeline culled objects using the hierarchical depth culling method; the second one used CPU-side frustum culling. We used a Radeon HD 2400 with an Intel Q6600 CPU and 3GB of RAM as a hardware platform.

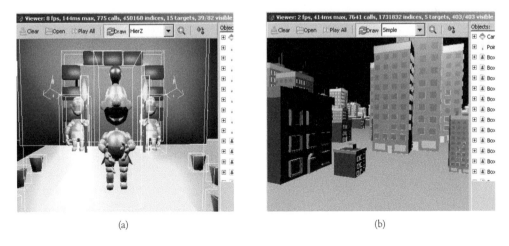

Figure 18.8. Rendered scenes: (a) soldiers scene, (b) city scene.

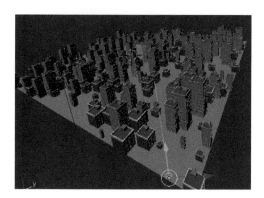

Figure 18.9. City scene screenshot from Blender.

We can see from the numbers that the cost of the hierarchical depth culling stage is minimal, while the construction of the depth buffer mipmap set is comparable to the time spent on the early depth pass. In the Soldiers scene, CPU-side culling proved to be slightly more effective. In the City scene, however, hierarchical depth culling performed significantly better, reducing the frame time by almost a factor of three.

Pipeline stage		Soldiers	City
	(omni lights)	9	1
Hierarchical depth culling pipeline			
	(visible)	39/82	53/403
	(draw calls)	775	1038
	EarlyDepth	517 μs	1644 μs
	ZMipMap	535 μs	533 μs
	HierZcull	22 μs	48 μs
	Lighting	33828 μs	6082 μs
Total		**34902 μs**	**8307 μs**
CPU-side culling pipeline			
	(visible)	42/82	231/403
	(draw calls)	865	4415
	EarlyDepth	470 μs	5070 μs
	Lighting	30867 μs	16989 μs
Total		**31337 μs**	**22059 μs**

Table 18.1. Soldiers scene and city scene rendered with different pipelines.

18.5 Conclusion and Future Work

I have presented a culling pipeline that effectively marks occluded objects according to the depth buffer mipmap set. The pipeline runs mostly on the GPU and requires minimal DMA transfer. It is designed to support skinning, morphing, and any other GPU-side mesh modifications. This feature is helpful for graphics engines that try not to keep synchronized copies of meshes in main memory and perform all mesh-related transformations on the GPU.

Using hierarchical depth culling makes classical frustum culling partially obsolete. Objects outside the far plane are culled by the depth buffer clear value (1.0). Objects outside of the side planes are culled by the border value (0.0). Only objects in front of the near plane are not culled by this method. We can skip frustum intersection checks on the CPU completely, allowing bounding-box data to live only on the GPU memory side.

Implementation of this pipeline is presented as one of the rendering modes of KRI Viewer [Malyshau 10], which is available on the book's website. By using the Blender exporter included in the demo, one can export any dynamic scene into KRI format and open it with Viewer. Switching to HierZ mode will show the up-to-date bounding boxes of objects and the number of occluded objects by the hierarchical depth buffer check. The demo also includes full versions of GLSL core profile shaders used for all stages of the culling pipeline. It is also possible to see the amount of time per frame being spent on a particular stage in comparison to the performance with nonculling, alternative rendering modes.

A lot of research remains to be done in order to utilize new highly parallelized graphics processors. The bounding box update procedure is the bottleneck in the current implementation and, therefore, requires some structural optimizations. We are also going to look into the latest OpenGL 4+ features in order to completely remove read-back operations (reading the culling results) by the conditional execution of draw calls on the GPU.

Bibliography

[Cozzi 09] Patrick Cozzi. "Z Buffer Optimizations." http://www.slideshare.net/pjcozzi/z-buffer-optimizations, 2009.

[Fernando 04] Randima Fernando. "Efficient Occlusion Culling." Reading, MA: Addison-Wesley Professional, 2004.

[Group 10] Khronos Group. "OpenGL 3.3 Core Profile Specification." http://www.opengl.org/registry/doc/glspec33.core.20100311.pdf, March 11, 2010.

[Malyshau 10] Dzmitry Malyshau. "KRI Engine Wiki." http://code.google.com/p/kri/w/list, 2010.

Massive Number of 19
Shadow-Casting Lights with
Layered Rendering

Daniel Rákos

19.1   Introduction

Shadow map generation is one of the most time-consuming rendering tasks that today's graphics applications have to deal with due to the high number of dynamic light sources used. Deferred rendering techniques have provided a reasonable answer for handling a large number of dynamic light sources in linear time because they work independently of the scene complexity. However, shadow map generation is still an $O(nm)$ time complexity task where n is the number of light sources and m is the number of objects.

This chapter explores the possibility of taking advantage of some of the latest GPU technologies to decrease this time complexity by using *layered rendering* to render multiple *shadow maps* at once using the same input geometry. Layered rendering will enable us to decrease the vertex attribute–fetching bandwidth requirements and the vertex processing time to $O(m)$ time complexity.

While this approach will still require $O(nm)$ time complexity for rasterizing and fragment processing, this generally takes far less time in practice, as usually, the light volumes don't overlap completely, so most of the geometric primitives will be culled early by the rasterizer. We will also investigate whether the required rasterizer throughput can be further decreased by doing view-frustum culling in the *geometry shader* performing the layered rendering.

I will present a reference implementation for both traditional and *layered shadow map rendering* that enables us to provide performance comparison results for the two approaches in different scenes with various scene complexities and various numbers of light sources and types. In addition, I will provide measurements about how the shadow map resolution affects the performance of the traditional method and our new technique.

Performance measurements are executed both for client-side and server-side workloads because, besides decreasing the geometry processing requirements of shadow rendering, the technique also drastically decreases the number of necessary state changes and draw commands to render multiple shadow maps, thus providing an edge for CPU-bound applications.

While the technique primarily targets OpenGL 4.x–capable GPUs, we present how the same technique can be implemented with some caveats for GPUs with only OpenGL 3.x capabilities.

Further, I will present some special use cases of layered shadow map rendering that can be used to render *shadow cube maps* and *cascaded shadow maps* with a single draw call, and I will briefly present how the technique can be altered to accelerate the generation of reflection maps and reflection cube maps in a similar fashion.

Finally, I will discuss the limitations of the presented algorithm, explicitly mentioning those imposed by hardware limitations of GPU implementations.

19.2   Traditional Shadow Map Rendering in OpenGL

Shadow mapping or projective shadowing is an image-space rendering technique introduced by [Williams 78] that became the de facto standard for performing shadow rendering in real time and offline graphics applications.

The principle of shadow mapping is that if we view the scene from a light source's position, all the object points we can see from there appear in light and anything behind those is in shadow. Based on this, the algorithm works in the following way:

- We render the scene from the light source's point of view to a depth buffer using the well-known z-buffer visibility algorithm.

- When we render the scene from the camera's point of view, by comparing the distance of the light source to any point of the surface with the sampled value from the depth buffer corresponding to the point, we can decide whether the given point is in light or in shadow. See Figure 19.1.

Modern graphics processors provide hardware support for this technique in the form of two features:

- Providing a mechanism to store depth-buffer images in textures.

- Providing a mechanism to compare a reference depth value with a depth value stored in a depth texture.

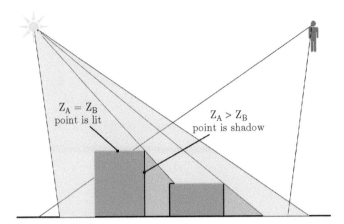

Figure 19.1. Illustration of the shadow mapping algorithm where Z_A is the distance of the fragment from the light source and Z_B is the value stored in the depth buffer generated in the first pass.

Both of these features are available as extensions [Paul 02] and have been part of the OpenGL specification since Version 1.4. These extensions provide a fixed-function mechanism that returns the boolean result of a comparison between the depth texture texel value and a reference value derived from the texture-coordinate set used for the fetch. Although in modern OpenGL these are all done with shaders, GLSL provides depth comparison texture lookup functions to perform the fixed-function comparison of the depth values.

Putting everything together, in order to implement shadow mapping for a single light source, we have to use a two-pass rendering algorithm. In the first pass, we set up the light's view-projection matrix for use in our shadow rendering *vertex shader*. Then we prepare the framebuffer for depth-texture rendering. Finally, we simply draw our scene without textures, materials, or any additional configuration, as we are interested only in the generated depth values (see Listing 19.1). There are no special requirements about the shaders used in the shadow map generation pass; we only need a single vertex shader, with no further shader stages, that performs the exact same transformations as it would do in case of regular scene rendering.

The framebuffer object used in Listing 19.1 is configured with only a single depth attachment with no color attachments. The code needed to set up the depth texture and the framebuffer object used in Listing 19.1 is presented in Listing 19.2.

In the second pass, we use the depth texture generated in the first pass as a texture input, and we will also need the light's view-projection matrix to reconstruct each fragment's position in the light view's clip space to perform the texture lookup and the depth comparison (see Listing 19.3). Obviously, this pass differs based on whether a forward renderer or a deferred renderer is in use, as the rendered geometry is either

```
/* bind the framebuffer that has only a depth texture attachment */
glBindFramebuffer(GL_FRAMEBUFFER, depth_fbo);

/* we must ensure that depth testing and depth writes are enabled */
glEnable(GL_DEPTH_TEST);
glDepthMask(GL_TRUE);

/* clear the depth buffer before proceeding */
glClear(GL_DEPTH_BUFFER_BIT);

/* bind the shadow map rendering program which has only a vertex shader attached */
glUseProgram(shadow_po);

/* bind the uniform buffer containing the view-projection matrix of the light */
glBindBufferBase(GL_UNIFORM_BUFFER, 0, lightVP_ubo);

/* render the scene as usual */
.................
```

Listing 19.1. Traditional shadow map generation pass using OpenGL 3.3+.

the whole scene or a primitive that represents the light (a light volume or a full screen quad), respectively.

Usually, when we have multiple light sources, we need to execute both passes for each light source separately. Sometimes, the first pass needs to be executed multiple times even for a single light source, as in the case of omnidirectional light sources or if we would like to use cascaded shadow maps as presented by [Dimitrov 07] for directional light sources.

```
/* create the depth texture with a 16-bit depth internal format */
glGenTextures(1, &depth_texture);
glBindTexture(GL_TEXTURE_2D, depth_texture);
glTexImage2D(GL_TEXTURE_2D, 0, GL_DEPTH_COMPONENT16, width, height, 0,
GL_DEPTH_COMPONENT, GL_FLOAT, NULL);

/* set up the appropriate filtering and wrapping modes */
glTexParameteri(GL_TEXTURE_2D, GL_TEXTURE_WRAP_S,    GL_CLAMP_TO_EDGE);
glTexParameteri(GL_TEXTURE_2D, GL_TEXTURE_WRAP_T,    GL_CLAMP_TO_EDGE);
glTexParameteri(GL_TEXTURE_2D, GL_TEXTURE_MAG_FILTER, GL_NEAREST);
glTexParameteri(GL_TEXTURE_2D, GL_TEXTURE_MIN_FILTER, GL_NEAREST);

/* create the framebuffer object and bind it */
glGenFramebuffers(1, &depth_fbo);
glBindFramebuffer(GL_FRAMEBUFFER, depth_fbo);

/* disable all color buffers */
glDrawBuffer(GL_NONE);

/* attach the depth texture as depth attachment */
glFramebufferTexture(GL_FRAMEBUFFER, GL_DEPTH_ATTACHMENT, depth_texture, 0);
```

Listing 19.2. Setting up a framebuffer object for shadow map rendering.

```
/* bind the target framebuffer that we want the lit scene to be rendered to */
glBindFramebuffer(GL_FRAMEBUFFER , final_fbo);
/* bind the shadow map as texture input */
glBindTexture(GL_TEXTURE_2D , depth_texture);
/* bind the light shader program with shadow mapping support */
glUseProgram(light_po);
/* bind the uniform buffer containing the view-projection matrix of the light */
glBindBufferBase(GL_UNIFORM_BUFFER, 0, lightVP_ubo);
/* render the scene or light as usual */
.................
```

Listing 19.3. Traditional shadow mapping pass using OpenGL 3.3+.

While shadow map generation is a lightweight rendering pass, especially for fragment processing as we don't have to compute per-fragment shading or other sophisticated effects, it still has a significant overhead for vertex and command processing. This is why we need a more streamlined algorithm for rendering shadow maps for multiple light sources.

19.3 Our Shadow Map Generation Algorithm

The latest generations of GPUs brought several hardware features that can be used to decrease the vertex processing and API overhead of the generation of multiple shadow maps. One of these features is the support for 1D and 2D *texture arrays* [Brown 06]. A texture array is actually an array of textures that have the same properties (internal format, size, etc.) and allows a programmable shader to access them through a single texture unit using a single coordinate vector. This means that we can access a 2D texture array with an (S, T, L) coordinate set where L selects the layer of the texture array and the (S, T) coordinate set is used to access that single layer of the array texture as if it were a regular 2D texture. This GPU generation does not allow us just to sample texture arrays but also to render to them.

From our point of view, the other important feature that was introduced with this hardware generation is the geometry shader [Brown and Lichtenbelt 08]. This new shader stage allows us to process OpenGL primitives as a whole, but it is capable of more: it can generate zero, one, or more output primitives based on the input primitive and also allows us to select the target texture layer to use for rasterization in the case of a layered rendering target. These features enable us to implement a more sophisticated shadow map generation algorithm.

In order to implement our shadow map generation algorithm, only small changes are required to be made to the traditional method. The first thing is to replace our 2D depth texture with a 2D depth texture array and to set up the framebuffer for layered rendering (this later step actually does not need any change compared to the code presented in Listing 19.2). The modified code is shown in Listing 19.4.

```
/* create the depth texture with a 16-bit depth internal format */
glGenTextures(1, &depth_texture);
glBindTexture(GL_TEXTURE_2D_ARRAY, depth_texture);
glTexImage3D(GL_TEXTURE_2D_ARRAY, 0, GL_DEPTH_COMPONENT16, width, height,
number_of_shadow_maps, 0, GL_DEPTH_COMPONENT, GL_FLOAT, NULL);

/* set up the appropriate filtering and wrapping modes */
glTexParameteri(GL_TEXTURE_2D, GL_TEXTURE_WRAP_S, GL_CLAMP_TO_EDGE);
glTexParameteri(GL_TEXTURE_2D, GL_TEXTURE_WRAP_T, GL_CLAMP_TO_EDGE);
glTexParameteri(GL_TEXTURE_2D, GL_TEXTURE_MAG_FILTER, GL_NEAREST);
glTexParameteri(GL_TEXTURE_2D, GL_TEXTURE_MIN_FILTER, GL_NEAREST);

/* create the framebuffer object and bind it */
glGenFramebuffers(1, &depth_fbo);
glBindFramebuffer(GL_FRAMEBUFFER, depth_fbo);

/* disable all color buffers */
glDrawBuffer(GL_NONE);

/* attach the depth texture as depth attachment */
glFramebufferTexture(GL_FRAMEBUFFER, GL_DEPTH_ATTACHMENT, depth_texture, 0);
```

Listing 19.4. Setting up a framebuffer object for layered shadow map rendering.

In order to emit all incoming geometric primitives to all the layers of the depth texture array, we have to inject a geometry shader into our shadow map rendering program that will do the task. We would like to use a separate view-projection matrix for each render target layer because they belong to different light sources; thus, the view-projection transformation has to be postponed to the geometry shader stage.

Here, we can take advantage of one more feature introduced with OpenGL 4–capable GPUs: *instanced geometry shaders*. With traditional OpenGL 3 geometry shaders, we could only emit multiple output primitives sequentially. As usual, sequential code is not really well suited for highly parallel processor architectures like the modern GPUs. Instanced geometry shaders allow us to execute multiple instances of the geometry shader on the same input primitive, thus making it possible to process and emit the output primitives in parallel. The implementation of such a geometry shader for emitting the incoming geometry to a total of 32 output layers is presented in Listing 19.5. This means that we can render with it to 32 depth textures at once. While this code contains a loop, the loop is very likely to be unrolled by the shader compiler, but more cautious developers can unroll the loop.

Let's discuss the effect the postponement of the view-projection transformation to the geometry shader can have on the usability of the presented algorithm. One may say that this can introduce performance issues because the transformation is executed multiple times on a single vertex; this can be especially problematic when skeletal animation or another sophisticated vertex transformation algorithm is used. While it is true that the light's view-projection may be executed multiple times on the same vertex, this is a fixed cost, and it may be done anyway multiple times even if we want to generate our shadow maps in the traditional way because of the limited storage

```
#version 420 core

layout(std140, binding = 0) uniform lightTransform {
    mat4 VPMatrix[32];
} LightTransform;

layout(triangles, invocations = 32) in;
layout(triangle_strip, max_vertices = 3) out;

layout(location = 0) in vec4 vertexPosition[];

out gl_PerVertex {
    vec4 gl_Position;
};

void main() {
    for (int i=0; i<3; ++i) {
        gl_Position = LightTransform.VPMatrix[gl_InvocationID] * vertexPosition[i];
        gl_Layer = gl_InvocationID;
        EmitVertex();
    }
    EndPrimitive();
}
```

Listing 19.5. OpenGL 4.2 instanced geometry shader that renders input geometry to 32 output layers.

of the post-transform vertex cache. However, model transformations like skeletal animation don't have to be moved to the geometry shader, as they are independent of the view and the projection, so those should be kept in the vertex shader.

So what else do we need to change in our code to make the layered shadow map generation algorithm work? Nothing, except that when rendering the scene to the shadow maps, our culling algorithms have to be aware that we are rendering our geometry not only from a single view but from multiple views; thus, these algorithms should skip the rendering of a scene node only when it is not visible from any of these views.

19.4 Performance

We use a Radeon HD5770 and an Athlon X2 4000+ for performance testing. The basic scenario is to render the shadow of the Stanford dragon model, which has a total of 35,577 triangles in our case.

The scene is rendered to up to 32 shadow maps, including the depth buffer clear, making the whole scene visible in the depth texture with traditional and layered shadow map generation. The resulting shadow maps will look like the one shown in Figure 19.2. Also, we try multiple shadow map resolutions to see how they affect the rendering performance.

The vertex shader is shown in Listing 19.6; the preprocessor directive **LAYERED** is defined only in the case of our layered shadow map generation algorithm. The

Figure 19.2. Sample depth maps of the Stanford dragon model consisting of 35,577 triangles from various light positions and directions.

geometry shader used is equivalent to the one presented earlier in Listing 19.5 with the number of geometry shader invocations set to the number of shadow maps that have to be rendered. The results of the GPU time needed to render the shadow maps for each particular resolution were measured using timer queries [Daniell 10] and can be seen in Figure 19.3.

```
#version 420 core

layout(location = 0) in vec3 inVertexPosition;

#ifdef LAYERED
layout(location = 0) out vec4 vertexPosition;
#endif

layout(std140, binding = 1) uniform transform {
    mat4 ModelMatrix;
} Transform;

#ifndef LAYERED
layout(std140, binding = 0) uniform lightTransform {
    mat4 VPMatrix;
} LightTransform;
out gl_PerVertex {
    vec4 gl_Position;
};
#endif

void main(void) {
#ifdef LAYERED
    vertexPosition = Transform.ModelMatrix * vec4(inVertexPosition, 1.f);
#else
    gl_Position = LightTransform.VPMatrix * (Transform.ModelMatrix * vec4(←
        inVertexPosition, 1.f));
#endif
}
```

Listing 19.6. Shadow rendering vertex shader used for performance measurements.

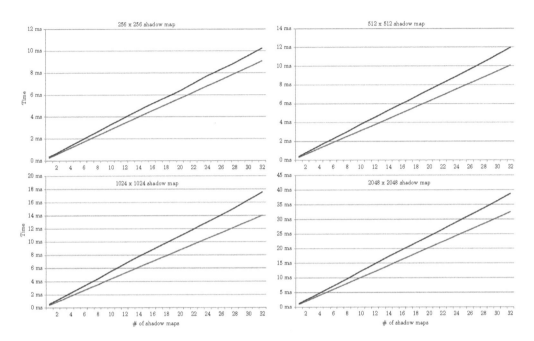

Figure 19.3. The GPU time required to render 1 to 32 shadow maps using traditional shadow map generation (blue) and our layered method (red). The resulting shadow maps are of size 256 × 256 (top left), 512 × 512 (top right), 1024 × 1024 (bottom left), and 2048 × 2048 (bottom right). Lower values are better.

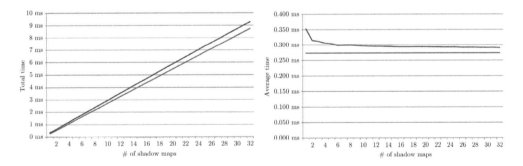

Figure 19.4. The total GPU time required to render 1 to 32 shadow maps (left) and the average GPU time required per shadow map (right) using traditional shadow map generation (blue) and our layered method (red). Lower values are better.

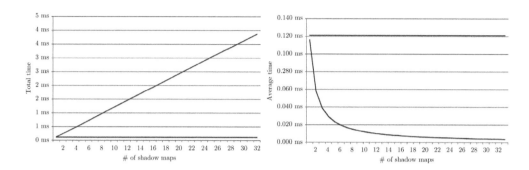

Figure 19.5. The total CPU time required to render 1 to 32 shadow maps (left) and the average CPU time required per shadow map (right) using traditional shadow map generation (blue) and our layered method (red). Lower values are better.

Figure 19.3 shows that when using such a simple vertex shader, the amount of GPU work saved by using layered rendering does not outweigh the overhead of the introduced geometry shader stage. Actually, it has roughly 10% lower performance than the traditional method. Also, the shadow map resolution has very little effect on the relative performance of the two techniques. The reason for this is that the fragment processing cost is equivalent in both cases. We will disable rasterization in our further measurements so that we can concentrate on the geometry processing time. This can be easily done by using the following command before our shadow map rendering:

```
glEnable(GL_RASTERIZER_DISCARD);
```

Figure 19.4 shows the performance results of the shadow map generation without rasterization. We also provide a separate chart to present the average GPU time required for generating a single shadow map.

When using such a simple vertex shader, the overhead of layered shadow map rendering makes the technique suboptimal from a GPU-resource point of view, but the time savings on the CPU side show the strength of layered rendering. As can be seen in Figure 19.5, the CPU time required to generate multiple shadow maps can go off the charts even though there is only a single draw command that renders the whole scene. Contrarily, our layered method has a constant CPU cost indifferent of the number of shadow maps generated.

19.4.1   Performance with Complex Vertex Shaders

The vertex processing requirements in our tests were too optimistic because we used a minimal vertex attribute setup of 12 bytes per vertex (3 floats for vertex position), and our shaders only perform two matrix-vertex multiplications, one for the model

```
#version 420 core

layout(location = 0) in vec3 inVertexPosition;
layout(location = 1) in ivec4 inBoneIndex;
layout(location = 2) in vec4 inBoneWeight;

#ifdef LAYERED
layout(location = 0) out vec4 vertexPosition;
#endif

layout(std140, binding = 1) uniform boneTransform {
    mat3 BoneMatrix[64];
} BoneTransform;

#ifndef LAYERED
layout(std140, binding = 0) uniform lightTransform {
    mat4 VPMatrix;
} LightTransform;
out gl_PerVertex {
      vec4 gl_Position;
};
#endif

void main(void) {
    vec3 vertex = (BoneTransform.BoneMatrix[inBoneIndex.x] * inVertexPosition) * ←
        inBoneWeight.x;
    if (inBoneIndex.y != 0xFF) {
        vertex += (BoneTransform.BoneMatrix[inBoneIndex.y] * inVertexPosition) * ←
            inBoneWeight.y;
        if (inBoneIndex.z != 0xFF) {
            vertex += (BoneTransform.BoneMatrix[inBoneIndex.z] * inVertexPosition) *←
                inBoneWeight.z;
            if (inBoneIndex.w != 0xFF) {
                vertex += (BoneTransform.BoneMatrix[inBoneIndex.w] * ←
                    inVertexPosition) * inBoneWeight.w;
            }
        }
    }
#ifdef LAYERED
    vertexPosition = vec4(vertex, 1.f);
#else
    gl_Position = LightTransform.VPMatrix * vec4(vertex, 1.f));
#endif
}
```

Listing 19.7. Shadow rendering vertex shader that performs skeletal animation with up to four bones per vertex.

transformation and one for the view-projection transformation. Now, let's try a real-life scenario by implementing a vertex shader that performs simple *skeletal animation*. We will provide a maximum of 64 bone matrices and a vertex attribute setup of 32 bytes per vertex (3 floats for vertex position, 4 bytes for bone indices, and 4 floats for bone weights), which provides us up to four bone matrices per vertex with no model transformation. Based on this, our vertex shader will look like the one presented in Listing 19.7.

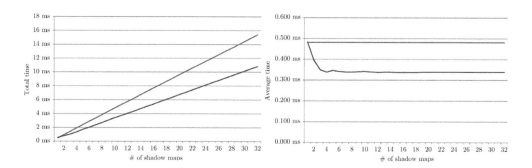

Figure 19.6. The total GPU time required to render 1 to 32 shadow maps (left) and the average GPU time required per shadow map (right) using traditional shadow map generation (blue) and our layered method (red) when using a vertex shader that performs skeletal animation. Lower values are better.

When we use the skeletal animation implementation instead of the simple vertex shader, layered shadow map generation outperforms the traditional method when rendering to more than two depth textures, saving about 30% of GPU time when we render three or more depth textures at once. It has diminishing performance difference compared to the traditional method even in the case of a single shadow map. See Figure 19.6.

Of course, one may say that skeletal animation is usually not applied to all the geometry rendered in a scene. But we also assume one more thing: the whole geometry is visible in the final rendering. While modern visibility-determination algorithms are very efficient, the CPU-based culling algorithms are usually rather coarse and conservative. This means that in many cases, a reasonable amount of geometry fed to the GPU does not contribute to the final image either due to occlusion or because the geometry falls out of the view's frustum.

19.4.2   View Frustum Culling Optimization

In the next test, we render the Stanford dragon model four times using *geometry instancing*, from which only one instance is visible from the light's perspective. With this, we can simulate a more realistic scenario when the input geometry is just partially visible. We won't do any sophisticated vertex transformation techniques like skeletal animation but simply use a per-instance model transformation matrix. The source code for the vertex shader is shown in Listing 19.8.

In addition to the geometry shader presented in Listing 19.5, used earlier for performing the layered rendering, we also perform tests with an alternative geometry shader shown in Listing 19.9 that performs conservative *view frustum culling* and emits the incoming triangles only when the triangle lies in the light's frustum.

```
#version 420 core

layout(location = 0) in vec3 inVertexPosition;

#ifdef LAYERED
layout(location = 0) out vec4 vertexPosition;
#endif

layout(std140, binding = 1) uniform transform {
    mat4 ModelMatrix[4];
} Transform;

#ifndef LAYERED
layout(std140, binding = 0) uniform lightTransform {
    mat4 VPMatrix;
} LightTransform;

out gl_PerVertex {
    vec4 gl_Position;
};
#endif

void main(void) {
#ifdef LAYERED
    vertexPosition = Transform.ModelMatrix[gl_InstanceID] * vec4(inVertexPosition, ↩
        1.f);
#else
    gl_Position = LightTransform.VPMatrix * (Transform.ModelMatrix[gl_InstanceID] * ↩
        vec4(inVertexPosition, 1.f));
#endif
}
```

Listing 19.8. Simplistic shadow rendering vertex shader with geometry instancing support.

As geometry shaders are usually output bound, we expect to get a reasonable performance increase from our new geometry shader. This optimization can reduce the

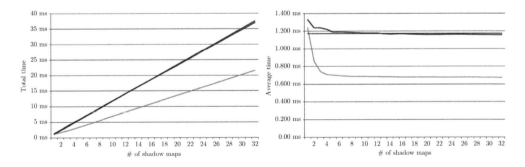

Figure 19.7. The total GPU time required to render 1 to 32 shadow maps (left) and the average GPU time required per shadow map (right) using traditional shadow map generation (blue), our layered method without view frustum culling (red) and our layered method with view frustum culling (green) using four instances of the scene. Lower values are better.

```
#version 420 core

layout(std140, binding = 0) uniform lightTransform {
    mat4 VPMatrix[32];
} LightTransform;

layout(triangles, invocations = 32) in;
layout(triangle_strip, max_vertices = 3) out;

layout(location = 0) in vec4 vertexPosition[];

out gl_PerVertex {
    vec4 gl_Position;
};

void main() {
    vec4 vertex[3];
    int outOfBound[6] = int[6]{ 0, 0, 0, 0, 0, 0 };
    for (int i=0; i<3; ++i) {
        vertex[i] = LightTransform.VPMatrix[gl_InvocationID] * vertexPosition[i];
        if (vertex[i].x > +vertex[i].w) ++outOfBound[0];
        if (vertex[i].x < -vertex[i].w) ++outOfBound[1];
        if (vertex[i].y > +vertex[i].w) ++outOfBound[2];
        if (vertex[i].y < -vertex[i].w) ++outOfBound[3];
        if (vertex[i].z > +vertex[i].w) ++outOfBound[4];
        if (vertex[i].z < -vertex[i].w) ++outOfBound[5];
    }

    bool inFrustum = true;
    for (int i=0; i<6; ++i)
        if (outOfBound[i] == 3) inFrustum = false;

    if (inFrustum) {
        for (int i=0; i<3; ++i) {
            gl_Position = vertex[i];
            gl_Layer = gl_InvocationID;
            EmitVertex();
        }
        EndPrimitive();
    }
}
```

Listing 19.9. OpenGL 4.1 instanced geometry shader that performs view frustum culling to determine whether the incoming triangle has to be emitted to a particular layer.

number of vertices emitted by the geometry shader performing the layered rendering by a factor of four. The measurements from this combined performance are shown in Figure 19.7.

Even the naive layered shadow map rendering approach that does not perform view frustum culling reaches the performance of the traditional method when we render at least five to ten shadow maps simultaneously. This is most probably the result of performing geometry instancing in this case so our vertex shader accesses the gl_InstanceID built-in variable. This shows how easily vertex shader costs can increase when using even such simple techniques like instancing.

While our original layered rendering geometry shader already provides adequate performance in this use case, what is even more impressive is that performing view frustum culling in the geometry shader almost doubles the performance of our layered shadow map generation algorithm despite the additional cost of the actual culling algorithm.

We've seen that the proposed shadow map generation technique offers a clear performance advantage compared to the traditional method when complex vertex shaders are used or when the visibility determination algorithms performed on the CPU provide only conservative results, but what if neither applies to our case? We still have one more thing that we haven't taken advantage of: *back-face culling*.

19.4.3   Back-Face Culling Optimization

When rendering uniformly tessellated closed and opaque geometry, back-face culling usually halves the amount of geometry rasterized. While OpenGL supports fixed-function back-face culling, it is done after the geometry shader stage, and that is already too late, as our algorithm is usually geometry-shader output-bound. Still, back-face culling can be used for our advantage to further decrease the number of triangles emitted by the layered rendering geometry shader if we perform it manually within the shader itself. Thus, the last version of the performance tests uses the

```
#version 420 core

layout(std140, binding = 0) uniform lightTransform {
  mat4 VPMatrix[32];
  vec4 position[32];
} LightTransform;

layout(triangles, invocations = 32) in;
layout(triangle_strip, max_vertices = 3) out;

layout(location = 0) in vec4 vertexPosition[];

out gl_PerVertex {
  vec4 gl_Position;
};

void main() {
  vec3 normal = cross(vertexPosition[2].xyz - vertexPosition[0].xyz, vertexPosition←
    [0].xyz - vertexPosition[1].xyz);
  vec3 view = LightTransform.position[gl_InvocationID].xyz - vertexPosition[0].xyz;

  if (dot(normal, view) > 0.f) {
    for (int i=0; i<3; ++i) {
      gl_Position = LightTransform.VPMatrix[gl_InvocationID] * vertexPosition[i];
      gl_Layer = gl_InvocationID;
      EmitVertex();
    }
    EndPrimitive();
  }
}
```

Listing 19.10. OpenGL 4.1 instanced geometry shader that performs back-face culling to determine whether the incoming triangle has to be emitted to a particular layer.

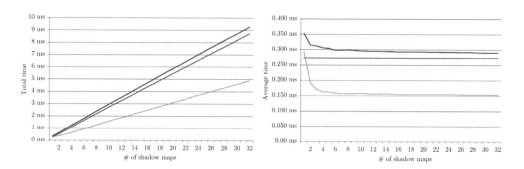

Figure 19.8. The total GPU time required to render 1 to 32 shadow maps (left) and the average GPU time required per shadow map (right) using traditional shadow map generation (blue), our layered method without back-face culling (red) and our layered method with back-face culling (green). Lower values are better.

geometry shader in Listing 19.10. The rest of the configuration is equivalent to the one used in the first test; we use the minimalistic vertex shader show in Listing 19.6 and only a single instance of the scene.

As shown in Figure 19.8, if we use back-face culling, the rendering time is almost halved, and the GPU time required by layered shadow map generation can be more than 40% lower than that of the traditional method, even in the case of a simple vertex shader and no other optimizations.

When layered shadow map rendering is properly implemented, it will outperform the traditional method despite the added overhead of using a geometry shader. The rule of thumb for the geometry shader applies to this technique: it's always worth spending even a lot of ALU instructions to decrease the number of output components emitted by the geometry shader.

In summary, the case of a slightly expensive vertex shader layered shadow map generation is about 30% faster; with a coarsely culled scene, view frustum culling brings roughly 40% speed advantage, and using back-face culling makes our layered technique more than 40% faster than the traditional method even for simple shaders. Obviously, these use cases may happen in combination; thus, we've executed a final test that renders four instances of the scene with skeletal animation done in the vertex shader, and with back-face culling and view frustum culling performed in the geometry shader in the case of layered shadow map generation. The results are shown on Figure 19.9.

The combined results show that our layered technique can take 60% less GPU time to render shadow maps if more than four depth textures are rendered at once. Further, even if in a special configuration, the presented technique does not provide any advantage over the traditional method from the GPU-time point of view, the amount of CPU time saved by batching the shadow map generation passes into a single pass can be a good enough reason to implement it.

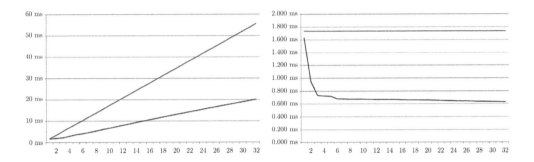

Figure 19.9. The total GPU time required to render 1 to 32 shadow maps (left) and the average GPU time required per shadow map (right) using traditional shadow map generation (blue) and our layered method (red) with back-face culling and view frustum culling. The scene is rendered four times using geometry instancing. Lower values are better.

19.5   Advanced Techniques

The shadow map generation technique we've presented can be directly used to render shadows for spot lights, but the technique can be applied in a similar manner for omnidirectional lights and directional light sources.

For omnidirectional lights, we can choose from several alternatives. We can split the omnidirectional light and use, for example, six 2D shadow maps from the shadow map array for rendering. Our technique naturally extends to omnidirectional light sources. We can also use cube shadow maps, in which case, we will use a cube-map texture array [Haemel 09] instead of a 2D one. Luckily, this does not affect the implementation of the layered shadow map generation algorithm, as each element of a cube-map texture array is actually seen as six 2D layers, and a single layer index can be used to address a specific side of a specific element in the cube-map texture array.

For directional light sources, layered rendering can be used to accelerate cascaded shadow map rendering. Usually, each layer of the cascaded shadow map has the same size because objects farther from the eye's position don't require that much resolution; all of the layers of the cascaded shadow map can be rendered in a single run using the very same algorithm. Actually, it is even possible to render multiple cascaded shadow maps in a single pass using our technique.

The presented algorithm also trivially handles other advanced shadow map generation techniques like the ones presented in [Martin and Tan 04, Stamminger and Drettakis 02, Wimmer et al. 04, Zhang et al. 06]. These techniques tackle the aliasing artifacts of shadow mapping resulting from undersampling by performing various transformations on the scene geometry before rendering it to the shadow map.

Layered rendering is not restricted to rendering shadow maps; it can be used to generate arbitrary textures. This enables us to use the presented rendering technique for the batched generation of reflection maps or reflection cube maps analogous to the shadow map generation for spot lights or omnidirectional light sources. The only difference is that we need to accompany our depth texture array with a color texture array that will be used as the color buffer of the framebuffer object and attach the appropriate fragment shaders to the pipeline.

Also, layered rendering can be advantageous for *stereoscopic rendering*. The only difference is that the view-projection matrices used will be those of the two eyes; the same geometry shaders presented could be used without any significant modification. This use case is a particularly good candidate to take advantage of the performance benefits of layered rendering, as the two eyes' position and orientation are roughly the same at any given time; thus, the list of triangles inside the view frustra are also more or less identical in the two cases.

Finally, layered rendering can be beneficial also for CAD software, which usually display multiple views of the same scene that can be rendered in a single pass this way.

19.6   Limitations

Though layered shadow map generation is very promising, it has limitations, many of them arising from certain hardware restrictions.

One of these limitations is that the layers of an array texture must have the same size. This means that multiple shadow maps, reflection maps, or other textures can be generated in a single pass using our technique only if they have the same size. We'll probably have to wait quite some time until hardware and APIs relax this restriction or provide other means to dispatch rendering to separate, different-sized texture images. Further, this also requires us to be able to select between different viewports besides target layers. While both viewport selection and layer selection is possible on the OpenGL 3.x hardware and API, support is limited to using only one of them at a time, not both. Until these issues are addressed by the hardware vendors, we need to use separate passes for each particular shadow map resolution. As an alternative, a possible solution on current hardware could be the use of a texture atlas that holds multiple depth images. In this case, the shaders should perform the appropriate viewport transformations and manually discard the fragments lying outside the intended viewport.

Another inherent limitation of the presented algorithm is the maximum number of parallel geometry shader invocations supported by hardware. At the time of this writing, this is capped at 32, although this may change in the near future. However, this is not a hard limit on the number of shadow maps our algorithm can handle, as more instances of an incoming primitive can be emitted to separate target layers even from within a single geometry shader invocation using a loop. While we lose some concurrency, we can somewhat increase the upper limit of the number of shadow maps that can be generated in a single run.

There is, however, also a performance perspective on the practical upper limit of the number of shadow maps that should be generated in a single pass. As we've seen in the performance-result charts, on a Radeon HD5770, our technique does not scale that nicely when rendering to more than six shadow maps. The average time per shadow map does still decrease somewhat above this limit, though we don't see as nice a slope as we see for lower number of layers. However, this may be different on other current or future hardware, including higher-end GPUs or hardware from other vendors.

There is also another practical limitation on the number of shadow maps that should be rendered in a single pass. Our technique performs best when there are many primitives that lie in more than one light source's frustum. This means that in the case where the light sources don't overlap well or, in other words, most of the triangles are visible only from a single light source's point of view, the added overhead of executing a geometry shader for every incoming primitive with an invocation count equal to the number of light sources will outweigh the eliminated vertex attribute fetching and vertex processing costs. Thus, care must be taken to group light sources in an appropriate way when their shadow maps are generated with the technique presented here.

19.7   Conclusion

I've presented a rendering technique that takes advantage of OpenGL's layered rendering capability to accelerate the generation of multiple shadow maps. I provided a reference implementation and performance measurements on OpenGL 4.x–capable hardware for both traditional shadow map generation and the layered technique. The layered technique outperforms traditional shadow map generation in most use cases on the GPU and can also reduce the CPU overhead of the generation process to constant time. While this technique primarily targets OpenGL 4.x–capable hardware, I've noted that an implementation is possible for OpenGL 3.x capable hardware.

Visibility determination algorithms like view frustum culling and back-face culling can be used to increase the efficiency of layered rendering and of geometry shaders in general. I've also presented how layered rendering can be used to increase the performance of other advanced rendering techniques like reflection map generation and stereoscopic rendering.

While layered rendering of shadow maps is not popular in the industry yet, I expect that it will soon gain attention, and developers will see more implementations taking advantage of it in the domains of video games, CAD software, and other computer graphics applications.

Bibliography

[Paul 02]   Brian Paul. "ARB_depth_texture and ARB_shadow." OpenGL extension specifications, 2002.

[Brown 06]   Pat Brown. "EXT_texture_array." OpenGL extension specification, 2006.

[Brown and Lichtenbelt 08]   Pat Brown and Barthold Lichtenbelt. "ARB_geometry" "_shader4." OpenGL extension specification, 2008.

[Daniell 10]   Piers Daniell. "ARB_timer_query." OpenGL extension specification, 2010.

[Dimitrov 07]   Rouslan Dimitrov. "Cascaded Shadow Maps." NVIDIA Corporation, 2007.

[Haemel 09]   Nick Haemel. "ARB_texture_cube_map_array." OpenGL extension specification, 2009.

[Martin and Tan 04]   Tobias Martin and Tiow-Seng Tan. "Antialiasing and Continuity with Trapezoidal Shadow Maps." School of Computing, National University of Singapore, 2004.

[Stamminger and Drettakis 02]   Marc Stamminger and George Drettakis. "Perspective Shadow Maps." REVES-INRIA, 2002.

[Williams 78]   Lance Williams. "Casting Curved Shadows on Curved Surfaces." Computer Graphics Lab, Old Westbury, New York: New York Institute of Technology, 1978.

[Wimmer et al. 04]   Michael Wimmer, Daniel Scherzer and Werner Purgathofer. "Light Space Perspective Shadow Maps." Eurographics Symposium on Rendering, 2004.

[Zhang et al. 06]   Fan Zhang, Hanqiu Sun, Leilei Xu and Lee Kit Lun. "Parallel-Split Shadow Maps for Large-scale Virtual Environments." Department of Computer Science and Engineering, The Chinese University of Hong Kong, 2006.

Efficient Layered Fragment Buffer Techniques   20

Pyarelal Knowles, Geoff Leach, and Fabio Zambetta

20.1   Introduction

Rasterization typically resolves visible surfaces using the depth buffer, computing just the front-most layer of fragments. However, some applications require all fragment data, including those of hidden surfaces. In this chapter, we refer to these data and the technique to compute them as a *layered fragment buffer* (LFB). LFBs can be used for order-independent transparency, multilayer transparent shadow maps, more accurate motion blur, indirect illumination, ambient occlusion, CSG, and relief imposters.

With the introduction of atomic operations and random access to video memory exposed via image units in OpenGL 4.2, it is now possible to capture all fragments in a single rendering pass of the geometry. This chapter describes and compares two approaches to packing this data: linked list–based and linearized array–based approaches.

Transparency is a well-known effect that requires data from hidden surfaces. It is used here to demonstrate and compare different LFB techniques. To render transparency, an LFB is constructed, and the fragments at each pixel are sorted. Figure 20.1 shows an example of fragment layers after sorting where each layer contains fragments of the same depth index. Note that surfaces are discretized and there is no fragment connectivity information. The sorted fragments are then blended in back-to-front order. Unlike polygon-sorting approaches to transparency, the LFB can resolve intersecting geometry and complex arrangements such as in Figure 20.2.

Previous approaches to capturing LFB data involve multiple rendering passes or suffer from read-modify-write problems, discussed in Section 20.2. OpenGL atomic

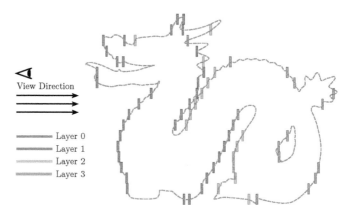

Figure 20.1. Fragment layers resulting from sorting fragments by depth.

operations allow the LFB to be accurately computed in a single rendering pass. The basic, *brute force LFB* technique for single-pass construction is to allocate a 3D array, storing a fixed number of layers in z for each pixel x, y. A per-pixel atomic counter is incremented to write fragments into the correct layer. Typical scenes have varying depth complexities, i.e., per-pixel fragment counts, so while the brute force LFB is fast, the fixed z dimension commonly wastes memory or overflows. The following are two general approaches to packing the data, solving this issue:

1. Dynamic linked list construction.

2. Array based linearization.

Both aim to pack the data with minimal overhead; however, there are some significant differences. Exploring these differences and comparing performance is the primary focus of this chapter.

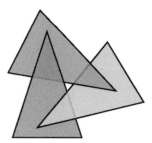

Figure 20.2. Cyclically overlapping geometry.

20.2   Related Work

There are a number of techniques to capture multiple layers of rasterized fragments. Before atomic operations in shaders were available, techniques used the depth buffer's fragment serialization and multiple rendering passes of the geometry. With the introduction of image units and atomic operations, techniques to capture fragments in a single pass have been proposed.

Depth peeling [Everitt 01, Mammen 89] is an established approach to capturing LFB data. The scene's geometry is rendered multiple times, capturing a single layer with each pass using the depth buffer. For complex geometry and high-depth complexities, this method is not practical for most real-time applications. Wei and Xu [Wei and Xu 06] use multiple framebuffer attachments to increase the speed of depth peeling by peeling multiple layers at once. This algorithm suffers from fragment collisions, i.e., concurrent read/write hazards; however, is guaranteed to resolve errors progressively with each pass. Dual depth peeling [Bavoil and Myers 08] improves the performance of depth peeling by peeling both front and back layers simultaneously using blending. Depth peeling via bucket sort [Liu et al. 09a] uses framebuffer attachments and blending to route fragments into buckets, defined by uniformly dividing the depth range. An adaptive approach that uses nonuniform divisions can be used to reduce artifacts caused by fragment collisions. Unlike the previous techniques, the k-buffer [Bavoil et al. 07] captures and sorts fragments in a single pass using insertion sort. Atomic operations were not available at the time, so this method suffers from fragment collisions that give rise to significant artifacts, although heuristics were described to reduce them.

Liu et al. [Liu et al. 09b] developed a CUDA rasterizer that atomically increments counters to push fragments onto constant-sized per-pixel arrays in one rendering pass. This is the brute force technique mentioned in Section 20.1. Yang et al. [Yang et al. 10] construct per-pixel linked lists of fragments dynamically on the GPU. We briefly describe this process in Section 20.3. The performance of this method originally suffered from atomic operation contention, discussed further in Section 20.5. Crassin [Crassin 10] presented a method to reduce atomic contention using "pages" of fragments. Around four to six fragments are stored in each linked-list node, thus reducing the atomic increments on the global counter at the cost of some overallocation of memory. Per-pixel counts are incremented for the index within the current page, and per-pixel semaphores are used to resolve which shader allocates new pages. We refer to this technique as the *linked pages LFB*.

An alternative to the linked-list approach is to pack the data into a linear array as described in Section 20.4. This technique is similar to the l-buffer concept [Lipowski 10], except for this method, packing is performed during rendering, reducing peak memory usage. A rudimentary implementation of this technique is included in the Direct3D 11 SDK [Microsoft Corporation 10]. The technique is also mentioned by Korostelev [Korostelev 10] and discussed by Lipowski [Lipowski 11], although this is the first detailed comparison as far as we are aware. Lipowski also packs the *lookup tables*, which reduces memory consumption by eliminating empty pixel entries.

20.3   The Linked-List LFB

The basic linked-list approach is relatively simple to implement. In one rendering pass, all fragments are placed in a global array using a single atomic counter for "allocation." Next, pointers are stored in a separate array of the same length to form linked lists. Each fragment is appended to the appropriate pixel's list via per-pixel head pointers. An atomic exchange safely inserts the fragment into the front of the list, following which, the fragment's next pointer is set to the previous head node:

```
node = atomicCounterIncrement(allocCounter);
head = imageAtomicExchange(headPtrs, pixel, node).r;
imageStore(nextPtrs, node, head);
imageStore(fragmentData, node, frag);
```

Figure 20.3 shows an example of the rendering result. The total number of fragments can be read from the atomic counter. Fragments in the same list are not guaranteed to be stored near each other in memory. Reading the fragment data is straightforward:

```
node = imageLoad(headPtrs, pixel).r;
while (node)
{
    frags[fragCount++] = imageLoad(fragmentData, node);
    node = imageLoad(nextPtrs, node).r;
}
```

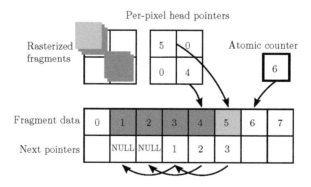

Figure 20.3. Per-pixel linked lists of fragments.

To determine the memory required for the global array, a preliminary fragment-counting pass can be performed, or the total memory required must be predicted. If insufficient memory is allocated in the latter case, data are discarded, or a complete rerender is needed.

20.4   The Linearized LFB

We now discuss the linearized LFB algorithm, which packs the fragment data into an array using an *offset* lookup table, as shown in Figure 20.4(a). This table is computed from per-pixel fragment counts, which is why a two-pass approach is used. The first pass calculates fragment counts, and the second regenerates and packs the fragment data. This produces a 1D array where all per-pixel fragments are grouped and stored one after the other, in contrast to the linked-list approach.

The linearized LFB rendering algorithm is summarized as follows:

1. Zero offset table.

2. First render pass: compute per-pixel fragment counts.

3. Compute offsets using parallel prefix sums.

4. Second render pass: capture and pack fragments.

An example of the count and offset data for three rasterized triangles is shown in Figure 20.5. In step 2, the count data is computed, for example, as shown in Figure 20.5(a). Only the fragment counts are needed, so additional fragment computation such as lighting is disabled.

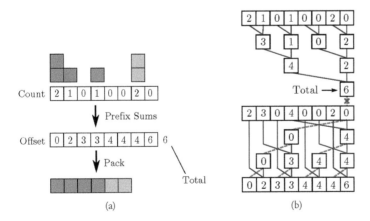

Figure 20.4. (a) Linearly packing fragment data and (b) the parallel prefix sum algorithm [Ladner and Fischer 80] used to create the offset table.

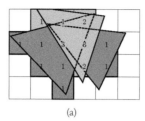

15	15	16	17	19	19	19	19
6	7	8	11	14	15	15	15
1	1	2	3	5	6	6	6
0	0	0	1	1	1	1	1

(a)   (b)

Figure 20.5. An example of (a) counts and (b) offsets for three triangles.

In step 3, offsets are computed, applying the parallel prefix sum algorithm [Ladner and Fischer 80] to the count data. The offsets are computed in place, overwriting the counts since the counts can be recalculated as the difference between consecutive offset values. This algorithm is visualized in Figure 20.4(b), and an example of the final offset table is shown in Figure 20.5(b). For simplicity, the input data for the parallel prefix sums is increased to the next power of 2, causing a maximum of double memory allocation for the offset data. Harris et al. [Harris et al. 07] describe methods for improving the speed of prefix sums using CUDA as well as handling non–power-of-2 data.

The total number of fragments is known from the prefix-sums computation. Thus, the exact memory needed is determined and allocated before packing during the main render.

In step 4, the second and main rendering pass of the scene is performed. Each incoming fragment atomically increments the offset value, giving a unique index that stores the fragment data. Figure 20.6 shows an example of the final linear LFB data. The data can be read using the difference in offsets, keeping in mind that they now mark the end of each fragment array:

```
fragOffset = 0;
if (pixel > 0)
    fragOffset = imageLoad(offsets, pixel - 1).r;
fragCount = imageLoad(offsets, pixel).r - fragOffset;

for (int i = 0; i < fragCount; ++i)
    frags[i] = imageLoad(fragmentData, fragOffset + i);
```

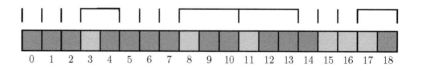

0   1   2   3   4   5   6   7   8   9   10 11 12 13 14 15 16 17 18

Figure 20.6. An example of linearized LFB fragment data. This, along with the offset table, Figure 20.5(b), is the algorithm's output.

20.4.1 Implementation Details

The LFB is a generic data structure, so having a cleanly accessible interface that multiple shaders can use is important. This is made more difficult with the two geometry
passes of the linearized LFBs. Our approach is to implement an external preprocessor
to parse the `#include` statement, which gives any shader access to the LFB interface. One could also use `ARB_shading_language_include`. The application's
LFB object then sets the uniform variables for each shader that `#includes` it. This
simplifies managing multiple LFB instances. Injecting `#define` values is also useful,
for example, for setting constants, removing unused code, or creating permutations
of shaders.

The following shows our basic linearized LFB rendering process, where `render`
`Program` and `transparencyProgram` are OpenGL shader programs:

```
lfb.init();              //zero lookup tables
lfb.setUniforms(renderProgram);
render();                //fragment count pass
lfb.count();             //parallel prefix sums
lfb.setUniforms(renderProgram);
render();                //capture and store fragments
lfb.end();               //cleanup. also pre-sort if needed
...
lfb.setUniforms(transparencyProgram);
fullScreenTriangle();    //draw LFB contents
```

In this example, `renderProgram` computes each fragment's color and calls
`addFragment(color, depth)`, defined in `"lfb.h"`. This call increments
the fragment count in the first rendering pass and writes fragment data in the
second. The transparent geometry drawn to the LFB in `render()` is then
blended into the scene, rendering a full-screen triangle. The fragment shader of
`transparencyProgram` calls `loadFragments()` and `sortFragments()`, defined in `"lfb.h"`, providing an array of sorted fragments to be blended.

We store the linearized LFB offset table and data in buffer objects and bind them
to `ARB_shader_image_load_store` image units via `glTexBuffer` for shader access. Memory barriers must be set between each LFB algorithm step and parallel
prefix sum pass with `glMemoryBarrier(GL_SHADER_IMAGE_ACCESS_BARRIER_`
`BIT)`. Memory barriers force previous operations on memory to finish before further operations start. This stops, for example, prefix sums from being computed
before the fragment-count pass has finished writing the results.

Fragment counts can be calculated in step 2 using either atomic increments or additive blending. Blending can be faster but is not supported with integer textures, so
either the prefix sums must be performed with floats or a copy is required. Care must
be taken to structure the implementation such that the fragment count between rendering passes matches exactly. For example, entire triangles intersecting the near- and
far-clipping planes are rasterized. We ignore fragments outside the clipping planes
by forcing the early depth test with `layout(early_fragment_tests) in;`.

If blending is used, the offset table can be zeroed with `glClear`. If blending is not used, zeroing a buffer object can be accomplished quickly using `glCopyBuffer SubData` to copy a preallocated block of zeroed memory. This gives a small performance boost over writing zeros from shaders, at the cost of additional memory overhead.

The prefix sums can be computed in a vertex shader by calling `glDraw Arrays(GL_POINTS, 0, n)` without client state attributes being bound. `gl_ VertexID` can be used as the thread ID for the computation. Enabling `GL_ RASTERIZER_DISCARD` prevents the point primitives proceeding to rasterization.

When reading the total fragment count during the prefix sums step, both `glGet BufferSubData` and `glMapBufferRange` are slow when operating directly on the offset table. As a workaround, we copy the total fragment count into a one-integer buffer and read from that instead. The same phenomenon occurs when reading the linked-list LFB atomic counter.

When rendering transparency, we sort the fragments in a local array in the shader, as access to global video memory is relatively slow. This imposes the limitation of a maximum number of fragments per pixel because the size of the local array is set at compile time. Saving the sorted data (or sorting in place for small depth complexities) may be beneficial for other applications that read fragments many times, for example, raycasting. The $O(n \log n)$ sorting algorithms perform worse than $O(n^2)$ algorithms for small n; the fastest sorting algorithm tested was insertion sort for up to 32 fragments. This is discussed further in Section 20.5.

We have found that shaders reading empty LFB fragment lists take an unexpectedly long time, so the stencil buffer is used to mask empty pixels. This provides a performance boost, especially when a significant fraction of the viewport is empty. We believe the cause is related to a slowdown from relatively large local arrays, in this case, the sorting array, for reasons about which we are uncertain.

20.5   Performance Results

We have implemented the brute force, linearized, linked-list, and linked-pages LFBs. Transparency is used as a benchmark, as other authors have done [Yang et al. 10, Crassin 10]. We compare performance and show that linearized and linked-list LFBs are competitive packing techniques. All timing experiments were performed using a Geforce GTX 460 at 1920 × 1080 resolution.

Updates to the OpenGL 4.2 implementation (late 2011) provide fast atomic counters. As such, there is no longer significant overhead from the atomic contention that originally hindered the linked-list approach. The basic linked-list LFB now performs better than the linked-pages variant [Crassin 10].

Two meshes, the dragon and atrium shown in Figures 20.7 and 20.8, are rendered to detail each algorithm's step times, given in Table 20.1. These scenes were chosen for their differing viewport coverage and depth complexities, shown in Figure 20.9.

Figure 20.7. The Stanford dragon model, 871,414 triangles, striped to better show transparency. 1.3M total fragments.

Reading and sorting LFB data quickly becomes the bottleneck with more fragments. A goal in linearizing the LFB data is to give better memory access patterns; however, we observe little performance benefit from the sequential access. Both techniques perform similarly for these scenes, to within 10% of each other.

Figure 20.8. Sponza atrium by Frank Meinl, 279,095 triangles. 17.5M total fragments.

Algorithm step	Dragon		Atrium	
	L	LL	L	LL
Zero tables or pointers	0.02	3.0	0.02	3.00
Fragment count render	3.97		10.60	
Compute prefix sums	4.47		4.67	
Main LFB render	3.79	5.99	30.00	30.99
Read & blend fragments	8.52	10.16	95.05	88.08
Sort in shader	1.3	0.93	43.68	42.14
Total	22.07ms	20.10ms	177.05ms	171.24ms

Table 20.1. Linearized (L) and linked-list (LL) LFB algorithm step times.

Results vary considerably depending on resolution and viewing direction compared to typical rasterization using the depth buffer. To better investigate these variables, we use a synthetic scene of transparent, layered tessellated grids, as shown in Figure 20.10. An orthographic projection is used, and the grid size, layers, and tessellation are varied. A linear relationship between rendering time and total fragments is observed in Figure 20.11, where fragments are increased by scaling ten layers of 20K triangle grids to fill the viewport. Rendering more grid layers to increase the total fragments gives similar results. The brute force LFB is faster than other techniques, although it has much higher memory requirements. The rendering times in the synthetic scene broadly match that of the dragon and atrium for their fragment counts.

Depth complexity, or rather, fragment distribution, impacts sorting performance significantly. In Figure 20.12, the linearized LFB is used to render increasing grid layers while reducing the viewport coverage, keeping the total fragments (8M) and

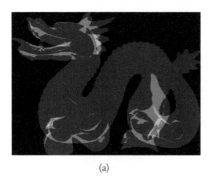

(a)

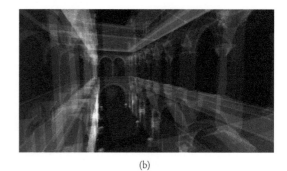

(b)

Figure 20.9. Depth complexities where black represents 0 fragments and white represents (a) 8 fragments and (b) 32 fragments.

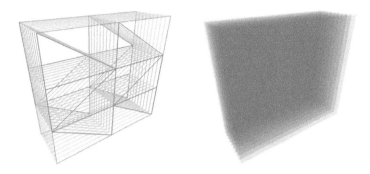

Figure 20.10. Transparent layered grids of polygons.

polygons (500–1000) approximately constant. Rendering times are similar for both linearized and linked-list LFBs, as sorting is a common operation. The sorting time becomes dominant after approximately 50 layers. Simply declaring and populating the sorting array (no sorting) with 256 **vec4** elements causes a 3–4× slowdown, compared to blending unsorted fragments directly from video memory (no local array). As expected, $O(n^2)$ insertion sort is faster for small n, for example, in the dragon and atrium scenes. We expect most scenes to have similar depth complexities; however, more complex scenes will benefit from $O(n \log n)$ sorting algorithms.

In terms of memory requirements, the overhead for the linearized LFB is the offset table, whereas the overhead for the linked-list LFB is both *head* and *next* pointers. In general, the linked-list LFB uses $\approx$ 25% more memory than the linearized LFB from the addition of **next** pointers, assuming 16 bytes of data per fragment.

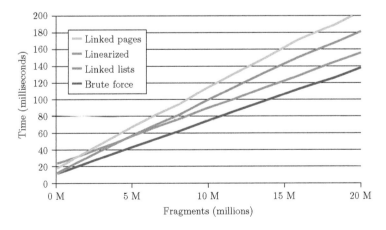

Figure 20.11. Comparing rendering times for different LFB techniques.

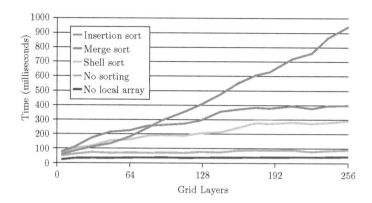

Figure 20.12. Varying depth complexity.

For 1920 × 1080 resolution, offsets are 8MB—in this case, 92KB more than **head** pointers, but potentially up to two times larger.

20.6   Conclusion

We have presented a comparison of linearized and linked-list LFBs, and results show both perform similarly for transparency. An expectation regarding the linearized LFB was that the sequential data layout would provide faster memory access. At this stage, this has not been observed to significantly affect the performance of transparency rendering.

The concept of capturing all output during rasterization, for example, in REYES [Carpenter 84], is well known, and the ability to do so in real time is becoming practical. In this chapter, we have focused on transparency; however, there are many applications that become possible or could be improved with the LFB. Screen-space effects such as ambient occlusion, indirect illumination [Yang et al. 10], motion blur, and depth of field suffer inaccuracies from missing data behind the front layer. Correct refraction and reflection [Davis and Wyman 07] require raycasting through multilayer data. Relief imposters [Hardy and Venter 10] produce incorrect results for concave objects, a problem that could be solved with the LFB.

Bibliography

[Bavoil and Myers 08] Louis Bavoil and Kevin Myers. "Order Independent Transparency with Dual Depth Peeling." Technical report, NVIDIA Corporation, 2008.

[Bavoil et al. 07] Louis Bavoil, Steven P. Callahan, Aaron Lefohn, João L. D. Comba, and Cláudio T. Silva. "Multi-Fragment Effects on the GPU Using the k-Buffer." In *Proceed-*

ings of the 2007 Symposium on Interactive 3D Graphics and Games, I3D '07, pp. 97–104. New York: ACM, 2007.

[Carpenter 84] Loren Carpenter. "The A-Buffer, an Antialiased Hidden Surface Method." *SIGGRAPH Computer Graphics* 18 (1984), 103–108.

[Crassin 10] Cyril Crassin. "Icare3D Blog: Linked Lists of Fragment Pages." http://blog. icare3d.org/2010/07/opengl-40-abuffer-v20-linked-lists-of.html, 2010.

[Davis and Wyman 07] Scott T Davis and Chris Wyman. "Interactive refractions with total internal reflection." In *Proceedings of Graphics Interface 2007, GI '07*, pp. 185–190. New York: ACM, 2007. Available online (http://doi.acm.org.ezproxy.lib.rmit.edu.au/ 10.1145/1268517.1268548).

[Everitt 01] Cass Everitt. "Interactive Order-Independent Transparency." Technical report, NVIDIA Corporation, 2001.

[Hardy and Venter 10] Alexandre Hardy and Johannes Venter. "3-View Impostors." In *Proceedings of the 7th International Conference on Computer Graphics, Virtual Reality, Visualisation and Interaction in Africa, AFRIGRAPH '10*, pp. 129–138. New York: ACM, 2010. Available online (http://doi.acm.org/10.1145/1811158.1811180).

[Harris et al. 07] Mark Harris, Shubhabrata Sengupta, and John D. Owens. "Parallel Prefix Sum (Scan) with CUDA." In *GPU Gems 3*, edited by Hubert Nguyen, Chapter 39, pp. 851–876. Reading, MA: Addison Wesley, 2007.

[Korostelev 10] Eugene Korostelev. "Order-Independent Transparency on the GPU Using Dynamic Lists." UralDev Programming Contest Articles 4, http://www.uraldev.ru/ articles/id/36, 2010.

[Ladner and Fischer 80] Richard E. Ladner and Michael J. Fischer. "Parallel Prefix Computation." *Journal of the ACM* 27 (1980), 831–838.

[Lipowski 10] Jarosław Konrad Lipowski. "Multi-Layered Framebuffer Condensation: The l-Buffer Concept." In *Proceedings of the 2010 International Conference on Computer Vision and Graphics: Part II, ICCVG'10*, pp. 89–97. Berlin, Heidelberg: Springer-Verlag, 2010.

[Lipowski 11] Jarosław Konrad Lipowski. "d-Buffer: Letting a Third Dimension Back In..." http://jkl.name/~jkl/rnd/, 2011.

[Liu et al. 09a] Fang Liu, Meng-Cheng Huang, Xue-Hui Liu, and En-Hua Wu. "Efficient Depth Peeling via Bucket Sort." In *Proceedings of the Conference on High Performance Graphics 2009, HPG '09*, pp. 51–57. New York: ACM, 2009.

[Liu et al. 09b] Fang Liu, Meng-Cheng Huang, Xue-Hui Liu, and En-Hua Wu. "Single Pass Depth Peeling via CUDA Rasterizer." In *SIGGRAPH 2009: Talks, SIGGRAPH '09*, pp. 79:1–79:1. New York: ACM, 2009. Available online (http://doi.acm.org/10.1145/ 1597990.1598069).

[Mammen 89] A. Mammen. "Transparency and Antialiasing Algorithms Implemented with the Virtual Pixel Maps Technique." *Computer Graphics and Applications, IEEE* 9:4 (1989), 43–55.

[Microsoft Corporation 10] Microsoft Corporation. "DirectX Software Development Kit Sample." http://msdn.microsoft.com, 2010.

[Wei and Xu 06] Li-Yi Wei and Ying-Qing Xu. "Multi-Layer Depth Peeling via Fragment Sort." Technical report, Microsoft Research, 2006.

[Yang et al. 10] Jason C. Yang, Justin Hensley, Holger Grün, and Nicolas Thibieroz. "Real-Time Concurrent Linked List Construction on the GPU." *Computer Graphics Forum* 29:4 (2010), 1297–1304. Available online (http://dblp.uni-trier.de/db/journals/cgf/cgf29.html#YangHGT10).

Programmable Vertex Pulling   21

Daniel Rákos

21.1 Introduction

OpenGL and today's GPUs provide a high degree of flexibility for acquiring geometry-related information from auxiliary buffers using the shader built-in constants provided by GLSL based on data granularity. The name `gl_VertexID` provides the index of the currently processed vertex, `gl_PrimitiveID`, which provides the index of the currently processed geometric primitive, and `gl_InstanceID` provides the index of the currently processed instance of an instanced draw command. Still, there are restrictions on how object information can be passed to the graphics pipeline if we use traditional methods for specifying geometric information using attribute arrays and an optional element array.

This chapter explores the possibility of taking advantage of some of the latest GPU technologies to provide a method that enables completely programmable *vertex pulling*, i.e., a programmable approach to fetch vertex attributes.

The possibility of implementing programmable vertex pulling has been available in OpenGL and in hardware for some time now, but this technique is rarely used in practice. The main reason behind this is that developers assume that fixed-functionality vertex pulling uses dedicated hardware to execute this task and thus can provide better performance.

However, OpenGL 3.x–capable hardware's unified architecture shows that fixed-function vertex pulling has to go through the very same hardware path that programmable buffer fetching does, including the cache hierarchy that is shared among all fetching units, including attribute, buffer, and texture fetches.

The main goal of this chapter is to implement a simple programmable vertex pulling shader with a sample vertex attribute setup and compare its performance with a setup that uses fixed-function vertex attribute fetching to demonstrate the performance characteristics of programmable vertex pulling.

Further, I will present common use cases where programmable vertex pulling can provide additional flexibility and/or performance over the traditional approaches.

21.2   Implementation

The core of the implementation of programmable vertex pulling is built around the functionality provided by *buffer textures* [Brown 08]. These textures provide a method that allows every shader stage to fetch arbitrary data from buffer objects. Trivially, this functionality alone is enough to implement programmable vertex pulling, as the only change that has to be made compared to fixed-function vertex pulling is that all vertex attributes and, optionally, the indices are manually fetched in the vertex shader.

I will distinguish two types of programmable vertex pulling methods:

1. Programmable attribute fetching. In this case, we will still use fixed-function indexed primitive rendering, but the vertex attributes will be manually fetched in the vertex shader.

2. Fully programmable vertex pulling. Vertex indexing will be done in the vertex shader together with the vertex attribute fetching.

In our sample implementation, we use a simple vertex attribute setup of 32 bytes/vertex (3 floats for position, 3 floats for normal, and 2 floats for texture coordinates) all stored in an interleaved buffer format. In the case of fixed-function vertex pulling, we use an element array for *indexed primitive rendering*. In the case of our programmable vertex pulling implementation, the element array will be fed to the vertex shader as the only vertex attribute array, and we will implement indexed primitive rendering programmatically in the vertex shader (i.e., fully programmable vertex pulling).

The vertex shader used for both fixed-function and programmable vertex pulling is presented in Listing 21.1, where the preprocessor directive PROGRAMMABLE is defined only in the case of the latter. The shader transforms the vertex position into clip space, the normal to view space, and passes them together with the texture coordinate set to subsequent stages of the rendering pipeline.

Obviously, the client-side code setup for the vertex arrays and the buffer textures is different in both cases. This is presented in Listing 21.2 using the same preprocessor directive for selecting between the two rendering paths.

Now, in this example, there is no additional flexibility provided by programmable vertex pulling; however, if the information required by the vertex shader is not

```
#version 420 core

layout(std140, binding = 0) uniform transform {
    mat3 NormalMatrix;
    mat4 MVPMatrix;
} Transform;

#ifdef PROGRAMMABLE
layout(location = 0) in int inIndex;
layout(binding = 0) uniform samplerBuffer attribBuffer;
#else
layout(location = 0) in vec3 inVertexPosition;
layout(location = 1) in vec3 inVertexNormal;
layout(location = 2) in vec2 inVertexTexCoord;
#endif

layout out vec3 outVertexNormal;
layout out vec2 outVertexTexCoord;

out gl_PerVertex {
    vec4 gl_Position;
};

void main(void) {
#ifdef PROGRAMMABLE
    vec4 attrib0 = texelFetch(attribBuffer, inIndex * 2);
    vec4 attrib1 = texelFetch(attribBuffer, inIndex * 2 + 1);
    vec3 inVertexPosition = attrib0.xyz;
    vec3 inVertexNormal = vec3(attrib0.w, attrib1.xy);
    vec2 inVertexTexCoord = attrib1.zw;
#endif
    gl_Position = MVPMatrix * vec4(inVertexPosition, 1.f);
    outVertexNormal = NormalMatrix * inVertexNormal;
    outVertexTexCoord = inVertexTexCoord;
}
```

Listing 21.1. Sample vertex shader that can perform fixed-function or programmable vertex pulling.

```
#ifdef PROGRAMMABLE
/* setup index buffer as the only vertex attribute */
    glBindBuffer(GL_ARRAY_BUFFER, indexBuffer);
    glEnableVertexAttribArray(0);
    glVertexAttribIPointer(0, 1, GL_INT, 4, NULL);
/* configure the buffer texture to use the vertex attribute buffer as storage */
    glBindTexture(GL_TEXTURE_BUFFER, bufferTexture);
    glTexBuffer(GL_TEXTURE_BUFFER, GL_RGBA32F, vertexBuffer);
#else
/* use the index buffer as element array buffer */
    glBindBuffer(GL_ELEMENT_ARRAY_BUFFER, indexBuffer);
/* use the vertex buffer to set up interleaved vertex attributes */
    glBindBuffer(GL_ARRAY_BUFFER, vertexBuffer);
    glEnableVertexAttribArray(0);
    glVertexAttribPointer(0, 3, GL_FLOAT, GL_FALSE, 32, 0);
    glEnableVertexAttribArray(1);
    glVertexAttribPointer(1, 3, GL_FLOAT, GL_FALSE, 32, 12);
    glEnableVertexAttribArray(2);
    glVertexAttribPointer(2, 2, GL_FLOAT, GL_FALSE, 32, 24);
#endif
```

Listing 21.2. Client-side configuration of the vertex attributes for fixed-function and programmable vertex pulling.

different for every vertex, programmable vertex pulling can be advantageous. Fixed-function vertex pulling provides a mechanism via instanced arrays [Helferty et al. 08] that makes it possible to fetch some vertex attributes with a smaller frequency than every vertex, but it is limited to the possibility of fetching new attributes at every nth instance. With programmable vertex pulling, this frequency can be arbitrary.

One can use the built-in shader variables `gl_VertexID`, `gl_PrimitiveID`, and `gl_InstanceID` to control the rate of attribute fetches, but on OpenGL 4.x–capable hardware, even nonuniform fetching frequencies can be achieved by using custom shader logic and *atomic counters* [Licea-Kane et al. 11].

21.3   Performance

One of the preconceptions that scares off developers from using programmable vertex pulling where traditional fixed-function vertex pulling is simply not flexible enough to solve a particular problem is performance. In order to falsify this preconception, I've executed some tests that reveal the strengths and weaknesses and the relative performance of programmable vertex pulling compared to the fixed functionality. The tests were executed on OpenGL 3– and OpenGL 4–capable GPUs from different vendors and use the Stanford Dragon and Buddha models consisting of 871,414 and 1,087,716 indexed triangles, respectively.

The tests use the vertex shader and client-side setup presented in Listing 21.1 and Listing 21.2. In the case of fixed-function vertex pulling and programmable attribute fetching, we render the models using a single `glDrawElements` call, while in the case of fully programmable vertex pulling, the `glDrawArrays` command is used because, in this case, we don't intend to utilize fixed-function indexed primitive rendering.

The measurements have been done so that we can eliminate all the fragment processing overhead by rendering the models outside the view frustum, as we are primarily aiming to measure vertex-processing cost differences between the three techniques. We use timer queries [Daniell 10] to measure the GPU time required to render the models (see Figure 21.1). Unfortunately, based on our tests, timer queries return very dissimilar values in the case of the two hardware vendors, which may be either the result of driver implementation or hardware architecture differences. However, as we are only interested in the relative performance of the three vertex pulling techniques, this does not really affect us.

Table 21.1 shows that programmable attribute fetching is as fast as fixed-function vertex pulling on modern GPUs, even though we may have expected a slight performance penalty because of the possible additional latency incurred by performing the vertex attribute fetching inside the vertex shader. This shows us that the sophisticated latency-hiding mechanisms of current GPUs eliminate this cost.

The picture is a bit less bright when using fully programmable vertex pulling, though the Radeons provide acceptable performance there as well. The reason behind

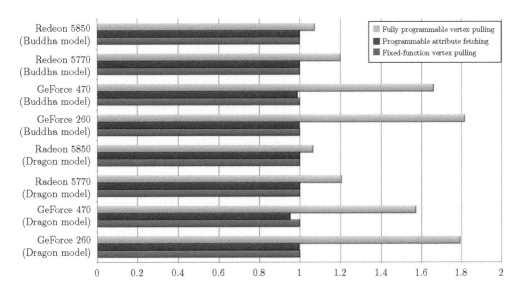

Figure 21.1. Relative GPU time of rendering the Stanford Dragon and Buddha models on various GPUs using programmable vertex pulling compared to fixed-function vertex pulling (lower values are better).

the performance penalty for fully programmable vertex pulling is the fact that it cannot take advantage of the *post-transform cache*, which can greatly increase the speed of indexed primitive rendering. I have to also mention that the models were not optimized for maximum post-transform cache usage, so the time difference may be even higher in real-life scenarios. The advantage of the Radeon GPUs when

GPU	Model	Fixed-function vertex pulling	Programmable attribute fetching		Fully programmable vertex pulling	
GPU time		**Absolute**	**Absolute**	**Relative**	**Absolute**	**Relative**
GeForce 260	Dragon	3.291 ms	3.281 ms	-0.3 %	5.902 ms	+79.3 %
(GL3)	Buddha	4.056 ms	4.047 ms	-0.2 %	7.366 ms	+81.6 %
GeForce 470	Dragon	0.786 ms	0.748 ms	-4.8 %	1.234 ms	+57.0 %
(GL4)	Buddha	0.928 ms	0.918 ms	-1.1 %	1.540 ms	+65.9 %
Radeon 5770	Dragon	10.287 ms	10.288 ms	0.0 %	12.393 ms	+20.5 %
(GL4)	Buddha	13.377 ms	13.381 ms	0.0 %	16.034 ms	+19.9 %
Radeon 5850	Dragon	8.896 ms	8.897 ms	0.0 %	9.471 ms	+6.5 %
(GL4)	Buddha	11.177 ms	11.177 ms	0.0 %	12.009 ms	+7.4 %

Table 21.1. Absolute and relative GPU time for rendering the Stanford Dragon and Buddha models on various GPUs using programmable vertex pulling compared to fixed-function vertex pulling (lower values are better).

using fully programmable vertex pulling makes me believe that AMD GPUs are less dependent on efficient post-transform cache usage.

Based on the results, my verdict is that programmable vertex pulling has no overhead compared to fixed-function vertex pulling in the following cases:

- When rendering nonindexed primitives (e.g., triangle strips).

- When rendering indexed primitives using fixed-function index handling.

While programmable index handling is also an option, when the meshes rely heavily on the usage of the post-transform cache, the performance of fully programmable vertex pulling can be prohibitive.

21.4   Application

We've already mentioned that programmable vertex pulling can enable us to control the frequency of vertex attribute consumption. This means that we can, for example, pass normals on a per-triangle basis instead of per-vertex; in a similar fashion, we can select a single layer of a texture array, again, on a per-primitive basis. Additionally, there might be attributes that have to be consumed from the attribute buffer only in certain cases, in which case, we can use an atomic counter to supervise our current position in the buffer. This can decrease memory size and bandwidth requirements of storing and fetching attributes, thus resulting in better overall performance.

Programmable vertex pulling can handle interleaved and separate data buffers as well, but it also makes possible the use of arbitrary data structures to store the vertex attributes or other information that may be needed by the vertex shader. This can include even multiple indirections, though performance may be a concern when doing an excessive number of buffer lookup indirections. This also enables the possibility of handling multiple vertex formats in a single vertex shader and thus can reduce the number of vertex format setups at the cost of a fairly low runtime overhead in most cases. While at the time of this, writing OpenGL does not support structure fetches, the introduction of POD (plain old data structure) fetches can further simplify the use of programmable vertex pulling in these cases.

Another application of programmable vertex pulling can be attribute-less rendering. This can come handy when rendering simple primitives like full-screen triangles for postprocessing or simple light-volume primitive rendering in the case of deferred rendering methods, but it can also be used to dynamically generate parametric curves and surfaces in the vertex shader. Neither of these require any vertex attribute arrays, as all of them can be implemented using a few uniform variables as parameters. Considering that ALU capacity is usually higher than memory bandwidth, programmable vertex pulling can greatly increase the rendering performance in these situations.

Besides performance-critical applications, where certain types of data structures would simply not be feasible, CAD software can benefit from programmable vertex pulling. CAD software, depending on the target domain, uses various data structures for storing the topology of the mesh internally. These internal representations can be based on, e.g., the winged edge model [Baumgart 75], quad-edge data structure [Guibas and Stolfi 85], combinatorial maps or boundary representation models. As CAD software, in general, uses fixed-function vertex pulling, it usually has to maintain two copies of the data, one for internal usage and one for rendering. Taking advantage of programmable vertex pulling can potentially eliminate the need for the second copy by enabling the rendering pipeline to parse and display the mesh data in its original form, used internally by the CAD software.

21.5 Limitations

The biggest issue with fully programmable vertex pulling is that we cannot take advantage of the post-transform vertex cache that otherwise greatly increases the speed of indexed primitive rendering. In order to take advantage of this optimization, we require new hardware and APIs to be able to explicitly tag vertices emitted by a vertex shader invocation.

In fixed-function vertex pulling, this is done up front by tagging the vertices with their indices. My proposal is to introduce a new output parameter called `gl_VertexTag` to the vertex shader language that would be used by the post-transform vertex cache to tag the received vertices. While this approach would still not allow us to discard vertices that are already processed on a wavefront, in practice, it could potentially increase the performance of fully programmable vertex pulling to as close as possible to the speed of its fixed-function counterpart. This feature would also allow the post-transform cache to function efficiently in other cases where the system disables it because the vertex shader can have side effects, as in the case where the vertex shader uses atomic counters or load/store images [Bolz et al. 11].

Another approach to optimize programmable vertex pulling in the case of programmatically indexed primitives is to implement a sort of post-transform vertex cache in the vertex shader. This option is actually possible using OpenGL 4.2 by taking advantage of atomic counters and load/store images to store already processed vertices, although the performance of such an approach may still be much lower than that of the fixed-function post-transform vertex cache.

A further limitation of programmable vertex pulling is that manual format conversion may be needed in the vertex shader when we would like to use interleaved attribute arrays that contain attributes with multiple different data formats. For such cases, our proposal is to attach the same buffer object to multiple buffer textures using different internal formats and access the appropriate buffer texture in the vertex shader that is as close to the target format as possible to minimize the ALU cost required to convert the values to the intended representation.

21.6   Conclusion

Based on the performance results, I can say that programmable attribute fetching is a viable alternative to fixed-function vertex pulling even in the case when the fixed-function method could be applied as well, considering that there is no latency incurred by manual attribute fetching on most GPUs. However, the strength of programmable vertex pulling appears when storing the attributes in a structure that is suitable for traditional rendering is simply not feasible due to the size of the data set or in cases in which we already have an internal representation that we would like to work with that does not map well to any of the fixed-function attribute-specification methods.

As we've seen, it is pretty straightforward to implement programmable vertex pulling using the existing tool set provided by OpenGL, and the required hardware is only an OpenGL 3.x–capable GPU, though a much greater level of flexibility is available on OpenGL 4.x–capable GPUs. Actually, in theory, even earlier GPUs can take advantage of this technique if they support vertex texture fetches by storing the vertex attributes in a traditional 1D texture.

I've also shown that programmable vertex pulling can only be prohibitive from a performance point of view if we are using programmable indexed primitive rendering, as in this case the lack of post-transform vertex cache utilization can dramatically decrease the performance. I also proposed a few possible solutions to circumvent this issue.

Finally, I also discussed a few potential applications of the presented technique, both regarding interactive rendering and CAD software, and I also discussed the key limitations of programmable vertex pulling compared to its fixed-function counterpart.

There is need for a much longer and more in-depth study in order to be able to get a better picture of the capabilities and weaknesses of programmable vertex pulling, although I hope that this brief preview of the technique's potential captures the attention of readers to seek and find their own best use cases for it.

Bibliography

[Baumgart 75] Bruce G. Baumgart. "Winged-Edge Polyhedron Representation for Computer Vision." National Computer Conference, 1975.

[Bolz et al. 11] Jeff Bolz, Pat Brown, Barthold Lichtenbelt, Bill Licea-Kane, Eric Werness, Graham Sellers, Greg Roth, Nick Haemel, Pierre Boudier, and Piers Daniell. "ARB_shader_image_load_store." OpenGL extension specification, 2011.

[Brown 08] Pat Brown. "ARB_texture_buffer_object." OpenGL extension specification, 2008.

[Daniell 10] Piers Daniell. "ARB_timer_query." OpenGL extension specification, 2010.

[Guibas and Stolfi 85] Leonidas J. Guibas and Jorge Stolfi. "Primitives for the Manipulation of General Subdivisions and the Computation of Voronoi Diagrams." *ACM Transactions on Graphics*, New York: ACM Press, 1985.

[Helferty et al. 08] James Helferty, Daniel Koch, Michael Gold, and John Rosasco. "ARB_instanced_arrays." OpenGL extension specification, 2008.

[Licea-Kane et al. 11] Bill Licea-Kane, Barthold Lichtenbelt, Chris Dodd, Eric Werness, Graham Sellers, Greg Roth, Jeff Bolz, Nick Haemel, Pat Brown, Pierre Boudier, and Piers Daniell. "ARB_shader_atomic_counters." OpenGL extension specification, 2011.

Octree-Based Sparse Voxelization Using the GPU Hardware Rasterizer

22

Cyril Crassin and Simon Green

22.1 Introduction

Discrete voxel representations are generating growing interest in a wide range of applications in computational sciences and particularly in computer graphics. Applications range from fluid simulation [Crane et al. 05], collision detection [Allard et al. 10], and radiative transfer simulation to detail rendering [Crassin et al. 09, Crassin et al. 10, Laine and Karras 10] and real-time global illumination [Kaplanyan and Dachsbacher 10, Thiedemann et al. 11, Crassin et al. 11]. When used in real-time contexts, it becomes critical to achieve fast *3D scan conversion* (also called *voxelization*) of traditional triangle-based surface representations [Eisemann and Décoret 08, Schwarz and Seidel 10, Pantaleoni 11].

In this chapter, we will first describe an efficient OpenGL implementation of a simple surface voxelization algorithm that produces a regular 3D texture (see Figure 22.1). This technique uses the GPU hardware rasterizer and the new image load/store interface exposed by OpenGL 4.2. This section will allow us to familiarize the reader with the general algorithm and the new OpenGL features we leverage.

In the second part, we will describe an extension of this approach, which enables building and updating a sparse voxel representation in the form of an octree structure. In order to scale to very large scenes, our approach avoids relying on an intermediate-full regular grid to build the structure and constructs the octree directly. This second approach exploits the draw indirect features standardized in OpenGL 4.0 in order to allow synchronization-free launching of shader threads during the octree construction, as well as the new *atomic counter* functions exposed in OpenGL 4.2.

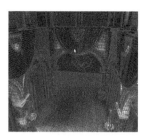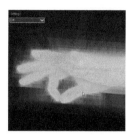

Figure 22.1. Real-time voxelization of dynamic objects into a sparse voxel octree (Wald's hand 16K triangles mesh voxelized sparsely in approximately 5.5 ms) and use of the technique for a voxel-based global illumination application.

One of our main motivations in this work has been to investigate the usability of the hardware graphics pipeline for fast and real-time voxelization. We will compare the performance of our approach to the recent work of Pantaleoni [Pantaleoni 11], which uses CUDA for regular-grid thin voxelization, and detail the performance of our sparse-octree building approach. A typical real-time usage of our dynamic voxelization inside a sparse voxel octree has been demonstrated recently as part of the voxel-based global illumination approach described in [Crassin et al. 11].

22.2   Previous Work

Previous work on 3D voxelization makes a distinction between two kinds of surface voxelization: *thin voxelization*, which is a *6-separating* representation of a surface (cf. [Huang et al. 98]) and fully *conservative voxelization*, where all voxels overlapped by a surface are activated, or *26-separating* (Figure 22.2). Although our method could easily be extended to fully conservative voxelization, in this chapter we will only describe the case of thin voxelization. Thin voxelization is cheaper to compute and is often more desirable in computer graphics applications.

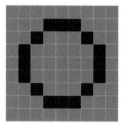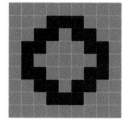

Figure 22.2. Examples of a 4-separating (left) and an 8-separating (right) 2D line rasterization equivalent to 6-separating and 26-separating surface voxelizations in 3D.

In recent years, many algorithms have been proposed that exploit GPUs by performing triangle mesh voxelization. Early approaches used the fixed-function pipeline found in commodity graphics hardware of the time. Previous hardware-based approaches [Fang et al. 00, Crane et al. 05, Li et al. 05] were relatively inefficient and suffered from quality problems. Due to the lack of random write access, these approaches had to use a multipass rendering technique, processing the volume slice by slice and retransforming the entire geometry with each pass. In contrast, [Dong et al. 04, Zhang et al. 07, Eisemann and Décoret 08] process multiple slices at a time by encoding voxel grids with a compact binary representation, achieving higher performance but limited to binary voxelization (only storing a single bit to represent an occupied voxel).

Newer voxelization approaches take advantage of the freedom offered by the *compute mode* (CUDA or OpenCL) available on modern GPUs [Schwarz and Seidel 10, Pantaleoni 11]. Instead of building on the fixed-function hardware, these approaches propose pure data-parallel algorithms, providing more flexibility and allowing new original voxelization schemes like direct voxelization into a *sparse octree*. However, using only the compute mode of the GPU means that these approaches don't take advantage of the powerful fixed-function graphics units, particularly the hardware rasterizer, that effectively provide a very fast point-in-triangle test function and sampling operation. With increasing industry focus on power efficiency for mobile devices, utilizing efficient fixed-function hardware is increasingly important. Our method combines the advantages of both approaches, taking advantage of the fast fixed-function graphics units while requiring only a single geometry pass and allowing sparse voxelization thanks to the most recent evolutions of the GPU hardware.

22.3 Unrestricted Memory Access in GLSL

Previous graphics-based approaches (not using compute) were limited by the fact that all memory write operations had to be done through the ROP (fragment operation) hardware, which does not allow random access and 3D-addressing because only the current pixel could be written. Recently, the programming model offered by OpenGL shaders has changed dramatically, with GLSL shaders acquiring the ability to generate side effects and to dynamically address arbitrary buffers and textures, for example, the OpenGL 4.2 specification standardized *image units* access in GLSL (previously exposed through the `EXT_shader_image_load_store` extension). This feature, only available on Shader Model 5 (SM5) hardware, gives us the ability to perform read/write access as well as atomic read-modify-write operations into a single mipmap level of a texture from any GLSL shader stage. Beyond textures, linear memory regions (*buffer objects* stored in GPU global memory) can also be easily accessed with this feature using "buffer textures" bound to a GLSL `imageBuffer`.

In addition, the NVIDIA-specific extensions `NV_shader_buffer_load` and `NV_shader_buffer_store` (supported on Fermi-class SM5 hardware), provide similar functionality on linear memory regions, but they do this through C-like pointers in GLSL, and the ability to query the global memory address of any buffer object. This approach simplifies the access to buffer objects and allows arbitrary numbers of discontinuous memory regions (different buffer objects) to be accessed from the same shader invocation, while only a limited number of image units can be accessed by a given shader (this number is implementation dependent and can be queried using `GL_MAX_IMAGE_UNITS`).

These new features dramatically change the computation model of GPU shaders and give us the ability to write algorithms with much of the same flexibility as CUDA or OpenCL, while still taking advantage of the fast fixed-function hardware.

22.4   Simple Voxelization Pipeline

In this section we will present an initial simple approach to directly voxelize into a regular grid of voxels stored in a 3D texture. Our voxelization pipeline is based on the observation that, as shown in [Schwarz and Seidel 10], a *thin surface voxelization* of a triangle B can be computed for each voxel V by testing if (1) B's plane intersects V, (2) the 2D projection of the triangle B along the dominant axis of its normal (one of the three main axes of the scene that provides the largest surface for the projected triangle) intersects the 2D projection of V.

Based on this observation, we propose a very simple voxelization algorithm that operates in four main steps inside a single draw call (illustrated in Figure 22.3). First, each triangle of the mesh is projected orthographically along the dominant axis of its normal, which is the one of the three main axes of the scene that maximizes the projected area and thus maximizes the number of fragments that will be generated during the conservative rasterization. This projection axis is chosen dynamically on a per-triangle basis inside a geometry shader (see Figure 22.4), where information about the three vertices of the triangle is available. For each triangle, the selected axis

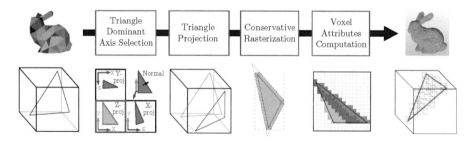

Figure 22.3. Illustration of our simple voxelization pipeline.

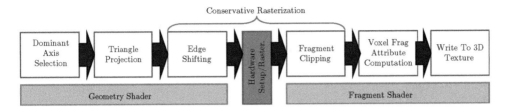

Figure 22.4. Implementation of our voxelization pipeline on top of the GPU rasterization pipeline.

is the one that provides the maximum value for $l_{\{x,y,z\}} = |\mathbf{n} \cdot \mathbf{v}_{\{x,y,z\}}|$, with $\mathbf{n}$ the triangle normal and $\mathbf{v}_{\{x,y,z\}}$ the three main axes of the scene. Once the axis selected, the projection along this axis is simply a classical orthographic projection, and this is calculated inside the geometry shader.

Each projected triangle is fed into the standard setup and rasterization pipeline to perform 2D scan conversion (rasterization, see Figure 22.4). In order to get fragments corresponding to the 3D resolution of the destination (cubical) voxel grid, we set the 2D viewport resolution (glViewport(0, 0, x, y)) to correspond to lateral resolution of our voxel grid (for instance 512×512 pixels for a 512^3 voxel grid). Since we rely on image access instead of the standard ROP path to the framebuffer to write data into our voxel grid, all framebuffer operations are disabled, including depth writes, depth testing (glDisable(GL_DEPTH_TEST)) and color writes (glColorMask(GL_FALSE, GL_FALSE, GL_FALSE, GL_FALSE)).

During rasterization, each triangle generates a set of 2D fragments. Each of these fragments can correspond to the intersection of the triangle with one, two or three voxels along its direction of projection. Indeed, due to our choice of the dominant triangle axis for projection (and the use of cubic voxels), the depth range of a triangle across a 2D pixel can only span a maximum of three voxels in depth. For each 2D fragment, the voxels actually intersected by the triangle are computed within the fragment shader, based on position and depth information interpolated from vertices' values at the pixel center, as well as screen-space derivatives provided by GLSL (dFdx()/dFdy()).

This information is used to generate what we call *voxel fragments*. A voxel fragment is the 3D generalization of the classic 2D fragment and corresponds to a voxel intersected by a given triangle. Each voxel fragment has a 3D integer coordinate inside the destination voxel grid, as well as multiple attribute values.

Voxel-fragment attributes are usually a color, a normal, and any other useful attribute one would want to store per voxel, depending on the application. As usual, these values can be either interpolated on pixel centers from vertex attributes by the rasterization process or sampled from the traditional 2D surface textures of the model using interpolated texture coordinates. In our demo implementation, we only store one color value as well as one normal vector (used for shading during the rendering of the voxel grid) per voxel.

Finally, voxel fragments are written directly from the fragment shader into their corresponding voxel inside the destination 3D texture, where they must be combined. This is done using image load/store operations as detailed in Section 22.4.2.

22.4.1   Conservative Rasterization

Although it is very simple, this approach does not ensure a correct thin (6-separating planes [Schwarz and Seidel 10]) voxelization. This is due to the fact that only the coverage of the center of each pixel is tested against the triangles to generate fragments during the rasterization step. Thus, a more precise *conservative rasterization* must be employed to ensure that a fragment will be generated for each pixel touched by a triangle. The precision of the coverage test could be enhanced by relying on multisample antialiasing (MSAA), but this solution only delays the problem a little further and still misses fragments in the case of small triangles. Instead, and similarly to [Zhang et al. 07], we build upon the second conservative rasterization approach proposed in [Hasselgren et al. 05]. We will not detail the technique here, and we invite the reader to refer to [Hasselgren et al. 05] for more details.

The general idea is to generate, for each projected triangle, a slightly larger bounding polygon that ensures that any projected triangle touching a pixel will necessarily touch the center of this pixel and thus will get a fragment emitted by the fixed-function rasterizer. This is done by shifting each triangle edge outward in order to enlarge the triangle using the geometry shader (Figure 22.4). Since the exact bounding polygon that does not overestimate the coverage of a given triangle is not triangle-shaped (Figure 22.5), the excess fragments outside the bounding box are killed in the fragment shader after rasterization. This approach entails more work in the fragment shader but, in practice, is faster than computing and generating exactly the correct bounding polygon inside the geometry shader.

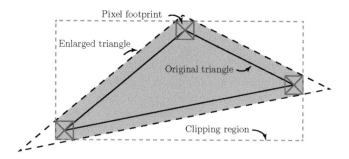

Figure 22.5. Bounding polygon of a triangle used for conservative rasterization.

22.4.2   Compositing Voxel Fragments

Once voxel-fragments have been generated in the fragment shader, their values can be written directly into the destination 3D texture using image load/store operations. However, multiple voxel fragments from different triangles can fall into the same destination voxel in arbitrary order. Since voxel fragments are created and processed in parallel, the order in which they will be written is not predictable, which leads to write-ordering issues and can create flickering and non–time-coherent results when dynamically revoxelizing a scene. In standard rasterization, this problem is handled by the ROP units, which ensure that fragments are composed in the framebuffer in the same order as their source primitives have been issued.

In our case, we have to rely on atomic operations. Atomic operations guarantee that the read-modify-write cycle is not interrupted by any other thread. When multiple voxel fragments end up on the same voxel, the most simple desirable behavior is averaging all incoming values. For specific applications, one may want to use more sophisticated combination schemes like coverage-based combination, but this goes beyond the scope of this chapter.

Averaging values using atomic operations.   To average all values falling into the same voxel, the simplest way is to first sum all values using an atomic add operation and then divide this sum by the total number of values in a subsequent pass. To do so, a counter must be maintained per voxel, and we rely on the *alpha channel* of the RGBA color values we store per voxel for this purpose.

However, image-atomic operations are restricted to 32-bit signed/unsigned integer types in OpenGL 4.2 specification, which will rarely correspond to the texel format used in the voxel grid. We generally want to store **RGBA8** or **RGBA16F/32F** color components per voxel. Thus, the **imageAtomicAdd** function cannot be used directly as is to do the summation.

We emulate an *atomic add* on such types by relying on a compare-and-swap **atomicCompSwap()** operation using the function detailed in Listing 22.1. The idea is to loop on each write until there are no more conflicts and the value, with which we have computed the sum has not been changed by another thread. This approach is a lot slower than a native **atomicAdd** would be but still allows a functionally correct behavior while waiting for the specification to evolve. On NVIDIA hardware, an **atomicCompSwap64** operating on 64-bit values can be used on global memory addresses (NV_shader_buffer_store), which allows us to cut by half the number of operations and thus provides a two times speedup over the cross-vendor path. Unfortunately, this process is not exposed for image access, which requires the voxel grid to be stored inside the global memory instead of the texture memory.

A second problem appears when using an **RGBA8** color format per voxel. With such a format, only 8 bits are available per color component, which quickly causes overflow problems when summing the values. Thus, the average must be computed incrementally each time a new voxel fragment is merged into a given voxel. To do

```
void imageAtomicFloatAdd(layout(r32ui) coherent volatile uimage3D imgUI, ivec3 ←
    coords, float val)
{
  uint newVal = floatBitsToUint(val);
  uint prevVal = 0; uint curVal;

  //Loop as long as destination value gets changed by other threads
  while( (curVal = imageAtomicCompSwap(imgUI, coords, prevVal, newVal)) != prevVal)
  {
    prevVal = curVal;
    newVal = floatBitsToUint((val + uintBitsToFloat(curVal)));
  }
}
```

Listing 22.1. AtomicAdd emulation on 32-bit floating point data type using a compare-and-swap operation.

this, we simply compute a *moving average* using the following formula:

$$C_{i+1} = \frac{iC_i + x_{i+1}}{i + 1}.$$

This can be done easily by slightly modifying the previous swap-based atomic add operation as shown in Listing 22.2. Note that this approach will only work if all data to be stored, including the counter, can be swapped together using one single atomic operation.

```
vec4 convRGBA8ToVec4(uint val){
  return vec4( float((val&0x000000FF)), float((val&0x0000FF00)>>8U), float((val&0←
    x00FF0000)>>16U), float((val&0xFF000000)>>24U) );
}
uint convVec4ToRGBA8(vec4 val){
  return (uint(val.w)&0x000000FF)<<24U | (uint(val.z)&0x000000FF)<<16U | (uint(val.y←
    )&0x000000FF)<<8U | (uint(val.x)&0x000000FF));
}

void imageAtomicRGBA8Avg(layout(r32ui) coherent volatile uimage3D imgUI, ivec3 ←
    coords, vec4 val) {
  val.rgb*=255.0f;                    //Optimise following calculations
  uint newVal = convVec4ToRGBA8(val);
  uint prevStoredVal = 0;  uint curStoredVal;
  //Loop as long as destination value gets changed by other threads
  while( (curStoredVal = imageAtomicCompSwap(imgUI, coords, prevStoredVal, newVal)) ←
    != prevStoredVal) {
    prevStoredVal = curStoredVal;
    vec4 rval=convRGBA8ToVec4(curStoredVal);
    rval.xyz=(rval.xyz*rval.w);       //Denormalize
    vec4 curValF=rval+val;            //Add new value
    curValF.xyz/=(curValF.w);         //Renormalize
    newVal = convVec4ToRGBA8(curValF);
  }
}
```

Listing 22.2. AtomicAvg on RGBA8 pixel type implemented with a moving average and using a compare-and-swap atomic operation.

22.4.3 Results

Table 22.1 shows execution times (in milliseconds) of our voxelization algorithm on the Stanford dragon mesh (871K triangles, Figure 22.6), for 128^3 and 512^3 voxel resolutions, with and without conservative rasterization, and with direct write or merging of values (Section 22.4.2). All timings have been done on an NVIDIA GTX480.

Figure 22.6. Stanford dragon voxelized into a 128^3 voxels grid.

Fermi and Kepler hardware support 32-bit floating point (FP32) atomic add operation on both images and global memory pointers, which is exposed through the NV_shader_atomic_float extension. Times marked with a star correspond to the results obtained with this native atomicAdd operation instead of our emulation. The right table compares our results using an FP32 voxel grid with VoxelPipe [Pantaleoni 11].

As can be seen, our approach provides as good or even better results than [Pantaleoni 11] when no merging is done (which does not give the same voxelization result) or when native atomic operations can be used (as is the case for R32F and RG16 voxel formats). For RG16 voxel formats (two normalized short integers), we perform the merging inside each voxel using the native atomicAdd operating on an unsigned int value, which works as long as the 16 bits per component do not overflow.

However, performance drops dramatically when we use our atomic emulation in floating-point format (R32F, nonstarred results) or our atomic moving average on RGBA8 formats (Section 22.4.2). Our FP32 atomicAdd emulation appears up to 25 times slower than the native operation when a lot of collisions occur. Paradoxically

Format	Res	Std. raster.		Cons. raster.		VoxelPipe	
		Write	Merge	Write	Merge	Write	Merge
R32F	128	1.19	1.24* /1.40	1.63	2.41* /62.1	4.80	5.00
	512	1.38	2.73* /5.15	1.99	5.30* /30.74	5.00	7.50
RG16	128	1.18	1.24	1.63	2.16		
	512	1.44	2.38	2.03	4.46		
RGBA8	128	1.18	1.40	1.63	69.80		
	512	1.47	5.30	2.07	31.40		

Table 22.1. Execution time (in milliseconds) of our voxelization algorithm and comparison with VoxelPipe on the Stanford dragon mesh. Times marked with a star correspond to the results obtained with the hardware atomicAdd operation instead of our emulation.

in these cases, lower resolution voxelization ends up slower than higher resolution, due to the increase in the number of collisions encountered per voxel.

22.5   Sparse Voxelization into an Octree

The goal of our sparse voxelization is to store only the voxels that are intersected by mesh triangles instead of a full grid in order to handle large and complex scenes and objects. For efficiency, this representation is stored in the form of a sparse-voxel octree in the spirit of [Laine and Karras 10] and [Crassin et al. 09]. To simplify explanations in the following sections, we will use the compute terminology and describe our algorithm in terms of *kernels* and launching of *threads*. The way we actually perform such compute-like thread execution in OpenGL will be described in Section 22.5.6.

22.5.1   Octree Structure

Our sparse-voxel octree is a very compact pointer-based structure, implemented similarly to [Crassin et al. 09]. Its memory organization is illustrated in Figure 22.7. The root node of the tree represents the entire scene; each of its children represents an eighth of its volume and so forth for every node.

Octree nodes are stored in linear video memory in a buffer object called the *octree pool*. In this buffer, nodes are grouped into $2 \times 2 \times 2$ *node tiles*, which allows us to store a single *pointer* in each node (actually an *index* into the buffer) pointing to eight child nodes. Voxel values can be stored directly into the nodes in linear memory or can be kept in *bricks* associated with the node tiles and stored in a big 3D texture. This node-plus-brick scheme is the one used in [Crassin et al. 11] to allow fast trilinear sampling of voxel values.

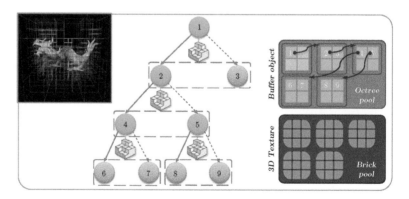

Figure 22.7. Illustration of our octree structure with bricks and its implementation in video memory.

This structure contains values for all levels of the tree, which allows querying filtered voxel data at any resolution and with increasing detail by descending the tree hierarchy. This property is highly desirable and was strongly exploited in our global illumination application [Crassin et al. 11].

22.5.2 Sparse-Voxelization Overview

In order to build the octree structure, our sparse-voxelization algorithm builds upon the regular grid voxelization we presented earlier. Our entire algorithm is illustrated in Figure 22.8. The basic idea of our approach is very simple.

We build the structure from top to bottom, one level at a time, starting from the 1-voxel root node and progressively subdividing nonempty nodes (intersected by at least one triangle) in each successive octree level of increasing resolution (step 2 in Figure 22.8). For each level, nonempty nodes are detected by voxelizing the scene at the resolutions corresponding to the resolution of the level, and a new tile of 2^3 subnodes is created for each of them. Finally, voxel-fragment values are written into the leaves of the tree and mipmapped into the interior nodes (steps 3 and 4 in Figure 22.8).

Figure 22.8. Illustration of our octree-building steps.

22.5.3 Voxel-Fragment List Construction Using an Atomic Counter

Actually revoxelizing the entire mesh multiple times, once for each level of the octree, would be very costly. Instead, we chose to voxelize it only once at the maximum resolution, the resolution of the deepest octree level, and to write generated voxel fragments into a *voxel fragment list* (step 1 in Figure 22.8). This list is then used instead of the triangle mesh to subdivide the octree during the building process.

Our voxel-fragment list is a linear vector of entries stored inside a preallocated buffer object. It is made up of multiple arrays of values, one containing the 3D coordinate of each voxel fragment (encoded in one 32-bit word with 10 bits per component and 2 unused bits) and the others containing all the attributes we want to store. In our demo implementation we only keep one color per voxel fragment.

In order to fill this voxel-fragment list, we voxelize our triangle scene similarly to how we did in the first part of this chapter. The difference here is that instead of directly writing voxel fragments into a destination 3D texture, we append them to our voxel fragment list. To manage the list, we store the index of the next available entry (that is also a counter of the number of voxel fragments in the list) as a single 32-bit value inside another buffer object.

This index needs to be accessed concurrently by thousands of threads appending voxel values, so we implement it with a new atomic counter (introduced with OpenGL 4.2). Atomic counters provide a highly optimized atomic increment/decrement operation on 32-bit integer variables. In contrast to the generic `atomicInc` or `atomicAdd` operations that allow dynamic indexing, atomic counters are designed to provide high performance when all threads operate on the same static memory region.

22.5.4   Node Subdivision

The actual subdivision of all nodes of a given octree level is done in three steps as illustrated in Figure 22.9. First, the nodes that need to be subdivided are flagged, using one thread per entry of the voxel-fragment list. Each thread simply traverses the octree from top to bottom, down to the current level (where there is no node linking subnodes), and *flags* the node in which the thread ended. Since multiple threads will end up flagging the same octree nodes, this allows us to gather all subdivision requests for a given node. This flag is implemented simply by setting the most significant bit of the children pointer of the node.

Whenever a node is flagged to be subdivided, a set of $2 \times 2 \times 2$ subnodes (a tile) needs to be allocated inside the octree pool and linked to the node. Thus, in a second step, the actual allocation of these subnode tiles is performed by launching one thread per node of the current octree level. Each thread first checks the flag of its assigned node, and if it is marked as touched, a new node tile is allocated and its index is assigned to the `childNode` pointer of the current node. This allocation of

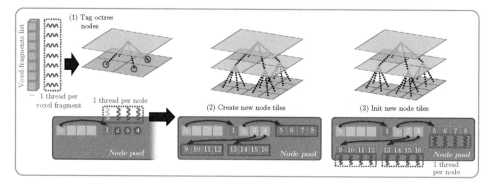

Figure 22.9. Illustration of the three steps performed for each level of the octree during the top-down construction with thread scheduling.

new node tiles inside the octree pool is done using a shared atomic counter, similarly to what we do for the voxel-fragment list (Section 22.5.3).

Finally, these new nodes need to be initialized, essentially to *null* child node pointers. This is performed in a separate pass so that one thread can be associated with each node of the new octree level (Figure 22.9, step 3).

22.5.5 Writing and Mipmapping Values

Once the octree structure has been built, the only remaining task is to fill it with the values from the voxel fragments. To do so, we first write the high-resolution voxel fragment values into the leaf nodes of the octree. This is achieved using one thread per entry of the voxel-fragment list. Each thread uses a similar scheme to the regular grid to splat and merge voxel-fragment values into the leaves (Section 22.4.2).

In a second step, we mipmap these values into the interior nodes of the tree. This is done level-per-level from bottom to top, in $n - 1$ steps for an octree of n levels. At each step, we use one thread to average the values contained in the eight sub-nodes of each non-empty node of the current level. Since we built the octree level-by-level (Section 22.5.2), node tiles get automatically sorted per level inside the octree pool. Thus, it is easy to launch threads for all nodes allocated in a given level to perform the averaging. These two steps are illustrated in Figure 22.8 (steps 3 and 4).

22.5.6 Synchronization-Free Compute-Like Kernel Launch Using draw indirect

In contrast to using CUDA or OpenCL, launching kernels with a specific number of threads (as we described) is not trivial in OpenGL. We propose to implement such kernel launches by simply using a vertex shader triggered with zero input vertex attributes. With this approach, threads are identified within the shader using the `gl_VertexID` built-in variable that provides a linear thread index.

Since our algorithm is entirely implemented on the GPU, all data necessary for each step of our approach are present in video memory. In order to provide optimal performance, we want to avoid reading back these values to the CPU to be able to launch new kernels since any readback will stall the pipeline. Instead, we rely on indirect draw calls (`glDrawArraysIndirect`) that read the call parameters from a structure stored within a buffer object directly in video memory.

This allows us to batch multiple kernel launches for successive steps of our algorithm with the actual thread configuration (the number of threads to launch and the starting offset) depending on the result of previous launches with absolutely zero CPU synchronization. Such GPU-driven kernel launch is currently not possible either in CUDA or in OpenCL.

We modify launch parameters using lightweight kernel launches with only one thread in charge of writing correct values into the draw indirect structure through global memory pointers.

With this approach, different kernels launched successively can potentially get scheduled at the same time on the GPU, and read/write ordering between two kernels is not ensured. When one kernel depends on the result of a previous kernel for its execution, we ensure that the data will be available to the threads of the second kernel by using *memory barriers* (`glMemoryBarrier()` command).

22.5.7   Results and Discussion

Table 22.2 shows computation time (in milliseconds) for the different steps of our algorithm on three representative scenes. Times marked with a star correspond to the results when atomic-based fragment merging is activated. The maximum voxelization resolution is 512^3 (9 octree levels). We use `RGBA32F` voxel values stored into a buffer object in global memory, and all timings have been done on a Kepler-based NVIDIA GTX680. We can observe that most of the time is spent in the octree construction, especially flagging the nodes (Section 22.5.4). Overall performance is 30% to 58% faster compared to a Fermi-based GTX480, and the atomic fragment merging is up to 80% faster.

Figure 22.10. The Sponza scene voxelized into our octree structure at a maximum resolution of respectively 512^3, 256^3, and 64^3 voxels and rendered without filtering.

Scene	Frag list	Octree Construction				Write	Mipmap	Total
		Flag	Create	Init	Total			
Hand	0.17	0.89	0.18	0.35	1.42	0.35/ 0.9*	0.55	2.49/ 3.04*
Dragon	3.51	4.93	0.22	0.49	5.64	2.01/ 3.05*	0.78	11.94/ 12.98*
Sponza	2.07	5.65	0.37	1.32	7.34	2.25/ 3.94*	2.09	13.75/ 15.44*

Table 22.2. Step-by-step execution time (in milliseconds) of our sparse octree voxelization for three different scenes. Times marked with a star correspond to the results when atomic-based fragment merging is activated.

Figure 22.10 shows the results of voxelizing the Sponza atrium scene into octree structures of different resolutions. We used this octree construction algorithm inside the voxel-based global illumination technique described in [Crassin et al. 11]. In this approach, a static environment must be quickly prevoxelized, and then at runtime, dynamic objects must be updated in real time inside the structure. Thanks to our fast voxelization approach, we were able to keep this structure update under 15% of the whole frame time.

Currently, one of the weakness of our approach is the requirement of preallocating the octree buffer with a fixed size. Although this may seem like a problem, it is in fact often desirable to manage this buffer as a cache, similar to what is proposed in [Crassin et al. 09].

22.6   Conclusion

In this chapter, we presented two approaches to voxelize triangle meshes, one producing a regular voxel grid and one producing a more compact sparse voxel octree. These approaches take advantage of the fast rasterization hardware of the GPU to implement efficient 3D sampling and scan conversion. Our approach dramatically reduces the geometrical cost of previous graphics-based approaches, while in most cases providing similar or slightly higher performance than state-of-the-art compute-based approaches. Although it was not detailed here, our approach supports a fast dynamic update of the octree structure, allowing us to merge dynamic objects inside a static prevoxelized environment, as demonstrated in [Crassin et al. 11]. Details can be found in the accompanying source code. Possible future work includes optimizing the voxel merging as well as the conservative rasterization implementation. In fact, the new NVIDIA Kepler architecture already improves atomic operation performance considerably.

Acknowledgments. We would like to thank Crytek for its improved version of the Atrium Sponza Palace model originally created by Marko Dabrovic. We would also like to thank the Stanford University Computer Graphics Laboratory for the Dragon model, as well as Ingo Wald for his animated hand model.

Bibliography

[Allard et al. 10] Jérémie Allard, François Faure, Hadrien Courtecuisse, Florent Falipou, Christian Duriez, and Paul Kry. "Volume Contact Constraints at Arbitrary Resolution." In *ACM Transactions on Graphics, Proceedings of SIGGRAPH 2010*, pp. 1–10. New York: ACM, 2010. Available online (http://hal.inria.fr/inria-00502446/en/).

[Crane et al. 05] Keenan Crane, Ignacio Llamas, and Sarah Tariq. "Real-Time Simulation and Rendering of 3D Fluids." In *GPU Gems 2*, pp. 615–634. Reading, MA: Addison Wesley, 2005.

[Crassin et al. 09] Cyril Crassin, Fabrice Neyret, Sylvain Lefebvre, and Elmar Eisemann. "GigaVoxels: Ray-Guided Streaming for Efficient and Detailed Voxel Rendering." In *ACM SIGGRAPH Symposium on Interactive 3D Graphics and Games (I3D)*, 2009. Available online (http://artis.imag.fr/Publications/2009/CNLE09).

[Crassin et al. 10] Cyril Crassin, Fabrice Neyret, Miguel Sainz, and Elmar Eisemann. "Efficient Rendering of Highly Detailed Volumetric Scenes with GigaVoxels." In *GPU Pro*, pp. 643–676. Natick, MA: A K Peters, 2010. Available online (http://artis.imag.fr/Publications/2010/CNSE10).

[Crassin et al. 11] Cyril Crassin, Fabrice Neyret, Miguel Sainz, Simon Green, and Elmar Eisemann. "Interactive Indirect Illumination Using Voxel Cone Tracing." In *Computer Graphics Forum (Pacific Graphics 2011)*, 2011.

[Dong et al. 04] Zhao Dong, Wei Chen, Hujun Bao, Hongxin Zhang, and Qunsheng Peng. "Real-Time Voxelization for Complex Polygonal Models." In *Proceedings of the Computer Graphics and Applications, 12th Pacific Conference, PG '04*, pp. 43–50. Washington, DC: IEEE Computer Society, 2004. Available online (http://dl.acm.org/citation.cfm?id=1025128.1026026).

[Eisemann and Décoret 08] Elmar Eisemann and Xavier Décoret. "Single-Pass GPU Solid Voxelization for Real-Time Applications." In *Proceedings of graphics interface 2008, GI '08*, pp. 73–80. Toronto, Ont., Canada, Canada: Canadian Information Processing Society, 2008.

[Fang et al. 00] Shiaofen Fang, Shiaofen Fang, Hongsheng Chen, and Hongsheng Chen. "Hardware Accelerated Voxelization." *Computers and Graphics* 24:3 (2000), 433–442.

[Hasselgren et al. 05] Jon Hasselgren, Tomas Akenine-Mller, and Lennart Ohlsson. "Conservative Rasterization." In *GPU Gems 2*. Reading, MA: Addison Wesley, 2005.

[Huang et al. 98] Jian Huang, Roni Yagel, Vassily Filippov, and Yair Kurzion. "An Accurate Method for Voxelizing Polygon Meshes." In *Proceedings of the 1998 IEEE Symposium on Volume Visualization, VVS '98*, pp. 119–126. New York: ACM, 1998. Available online (http://doi.acm.org/10.1145/288126.288181).

[Kaplanyan and Dachsbacher 10] Anton Kaplanyan and Carsten Dachsbacher. "Cascaded Light Propagation Volumes for Real-time Indirect Illumination." In *Proceedings of I3D*, 2010.

[Laine and Karras 10] Samuli Laine and Tero Karras. "Efficient Sparse Voxel Octrees." In *Proceedings of ACM SIGGRAPH 2010 Symposium on Interactive 3D Graphics and Games*, pp. 55–63. New York: ACM Press, 2010.

[Li et al. 05] Wei Li, Zhe Fan, Xiaoming Wei, and Arie Kaufman. "Flow Simulation with Complex Boundaries." In *GPU Gems 2*, pp. 615–634. Reading, MA: Addison Wesley, 2005.

[Pantaleoni 11] Jacopo Pantaleoni. "VoxelPipe: A Programmable Pipeline for 3D Voxelization." In *Proceedings of the ACM SIGGRAPH Symposium on High Performance Graphics, HPG '11*, pp. 99–106. New York: ACM, 2011. Available online (http://doi.acm.org/10.1145/2018323.2018339).

[Schwarz and Seidel 10] Michael Schwarz and Hans-Peter Seidel. "Fast Parallel Surface and Solid Voxelization on GPUs." In *ACM SIGGRAPH Asia 2010 papers, SIGGRAPH ASIA*

'10, pp. 179:1–179:10. New York: ACM, 2010. Available online (http://doi.acm.org/ 10.1145/1866158.1866201).

[Thiedemann et al. 11] Sinje Thiedemann, Niklas Henrich, Thorsten Grosch, and Stefan Müller. "Voxel-Based Global Illumination." In *Symposium on Interactive 3D Graphics and Games, Proceedings of I3D*, pp. 103–110. New York: ACM, 2011.

[Zhang et al. 07] Long Zhang, Wei Chen, David S. Ebert, and Qunsheng Peng. "Conservative Voxelization." *The Visual Computer* 23 (2007), 783–792. Available online (http://dl.acm.org/citation.cfm?id=1283953.1283975).

IV Performance

When it comes to real-time graphics, performance is what defines the possible from the impossible; it is what sets the boundaries.

A lack of performance might come from a lack of understanding of the platform we are working on. This may have a dramatic negative impact on the tile-based GPUs leading the OpenGL ES world. In his chapter, "Performance Tuning for Tile-Based Architectures," Bruce Merry presents key tile-based GPU architecture features and how to take advantage of them. Jon McCaffrey follows this discussion in his chapter "Exploring Mobile vs. Desktop OpenGL Performance," which shows the performance-scale differences between the mobile and desktop worlds.

Performance is not only the concern of GPU architectures, it is also the direct result of how we write software. With GPUs whose performances increase at a faster rate than CPUs, we are more and more often CPU-bound, leaving us incapable to benefit from all the GPU power. Sébastien Hillaire, in his chapter "Improving Performance by Reducing Calls to the Drivers," introduces some fundamental concepts to reduce CPU overhead with a legacy flavor.

In his chapter "Indexing Multiple Vertex Arrays," Arnaud Masserann comes back to one of the most fundamental elements for GPU performance: how we submit vertex array data to the GPU. He provides a directly applicable method to ensure that vertex indexing will be used even on assets not organized this way, like COLLADA geometry.

Finally, sometimes we are left with no choice: to scale performance, we must scale the number of GPUs used for rendering. This is the topic of Shalini Venkataraman in her chapter "Multi-GPU Rendering on NVIDIA Quadro." She explains how to efficiently use multiple GPUs for rendering and integrate their work to build the final image.

Performance Tuning for Tile-Based Architectures 23

Bruce Merry

23.1 Introduction

The OpenGL and OpenGL ES specifications describe a virtual pipeline in which triangles are processed *in order*: the vertices of a triangle are transformed, the triangle is set up and rasterized to produce fragments, the fragments are shaded and then written to the framebuffer. Once this has been done, the next triangle is processed, and so on. However, this is not the most efficient way for a GPU to work; GPUs will usually reorder and parallelize things under the hood for better performance.

In this chapter, we will examine *tile-based rendering*, a particular way to arrange a graphics pipeline that is used in several popular mobile GPUs. We will look at what tile-based rendering is and why it is used and then look at what needs to be done differently to achieve optimal performance. I assume that the reader already has experience with optimizing OpenGL applications and is familiar with the standard techniques, such as reducing state changes, reducing the number of draw calls, reducing shader complexity and texture compression, and is looking for advice that is specific to tile-based GPUs.

Keep in mind that every GPU, every driver, and every application is different and will have different performance characteristics [Qua 10]. Ultimately, performance-tuning is a process of profiling and experimentation. Thus, this chapter contains very few hard-and-fast rules but instead tries to illustrate how to estimate the costs associated with different approaches.

This chapter is about maximizing performance, but since tile-based GPUs are currently popular in mobile devices, we will also briefly mention power consumption. Many desktop applications will simply render as many frames per second as possible, always consuming 100% of the available processing power. Deliberately throttling the frame rate to a more modest level and thus consuming less power can significantly extend battery life while having relatively little impact on user experience. Of course, this does not mean that one should stop optimizing after achieving the target frame rate: further optimizations will then allow the system to spend more time idle and hence improve power consumption.

The main focus of this chapter will be on OpenGL ES since that is the primary market for tile-based GPUs, but occasionally I will touch on desktop OpenGL features and how they might perform.

23.2   Background

While performance is the main goal for desktop GPUs, mobile GPUs must balance performance against power consumption, i.e., battery life. One of the biggest consumers of power in a device is memory bandwidth: computations are relatively cheap, but the further data has to be moved, the more power it takes.

The OpenGL virtual pipeline requires a large amount of bandwidth. For a fairly typical use-case, each pixel will require a read from the depth/stencil buffer, a write back to the depth/stencil buffer, and a write to the color buffer, say 12 bytes of traffic, assuming no overdraw, no blending, no multipass algorithms, and no multisampling. With all the bells and whistles, one can easily generate over 100 bytes of memory traffic for each displayed pixel. Since at most 4 bytes of data are needed per displayed pixel, this is an excessive use of bandwidth and hence power. In reality, desktop GPUs use compression techniques to reduce the bandwidth, but it is still significant.

To reduce this enormous bandwidth demand, many mobile GPUs use *tile-based rendering*. At the most basic level, these GPUs move the framebuffer, including the depth buffer, multisample buffers, etc., out of main memory and into high-speed on-chip memory. Since this memory is on-chip, and close to where the computations occur, far less power is required to access it. If it were possible to place a large framebuffer in on-chip memory, that would be the end of the story; but unfortunately, that would take far too much silicon. The size of the on-chip framebuffer, or *tile buffer*, varies between GPUs but can be as small as 16×16 pixels.

This poses some new challenges: how can a high-resolution image be produced using such a small tile buffer? The solution is to break up the OpenGL framebuffer into 16×16 *tiles* (hence the name "tile-based rendering") and render one at a time. For each tile, all the primitives that affect it are rendered into the tile buffer, and once the tile is complete, it is copied back to the more power-hungry main memory, as shown in Figure 23.1. The bandwidth advantage comes from only having to write back a minimum set of results: no depth/stencil values, no overdrawn pixels, and no multisample buffer data. Additionally, depth/stencil testing and blending are done entirely on-chip.

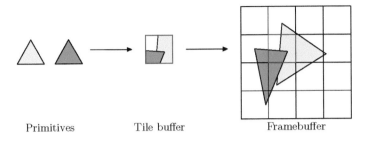

Primitives   Tile buffer   Framebuffer

Figure 23.1. Operation of the tile buffer. All the transformed primitives for the frame are stored in memory (left). A tile is processed by rendering the primitives to the tile buffer (held on-chip, center). Once a tile has been rendered, it is copied back to the framebuffer held in main memory (right).

We now come back to the OpenGL API, which was not designed with tile-based architectures in mind. The OpenGL API is *immediate-mode*: it specifies triangles to be drawn in a current state, rather than providing a scene structure containing all the triangles and their states. Thus, an OpenGL implementation on a tile-based architecture needs to collect all the triangles submitted during a frame and store them for later use. While early fixed-function GPUs did this in software, more recent programmable mobile GPUs have specialized hardware units to do this. For each triangle, they will use the `gl_Position` outputs from the vertex shader to determine which tiles are potentially affected by the triangle and enter the triangle into a spatial data structure. Additionally, each triangle needs to be packaged with its current fragment state: fragment shader, uniforms, depth function, etc. When a tile is rendered, the spatial data structure is consulted to find the triangles relevant to that tile together with their fragment states.

At first glance, we seem to have traded one bandwidth problem for another: instead of vertex attributes being used immediately by a rasterizer and fragment shading core, triangles are being saved away for later use in a data structure. Indeed, storage is required for vertex positions, vertex shader outputs, triangle indices, fragment state, and some overhead for the spatial data structure. We will refer to these collective data as the *frame data* (ARM documentation calls them *polygon lists* [ARM 11], while Imagination Technologies documentation calls them the *parameter buffer* [Ima 11]). Tile-based GPUs are successful because the extra bandwidth required to read and write these data is usually less than the bandwidth saved by keeping intermediate shading results on-chip. This will be true as long as the number of post-clipping triangles is kept to a reasonable level. Excessive tessellation into micropolygons will bloat the frame data and negate the advantages of a tile-based GPU.

Figure 23.2(a) shows the flow of data. The highest bandwidth data transfers are those between the fragment processor and the tile buffer, which stay on-chip. Contrast this to Figure 23.2(b) for an immediate-mode GPU, where multisample color, depth, and stencil data are sent across the memory bus.

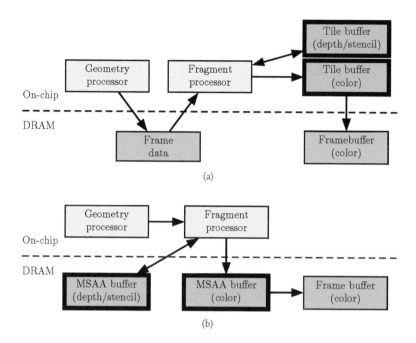

Figure 23.2. Data flow in (a) tiled-based and (b) immediate-mode GPUs for multisampled rendering. Yellow boxes are computational units, blue boxes are memory, and thick borders indicate multisampled buffers. The immediate-mode GPU moves multisampled pixel data on and off the chip, consuming a lot of bandwidth.

23.3   Clearing and Discarding the Framebuffer

When it comes to performance-tuning, the most important thing to remember about a tile-based GPU is that the representation of a frame that is currently being constructed is not a framebuffer but the frame data: lists of transformed vertices, polygons, and state necessary to produce the framebuffer. Unlike a framebuffer, these data grow as more draw calls are issued in a frame. It is thus important to ensure that frames are properly terminated so that the frame data do not grow indefinitely.

When swapping a double-buffered window, the effect on the back buffer depends on the window system bindings used. Both EGL and GLX allow the implementation to invalidate the contents of the back buffer. Thus, the driver can throw away the frame data after each swap and start with a blank slate (with EGL, applications can opt to have the back buffer preserved on a swap; see Section 23.4 for more details).

Things become more difficult when using framebuffer objects, which do not have a swap operation. Specifically, consider the use of `glClear`. Typical desktop GPUs are immediate-mode architectures, meaning that they draw fragments as soon as all the data for a triangle are available. On an immediate-mode GPU, a call to `glClear`

```
glDisable(GL_SCISSOR_TEST);
glColorMask(GL_TRUE, GL_TRUE, GL_TRUE, GL_TRUE);
glDepthMask(GL_TRUE);
glStencilMask(0xFFFFFFFF);
glClear(GL_COLOR_BUFFER_BIT | GL_DEPTH_BUFFER_BIT | GL_STENCIL_BUFFER_BIT);
```

Listing 23.1. Clearing the screen correctly for a tile-based GPU.

actually writes values into the framebuffer and thus can be expensive. Programmers use assorted tricks to avoid this, such as not clearing the color buffer if they know it will be completely overwritten and using half the depth range on alternate frames to avoid clearing the depth buffer. While these tricks were useful in the past, they have been surpassed by hardware-level optimizations, and can even reduce performance by working against these hardware optimizations.

On a tile-based architecture, avoiding clears can be disasterous for performance: since the frame is built up in frame data, clearing all buffers will simply free up the existing frame data. In other words, not only is `glClear` very cheap, it actually improves performance by allowing unneeded frame data to be discarded.

To get the full benefit of this effect, it is necessary to clear everything: using a scissor or a mask or only clearing a subset of color, depth, and stencil will prevent the frame data from being freed. While drivers may detect more cases where clearing can free the frame data, the safest and most portable approach is shown in Listing 23.1.

This should be done at the start of each frame,[1] unless the window system already takes care of discarding the framebuffer contents. Of course, the masks and scissor enable don't need to be set explicitly if they are already in the correct state.

The above discussion about clearing highlights a limitation of the API: `glClear` is a low-level command that specifies buffer contents rather than a high-level hint about how the application is using a buffer. OpenGL ES developers wanting portable performance should consider the **EXT_discard_framebuffer** extension, which provides this hint. The command `glDiscardFramebufferEXT` indicates to the driver that the application no longer cares about the contents of some buffers, allowing the driver to set the pixel values to whatever it wishes. Tiled-based architectures can use this hint to free up the frame data, while immediate-mode architectures can choose to ignore the hint. Listing 23.2 shows an example that can be used in place of Listing 23.1.

```
const GLenum attachments[3] = { COLOR_EXT, DEPTH_EXT, STENCIL_EXT };
glDiscardFramebufferEXT(GL_FRAMEBUFFER, 3, attachments);
```

Listing 23.2. Discarding framebuffer contents with **EXT_framebuffer_discard**.

---

[1] OpenGL does not define what a "frame" is, and it is a surprisingly slippery concept. In this context, we consider each framebuffer that is generated to constitute a separate frame, even if multiple framebuffer objects are combined to create a single onscreen image.

Discards have another use with framebuffer objects, i.e., render-to-texture. When rendering 3D geometry to a texture such as an environment map, a depth buffer is needed during the rendering but does not need to be preserved afterwards. The application can inform the driver of this by calling `glDiscardFramebufferEXT` after doing the rendering but before unbinding the framebuffer object, and a tile-based GPU may use this as a hint that depth values need not be copied back from the tile buffer to main memory. Although not yet available on desktop OpenGL, `EXT_discard_framebuffer` is likely to be useful for multisampled framebuffer objects as well, where the multisampled buffer may be discarded as soon as it has been resolved into a single-sampled target. At the time of this writing, `EXT_discard_framebuffer` is still relatively new, and some experimentation will be required to determine how effectively the hints are used by any particular implementation.

23.4   Incremental Frame Updates

For a 3D view with a moving camera, such as in a first-person shooter game, it is reasonable to expect every pixel to change from frame to frame, and so clearing the framebuffer will not destroy any useful information. For more GUI-like applications, there may be assorted controls or information views that do not change from frame to frame and which do not need to be regenerated. Application developers using EGL on a tile-based GPU are often surprised to find that the color buffer does not persist from frame to frame. EGL 1.4 allows this to be explicitly requested by setting `EGL_SWAP_BEHAVIOR` on the surface, but it is not the default on a tile-based GPU since it reduces performance.

To understand why back-buffer preservation reduces performance, consider again how a tile-based GPU composes fragments for a single tile. If the framebuffer is cleared at the start of a frame, the tile buffer need only be initialized to the clear color before fragments are drawn, but if the framebuffer is preserved from the previous frame, then the tile buffer needs to be initialized with the corresponding section of the framebuffer before any new fragments are rendered, and this requires bandwidth. The bandwidth cost is comparable to treating the previous framebuffer as a texture and drawing it into the current frame. Although it will depend on the complexity of the scene, it can be faster just to redraw the entire frame than to try to preserve regions from the previous frame.

Qualcomm provides a vendor extension (`QCOM_tiled_rendering`) that addresses this use-case. The application explicitly indicates which region it is going to update, and all rendering is clipped to this region. The GPU then only needs to process the tiles intersecting this region, and the rest of the framebuffer can remain untouched. This extension also includes features similar to `EXT_discard_framebuffer` to allow the user to indicate whether the existing contents of the target region need to be preserved. For example, suppose an application contains a 3D view in the region with offset x, y and dimensions $w \times h$, which is going to be com-

```
glStartTilingQCOM(x, y, width, height, GL_NONE);
glClear(GL_COLOR_BUFFER_BIT | GL_DEPTH_BUFFER_BIT | GL_STENCIL_BUFFER_BIT);
glViewport(x, y, width, height);
// Draw the scene
glEndTilingQCOM(GL_COLOR_BUFFER_BITO_QCOM);
eglSwapBuffers(dpy, surface);
```

Listing 23.3. Replacing a portion of the framebuffer using QCOM_tiled_rendering. GL_NONE indicates that the previous contents of the framebuffer for the affected region may be discarded. GL_COLOR_BUFFER_BITO_QCOM indicates that the rendered color data must be written back to the framebuffer. Depth and stencil may be discarded.

pletely replaced, while the rest of the window is static and does not need to be updated. This can be achieved using the code in Listing 23.3 in addition to setting EGL_SWAP_BEHAVIOR to EGL_BUFFER_PRESERVED.

23.5 Flushing

Tile-based GPUs are sometimes referred to as *deferred* because the driver will try to avoid performing fragment shading until it is required. Eventually, of course, the pixel values will be needed. The following operations will all force the framebuffer contents to be brought up to date:

- eglSwapBuffers and its equivalents in other window systems;

- glFlush and glFinish;

- glReadPixels, glCopyTexImage, and glBlitFramebuffer;

- querying an occlusion query result from an occlusion query in the current frame;

- using the result of render-to-texture for texturing.

Changing framebuffer attachments using either glFramebufferRenderbuffer or glRenderbufferStorage, or the texture equivalents is also likely to cause a flush, as the frame data will only be applicable to the old attachment.

The following pattern will have very poor performance:

1. Draw some triangles.

2. Use the framebuffer contents.

3. Draw another triangle.

4. Use the framebuffer contents.

5. Draw another triangle....

Each time the framebuffer contents are needed, there will be another fragment-shading pass, which in the worst case could involve a read and a write for every framebuffer pixel just to draw one triangle. Because the cost of each pass is so high, the goal is to have only one pass per frame.

This is true even if the accesses to the framebuffer contents are done entirely on the GPU, such as by accessing the results of render-to-texture or by calling `glReadPixels` with a pixel pack buffer, because each draw-then-access requires the fragment shading to be rerun. Compare this to an immediate-mode GPU, where the cost of `glReadPixels` with a pixel pack buffer will be essentially the same regardless of when it is performed.

In some drivers, `glBindFramebuffer` also starts fragment shading for the framebuffer that has just been unbound. Thus, it is best to bind each framebuffer only once per frame. As an example, consider a scene in which some objects are made shiny by using generated environment maps. A naïve walk of the scene graph might cause each environment map to be generated immediately before drawing the object itself, but it would be better to first generate all the environment maps before binding the window system framebuffer to render the final scene.

Apart from the commands above, there is another situation in which flushing happens. Because the memory usage for the frame data scales with the amount of geometry in the frame, an application that just keeps drawing more geometry without swapping or clearing would eventually run out of memory. To prevent this from happening, the driver will eventually force a flush. This is very expensive because unlike a swap operation, all the buffers, including multisample buffers, are written out to memory and then reloaded for rendering to continue, which can easily consume 16 times the bandwidth of a regular flush.

This means that performance does not scale linearly with the number of vertices. Once an application has sufficiently simple geometry to run at interactive rates, it should be well clear of this performance cliff, but when starting optimization, it is worth checking for this case before estimating a target vertex count from current throughput.

23.6   Latency

Since vertex and fragment processing for a frame happen in separate phases, an application that has balanced demands on the CPU, vertex processor, and fragment processor will have three frames in flight at any time, as shown in Figure 23.3. The exact latency between command submission and completion will depend on which resources are most limited and will also vary over time.

Apart from impacting responsiveness to user input, latency is a concern when results of rendering are read back to the CPU. Synchronous queries such as `glRead Pixels` without a pixel pack buffer will stall the CPU until results are available and should almost never be used. But even with asynchronous queries such as occlu-

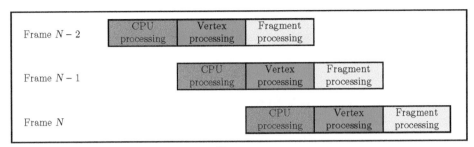

Figure 23.3. Processing pipeline in a tile-based GPU. At any point in time, there can be three frames in different stages of processing. This shows an idealized case with no pipeline bubbles.

sion queries, the result must eventually be read, and doing so too soon will stall the pipeline. If it is acceptable to just wait until the query result is available, then a periodic check of GL_QUERY_RESULT_AVAILABLE is sufficient. Code that is written for an immediate-mode GPU that assumes the query result will be available within a fixed number of frames may need to be retuned, either to wait for a larger number of intervening frames or to poll for the result becoming available. Similarly, if glReadPixels must be used, performance can be greatly improved at the cost of some latency by rotating between multiple framebuffer objects and reading not the just-rendered frame but a previous one, which is more likely to have completed rendering.

Latency also plays a role when objects are modified since commands bind their resources at the time they are issued. A common example is an animated mesh, where the vertex positions are updated every frame. The previous vertex positions may still be in use for vertex shading in the previous frame, so when the application updates the vertex buffer, the memory the GPU is reading from cannot be touched until the previous frame is complete. In most cases, drivers handle this by making an extra copy of the resource "under the hood" to avoid stalling the pipeline, but on a memory- and bandwidth-constrained mobile device, it is still worth being aware that this *copy-on-write* is happening. The problem becomes worse if a single resource is used multiple times during a frame, interspersed with partial updates, leading to multiple copy-on-writes. If possible, all the updates should be done as a block before the resource is used.

Be particularly careful when using extensions such as EGL_KHR_image_pixmap or GLX_EXT_texture_from_pixmap to modify operating system pixmaps. Drivers usually have less freedom to move these resources around in memory and may need to stall the pipeline or even flush partial results to the framebuffer and reload them.

The three-phase processing shown in Figure 23.3 means that tile-based GPUs will typically have a higher latency than immediate-mode GPUs, and thus, code that has been tuned for an immediate-mode GPU may need retuning. For some tile-based GPUs, vertex shading for a frame finishes much earlier than fragment shading (in fact, before fragment shading starts), so the latency for vertex shading will be lower. However, in some cases, parts of vertex shading will be delayed until needed during fragment shading.

23.7   Hidden Surface Removal

When objects overlap in an immediate-mode GPU, causing one pixel to be overwritten by another, there are two costs associated with this: the cost of shading the hidden pixels and the extra bandwidth consumed by the associated framebuffer accesses. In a tile-based GPU, the latter cost is eliminated because only fully rendered tiles are emitted to memory, but the shading cost remains. It is thus still important to do high-level culling and to submit opaque objects in front-to-back order to take advantage of hardware early depth tests. Because the costs are different, however, the optimal balance of CPU load for sorting and GPU load for shading may be different compared to an immediate-mode GPU.

An exception to the above is the PowerVR family of GPUs, which feature per-pixel hidden surface removal during fragment shading [Ima 11]. Before running any fragment shaders, the polygons are preprocessed to determine which fragments potentially contribute to the final result, and only those are shaded. This removes the need to sort opaque geometry. To take full advantage of this, the fragment shader must be guaranteed to replace occluded pixels. The presence of the GLSL `discard` keyword as well as sample masking, alpha testing, alpha-to-coverage, and blending will all disable the optimization as the occluded pixel may potentially impact the final image. Thus, these features should only be enabled for the objects that require them, even at the cost of extra state changes.

Where PowerVR-style hardware hidden-surface removal is not available, another option is to use an initial *depth-only pass*: submit all the geometry once with an empty fragment shader and color writes disabled to populate the depth buffer, and then draw everything again with the real fragment shader. The depth pass will determine the depth of the visible surfaces, and the color pass will then perform fragment shading only for the those surfaces (assuming early depth culling).

This depth-only pass technique can be effective on either an immediate-mode GPU or a tile-based GPU when it eliminates expensive shading computations, but the trade-offs are different. In both cases, the depth pass incurs all the vertex processing and rasterization costs of the color pass (however, the Adreno 200 and possibly others have higher fragment throughput in a depth-only pass [Qua 10]). On an immediate-mode GPU, a depth-only pass incurs a bandwidth penalty since the depth buffer is accessed during both passes. On a tile-based GPU, the depth buffer accesses have no main memory bandwidth penalty, but there is the smaller penalty of duplicating all the geometry in the frame data. Thus, for bandwidth-limited applications a depth-only pass may be effective on a tile-based GPU even when it is not effective on an immediate-mode GPU.

23.8   Blending

On immediate-mode GPUs, blending is usually expensive because it requires a read-modify-write cycle to the framebuffer, which is held in relatively slow memory. On a tile-based CPU, this read-modify-write cycle occurs entirely on-chip and so is very cheap. Some GPUs have dedicated blending hardware which makes the blending operation essentially free, while others use shader instructions to implement blending; hence, blending will reduce fragment shading throughput.

Note that this only addresses the direct cost of the blending operation compared to other transparency or translucency techniques such as alpha tests or alpha-to-coverage. Making an object partially transparent or translucent has indirect costs, as the object can no longer be treated as an occluder for hidden-surface removal. The fragments behind the translucent object must now be processed, whereas previously they could be eliminated by optimizations such as hardware hidden-surface removal or early depth testing.

23.9   Multisampling

Multisampling is an effective technique to improve visual quality without sacrificing as much performance as supersampling. Each framebuffer pixel stores multiple samples, which are averaged together to produce an antialiased image, but fragments generated by rasterization need only be shaded once per pixel. While this keeps fragment shading costs largely the same, it has an enormous bandwidth impact on immediate-mode GPUs: with 4 times multisampling (a common choice), the bandwidth of all framebuffer accesses increases by a factor of 4. Various hardware optimizations reduce this bandwidth overhead to the point where multisampling is practical, but it is still expensive.

In contrast, multisampling in a tile-based GPU can be very cheap, as the multiple samples need only be retained in the on-chip tile buffer, with only the averaged color value written out to framebuffer memory. Thus, multisampling has no impact on framebuffer bandwidth.

There are, nevertheless, two costs: firstly, 4 times multisampling will require four times as much tile buffer memory. Since tile buffer memory is expensive in terms of silicon area, some GPUs compensate for this by reducing the tile size when multisampling is in effect. A reduction in tile size has some impact on performance, but halving the tile size will not halve the performance, and applications limited by fragment shading throughput will see only a minor impact.

The second cost for multisampling (which also affects immediate-mode GPUs) is that more fragments will be generated along object silhouettes. Each polygon will hit more pixels as shown in Figure 23.4. Furthermore, where both the foreground and background geometry contribute to a single pixel, both fragments must be shaded, and so hardware hidden surface removal will cull fewer fragments. The cost of these

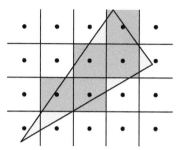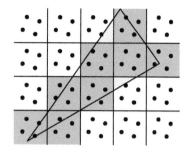

Figure 23.4. The effect of multisampling on fragment shader load. Without multisampling, only pixels whose centers are covered generate fragments (left; blue). If any of the sample points are covered, a fragment is generated, thus leading to slightly more fragments along edges (right).

extra fragments will depend on how much of the scene is made up of silhouettes, but 10% is a good first guess.

23.10   Performance Profiling

On an immediate-mode GPU, the `ARB_timer_query` extension can be used to gauge the cost of rendering some part of the scene: a range of commands to profile is bracketed by `glBeginQuery` and `glEndQuery`, and the time elapsed between these commands in the command stream is measured. This functionality is described in more detail in Chapter 34.

While it is possible to implement this extension on a tile-based GPU, the results will not be useful for anything less than frame granularity. This is because commands are not processed in the order they are submitted: the vertex processing is all done in a first pass, and then fragment processing is ordered by tiles. Thus, profiling will need to rely on more intrusive techniques, such as turning parts of the scene on or off to determine the performance impact. Vendor-specific tools for accessing internal performance counters can also be a great help in identifying which parts of the pipeline are causing bottlenecks.

Apart from post hoc profiling, it is often a good idea to start development with microbenchmarks that measure the performance of specific aspects of the system to determine a budget for triangles, textures, shader complexity, etc. When doing so, keep in mind that submitting too much geometry without swapping will lead to a performance cliff as described in Section 23.5. It is also important to ensure that the commands do actually get executed—placing a `glClear` after draw calls may well cancel those draw calls before they reach the GPU.

23.11 Summary

Every GPU and every driver is different, and different choices in optimizations and heuristics mean that the only way to truly determine the performance impact of design choices on a specific system is to test it. Nevertheless, the following rules of thumb are a good starting point to obtain high performance from a tile-based GPU:

- Clear or discard the entire contents of the color, depth, and stencil buffers at the start of each frame.

- For each framebuffer, bind it once during the frame, and submit all the commands for the frame before unbinding it or using the results.

- Keep latency in mind when using occlusion queries or other mechanisms to retrieve the results of commands, and if an application was previously tuned for the latencies of an immediate-mode GPU, it may need to be retuned.

- Keep polygon counts to a reasonable level, and in particular avoid micropolygons.

- On hardware with built-in hidden surface removal (PowerVR), there is no need to sort opaque objects front to back; on other hardware, this should be done. Also consider using a depth-only pass.

- Take advantage of cheap multisampling.

- Remember that on mobile devices, performance must be balanced against power consumption.

Bibliography

[ARM 11] ARM. *Mali GPU Application Optimization Guide*, 2011. Version 1.0.

[Ima 11] Imagination Technologies Ltd. *POWERVR Series5 Graphics SGX Architecture Guide for Developers*, 2011. Version 1.0.8.

[Qua 10] Qualcomm Incorporated. *Adreno™ 200 Performance Optimization: OpenGL ES Tips and Tricks*, 2010.

Exploring Mobile vs. Desktop OpenGL Performance

24

Jon McCaffrey

24.1 Introduction

The stunning rise of mobile platforms has opened a new market for new 3D applications and games where, excitingly, OpenGL ES is the lingua franca for graphics. However, mobile platforms and GPUs have performance profiles and characteristics that may be unfamiliar to desktop developers. Developers making the transition from desktop to mobile need to be aware of the limits and capabilities of mobile devices to create the best experience possible for the given hardware resources. This chapter surveys mobile GPU design decisions and constraints, and then explores how these affect classic rendering paradigms.

First, we examine how mobile and desktop GPUs differ in design goals, scale and architecture. We then look at memory bandwidth, which greatly affects performance and device power consumption, and break down the contributions of display, rendering, composition, blending, texture access, and antialiasing. After that, our focus shifts towards optimizing fragment shading for limited compute power. We will look at ways to eliminate shading work entirely if we can or perform operations more efficiently if we can't

Finally, we will discuss the relationship between vertex and fragment shaders and how it is affected by different mobile GPU architectures and will end with some tips for optimizing vertex data for efficient reads and updates.

24.2 Important Differences and Constraints

24.2.1 Differences in Scale

Modern mobile devices are very capable, but they face greater limitations than desktop systems in terms of cost, chip die size, power consumption, and heat dissipation.

Power consumption is a major concern for mobile platforms that is much less pressing on the desktop. Mobile devices must run off batteries small enough to fit in the body of the device, and a short battery life is frustrating and inconvenient to the user. Mobile hardware is built to use less power than desktop hardware via lower clock frequencies, narrower busses, smaller chips, smaller data formats, and by limiting redundant and speculative work. Display and radio take a great deal of power, but OpenGL applications contribute to power consumption, especially through computation and through off-chip memory accesses.

Power consumption is doubly impactful on mobile devices since power consumed by the processor, GPU, and memory is largely dissipated as heat. Unlike desktop systems with active air cooling, good air circulation, and large heat sinks, mobile systems are usually passively cooled and have contrained bodies with little room for large sinks or radiating fins. Excess heat generation is not only potentially damaging to components, it's also noticeable and irritating to users of handheld products.

Die size and cost are also greatly different between mobile and desktop. High-end desktop GPUs are some of the largest mainstream chips made, with over three billion transistors on recent models [Walton 10]. The large area and the effect of area on yield mean increased cost. A discrete GPU also means a separate package and mounting and the expected cost increase. In mobile systems, however, the GPU is usually one component on an integrated *system on a chip* (SoC) designed for mobile and embedded applications, which means that a mobile GPU is a fraction of the cost and area of a desktop GPU.

24.2.2 Differences in Rendering Architecture

Mobile and desktop GPUs don't differ only in scale. Mobile GPUs such as the Imagination Tech SGX543MP2 used in the Apple iPhone 4S/iPad 2 and the ARM Mali-400 used in the Samsung Galaxy S2 use a tile-based rendering architecture [Klug and Shimpi 11b]. In contrast, desktop GPUs from NVIDIA and ATI and mobile GPUs like the GeForce ULV GPU used in the Samsung Galaxy Tab 10.1 use *immediate-mode rendering* (IMR).

In IMRs, vertices are transformed once and primitives are rasterized essentially in order (see Figure 24.1). If a fragment passes depth testing (assuming the platform has early-z), it will be shaded and its output color will be written to the framebuffer. However, a later fragment may overwrite this pixel, nullifying the earlier work done and writing the framebuffer again. This behavior is known as overdraw. If the frame-

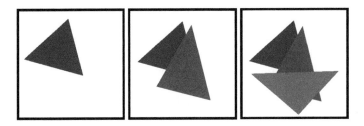

Figure 24.1. IMRs render each primitive only once and render the entire framebuffer in a single pass.

buffer is stored in DRAM external to the GPU, this means a relatively costly and slow memory access was wasted. Even without overdraw, the depth buffer still must be read for later fragments generated at a pixel location in order to reject them.

Tilers instead divide the framebuffer into tiles of pixels (see Figure 24.2). All draw commands are buffered. At the end of the frame, for each tile, all geometry overlapping that tile is transformed, clipped, and rasterized into a framebuffer cache. Once the final values for all pixels have been resolved, the entire tile is written out to memory from the framebuffer cache. This saves redundant framebuffer writes and allows for fast depth-buffer access since depth testing and depth and color writes can be performed with the local framebuffer cache. The end goal is to limit the memory bandwidth consumed by color- and depth-buffer access.

There is an additional group of tilers which use *tile-based deferred rendering* (TBDR), for example, the Imagination Tech SGX family. The idea is to rasterize all primitives in a tile before performing any fragment shading. This allows *hidden surface removal* (HSR) and depth testing to be performed in a fast framebuffer cache before any fragment shading work is done. Assuming opaque geometry, each pixel is then shaded and written to the framebuffer exactly once.

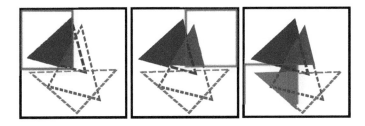

Figure 24.2. Tiling architectures divide the scene into tiles and render all primitives into each tile using a fast framebuffer cache.

Tiling doesn't come for free. The scene geometry must be retransformed and clipped for each tile, so, to maintain a balanced pipeline, additional vertex processing power is needed. Bandwidth will also be spent rereading vertex data for each tile. The digital logic for tiling, repeated vertex shading, and a fast framebuffer cache also takes transistors from raw fragment-shading horsepower. Tiling also requires buffering commands deeply, leading to a more complicated hardware and driver implementation, and the fact that the rendering of each primitive cannot be neatly placed in a single interval of time makes performance analysis more difficult. For more tips on performance-tuning specific to tiling architectures, see Chapter 23.

Architecturally, the mobile GPU landscape is not homogenous. Optimizations may affect the different architectures very differently, so it is important to test on multiple devices for cross-platform releases.

24.2.3   Differences in Memory Architecture

On desktop systems, middle to high-end GPUs are discrete devices that communicate with the rest of the system via a peripheral bus like PCI-e, although some desktop CPUs are now shipping with capable integrated GPUs, for example, the AMD Llano processors. For good performance, this means that GPUs must include their own dedicated memory since accessing system memory through a peripheral bus for all memory accesses would be too slow in terms of bandwidth and latency. While this increases cost, it is an optimization opportunity since this memory and its configuration, controller, caching, and geometry can be optimized for graphics workloads.

For example, the NVIDIA Fermi architecture uses GDDR5 memory that is heavily partitioned [Walton 10] to allow for a wide memory interface. There are no other components competing for this bandwidth except for uploads from the rest of the system and scan-out for output devices; the GPU is the only user of this memory.

In mobile devices, on the other hand, the GPU is usually integrated into the same SoC as the CPU and other components. To save cost, power, die size, and package complexity, the GPU shares the RAM and memory interface with the other components. This is known as a *unified memory architecture* (UMA). A common memory type is the low-power LPDDR2, which has a 32-bit-wide interface [Klug and Shimpi 11a]. Not only is this memory general purpose, the GPU now shares bandwidth with other parts of the system like the CPU, network, camera, multimedia, and display, leaving less dedicated bandwidth available for rendering and composition.

There are some performance advantages to a unified memory architecture besides the savings in cost and complexity. With discrete GPUs the peripheral bus could become a bottleneck for transfers, especially for non–PCI-e buses with asymmetric speeds [Elhasson 05]. With a UMA, OpenGL client and server data are in fact stored in the same RAM. Even when it is not possible to directly access server-side data with `glMapBufferOES`, there are fewer performance cliffs lurking in transfers between

OpenGL client and server data, and using client-side data for dynamic vertices or indices may not have as great a performance penalty. Data transfer and command latencies from the GPU to the CPU are also likely to be lessened.

One current limitation is that OpenGL ES does not yet have an extension for *pixel buffer objects* (PBO), meaning that pixel and texture data must be transferred synchronously. This makes the comparatively cheap bandwidth between client and server data less useful and also makes streaming assets during runtime more difficult.

24.3 Reducing Memory Bandwidth

As shown in Table 24.1, memory bandwidth pressure is one of the major performance pressures on mobile devices, especially on games and other applications that also perform heavy amounts of CPU-side work during the frame, or in multimedia applications which have additional bandwidth clients besides the GPU and display.

Besides limiting performance, memory accesses external to the GPU consume a great deal of power, sometimes more than the computation itself [Antochi et al. 04].

Device	CPU Write Bandwidth (GB/s)	GPU Write Bandwidth (GB/s)
Motorola Xoom	2.6	1.252
Motorola Droid X	1.4	6.8
LG Thunderbolt	0.866	0.518
Dell Inspiron 520	4.8	3.8
Desktop System	14.2	25.7

Table 24.1. Write bandwidth for CPU and GPU on different devices. CPU write bandwidth estimated by memset. GPU bandwidth estimated by glClear followed by glFinish. Desktop system has an Intel Core 2 Quad and NVIDIA GeForce 8800 GTS. The desktop system has significantly more bandwidth available to the GPU than to the CPU, and CPU and GPU memory accesses do not interfere with each other. The Droid X GPU write bandwidth score is high enough that it may not actually be writing the framebuffer each time (i.e., coalescing redundant clears or setting a cleared flag).

24.3.1 Relative Display Sizes

Despite the tight power and cost constraints for mobile devices, the display resolutions of modern mobile devices are a considerable fraction of the resolutions of desktop displays. Even though the display sizes are smaller, mobile devices often have a higher pixel density to be viewable at a close distance (see Table 24.2).

With the limited fragment shading throughput and memory bandwidth of mobile devices, these comparatively large display sizes mean that fragment shading and

Device	Resolution	% of 1280×1024	% of 1920×1080
Motorola Xoom	1280×800	78.13	49.38
Apple iPad 2	1024×768	58.63	37.06
Apple iPhone 4S	960×640	46.89	29.63
Samsung Galaxy S2	800×480	30.00	18.52

Table 24.2. Resolution comparison of desktop and mobile panels.

full-screen or large-quad operations can easily become a bottleneck since these requirements scale proportionally with the number of output pixels. Memory bandwidth is also a major power drain, making limiting bandwidth doubly important. Common large-quad operations include postprocessing effects and user-interface composition.

Within mobile devices, there is also a large spread of resolution sizes, especially between tablets and phone form factors, so testing on multiple devices is important for performance testing as well as application useabilty.

24.3.2   Framebuffer Bandwidth

Basic rendering can consume surprisingly significant amounts of memory bandwidth. Assume the framebuffer has 16-bit color with 16-bit depth [Android 11] and a 1024×768 resolution. Accessing every pixel in the framebuffer 60 times a second takes 94MB/s of bandwidth, so to write all the pixels' colors every frame at 60 frames a second with 0% overdraw, takes 94MB/s of bandwidth.

However, assuming an IMR architecture, to be able to render a scene, we also usually perform a depth-buffer read for each rendered pixel. Both the depth buffer and the color buffer are also usually cleared each frame, and when applications write to the color buffer while rendering the scene, they also generally write the fragment depth to the depth buffer.

The memory bandwidth consumption of the final framebuffer doesn't end when the application is done writing it either. After `eglSwapBuffers`, it may need to be composited by the platform-specific windowing system and then scanned out to the display. Unlike desktop systems which often have dedicated graphics or framebuffer memory, this will also consume system memory bandwidth. This will consume 94MB/s of bandwidth just for scanout, or at least 288MB/s with composition (read, write to composited framebuffer, and scanout).

Thus, with a depth and color clear, one depth-buffer read, a depth- and color-buffer write, and display scanout, a basic clear-fill-and-display operation on an IMR consumes 564–752MB/s of bandwidth, so even simple-use cases consume a significant amount of memory bandwidth; anything interesting the application does only costs more bandwidth. If a 32-bit framebuffer is used, this number will be even greater. This can be a significant portion of the bandwidth available on a mobile device (see Table 24.1 for bandwidth measurements for some devices).

Tile-based architectures can consume less bandwidth for this basic operation since they ideally handle the depth and color clears and the depth buffer reads within the framebuffer cache. Use of the `EXT_discard_framebuffer` [Bowman 09] extension saves additional bandwidth because it means the calculated depth buffer never needs to be written back to external memory from the framebuffer cache once the frame is complete. So a tile-based architecture will consume at least 188–377MB/s for basic clear-fill-and-display operation.

Applications using a 32-bit framebuffer that may be bandwidth-bound should experiment with a lower-precision format. Since the output framebuffer is not often used in subsequent calculations, the loss of numerical precision is not propagated and magnified. One valid concern is banding or quantization of smooth gradients [Guy 10]. However, this may be more of an issue in photography and media applications rather than games and 3D applications because of the nature of the produced content.

24.3.3 Antialiasing

Antialiasing improves image quality by refining edges that are jagged when rendered. *Supersampling antialiasing* (SSAA) consumes a large amount of extra bandwidth and fragment-shading load since it must render the scene to a larger, high-resolution buffer and then downsample to the final image. *Multisample antialiasing* (MSAA), on the other hand, rasterizes multiple samples per pixel and stores a depth and color for each sample. If all samples in a pixel are covered by the same primitive, the fragment shader will only be run once for that pixel, and the same color value will be written for all samples in that pixel. These samples are then blended to compute the final image [aths 03].

Though using MSAA creates little if any additional fragment-shading work or texture-read bandwidth consumption, it does use a significant amount of bandwidth to read and write the multiple samples for pixels. Tiling architectures may be able to store the samples in the framebuffer cache and perform this blending before write-back to system memory [Technologies 11]. Vendors may perform other optimizations like only storing multiple samples when there is nontrivial coverage information.

24.3.4 Texture Bandwidth

Since texture accesses are often performed at least once per-pixel, these can be another large source of bandwidth consumption.

One simple way to reduce bandwidth is to lower the texture resolution. Fewer texels, besides a smaller memory footprint, means better texture cache utilization and more efficient filtering. The framebuffer resolution usually can't be lowered, since native resolution is expected. Texture sizes are more flexible, particularly if they represent low-frequency signals like illumination. Low-frequency textures could even be demoted to vertex attributes, and interpolated. If assets have been ported from desktop, there may be room for optimization here.

For static textures, as opposed to textures drawn by frequent offscreen rendering, texture compression is another great way to save bandwidth, loading time, memory footprint, and disk space. Even though work must be done to decompress the texture data when they are used, the smaller size of compressed textures makes them friendlier to texture caching and memory bandwidth, increasing runtime performance.

One complication is that there are multiple incompatible formats for texture compression supported via OpenGL ES 2 extensions. Example formats are ETC, available on most Android 2.2 devices, S3TC, available on NVIDIA Tegra, and PVRTC, available on ImaginationTech SGX [Motorola 11].

To support texture compression formats on multiple devices, an application must either package multiple versions of its assets and dynamically choose the correct ones or perform the compression at runtime, loadtime, or install-time. Performing the compression at runtime or install-time must be done carefully to avoid slowing down the application and gives up the benefits of improved loading time and disk space, as well as reduced network bandwidth required to download the application. S3TC has compression ratios between 4:1 and 8:1, so the space and download savings lost are substantial [Domine 00].

As for framebuffer bandwidth, using a texture format with lower precision like RGB565 saves read bandwidth. Unlike texture compression, this applies to textures used as render targets as well.

24.3.5   Texture Filtering and Bandwidth

The texture filtering mode used can also have a significant impact on the memory bandwidth consumed, though texture caching can greatly mitigate these costs. GL_NEAREST only needs a single value from the texture. GL_LINEAR requires four values for bilinear filtering, but it is unlikely that all four samples will have to be read from external memory since, due to the locality of texture coordinates of neighboring fragments, those samples are possibly already in the texture cache. Trilinear filtering with mipmaps via GL_LINEAR_MIPMAP_LINEAR requires eight values per sample, but it can actually increase performance since, for faraway pixels, samples from the smaller mip levels are very likely to hit in texture cache.

Anisotropic filtering via EXT_texture_filter_anisotropic prevents surfaces oblique to the viewer from appearing blurry. However, it requires between 2 and 16 taps into a mipmapped texture for each sample. Even if the majority of these taps hit in texture cache, high levels of anistropic filtering stress memory bandwidth and texture filtering hardware.

24.4 Reducing Fragment Workload

Due to the limited compute and bandwidth available on mobile devices with respect to the large number of pixels and the complexity of modern rendering, fragment shading is often a bottleneck for mobile GPUs. However, fragment shading can be improved in other ways than just simplifying shading.

24.4.1 Overdraw and Blending

Overdraw is when pixels that have previously been shaded are overwritten by later fragments in a scene (see Figure 24.3). On IMRs and tiling immediate-mode renderers, overdraw wastes completed fragment shading since the previous computed pixel value is overwritten and lost. On IMRs, this also results in an additional framebuffer write, when only one final pixel color needs to be written.

On IMR GPUs, this extra bandwidth consumption and fragment work can be limited by sorting and rendering geometry from front to back (see Figure 24.4). This is especially practical for static geometry, which can be processed into a spatial data structure during an asset export step. An additional heuristic for games is to render the player character first and the sky-box last [Pranckevicius and Zioma 11].

For batches where front-to-back object sorting is not practical, for example, with complicated, interlocking geometry or heavy use of alpha testing, a depth prepass can be used to eliminate redundant pixel calculations, at the cost of repeated vertex shading work, primitive assembly, and depth-buffer access (see Figure 24.5).

The idea of a depth prepass is to bind a trivial fragment shader and render the scene with color writes disabled. Depth calculation, testing, and writes proceed as normal, and the final pixel depth is resolved. The normal fragment shader is then bound, and the scene is rerendered. In this manner, only the final fragments that affect the scene color are rendered. This only works for opaque objects.

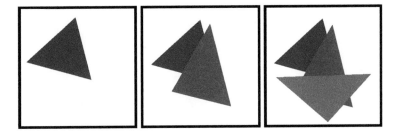

Figure 24.3. In this overdraw case, pixels that are covered by later primitives are shaded more than once

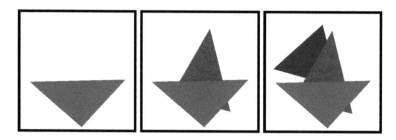

Figure 24.4. By ordering front to back, we no longer shade the covered pixels more than once

Even without overdraw, on IMRs, heavy amounts of overlapping geometry can still be expensive because of the depth-buffer reads needed to reject pixels. Primitive assembly, rasterization, and the pixel reject rate can also become limiting for large primitives like sky-boxes [Pranckevicius and Zioma 11].

One type of effect that can be particular expensive in terms of fragment shading and framebuffer bandwidth is particle effects rendered via multiple overlapping quads with blending. On IMRs, each layer of overlap requires a read and write of the existing framebuffer value. For all mobile GPUs, each layers adds additional fragment computation and blending. Some simple effects like a torch flame can be converted into an animated shader, for example, by changing a texture offset each frame. Other effects, like a candle flame, can be done by rendering a mesh of dynamic data instead of many overlapping billboarded quads. This reduces overlap and the resultant blending. When applicable, using opaque, alpha-tested sprites also eliminates the cost of blending.

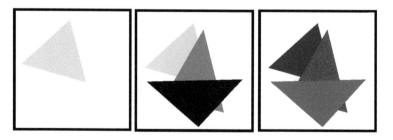

Figure 24.5. A depth prepass resolves ordering in the depth buffer before performing nontrivial fragment shading.

24.4.2 Full-Screen Effects

Full-screen postprocessing effects are a major tool for visual effects in modern games and graphics applications and have been an area of innovation in recent years. Common applications of full-screen postprocessing in games are motion blur, depth of field, screen-space ambient occlusion, light bloom, color filtering, and tone-mapping. Other applications such as photo-editing tools may use full-screen or large-area effects for composition, blending, warping, and filtering.

Full-screen postprocessing is a powerful tool to create effects, but it is an easy way to consume large amounts of bandwidth and fragment processing. Such effects should be carefully weighed for their worth and are prime candidates for optimization.

A full-screen pass implies at least a read and write of the framebuffer at full resolution, which at 16-bit color and a 1024×768 resolution means 188MB/s bandwidth. Even with tiling architectures, a post-processing pass means a roundtrip to external memory. One way to optimize these effects is to remove the extra full-screen pass. Some postprocessing effects such as color filtering or tone mapping that don't require knowledge of neighboring pixels or feedback from rendering may be merged into the fragment shaders for the objects themselves. This may require the use of *uber-shaders* or shader generation, to allow for natural editing of object fragment shaders while programmatically appending postprocessing effects.

If the additional pass cannot be eliminated, then all layered full-screen postprocessing effects can be coalesced into a single additional pass. Instead of multiple passes that each read the previous result from a texture and write out a new filtered value, each effect can pass its computed value to the next effect in the same shader. This saves redundant roundtrips to framebuffer memory.

One limitation of OpenGL ES 2.0 is poor support for *multiple render targets* (MRT), which allow multiple output buffers from a fragment shader. This makes deferred shading impractical: it relies on separate *geometry buffers* to store different geometry attributes, but without MRTs, this requires rendering a full pass of the scene for each. Even if MRTs were available, however, the additional bandwidth cost of reading and writing multiple full-screen intermediate buffers make deferred shading prohibitively expensive.

24.4.3 Offscreen Passes

Similar to full-screen effects are effects requiring offscreen render targets like environmental reflections, depth-map shadows, and light bloom.

Many of these effects require multiple samples of the offscreen image for a soft effect. Since these textures are rendering targets, they probably don't have full mipmap levels or optimal internal texture layouts for coherent read access, so eliminating the cost of multiple samples of a large texture is particularly important. One way to optimize offscreen effects that require a blurred image is to take advantage of

Device	GPU Arch	MP/s				
		clear	vtx_lgt	frg_lgt	one_tap	five_tap
Motorola Xoom	IMR	626	52.4	24.08	26.13	3.17
Motorola Droid X	TBDR	3670	234	62.9	5.36	5.7
LG Thunderbolt	TB IMR	305	48.7	–	30	20.36
Dell Inspiron 520	IMR	1920	231	204	139	120
Desktop System*	IMR	1380	2950	1920	1730	1290

*Desktop system has an Intel Core 2 Quad and NVIDIA 8800 GTS.

Table 24.3. Performance for different shading and pass configurations. All tests used 1024 × 1024 16-bit offscreen depth and color buffers as the main framebuffer, with a 32-bit RGBA intermediate color buffer and 16-bit depth buffer where applicable. clear performs color buffer clear operations. vtx_lgt renders a synthetic scene with lighting computed per-vertex, a per-pixel texture lookup, and 39,200 triangles with 0% overdraw. frg_lgt uses the same scene and calculates the diffuse illumination in the fragment shader. five_tap and one_tap draw the vertex lighting scene with five- and one- sample full-screen postprocessing passes, respectively. All units are pixels per second. The Droid X clear scores are high enough that it may not actually be writing the framebuffer each time (i.e., coalescing redundant clears, setting a cleared flag, or color compression).

texture-filtering hardware. Rather than rendering a large offscreen image, and then taking multiple samples of a fragment shader, the scene can be rendered into a low-resolution offscreen target and blurred via texture filtering.

The main fragment shader for the scene can then bind that target as a texture and read from it with an appropriate texture-filtering mode such as GL_LINEAR. The smaller size of the offscreen target makes this strategy particularly cache-friendly. This may work well for light bloom and environmental reflection, for example. Depending on the effect, an additional Gaussian blurring pass on the offscreen target may be needed, but these can also be accelerated with texture filtering and separable kernels as well [Rideout 11].

Even when blurring due to texture filtering is not beneficial, reducing offscreen target resolution is an easy way to reduce the fragment workload and memory bandwidth without a serious visual impact for effects that only need low-frequency signals like environmental reflections.

Whenever moving additional computations from a separate full-screen pass into the fragment shader of objects in the scene, it is important on non-TBDR architectures to minimize overdraw to avoid wasted work. One advantage of full-screen postprocessing in a separate pass is that each pixel is computed exactly once. Performance of various configurations can be seen in Table 24.3.

24.4.4 Shaving Fragment Work

One area of optimization with a significant amount of leverage is optimizing fragment shaders. Shaders tend to be fairly small and simple, but the sheer number of fragments and amount of floating-point computation makes nontrivial fragment shading a major bottleneck on both tiling and IMR GPUs. Optimizations here will probably have some effect on visual quality, but it may well be worth the gain in performance.

For static geometry and lighting, baking most of the illumination into light maps saves computation at runtime and allows the use of more advanced lighting techniques than would otherwise be affordable [Miller 99, Unity 11]. Light-map generation and export does require a well-developed asset pipeline.

Another classic trick to avoid floating-point work and special functions in fragment shaders is to approximate a complicated function with a lookup texture [Pranckevicius 11]. This allows the use of much more elaborate BDRFs. This also allows for effects that would be difficult to achieve purely procedurally [Jason Mitchell 07]. One-dimensional look-up textures may be particular cache-friendly and with a smooth input parameter, should have good locality of reference.

Fragment shaders with multiple texture fetches, however, may already be bound by texture fetch. Large amounts of state for each fragment shader may also limit the maximum number of in-flight fragments due to register pressure, which affects the ability of the GPU to hide the latency of texture lookups.

24.5 Vertex Shading

24.5.1 Vertex vs. Fragment Work

Traditional IMR wisdom states that lifting computations like lighting, specularity, and normalization from per-fragment to per-vertex and then interpolating the results can save performance at the cost of image quality, and this is still true for IMRs.

However, for tiling architectures, this performance wisdom is more dubious because tilers must perform all vertex computations for each tile [Apple 11]. Tilers are more likely to be vertex-bound, and Unity recommends 40K or fewer vertices on recent iOS devices, which use Imagination Tech SGX GPUs [Unity 11].

This means that heavy vertex shaders, even if they save fragment work, may be a performance drag on tiling architectures. This is particularly true for TBDRs since they perform little-to-no redundant fragment work. When working with IMRs, lifting computation from the fragment shader to the vertex shader is likely a performance win, and becoming vertex-bound is less of a concern.

Another consideration to the relationship between vertex and fragment shaders is that adding too many additional varyings can be a drag on performance since they must all be interpolated, and a large amount of per-fragment memory to store varyings may limit the number of fragments that can be in flight at once. A large number of varyings may also thrash the post-transform cache, which stores the results of vertex shading, making vertex processing more expensive. So, thinning the interface between vertex and fragment shading can be valuable.

Vertex processing is more of a bandwidth drain on tiling architectures since the attributes are probably pulled again for each tile unless they hit in a pre- or post-transform cache. To lower this bandwidth, use a lower-precision buffer format such as `OES_vertex_half_float`.

Interleaved vertex data, which interleaves the attributes for each vertex in the same buffer, is also more efficient for attribute fetch since an entire vertex can be fetched in one linear read [Apple 11]. Since memory reads have some granularity, interleaving all the data for a vertex means less unnecessary data will be transferred because it was adjacent to a fetched attribute. If there is a pretransform vertex attribute cache, which stores fetched vertex attributes and the surrounding data, this will make more efficient use of it.

One caveat to interleaving vertex data is if the vertex data is partially dynamic. The most common case is when only positions are updated. A solution is to separate the vertex data into "hot" attributes that are frequently updated and "cold" ones which are mostly static, and store them in separate buffers. This avoids inefficient updates to the "hot" attributes because of a large stride between vertices.

24.6 Conclusion

OpenGL ES is a fundamental component of the modern mobile experience for UI rendering and composition [Guy and Haase 11] and presents a huge market and potential impact for OpenGL developers. However, driven by explicit consumer demand for long battery life and slender devices on the one hand and large, brilliant displays with perfectly smooth rendering on the other, performance must be a dominant consideration during development. The wide range of devices in the market, differing in age, resolution, and capability, only make this more difficult.

One important question is if the significant difference in performance between mobile and desktop GPUs will continue to be a dominant consideration in application development or if it is something that the steady march of semiconductor process and architectural improvements will soon make irrelevant. Looking at the projected roadmaps for mobile GPU vendors, the compute power of mobile GPUs should indeed climb over the next few years. However, other limits, including bandwidth and power consumption, are more fundamental and cannot be conquered as easily. Desktop and even laptop systems are less tightly constrained on those dimensions.

The expected workloads of mobile devices are also changing. Sprite-based games and 2D workloads are still very important, but several publishers have produced mobile ports of desktop game engines, and games with console or desktop levels of rich game worlds and visual quality. These games raise the bar for what is considered possible and now expected on mobile systems and present challenges in terms of the amount of geometry, assets, and visual effects they require. The main strategy to deliver on these promises is a measured assessment of a platform's capabilities and limitations paired with an understanding and quantification of the costs of different effects and rendering techniques.

While developing a fast and efficient application for mobile devies takes thought, careful measurement and budgeting, and creative corner cutting, with a consciousness to the costs and limitations involved, developers can deliver beautiful and compelling graphics and an experience users can barely believe is possible.

Bibliography

[Android 11] Google Android. "GLSurfaceView." http://developer.android.com/reference/android/opengl/GLSurfaceView.html, 2011.

[Antochi et al. 04] Iosif Antochi, Ben H. H. Juurlink, Stamatis Vassiliadis, and Petri Liuha. "Memory Bandwidth Requirements of Tile-Based Rendering." In *SAMOS*, *Lecture Notes in Computer Science*, edited by Andy D. Pimentel and Stamatis Vassiliadis, pp. 323–332. Springer, 2004.

[Apple 11] Apple. "Best Practices for Working with Vertex Data." http://developer.apple.com/library/ios/#documentation/3DDrawing/Conceptual/OpenGLES_ProgrammingGuide/TechniquesforWorkingwithVertexData/TechniquesforWorkingwithVertexData.html#//apple_ref/doc/uid/TP40008793-CH107-SW1, 2011.

[aths 03] aths. "Multisampling Anti-Aliasing: A Closeup View." http://alt.3dcenter.org/artikel/multisampling_anti-aliasing/index_e.php, 2003.

[Bowman 09] Benji Bowman. "EXT_discard_framebuffer." http://www.khronos.org/registry/gles/extensions/EXT/EXT_discard_framebuffer.txt, 2009.

[Domine 00] Sebastian Domine. "Using Texture Compression in OpenGL." http://www.oldunreal.com/editing/s3tc/ARB_texture_compression.pdf, 2000.

[Elhasson 05] Ikrima Elhasson. "Fast Texture Downloads and Readbacks using Pixel Buffer Objects in OpenGL." http://developer.download.nvidia.com/assets/gamedev/docs/Fast_Texture_Transfers.pdf?display=style-table, 2005.

[Guy and Haase 11] Romain Guy and Chet Haase. "Android 4.0 Graphics and Animations." http://android-developers.blogspot.com/2011/11/android-40-graphics-and-animations.html, 2011.

[Guy 10] Romain Guy. "Bitmap Quality, Banding, and Dithering." http://www.curious-creature.org/2010/12/08/bitmap-quality-banding-and-dithering/, 2010.

[Jason Mitchell 07] Dhabih Eng Jason Mitchell, Moby Francke. "Illustrative Rendering in Team Fortress 2." International Symposium on Non-Photorealistic Animation and Rendering, 2007.

[Klug and Shimpi 11a] Brian Klug and Anand Lal Shimpi. "LG Optimus 2X & NVIDIA Tegra 2 Review: The First Dual-Core Smartphone." http://www.anandtech.com/show/4144/lg-optimus-2x-nvidia-tegra-2-review-the-first-dual-core-smartphone/5, 2011.

[Klug and Shimpi 11b] Brian Klug and Anand Lal Shimpi. "Samsung Galaxy S 2 (International) Review—The Best, Redefined." http://www.anandtech.com/Show/Index/4686?cPage=13&all=False&sort=0&page=15&slug=samsung-galaxy-s-2-international-review-the-best-redefined, 2011.

[Miller 99] Kurt Miller. "Lightmaps (Static Shadowmaps)." http://www.flipcode.com/archives/Lightmaps_Static_Shadowmaps.shtml, 1999.

[Motorola 11] Motorola. "Understanding Texture Compression." http://developer.motorola.com/docstools/library/understanding-texture-compression/, 2011.

[Pranckevicius and Zioma 11] Aras Pranckevicius and Renaldas Zioma. "Fast Mobile Shaders." http://blogs.unity3d.com/2011/08/18/fast-mobile-shaders-talk-at-siggraph/, 2011.

[Pranckevicius 11] Aras Pranckevicius. "iOS Shader Tricks, or It's 2001 All Over Again." http://aras-p.info/blog/2011/02/01/ios-shader-tricks-or-its-2001-all-over-again/, 2011.

[Rideout 11] Philip Rideout. "OpenGL Bloom Tutorial." http://prideout.net/archive/bloom/, 2011.

[Technologies 11] Imagination Technologies. "POWERVR Series5 Graphics SGX Architecture Guide for Developers." http://www.imgtec.com/powervr/insider/docs/POWERVR%20Series5%20Graphics.SGX%20architecture%20guide%20for%20developers.1.0.8.External.pdf, 2011.

[Unity 11] Unity. "Optimizing Graphics Performance." http://unity3d.com/support/documentation/Manual/Optimizing%20Graphics%20Performance.html, 2011.

[Walton 10] Steven Walton. "NVIDIA GeForce GTX 480 Review: Fermi Arrives." http://www.techspot.com/review/263-nvidia-geforce-gtx-480/page2.html, 2010.

Improving Performance by   25
Reducing Calls to the Driver

Sébastien Hillaire

25.1   Introduction

Rendering a scene can involve several rendering passes such as shadow map construction, light contribution accumulation, and framebuffer postprocessing. OpenGL is a state machine, and each of these passes requires changing state several times. Rendering requires two main steps:

1. Modify OpenGL states and objects in order to set up the assets used for rendering.

2. Issue a draw call to draw triangles and effectively change some pixel values.

These two steps require multiple calls to the driver. The driver is responsible for translating these function calls into commands to be sent to the GPU. The driver is provided by the GPU vendor and could be considered as a black box where only the vendor knows what is being done by each function call. At first, it seems reasonable to think that the drivers are filling a FIFO command queue that will be used to render the next frame. However, the driver's behavior can be very different depending on the vendor and/or platform. For example, a GPU driver for desktop computers has to take into account the wide variety of hardware that makes drivers a lot more complex than their counterpart on consoles, for which the platform is entirely and reliably known [Carmack 11]. Indeed, on such a platform, the driver can be specifically optimized for the installed hardware, whereas on the PC, the API requires a higher level of abstraction. Therefore, we should assume that each call to the OpenGL API will result in costly driver operations such as resource management, current state error checking, or multiple shared context threads synchronizations.

This chapter presents solutions that can be used to reduce the number of calls to the graphic driver in order to improve the performance. These solutions allow us to reduce the CPU overhead and hence increase rendering complexity.

25.2 Efficient OpenGL States Usage

Accessing and modifying OpenGL states can only be done through multiple calls to the API functions. Each call can potentially consume a lot of processing power. As a result, care must be taken to efficiently change OpenGL states using as few API calls as possible. In the OpenGL 1.0 days, state change operations could be accelerated using display lists which stored precompiled commands that could be executed in a single call. Despite being static, display lists were used as a fast way to change OpenGL states. However, they were removed from the OpenGL 3.2 core profile but are still available in the compatibility profile.

This section presents ways of detecting and avoiding unnecessary API calls. We also present recent OpenGL features that allow us to increase the efficiency of each call intended to change the current OpenGL states.

25.2.1 Detecting Redundant State Modifications

Debugging and optimizing an OpenGL application can be made easier by using some specific existing software. *gDEBugger* [Remedy 11] is a free tool that can record the OpenGL function call sequence for each frame independently. An important feature of this software is the *Statistics and Redundant Function Calls Viewer*, as seen in Figure 25.1, accessible using Ctrl+Shift+S. It allows us to count the number of

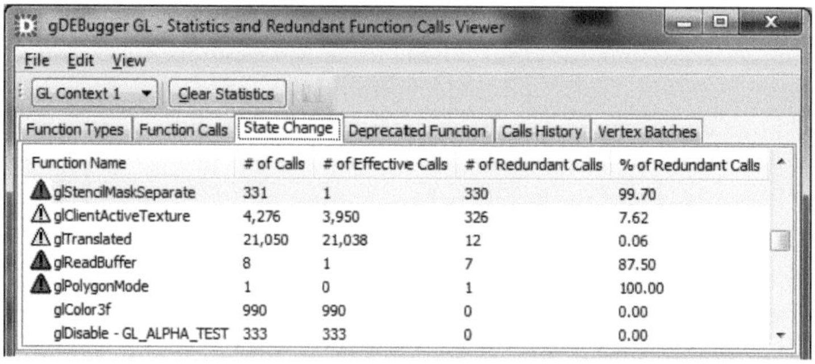

Figure 25.1. Using gDEBugger statistics to detect redundant OpenGL calls.

redundant calls to the driver that do not change its state. These calls are hence useless and should be avoided for the benefit of performance on the CPU/application side.

gDEBugger can also be used to verify that no deprecated functions are called. One of its drawbacks is that it is currently limited to OpenGL 3.2. However, more runtime debugging possibilities are offered such as OpenGL data/states viewing, global statistics, and performance analysis.

25.2.2 General Methods for Efficient State Modification

To avoid redundant calls, a solution would be to rely on the `glGet*` functions in order to query an OpenGL state's value before each API call that might modify it. This approach must must be avoided, as it is not efficient. This is due to the fact that the driver may have to look for the value resulting from previous commands appended to the command queue. Instead, two software solutions should be preferred: *return-to-default-state* or *state tracking*.

The return-to-default-state method is a straightforward one. OpenGL is first initialized to what is called the *default states*. When rendering is required, OpenGL states are modified. After draw calls corresponding to this state has been issued, default OpenGL states are restored so that others parts of the program start from the same point when modifying the default OpenGL states assumed. This widely used approach, often in old maintained projects and demos, has the advantage of avoiding checking all OpenGL states before changing only a few of them. The drawback is that it potentially issues twice as many API calls unless you rely on `glPushAttrib`/`glPopAttrib`, which is not a recommended approach.

The widely used alternative method called state tracking avoids redundant calls by keeping the OpenGL states up-to-date on the CPU side and keeping track of changes. This enables runtime evaluation of which driver calls are required to change the current states to the desired one. A very efficient implementation of this behavior is available in the game Quake 3 Arena [IdSoftware 05].[1] OpenGL states are kept in a single unsigned long value (Listing 25.1). Each bit of this double word stores whether or not an OpenGL state is activated. This enables the application to keep track of binary OpenGL states.

More complex states can also be tracked. As an example, the source and destination blend modes are kept in the lowest significant byte of the double word. If this byte is 0×00, then blending is disabled, else the first and second hexadecimal are custom values representing the source and destination blend mode. When rendering the scene, each time a new material, e.g., shader, is selected to render surfaces, the `GL_State` function is called with the desired OpenGL states as a parameter (Listing 25.1). The differences as compared to current OpenGL states are first computed using `XOR`. This is used to check, for each OpenGL state, whether a change needs to be applied. If the result is not zero, then, the state needs to be changed and an

---

[1] See `GL_State` function in `tr_backend.c`.

```
void GL_State(unsigned long stateBits)
{
  // Xor operation to compute state that need to be changed
  unsigned long diff = stateBits ^ glState.glStateBits;

  // Check depthFunc bits
  if (diff & GLS_DEPTHFUNC_EQUAL_BITS)
  {
    if (stateBits & GLS_DEPTHFUNC_EQUAL)
    {
      glDepthFunc( GL_EQUAL );
    }
    else
    {
      glDepthFunc( GL_LEQUAL );
    }
  }

  // [Process other states...]

  // Store current state
  glState.glStateBits = stateBits;
}
```

Listing 25.1. Avoiding redundant OpenGL calls by storing current state on the CPU.

API call needs to be issued. At the end of this method, the current tracked state is replaced with the new one. The Quake 3 engine also tracks OpenGL objects that can be bound such as textures and the associated environment parameter for the first two texture units.

We have modified the Quake 3 rendering engine to compare the return-to-default-state approach to the state tracking one used in Quake 3. The performance was measured on a replayed session of the game with 32 bots playing against a human on the Q3DM7 map. The computer was equipped with an Intel Core i5 processor, 4GB of memory, and an NVIDIA GeForce 275 GTX. Results show that for a complex scene with surfaces ordered by material, the state tracking method is 11% faster than the return-to-default-state approach (Table 25.1). We must keep in mind that the difference would have been much higher on a computer from 1999 because of lower CPU frequency. Also, OpenGL now requires the use of shaders, uniform values, buffer objects, etc. These increase the number of states that must be tracked.

	Frames per second	milliseconds
states-tracking	714	1.4
return-to-default-states	643	1.55

Table 25.1. Mean performance measured when replaying 20 recorded sessions of Quake 3 arena with and without OpenGL states check on the CPU.

It is important to understand that the state-tracking method alone will not dramatically improve performance if meshes are rendered in a random order. It should only be seen as an additional component to more generalized optimization approaches. Indeed, the performance of an application will benefit more from the a priori knowledge we have when rendering meshes. For example, the Quake 3 engine sorts meshes per material so that they are drawn in a specific order, e.g., opaque, sky box, then transparent geometry. This helps us apply fewer changes to states related to material such as textures or alpha blending. Furthermore, state tracking can also be applied only when a material needs to be changed. You can also group some common states together to look for state differences at a coarse level first and then apply fine-grained state checks. Instead of material, grouping state changes as a function of their modification frequency can also be a good choice. To sum up, a priori knowledge, coarse state grouping, and fine-grained state changes are three methods that can be combined, or used independently, for efficient state tracking and modifications.

Another example of the use of such methods can be found in recent opensource game engines such as the engines used for games Penumbra Overture [Frictional-Game 10] and Doom 3 [IdSoftware 11]. Unified lighting is achieved in the Doom 3 renderer by using a common set of shaders to render all surfaces. As in Quake 3, an a priori knowledge is used to sort meshes according to their material. The state tracking method is also used to modify OpenGL states at specific stages of each code path for the unified lighting and shadowing methods. This reveals that these methods are timeless and should always be considered when developing any renderer.

25.3   Batching and Instancing

The performance of a rendering system will not only be driven by the number of triangles an application need to draw. The number of draw calls issued for each frame also plays a crucial role. Indeed, this is a very complex metric that depends a lot on the hardware [Wloka 03], i.e., CPU/GPU, and software, i.e., the driver [Hardwidge 03]. Thus, if CPU bound, the performance of an application will be mostly influenced by the number of batches per frame, a batch representing a draw call (`glDraw*`) that is often accompanied with state changes. If GPU bound, the performance will be influenced by the number of triangles drawn and pixel-shader complexity. Reducing the number of draw calls is mostly a CPU-only optimization. Thus, such reduction will not influence the performance of an application that is GPU bound because of complex geometry or shaders.

On a PC, the number of batches that can be submitted every frame is very limited when compared to consoles because of higher driver overhead [Hardwidge 03]. Wloka [Wloka 03] has shown that the number of batches that can be issued per frame highly depends on the CPU when there are few triangles because of the overhead resulting from the setup and commands submission to the driver (CPU-bound application). As a result, we can, to some extent, freely render more triangles per batch without hurting the overall performance of the application. It shows that performance depends a lot on the CPU and GPU performance and the way they are tied together. Despite being old, the presentation of Wloka is a good starting point to begin understanding the cost of batches. We have to keep in mind that performance will be closely linked to our hardware and context of execution, and it can evolve with hardware. However, there are still some guidelines that can be followed to improve draw-call size and reduce the number of draw calls.

25.3.1 Batching

Batching refers to the general activity of grouping primitives together to render them all using as few draw call as possible. The larger the batches, the less the cumulative batch-submission overhead, i.e., fewer draw calls for fewer driver calls and CPU usage. Changes in transformation, material, or texture are the major batch breakers as these operations require changing OpenGL states. Several batching methods exist to reduce the number of draw calls: *combine*, *combine+element*, and *dynamic*.

The combine method packs together several geometry objects in a single set of buffer arrays (vertices and their attributes, indices) and renders them in a single draw call. The combination can be done based on object-appearance similarity. For example, small rocks could be combined and drawn together in a single draw call. The drawbacks are that objects can no longer move relative to each other, and culling will be limited. However, a certain amount of culling can be maintained if we take into account the relative position of objects in order to not pack together objects that are far away. You can also group together object that are in the same room or area of your scene.

The combine+element method consists of packing together geometry objects in a single set of buffer arrays (vertices and their attributes) but keeping the element array (indices) dynamic. As compared to combine, this approach allows us to have full control over object culling. It can be used for small-to-large static objects, as copying element indices can be done very fast. However, the combined array buffers containing geometry can take a lot of memory because they must contain all transformed geometry of all objects in the scene. The drawback of this method is that it can only be used to group nonanimated meshes.

The last method, dynamic, proposes to preallocate vertex and element buffers and to fill them dynamically at runtime. This approach can be used for objects sharing the same rendering state (shaders, textures, uniforms, blending, etc.) but potentially different vertex buffers over time, e.g., objects resulting from transformation or skinning. This approach is efficient for a lot of relatively small objects when computing vertex transformation on the CPU is faster than issuing more draw calls. Also, it takes some memory bandwidth to fill dynamic buffers, so performance tests must be conducted before choosing this method instead of issuing more draw calls.

In the case where different objects packed in a single array require different textures for their appearance, a texture atlas can be used. A texture atlas refers to a single

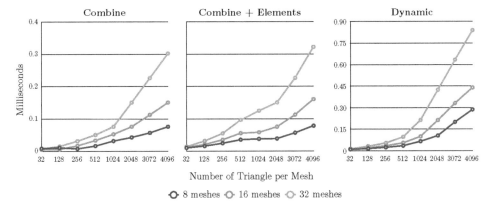

Figure 25.2. Batching performance for three different methods.

large texture containing several textures [NVIDIA 04]. Thus, changing appearance no longer requires changing the currently bound texture object. This method still suffers from the need to preprocess texture coordinates to match the texture atlas. Also, texture repetition cannot be used unless handled specifically in the fragment shader using more ALU operations. A more efficient approach on today's hardware would be to use texture arrays through the extension `ARB_texture_array`. In this case, a single texture object can address different textures of the same size according to a single index and without the need to process texture coordinates.

The performance of each method is presented in Figure 25.2 for 8, 16, and 32 meshes rendered. Performance is presented as a function of the number of triangles per mesh with each vertex attribute having 2-component texture coordinates and a 3-component normal. We can notice that the combine+element method has an overhead because it needs to send the element array before each draw call. That cost disappears when the number of triangles to draw increases. As expected, the dynamic method is the most costly one, as all data need to be sent to the GPU before each draw call.

The methods presented in this section effectively reduce the number of draw calls. However, they also require either a lot of preprocessing, making them harder to use in dynamically generated content environments. These solutions fit perfectly for most of the use cases. However, they would not be able to efficiently render a huge number of instances of an object with specific per-instance data. A solution for such a case is to use *instancing*.

25.3.2   OpenGL Instancing

The efficient rendering of a huge number of instances of objects having different positions and appearance is a complex task. With OpenGL, two methods can be used to achieve instancing.

The first instancing method relies on the memory available through shader uniforms to store arrays of parameters. This array can be indexed through an additional per-instance vertex attribute. Thus, a large batch of geometry can be rendered in a single draw call, and each vertex will automatically read the input it needs to achieve a specific appearance and transformation in a way similar to indexed vertex skinning [Beeson 04]. With this method, we do not need any OpenGL extensions. The downside is that we are limited by the number of uniforms that can be allocated for each vertex shader. An extension to this method is to use vertex texture fetch to read data from textures. However, this requires having a graphic card supporting at least the OpenGL 2.0 core and, if we require floating point values, to check that the `GL_ARB_texture_float` extension is defined unless we use the OpenGL core 3.0. This methods has the advantage of being usable on old hardware, but the number of instances drawn per draw call will be limited.

True instancing [Carucci 05] can be achieved with OpenGL 3.1 or through the `GL_ARB_instanced_array` extension. It is achieved using three specific steps: (1) bind array buffers to the attribute input of the vertex shader; (2) for each attribute input, specify the frequency at which vertex attributes need to be updated using the divisor value (attribute array pointer will be incremented every "*divisor*" instance); (3) call a draw function that takes as input the number of instances to draw, e.g., `glDrawElementsInstanced`. Additionally, the constant `gl_instanceID` representing the number of instances already drawn is available in the shaders. It allows us to compute specific data for the current instance being rendered.

Concerning visual diversity, instancing is more limited than multiple independent draw calls. However, OpenGL extensions such as `ARB_base_vertex`, `ARB_base_instance`, or `ARB_texture_array` were designed to help developers restore that diversity on all instances, e.g., material parameters and textures.

To show the importance of instancing on GPU performance, I measured the cost of rendering different number of instances with a varying number of per-instance data. To get the raw performance, each instance consisted of a single triangle. I compared one draw call per instance, `glDrawElements`, to one single call for all instances, `glDrawElementsInstanced`. In the first case, per-instance parameters were sent through shader uniforms. In the second case, the divisor value is used with array buffers, as described previously, to get different input values for each instance (divisor = 1). Figure 25.3 presents the measured performance for several instances and per-instance vec3 parameters. All triangles were rendered outside the view frustrum to avoid rasterization cost. Performance was measured on a Intel i5 processor, with 4GB of memory and a NVIDIA GeForce 275 GTX. This table reveals a cost overhead for the instancing method when there are fewer than 768 instances. Above that limit, the more per-instance parameters we add, the more interesting it is to use instancing. Also, 768 instances is a worst-case scenario as we are only instancing a single triangle. As revealed by Wloka [Wloka 03], we could also draw more triangles per instance without hurting performance: the more triangles per instance, the lower

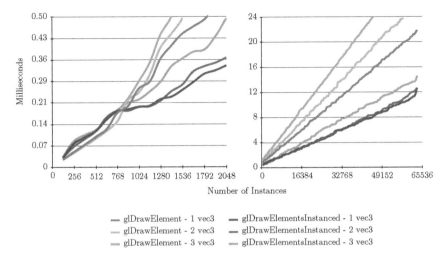

Figure 25.3. Performance comparison for one draw call per instance (`glDrawElements`) to one single call for all instances (`glDrawElementsInstanced`) for 1–3 per-instance vec3 attributes.

the instancing initialization overhead. Also, the GPU rendering cost grows linearly with the number of instances drawn.

Instancing is an interesting method, but we must keep in mind that the cost overhead of each batch is much higher than a standard draw call. We have conducted another performance experiment when rendering volumetric lines filled with

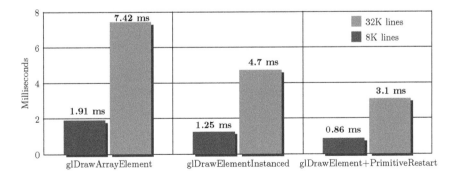

Figure 25.4. Performance when rendering volumetric lines using three different approaches: one draw call per line, instancing, and multiple lines drawn using a primitive restart element.

a single color using the vertex extrusion method presented in Chapter 11. Performance is visible in Figure 25.4. In this case, the color is the parameter that needs to be modified for each line instance. As expected, the slowest method is again the one that issues a draw call for each line after having modified the uniform color value (Figure 25.4, `glDrawElement`). Using instancing, performance is 50% higher (Figure 25.4, `glDrawElementsInstanced`). In this case, an array buffer object is updated once per frame with colors of each instance. The color attribute is updated once per instance using the per-vertex attribute divisor. Surprisingly, the fastest method is the one relying on a dynamically filled array buffer object as illustrated in Chapter 11 (Figure 25.4, `glDrawElements+PrimitiveRestart`). In this implementation, the triangle strip vertices are generated on the CPU and sent into a vertex buffer object on the GPU. All strips are drawn using an preallocated element buffer that contains a special index value used to restart the strip primitives. This method indeed consumes a lot more memory than the one relying on instancing. However, because the cost of a primitive restart is negligible when compared to the overhead of using instancing, this method is actually the fastest. However, although Figure 25.4 does not show such a trend, we must keep in mind that the CPU might become the bottleneck when too many lines have to be processed. This last example shows that we must stay imaginative and try multiple approaches: the latest technology may not be the right choice in some cases and on some hardwares. As in this example, the choice of an implementation can often be regarded as a quality/memory/computation complexity trade-off but not a technology decision.

25.4 Conclusion

Over the last several years, the OpenGL API has been heavily modified in order to make certain high-frequency calls more efficient for better overall performance. There is no doubt that upcoming years will reveal more API modification for the purpose of simplicity and efficiency. However, even with all these new tempting technologies, we must also keep in mind that traditional brute force approaches can still be faster under certain circumstances.

Acknowledgments. I would like to thank the editors, Randall Hopper, Aras Pranckevičius, Emil Persson, and an anonymous reviewer for their insightful comments during the review process of this article.

Bibliography

[Beeson 04] Curtis Beeson. "Animation in the Dawn Demo." In *GPU Gems*. Reading, MA: Addison-Wesley, 2004.

[Carmack 11] John Carmack. "QuakeCon Keynote." QuakeCon Conference, Dallas, 2011.

[Carucci 05] Francesco Carucci. "Inside Geometry Instancing." In *GPU Gems 2*. Reading, MA: Addison-Wesley, 2005.

[FrictionalGame 10] FrictionalGame. "Penumbra Overture Engine." http://frictionalgames. blogspot.com/2010/05/penumbra-overture-goes-open-source.html, 2010.

[Hardwidge 03] Ben Hardwidge. "Farewell to DirectX?" http://www.bit-tech.net/hardware/ graphics/2011/03/16/farewell-to-directx/1, 2003.

[IdSoftware 05] IdSoftware. "IdTech3 Source Code." http://en.wikipedia.org/wiki/Id_Tech_3, 2005.

[IdSoftware 11] IdSoftware. "IdTech4 Source Code." http://github.com/TTimo/doom3.gpl, 2011.

[NVIDIA 04] NVIDIA. "Improve Batching Using Texture Atlases." http://http.download. nvidia.com/developer/NVTextureSuite/Atlas_Tools/Texture_Atlas_Whitepaper.pdf, 2004.

[Remedy 11] Graphic Remedy. "gDEBugger." http://www.gremedy.com, 2011.

[Wloka 03] Matthias Wloka. "Batch, Batch, Batch, What Does It Really Mean?" Game Developer's Conference, San Francisco, 2003.

Indexing Multiple Vertex Arrays   26

Arnaud Masserann

26.1   Introduction

One of OpenGL's features is vertex buffer object (VBO) indexing, which allows developers to reuse a single vertex in several primitives. Since vertex attributes don't need to be duplicated, indexing saves memory and bandwidth. Given that the GPU is often memory-bound, most of the time we can get extra speed with indexing.

Indexing requires having a single index for positions, texture coordinates, normals, and so on. Unfortunately, this is not how many 3D file formats work: for instance, COLLADA has different indices for each vertex attribute. This is problematic in asset pipelines, where models can come from a variety of sources.

This chapter shows a simple algorithm that transforms several attribute buffers, each using different indices, into a format that is directly usable by OpenGL. For applications that do not use indexing, this chapter provides a simple way to improve run-time performance. In practice, speedups of about 1.4 times can be expected, and this format opens possibilities for further optimizations.

26.2   The Problem

With nonindexed VBOs (see Figure 26.1), we need to specify all attributes for each vertex: position, color, and all needed UV coordinates, normals, tangents, bitangents, etc.

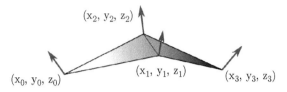

Vertex Array Buffer:
(x_0, y_0, z_0), (x_1, y_1, z_1), (x_2, y_2, z_2),
(x_2, y_2, z_2), (x_1, y_1, z_1), (x_3, y_3, z_3)

Normal Array Buffer:
(x'_0, y'_0, z'_0), (x'_1, y'_1, z'_1), (x'_2, y'_2, z'_2),
(x'_2, y'_2, z'_2), (x'_1, y'_1, z'_1), (x'_3, y'_3, z'_3)

Figure 26.1. A nonindexed VBO.

Nonindexed VBOs suffer from two performance penalties. First, on most meshes this method uses more memory. For instance, on a sphere with 1000 vertices, all vertices are shared by three triangles. A nonindexed VBO with **GL_FLOAT** attributes for positions, UVs, and normals will take $3 \times 1,000 \times (3 \times 4 + 2 \times 4 + 3 \times 4) = 3 \times 1,000 \times 32 = 96,000$ bytes. A similar, indexed VBO will take $96,000/3$ bytes, plus $3 \times 1,000 \times 4 = 12,000$ for the index buffer, totaling 44,000 bytes. In this ideal case, the indexed VBO only takes 45% of the size of the nonindexed VBO. Indexing thus reduces both the memory footprint and the PCI-e transfers.

The second performance penalty comes from the difference in cache usage. There are two kinds of vertex caches:

- AMD GPUs have a pretransform vertex cache that contains a part of the raw VBO. This cache is used to feed the vertex shader.

- The post-transform cache is used to store the ouput variables of the vertex shader. This is useful because most of the time, a vertex is used by several triangles. The cache avoids the cost of re-executing the same computations for each vertex shared by several triangles. However, it uses the index of the vertex as a key, so if primitives are drawn without indexing, the cache has no effect.

There are two consequences. First, simple indexing will natively improve performance. Second, the use of both of these caches can be optimized:

- If the element buffer contains indices to vertices that have a good spatial locality, the pretransform cache will make a large number of hits. In other words, indices 0-1-2 are better than 0-50-99.

- If neighboring triangles are drawn consecutively, most of the used vertices will be in the post-transform cache, available for immediate reuse. A number of algorithms can be found in the literature for reorganizing the indices in order to get a better post-transform cache usage. In particular, I recommend **nvTriStrip**, which is slow but ready-to-use, and Tom Forsyth's algorithm [Forsyth 06], which runs in linear time.

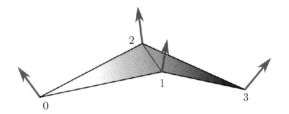

Vertex Array Buffer:
(x_0, y_0, z_0),
(x_1, y_1, z_1),
(x_2, y_2, z_2),
(x_3, y_3, z_3)

Normal Array Buffer:
(x'_0, y'_0, z'_0),
(x'_1, y'_1, z'_1),
(x'_2, y'_2, z'_2),
(x'_3, y'_3, z'_3)

Element Array Buffer:
0 1 2, 2 1 3

Figure 26.2. An indexed VBO.

Figure 26.2 shows what an indexed VBO looks like, along with the associated attributes. Note that both coordinates and normals are shared for vertices 1 and 2.

For these reasons, indexing is recommended by all major GPU vendors [NVIDIA 08, Hart 04, Imagination Technologies 09]. However, Figure 26.3 shows an excerpt of the COLLADA export of a similar mesh.

```
1  <mesh>
2      <source id="Plane-mesh-positions">
3          <float_array id="Plane-mesh-positions-array" count="12">
4              1 1 0 1 -1 -0.5 -1 -0.9999998 0 -0.9999997 1 -0.5
5          </float_array>
6      </source>
7      <source id="Plane-mesh-normals">
8          <float_array id="Plane-mesh-normals-array" count="12">
9              0 0 1 -0.2356944 0.2356944 0.9428083 0 0 1 0.2356944
10             -0.2356944 0.9428083
11         </float_array>
12     </source>
13     <polylist count="2">
14         <input semantic="VERTEX" source="#Plane-mesh-vertices" offset="0"/>
15         <input semantic="NORMAL" source="#Plane-mesh-normals" offset="1"/>
16         <vcount>3 3 </vcount>
17         <p>
18             0 0 3 1 2 2 0 0 2 2 1 3
19         </p>
20     </polylist>
21  </mesh>
```

Figure 26.3. A COLLADA mesh.

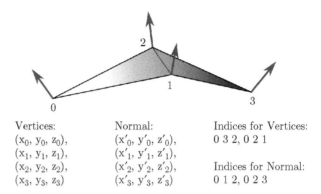

Figure 26.4. COLLADA representation of the mesh.

As shown in Figure 26.4, several index buffers, or element array buffers in OpenGL terminology, are needed—one for each attribute. This is not possible in OpenGL, where all attributes must be indexed by the same element array buffer.

This chapter shows a simple solution to convert nonindexed data into an indexed form, allowing its use in an efficient way with many file formats such as OBJ, X, VRML, and COLLADA.

26.3   An Algorithm

The trick is to only reuse a vertex if all of its attributes match. We can simply iterate through all input vertices and append them to the output buffer when it doesn't already contain a matching vertex.

In Listing 26.1, `in_vertices` and `out_vertices` are arrays. It is important that `getSimilarVertexIndex` is as fast as possible since it is called once for each input vertex. This can be done using a data structure like a `std::map`, which limits the complexity of the algorithm to $O(n \log n)$, or a `std::hash_map`, with a theoretical complexity of $O(n)$.

An important detail is that this version of the code assumes that `in_vertices` and `out_vertices` contain packed vertices, so comparing two vertices takes all attributes into account.

```
// Reserve space in output vectors
out_indices.reserve(in_vertices.size());
// ...

std::map<PackedVertex,unsigned short> VertexToOutIndex;

// For each input vertex
for (unsigned int i = 0; i < in_vertices.size(); i++ )
{
  PackedVertex packed(in_vertices[i], in_uvs[i], in_normals[i]);

  unsigned short index;
  bool found = getSimilarVertexIndex(packed, VertexToOutIndex, index);

  if (found)
  {
    // A matching vertex is already in the VBO, use it instead.
    out_indices.push_back(index);
  }
  else
  {
    // If not, it needs to be added in the output data.
    out_vertices.push_back(in_vertices[i]);
    out_uvs.push_back(in_uvs[i]);
    out_normals.push_back(in_normals[i]);
    unsigned short newindex = (unsigned short)out_vertices.size() - 1;
    out_indices.push_back(newindex);
    VertexToOutIndex[packed] = newindex;
  }
}

// Downsize the output vectors to the exact needed size
std::vector<unsigned short>(out_indices).swap(out_indices);
// ...
```

Listing 26.1. The indexing algorithm.

26.4 Vertex Comparison Methods

The containers need a comparison function in order to create their internal tree. This function does not need to have a real meaning; the only requirement is that for two equal vertices, v1 and v2, compare(v1,v2) == false and compare(v2,v1) == false (no vertex is greater than the other).

26.4.1 If/Then/Else Version

The comparison function can be implemented as shown in Listing 26.2. This is the most generic version, and it will work on any platform. What's more, we can tweak isEqual depending on our needs. If we know that similar vertices will have exactly the same coordinates, we can implement isEqual with the == operator. This is usually the case, because the coordinates are not modified with floating-point operations during the export and import phases. On the other hand, we may want to weld vertices with slight differences in their normals to reduce the size of the VBO or to smooth out the rendering. This can be done by using an epsilon in isEqual.

```
if (isEqual(v1.x,v2.x))
{
  // Can't sort on this criterion, try another
  if (isEqual(v1.y,v2.y))
  {
    if (isEqual(v1.z,v2.z))
    {
      // Same for UVs, normals, ...
      // Vertices are equal
      return false;
    }
    else
    {
      return v1.z > v2.z;
    }
  }
  else
  {
    return v1.y > v2.y; // Can't sort on x, but y is ok
  }
}
else
{
  return v1.x > v2.x; // x is already discriminant, sort on this axis
}
```

Listing 26.2. Comparison function 1.

26.4.2   memcmp() Version

If the vertices are packed and we only want to weld vertices with perfectly equal co-ordinates, this function can be greatly simplified by using memcmp instead, as shown in Listing 26.3.

```
return memcmp((void*)this, (void*)&that, sizeof(PackedVertex))>0;
```

Listing 26.3. Comparison function 2.

This will work if the structure is tightly packed (aligned on 8 bits, which may not be a good idea since the driver will probably realign it on 32 bits internally), or if all unused zones are always set to the same value. This can be done by zeroing the whole structure with memset, for instance in the constructor, as shown in Listing 26.4.

```
memset((void*)this, 0, sizeof(PackedVertex));
```

Listing 26.4. Dealing with alignment.

26.4.3   Hashing Function

We can also implement the algorithm using a `Dictionary`, or `std::hash_map` in C++, instead. Such a container requires two functions: a hash function, which converts our vertex into an integer and an equality function. The equality function is straightforward: all attributes must be equal. The hash function can be implemented in a variety of ways; the main constraint is that if two vertices are considered equal, their hash must be equal. This actually heavily restricts our possibilities of using an epsilon-based equality function.

Listing 26.5 shows a simplistic implementation. It groups the vertices in a uniform grid of 0.01 units and computes the hash by multiplying each new coordinate by a prime number, which avoids clustering vertices in common planes. Finally, the hash is modulated by 2^{16}, which creates 65,536 bins in the hashmap. Other attributes are not used, because position is usually the most separating criterion, and they will be taken into account by the equality function.

For a more detailed analysis of hashing functions for 3D vertices, see, for instance [Hrádek and Skala 03].

```
class hash<PackedVertex>
{
  public size_t operator()(const PackedVertex & v)
  {
    size_t x = size_t(v.position.x) * 100;
    size_t y = size_t(v.position.y) * 100;
    size_t z = size_t(v.position.z) * 100;
    return (3 * x + 5 * y + 7 * z) % (1 << 16);
  }
}
```

Listing 26.5. Hashing function.

26.5   Performance

Table 26.1 and Figure 26.5 give indexing times (in milliseconds) for models of various complexities. A standard `std::map` is used, with the `memcmp` version of the

Model	# vertices	# triangles	Indexing time (ms)
Suzanne	500	1,000	0.7
Plane	10,000	20,000	14
Sponza	153,000	279,000	820

Table 26.1. Indexing times for various models.

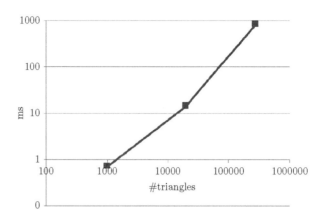

Figure 26.5. Indexing time w.r.t. triangles count.

comparison operator. The vertices are packed and have floating-point UVs and normals. Times are given for an Intel i5 2.8GHz CPU.

Table 26.2 gives rendering speeds (in milliseconds) for the same three models.
Each model is rendered 100 times per frame in different positions, with a vertex
shader that outputs five varyings and a Blinn-Phong fragment shader with one texture
fetch.

Indexed versions are at least as fast, and up to 1.8 times faster than their nonindexed equivalents. This number is mostly valid for meshes with a topology that
is already cache-friendly; other models will usually require a post-transform cache-
optimization pass, as mentioned above. For instance, a Standford Bunny model

Model		ms/frame			
		Indexed interleaved	Indexed noninterleaved	Nonindexed interleaved	Nonindexed noninterleaved
NVIDIA	Suzanne	1.6	1.6	1.6	1.6
GTX	Plane	6.2	6.3	11.5	11.5
470	Sponza	154	154	161	161
AMD	Suzanne	4.8	4.8	5.1	5.1
HD	Plane	25	25	31	32
6570	Sponza	281	277	282	304
Intel	Suzanne	16	15	16	16
GMA	Plane	77	74	128	129
3000	Sponza	1170	1166	1228	1229

Table 26.2. Rendering performance.

Method	Rendering time (ms/frame)
Nonindexed interleaved	0.70
Indexed interleaved	0.58
Indexed interleaved and optimized	0.50

Table 26.3. Rendering performance for an optimized model.

with 35,000 vertices is rendered 1.4 times faster when indexed and optimized with `nvTriStrip`, as shown in Table 26.3.

26.6   Conclusion

The proposed algorithm has some key advantages:

- it is simple to implement;

- it is cross-platform, and works with any CPU, OpenGL version, programming language, and OS;

- it is simple to customize and to integrate into existing code;

- it can either generate one interleaved array or separate arrays, depending on our needs;

- it can be integrated directly into our asset pipeline so that we have no runtime performance penalty;

- it opens possibilities for further performance gains through pre- and post-transform cache optimizations;

- most importantly, it can get us extra milliseconds for free.

An example implementation using interleaved arrays and an `std::map` with the `memcmp` comparison function can be found on the OpenGL Insights website, www.openglinsights.com.

Bibliography

[Forsyth 06] Tom Forsyth. "Linear-Speed Vertex Cache Optimisation." http://home.comcast.net/~tom_forsyth/papers/fast_vert_cache_opt.html, September 28, 2006.

[Hart 04] Even Hart. "OpenGL Performance Tuning." http://developer.amd.com/media/gpu_assets/PerformanceTuning.pdf, 2004.

[Hrádek and Skala 03] Jan Hrádek and Václav Skala. "Hash Function and Triangular mesh Reconstruction." *Computers & Geosciences* 29:6 (2003), 741–751.

[Imagination Technologies 09] Imagination Technologies. "PowerVR Application Development Recommendations." http://www.imgtec.com/powervr/insider/sdk/KhronosOpenGLES2xSGX.asp, 2009.

[NVIDIA 08] NVIDIA. *NVIDIA GPU Programming Guide*, 2008.

Multi-GPU Rendering on NVIDIA Quadro 27

Shalini Venkataraman

27.1   Introduction

Multi-GPU configurations are becoming a common and affordable option for OpenGL applications to scale performance, data size, display size, image quality, and the number of users per GPU in server-based environments. Current technologies targeted for multi-GPU configurations like NVIDIA SLI or ATI Crossfire require no application changes; the OpenGL driver transparently handles command dispatch to all GPUs. However, this limits scalability as applications are still single threaded, which requires a single CPU core to keep the multiple GPU hardware queues busy. This is particularly evident in scene-graph based applications where the scene traversal is typically done on the CPU. Moreover, both commands and data are replicated across all GPUs. To achieve maximum performance, applications require fine-grained programmability to manage individual GPU workloads as well as to optimize communication between GPUs.

Currently, targeting specific GPUs for OpenGL rendering on Windows is vendor specific. This article focuses on NVIDIA's `WGL_NV_gpu_affinity` extension, with details on how to enumerate the graphics resources on a system, and allocate contexts per GPU and the cross-platform `NV_copy_image` extension, which is used for optimized data transfer between GPUs. Both of these extensions are only available on NVIDIA Quadro cards. I also show the best practices for multi-GPU programming

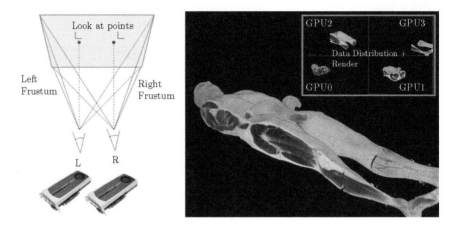

Figure 27.1. Using two GPUs for stereoscopic rendering, giving linear scaling (left). Rendering the 14GB Visible Human dataset across four GPUs (right).

by using multiple threads, GL contexts, and managing synchronization. I conclude with common application scenarios and programming pointers to implement:

- Onscreen rendering. Each GPU is responsible for rendering the view frustum and displaying the viewport for its attached display such as in multitiled display and projector configurations. The application does not do any explicit communication between the GPUs. Another example is passive stereoscopic configurations, where each GPU renders one eye and feeds the information to a projector (Figure 27.1 (left)).

- Offscreen rendering and readback. Each GPU is treated as a separate rendering resource that can communicate with other GPUs to implement complex task decomposition and load balancing schemes. For example, large data sets that cannot fit into a single GPU's memory are split across multiple GPUs, rendered, read back, and then composited for final display. Figure 27.1 (right) shows this scaling approach for the 14GB Visible Human Dataset [NLM 03] that cannot fit into the texture memory of a single GPU. Another example is for fill-rate intensive applications like raytracing, where each GPU works on a tile of the final image.

27.2   Previous Scaling Approaches

In transparent mechanisms like NVIDIA SLI [NVIDIA 11] and AMD Crossfire [AMD 11], multiple cards are connected through a hardware bridge so that they appear as one virtual graphics resource to the OS and the application. In this case, only one graphics card is connected to the monitor, and the other card is used as a slave for extra processing power. Rendering work is split in a predefined way between the two GPUs and cannot be changed at runtime. OpenGL commands and application data are replicated on all GPUs. This approach provides a quick seamless way to increase the overall pixel fill rate but creates a potential bottleneck at the application level since a single stream of OpenGL commands must now saturate multiple graphics cards. Furthermore, since all the commands and data are replicated across GPUs, any application-specific parallelism such as distributing the data or load balancing cannot be programmed.

27.3   Targeting a Specific GPU for Rendering

OpenGL behavior on multi-GPU configurations is OS specific. On Linux with separate X screen configuration, the default behavior is for OpenGL calls to be sent only to the GPU attached to the screen that was used to open the display connection. On Windows XP, the default behavior is for OpenGL commands to be sent to all GPUs, causing the performance to be gated by the slowest GPU. Windows 7, meanwhile, defaults to the most powerful GPU to execute all the OpenGL commands, and the resulting image is copied by the drivers to the the the other GPU's framebuffer for final display. Applications, however, require a deterministic way of selecting which GPU(s) in the system OpenGL calls should be directed to, which is the focus of this section.

On Linux, this is easily achieved by configuring each GPU to have its separate X screen without Xinerama. In this case, the windows cannot be moved across screens. Typically, one X server is used for all cards, and to address each GPU, the corresponding X screen is specified using `XOpenDisplay:0.[screen]`. On Windows, the `WGL_NV_gpu_affinity` [ARB 09c] extension provides the mechanism to select specific NVIDIA Quadro GPUs for rendering. On AMD GPUs, the alternative is to use the `WGL_AMD_gpu_association` [ARB 09d].

The `WGL_NV_gpu_affinity` extension, which is the focus of this section, introduces the concept of a *GPU affinity mask* that specifies the GPUs the OpenGL commands should be sent to. In addition, there is the concept of an *affinity device context*, which is simply a device context (DC) with the GPU affinity mask embedded. When an OpenGL context is created from this affinity DC, it inherits the GPU affinity mask, and subsequent calls made in that context are only sent to the GPUs in the mask.

This OpenGL affinity context can be used in two ways:

- Onscreen rendering. When the affinity context is associated with a window DC, the GPUs specified in its affinity mask are responsible for that window's drawing. Figure 27.2 shows this for a two-display configuration where each GPU is responsible for rendering its view frustum and viewport to its

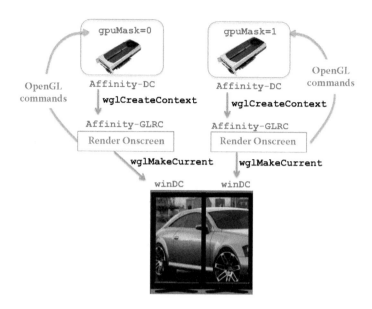

Figure 27.2. Drawing onscreen with WGL_NV_gpu_affinity.

attached display with no inter-GPU communication. The application has full control of each GPU's OpenGL command stream and can do any viewing-based optimizations at runtime such as view-frustum culling.

- Offscreen rendering. There is no window DC, and the affinity context is associated with its affinity DC instead. The application uses a framebuffer object (FBO) for offscreen rendering to texture. Figure 27.3 shows an example for this case where the rendered subimage is now copied over PCI-express to the primary GPU where it is composited with the primary GPU's intermediate result and then displayed onscreen, for which the primary window DC is still used. The offscreen method provides the maximum flexibility in terms of distributing render workloads and implementing various composition methods for final image assembly.

The simplest way to access the WGL_NV_gpu_affinity functions is using extension wrapper libraries such as GLEW [GLEW 11] and GLee [GLee 09]. Alternatively, the function handles can be retrieved using wglGetProcAddress as defined in wglext.h [Khronos 11]. A valid OpenGL context must be created and made current before doing this.

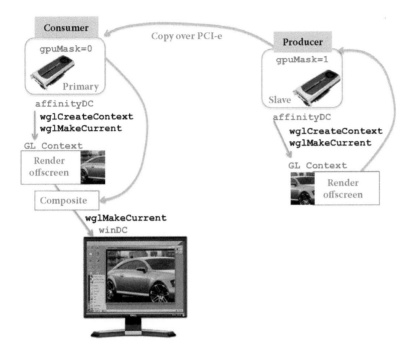

Figure 27.3. Offscreen drawing showing communication between GPUs

27.3.1 Enumerating GPUs and Displays

Before targeting a specific GPU for rendering, the first step is to enumerate all the GPUs in the system along with their capabilities. Handles for the GPUs present in a system are enumerated with `wglEnumGpusNV`:

```
BOOL wglEnumGpusNV(UINT iGpuIndex, HGPUNV *phGPU)
```

By looping over `wglEnumGpusNV` and incrementing `iGPUIndex` starting at 0, the corresponding GPU handle is returned in **phGPU**. For each GPU handle, the attached displays can be enumerated using the `wglEnumGpuDevicesNV` call:

```
BOOL wglEnumGpuDevicesNV(HGPUNV hGpu,UINT iDeviceIndex, PGPU_DEVICE lpGpuDevice)
```

Again, by looping over `wglEnumGpuDevicesNV` and incrementing `iDevice Index` starting at 0, all the display devices attached to a GPU can be queried. This will populate the **GPU_DEVICE** structure shown in Listing 27.1 and explained further in Table 27.1. The complete enumeration code for GPUs and displays is shown in Listing 27.2.

```
typedef struct _GPU_DEVICE
{
  DWORD cb;
  CHAR DeviceName[32];
  CHAR DeviceString[128];
  DWORD Flags; //
  RECT rcVirtualScreen;
} GPU_DEVICE, *PGPU_DEVICE;
```

Listing 27.1. GPU_DEVICE structure.

Finally, the affinity-DC is created with `wglCreateAffinityDCNV`:

```
HDC wglCreateAffinityDCNV(const HGPUNV *phGpuList)
```

The GPU handles that were retrieved earlier are passed into a NULL-terminated array in `phGpuList`. An OpenGL context can be created with this affinity DC using `wglCreateContext`, and rendering will now be restricted to the GPUs specified in `phGpuList`.

Listing 27.2 shows the affinity DC creation, which corresponds to the scenario in Figure 27.3 that we use throughout the chapter to show a simple multi-GPU producer-consumer example. The slave GPU acts as the producer that generates its portion of the final image, which is then copied over to the primary GPU that "consumes" the image by compositing with its subimage and then displays the final result onscreen. The primary GPU has two DCs: (1) the affinity DC, `destDC`, that is used for offscreen rendering to generate its subimage and (2) the window DC,

cb	Size of the GPU_DEVICE structure
DeviceName	String identifying the display device, e.g., DISPLAY1
DeviceString	String identifying the GPU driving this display, e.g., Quadro 4000
Flags	Indicates the state of the display device, which can be a combination of any of the following: • DISPLAY_DEVICE_ATTACHED_TO_DESKTOP: If set, the device is part of the desktop. • DISPLAY_DEVICE_PRIMARY_DEVICE: If set, the primary desktop is on this device. Only one device in the system can have this set.
rcVirtualScreen	Specifies the display device rectangle in virtual screen coordinates. The value of rcVirtualScreen is undefined if the device is not part of the desktop, i.e., DISPLAY_DEVICE_ATTACHED_TO_DESKTOP is not set in the Flags field.

Table 27.1. Fields in the GPU_DEVICE structure.

```
HGPUNV hGPU, gpuMask[2];
GPU_DEVICE gpuDevice;

HDC winDC = GetDC(hWnd); // Assume window is created
pixelFormat = ChoosePixelFormat(winDC, &pfd);
SetPixelFormat(winDC, pixelFormat, &pfd)
// Create a dummy context just to get function handles
HGLRC winRC = wglCreateContext(winDC);
wglMakeCurrent(winDC, winRC)
// Assume all the function handles have been retrieved with wglGetProcAddress
wglDeleteContext(winRC); // Dummy context is no longer needed

gpuDevice.cb = sizeof(gpuDevice);
// First call this function to get a handle to the gpu
UINT GPUIdx = 0;
while(wglEnumGpusNV(GPUIdx, &hGPU))
{
  printf("Device# %d:\n", GPUIdx);
  bool bDisplay = false;
  bool bPrimary = false;
  // Now get the detailed information about this device:
  // how many displays it's attached to
  UINT displayDeviceIdx = 0;
  while(wglEnumGpuDevicesNV(hGPU, displayDeviceIdx, &gpuDevice))
  {
    bDisplay = true;
    bPrimary |= (gpuDevice.Flags & DISPLAY_DEVICE_PRIMARY_DEVICE) != 0;

    printf("Display# %d:\n", displayDeviceIdx);
    printf("Name: %s\n", gpuDevice.DeviceName);
    printf("String: %s\n", gpuDevice.DeviceString);

    if(gpuDevice.Flags & DISPLAY_DEVICE_ATTACHED_TO_DESKTOP)
    {
      printf("Attached to the desktop: LEFT=%d, RIGHT=%d, TOP=%d, BOTTOM=%d\n", ←
          gpuDevice.rcVirtualScreen.left,gpuDevice.rcVirtualScreen.right, gpuDevice↩
          .rcVirtualScreen.top,gpuDevice.rcVirtualScreen.bottom);
    }
    else
    {
      printf("Not attached to the desktop\n");
    }

    // See if it's the primary GPU
    if(gpuDevice.Flags & DISPLAY_DEVICE_PRIMARY_DEVICE)
    {
      printf("  This is the PRIMARY Display Device\n");
    }
    displayDeviceIdx++;
  } // End of while (wglEnumGpuDevicesNV)
  // At this point all the attached displays are queried for GPUIdx
  if(bPrimary)
  {
    // Primary GPU is the destination
    gpuMask[0] = hGPU;
    gpuMask[1] = NULL;
    destDC = wglCreateAffinityDCNV(gpuMask);
  }
```

```
 else
 {
    // Non-primary gpu is the source
    gpuMask[0] = hGPU;
    gpuMask[1] = NULL;
    srcDC = wglCreateAffinityDCNV(gpuMask);
 }
 GPUIdx++;
} // End of while (wglEnumGpusNV)
```

Listing 27.2. Enumerating multiple GPUs and their associated displays.

winDC, that is used to render the final composited image onscreen, and they both use the same GL context. Like a regular window DC, the affinity DC also requires a valid pixel format to be set before a GL context can be created.

27.4   Optimized Data Transfer between GPUs

In the producer-consumer case introduced earlier, textures need to be shared between GPUs. Typically, textures are shared between multiple contexts using **ARB_create_context**, which only works when both contexts are on the same physical device. With contexts across multiple GPUs, one method is to download from the producer to main memory using **glReadPixels** or **glGetTexImage** and then upload to the destination GPU using **glTexSubImage**.

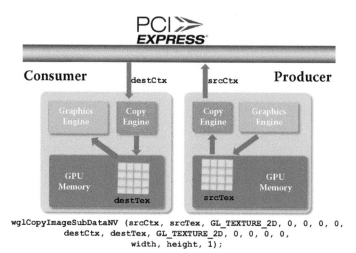

```
wglCopyImageSubDataNV (srcCtx, srcTex, GL_TEXTURE_2D, 0, 0, 0, 0,
             destCtx, destTex, GL_TEXTURE_2D, 0, 0, 0, 0,
                     width, height, 1);
```

Figure 27.4. Inter-GPU texture transfer with NV_copy_image.

This method, if implemented naively, could trigger multiple copies between driver pinned memory and application during download and upload increasing latency. The `NV_copy_image` [ARB 09b] extension that works in tandem with `WGL_NV_gpu_affinity` was created to avoid this latency and additional programming complexity. This extension exposes the `wglCopyImageSubDataNV` function on Windows and `glXCopyImageSubDataNV` on Linux, enabling efficient image data transfer between image objects without the need to bind the objects or perform any other state changes. An image object may be either a texture or a renderbuffer. In addition to 2D textures, 3D textures and cube maps are also supported. Figure 27.4 shows how in a single call, the source texture, `srcTex`, is copied to the destination texture, `destTex`, on the primary GPU. On Fermi and later Quadros, this transfer happens asynchronously using the copy engine (Chapter 29). On previous-generation hardware, this call would stall the GPU until the transfer is completed.

27.5 Application Structure for Multi-GPU

This section explains how to put together all the concepts introduced into an application framework using the producer-consumer example outlined earlier. This example shows a 1:1 mapping between the producer and consumer; however, this can be scaled to multiple producing GPUs. The full source code for this example is available on the OpenGL Insights website, www.openglinsights.com.

To scale across multiple GPUs, it is recommended that the application be multithreaded with a thread per GPU so that multiple CPU cores can, in parallel, keep the GPU hardware queue busy. While pipelining without threading can provide some speedup, especially for GPU-bound applications, it requires that a single core keep all GPUs fully busy, and scalability may be limited or even negative as more GPUs are added.

Separate OpenGL contexts for the producer and consumer are created in the main application thread and made current to their affinity DCs (for Windows) or open X11 Displays (for Linux). The main thread then spawns off the producer and consumer threads that operate with their GL contexts. Multiple textures per GPU context are used to increase overlap between transfer and texture access on the consumer. Figure 27.5 shows this overlap where the producer GPU has completed rendering to texture, `srcTex[1]`, and is transfering across PCI-e while the consumer thread is concurrently reading and compositing from texture, `destTex[0]`.

The producer thread does the offscreen render of its assigned region to texture, `srcTex`, and is also responsible for triggering the copy of this texture across the PCI-e using `NV_copy_image`. It then signals the consumer once the copy has completed. On Fermi and later hardware, this copy can happen asynchronously so that further rendering commands can be added to the producer stream before the consumer is done.

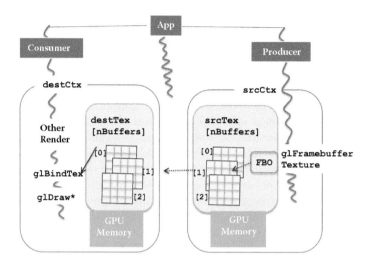

Figure 27.5. Multithreaded application structure.

Meanwhile, the consumer runs on the primary GPU attached to the display and is responsible for rendering its portion of the final image. It then waits for the producer to signal completion of texture transfer before using that texture, `destTex`, to composite with its intermediate image and display the final result onscreen. Figure 27.5 shows this process.

27.5.1   Synchronization between Multiple OpenGL Contexts

The multicontext producer-consumer example requires the producer to notify the consumer when it has finished the transfer of its current frame. Likewise, the consumer notifies the producer when it has finished using a texture, and the producer is free to copy into that. OpenGL rendering commands, however, are assumed to be asynchronous in the sense that when a GL call is issued, it is not guaranteed to be completed by the time the call returns. To signal GPU completion of a specific GL command, we use the OpenGL fence objects defined in the `GL_ARB_sync` [ARB 09a] available in OpenGL 3.2 and above. In addition, a CPU event is created to signal when the fence is valid to be waited upon by another thread. The GPU fences and CPU events are created for each texture in the array.

Figure 27.6 shows the synchronization mechanism for our case. The producer queues the fence, `producedFence`, after rendering and copying its texture to the consumer's texture across the bus. The consumer waits on this fence after it has done its rendering portion. Once signalled, it uses the texture for composition and queues

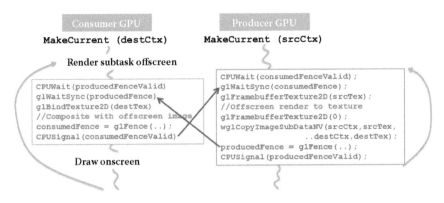

Figure 27.6. Synchronization between producer and consumer GPU.

the `consumedFence` to notify the producer. The consumer then proceeds to draw the final result onscreen.

27.6   Parallel Rendering Methodologies

There are many ways to scale rendering with each having its benefits for different problem domains. Here, we focus on implementing some common parallel rendering methodologies with multiple GPUs. All the following approaches are orthogonal to each other and can be combined for increased parallelism. For instance, multiple GPUs can be used for data decomposition while a subset of the GPUs are used for rendering each eye in a stereo configuration. Results shown are for a full-HD resolution final image (1920 × 1200) generated on a workstation running Windows 7 with two Quadro 5000s attached to the PCI-e 16X slots.

For larger installations, programming using a higher-level middleware abstraction may be desired, which helps the developer focus on the application rather than the low-level GPU intricacies that can quickly get unwieldy. Equalizer [Eilemann et al. 09] is a cross-platform and opensource framework for an OpenGL application to scale from single GPU to a multisystem graphics cluster. Equalizer implements a large set of parallelization, composition, and load-balancing schemes. CompleX [CompleX 09] is reference framework that runs on NVIDIA hardware in a single-system multi-GPU configuration.

27.6.1   Sort-First Image Decomposition

Parallelism occurs in screen space; each GPU focuses on its view frustum corresponding to the image subregion. Adding more GPUs lets each GPU work on a smaller

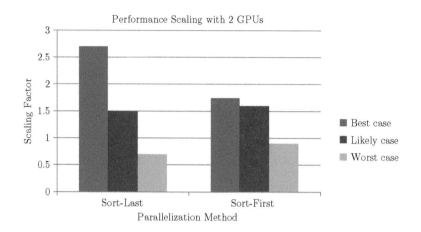

Figure 27.7. Results comparing scaling with two GPUs.

subregion, thereby increasing performance. If each subregion is directly mapped to an associated screen, the onscreen rendering approach described earlier is used with no inter-GPU communication. Powerwalls with multiple LCD panels or projectors as well as CAVEs are some of the applications. If the subregions are to be read back and composited into one final image, the offscreen approach using the producer-consumer example can be simply extended to have multiple producers corresponding to the number of slave GPUs. This tiling approach works well for fill-rate limited applications such as raytracing. Figure 27.7 shows the likely best- and worst-case scenarios. An example of the worst-case scenario is encountered when all the rendering lands on one GPU, but the other GPUs are still transmitting empty images, causing a slowdown. The best-case scenario is generally found when fragment-intensive tasks are divided in a balanced way such that the transfer overhead is mitigated by the high processing time. There is still some synchronization overhead in the drivers that limit scaling to around 75%. As more GPUs are added, the transfer requirements per GPU decrease proportionally, making this a good candidate for parallelization when the data can fit into GPU memory.

27.6.2   Sort-Last Data Decomposition

This parallelism approach is most useful when the application data exceeds the memory on the GPU. Each GPU renders part of the data set, and the intermediate results are read back and composited for final display. Figure 27.8 shows a volume-rendering example with a 3D texture distributed across four GPUs. There are three slave GPUs, and the primary GPU, along with rendering its portion of the data, does the alpha compositing. The intermediate images are sorted and blended along the viewing direction. For opaque geometry, the depth buffers are also transferred, and depth

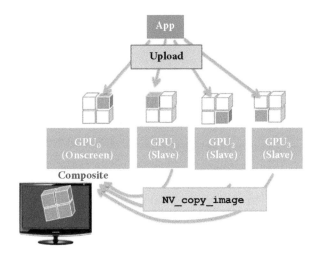

Figure 27.8. Data decomposition approach.

composition takes place, requiring twice the transfer bandwidth compared to the volumetric case. This is manifested in the worst-case scenario shown in Figure 27.7, where the transfer is the bottleneck compared to the rendering time causing the slowdown when scaling the number of GPUs. The best-case for sort-last is realized where superlinear scaling can be achieved since both processing cores and available memory are scaled. In contrast to sort-first, the bandwidth requirements increase proportionally with the number of GPUs since the full image resolution has to be transferred.

27.6.3 Stereo

Each GPU is responsible for rendering each eye in a stereo pair and can be considered a special case of sort-first with two GPUs. In the case of passive stereoscopy, the left-right images can be directly fed into the projector for each eye using the onscreen approach with some hardware-level synchronization. If the streams need to be combined into one stereo left-right signal, the offscreen approach can be used, where one view is copied to the consumer and used in the GL_BACK_LEFT or GL_BACK_RIGHT buffer, depending on the eye.

27.6.4 Server-Side Rendering

In this case, there is one master acting as the broker (consumer) spawning render tasks on the slave GPUs (producers) and reading back the results to be sent across the network. The master decides the GPU for each task depending on current GPU loads for which the NVIDIA-specific extension GL_NVX_mem_info (Chapter 38) is used. This approach can be extended to a cluster or cloud environment where each node is attached to multiple GPUs and message-passing mechanisms like MPI are used for intersystem communication.

27.7   Conclusion

This article introduced the building blocks of a scalable rendering system. Using the `WGL_NV_affinity` extension, an application can target specific graphics resources for rendering tasks depending on current GPU load and application metrics. This allows for dynamic load balancing where the GPU can be thought of and programmed as a coprocessor. The `NV_copy_image` extension provides a path for direct image transfer between GPUs. I discussed the application restructuring that is required to get the maximum performance out of multiple GPUs and the synchronization required using a simple producer-consumer example. This simple example can be extended to implement complex parallel rendering topologies, and I concluded with a discussion of some of the expected performance improvement with each of them.

Bibliography

[AMD 11] AMD. "AMD CrossFire." http://www.amd.com/us/PRODUCTS/ WORKSTATION/GRAPHICS/CROSSFIRE-PRO/Pages/crossfire-pro.aspx, 2011.

[ARB 09a] OpenGL ARB. "OpenGL ARB_Sync Specification." http://www.opengl.org/ registry/specs/ARB/sync.txt, 2009.

[ARB 09b] OpenGL ARB. "OpenGL NV_copy_image Specification." http://developer. download.nvidia.com/opengl/specs/GL_NV_copy_image.txt, 2009.

[ARB 09c] OpenGL ARB. "OpenGL WGL_NV_gpu_affinity." http://developer.download. nvidia.com/opengl/specs/WGL_nv_gpu_affinity.txt, 2009.

[ARB 09d] OpenGL ARB. "WGL_AMD_gpu_association specification." http://www.opengl. org/registry/specs/AMD/wgl_gpu_association.txt, 2009.

[CompleX 09] CompleX. "NVIDIA." http://developer.nvidia.com/complex, 2009.

[Eilemann et al. 09] Stefan Eilemann, Maxim Makhinya, and Renato Pajarola. "Equalizer: A Scalable Parallel Rendering Framework." *IEEE Transactions on Visualization and Computer Graphics* 15:3 (2009), 436–452.

[GLee 09] GLee. "GLee (GL Easy Extension library)." http://elf-stone.com/glee.php, 2009.

[GLEW 11] GLEW. "The OpenGL Extension Wrangler Library." http://glew.sourceforge. net/, 2011.

[Khronos 11] Khronos. "wglext.h." http://opengl.org/registry/api/wglext.h, 2011.

[NLM 03] NIH NLM. "The Visible Human Project." http://www.nlm.nih.gov/research/ visible/visible_human.html, 2003.

[NVIDIA 11] NVIDIA. "NVIDIA SLI Technology." http://www.nvidia.com/object/quadro_ sli.html, 2011.

V   Transfers

OpenGL applications transfer a lot of data. Data is transferred between machines, between disk and system memory, between system and video memory, between video memory and video memory, and so on. Optimizing these transfers improves performance. In this section, we look at optimizing asynchronous transfers between the CPU and GPU; compressing models for use with WebGL; compressing textures on the GPU for video creation; and an efficient geometry file format.

Although general computations like particle systems are being pushed to the GPU, there is still a need to do many computations or IO on the CPU and then efficiently stream data to the GPU. In Chapter 28, "Asynchronous Buffer Transfers," Ladislav Hrabcak and Arnaud Masserann share best practices for maximizing performance when using buffer objects to transfer data between the CPU and GPU in either direction. With detailed performance analysis, they cover direct memory access (DMA), buffer usage hints, implicit synchronization with draw calls, pinned memory, and multithreading. Shalini Venkataraman continues the asynchronous transfers discussion in the following chapter, "Fermi Asynchronous Texture Transfers," where she discusses how the NVIDIA Fermi architecture allows transfer and rendering to occur at the same time when using multiple threads and OpenGL contexts.

The discussion of transfers moves from within a system to across systems in Chapter 30, "WebGL Models: End-to-End." Won Chun presents the techniques, including a detailed analysis, used in Google Body to compress and transfer models to a web browser for rendering with WebGL. Continuing on the compression theme, Brano Kemen demonstrates real-time image compression on the GPU in Chapter 31, "In-Game Video Capture with Real-Time Texture Compression." He applies his method to video compression using a DXT fixed-rate compression format to reduce bandwidth consumption, and he explores various decoloration methods to enhance image compression quality.

In graphics, content is king. A smooth content-creation pipeline empowers artists, and a format that requires minimal runtime processing improves load times. In the last chapter of this section, "An OpenGL Friendly Geometry File Format and its Maya Exporter," Adrien Herubel and Venceslas Biri present the Drone format, a binary geometry file format suitable for use with OpenGL.

Asynchronous Buffer Transfers 28

Ladislav Hrabcak and Arnaud Masserann

28.1 Introduction

Most 3D applications send large quantities of data from the CPU to the GPU on a regular basis. Possible reasons include

- streaming data from hard drive or network: geometry, clipmapping, level of detail (LOD), etc.;

- updating skeletal and blend-shapes animations on the CPU;

- computing a physics simulation;

- generating procedural meshes;

- data for *instancing*;

- setting uniform parameters for shaders with *uniform buffers*.

Likewise, it is often useful to read generated data back from the GPU. Possible scenarios are

- video capture [Kemen 10];

- physics simulation;

- page resolver pass in virtual texturing;

- image histogram for computing HDR tonemapping parameters.

While copying data back and forth to the GPU is easy, the PC architecture, without unified memory, makes it harder to do it fast. Furthermore, the OpenGL API specification doesn't tell how to do it efficiently, and a naive use of data-transfer functions wastes processing power on both the CPU and the GPU by introducing pauses in the execution of the program.

In this chapter, for readers familiar with buffer objects, we are going to explain what happens in the drivers and then present various methods, including unconventional ones, to transfer data between the CPU and the GPU with maximum speed. If an application needs to transfer meshes or textures frequently and efficiently, these methods can be used to improve its performance. In this chapter, we will be using OpenGL 3.3, which is the Direct3D 10 equivalent.

28.1.1   Explanation of Terms

First, in order to match the OpenGL specification, we refer to the GPU as the *device*.

Second, when calling OpenGL functions, the drivers translate calls into commands and add them into an internal queue on the CPU side. These commands are then consumed by the device asynchronously. This queue has already been refered to as the command queue, but in order to be clear, we refer to it as the *device command queue*.

Data transfers from CPU memory to device memory will be consistently referred to as *uploading* and transfers from the device memory to CPU memory as *downloading*. This matches the client/server paradigm of OpenGL.

Finally, *pinned memory* is a portion of the main RAM that can be directly used by the device through the PCI express bus (PCI-e). This is also known as *page-locked memory*.

28.2   Buffer Objects

There are many buffer-object targets. The most well-known are `GL_ARRAY_BUFFER` for vertex attributes and `GL_ELEMENT_ARRAY_BUFFER` for vertex indices, formerly known as vertex buffer objects (VBOs). However, there are also `GL_PIXEL_PACK_BUFFER` and `GL_TRANSFORM_FEEDBACK_BUFFER` and many other useful ones. As all these targets relate to the same kind of objects, they are all equivalent from a transfer point of view. Thus, everything we will describe in this chapter is valid for any buffer object target.

Buffer objects are linear memory regions allocated in device memory or in CPU memory. They can be used in many ways, such as

- the source of vertex data,

- texture buffer, which allows shaders to access large linear memory regions (128–256 MTexels on GeForce 400 series and Radeon HD 5000 series) [ARB 09a],

- uniform buffers,

- pixel buffer objects for texture upload and download.

28.2.1 Memory Transfers

Memory transfers play a very important role in OpenGL, and their understanding is a key to achieving high performance in 3D applications. There are two major desktop GPU architectures: discrete GPUs and integrated GPUs. Integrated GPUs share the same die and memory space with the CPU, which gives them an advantage because they are not limited by the PCI-e bus in communication. Recent APUs from AMD, which combine a CPU and GPU in a single die, are capable of achieving a transfer rate of 17GB/s which is beyond the PCI-e ability [Boudier and Sellers 11]. However, integrated units usually have mediocre performance in comparison to their discrete counterparts. Discrete GPUs have a much faster memory on board (30–192 GB/s), which is a few times faster than the conventional memory used by CPUs and integrated GPUs (12–30 GB/s) [Intel 08].

The direct memory access (DMA) controller allows the OpenGL drivers to asynchronously transfer memory blocks from user memory to device memory without wasting CPU cycles. This asynchronous transfer is most notably known for its widespread usage with pixel buffer objects [ARB 08], but can actually be used to transfer any type of buffer. It is important to note that the transfer is asynchronous from the CPU point of view only: Fermi (GeForce 400 Series) and Nothern Islands (Radeon HD 6000 Series) GPUs can't transfer buffers and render at the same time, so all OpenGL commands in the command queue are processed sequentially by the device. This limitation comes partially from the driver, so this behavior is susceptible to change and can be different in other APIs like CUDA, which exposes these GPU-asynchronous transfers. There are some exceptions like the NVIDIA Quadro, which can render while uploading and downloading textures [Venkataraman 10].

There are two ways to upload and download data to the device. The first way is to use the `glBufferData` and `glBufferSubData` functions. The basic use of these functions is quite straightforward, but it is worth understanding what is happening behind the scenes to get the best functionality.

As shown in Figure 28.1, these functions take user data and copy them to pinned memory directly accessible by the device. This process is similar to a standard `memcpy`. Once this is done, the drivers start the DMA transfer, which is asynchronous, and return from `glBufferData`. Destination memory depends on usage hints, which will be explained in the next section, and on driver implementation. In some cases, the data stay in pinned CPU memory and is used by the GPU directly from this memory, so the result is one hidden `memcpy` operation in every `glBufferData` function. Depending on how the data are generated, this `memcpy` can be avoided [Williams and Hart 11].

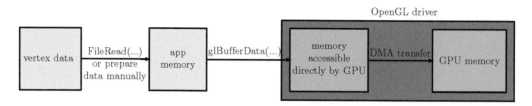

Figure 28.1. Buffer data upload with `glBufferData` / `glBufferSubData`.

A more efficient way to upload data to the device is to get a pointer to the internal drivers' memory with the functions `glMapBuffer` and `glUnmapBuffer`. This memory should, in most cases, be pinned, but this behavior can depend on the drivers and available resources. We can use this pointer to fill the buffer directly, for instance, using it for file read/write operations, so we will save one copy per memory transfer. It is also possible to use the `ARB_map_buffer_alignment` extension, which ensures that the returned pointer is aligned at least on a 64-byte boundary, allowing SSE and AVX instructions to compute the buffer's content. Mapping and unmapping is shown in Figure 28.2.

The returned pointer remains valid until we call `glUnmapBuffer`. We can exploit this property and use this pointer in a worker thread, as we will see later in this chapter.

Finally, there are also `glMapBufferRange` and `glFlushMappedBuffer Range`, similar to `glMapBuffer`, but they have additional parameters which can be used to improve the transfer performance and efficiency. These functions can be used in many ways:

- `glMapBufferRange` can, as its name suggests, map only specific subsets of the buffer. If only a portion of the buffer changes, there is no need to reupload it completely.

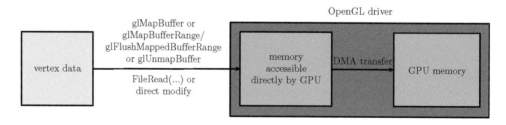

Figure 28.2.   Buffer data upload with `glMapBuffer` / `glUnmapBuffer` or `glMapBufferRange` / `glFlushMappedBufferRange`.

- We can create a big buffer, use the first half for rendering, the second half for updating, and switch the two when the upload is done (manual double buffering).

- If the amount of data varies, we can allocate a big buffer, and map/unmap only the smallest possible range of data.

28.2.2   Usage Hints

The two main possible locations where the OpenGL drivers can store our data are CPU memory and device memory. CPU memory can be page-locked (pinned), which means that it cannot be paged out to disk and is directly accessible by device, or paged, i.e., accessible by the device too, but access to this memory is much less efficient. We can use a hint to help the drivers make this decision, but the drivers can override our hint, depending on the implementation.

Since Forceware 285, NVIDIA drivers are very helpful in this area because they can show exactly where the data will be stored. All we need is to enable the GL_ARB_debug_output extension and use the WGL_CONTEXT_DEBUG_BIT_ARB flag in wglCreateContextAttribs. In all our examples, this is enabled by default. See Listing 28.1 for an example output and Chapter 33 for more details on this extension.

It seems that NVIDIA and AMD use our hint to decide in which memory to place the buffer, but in both cases, the drivers uses statistics and heuristics in order to fit the actual usage better. However, on NVIDIA with the Forceware 285 drivers, there are differences in the behavior of glMapBuffer and glMapBufferRange: glMapBuffer tries to guess the destination memory from the buffer-object usage, whereas glMapBufferRange always respects the hint and logs a debug message (Chapter 33) if our usage of the buffer object doesn't respect the hint. There are also differences in transfer rates between these functions; it seems that using

```
Buffer detailed info: Buffer object 1 (bound to GL_TEXTURE_BUFFER, usage hint is ←
    GL_ENUM_88e0) has been mapped WRITE_ONLY in SYSTEM HEAP memory (fast).
Buffer detailed info: Buffer object 1 (bound to GL_TEXTURE_BUFFER, usage hint is ←
    GL_ENUM_88e0) will use SYSTEM HEAP memory as the source for buffer object ←
    operations.
Buffer detailed info: Buffer object 2 (bound to GL_TEXTURE_BUFFER, usage hint is ←
    GL_ENUM_88e4) will use VIDEO memory as the source for buffer object operations.
Buffer info:
Total VBO memory usage in the system:
 memType: SYSHEAP, 22.50 Mb Allocated, numAllocations: 6.
 memType: VID, 64.00 Kb Allocated, numAllocations: 1.
 memType: DMA_CACHED, 0 bytes Allocated, numAllocations: 0.
 memType: MALLOC, 0 bytes Allocated, numAllocations: 0.
 memType: PAGED_AND_MAPPED , 40.14 Mb Allocated, numAllocations: 12.
 memType: PAGED , 142.41 Mb Allocated, numAllocations: 32.
```

Listing 28.1. Example output of GL_ARB_debug_output with Forceware 285.86 drivers.

Function	Usage hint	Destination memory	Transfer rate (GB/s)
glBufferData / glBufferSubData	GL_STATIC_DRAW	device	3.79
glMapBuffer / glUnmapBuffer	GL_STREAM_DRAW	pinned	n/a (pinned in CPU memory)
glMapBuffer / glUnmapBuffer	GL_STATIC_DRAW	device	5.73

Table 28.1. Buffer-transfer performance on an Intel Core i5 760 and an NVIDIA GeForce GTX 470 with PCI-e 2.0.

glMapBufferRange for all transfers ensures the best performance. An example application is available on the OpenGL Insights website, www.openglinsights.com, to measure the transfer rates and other behaviors of buffers objects; a few results are presented in Tables 28.1 and 28.2.

Pinned memory is standard CPU memory and there is no actual transfer to device memory: in this case, the device will use data directly from this memory location. The PCI-e bus can access data faster than the device is able to render it, so there is no performance penalty for doing this, but the driver can change that at any time and transfer the data to device memory.

Transfer	Source memory	Destination memory	Transfer rate (GB/s)
buffer to buffer	pinned	device	5.73
buffer to texture	pinned	device	5.66
buffer to buffer	device	device	9.00
buffer to texture	device	device	52.79

Table 28.2. Buffer copy and texture transfer performance on an Intel Core i5 760 and an NVIDIA GeForce GTX 470 with PCI-e 2.0 using glCopyBufferSubData and glTexImage2D with the GL_RGBA8 format.

28.2.3   Implicit Synchronization

When an OpenGL call is done, it usually is not executed immediately. Instead, most commands are placed in the device command queue. Actual rendering may take place two frames later and sometimes more depending on the device's performance and on driver settings (triple buffering, max prerendered frames, multi-GPU configurations, etc.). This lag between the application and the drivers can be measured by the timing functions glGetInteger64v(GL_TIMESTAMP,&time) and glQueryCounter(query,GL_TIMESTAMP), as explained in Chapter 34. Most of

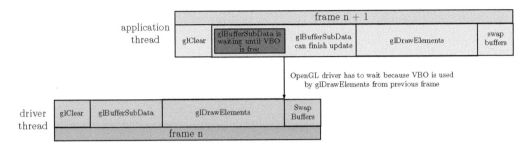

Figure 28.3. Implicit synchronization with `glSubBufferData`.

the time, this is actually the desired behavior because this lag helps drivers hiding latency in device communication and providing better overall performance.

However, when using `glBufferSubData` or `glMapBuffer[Range]`, nothing in the API itself prevents us from modifying data that are currently used by the device for rendering the previous frame, as shown in Figure 28.3. Drivers have to avoid this problem by blocking the function until the desired data are not used anymore: this is called an *implicit synchronization*. This can seriously damage performance or cause annoying jerks. A synchronization might block until all previous frames in the device command queue are finished, which could add several milliseconds to the performance time.

28.2.4 Synchronization Primitives

OpenGL offers its own synchronization primitives named *sync objects*, which work like fences inside the device command queue and are set to *signaled* when the device reaches their position. This is useful in a multithreaded environment, when other threads have to be informed about the completeness of computations or rendering and start downloading or uploading data.

The `glClientWaitSync` and `glWaitSync` functions will block until the specified fence is signaled, but these functions provide a timeout parameter which can be set to 0 if we only want to know whether an object has been signaled or not, instead of blocking it. More precisely, `glClientWaitSync` blocks the CPU until the specified sync object is signaled, while `glWaitSync` blocks the device.

28.3 Upload

Streaming is the process in which data are uploaded to the device frequently, e.g., every frame. Good examples of streaming include updating instance data when using instancing or font rendering. Because these tasks are processed every frame, it is important to avoid implicit synchronizations. This can be done in multiple ways:

- a round-robin chain of buffer objects,

- buffer respecification or "orphaning" with `glBufferData` or `glMapBuffer Range`,

- fully manual synchronization with `glMapBufferRange` and `glFenceSync / glClientWaitSync`.

28.3.1   Round-Robin Fashion (Multiple Buffer Objects)

The idea of the round-robin technique is to create several buffer objects and cycle through them. The application can update and upload buffer N while the device is rendering from buffer $N-1$, as shown on Figure 28.4. This method can also be used for download, and it is useful in a multithreaded application, too. See Sections 28.6 and 28.7 for details.

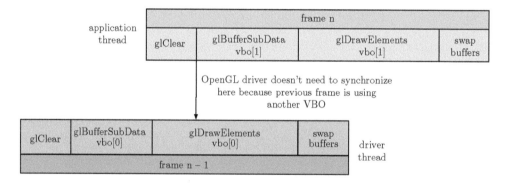

Figure 28.4. Avoiding implicit synchronizations with a round-robin chain.

28.3.2   Buffer Respecification (Orphaning)

Buffer respecification is similar to the round-robin technique, but it all happens inside the OpenGL driver. There are two ways to respecify a buffer. The most common one is to use an extra call to `glBufferData` with NULL as the data argument and the exact size and usage hint it had before, as shown in Listing 28.2. The driver will detach the physical memory block from the buffer object and allocate a new one. This operation is called *orphaning*. The old block will be returned to the heap once it is not used by any commands in the command queue. There is a high probability that

```
glBindBuffer(GL_ARRAY_BUFFER, my_buffer_object);

glBufferData(GL_ARRAY_BUFFER, data_size, NULL, GL_STREAM_DRAW);
glBufferData(GL_ARRAY_BUFFER, data_size, mydata_ptr, GL_STREAM_DRAW);
```

Listing 28.2. Buffer respecification or orphaning using `glBufferData`.

this block will be reused by the next **glBufferData** respecification call [OpenGL Wiki 09]. What's more, we don't have to guess the size of the round-robin chain, since it all happens inside the driver. This process is shown in Figure 28.5.

The behavior of **glBufferData** / **glBufferSubData** is actually very implementation dependent. For instance, it seems that AMD's driver can implicitly orphan the buffer. On NVIDIA, it is slightly more efficient to orphan manually and then upload with **glBufferSubData**, but doing so will ruin the performance on Intel. Listing 28.2 gives the more "coherent" performance across vendors. Lastly, with this technique, it's important that the size parameter of **glBufferData** is always the same to ensure the best performance.

The other way to respecify the buffer is to use the function **glMapBufferRange** with the **GL_MAP_INVALIDATE_BUFFER_BIT** or **GL_MAP_INVALIDATE_RANGE_BIT** flags. This will orphan the buffer and return a pointer to a freshly allocated memory block. See Listing 28.3 for details. We can't use **glMapBuffer**, since it doesn't have this option.

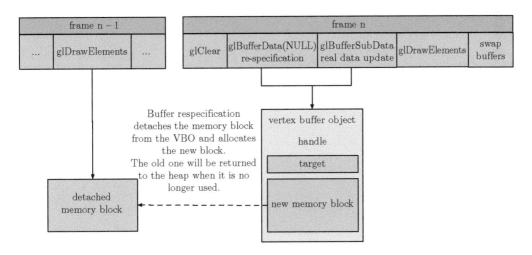

Figure 28.5. Avoiding implicit synchronizations with orphaning.

```
glBindBuffer(GL_ARRAY_BUFFER , my_buffer_object);
void *mydata_ptr = glMapBufferRange(
  GL_ARRAY_BUFFER , 0, data_size ,
  GL_MAP_WRITE_BIT | GL_MAP_INVALIDATE_BUFFER_BIT);

// Fill mydata_ptr with useful data

glUnmapBuffer(GL_ARRAY_BUFFER);
```

Listing 28.3. Buffer respecification or invalidation using glMapBufferRange.

However, we found that, at least on NVIDIA, `glBufferData` and `glMap` `BufferRange`, even with orphaning, cause expensive synchronizations if called concurrently with a rendering operation, even if the buffer is not used in this draw call or in any operation enqueued in the device command queue. This prevents the device from reaching 100 percent utilization. In any case, we recommend not using these techniques. On top of that, flags like GL_MAP_INVALIDATE_BUFFER_BIT or GL_MAP_INVALIDATE_RANGE_BIT involve the driver memory management, which can increase the call duration by more than ten times. The next section will present unsynchronized mapping, which can be used to solve all these synchronization problems.

28.3.3   Unsynchronized Buffers

The last method we will describe here gives us absolute control over the buffer-object data. We just have to tell the driver not to synchronize at all. This can be done by passing the GL_MAP_UNSYNCHRONIZED_BIT flag to `glMapBufferRange`. In this

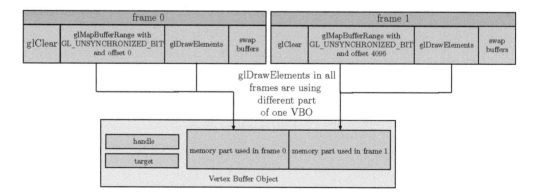

Figure 28.6. Possible usage of unsynchronized glMapBufferRange.

```
const int buffer_number = frame_number++ % 3;

// Wait until buffer is free to use, in most cases this should not wait
// because we are using three buffers in chain, glClientWaitSync
// function can be used for check if the TIMEOUT is zero
GLenum result = glClientWaitSync(fences[buffer_number], 0, TIMEOUT);
if (result == GL_TIMEOUT_EXPIRED || result == GL_WAIT_FAILED)
{
    // Something is wrong
}

glDeleteSync(fences[buffer_number]);
glBindBuffer(GL_ARRAY_BUFFER, buffers[buffer_number]);
void *ptr = glMapBufferRange(GL_ARRAY_BUFFER, offset, size, GL_MAP_WRITE_BIT | ←
    GL_MAP_UNSYNCHRONIZED_BIT);

// Fill ptr with useful data
glUnmapBuffer(GL_ARRAY_BUFFER);

// Use buffer in draw operation
glDrawArray(...);

// Put fence into command queue
fences[buffer_number] = glFenceSync(GL_SYNC_GPU_COMMANDS_COMPLETE, 0);
```

Listing 28.4. Unsynchronized buffer mapping.

case, drivers just return a pointer to previously allocated pinned memory and do no synchronization and no memory re-allocation. This is the fastest way to deal with mapping (see Figure 28.6).

The drawback is that we really have to know what we're doing. No implicit sanity check or synchronization is performed, so if we upload data to a buffer that is currently being used for rendering, we can end up with an undefined behavior or application crash.

The easiest way to deal with unsynchronized mapping is to use multiple buffers like we did in the round-robin section and use GL_MAP_UNSYNCHRONIZED_BIT in the glMapBufferRange function, as shown in Listing 28.4. But we have to be sure that the buffer we are going to use is not used in a concurrent rendering operation. This can be achieved with the glFencSync and glClientWaitSync functions. In practice, a chain of three buffers is enough because the device usually doesn't lag more than two frames behind. At most, glClientWaitSync will synchronize us on the third buffer, but it is a desired behavior because it means that the device command queue is full and that we are GPU-bound.

28.3.4   AMD's pinned_memory Extension

Since Catalyst 11.5, AMD exposes the AMD_pinned_memory extension [Mayer 11, Boudier and Sellers 11], which allows us to use application-side memory allocated

```
#define GL_EXTERNAL_VIRTUAL_MEMORY_AMD 37216 // AMD_pinned_memory

char *_pinned_ptr = new char[buffer_size + 0x1000];
char *_pinned_ptr_aligned = reinterpret_cast<char *>(unsigned(_pinned_ptr + 0xfff) &←
    (~0xfff));

glBindBuffer(GL_EXTERNAL_VIRTUAL_MEMORY_AMD, buffer);
glBufferData(GL_EXTERNAL_VIRTUAL_MEMORY_AMD, buffer_size, _pinned_ptr_aligned, ←
    GL_STREAM_READ);
glBindBuffer(GL_EXTERNAL_VIRTUAL_MEMORY_AMD, 0);
```

Listing 28.5. Example usage of `AMD_pinned_memory`.

with `new` or `malloc` as buffer-object storage. This memory block has to be aligned to the page size. There are a few advantages when using this extension:

- Memory is accessible without OpenGL mapping functions, which means there is no OpenGL call overhead. This is very useful in worker threads for geometry and texture loading.

- Drivers' memory management is skipped because we are responsible for memory allocation.

- There is no internal driver synchronization involved in the process. It is similar to the `GL_MAP_UNSYNCHRONIZED_BIT` flag in `glMapBufferRange`, as explained in the previous section, but it means that we have to be careful which buffer or buffer portion we are going to modify; otherwise, the result might be undefined or our application terminated.

Pinned memory is the best choice for data streaming and downloading, but it is available only on AMD devices and needs explicit synchronization checks to be sure that the buffer is not used in a concurrent rendering operation. Listing 28.5 shows how to use this extension.

28.4 Download

The introduction of the PCI-e bus gave us enough bandwidth to use data download in real-life scenarios. Depending on the PCI-e version, the device's upload and download performance is approximately 1.5–6 GB/s. Today, many algorithms or situations require downloading data from the device:

- procedural terrain generation (collision, geometry, bounding boxes, etc.);

- video recording, as discussed in Chapter 31;

- page resolver pass in virtual texturing;

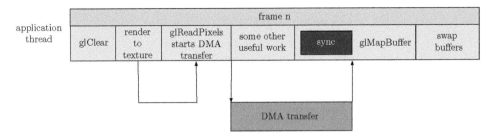

Figure 28.7. Asynchronous DMA transfer in download.

- physics simulation;

- image histogram.

The asynchronous nature of OpenGL drivers brings some complications to the download process, and the specification is not very helpful regarding how to do it fast and without implicit synchronization. OpenGL currently offers a few ways to download data to the main memory. Most of the time, we want to download textures because rasterization is the most efficient way to generate data on the GPU, at least in OpenGL. This includes most of the use-cases above.

In this case, we have to use `glReadPixels` and bind a buffer object to the `GL_PIXEL_PACK_BUFFER` target. This function will start an asynchronous transfer from the texture memory to the buffer memory. In this case, it is important to specify a `GL_*_READ` usage hint for the buffer object because the OpenGL driver will copy the data to the driver memory, which can be accessed from the application. Again, this is only asynchronous for the CPU: the device has to wait for the current render to complete and process the transfer. Finally, `glMapBuffer` returns a pointer to the downloaded data. This process is presented in Figure 28.7.

In this simple scenario, the application thread is blocked because the device command queue is always lagging behind, and we are trying to download data which aren't ready yet. Three options are available to avoid this waiting:

- do some CPU intensive work after the call to `glReadPixels`;

- call `glMapBuffer` on the buffer object from the previous frame or two frames behind;

- use fences and call `glMapBuffer` when a sync object is signaled.

The first solution is not very practical in real applications because it doesn't guarantee that we will not be waiting at the end and makes it harder to write efficient code. The second solution is much better, and in most cases, there will be no wait

```
if (rb_tail != rb_head)
{
  const int tmp_tail = (rb_tail + 1) & RB_BUFFERS_MASK;
  GLenum res = glClientWaitSync(fences[tmp_tail], 0, 0);
  if (res == GL_ALREADY_SIGNALED || res == GL_CONDITION_SATISFIED)
  {
    rb_tail = tmp_tail;
    glDeleteSync(sc->_fence);
    glBindBuffer(GL_PIXEL_PACK_BUFFER, buffers[rb_tail]);
    glMapBuffer(GL_PIXEL_PACK_BUFFER, GL_READ_ONLY);
    // Process data
    glUnmapBuffer(GL_PIXEL_PACK_BUFFER);
  }
}
const int tmp_head = (rb_head + 1) & RB_BUFFERS_MASK;
if (tmp_head != rb_tail)
{
  glReadBuffer(GL_BACK);
  glBindBuffer(GL_PIXEL_PACK_BUFFER, buffers[rb_head]);
  glReadPixels(0, 0, width, height, GL_BGRA, GL_UNSIGNED_BYTE, (void*)offset);
}
else
{
  // We are too fast
}
```

Listing 28.6. Asynchronous pixel data transfer.

because the data is already transferred. This solution needs multiple buffer objects as presented in the round-robin section. The last solution is the best way to avoid implicit synchronization because it gives exact information on the completeness of the transfer; we still have to deal with the fact that the data will only be ready later, but as developers, we have more control over the status of the transfer thanks to the fences. The basic steps are provided in Listing 28.6.

However, on AMD hardware, `glUnmapBuffer` will be synchronous in this special case. If we really need an asynchronous behavior, we have to use the `AMD_pinned_memory` extension.

On the other hand, we have found that on NVIDIA, it is better to use another intermediate buffer with the `GL_STREAM_COPY` usage hint, which causes the buffer to be allocated in device memory. We use `glReadPixels` on this buffer and finally use `glCopyBufferSubData` to copy the data into the final buffer in CPU memory. This process is almost two times faster than a direct way. This copy function is described in the next section.

28.5 Copy

A widespread extension is `ARB_copy_buffer` [NVIDIA 09], which makes it possible to copy data between buffer objects. In particular, if both buffers live in device

```
glBindBuffer(GL_COPY_READ_BUFFER, source_buffer);
glBindBuffer(GL_COPY_WRITE_BUFFER, dest_buffer);
glCopyBufferSubData(GL_COPY_READ_BUFFER, GL_COPY_WRITE_BUFFER, source_offset, ←
    write_offset, data_size);
```

Listing 28.7. Copying one buffer into another using ARB_copy_buffer.

memory, this is the only way to copy data between buffers on the GPU side without CPU intervention (see Listing 28.7).

As we pointed out at the end of previous section, on NVIDIA GeForce devices, copy is useful for downloading data. Using an intermediate buffer in device memory and reading the copy back to the CPU is actually faster than a direct transfer: 3GB/s instead of 1.5GB/s. This is a limitation of the hardware that is not present on the NVIDIA Quadro product line. On AMD, with Catalyst 11.12 drivers, this function is extremely unoptimized, and in most cases, causes expensive synchronizations.

28.6   Multithreading and Shared Contexts

In this section, we will describe how to stream data from another thread. In the last few years, single-core performance hasn't been increasing as fast as the number of cores in the CPU. As such, it is important to know how OpenGL behaves in a multithreaded environment. Most importantly, we will focus on usability and performance considerations. Since accessing the OpenGL API from multiple threads is not very well known, we need to introduce shared contexts first.

28.6.1   Introduction to Multithreaded OpenGL

OpenGL can actually be used from multiple threads since Version 1.1, but some care must be taken at application initialization. More precisely, each additional thread that needs to call OpenGL functions must create its own context and explicitly connect that context to the first context in order to share OpenGL objects. Not doing so will result in crashes when trying to execute data transfers or draw calls. Implementation details vary from platform to platform. The recommended process on Windows is depicted in Figure 28.8, using the WGL_ARB_create_context extensions available in OpenGL 3.2 [ARB 09b]. A similar extension, GLX_ARB_create_context, is available for Linux [ARB 09c]. Implementation details for Linux, Mac, and Windows can be found in [Supnik 08].

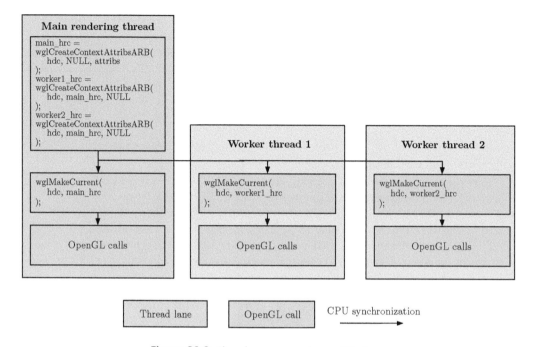

Figure 28.8. Shared-context creation on Windows.

28.6.2   Synchronization Issues

In a single-threaded scenario, it is perfectly valid to respecify a buffer while it is currently in use: the driver will put `glBufferData` in the command queue, and upon processing, wait until draw calls relying on the same buffer are finished.

When using shared contexts, however, the driver will create one command queue for each thread, and no such implicit synchronization will take place. A thread can thus start a DMA transfer in a memory block that is currently used in a draw call by the device. This usually results in partially updated meshes or instance data.

The solution is to use the above-mentioned techniques, which also work with shared contexts: multibuffering the data or using fences.

28.6.3   Performance Hit due to Internal Synchronization

Shared contexts have one more disadvantage: as we will see in the benchmarks below, they introduce a performance hit each frame.

In Figure 28.9, we show the profiling results of a sample application running in Parallel Nsight on a GeForce GTX 470 with the 280.26 Forceware drivers. The first timeline uses a single thread to upload and render a 3D model; the second

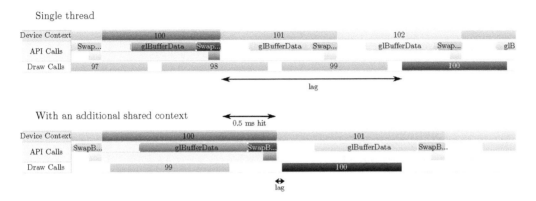

Figure 28.9. Performance hit due to shared contexts.

timeline does exactly the same thing but with an extra shared context in an idle thread. This simple change adds 0.5 ms each frame, probably because of additional synchronizations in the driver. We also notice that the device only lags one frame behind instead of two.

At least on NVIDIA, this penalty usually varies between 0.1 and 0.5 ms; this mostly depends on the CPU performance. Remarkably, it is quite constant with respect to the number of threads with shared contexts. On NVIDIA Quadro hardware, this penalty is usually lower because some hardware cost optimizations of the GeForce product line are not present.

28.6.4   Final Words on Shared Context

Our advice is to use standard working threads when possible. Since all the functionality that shared contexts offers can be obtained without them, the following do not usually cause a problem:

- If we want to speed up the rendering loop by offloading some CPU-heavy task in another thread, this can be done without shared contexts; see the next section for details.

- If we need to know if a data transfer is finished in a single-threaded environment, we can use fences, as defined in the GL_ARB_sync extension; see Listing 28.8 for details.

We have to point out that shared contexts won't make transfers and rendering parallel, at least in NVIDIA Forceware 285 and AMD Catalyst 11.12, so there is usually minimal performance advantage for using them. See Chapter 29 for more details on using fences with shader contexts and multiple threads.

```
glUnmapBuffer(...);

GLsync fence = glFenceSync(GL_SYNC_GPU_COMMANDS_COMPLETE, 0);

// Other operations

int res = glClientWaitSync(fence, 0, TIMEOUT);
if (res == GL_ALREADY_SIGNALED || res == GL_CONDITION_SATISFIED)
{
  glDeleteSync(fence);
  // Transfer finished
}
```

Listing 28.8. Waiting for a transfer completion with GL_ARB_sync.

28.7   Usage Scenario

In this last section, we will now present a scenario in which we will stream some scene object data to the device. Our scene is represented by 32,768 objects representing a building structure. Each object is generated in a GPU shader, and the only input is the transformation matrix, which means 2MB of data per frame for the whole scene. For rendering, we use an instanced draw call that minimizes the CPU intervention.

This scenario is implemented in three different methods: a single-threaded version, a multithreaded version without shared contexts, and a multithreaded version with shared contexts. All the source code is available for reference on the OpenGL Insights website, www.openglinsights.com.

In practice, these methods can be used to upload, for instance, frustum culling information, but since we want to measure the transfer performance, no computation is actually done: the work consists simply in filling the buffer as fast as possible.

28.7.1   Method 1: Single Thread

In this first method, everything is done in the rendering thread: buffer streaming and rendering. The main advantage of this implementation is its simplicity. In particular, there is no need for mutexes or other synchronization primitives.

The buffer is streamed using **glMapBufferRange** with the **GL_MAP_WRITE_BIT** and **GL_MAP_UNSYNCHRONIZED_BIT** flags. This enables us to write transformation matrices directly into the pinned memory region, which will be used directly by the device, saving an extra memcpy and a synchronization compared to the other methods.

In addition, **glMapBufferRange** can, as the name suggests, map only a subset of the buffer, which is useful if we don't want to modify the entire buffer or if the size of the buffer changes from frame to frame: as we said earlier, we can allocate a big buffer and only use a variable portion of it. The performance of this single-threaded implementation method is shown in Table 28.3.

Architecture	Rendering time (ms/frame)
Intel Core i5, NVIDIA GeForce GTX 470	2.8
Intel Core 2 Duo Q6600, AMD HD 6850	3.6
Intel Core i7, Intel GMA 3000	16.1

Table 28.3. Rendering performance for Method 1.

28.7.2 Method 2: Two Threads and One OpenGL Context

The second method uses another thread to copy the scene data to a mapped buffer. There are a number of reasons why doing so is a good idea:

- The rendering thread doesn't stop sending OpenGL commands and is able to keep the device busy all the time.

- Dividing the processing between two CPU cores can shorten the frame time.

- OpenGL draw calls are expensive; they are usually more time consuming than simply appending a command in the device command queue. In particular, if the internal state has changed since the last draw call, for instance, due to a call to `glEnable`, a long state-validation step occurs [2]. By separating our computations from the driver's thread, we can take advantage of multicore architectures.

In this method (see Figure 28.10), we will use two threads: the application thread and the renderer thread. The application thread is responsible for

- handling inputs,

- copying scene instance data into the mapped buffer,

- preparing the primitives for font rendering.

The renderer thread is responsible for

- calling `glUnmapBuffer` on the mapped buffers that were filled in the application thread,

- setting shaders and uniforms,

- drawing batches.

We use a queue of frame-context objects that helps us avoid unnecessary synchronizations between threads. The frame-context objects hold all data required for a frame, such as the camera matrix, pointers to memory-mapped buffers, etc. This design is very similar to the round-robin fashion because it uses multiple unsynchronized buffers. It is also used with success in the Outerra Engine [Kemen and

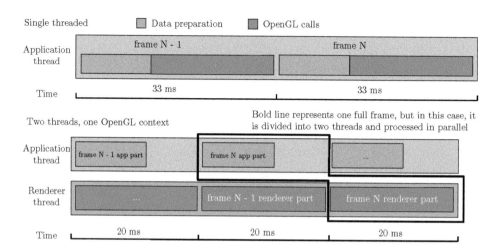

Figure 28.10. Method 2: improving the frame rate with an external renderer thread.

Hrabcak 11]. The performance results are shown in Table 28.4. For simplicity, we used only two threads here, but we can of course add more, depending on the tasks and the dependencies in the computations.

Architecture	Performance	
	(ms/frame)	improvement vs. Method 1
Intel Core i5, NVIDIA GeForce GTX 470	2.0	×1.4
Intel Core 2 Duo Q6600, AMD HD 6850	3.2	×1.25
Intel Core i7, Intel GMA 3000	15.4	×1.05

Table 28.4. Rendering performance for Method 2.

28.7.3   Method 3: Two Threads and Two OpenGL Shared Contexts

In this last method, the scene-data copy is done in an OpenGL-capable thread. We thus have two threads: the main rendering thread and the additional rendering thread. The main rendering thread is responsible for the following tasks:

- handling inputs,

- calling `glMapBufferRange` and `glUnmapBuffer` on buffers,

- copying scene instance data into the mapped buffer,

- preparing primitives for font rendering.

Architecture		Performance	
	(ms/frame)	improvement vs. Method 1	hit due to shared contexts (ms/frame)
Intel Core i5, NVIDIA GeForce GTX 470	2.1	×1.33	+0.1
Intel Core 2 Duo Q6600, AMD HD 6850	7.5	×0.48	+4.3
Intel Core i7, Intel GMA 3000	15.3	×1.05	-0.1

Table 28.5. Rendering performance for Method 3.

The renderer thread is responsible for

- setting shaders and uniforms,

- drawing batches.

In this method, buffers are updated in the main thread. This includes calling `glMapBufferRange` and `glUnmapBuffer` because the threads are sharing the OpenGL rendering context. We get most of the benefits from the second method (two threads and one OpenGL context) as compared to the single-threaded version: faster rendering loop, parallelization of some OpenGL calls, and better overall performance than Method 1, as shown in Table 28.5. However, as mentioned earlier, there is a synchronization overhead in the driver, which makes this version slower than the previous one. This overhead is much smaller on professional cards like NVIDIA Quadro, on which such multithreading is very common, but is still present.

The performance drop of AMD in this case should not be taken too seriously, because unsynchronized buffers are not ideal with shared contexts on this platform. Other methods exhibit a more reasonable 1.1 times performance improvement over the first solution, as shown in the next section.

28.7.4 Performance Comparisons

Table 28.6 shows the complete performance comparisons of our scenarios with several upload policies on various hardware configurations. All tests use several buffers in a round-robin fashion; the differences lie in the way the data is given to OpenGL:

- InvalidateBuffer. The buffer is mapped with `glMapBufferRange` using the `GL_MAP_WRITE_BIT | GL_MAP_INVALIDATE_BUFFER_BIT` flags, and unmapped normally.

- FlushExplicit. The buffer is mapped with `glMapBufferRange` using the `GL_MAP_WRITE_BIT | GL_MAP_FLUSH_EXPLICIT_BIT` flags, flushed, and unmapped. The unmapping must be done because it is not safe to keep the buffer mapped permanently, except when using `AMD_pinned_memory`.

CPU	Intel Q6600		Intel i7 2630QM		Intel i5 760	
GPU	AMD HD 6850	NV GTX 460	Intel HD 3000	NV GT 525M	AMD HD 6570	NV GTX 470
Scenario 1						
InvalidateBuffer	3.6	5.0	16.1	12.6	12.0	3.5
FlushExplicit	4.9	4.9	16.1	12.5	18.4	3.5
Unsynchronized	3.6	3.7	16.1	11.2	9.0	2.8
BufferData	5.2	4.3	16.2	11.7	6.7	3.1
BufferSubData	4.4	4.3	17.3	11.6	9.5	3.1
Write	8.8	4.9	16.1	12.4	19.5	3.5
AMD Pinned	3.7	n/a	n/a	n/a	8.6	n/a
Scenario 2						
InvalidateBuffer	5.5	3.2	15.3	10.3	9.5	2.1
FlushExplicit	7.2	3.1	15.3	10.3	16.3	2.1
Unsynchronized	**3.2**	**2.9**	15.4	**9.9**	8.0	**2.0**
BufferData	4.6	3.5	15.2	10.4	**5.5**	2.3
BufferSubData	4.0	3.5	**15.1**	10.5	8.3	2.3
Write	7.4	3.1	15.3	10.3	17.0	2.1
AMD Pinned	**3.2**	n/a	n/a	n/a	8.1	n/a
Scenario 3						
InvalidateBuffer	5.3	3.8	15.2	10.6	9.4	2.4
FlushExplicit	7.4	3.7	15.2	10.6	17.1	2.3
Unsynchronized	7.5	3.2	15.3	10.2	17.9	2.1
BufferData	broken	4.5	15.3	11.0	broken	2.5
BufferSubData	4.5	3.9	**15.1**	11.0	8.6	2.5
Write	7.5	3.5	15.2	10.5	17.9	2.3
AMD Pinned	**3.2**	n/a	n/a	n/a	8.0	n/a

Table 28.6. Our results in all configurations. All values are expressed in ms/frame (smaller is better).

- Unsynchronized. The buffer is mapped with `glMapBufferRange` using the `GL_MAP_WRITE_BIT | GL_MAP_UNSYNCHRONIZED_BIT` flags and unmapped normally.

- BufferData. The buffer is orphaned using `glBufferData(NULL)`, and updated with `glBufferSubData`.

- BufferSubData. The buffer is not orphaned and is simply updated with `glBufferSubData`.

- Write. The buffer is mapped with `glMapBufferRange` using only the `GL_MAP_WRITE_BIT` flag.

Tests on the Intel GMA 3000 were performed with a smaller scene because it wasn't able to render the larger scene correctly.

The Intel GMA 3000 has almost the same performance in all cases. Since there is only standard RAM, there is no transfer and probably fewer possible variations for accessing the memory. Intel also seems to have a decent implementation of shared contexts with a minimal overhead.

NVIDIA and AMD, however, both have worse performance when using shared contexts. As said earlier, the synchronization cost is relatively constant but not negligible.

For all vendors, using a simple worker thread gets us the best performance, provided that synchronizations are done carefully. While the unsynchronized version is generally the fastest, we notice some exceptions: in particular, `glBufferData` can be very fast on AMD when the CPU can fill the buffer fast enough.

28.8 Conclusion

In this chapter, we investigated how to get the most out of CPU-device transfers. We explained many available techniques to stream data between the CPU and the device and provided three sample implementations with performance comparisons.

In the general case, we recommend using a standard worker thread and multiple buffers with the `GL_MAP_UNSYCHRONIZED_BIT` flag. This might not be possible because of dependencies in the data, but this will usually be a simple yet effective way to improve the performance of an existing application.

It is still possible that such an application isn't well suited to parallelization. For instance, if it is rendering-intensive and doesn't use much CPU, nothing will be gained from multithreading it. Even there, better performance can be achieved by simply avoiding uploads and downloads of currently used data. In any case, we should always upload our data as soon as possible and wait as long as possible before using new data in order to let the transfer complete.

We believe that OpenGL would benefit from a more precise specification in buffer objects, like explicit pinned memory allocation, strict memory destination parameters instead of hints, or a replacement of shared contexts by streams, similar to what CUDA and Direct3D 11 provide. We also hope that future drivers provide real GPU-asynchronous transfers for all buffer targets and textures, even on low-cost gaming hardware, since it would greatly improve the performance of many real-world scenarios.

Finally, as with any performance-critical piece of software, it is very important to benchmark the actual usage on our target hardware, for instance, using NVIDIA Nsight because it is easy to leave the "fast path."

Bibliography

[ARB 08] OpenGL ARB. "OpenGL EXT_framebuffer_object Specification." www.opengl. org/registry/specs/EXT/framebuffer_object.txt, 2008.

[ARB 09a] OpenGL ARB. "OpenGL ARB_texture_buffer_object Specification." www. opengl.org/registry/specs/EXT/texture_buffer_object.txt, 2009.

[ARB 09b] OpenGL ARB. "OpenGL GLX_create_context Specification." www.opengl.org/ registry/specs/ARB/glx_create_context.txt, 2009.

[ARB 09c] OpenGL ARB. "OpenGL WGL_create_context Specification." www.opengl.org/ registry/specs/ARB/wgl_create_context.txt, 2009.

[Boudier and Sellers 11] Pierre Boudier and Graham Sellers. "Memory System on Fusion APUs: The Benefit of Zero Copy." developer.amd.com/afds/assets/presentations/1004_ final.pdf, 2011.

[Intel 08] Intel. "Intel X58 Express Chipset." http://www.intel.com/Assets/PDF/prodbrief/ x58-product-brief.pdf, 2008.

[Kemen and Hrabcak 11] Brano Kemen and Ladislav Hrabcak. "Outerra." outerra.com, 2011.

[Kemen 10] Brano Kemen. "Outerra Video Recording." www.outerra.com/video, 2010.

[Mayer 11] Christopher Mayer. "Streaming Video Data into 3D Applications." developer. amd.com/afds/assets/presentations/2116_final.pdf, 2011.

[NVIDIA 09] NVIDIA. "OpenGL ARB_copy_buffer Specification." http://www.opengl.org/ registry/specs/ARB/copy_buffer.txt, 2009.

[OpenGL Wiki 09] OpenGL Wiki. "OpenGL Wiki Buffer Object Streaming." www.opengl. org/wiki/Buffer_Object_Streaming, 2009.

[Supnik 08] Benjamin Supnik. "Creating OpenGL Objects in a Second Thread—Mac, Linux, Windows." http://hacksoflife.blogspot.com/2008/02/ creating-opengl-objects-in-second.html, 2008.

[Venkataraman 10] Shalini Venkataraman. "NVIDIA Quadro Dual Copy Engines." www. nvidia.com/docs/IO/40049/Dual_copy_engines.pdf, 2010.

[Williams and Hart 11] Ian Williams and Evan Hart. "Efficient Rendering of Geometric Data Using OpenGL VBOs in SPECviewperf." www.spec.org/gwpg/gpc.static/ vbo_whitepaper.html, 2011.

Fermi Asynchronous Texture Transfers   29

Shalini Venkataraman

29.1   Introduction

Many real-world graphics applications need to transfer textures efficiently in and out of the GPU memory in the form of 2D images, 2.5D terrains, or 3D volumes and their time-varying counterparts. In the pre-Fermi generation of NVIDIA hardware, any data transfer would stall the GPU from rendering because the GPU had a single hardware execution thread that could either execute transfers or rendering. The OpenGL pixel buffer object (PBO) [ARB 04] provides a mechanism to optimize transfers, but it is CPU asynchronous in that it allows for concurrent CPU processing while the GPU performs uploads and downloads. However, the GPU is still blocked from rendering OpenGL commands while the actual data transfers occur. As discussed in Chapter 28, many applications go a step further to use multiple threads for resource preparation such that the GPU is always kept busy. At the hardware-execution level, however, the GPU will end up serializing the transfer and the draw command queues.

This chapter explains how this limitation is overcome by the *copy engine hardware* found in the NVIDIA Fermi architecture [NVIDIA 10] generation and later GPUs. A copy engine is a dedicated controller on the GPU that performs DMA transfers of data between CPU memory and GPU memory independent of the graphics engine (Figure 29.1). Each copy engine allows one-way-at-a-time bidirectional transfer. The NVIDIA Fermi GeForce and the low-end Quadro cards[1] have one copy engine such

---

[1] Quadro 2000 and below.

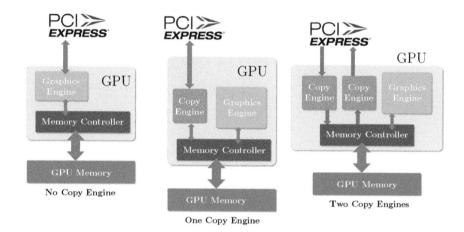

Figure 29.1. Copy engine and graphics engine layout for various GPUs.

that unidirectional transfers can be concurrently performed with rendering, allowing for two-way overlap. The Quadro mid-higher level cards[2] have two copy engines so that bidirectional transfers can be done in parallel with rendering. This three-way overlap means that the current set of data can be processed while the previous set is downloaded from the GPU and the next set is uploaded.

Figure 29.1 shows the block diagrams comparing GPUs with (left) no copy engine, where the graphics engine handles transfers and drawing; (center) a single copy engine that handles transfers in both directions; and finally, (right) two copy engines, each dedicated to transfers in a single direction.

Some examples for overlapped transfers include the following:

- **Video or time-varying geometry and volumes.** This includes transcoding, visualizing time-varying numerical simulations, and scanned medical data such as 4D ultrasound.

- **Remoting graphics.** Powerful GPU servers are used for offscreen rendering, and the results are downloaded to the server's main memory, which is sent over the network to thin clients such as phones and tablets.

- **Parallel rendering.** When a scene is divided and rendered across multiple GPUs and the color and depth are read back for composition, parallelizing readback will speed up the pipeline. This is likewise the case for a sort-first implementation, where at every frame, the data have to be streamed to the GPU based on the viewpoint.

---

[2]Quadro 4000, 5000, 6000, and Quadro Plex 7000.

- Data bricking for large images, terrains, and volumes. Bricks or LODs are paged in and out as needed in another thread without disrupting the rendering thread.

- OS cache. Operating systems can page in and out textures as needed, eliminating shadow copies in RAM.

This chapter starts by covering existing methods for texture transfers, such as synchronous and CPU-asynchronous methods like PBOs, and explains their limitations. Then, GPU-asynchronous methods using the Fermi copy engines are introduced where transfers can occur concurrently with GPU rendering. Achieving this parallelism on the GPU hardware requires application restructuring into multiple threads with a context per thread and use of OpenGL fences to manage the synchronization. Finally, it concludes with results showing the speedup achieved for various data sizes, application characteristics, and GPUs with different overlap capabilities. The complete source code that is used to generate the results is available on the OpenGL Insights website, www.openglinsights.com.

29.2   OpenGL Command Buffer Execution

Before diving into transfers, I will lay the groundwork for understanding OpenGL command buffers, specifically the interplay between the drivers and the OS and how it is all finally executed by the graphics hardware. I use GPUView [Fisher and Pronovost 11], a tool developed by Microsoft and available as part of the Windows 7 SDK. GPUView will allow us to see, as a function of time, the state of all the context-specific CPU queues as well as the queue for the graphics card.

Figure 29.2 shows the trace for an OpenGL application with multiple contexts. The application thread continuously submits work to the CPU command queue from where the OS uploads to the GPU hardware queue. The CPU command queue exists per OpenGL context. OpenGL calls for a context are batched in a list of commands for that context, and when enough commands are built up, they are flushed to the CPU command queue. Each CPU command queue has its own color so that it is easy to see which queue the graphics hardware is currently working on. Periodically, when there is room, the graphics scheduler will add a task from the CPU context command queue onto the GPU hardware queue. The GPU hardware queue shows the work that is currently being processed by the graphics card and queue of tasks it is working on. There are two GPU hardware queues in this example showing some of the packets that are processed in parallel and others in serial. The arrows follow a series of command packets as they are flushed to the CPU command queue, and then wait in the queue and are executed on the GPU. When the GPU has finished executing the final packets, the CPU command queue can return and the next frame begins. Throughout this chapter, we use GPUView traces to understand what happens under the hood for the various transfer approaches.

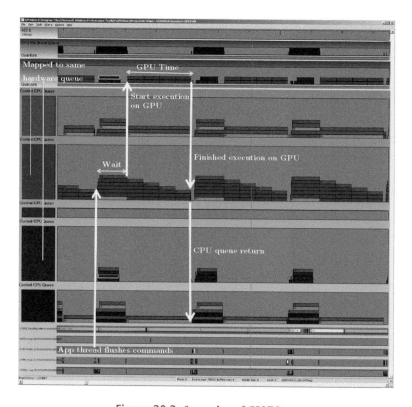

Figure 29.2. Screenshot of GPUView.

29.3   Current Texture Transfer Approaches

A typical upload-process-download pipeline can be broken down into the following:

- Copy. The CPU cycles spent for data conversion, if any, to native GPU formats; use `memcpy` from application space to driver space for upload and vice versa for download.

- Upload. The time for the actual data transfer on the PCI-e bus from host to GPU.

- Process. The GPU cycles for rendering or processing.

- Download. The time for the data transfer from the GPU back to host.

To achieve maximum end-to-end throughput on the GPU, maximum overlap is required between these various stages in the pipeline.

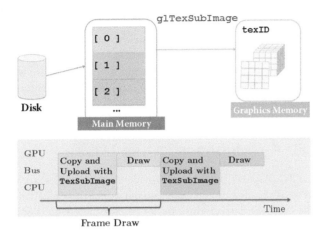

Figure 29.3. Synchronous texture uploads with no overlap.

29.3.1 Synchronous Texture Transfers

For simplicity, we start by analyzing an upload-render pipeline. The straightforward upload method for textures is to call `glTexSubImage`, which uses the CPU for copying data from user space to driver pinned memory and blocks it during the subsequent data transfer on the bus to the GPU. Figure 29.3 illustrates the inefficiency of this method as the GPU is blocked during the CPU copy. The corresponding

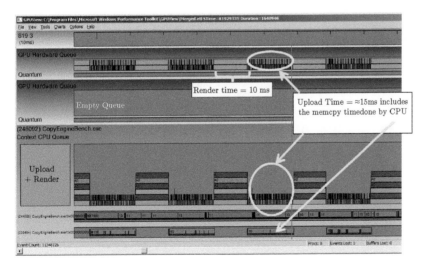

Figure 29.4. GPUView timeline showing synchronous texture uploads.

GPUView trace is shown in Figure 29.4, and shows that upload and render are handled sequentially and the additional GPU hardware queue is unused. This graph also shows that the `memcpys` are in fact interspersed with the transfer, causing the spikes and gaps in the CPU and GPU command queues. Ideally, we would like the execution timeline of a packet to be solid until completion to show that the GPU is kept fully busy, as is shown by the render.

29.3.2 CPU Asynchronous Texture Transfers

The OpenGL PBO [ARB 04] mechanism provides for transfers that are asynchronous on the CPU if an application can schedule enough work between initiating the transfer and actually using the data. In this case, `glTexSubImage`, `glReadPixels`, and `glGetTexImage` operate with little CPU intervention. PBOs allow direct access into GPU driver-pinned memory, eliminating the need for additional copies. After the copy operation, the CPU does not stall while the transfer takes place and continues on to process the next frame. Ping-pong PBOs can further increase parallelism where one PBO is mapped for `memcpy` while the other feeds to the texture.

Figure 29.5 shows the workflow along with the timeline for the same upload-render workflow, and Listing 29.1 shows the code snippets to map the PBOs and populate or "unpack" them. Multiple threads can be used to feed the data for transfer (see Chapter 28); however, at the hardware-execution level, there is only one thread of execution causing transfers to be serialized with the drawing as shown in the GPUView trace in Figure 29.6. The trace also shows solid lines for upload and render, signifying 100% GPU utilization without any CPU intervention.

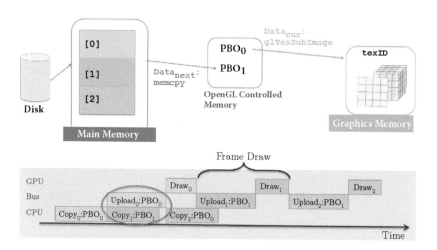

Figure 29.5. CPU asynchronous uploads with ping-pong PBOs.

```
GLuint pbo[2]; // The ping-pong pbo's
unsigned int curPBO = 0;
// Bind current pbo for app->pbo transfer
glBindBuffer(GL_PIXEL_UNPACK_BUFFER, pbo[curPBO]);
GLubyte *ptr;
ptr = (GLubyte *)glMapBufferRange(GL_PIXEL_UNPACK_BUFFER_ARB, 0, size, ←
    GL_MAP_WRITE_BIT | GL_MAP_INVALIDATE_BUFFER_BIT);
memcpy(ptr, pData, width * height * sizeof(GLubyte) * nComponents);
glUnmapBuffer(GL_PIXEL_UNPACK_BUFFER);
glBindTexture(GL_TEXTURE_2D, texId);
// Bind next pbo for upload from pbo to texture object
glBindBuffer(GL_PIXEL_UNPACK_BUFFER, pbo[1 - curPBO]);
glTexSubImage2D(GL_TEXTURE_2D, 0, 0, 0, width, height, GL_RGBA, GL_UNSIGNED_BYTE,←
    0);
glBindBuffer(GL_PIXEL_UNPACK_BUFFER, 0);
glBindTexture(GL_TEXTURE_2D, 0);
curPBO = 1 - curPBO;
```

Listing 29.1. CPU asynchronous upload using ping-pong PBOs.

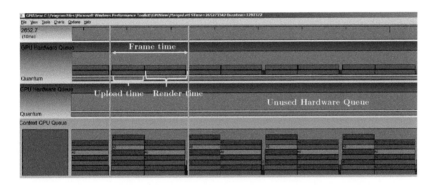

Figure 29.6. CPU asynchronous transfers using PBOs in the same thread as render.

29.4   GPU Asynchronous Texture Transfers

The GPUView diagrams show that only one GPU hardware queue was used and the additional GPU hardware queues signifying tasks for the copy engines are empty. The copy engines are not used by default, as there is some additional overhead in initialization and synchronization, which is not warranted for small transfers as the results later show (Section 29.6). In order to trigger the copy engine, the application has to provide a heuristic to the drivers, and it does this by separating the transfers in a separate thread. When the transfers are partitioned this way, the GPU scheduler ensures that the OpenGL commands issued in the render thread will map and run on the graphics engine and the commands in the transfer threads on the copy engines in parallel and completely asynchronously. This is what I refer to as GPU asynchronous transfers.

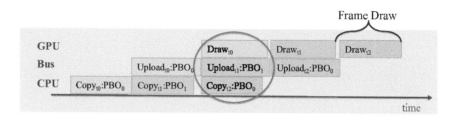

Figure 29.7. GPU asynchronous transfer showing overlap of upload and draw.

Figure 29.7 shows the end-to-end frame time amortized over three frames for an upload-render case. The current frame upload ($t1$) is overlapped with the render of the previous frame ($t0$) and CPU `memcpy` of the next frame ($t2$). Figure 29.8 shows the GPUView trace on a Quadro 6000 card where three separate GPU command queues are exposed, although the download queue is currently unused. The upload here is hidden by the render time.

So far in this chapter, I have touched mostly on the upload-render case for the sake of simplicity in illustration. However, the same principles apply for a render-download and a upload-render-download overlap case.

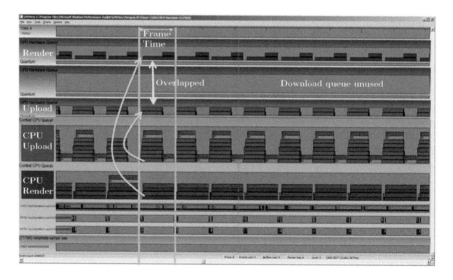

Figure 29.8. GPUView timing diagram showing the overlap of upload and draw at the GPU hardware queues.

29.5   Implementation Details

29.5.1   Multiple OpenGL Contexts

A separate thread with its associated OpenGL context is created for each stage applicable in the pipeline: upload, render, and download. Figure 29.9 shows the schematic for a upload-render pipeline. The upload thread is responsible for streaming source data from main memory into a shared texture that the render thread subsequently accesses for drawing.

Likewise, as shown in Figure 29.10, the render thread renders to a framebuffer-object attachment that the download thread is waiting on to transfer back to main memory. The offscreen rendering is done via FBOs [ARB 08]. All the transfers are still done using PBOs, as was explained in Section 29.3.2. Multiple textures for both source and destinations are used to ensure sufficient overlap such that uploads and downloads are kept busy while the GPU is rendering to or with a current texture.

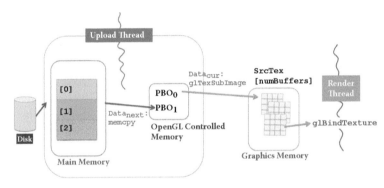

Figure 29.9. Schematic showing upload and render threads with shared textures.

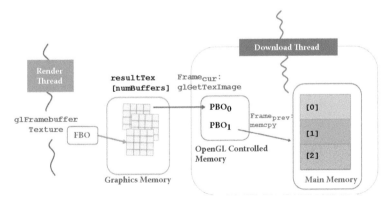

Figure 29.10. Render and download threads accessing shared offscreen textures.

The textures are shared between multiple contexts using WGL_ARB_create _context [ARB 09c] on Windows and GLX_ARB_create_context on Linux [ARB 09b]. Threads are then spawned to handle the upload, render, and download processes. To manage concurrent access from threads to shared textures, synchronization primitives like CPU events and GPU fences are created per texture.

29.5.2 Synchronization

OpenGL rendering commands are assumed to be asynchronous. When a glDraw* call is issued, it is not guaranteed that the rendering is done by the time the call returns. When sharing data between OpenGL contexts bound to multiple CPU threads, it is useful to know that a specific point in the command stream was fully executed. For example, the render thread needs to know when the texture upload has completed in order to use the texture. This handshaking is managed by synchronization objects as part of the GL_ARB_Sync mechanism [ARB 09a]. Synchronization objects can be shared between different OpenGL contexts, and an object created in a context can be waited on by another context. Specifically, we use a fence, which is a type of synchronization object that is created and inserted in the command stream (in a nonsignaled state) and when executed, changes its state to signaled. Due to the in-order execution of OpenGL, if the fence is signaled, then all commands issued before the fence in the current context have also been completed. In an upload-render scheme, as shown in Figure 29.11, the render waits on the fence, endUpload, inserted after texture upload to start the drawing while the upload waits on the startUpload fence, which the render queues after the drawing. These fences are created per texture. Corresponding CPU events are used to signal the GPU fence creation to avoid busy waiting. For example, the endUploadValid event is set by the upload thread to signal to the render thread to start the glWaitSync for the endUpload fence before rendering to that texture.

Likewise, in a render-download scheme, as shown in Figure 29.12, the download waits on the fence startDownload inserted after render to start reading from the texture, and the render waits for download to complete before using the endDown load fence.

Figure 29.11. Upload thread produces to srcTex[2] while render thread consumes from srcTex[0].

Figure 29.12. Render thread produces resulting image to `resultTex[3]` while download thread consumes from `resultTex[2]`.

29.5.3   Copy Engine Considerations

An OpenGL context attached to a copy engine is a fully functional GL context so that non-DMA commands can be issued in the transfer threads. However, some of these calls may time-slice with the rendering thread, causing us to lose parallelism. In the event that the driver has to serialize calls between the transfer and render context, it generates a debug message, "Pixel transfer is synchronized with 3D rendering," which the application can query using the `GL_ARB_debug_output` extension (Chapter 33). Another limitation of Fermi's copy engine is that it is only limited to pixel transfers and not vertex transfers.

When FBOs are used in conjunction with copy engines, there is some over-head in doing the FBO validation during texture and renderbuffer attachments. For this reason, `glGetTexImage` is the prefered path for download rather than using `glReadPixels` to read from a renderbuffer or texture. Lastly, the optimal number of shared textures should be set based on the ratio of render time to transfer time; this requires some experimentation. When both the times are balanced, a double-buffered texture is sufficient.

29.6   Results and Analysis

The following tests were done on a Dell T7500 Workstation with Intel Xeon Quad Core E5620 at 2.4GHz and 16GB RAM. The test boards used were NVIDIA Quadro 6000 and NVIDIA GeForce GTX 570 attached to the PCI-e x16 slot with Quadro and Forceware 300.01 drivers. As the PCI transfer rates are highly sensitive to the chipset, a workstation-class motherboard is used to achieve the best results.

The results compare the performance gain achieved on the GeForce and Quadro with various texture sizes for applications that range from transfer-heavy to balanced to render-heavy. The horizontal axis shows the ratio of render to transfer time on a logarithmic scale. The baseline for each series is the time taken for CPU-asynchronous transfers (Section 29.3.2) on that card.

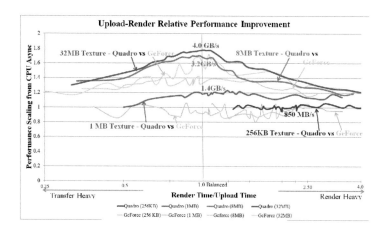

Figure 29.13. Comparing upload-render performance improvement.

For the upload-render overlap in Figure 29.13, the performance improvement on Quadro is higher than GeForce (lighter colored lines) for all data sizes. The overlap performance on the Quadro is also more deterministic as compared to the GeForce, which shows a lot of jitter between runs. It is also seen that for texture

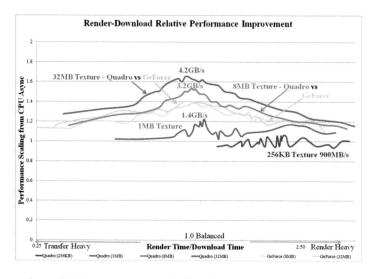

Figure 29.14. Comparing render-download performance improvement.

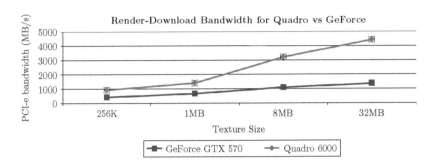

Figure 29.15. Quadro download performance is 3X higher than GeForce.

sizes less than 1MB invoking the copy engine shows very little gain. There are only significant gains, 50% or more, which warrant the extra programming effort, from using the copy engine for textures bigger than 1MB. Using the copy engine also favors applications that are balanced between transfer and rendering time. For example, we see close to linear scaling at around 1.8X for the 32MB texture in the balanced case, which sustains a bandwidth of 4GB/s.

Figure 29.14 shows the performance improvement in the render-download overlap case. The bandwidth for the peaks are comparable to the upload case. For

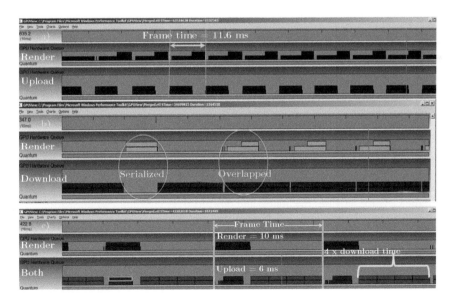

Figure 29.16. GeForce GTX 570 trace for upload, download, and bidirectional overlap.

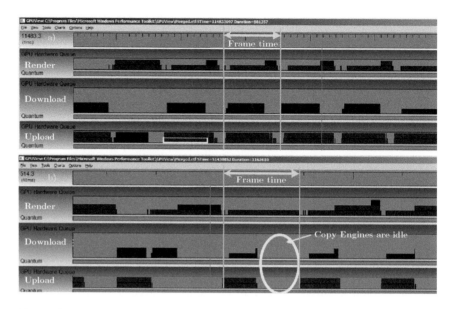

Figure 29.17. Ideal case of bidirectional transfers where upload, render, and download take the same time (top). Render-bottlenecked applications where the copy engines are idle 50% of the time (bottom).

the GeForce, although using the copy engine gives a 40% improvement in render-download overlap performance for the 8MB and 32MB texture, the absolute download performance is significantly better on the Quadro, peaking at more than 3X, as shown in Figure 29.15.

The behavior on GeForce cards is verified by the GPUView trace in Figure 29.16 (top), which shows the upload-render overlap working as expected, and Figure 29.16 (middle), which shows the render-download overlap but with much larger download times for the same texture size. The GeForce boards are only optimized for the upload path, as that is the use case for many consumer applications and games that do bricking and paging. Figure 29.16 (bottom) shows how doing bidirectional transfers on the GeForce serializes the upload and download, as they now end up sharing one copy engine.

Figure 29.17 shows the bidirectional transfer overlap with rendering that is available on mid- to high-end Quadros. Figure 29.17 (top) shows the ideal case where there is maximum overlap and very little idle time in any of the three queues. Figure 29.17 (bottom), on the other hand, shows a render-heavy case where the copy engines are idle half the time.

29.6.1   Previous Generation Architecture

Figure 29.18 shows the same application running on a Quadro 5800 based on the GT 200 chip and the NVIDIA Tesla architecture. The number of threads and the CPU command queues remain the same, but at the hardware level, the GPU scheduler serializes the different command queues, and therefore, no overlap is seen. The length of the CPU command queue for the download shows the latency from the time when the download commands were queued by the application to when the GPU has completed execution.

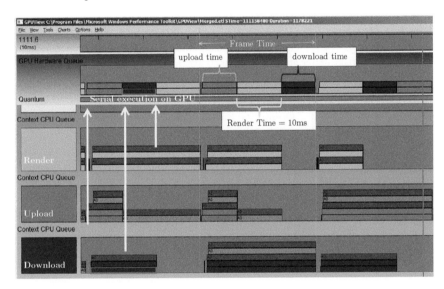

Figure 29.18. The same multithreaded application on a Tesla card (Quadro 5800) is serialized in the GPU hardware queue.

29.7   Conclusion

The GPU asynchronous texture-transfer mechanism enabled by the copy engines in NVIDIA's Fermi and above generation provides for the best transfer performance for applications that (1) are balanced in terms of render and transfers and (2) have significantly large data (more than 1MB) to transfer. I also illustrated how to use multiple threads and synchronization primitives to invoke the copy engines using a 2D texture streaming example. Results with the aid of GPUView show the two-way overlap that takes place on the GeForce and low-end Quadros and three-way overlap on the higher-end Quadros. This example can be easily applied to a terrain-paging system where the different LODs are uploaded concurrently with the rendering depending on view parameters. Other extensions could include large volumetric rendering by bricking 3D textures for applications in medical imaging, oil and gas, and numerical simulations. The render-download usage case maps directly to server-based OpenGL rendering that is rampant with the proliferation of thin clients like phones and tablets.

Bibliography

[ARB 04] OpenGL ARB. "OpenGL PBO Specification." http://www.opengl.org/registry/specs/ARB/pixel_buffer_object.txt, 2004.

[ARB 08] OpenGL ARB. "OpenGL FBO Specification." http://www.opengl.org/registry/specs/EXT/framebuffer_object.txt, 2008.

[ARB 09a] OpenGL ARB. "OpenGL ARB_Sync Specification." http://www.opengl.org/registry/specs/ARB/sync.txt, 2009.

[ARB 09b] OpenGL ARB. "OpenGL GLX_ARB_create_context." http://www.opengl.org/registry/specs/ARB/glx_create_context.txt, 2009.

[ARB 09c] OpenGL ARB. "OpenGL WGL_ARB_create_context." http://www.opengl.org/registry/specs/ARB/wgl_create_context.txt, 2009.

[Fisher and Pronovost 11] Mathew Fisher and Steve Pronovost. "GPUView." http://graphics.stanford.edu/~mdfisher/GPUView.html, 2011.

[NVIDIA 10] NVIDIA. "Fermi White Paper." http://www.nvidia.com/content/PDF/fermi_white_papers/NVIDIA_Fermi_Compute_Architecture_Whitepaper.pdf, 2010.

WebGL Models: End-to-End   30

Won Chun

30.1   Introduction

When we were making Google Body in 2010 (see Figure 30.1), WebGL was new technology. It wasn't entirely clear what we'd be able to accomplish; indeed, the uncertainty was one of the reasons for building it in the first place. Adopting a new technology like WebGL was a leap of faith. Even if the idea made perfect sense to us, so many things outside of our control needed to go right. We eventually open sourced Google Body,[1] and unequivocally demonstrated that it is possible to build a rich, 3D application using WebGL. Google Body made the use of WebGL less an act of faith, and more an act of execution.

Figure 30.1. Google Body, a 3D anatomy browser for the web.

---

[1] The content is now available at zygotebody.com.

When we started, the simple act of loading a 3D model was its own little leap of faith. The source 3D model data was incredibly detailed; we ended up shipping a reduced version with 1.4 million triangles and 740 thousand vertices for 1,800 anatomical entities. Our first prototype simply loaded everything using COLLADA, but that took almost a minute to load from a local web server. That's a really long time to wait for a web page.

COLLADA was inefficient in its use of bandwidth and computation, but it wasn't immediately apparent how we could do better. There is no DOM node or MIME-type for 3D models. WebGL added TypedArray support to JavaScript, but `XMLHttpRequest` wouldn't get it for months. Fortunately, we devised a way to load Google Body's 1.4 million triangles much more efficiently than we expected using a surprising combination of standard web technologies.

I've shared WebGL Loader, http://code.google.com/p/webgl-loader/, as an open-source project so that other WebGL projects can benefit. This chapter describes how WebGL Loader works. WebGL Loader can compress a 6.3 MB OBJ file to under 0.5 MB, better than a 13:1 compression ratio. GZIP alone shrinks the same file to about 1.8 MB and yields a model file that is slower to parse and render. Taken apart, the techniques and concepts are actually quite simple to understand. I also hope to give insights into the process of how we went about making those choices so that we can be equipped with more than just faith for the next time we are spurred to delve into the depths of technical uncertainty.

30.2   Life of a 3D Model

Loading 3D models was the apparent challenge, but it is always important to keep the big picture in mind. When I joined Google, as part of orientation, I attended internal lectures about how the key internal systems at Google work. They all had titles like "Life of a [blank]." For example, "Life of a Query" walks through, step by step, what happens when a user performs a search on google.com. This end-to-end perspective is the key to building computer systems because it motivates what we build, even when we focus on a single component. I spent two years optimizing a tiny corner of web search by a few percent, but I knew the effort was worthwhile because it was in the critical path for every web search by all of our users. If "Life of a Query" teaches us anything, it is that there are lots of queries.

It doesn't make sense to think about loading 3D models outside the context of all the other steps a 3D model takes through an application. Each step informs the design. For Google Body, we thought of the model as it related to four key stages. They are general enough that they should apply to most other WebGL projects as well:

- Pipeline. Where does the 3D model data originate?
- Serving. How does the 3D model data arrive in users' browsers?
- Encoding. What format should the 3D model data use?
- Rendering. How does the 3D model data get to the screen?

30.2.1 Stage 1: Pipeline

Unless the application is a demo where 3D models are mere stand-ins to showcase some new technology, it is important to understand their creation process, called the art pipeline. The art pipeline can include many creative steps, like concept drawing or 3D modeling, but the key technological steps to understand are the tools that get models from the care of the artists to the application.

Art creation tools like Maya, Blender, Photoshop, or GIMP have their own file formats, but applications usually don't use them directly. The flexibility that is a necessity during creation ends up as baggage after the art is created. Contrast a Photoshop PSD file with a plain old JPG image. The PSD file can contain lots of extra sophistication like layers or color transforms that are essential for lossless, nondestructive editing, but that will never get used by something that simply needs to present the final image.

A similar thing happens with 3D models. For example, 3D modeling software keeps track of positions, normals, texture coordinates, or other vertex attributes in separate lists. A vertex is represented as a tuple of indices, one for each vertex attribute. This is an excellent choice for creation and editing; if an artist changes an attribute like a position or texture coordinate, all the vertices that share that attribute are implicitly updated. GPUs don't support these multi-indexed vertex lists; they must first be converted to a single-indexed vertex list. WebGL additionally enforces a limit of 65,536 unique vertices in a single `drawElements` call for maximum portability. Larger meshes must be split into batches.

Somewhere along the line, the model needs to be converted from a multipurpose, creation-appropriate form to a streamlined, render-appropriate form. The best time and place to do this is in the art pipeline. From the perspective of the application, everything that happens in the art pipeline appears to happen magically ahead of time. Since more time can be spent in the art pipeline than during loading, it is a great opportunity to offload work from the stages ahead. This is where to optimize the mesh for rendering and compress it for serving.

30.2.2 Stage 2: Serving

We don't have much control over what happens between the server and client because it is all governed by Internet standards; all we can do is understand how things work and how to best use them. I learned about high-performance web serving during my first project at Google, optimizing infrastructure behind iGoogle.[2] As it turns out, serving 3D models over HTTP is not that different from serving other kinds of static contents, such as stylesheets or images. Almost everything in this section applies equally to images and to meshes since it is all about how to send bits onto the client. Perhaps more accurately, this section is about how *not* to send bits to the client using that reliable system design workhorse: caching. The bits we never send are the fastest and cheapest of all.

---

[2]iGoogle is the customizable homepage for Google: http://www.google.com/ig.

HTTP caching fundamentals. Before a browser makes an HTTP GET request to download the data for a URL, it first checks the cache to see if the data corresponding to that URL are already present. If so, the browser potentially has a cache hit. The problem with simply using these data right away is that they might be stale; the data in the cache might not reflect what is actually being served anymore. This is the trouble with caches; they seem like a cheap and simple way to improve performance, but then we have to deal with the extra complexity of validation.

There are several ways a browser validates its cache data. The basic approaches use a conditional GET. The browser remembers when it originally fetched the data, so it uses an if-modified-since header in a GET request, and the server responds with a new version only if necessary. Another approach is to use ETags, which can act as a content fingerprint so the server can detect when a URL has changed since last requested.

These approaches work as we would expect, but both still require a round-trip communication with the server. These requests, while usually cheap, still consume connections, a limited resource on both the client and server, and can have unpredictable latencies depending on the state of the network. It is better to completely avoid this parasitic latency with a simple tweak in the server. Instead of forcing the browser to ask, "Is this stale?" for each request, the server can proactively tell the browser how long the data will be fresh by using an Expires header. With an explicit expiration, the browser can use locally cached data immediately.

A long Expires header (the longest supported is just under a year) improves caching performance, but makes updates less visible. My favorite approach to deal with this is to simply never update the data for a given URL by using unique URLs for each version of the data. One particularly simple way is to embed a content fingerprint in the URL—no need to maintain any extra state.

Fingerprinting works best if you control the references to your fingerprinted assets; otherwise, clients can end up with stale references. A hybrid approach is to have a small manifest file with a conventional URL and caching parameters referencing fingerprinted URLs. This way, we can have good caching performance for bulk data, amortizing validation, while maintaining freshness.

HTTP proxy caches. The most important cache is the browser cache, but in reality, there could be many between the user and the server. Companies use HTTP proxies as an intermediary between workstations and the Internet, and usually these include web caches to efficiently use available Internet bandwidth. ISPs, in the business of providing bandwidth, deploy many caching proxies to improve performance. Some web servers will have reverse proxies that are optimized for serving static content. It is an excellent idea to recruit these caches, especially because they are numerous and tend to be closer to users. Fortunately, all these caches understand the same HTTP conventions, so with some careful design, we can simultaneously optimize for all of them.

To enable proxy caching, the server should set the `Cache-control:  public` header. Since proxy caches are shared, a few more criteria must be met before the data is actually effectively cached. Some proxy caches ignore URLs with ? so don't use query strings. Cookies don't work in shared caches, and they also make every HTTP request header larger.

A good way to avoid performance problems with cookies is to use a separate, cookieless domain. Different domains need not be separate servers, but they could be, for example, if we used a content delivery network (CDN) service. To use multiple domains to serve content, we must also enable CORS, cross-origin resource sharing (http://enable-cors.org/), to add exceptions to the browser's same-origin security policy. CORS applies to resources fetched using `XMLHttpRequest` as well as HTML images destined to be WebGL texture data.

Compression. Caching is one way HTTP avoids sending bits, and compression is the other. Media files used on the web are already compressed. A raw true-color image uses 24-bits per pixel, but JPEG is typically able to compress that image using only 1 or 2 bits per pixel at high quality. Modern codecs like WebP perform even better [Banarjee and Arora 11].

For text files, like HTML, CSS, or JavaScript, HTTP allows for on-the-fly compression using GZIP. Unlike JPEG, GZIP is an exact, lossless encoding tuned for text. At a high level, GZIP is similar to many other text-compression algorithms. It starts with a phrase matcher, LZ77, to eliminate repeated character sequences and follows that with Huffman coding [Gailly and Adler 93]. Huffman coding, which uses fewer bits to encode frequently occurring bytes, is the workhorse statistical coder; it is also used as the final step of JPEG and PNG compression.

It turns out that it is also possible to use Huffman encoding as the final step for compressing 3D models by piggybacking on top of HTTP's GZIP encoding. Instead of writing our own compressor, all we need is to encode 3D models in a GZIP-friendly way.

30.2.3   Stage 3: Loading

Even before JavaScript gets to see the model's data, the browser has already performed quite a bit of work downloading it. As efficient as JavaScript implementations have gotten recently, it is a still a good idea to exploit as much native capability as possible. Fortunately, we can use GZIP to handle most of the compression and decompression work. The key to efficient loading is in finding a representation that is compact but easy to convert to WebGL vertex buffers from what we can receive and process using JavaScript.

XML or JSON? `XMLHttpRequest` is the principle mechanism for downloading bulk application data in JavaScript, and until recently, it didn't even really support binary data. Despite the name, we don't actually have to use `XMLHttpRequest` for

XML data; we can grab the raw `responseText` string data and do pretty much what we want with it using JavaScript.

If not XML, could we use JSON? Working with JSON in JavaScript is simple because it is a tiny, data-only dialect of JavaScript. Every browser that supports WebGL has a fast and safe `JSON.parse` method. JSON may be a lighter and simpler alternative to XML, but it is still no panacea for 3D models. Sure, XML's tags are much larger than JSON's, but the tag sizes don't really matter if almost all of the bytes are consumed by giant float arrays. Besides, GZIP does a good job of compressing the redundancy in XML tags. We'll leave the XML versus JSON war alone.

Quantization. For models, the real problem isn't XML versus JSON at all. The key is avoiding the storage, transmission, and parsing of the vertex attributes and triangle indices. As a human-readable string, a 32-bit, 4-byte floating-point value requires up to seven decimal digits, not including the sign (another byte), decimal point (another byte), and possibly the scientific notation exponent (yet more bytes): -9.876543e+21, for example. Since floating-point numbers do not always have exact decimal representations, algorithms for parsing decimal values are exceedingly fussy, challenging, and slow. Quantizing the source floating-point format to a fixed-point format in the art pipeline would greatly help. Since 32-bit floating point is more than you need for most situations,[3] we can save space and time by using only as much precision as necessary.

The fixed-point resolution depends on the attribute: 10 bits (1,024 values) per channel is generally considered adequate for normals, and it works well for texture coordinates as well. Google Body was very sensitive to positions, since our models included many small anatomical details. We settled on 14 bits (16,384 levels) per channel. For a six-foot human, this was nearly 1/250'' resolution; for a two-meter human, this was better than 1/8 mm resolution. Google Body had very high quality requirements, and analyses later in this chapter use this fine level of quantization. Most models could manage with less, and compression rates will improve accordingly.

After quantizing, both the vertex attributes and triangle indices can be encoded within short, 16-bit integers. Small integers are faster on many JavaScript virtual machines; Chrome's V8 engine is particularly efficient with integers that fit within 31-bits [Wingo 11]. And, as it turns out, JavaScript has always had a fast, compact, and convenient way of representing arrays of 16-bit values: strings.

With this key insight, `XMLHttpRequest.responseText` suddenly looks quite well suited for the job. JavaScript uses UTF-16 for its internal string representation, and we index a string by simply using the `String.charCodeAt` method. The art pipeline could encode all the attributes and indices as "characters" in a string, serve them up GZIP compressed, and then decode them into TypedArrays destined to become vertex and index buffer objects.

---

[3]Sometimes, 32-bit floating point is not enough! See [Cozzi and Ring 11].

Code Points	Byte 1	Byte 2	Byte 3
[0 ... 127]	0XXXXXXX		
[128 ... 2,047]	110YYYXX	10XXXXXX	
[2,048 ... 65,535]	1110YYYY	10YYYYXX	10XXXXXX

Table 30.1. Table of UTF-8 encodings for 16-bit Unicode code points. XXXXXXXX represents the bottom 8 bits of the code point, and YYYYYYYY represents the top 8 bits.

Unicode, UTF-16, and UTF-8. This works aside from one detail: surrogate pairs. As of Unicode 6.0, there are over one million code points[4] defined; only the most common code points, the basic multilingual plane (BMP), can be encoded by a single 16-bit value. Code points outside the BMP are encoded using a pair of 16-bit values,[5] both of which are in the 2,048 code surrogate-pair range from 0xD800 (55,296) to 0xDFFF (57,343). The surrogate-pair range is at the high end of 16-bit values, so it is reasonable to avoid it by ensuring that all the encoded values are small enough. In fact, we encoded many meshes in blissful ignorance before encountering one that hit the surrogate-pair range. In practice, this is not a problem (see Table 30.1).

Even though JavaScript uses UTF-16 for strings, UTF-8 is the strongly preferred encoding for HTTP data, and is transparently decoded by the browser. UTF-8 is a very well-designed character encoding. It uses a clever byte-oriented variable-length encoding, so it maintains backwards compatibility with ASCII, compresses well with GZIP, and is endian-independent. Like UTF-16, UTF-8 is designed to transmit smaller Unicode code points more efficiently than larger ones. Because most 16-bit Unicode code points require a 3-byte encoding, variable-length encoding seems like a disadvantage, but if most values are small, then it is a significant advantage.

30.2.4   Stage 4: Rendering

Used correctly, indexed triangle lists are one of the fastest methods used to draw triangles in most GPU-accelerated 3D graphics libraries, including WebGL. Indexed triangle lists are intrinsically faster because they contain the most information about how vertices are shared between triangles. Triangle strips and fans also share vertices between triangles, but not as effectively. Strips are also inconvenient to draw in WebGL; to save on draw calls, triangle strips must be joined together by degenerate triangles.

Optimizing for the post-transform vertex cache. To render a triangle, the GPU must first transform its vertices. Vertex shading is programmable in WebGL, so these transforms have the potential to be expensive. Fortunately, the results are

---

[4]"Code point" is rigorous Unicode specification language for what we consider to be a "character" [Unicode 11].

[5]Unicode makes a distinction between characters and encodings, so technically, values within the surrogate-pair range are "code units," not "code points."

strictly determined by the inputs. If the GPU knows when a vertex is shared between triangles, it can also share the transformation for that vertex. To do this, the GPU stores recently transformed vertices in the post-transform vertex cache.

The post-transform vertex cache can be quite effective in reducing the number of vertex transforms. In a normal model, most vertices are shared by 6 triangles. In this idealized case, there are only 0.5 vertices per triangle, so the vertex shader would only execute every other triangle—an ACMR (average cache miss ratio) of 0.5. These are compulsory misses; each vertex needs to be transformed at least once, no matter how often it is shared. Idealized triangle strips only achieve a best-case ACMR of 1.0. It is rare to actually achieve these ideal values. In practice, good ACMRs for indexed triangle lists are in the 0.6 to 0.7 range,[6] which is still considerably better than the theoretical ideal ACMR for triangle strips.

Unlike the caches used in HTTP, which operate in millisecond timescales, the post-transform vertex cache is a tight piece of hardware that operates on nanosecond timescales. In order for it to help, it must be very fast, and in order for it to be fast, it must be small. As a result, the post-transform vertex cache can only store a fixed number of vertices at a time, introducing the possibility of capacity misses. We can help avoid capacity misses by optimizing the triangle order so that vertex references are locally clustered.

There is a great deal of existing literature written on optimizing triangle orders to minimize ACMR. The key to all triangle optimization approaches is in how they model the post-transform vertex cache. The problem is that there are too many different kinds of post-transform vertex caches. GPUs with separate vertex shaders generally used FIFOs with 16 to 32 elements, Modern unified-shader GPUs do something completely different. And who knows what might change in the future?

Instead of trying to model all of these variants precisely, a better approach is to use a cache-oblivious model that does a reasonable job of approximating them all. WebGL Loader uses my favorite approach, Tom Forsyth's "Linear Speed Vertex Optimization." It is fast, simple, and generally gets as close to ideal results as more specific or sophisticated approaches. More crucially, it never performs badly.

Forsyth's algorithm is greedy and does no backtracking; it simply finds the best triangle at any given moment and adds that to the triangle list [Forsyth 06]. Determining the "best" triangle trades off between greedily maximizing cache use and ensuring that triangles are added promptly so that the last few triangles are not left scattered around the mesh. Forsyth's algorithm uses simple heuristics to address both factors. Vertex references are tracked using a 32-entry LRU list where more recently referenced vertices have higher scores. The algorithm also tracks the number of remaining triangles that share a vertex; vertices with fewer triangles remaining have higher scores. The best triangle is the triangle with the highest vertex score sum.

---

[6]Unfortunately, perfect ACMR depends on the mesh, specifically the actual ratio of vertices to triangles. An alternative metric is ATVR, average transform to vertex ratio, which was first described by Ignacio Castaño. Naturally, a perfect ATVR is 1 [Castano 09].

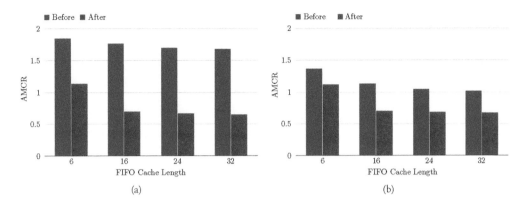

Figure 30.2. Post-transform vertex cache optimization on (a) hand_00 and (b) ben_00.

We quantify the improvements that post-transform vertex cache optimization makes by modeling FIFO caches of various common sizes on meshes before and after optimization. We use two models from the Utah 3D Animation Repository [SCI Institute 11]: hand_00, the first keyframe of a wiggling hand animation with 9,740 vertices and 17,135 triangles, an ideal ACMR of 0.568, and ben_00, the first keyframe of a running man animation with 44,915 vertices and 78,029 triangles, an ideal ACMR of 0.575 (see Figure 30.2).

For both models and all modeled FIFO cache lengths, Forsyth's algorithm improves ACMR. Larger caches have greater benefit, but these benefits are marginal beyond 16 or 24 entries, so the choice of a 32-entry LRU cache is well justified [Hoppe 99].

Optimizing for the pretransform vertex cache. Just as there is a cache at the output of the vertex shaders, there is also one buffering the input loads. To optimize for the pretransform vertex cache, we must try to make these loads occur as sequentially as possible. The index array is accessed sequentially no matter what, so nothing needs to be done there. For static geometry, it is slightly more efficient to interleave all the vertex attributes needed for rendering so that the vertex shader can load them together.

The remaining variable is the actual ordering of the vertex accesses, which are indirectly indexed. We don't want to actually change the order of the triangles established by the post-transform vertex optimization, but it is possible to change the order of the vertices without changing the order of the triangles. Simply order the vertices by their first reference in the index buffer, and update the index buffer to reference its new location.

Figure 30.3 is an illustration of an indexed triangle list before and after the pretransform vertex cache optimization. On the left, the vertex indices have been

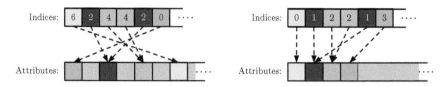

Figure 30.3. Before (left) and after (right) vertex reordering.

optimized using the post-transform vertex cache but not the pretransform vertex cache. Attributes are shared between nearby triangles, but appear in an arbitrary order, causing random reads by the vertex shader. After the pretransform vertex-cache optimization (on the right), the attributes are ordered by first appearance, yielding mostly sequential reads by the vertex shader. The triangle order is preserved.

Analysis. We can visualize the effect of vertex cache optimization by plotting indices and attributes before and after. We examine the first 2,000 indices and x positions of the Happy Buddha, a large, greater than one-million triangle model from the Stanford 3D Scanning Repository[7] (see Figure 30.4).

In general, indices follow a linear trend upwards. The slope represents the average number of times a vertex is shared—in this case, roughly 5.5 times (there are 361 unique values in the first 2,000 indices). Before optimization, index values jump around both forwards and backward by hundreds. Around position 1,600, there is

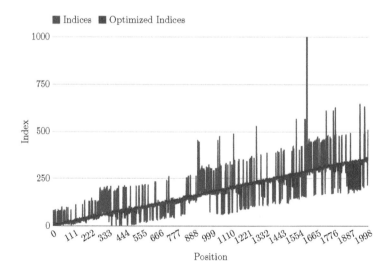

Figure 30.4. Effect of optimization on indices.

---

[7]http://graphics.stanford.edu/data/3Dscanrep/

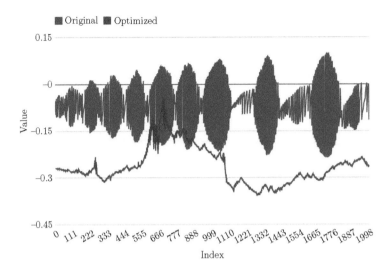

Figure 30.5. Effect of optimization on x position.

even an index that goes off the charts. After optimization, the indices form a much smoother line. Because of pretransform vertex-cache optimization, there are no large forward jumps, and because of post-transform vertex-cache optimization, backwards jumps are relatively small.

Vertex-cache optimization also affects attributes. There is a definite pattern to the original data; they were originally captured by laser, so the periodic scanning is apparent. The value units are in the original floating-point data, although the actual data have been quantized. After vertex-cache optimization, attributes are ordered by use. Instead of rapidly scanning back and forth, x positions are more correlated, forming a random-looking, but connected line (see Figure 30.5). We will see that while this line appears random, it has structure that can be exploited for compression.

30.3   A Coherent Whole

WebGL and HTTP are calling the shots in the life of a 3D model, and all we can do is find the best way to do as much work as possible ahead of time during the art pipeline without placing too large of a burden on browser JavaScript. Fortunately, even if WebGL and HTTP apply constraints on what we can do, they also provide the tools and guidance to make everything work together.

Part of the problem is solved: we will encode attributes and indices as Unicode code points. Let us now revisit UTF-8 encoding. On one hand, as a byte-oriented encoding, UTF-8 interacts well with GZIP; on the other hand, only a small range of

UTF-8 is encoded compactly. It is a waste and missed opportunity to use GZIP to counteract this expansion, especially when it is avoidable.

Optimizing the mesh for vertex caches introduces an exploitable structure to the vertex indices and attributes. Because of post-transform vertex-cache optimizations, vertex index references are clustered. Because of pretransform vertex-cache optimizations, index values increase gradually and sort related vertex attributes together. Introducing coherence in the mesh not only makes it faster to render, it makes it more compressible too!

30.3.1 Delta Coding

GZIP is designed for text compression, so it needs a little help compressing signals like vertex attributes and indices. It is unreasonable to expect LZ77 phrase matching to help something that isn't structured like words, but Huffman coding should certainly help. An easy approach is to first transform the data using delta coding. Delta coding is a simple predictive filter that sends differences within the data instead of the data themselves. If the most recent value is a good predictor of the next value, then the difference will be cheaper to encode than the next value. Delta coding can be implemented like this in JavaScript:

```
var prev = 0;
for (var i = 0; i < original.length; i++) {
    delta[i] = original[i] - prev;
    prev = original[i];
}
```

Given an `original` array of [100, 110, 107, 106, 115], the `delta` array will be [100, 10, −3, −1, 9]. Delta decoding to reverse this is also really simple. This is good news because it is the innermost loop of the JavaScript decompressor:

```
var prev = 0;
for (var i = 0; i < delta.length; i++) {
    prev += delta[i];
    original[i] = prev;
}
```

From this example, we can see that even if the original data are in the hundreds range, the differences are much smaller in magnitude. This effect will help both UTF-8 and Huffman coding. Smaller values will use fewer bytes in UTF-8. Smaller values also skew the distribution of bytes so that Huffman coding can use fewer bits to encode them.

When delta encoding or decoding a vector quantity, such as a vertex attribute, you want to make sure to compute differences across like values, rather than adjacent interleaved values—x positions with x positions, and not x positions with y positions or even x normals. In general, this means you need a different `prev` for each scalar attribute value. For example, if your vertex format contains both a position and a normal, you will need to keep track of six values in the decoder (the encoder is left as an exercise to the reader):

```
var prev = new Array(6);
for (var i = 0; i < delta.length;) {
    for (var j = 0; j < 6; j++) {
        prev[j] += delta[i];
        original[i] = prev[j]
        ++i;
    }
}
```

30.3.2 Delta Coding Analysis

We can visualize the effects of delta coding using the Happy Buddha x position data. Compared to the original signal, the delta coded signal is centered on zero, and has smaller variation. These qualities make it more compressible (see Figure 30.6).

Delta coding doesn't always help. For example, the original data do not have coherence easily exploitable by delta coding, as shown in Figure 30.7. Even though delta coding manages to center values around zero, the difference signal varies *more* than the original, unoptimized data.

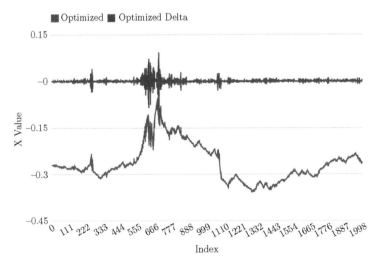

Figure 30.6. Delta coding optimized positions.

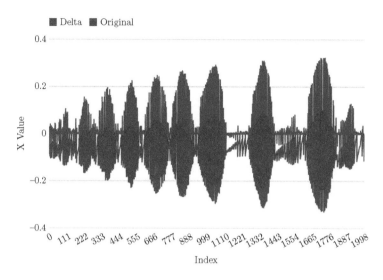

Figure 30.7. Delta coding original positions.

30.3.3   ZigZag Coding

Delta coding generates negative values roughly half the time. Unlike floating-point numbers, which have a dedicated sign bit, fixed-point values normally use a two's complement representation. In two's complement, small negative numbers map to large unsigned values, which spoils the skew distribution we were hoping to achieve with delta coding. Ideally, we'd like the bottom bit to act like a sign bit so that small negative numbers are interleaved with small positive numbers, as shown in Table 30.2.

At Google, we call this zigzag coding, although it is a much older idea that follows naturally from delta coding. It's defined in the open-source Protocol Buffer library [Proto 11], which uses a variable-length encoding for integer values. Since zigzag

Delta	Unsigned	ZigZag
−3	0xFFFD	0x0005
−2	0xFFFE	0x0003
−1	0xFFFF	0x0001
0	0x0000	0x0000
1	0x0001	0x0002
2	0x0002	0x0004
3	0x0003	0x0006

Table 30.2. Two's complement and zigzag coding.

encoding and decoding are in the inner loop for the compressor and decompressor, it is worth using some bit-twiddling magic to make sure it is as fast as possible. Encoding a 16-bit signed value uses the following incantation:

```
((input << 1) ^ (input >> 15)) & 0xFFFF;
```

The 0xFFFF might be implicit if you know it will be stored in a 16-bit value (e.g. a uint16_t in C/C++ or within a Uint16Array in JavaScript). Decoding is also funky: In both cases, you want to make sure to use signed right shifts.

```
(input >> 1) ^ (-(input & 1));
```

30.3.4   Delta + ZigZag Coding Analysis

We can visualize the effectiveness of delta + zigzag coding by examining the distribution of encoded values, as shown in Figure 30.8. A semi-log plot of the first 128 values, shown in Figure 30.9, shows that delta values have a small magnitude bias. These are the values that will be encoded in a single UTF-8 byte and account for 92.8% of the total. Aside from some periodic spikes, the plot is linear with a negative slope, indicating an exponential decay. The spikes, which occur at multiples of 41, are artifacts of the discrete scanning resolution of the original model.

The trend continues for the first 2,048 values, the values that can be encoded in UTF-8 using up to 2 bytes. The exponential decay and the periodic spikes continue.

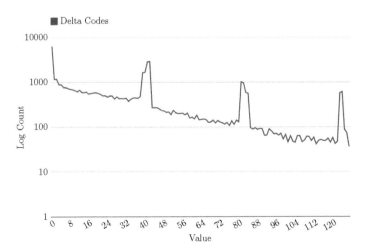

Figure 30.8. UTF-8 single byte encoding.

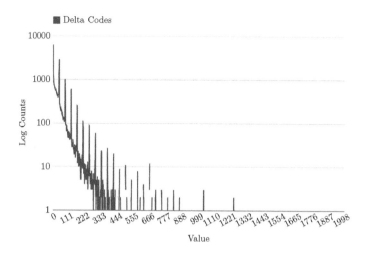

Figure 30.9. UTF-8 single and double byte encoding.

This plot accounts for 99.98% of the total values. Values larger than 1,000 are very rare.

30.3.5 The Compression Pipeline

We finally have all the details we need to build a model compressor. Google Body followed exactly these steps:

1. **Quantize attributes.** Encode attributes such that each value can be read as a single small integer value from JavaScript, avoiding expensive client-side parsing. We may reconstitute the original values at load time or delay that to the vertex shader; position scales and offsets are easy to fold into the model transformation.

2. **Optimize models for vertex-cache performance.** Forsyth's "Linear Speed Vertex Optimizer" simultaneously improves rendering performance while making the model data more compressible by making the data more coherent.

3. **Delta coding.** Expose coherence to later coding stages.

4. **ZigZag coding.** Fix two's complement mapping so that small negative numbers are encoded using small values.

5. **UTF-8 encoding.** This is how HTTP likes to send text data. As a bonus, it uses fewer bytes to send smaller values, an excellent follow-up to delta and zigzag coding.

6. GZIP compression. Standard HTTP compression provides the final statistical coder in the form of Huffman coding.

30.4   Key Improvements

After open-sourcing WebGL Loader, we discovered a few improvements over Google Body's original mesh-compression algorithm. The first was an ordering that improved attribute compression, and the second was a new technique for encoding vertex indices that improved on basic delta coding.

30.4.1   Interleaving vs. Transposing

WebGL prefers storing vertex attributes in interleaved form because that is how they are accessed by the vertex shader. This is not ideal for Huffman coding, which dynamically adapts to the input statistics. If the data is interleaved, then Huffman coding will see a mix of deltas for disparate attributes like positions, normals, and texture coordinates. Even different dimensions of the same attribute can have different behavior (see Figure 30.10).

In the above semi-log chart, we plot the value distributions of both x position and x normal. While both show a characteristic exponential decay, their lines have different slopes and thus different decay rates. Furthermore, normals don't have the periodic frequency spikes exhibited in the positions.

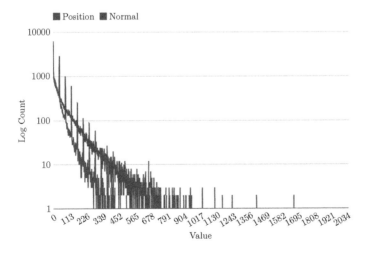

Figure 30.10. Attribute distributions.

If we use a transposed format for compression (*xxx...yyy...zzz...* instead of *xyzxyz xyz...*), then Huffman coding will see long runs of values that come from a single attribute dimension, allowing it to adapt and encode to their distribution more efficiently. Interleaving doesn't have a significant additional cost for decoding in JavaScript, because all the data need to be copied from the `XMLHttpRequest`. `responseText` to a TypedArray anyway. Compared to the interleaved representation, the transposed representation has slightly worse memory locality, but achieves approximately 5% better GZIP compression.

30.4.2   High-Water Mark Prediction

Another significant improvement was in the delta and zigzag coding for vertex indices. There is a better predictor for the next index than the previous index: the highest seen index to that point, or the high-water mark. When a model is optimized for the post-transform vertex cache, vertex indices tend to be clustered. When a model is optimized for the pretransform vertex cache, vertex indices slowly increase. Specifically, the only time a vertex index larger than the current high-water mark appears, it is exactly one larger. Contrast this with delta coding, where differences are positive or negative with roughly equal probability.

High-water mark prediction works by encoding the difference from the potential next high-water mark. Differences will never be negative and will be zero if and only if a new vertex index is referenced. This encoding is about as simple as delta coding:

```
var nextHighWaterMark = 0;
for (var i = 0; i < original.length; i++) {
    var index = original[i];
    delta[i] = nextHighWaterMark - index;
    if (index === nextHighWaterMark) {
        nextHighWaterMark++;
    }
}
```

Since differences are never negative, there is no need for zigzag coding. Decoding correspondingly looks like this:

```
var nextHighWaterMark = 0;
for (var i = 0; i < delta.length; i++) {
    var code = delta[i];
    original[i] = nextHighWaterMark - code;
    if (code === 0) {
        nextHighWaterMark++;
    }
}
```

We can visualize the effectiveness of delta coding with and without high-water mark prediction by examining the effect on the distribution of encoded values on the

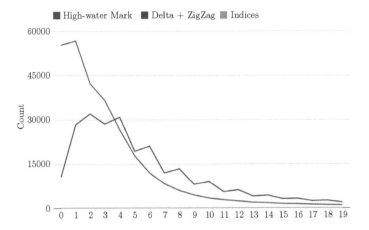

Figure 30.11. Top 20 references.

first 55,000 vertices of the Happy Buddha model. First, a close-up of the 20 smallest, most frequently referenced values, as shown in Figure 30.11.

The original index data are the yellow line along the bottom that plots the number of times the first 20 vertex indices are referenced. In this scale, it is difficult to see that each index is referenced about six times on average, as expected. High-water mark prediction yields the blue line, and delta + zigzag coding is the red line. They each plot the number of times an encoded value is sent. Both high-water mark and delta + zigzag strongly bias the distribution of values sent to be small; this effect

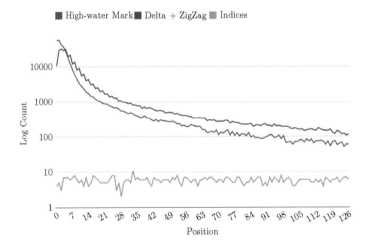

Figure 30.12. UTF-8 single byte encoding.

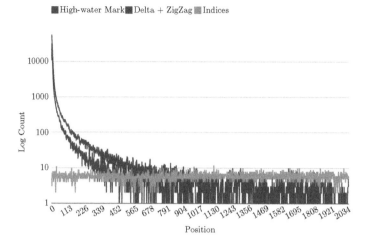

Figure 30.13. UTF-8 single- and double-byte encoding.

allows Huffman coding to compress well. However, high-water mark coding does a better job, yielding smaller values with a steeper distribution. Delta + zigzag coding reveals a slight sawtooth character; there are slight peaks at even values, indicating a slight skew towards positive deltas. These trends continue as we examine the set of values encoded by a single byte in UTF-8, as shown in Figure 30.12.

Using a semi-log plot, the original index data are actually visible. The gap between high-water mark and delta + zigzag coding persists. Over 95.7% of high-water mark–predicted values are encoded by one byte, compared to just over 90.9% for delta + zigzag, a nearly 5% improvement. We can see that the tail is substantially longer for delta + zigzag by zooming out to the set of values encoded in up to two bytes in UTF-8, as shown in Figure 30.13.

For delta + zigzag, 6.54% of the values require two bytes in UTF-8. High-water mark reduces this to 2.88%. Cumulatively, 98.6% of high-water mark–predicted values are encoded using 2 bytes or fewer, slightly better than 97.4% for delta + zigzag.

30.4.3 Performance

Most of the computation in this model-compression technique is actually done by UTF-8 and GZIP, so JavaScript doesn't have to do very much to the data. The time actually spent doing delta, zigzag, and high-water mark decoding is quite low. Consider the Happy Buddha model, which is 1,087,716 triangles and 543,652 vertices (position and normal) and compresses to 5,148,735 bytes ($\sim$ 4.73 bytes per triangle). We must delta + zigzag decode 3,261,912 16-bit vertex attributes and 3,263,148

16-bit indices. On my oldest working laptop, a 2.4 GHz Core 2 Duo running Mac OS 10.5.8, the time spent in JavaScript is a fraction of a second.

The performance depends on the browser. Prior to Chrome 17, Firefox 8 is faster, but Chrome 17 makes some important performance improvements for handling strings from `XMLHttpRequest`:

Browser	Time
Chrome 16.0.912.41	383 ms
Firefox 8.01	202 ms
Chrome 17.0.949.0	114 ms

Churning through 5,148,735 bytes in 114 ms is a throughput better than 45MB/sec, closer to local storage bandwidth than broadband Internet bandwidth.

The current implementation in WebGL loader uses progress events to incrementally decode, so transfer and compute latency can overlap. WebWorkers will soon support fast, zero-copy transfers of TypedArrays [Herman and Russell 2011], so multiple models could be decoded in parallel. Since decoding is pure JavaScript and doesn't actually require a WebGL context, it is possible to overlap parallel model downloads with operations like WebGL context and shader initialization.

30.4.4 Future Work

There are a few more improvements we have not yet implemented that should improve compression. One notable improvement is to use indexed triangle strips instead of indexed triangle lists. Indexed triangle strips are not very popular, because they aren't faster than indexed triangle lists on desktop GPUs (strips may be faster on mobile GPUs). They would help for compression in two ways: directly, by making index buffers smaller, and indirectly, by making parallelogram prediction simple.

Parallelogram prediction (Figure 30.14) is a technique that can be used to predict vertex attributes on triangles that share an edge, as adjacent triangles in a triangle strip implicitly do. In the figure to the right, the

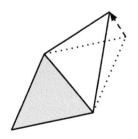

Figure 30.14. Parallelogram prediction.

shaded triangle is the current triangle in a triangle strip and so shares an edge with the next triangle. Parallelogram prediction assumes that the next triangle looks like the previous one, so it guesses that the next vertex can be computed by reflecting the unshared vertex (at the bottom-left) across the shared edge, yielding the dotted triangle. The guess is usually close to the actual triangle (solid, unshaded triangle), so only a small correction vector needs to be stored (dashed arrow).

30.5 Conclusion

Web browsers are evolving at a rapid pace. WebGL is a welcome addition, but it has brought its share of unsolved problems. Google Body's model-compression technique described how to close a key gap: how to load high-quality meshes in WebGL without direct browser support. Thanks to existing web infrastructure and quantum leaps in JavaScript performance, meshes can be compressed compactly and efficiently without a severe impact on loading time while simultaneously optimizing for GPU rendering performance. We eagerly anticipate the pervasive deployment of 3D content on the Web using WebGL.

Acknowledgments. I would first like to thank the Zygote Media Group, who was an excellent partner during the Google Body endeavor. Preserving the quality of their artistically fashioned models of human anatomy was a significant motivation for the work in this chapter. I would like to thank the people at Google who helped make this happen: my 80% team who was always patient even when this 20% activity became all consuming; Thatcher Ulrich, who tells me which of my ideas are any good; and Ken Russell, who was always generous with his knowledge of browser and WebGL performance. Finally, I reserve my greatest thanks forthe Google Body team, especially Arthur Blume, David Kogan, Vangelis Kokkevis, Rachel Weinstein Petterson, Nico Weber, and Dr. Roni Zeiger.

Bibliography

[Banarjee and Arora 11] Somnath Banerjee and Vikas Arora. "WebP Compression Study." code.google.com/speed/webp/docs/webp_study.html, May 18, 2011.

[Castano 09] Ignacio Castaño, "ACMR." http://www.ludicon.com/castano/blog/2009/01/acmr-2/, January 29, 2009.

[Cozzi and Ring 11] Patrick Cozzi and Kevin Ring. *3D Engine Design for Virtual Globes.* Natick, MA: A K Peters, 2011. http://www.virtualglobebook.com/.

[Forsyth 06] Tom Forsyth. "Linear-Speed Vertex Cache Optimization." http://home.comcast.net/~tom_forsyth/papers/fast_vert_cache_opt.html, September 28, 2006.

[Gailly and Adler 93] Jean-Loup Gailly and Mark Adler. "A Brief Description of the Algorithms used by GZIP." http://www.gzip.org/algorithm.txt,August 9, 1993.

[Herman and Russell 2011] David Herman and Kenneth Russell. "Typed Array Specification." http://www.khronos.org/registry/typedarray/specs/latest/#9, December 8, 2011.

[Hoppe 99] Hughes Hoppe. "Optimization of Mesh Locality for Transparent Vertex Caching." *ACM SIGGRAPH Proceedings* (1999) 269–276.

[Proto 11] Proto. "Encoding." http://code.google.com/apis/protocolbuffers/docs/encoding.html#types,retrieved December 14, 2011.

[SCI Institute 11] SCI Institute. *The Utah 3D Animation Respository.* http://www.sci.utah.edu/~wald/animrep/.

[Unicode 11] Unicode. "Unicode 6.0.0." http://www.unicode.org/versions/Unicode6.0.0/, September 26, 2011.

[Wingo 11] Andy Wingo. "Value Representation in JavaScript Implementations." http://wingolog.org/archives/2011/05/18/value-representation-in-javascript-implementations, May 11, 2011.

In-Game Video Capture with   31
Real-Time Texture Compression

Brano Kemen

31.1   Introduction

This chapter discusses techniques for real-time compression of images on the GPU for use with various types of procedurally or dynamically generated images and virtual texturing. The techniques are designed to achieve lower memory and bandwidth requirements while providing high quality. We also describe the use of this technique in capturing high-quality video directly from the application without significantly impairing the overall performance.

Figure 31.1. Procedural tree generator in Outerra using real-time compression for clusters of leaves.

31.2   Overview of DXT Compression

DXT compression, also S3 Texture Compression, S3TC [S3TC 12], refers to a group of lossy, fixed-rate image-compression algorithms that are now widely supported in graphics hardware, as they are well suited for hardware-accelerated texture decompression for 3D graphics.

The compression ratio is fixed, either 8:1 or 6:1 for the DXT1 format with 1-bit transparency or without alpha, respectively. Formats with higher quality alpha encoding have 4:1 compression ratios.

All compression schemes encode the RGB part in the same way by compressing blocks of 4 × 4 input pixels in 64 bits of color output. The output consists of two 16-bit RGB 5:6:5 quantized color values, followed by 16 2-bit values that determine how the corresponding pixel color is computed: either one of the two colors or a blend between them.

The alpha component can be encoded in several ways depending on the mode. For DXT4 and DXT5, it's encoded using a scheme similar to the color part but with two 8-bit alpha values and 3-bit interpolation values for each pixel.

DXT compression has some limitations, and the image quality can be degraded if used naively on some images with sharp changes in colors (Figure 31.3). However, it is well suited for most of the textures used in 3D graphics, as these are usually more homogenous.

The quality loss is offset by the significantly reduced memory and bandwidth requirements; compressed textures of the same dimensions render faster as the result. Alternatively, a gain in quality can be achieved by using higher-resolution textures for the same amount of memory.

31.3   DXT Compression Algorithms

While the decompression algorithm is defined exactly, there are multiple compression algorithms with different quality output. The quality mainly depends on the way the two endpoint color values are selected [Brown 06]. High-quality compression algorithms try to find the best endpoints for the given set of pixels. Testing all possible endpoints by a bruteforce method is very time consuming, so the goal is to reduce the number of combinations to be tested.

Colors in a 4 × 4 block can be considered points in 3D RGB space. Resulting compressed colors must lie on a line between two selected endpoints in this space. The direction along which the points vary the most can be found using the technique of principal components analysis. It is likely that this direction, called the principal axis, is very close to the direction of the line through the optimal endpoints, and it can be used to seed the search.

Nevertheless, these algorithms are still too slow for real-time compression, for which we need a fast selection of the compression line. We can use the extents of the bounding box of RGB color subspace in which the colors from given 4×4 pixel block are contained. The line spans the complete dynamic range and tends to line up with the luminance distribution. The selection process then reduces to finding out which diagonal of the bounding box is the best. This can be done by testing the sign of the covariance of the color values relative to the center of the bounding box, which can be done easily on the GPU.

For each texel in the 4×4 block, the algorithm finds the closest color representable on the selected line and outputs a coded-color index. More details about the algorithm can be found in [van Waveren 06] and [van Waveren and Castaño 07].

31.3.1 Creating Compressed Textures Dynamically

To create a compressed texture from another source texture, we use the render-to-texture technique, setting up a framebuffer and binding an auxiliary integer texture in GL_RGBA32UI format (128-bits/texel, same size as 1 DXT5 block) or in GL_RG32UI (64-bits/texel, same size as 1 DXT1 block). The encoding shader compresses each 4×4 block of input texels into one pixel of the target. The width and height of the target texture will be a quarter of the size of the source texture. If the input size is not a multiple of four, we need an additional row or column in the target, and the texel fetch operation has to be clamped to the edges of the source texture.

The auxiliary texture is then loaded into a buffer object using glReadPixels, which is in turn used as the source buffer in texture upload via glCompressedTex SubImage2D. The command sequence is shown in Listing 31.1.

The transfer happens on the GPU side, so it's quite fast. Unfortunately, OpenGL doesn't provide a mechanism to reinterpret a block of memory under a different format to avoid the copying. We cannot use glCopyTexImageSubDataNV to avoid one copy operation, as it requires the pixel format to be the same for the source and destination textures.

```
// The compressed DXT image is assumed to be in the first
// color attachment of the currently bound FBO
glReadBuffer(GL_COLOR_ATTACHMENT0);
glBindBuffer(GL_PIXEL_PACK_BUFFER, bo_aux);
glReadPixels(0, 0, (w + 3) / 4, (h + 3) / 4, GL_RGBA_INTEGER , GL_UNSIGNED_INT , 0);

glBindBuffer(GL_PIXEL_PACK_BUFFER, 0);
glBindFramebuffer(GL_DRAW_FRAMEBUFFER, 0);

// Copy to dxt texture
glBindTexture(GL_TEXTURE_2D , tex_aux);
glBindBuffer(GL_PIXEL_UNPACK_BUFFER, bo_aux);

glCompressedTexSubImage2D(GL_TEXTURE_2D , 0, 0, 0, w, h,
    GL_COMPRESSED_RGBA_S3TC_DXT5_EXT, w * h, 0);
```

Listing 31.1. Flipping the framebuffer attachment into a compressed texture.

In case the mipmaps are needed on the resulting texture, there are two ways to get them: either by invoking `glGenerateMipmap` to automatically generate the mipmaps, or by creating and uploading all required mipmap levels in the same way we have created the top-level texture. While the first method is more convenient, it's important to verify whether the driver implements `glGenerateMipmap` effectively on the GPU. At the time of writing this, invoking automatic mipmap generation on a compressed texture incurs a pipeline stall under both major vendors, indicating that the texture gets pulled and processed on the CPU side. With AMD, we get the hit even with the uncompressed textures. Apparently, this functionality doesn't have the priority in most of the existing applications, but for the procedural rendering, it could save a few commands.

31.4 Transformation to YUV Style Color Spaces

DXT compression has some limitations and quality issues when we try to use it on arbitrary images. However, the perceived quality can be enhanced by using a different color space. The *YUV color space* is a color encoding scheme that takes human perception into account. Indeed, one of its goals is to mask and suppress the compression artifacts by dedicating more bandwidth to image attributes that are more significant in human perception.

Our eyes are much more sensitive to changes in luminance than to the changes in chrominance. Thus, if we convert the color values from the RGB color space to a color space based on luminance (Y) and two other chroma components, we can use a higher-quality encoding for the luminance while lowering the bandwidth for the chrominance and gaining a higher perceived quality overall.

As presented in [van Waveren and Castaño 07], this can be achieved using the DXT5 compression scheme. If we look at how the DXT5 scheme encodes RGBA color data, we can see that it uses 64 bits for the RGB components, and the same number of bits solely for the alpha component. This obviously lends itself to using the alpha for the luminance and to encoding the chroma channels in the RGB part.

31.4.1 YC_oC_g Color Space

Thus far, we were using a wider definition of the YUV color space, encompassing all color spaces that use either luminance (Y) or luma (Y') and two other channels used to encode the deviation from grey along a selected axis. There are several schemes and equations to compute the luminance and chrominance values in use, employed, for example, in analog and digital TV and elsewhere.

One of the color spaces of this class that can be used effectively with graphics hardware is YC_oC_g, with C_o standing for chroma-orange and C_g for chroma-green.

Since we are going to add a code that transforms from a YUV color space to RGB color space, we need something that is relatively cheap to execute in a fragment shader. With YC_oC_g, the conversion to RGB becomes quite simple:

$$R = Y + C_o - C_g,$$
$$G = Y + C_g,$$
$$B = Y - C_o - C_g.$$

With YC_oC_g, the Y value is stored in the alpha channel, and C_o and C_g are stored in the red and green channel, respectively. Because of the 5:6:5 quantization in DXT, the C_g channel uses 6 bits in comparison to 5 bits for the C_o channel. The value of C_g is present in all three equations when converting back to RGB, so the green channel can use a little better precision.

Nevertheless, the quantization of DXT colors in the RGB component can cause a loss of color in situations where the dynamic range of chroma components is narrow. For this reason, an extended YC_oC_g-S implementation utilizes also the third, so far unused blue channel to store a scaling factor. The C_o and C_g values are scaled up during the compression, and the scale factor is stored within the blue channel and then used in the decoder to scale the values back down.

Decoding now becomes slightly more complex:

$$Scale = \frac{1}{\frac{255}{8}B + 1},$$
$$Y = A,$$
$$C_o = (R - 0.5)Scale,$$
$$C_g = (G - 0.5)Scale.$$

$$R = Y + C_o - C_g,$$
$$G = Y + C_g,$$
$$B = Y - C_o - C_g.$$

This method adds some additional code to the decoder and consumes the third channel that could be used for other things.

Eric Lasota [Lasota 10] came up with a simplified scheme, named YC_oC_g-X in this chapter, and in the example, based on YC_oC_g with scaling. The reasoning behind the simplified scheme is that, with YC_oC_g being a YUV-style color space, the values for C_o and C_g are constrained to a range that's proportional to the value of the Y channel. Instead of using a separate scale factor and putting it into the blue channel, we can use the value of Y to normalize C_o and C_g channels. The C_o and C_g now reflect only the changes in the tone and saturation, leaving the information about intensity solely in the Y channel.

This scheme uses slightly different vectors for the computation of chromatic values to make the resulting math simple:

$$Y = (R + 2G + B)/4,$$
$$C_o = 0.5 + (2R - 2B)/4,$$
$$C_g = 0.5 + (-R + 2G - B)/4.$$

$$R = 2Y(2C_o - C_g),$$
$$G = 2YC_g,$$
$$B = 2Y(2 - 2C_o - C_g).$$

Like the YC_oC_g-S, this scheme addresses the problems of quantization in the non-scaled YC_oC_g mode; however, it's not a quality improvement over the YC_oC_g-S scheme, as the peak signal-to-noise ratio (PSNR) metrics indicate as well.

31.5 Comparison

The compression schemes have been tested on a few sample scenes using a visual test together with the commonly used PSNR metrics for comparison. Figure 31.2 shows some of the artifacts occurring with the selected compression schemes, using the image 03 from Kodak Lossless True Color Image Suite [Franzen 99].

Images compressed directly in the RGB color space show some obvious errors in the form of a discolored block of 4 × 4 pixels appearing in between the areas with different colors. Especially in this case, the error is higher and more visible for the runtime compressor in comparison to the higher quality offline compressor, that can invest much more time in the search of optimal endpoints. However, the runtime compressor used on the YC_oC_g color space easily outperforms even the offline one in terms of quality.

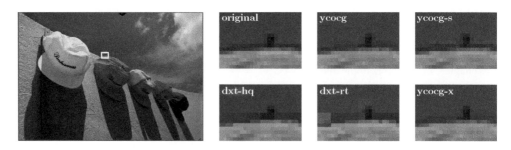

Figure 31.2. Comparison of the compression artifacts.

The difference between various YC_oC_g compressors can be observed mostly in some of the corner cases. The basic version without scaling shows a loss of color in shaded areas, where the chromacity values are low. The effect of 5:6 quantization of C_o and C_g values can be also observed in some notorious cases, like the compression of the sky gradient. The scaled scheme (YC_oC_g-S) achieves the best quality; however, it still doesn't have the full dynamic range to handle the sky gradient flawlessly. The simplified scaled scheme (YC_oC_g-X) can handle the shaded areas best, but it doesn't perform well in the bright areas with a gradual change in chromacity.

Errors in YC_oC_g color space are harder to spot and less intrusive than similar errors in RGB space. Figure 31.3 shows the differences between the encoding schemes and the original image, amplified 16 times. Errors along the edges of the image compressed with plain DXT are rather visible and disturbing; the differences in YUV-style schemes appear more like color tone changes and aren't that easily spotted.

Apart from the Kodak image used because of the wild chrominance and luminance changes, I tested the method on two images from planetary engine Outerra in two different lighting conditions (see Figure 31.4). The lower, darker half of Figure 31.4(b) was also tested separately as a last option.

PSNR error metrics for these sample images are shown in Table 31.1. Thanks to the division by luminance, YC_oC_g-X performs exceptionally well in darker areas, but it cannot match the results of the other two YC_oC_g schemes in bright ones with

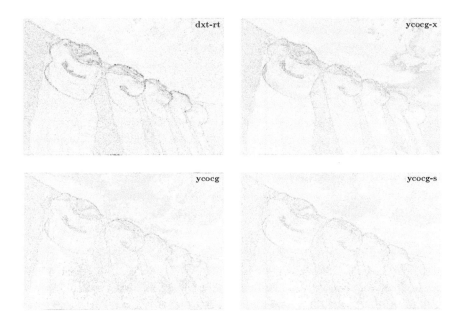

Figure 31.3. 16X amplified and inverted difference between compressed and original images.

Figure 31.4. (a) Bright and (b) dark scene used in the test.

a gradual hue change like a clean sky. Still, its properties can be used with advantage in some cases, for example, when compressing generated ground textures.

Raw PSNR doesn't represent well how the compression artifacts appear to the human eye, and metrics that would give different weights to luminance and chrominance channels would be probably better.

Scheme	PSNR			
	kodim03	light	dark	dark low
DXT real-time	38.7839	38.3560	44.9785	46.3247
YC_oC_g	42.3551	41.7667	45.0011	46.8363
YC_oC_g-S	42.7758	42.0848	45.3294	47.2720
YC_oC_g-X	40.6135	36.8699	41.7026	52.7532

Table 31.1. PSNR of various compression schemes: bigger is better. YC_oC_g-S wins in most situations, trumped by YC_oC_g-X only on the dark test scene.

31.6 Using Real-Time DXT Compression for Procedural Content and Video Capture

Where can real-time DXT encoding be used? Obviously, it's not necessary or even desired for static data, as offline compressors can usually achieve a higher-quality output, and the longer running time doesn't matter as much in that case.

Real-time compression can be used with advantage on the image data that are generated dynamically, for example, the output of various procedural generators that produce data on demand. In procedural engine Outerra, it can be found in several places, for example, in the terrain texture generator, lowering the memory requirements of the tile cache and speeding up terrain rendering as well by reducing the required bandwidth. Figure 31.1 shows the output of the procedural tree generator, where the real-time compression is used on the produced clusters of leaves. The generator creates the textures dynamically at startup using current quality settings. The ability to produce the data dynamically means that the quality can be adjusted as the hardware gets better over time. Another interesting area is the use of this technique for in-game video capture.

31.6.1 Video Capture Using YUYV-DXT Compression

When we or our users want to capture videos from our 3D application, there are relatively few options: we can use an external program such as Fraps or a special hardware for capturing the video as it goes out from the graphics card.

Both have their advantages and disadvantages. External programs are widely available and can be easily used by players, but they can considerably slow down the application, forcing it to use a lower resolution or reduced-quality modes. Capture cards will provide a high-quality output, but they aren't cheap, nor are they widely available.

However, there's another option: to endow the application with a native video capture support. It gives our users the ability to capture videos without any additional software or hardware. There are, of course, some complications.

31.6.2 Bandwidth Considerations

To capture a raw RGB video with 1080p resolution at 30 fps, we need a bandwidth of 187MB/s. However, since the memory on GPU is aligned, we can't effectively read 8-bit RGB directly and must read RGBA instead, making it 249MB/s.

This is still well below the peak download bandwidth between the GPU and CPU, which is around 2.5–6GB/s, but the problematic part here is the sustained write speed of hard disks. A typical modern 7200 rpm desktop SATA hard drive, like the Seagate Barracuda 7200.11, has a sustained data transfer rate up to 129MB/s. It's apparent we need to perform a compression to get below the limits.

A real-time on-GPU DXT-like compression would be an ideal candidate for this since we can utilize the parallel computing powers of the GPU, reducing both the GPU-CPU and CPU-disk bandwidth below the sustainable system speeds. Using YC_oC_g-DXT5 encoding, the bandwidth for the above scenario reduces to 62.2MB/s.

31.6.3 Format of the Video Stream

We have shown that a YUV-style transformation can enhance the quality of DXT-style compressed data so that they become usable for a light compression of image data. So far we have been ensuring that the derived YUV-formats we are using can be efficiently decoded in a fragment shader, limiting ourselves to the existing DXT schemes. However, since the captured video will be transcoded outside of our application, we should care also about the format that will be used for the video and adapt the encoding to it.

Since we are no longer constrained by the requirement to use an accelerated DXT decoding, the resulting format can be modified. For example, instead of using the 5:6:5 quantization from the original RGB block of DXT textures, we can use 8:8 quantization for the two chromatic values, utilizing the full dynamic range and avoiding the issues mentioned in Section 31.2 of using a custom and simplified software decoder for the video format.

From the available and well-supported video formats, one of the most used and available is YUYV422. It stores one pair of U and V chrominance values for every 2 luminance (Y) values. As has already been mentioned, the human eye is more sensitive to luminance than chrominance, so the loss of chrominance samples does not have a significant impact on image quality. In order to support the YUYV422 encoding, we can subsample the chromatic values by averaging values of U and V in

```
const vec3 TO_Y = vec3(0.2215, 0.7154, 0.0721);
const vec3 TO_U = vec3(-0.1145, -0.3855, 0.5000);
const vec3 TO_V = vec3(0.5016, -0.4556, -0.0459);

void ExtractColorBlockYY(out vec2 col[16], sampler2D image, ivec2 coord)
{
  for(inti=0;i<4;i++)
  {
    for(intj=0;j<4;j++)
    {
      vec3 color = texelFetch(image, coord + ivec2(j, i), 0).xyz;
      col[i * 4 + j].x = dot(TO_Y, color);
    }
  }

  for(inti=0;i<4;i++)
  {
    for(intj=4;j<8;j++)
    {
      vec3 color = texelFetch(image, coord + ivec2(j, i), 0).xyz;
      col[i * 4 + j - 4].y = dot(TO_Y, color);
    }
  }
}

void ExtractColorBlockUV(out vec2 col[16], sampler2D image, ivec2 coord)
{
  for (inti=0;i<4;i++)
  {
    for (intj=0;j<8;j+=2)
    {
      vec3 color0 = texelFetch(image, coord + ivec2(j, i), 0).xyz;
      vec3 color1 = texelFetch(image, coord + ivec2(j + 1, i), 0).xyz;
      vec3 color = 0.5 * (color0 + color1);
      col[i * 4 + (j >> 1)].x = dot(TO_U, color) + offset;
      col[i * 4 + (j >> 1)].y = dot(TO_V, color) + offset;
    }
  }
}
```

Listing 31.2. Extracting YY and UV blocks from 8 × 4 RGB input block.

two horizontal pixels. Two blocks of $4 \times 4 Y$ values and two blocks of U and V values can be encoded separately, each in its corresponding block equivalent to how the alpha component is being encoded in the DXT5 format, with two 8-bit boundary values and 16 3-bit interpolation indices. The GLSL code to extract YY and UV blocks from the input texture is in Listing 31.2.

31.6.4 Download of Video Frames from the GPU

The YUYV scheme still keeps the same 3:1 effective compression ratio as the DXT5-YC_oC_g mode, requiring a 62.2MB/s bandwidth in 1080p mode at 30 fps. It is less than half of the sustained write speed of the hard disk; nevertheless, it is still desirable to use a different drive than the one used by the system and our application for data loading to avoid potential clashes on the bus.

After the current frame is rendered into an offscreen buffer, it is used as a source texture for the real-time compression shader pass. The setup is the same as described in Section 31.3.1: a shader pass first generates an intermediate integer texture with compressed data, which is then flipped to a buffer object. The buffer is then down-loaded to the CPU.

As with all transfers from and to the GPU, we have to be careful to avoid pipeline stalls. It is important to download the buffers asynchronously. The process is described in depth in Chapter 28. The example code for the YUYV-DXT video capture is integrated into the example code for the asynchronous buffer downloads.

The remaining part of the capture process is writing the captured frame data to disk. For the best performance, we use asynchronous writes here, avoiding unnecessary caching. Otherwise, the implementation is pretty straightforward.

Captured videos will take quite a lot of disk space: one minute of a 1080p video at 30 fps consumes more than 3.7GB of disk space. We also need a custom decoder in order to play and convert the video stream. There already exists an unofficial decoder plugin for the libavcodec audio/video codec library used in FFmpeg [FFmpeg 07]. The decoder uses a custom YOG container file format described in [Kemen 10], which is quite simple to output: a simple header followed by the frames with compressed data.

With the plugin, all FFmpeg tools can recognize and play YOG videos. They can also be converted to another supported format, for example, to MJPEG with high-quality settings for further editing, or directly to an H264 format for high compression.

31.7 Conclusion

I described real-time DXT compression on the GPU and its use for dynamically generated content, comparing several quality enhancing schemes. I have shown that even with real-time compression, one can achieve high-quality results while saving memory and bandwidth.

We have also used the technique for real-time video capturing from our OpenGL application. Source code on the OpenGL Insights website, www.openglinsights.com, shows two examples for this chapter: one with the code for the real-time compression of textures and creation of DXT textures, together with the code used to decode it back to RGB color space. The second code example is integrated into the example for Chapter 28, capturing and saving the video from the example application.

Bibliography

[Brown 06] Simon Brown. "DXT Compression Techniques." http://www.sjbrown.co.uk/ 2006/01/19/dxt-compression-techniques/, 2006.

[FFmpeg 07] FFmpeg. "A Complete, Cross-Platform Solution to Record, Convert and Stream Audio and Video." http://ffmpeg.org/, 2007.

[Franzen 99] Rich Franzen. "Kodak Lossless True Color Image Suite." http://r0k.us/graphics/ kodak/, 1999.

[Kemen 10] Brano Kemen. "In-Game HD Video Capture using Real-Time YUYV-DXT Compression." http://www.outerra.com/video/, 2010.

[Lasota 10] Eric Lasota. "YCoCg DXT5: Stripped Down and Simplified." http://codedeposit. blogspot.com/2010/10/ycocg-dxt5-stripped-down-and- simplified.html, 2010.

[S3TC 12] S3TC. "S3 Texture Compression." http://en.wikipedia.org/wiki/S3_Texture_ Compression, 2012.

[van Waveren and Castaño 07] J. M. P. van Waveren and Ignacio Castaño. "Real-Time YCoCg-DXT Compression." http://www.nvidia.com/object/real-time- ycocg-dxt-compression.html, 2007.

[van Waveren 06] J. M. P. van Waveren. "Real-Time DXT Compression." id Software, Inc., 2006.

An OpenGL-Friendly 32
Geometry File Format and
Its Maya Exporter

Adrien Herubel and Venceslas Biri

32.1 Introduction

Geometry is at the heart of most computer graphics, whether film, video games, or tools. The vast majority of props, sets, and characters rendered to the screen come from geometry files stored in the computer hard drive.

Despite being the lowest common denominator of CG applications, there is no de facto standard for geometry files. On the contrary, there is a plethora of both proprietary and open formats. One of the many reasons for this state of affairs is that each application has different requirements that are not efficiently compatible. An out-of-core path tracer will have different needs for its geometry-storing solution than a 3D editor or a game. Of course a kitchen-sink approach will offer all the needed features, but probably at the cost of computational and storage efficiency.

The goal of this chapter is not to implement the ultimate geometry format. Instead, we will show how to tackle the problem by creating a file format suited to our needs along with the right tools. A file format is pointless without tools for exporting and importing but also for data-mining or conformation. Good tools enable rapid iterations on our asset production pipeline, thus increasing productivity and enabling better artistic impulse.

First we start by defining our feature requests for a file format suitable for the OpenGL API. We will then confront our use cases against the feature matrix of existing formats. In the second part, we will present the Drone format, a binary chunk-based format, designed for efficient deserialization and serialization of a 3D scene. Then, in the third part, we write our first tool, a Maya exporter, introducing the software API. Finally, a second tool is used to benchmark our file format.

32.2   Manifesto

32.2.1   Goals and Features

Computer graphics presents an interesting paradox stated by Blinn's law: "As technology advances, rendering time remains constant." Performance is and always will be a key requirement when building a CG application. Therefore, geometry storage is not an exception. We define a few key points for a geometry file format suitable for a typical OpenGL application. Generally geometry data is stored once and for all during the asset creation pipeline and potentially read many times at runtime, so the format should be optimized to follow this use case.

Full scene storage. A good format will offer the possibility either to use a file for each shape or to consolidate a full scene into only a few files. Therefore, a basic scene structure is required. A scene should at least feature, meshes, transforms, lights, and basic shading data like diffuse color and specular coefficient. Meshes can be either static, or animated, using keyframes or skinning.

No transformation at runtime. Data stored on the disk should be kept as close as possible as the data used to feed the OpenGL Vertex Buffer API. Ideally, the initial deserialized buffer should be enough. Runtime transformation of data should be kept for dynamic geometry only. For example, a mesh should be stored using only triangles, and vertices with multiple normals should be duplicated. This requires more computation when writing geometry but considerably reduces loading times. There are trade-offs when precomputing transformations directly into the file, as it increases file size. The cost of loading the file might surpass the cost of transforming geometry, especially if it is stored on a slow media or streamed across the network. Moreover, some transformations, like subdivision surfaces and level-of-detail, are generally not uniformly applied on the whole scene and therefore might not be suited for precomputation in the file.

Arbitrary access. The file-format-reading API should be able to only load part of the file. For example, we should allow it to quickly iterate on all the stored bounding boxes, then only load visible meshes. The other advantage for offering arbitrary access to shapes is to enable the use of out-of-core algorithms by loading and discarding data as needed.

Scene exporting. In game and film industries, sets and characters are generally built in commercial or homegrown editors, often using their own geometry formats. Thus, the asset-creation pipeline should be supported by robust exporting procedures from the editor format to the rendering-engine or game-engine format. Due to the sheer amount of produced data, per-shape tweaking, and human intervention in general should not be necessary during this stage.

Simplicity and extensibility. Writing and reading from a file format should not force the user to bear with huge dependencies on various frameworks. A format using small and consistent APIs is much easier to use and extend in a project.

32.2.2 Existing Formats

When writing a 3D engine, whether for a game, an editor, or a demo, developers are faced with a multitude of geometry file formats (Figure 32.1), coarsely divided in two categories. COLLADA and FBX are competing to become the standard file format when it comes to exchanging geometry between applications. The two formats implement a wide array of functionalities. However, they require huge frameworks for manipulation, and as exchange formats, performance is not the main focus. Moreover, the FBX SDK is closed source. Formats focused only on geometry assets are therefore more easily implemented, yet they often are ASCII-only and poorly standardized, or lack exporters in commercial editors.

Format	Autodesk 3DS Max	Autodesk Maya	Blender	Triangu-lation	Hard Edges Extraction	Storage	Anim-ations	Multiple Objects	Arbitrary Access	Shading
FBX	Builtin I/O	Builtin I/O	Plugin Export	Yes	Yes	Binary	Skinning and anim curves	Yes	No	Yes
COLLADA	Plugin	Plugin	Plugin	Yes	Yes	XML	Skinning and anim curves	Yes	No	Yes
MD5	Multiple plugins	Multiple plugins	Plugin Export	Yes	Not all plugins	ASCII	Animation in external file	Yes	No	Yes
Obj	Builtin I/O	Builtin I/O	Builtin I/O	Yes	No	ASCII	No	Non-standard	No	External non-standard

Figure 32.1. Geometry file-format feature matrix.

32.3 The Drone Format

We introduce a new geometry file format, meeting all the previously stated requirements. We design our format around two very simple APIs: the first is used to manage low-level data chunks, and the second is used to serialize and deserialize the scene. The code of the two APIs and a viewer is included in the companion code on the OpenGL Insights website, www.openglinsights.com.

32.3.1 Binary Layout

To achieve minimum runtime transformation, data will be stored in a binary form. The Drone format is based on the notions of chunks and chunk descriptors. A chunk

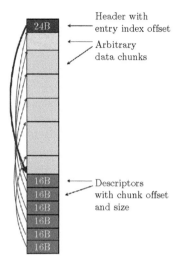

Header with
entry index offset

Arbitrary
data chunks

Descriptors
with chunk offset
and size

Figure 32.2. Binary layout for the Drone format.

is an arbitrarily sized contiguous array stored in the file and a descriptor of a small structure containing chunk metadata. A scene exported in the Drone format will be divided into many chunks.

The low-level layout (Figure 32.2) is straightforward: a 24-byte structure is serialized at the start of the file (Listing 32.1); it contains a version number corresponding to the Drone API version, an offset pointing to the start of the descriptor array, and the number of chunks. Then, raw data chunks are stored consecutively, and finally, the descriptors are serialized. Storing metadata at the end of the file enables us to write the chunks on the fly instead of keeping them in RAM until the end but at the cost of a file seek upon load. Each descriptor contains chunk offset and size. It is tempting to add additional data for each chunk, such as a type. However, many chunks will be stored, and the smaller the structure is, the greater the number of descriptors will fit in the CPU cache.

```c
typedef struct
{
  uint64_t version;
  uint64_t index_offset;
  uint64_t chunk_count;
} drone_header_data_t;

typedef struct
{
  uint64_t offset;
  uint64_t size;
} drone_desc_t;
```

Listing 32.1. Drone header and descriptor data structures.

32.3.2 Drone API

The low-level Drone API is divided in two parts, the writer and the reader. If we closely examine our use cases, we need to be able to write our scene once to the file and then read many times from it at runtime. To be efficient in both cases, we need different structures for writing and reading into the file. The API is in pure C without any dependency besides the libc. The full code is available in the lib/drone subdirectory of the code.

```
// Creates a writer object. Save place for the header in the file.
int32_t drone_open_writer(drone_writer_t *writer, const char *filename);
// Store the descriptor list in the file and closes file descriptor
int32_t drone_close_writer(drone_writer_t *writer);
// Write a chunk in the file. Add a descriptor to the list.
int32_t drone_writer_add_desc(drone_writer_t *writer, const void *data, uint64_t ←
    size);
// Get the last added descriptor ID
drone_desc_id_t drone_writer_get_last_desc(drone_writer_t *writer);
```

Listing 32.2. Drone writer API.

Writer API. The writer API (Listing 32.2) uses a writer object containing a file descriptor, various offset counters, and a descriptor list. Each time we add a chunk, the data are written to the disk, and the descriptor is added to the list in memory. When the writing is done, the list is transformed in an array and written at the end of the file, and the header is updated. See usage example in Listing 32.3.

```
float random_float_chunk[256];
const char *arbitrary_string = "34zh3t4tr34h3tr1h351e3h1zt53h13zt1hzr31hzt31htr3";
drone_writer_t writer_writer;
// Create a writer object. Open the file and seek to next writing location.
int32_t status = drone_open_writer(&writer_writer, "file.drn");
// Write chunk. Add descriptor to list.
status = drone_writer_add_desc(&writer_writer, random_float_chunk, sizeof(float) * ←
    256);
// Write chunk. Add descriptor to list.
status = drone_writer_add_desc(&writer_writer, arbitrary_string, strlen(←
    arbitrary_string));
// Write header. Convert list to array. Write descriptor array in the  file. Close ←
    file
status = drone_close_writer(&writer_writer);
```

Listing 32.3. Drone writer API usage.

Reader API. Reading a drone file (Listing 32.4) mostly consists in deserializing the header and the descriptor array and then using them to navigate in the data. The API

```
drone_t reader;
// Open the reader in load mode
int32_t status = drone_open(&reader, "file.drn", DRONE_READ);
// Get descriptor object of ID 0
drone_desc_t desc = drone_get_desc(&reader, 0);
// Get associated data
const float *data = (float *)drone_get_chunk(&reader, 0);
// Close reader
status = drone_close(&reader);
```

Listing 32.4. Drone reader API usage.

```
#define DRONE_READ_LOAD 0 // Load all the file into a single array
#define DRONE_READ_MMAP 1 // Mmap the file
#define DRONE_READ_NOLOAD 2 // Load only the header and descriptor array
// Creates a reader object. Load or mmap data if necessary.
int32_t drone_open(drone_t *reader, const char *filename,  uint32_t mode);
// Close the file descriptor of the reader. Deallocates or unmap  data if necessary.
int32_t drone_close(drone_t *reader);
// Read Drone API version
uint64_t drone_get_version(drone_t *reader);
// Get the number of registered chunk
uint64_t drone_get_chunk_count(drone_t *reader);
// Get the descriptor corresponding to the ID
drone_desc_t drone_get_desc(drone_t *reader, drone_desc_id_t desc_id);
// Get a pointer on the chunk referenced by the descriptor. Only works in load and ←
    mmap modes
const void *drone_get_chunk(drone_t *reader, drone_desc_id_t desc_id);
// Copy the chunk referenced by the descriptor into the array. Load data in NO_LOAD ←
    mode
int32_t *drone_copy_chunk(drone_t *reader, const void *data, drone_desc_id_t desc_id←
    );
```

Listing 32.5. Drone reader API.

(Listing 32.5) offers three choices for loading the data. The user can either decide to load them completely, to map them into RAM, or to load them on demand. The **LOAD** mode serves for the general case, when all the scene fits into RAM. The mapping approach is particularly suited for out-of-core algorithms and large files. Using either the `mmap` system call on Unix or the `MapViewOfFile` on Windows, the operating system will handle streaming the data from disk to RAM on demand and manage itself with the proper LRU queues depending on data usage. More details about the use of memory mappings regarding performance will be found in [Kamp 10]. Finally, when using the **NOLOAD** mode, data will be loaded on demand from the disk.

32.3.3 Scene API

The Scene API describes how to store and read a scene using the Drone API. For each type of object, the API features two structures. The *container* is stored directly into the file, it can contain scalars, statically allocated vectors, and chunk descriptor IDs pointing to other chunks. This type of structure is known as *plain-old-data*. The other structure is constructed when the file is loaded. It has the same fields as the container, except that descriptor IDs are replaced by pointers to the corresponding data. Using this mechanism, we can represent the various data hierarchies inherent in a 3D scene. The full code is available in the lib/scene subdirectory of the code, and an example of scene reading is available in the viewer source code in the tools/viewer subdirectory. Our scene API features a whole hierarchy of containers for describing meshes, dynamic mesh data, shading, transformations, and skeletons.

```
struct MeshDynamicDataContainer
{
  drone_desc_id_t vertices;
  drone_desc_id_t normals;
};

struct MeshDynamicData
{
  const float *vertices;
  const float *normals;
  const MeshDynamicDataContainer *d;
};

struct MeshContainer
{
  uint32_t numTriangles;
  uint32_t numVertices;
  drone_desc_id_t triangleList;
  drone_desc_id_t uvs;
  drone_desc_id_t dynamicData;
};

struct Mesh
{
  uint64_t dagNodeId;
  uint32_t numTriangles;
  uint32_t numVertices;
  const int *triangleList;
  const float *uvs;
  MeshDynamicData *dynamicData;
  const MeshContainer *d;
};
```

Listing 32.6. Scene container example.

In Listing 32.6, we can observe the dual-structure mechanism. The two containers are actually serialized in the drone file, and at runtime, each container is resolved in the corresponding structure.

One big advantage of separating the two APIs is that the scene is independent from the chunk-storing order. The layout of the chunks in the file is tremendously important performancewise. For example, the various chunks of vertex keyframes can be stored either per-object then per-frame, or per-frame then per-object. In the first case, reading the animations for the whole scene will be largely slower, and in the second case, reading the animation of only one object will be slower. The decoupling of both APIs enables us to optimize the files for each one of the reading scenarios without altering the format.

APIs are making it easy to write tools that manipulate and explore the geometry files. It is relatively simple to build small applications for data-mining purposes, for example, to analyze scene complexity. We can also write tools that reorder chunks offline to improve performances, merge multiple files into one, or filter animation data.

32.4   Writing a Maya File Translator

Autodesk Maya is one of the most popular 3D computer graphics software, offering a wide range of features, from modeling to animation, simulation, and rendering.

32.4.1   Maya SDK 101

Maya offers developers a huge C++/Python API, a solid scripting language called MEL, and flexible batch execution modes. Automating tasks and creating custom tools is extremely easy and common in production.

Each component and feature of the software can be derived and redefined using the API as described in the online documentation and the authoritative book [Gould 02]. Most of the terms written in `code font` can be directly looked up in the online Maya documentation [Autodesk 11].

32.4.2   Writing a Translator

To export a scene from Maya to an unsupported file format, it is necessary to implement a component called a **FileTranslator**. Our **FileTranslator** will be called the **DroneTranslator** (Listing 32.7) and will only have writing capabilities, as by default, a **FileTranslator** can also be used for import. Our translator supports exporting meshes, skeletons, locators, lights, and cameras. Transform matrices for objects and joints, baked vertices, and normals can be exported over an arbitrary number of frames in the same file. We also support basic shading nodes and embedded textures. The full code of the Maya plugin is available in the tools/mayadrone subdirectory of the code.

All Maya plugins have to define two functions, **initializePlugin**, and **uninitializePlugin**. In these two functions, nodes, commands, translators, or shaders are, respectively, registered and unregistered using an **MFnPlugin** object. We

```
class DroneTranslator : public MPxFileTranslator
{
public:
  DroneTranslator() {}
  virtual ~DroneTranslator() {}
  // Actual constructor
  static void *creator();
  // This function is called when the translator is used to export a scene
  MStatus writer(const MFileObject& file, const MString& optionsString,  ←
      FileAccessMode mode);
  bool haveReadMethod() const {return false; }
  bool haveWriteMethod() const { return true; }
  MString defaultExtension() const { return "drn"; }
};
```

Listing 32.7. A write-only custom `FileTranslator` declaration.

```
select -all;
file -f -type "DroneTranslator" -op "option string"  -es "mymodel.drn";
```

Listing 32.8. Selecting all the scene and calling the DroneTranslator.

register the translator using the `registerFileTranslator` function by passing it a pointer on the `DroneTranslator::creator` function.

Given that the plugin is correctly compiled and placed in the right directory, loading it will be accomplished using either the GUI or the `loadPlugin` MEL instructions. Using the script editor instead of the GUI enables the developer to quickly iterate while developing a plugin.

When a `FileTranslator` is registered, it will immediately appear in the export dialog box. A custom export interface can be shipped with the plugin using MEL. For now, we will only use the MEL script to call and pass options to the `DroneTranslator` (Listing 32.8). By default, the `FileTranslator` will grab the current selection. Then the `writer` function will finally be called.

32.4.3 Walking through the Maya DAG

When the `writer` function is called, the selection, the option string, and the file name are passed in parameters. It is then entirely up to the developer to iterate through the selection to search depth-first through the scene directed acyclic graph (DAG).

A simplified `writer` mechanism in a translator will generally follow those steps:

- Parse options, check if the file can be written, and write a header placeholder.

- Get the active selection or build it using the options. Consulting global Maya states like the active selection is done through the `MGlobal` header.

- Build an `MItSelectionList` to iterate on DAG nodes contained in the selection.

- For each given DAG node, build a depth-first DAG iterator object `MItDag` to traverse each subgraph.

- For each traversed node, build an `MDagPath` object. These objects are used to identify nodes through their position or path in the graph. Thus, they can be notably used to retrieve the transforms.

- Use the `MFn` API on the path to determine the underlying data type. The `MFn` API is the RTTI system of the Maya API; it tests if the end node of a path supports a given function set. For example, we can test if the node has `MFn::kMesh` support.

- If the node supports the `MFn::kMesh` function sets, we can build an `MFnMesh` function set to access the data in the node. Then, we write data accordingly to the format.

- Write metadata and close the file.

Transform nodes in Maya also support the function set of their child node; thus, a transform node can be mistakenly taken for a shape node if not properly tested.

32.4.4   Exporting OpenGL-Ready Meshes

The Maya API for meshes is able to triangulate polygons, but a bit of work is necessary to reorder all the vertex attributes like normals and texture coordinates along the triangles. Another source of trouble is that Maya is perfectly fine with having multiple normals and texture coordinates associated with the same vertex, as they are stored per-vertex and per-primitive. In order to obtain OpenGL-ready meshes, such vertices need to be duplicated.

- Gather base and triangulated topologies as well as vertex attributes using the `MFnMesh` previously obtained. The Maya API uses its own data containers such as `MIntArray` and `MPointArray`; they are tightly packed so the base C pointer is easily accessible.

- Prepare arrays for triangulated normal and texture coordinates.

- For each polygon and then for each triangle in the polygon, find the matching normal and texture coordinate ID; then, store it.

We now need to identify which vertices are associated with more than one normal or texture coordinate.

- For each triangle, and then for each vertex, build a tuple containing vertex ID, normal ID, and texture-coordinate ID.

- Use a hash table (or another similar structure) to find if the tuple is unique.

- If the tuple is unique, generate a new vertex ID and associate it with the tuple; then, store it in the hash table.

- Reorder vertices and vertex attributes along the new unique vertex IDs.

Triangulated geometry can be obtained more easily, for example, if the geometry has previously been triangulated using the `Mesh->triangulate` menu. However, if the mesh contains hard edges, the vertices still need to be duplicated, which can also been done by hand but much more tediously.

32.5 Results

The benchmarks were done on a Intel Core i7 920 2.67GHz, 7200 trpm HDD and an NVIDIA GeForce 295 GTX GPU. The scene (Figure 32.3) is the San Miguel [McGuire 11] model with a supplementary skinned and textured character. We measure file size for various part of the sets. Files are generated using Maya 2011. FBX and OBJ files are exported using Maya's own plugins, COLLADA files using the third party OpenCOLLADA plugin [OpenCOLLADA 12]. As shown in Table 32.1, triangulation, per-vertex normal options, are activated when available and texture embedding is deactivated.

Model	Number of shapes	Number of triangles
Character	5	13434
Wood table	11	2216
Plants only	1207	3.1M
Walls only	1385	0.66M
Full set	7102	6.1M

Table 32.1. Number of shapes and triangles in the benchmark scenes.

COLLADA and Wavefront OBJ are ASCII-based; thus, file size is significantly larger (Figure 32.4), FBX file size is sightly lower than the Drone file size, probably due to mesh data compression.

Figure 32.3. Side-by-side capture of the Drone viewer and the same scene in Maya.

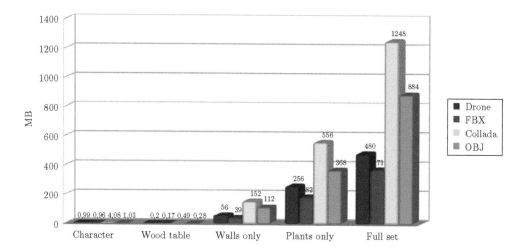

Figure 32.4. File size performance comparison between formats on the test scene.

Loading times (Figure 32.5) are measured using the Assimp library [Source-Forge 07] for COLLADA and OBJ and the official SDK [Autodesk 12] for FBX format. We define the loading time by calculating time elapsed between the beginning of the load and the first displayed frame containing the model. Despite using an efficient XML parser, COLLADA loading times drop significantly when the number of shapes increases. The Drone format clearly benefits from the layout optimization and the no-runtime transformation policy.

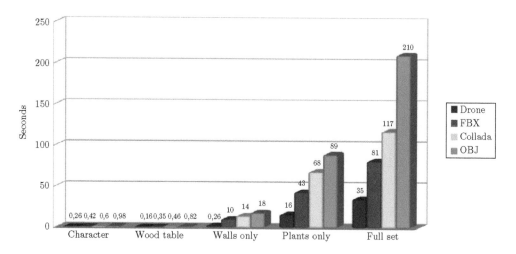

Figure 32.5. Loading performance comparison between formats on the test scene.

32.6 Conclusion

For simplicity's sake, a few features of both APIs presented in the source code were omitted from the previous description. Notably, in the Drone API, we added a dictionary mechanism so chunks can be tagged by an arbitrary number of strings, as it can be useful for data-mining purposes or for storing multiple scenes in the same file using different name spaces. Furthermore, it is very likely that we will add Drone support to other commercial and noncommercial 3D software packages, such as Autodesk 3DS Max and Blender.

Rather than presenting a fixed-function, definitive-geometry file format, we first presented our requirements and then defined a file format meeting these goals. The Drone file format is capable of representing a full 3D scene, animated and shaded, in a compact manner, with built-in out-of-core capabilities. The geometry data is prepared offline to be directly compatible with the OpenGL vertex buffer API. We also presented how to use the Maya API to write an geometry exporter suited to our requirements.

The format is meant to be expanded and modified to suit a wide range of interactive and noninteractive CG applications, as some choices made for the Drone format and exporter are not suited to some CG algorithms. Typically, an application dealing with subdivision surfaces will prefer using nonduplicated vertices: a Reyes renderer will need the base topology instead of triangles. When dealing with massive data, compression should be considered, either by chunk, by group of chunks, or by file. Notably, LZ4 and Google's snappy compression algorithms are relatively fast and provide good results for geometry data.

Bibliography

[Autodesk 11] Autodesk. "Auotdesk Maya API Documentation." http://download.autodesk. com/us/maya/2011help/API/, 2011.

[Autodesk 12] Autodesk. http://www.autodesk.com, 2012.

[Gould 02] D. A. D. Gould. *Complete Maya Programming: An Extensive Guide to MEL and the C++ API*, 1. San Francisco: Morgan Kaufmann, 2002.

[Kamp 10] P. H. Kamp. "You're Doing it Wrong." *Communications of the ACM* 53:7 (2010), 55–59.

[McGuire 11] Morgan McGuire. "Computer Graphics Archive." http://graphics.cs.williams. edu/data, 2011.

[OpenCOLLADA 12] OpenCOLLADA. http://opencollada.org/, 2012.

[SourceForge 07] SourceForge. "Assimp Open Asset Import Library." http://assimp. sourceforge.net/, 2007.

VI

Debugging and Profiling

We probably often underestimate how powerful the OpenGL API can be. However, programming is less about the result than the process to reach this result. The most impressive rendering is nothing but the end of a path that is, in a large part, debugging and profiling. Unfortunately, OpenGL doesn't have a great reputation on that side. Who really enjoys using `glGetError`?

This part of the OpenGL experience is now history since the release at SIGGRAPH 2010 of the `GL_ARB_debug_ouput` extension that revolutionizes every day of an OpenGL programmer's life. This revolution is captured by António Ramires and Bruno Oliveira in their chapter "ARB_debug_output: OpenGL's Solutions for Desperate Developers," which shows every aspect of this extension, how to break the program when an OpenGL error occurs, and even opens on interesting debugging perspectives.

Profiling knew an earlier take-off in the world of OpenGL programming thanks to the release of `GL_EXT_timer_query` in 2006, then standardized within OpenGL 3.3. Thanks to Christopher Lux and his chapter, "The OpenGL Timer Query," this primitive of OpenGL profiling won't hide any secrets any longer.

There are two kinds of profiler: the built-in and the external tools, which provide two different approaches to picture profiling. On one side, a profiler tightly connected to application designs and specific use-cases, on other side more generic tools that can embrace all sorts of scenarios and software. The first approach is perfectly reflected by Lionel Fuentes in his chapter "A Real-Time Profiling Tool," which deals with how a built-in real-time profiler can help the game programmer and also the artist creating game assets. Chris Dirks and Omar A. Rodriguez expose the second approach through their chapter "Browser Graphics Analysis and Optimizations," which discuss the utilization of Intel GPA to study WebGL performance.

Finally, Aleksandar Dimitrijević offers us two innovative profiling chapters, first introducing us to GPU P-States in his chapter "Performance State Tracking," where he calls our attention to how GPUs reach full speed and how this may affect our performance measurements. He backs his discussion with AMD and NVIDIA proprietary libraries. In his second chapter, he deals with the problem of GPU memory limits. OpenGL doesn't provide functionalities to determine the actual memory usage, but proprietary extensions provide the required information, and Dimitrijević helps us to go through them in his chapter "Monitoring Graphics Memory Usage."

ARB_debug_output: 33
A Helping Hand for
Desperate Developers

António Ramires Fernandes and Bruno Oliveira

33.1 Introduction

Since the inception of OpenGL, error handling has not been without some controversy, as the only available mechanism to provide feedback was the `glGetError` function. For each OpenGL command, the application had to explicitly query for possible errors, getting in return a single and very broad meaning error identifier for the latest error.

`ARB_debug_output` [Konttinen 10a], originally proposed by AMD [Konttinen 10b], introduces a new feedback mechanism. It allows developers to define a callback function that will be invoked by OpenGL to report events back to the application. The callback mechanism frees the developer from having to explicitly check for errors during execution, populating the code with `glGetError` function calls. Nevertheless, the extension specification does not force the definition of a callback function. When no callback is defined, the implementation will keep an internal log called the message log.

The nature of the reported events is very broad and can relate, for instance, to errors using the API, the usage of deprecated functionality, performance warnings, or GLSL compiler/linker issues. Event information contains a driver-implementation dependant message and other data such as its severity, type, and source.

The extension also allows user-defined filtering of the events that are reported by selecting only the ones of interest. Finally, the application, or any third-party library, may also generate custom events. In the following sections, we will show how to use the aforementioned extension and its features. We will also have a peek at the current implementation approaches.

33.2   Exposing the Extension

As stated in the specification, it is recommended that the extension is available only in an OpenGL debug context to avoid a potential performance impact; hence, it may be required to create such a context. Using *freeglut* as an example, this can be achieved with `glutInitContextFlags(GLUT_DEBUG)`. An example of the flags to create an OpenGL 4.1 core debug context using `WGL` and `GLX` is presented in Listing 33.1. To check if the extension is available, we can use `glGetStringi`.

```
int attribs[] =
{
#ifdef WIN32
  WGL_CONTEXT_MAJOR_VERSION_ARB, 4,
  WGL_CONTEXT_MINOR_VERSION_ARB, 1,
  WGL_CONTEXT_FLAGS_ARB, WGL_CONTEXT_DEBUG_BIT_ARB,
  WGL_CONTEXT_PROFILE_MASK, WGL_CONTEXT_CORE_PROFILE_BIT_ARB,
#endif
#ifdef __linux__
  GLX_CONTEXT_MAJOR_VERSION_ARB, 4,
  GLX_CONTEXT_MINOR_VERSION_ARB, 1,
  GLX_CONTEXT_FLAGS_ARB, GLX_CONTEXT_DEBUG_BIT_ARB,
  GLX_CONTEXT_PROFILE_MASK, GLX_CONTEXT_CORE_PROFILE_BIT_ARB,
#endif
  0
};
```

Listing 33.1. Flags to create a core debug context in WGL and GLX.

33.3   Using a Callback Function

The extension allows the definition of a callback function that will be invoked each time an event is issued. This directs the flow of generated events to the callback, and they will not be stored in the message log.

If working with multiple contexts, each one should have its own callback function. Multithreading applications are allowed to use the same callback for multiple threads, and the application is fully responsible for ensuring thread safety.

Listing 33.2 is an example of such a callback function; it prints the event passed by OpenGL in a human-readable form. The enumerations are defined in the extensions spec [Konttinen 10a]. The `getStringFor*` functions translates the enumeration value into a human readable format. The complete code can be found on the book's web site (www.openglinsights.com).

The function `glDebugMessageCallbackARB`, used to specify the callback function, takes two arguments: the name of the callback function and a pointer to the user data. The pointer to the user data can only be changed with a new call to `glDebugMessageCallbackARB`. This pointer allows the callback to receive user-

```
void CALLBACK DebugLog(GLenum source, GLenum type, GLuint id, GLenum severity, ←↩
    GLsizei length, const GLchar *message, GLvoid *userParam)
{
  printf("Type: %s; Source: %s; ID: %d; Severity: %s\n",
    getStringForType(type).c_str(),
    getStringForSource(source).c_str(),id,
    getStringForSeverity(severity).c_str());
  printf("Message: %s\n", message);
}
```

Listing 33.2. Example of a simple callback function.

defined data, in addition to the event data. Listing 33.3 shows a very simple, although useless, example. In that snippet of code, the last two OpenGL function calls should generate events. The callback function will receive a pointer to `myData`, which will hold the value 2 the first time, and 3 the second.

```
int myData;
...
// set myData as the user data
glDebugMessageCallbackARB(DebugLog, &myData);
...
//set the value of the variable myData
myData = 2
// Generate an event due to an invalid parameter to glEnable
glEnable(GL_UNIFORM_BUFFER);
// change the variable myData.
myData = 3;
// From now on events will carry the value 3 in the user param.
// Another event: parameter combination not available in core profile
glPolygonMode(GL_FRONT, GL_LINE);
```

Listing 33.3. Example of the user-data parameter usage facilities.

A more realistic and complete example of usage for the user data is to pass a struct holding pointers to the relevant subsystems of the application, such as the resource manager and the rendering manager.

Once set, the callback can be disabled by passing NULL as the first argument to `glDebugMessageCallbackARB`. From that point onwards, events will be directed to the message log. A final note: any call to an OpenGL or window-system function inside the callback function will have undefined behaviour and may cause the application to crash.

33.4 Sorting Through the Cause of Events

Getting events reported is only a part of the debugging process. The rest of the procedure involves pinpointing the issue's location and then acting upon it. Finding the cause of the event or the offending lines of code can be a very simple task with the extension *synchronous* mode.

The specification defines two event reporting modes: *synchronous* and *asynchronous*. The former will report the event before the function that caused the event terminates. The latter option allows the driver to report the event at its convenience. The reporting mode can be set by enabling or disabling GL_DEBUG_OUTPUT_SYNCHRONOUS_ARB. The default is asynchronous mode.

In synchronous mode, the callback function is issued while the offending OpenGL call is still in the call stack of the application. Hence, the simplest solution to find the code location that caused the event to be generated is to run the application in a debug runtime environment. This allows us to inspect the call stack from inside the IDE by placing a breakpoint at the callback function.

33.4.1   Accessing the Call Stack Outside the IDE

The other solution, harder to deploy but neater, is to implement a function within the application to get the call stack and print it out. While more complex, this solution is far more productive since there is no need to keep stopping the program at each event; it also allows us to filter from the call stack only the calls originated from the application, eliminating calls to the operating system's libraries, thereby providing a cleaner output. This output can be directed to a stream, allowing for maximum flexibility. The callback, when running in test machines, can produce a sort of a minidump file, pinpointing the error location, that later can be sent to the developer team.

The source code accompanying this chapter provides a small library that includes a function for Windows and Linux systems that retrieves the call stack. An example of a call stack is printed by the library as

```
function: setGLParams - line: 1046
function: initGL - line: 1052
function: main - line: 1300
```

33.5   Accessing the Message Log

As mentioned before, if no callback is defined, the events are stored in an internal log. In the extension specification, this log is referenced as the message log; however, it contains all the event's fields. Hence, *event log* would probably be a more descriptive name.

The log acts as a limited-size queue. The limited size causes new events to be discarded when the log is full; hence, the developer must keep cleaning the log to ensure that new events fit in, as any event that occurs often is bound to fill the log very rapidly. Also, being a queue, the log will provide the events in the order they were added. When retrieving an event, the oldest event is reported first.

```
GLint maxMessages, totalMessages, len, maxLen, lens[10];
GLenum source, type, id, severity, severities[10];
// Querying the log
glGetIntegerv(GL_MAX_DEBUG_LOGGED_MESSAGES_ARB, &maxMessages);
printf("Log Capacity: %d\n", maxMessages);

glGetIntegerv(GL_DEBUG_LOGGED_MESSAGES_ARB, &totalMessages);
printf("Number of messages in the log: %d\n", totalMessages);

glGetIntegerv(GL_MAX_DEBUG_MESSAGE_LENGTH_ARB, &maxLen);
printf("Maximum length for messages in the log: %d\n", maxLen);

glGetIntegerv(GL_DEBUG_NEXT_LOGGED_MESSAGE_LENGTH_ARB, &len);
printf("Length of next message in the log: %d\n", len);
char *message = (char *)malloc(sizeof(char) * len);
// Retrieving all data for the first event in the log. Placing NULL
//  in any of the fields is allowed and the field will be ignored.
glGetDebugMessageLogARB(1, len, &source, &type, &id, &severity, NULL, message);
// Retrieving the severity and messages for the first 10 events.
char *messages = (char *)malloc(sizeof(char) * maxLen * 10);
glGetDebugMessageLogARB(10, maxLen * 10, NULL, NULL, NULL, severities, lens, ←
    messages);
// Clearing the log
glGetIntegerv(GL_DEBUG_LOGGED_MESSAGES_ARB, &totalMessages);
glGetDebugMessageLogARB(totalMessages, 0, NULL, NULL, NULL, NULL, NULL, NULL);
```

Listing 33.4. Querying the log and retrieving messages.

The log's capacities and the length of the first message can be queried with **glGetInteger**. Multiple events can be retrieved with a single call using **glGetDebugMessageLogARB**. Listing 33.4 presents some examples of usage.

When retrieving multiple events, their associated messages are all concatenated in a string, separated by a null terminator. The array **lens** will store their individual lengths. If the maximum length (second parameter) is not sufficient to hold all the messages to retrieve, only those events whose messages do fit in **message** will actually be retrieved.

Each time an event is retrieved, it is removed from the log. Hence, to clear the log, one just needs to retrieve all events (Listing 33.4).

33.6   Adding Custom User Events to the Log

An application, or third-party library, can also take advantage of the debug facilities now available with this extension since it is possible to insert the application's own events into the log. The log can then be used as a centralized debug resource for all that is related to the graphics pipeline.

One note, though, regarding this approach. Developers of libraries have to be aware of possible clashes in the IDs of the events, although this could partially be

```
glDebugMessageInsertARB(GL_DEBUG_SOURCE_APPLICATION_ARB,
  GL_DEBUG_TYPE_ERROR_ARB,
  1111, GL_DEBUG_SEVERITY_LOW_ARB,
  -1, // null terminated string
  "Houston, there's some problem with my app...");
```

Listing 33.5. Extension function to add events to the event log.

solved by adding, in each event's message, an identification of the library who issued it.

Adding events to the log is very straightforward, with only one new function, **glDebugMessageInsertARB**. An example of usage can be found in Listing 33.5. The source field can only be GL_DEBUG_SOURCE_APPLICATION_ARB or GL_DEBUG_SOURCE_THIRD_PARTY_ARB. The specification states that low-severity events are not enabled by default. Next section will show how to enable and disable classes, or individual events.

33.7   Controlling the Event Output Volume

The extension provides a function, **glDebugMessageControlARB**, which can be used to filter the events that get reported. The function effectively filters out, GL_FALSE, or allows the inclusion, GL_TRUE, of any events that match the criteria specified. This does not affect events already in the log; it will only filter new events. Listing 33.6 shows some examples of usage.

To specify a particular combination of **source**, **type**, and/or **severity** (the first three parameters), just set them to either one of the defined enumeration values or use GL_DONT_CARE, i.e., no filter is applied to that field.

A set of event IDs can also be specified to set an array with the required values. This only works for pairs of **source** and **type**, both not being simultaneously GL_DONT_CARE, while **severity** must be set to GL_DONT_CARE. This is because an event is uniquely identified by its **type**, **source**, and **ID**.

This feature can become even more powerful if integrated with a dynamic debugging system. In conjunction with the callback function, or with a periodic inspection to the event log, it is possible to devise a mechanism by which some events are disabled after some number of occurrences.

33.8   Preventing Impact on the Final Release

As we begin to use this extension, its functions will start to appear here and there in our code. This brings up the next issue: how to get rid of all these function calls for the final release version. Building a library allows us to concentrate these calls in a

```
// Disabling events related to deprecated behaviour
glDebugMessageControlARB(GL_DONT_CARE,
  GL_DEBUG_TYPE_DEPRECATED_BEHAVIOR_ARB,
  GL_DONT_CARE,
  0, NULL, GL_FALSE);
// Enabling only two particular combinations of source, type and id.
// Note that first we had to disable all events.
GLuint id[2] = {1280, 1282};
glDebugMessageControlARB(GL_DONT_CARE, GL_DONT_CARE, GL_DONT_CARE,
  0, 0, FALSE);
glDebugMessageControlARB(GL_DEBUG_SOURCE_API_ARB,
  GL_DEBUG_TYPE_ERROR_ARB,
  GL_DONT_CARE,
  // 2 is the number of IDs
  2, id, GL_TRUE);
```

Listing 33.6. Filtering events.

particular class, yet this does not solve the issue, as now one has to call the library's functions instead.

A possible workaround for this issue is to use compilation flags, dealt by the preprocessor. A simple example is shown in Listing 33.7. With this approach, all calls related to the extension can be removed just by undefining the compilation flag.

```
#ifdef OPENGL_DEBUG
// do this for all extension functions
#define GLDebugMessageControl(source, type, sev, num, id, enabled) \\
  glDebugMessageControlARB(source, type, sev, num, id, enabled)
#else
// do this for all extension function
#define  GLDebugMessageControl(source, type, sev, num, id, enabled)
#endif
// now instead of calling glDebug... call GLDebug..., for instance
GLDebugMessageControl(NULL, NULL, NULL, -1, NULL, GL_TRUE);
```

Listing 33.7. Using compilation flags to prevent impact on the final release.

33.9 Clash of the Titans: Implementation Strategies

AMD and NVIDIA have started in different directions when implementing this extension. AMD had a head start since it already had an implementation for AMD_debug_output. This extension is very similar to ARB_debug_output and contains most of the features in it.

AMD drivers, Catalyst 11.11, are focused on giving more meaningful information to situations typically reported by glError. They also consider GLSL compiler/linker issues as events, providing the *info log* as the message. NVIDIA, on the other hand, started off paying little attention to these issues and went on to provide information on operations such as buffer binding and memory allocation. Starting from version 290.xx, NVIDIA also began to provide some more information to `glError` scenarios, starting to close the gap between their drivers and AMD drivers.

Regarding implementation constants, both drivers share the same log queue size, 128 events, and maximum message length, 1024 bytes.

As for events caused by OpenGL commands, consider binding a buffer to a non–buffer-object name. NVIDIA does not report any event on this, while AMD provides the following information:

```
glBindBuffer in a Core context performing invalid operation
with parameter <name> set to '0x5' which was removed
from Core OpenGL (GL_INVALID_OPERATION)
```

Note that, although the message is not entirely correct since it refers incorrectly to a deprecated feature, it provides the value of the offending parameter. Similar information detail is obtained when attempting to use a deprecated combination of parameters. For instance when using **glPolygonMode(GL_FRONT, GL_LINE)**, one gets

```
Using glPolygonMode in a Core context with parameter
<face> and enum '0x404' which was removed from
Core OpenGL (GL_INVALID_ENUM)
```

NVIDIA, on the other hand, reports

```
GL_INVALID_ENUM error generated. Polygon modes for <face> are
 disabled in the current profile.
```

Although not as complete as AMD, it is an improvement from its earlier implementations (285.62 drivers), where it reported only a **GL_INVALID_ENUM** error.

In a different scenario, when the name is actually bound and data are successfully sent to the buffer, the AMD driver keeps silent, while NVIDIA is kind enough to give information about the operation in low-severity messages:

```
Buffer detailed info: Buffer object 3 (bound to
GL_ELEMENT_ARRAY_BUFFER_ARB, usage hint
is GL_ENUM_88e4) will use VIDEO memory as
the source for buffer object operations.
```

This becomes particularly useful when too many buffers have been allocated and they do not fit in video memory anymore. In this situation, when calling **glBufferData**, the driver reports that system heap memory will be used instead.

NVIDIA also warns if something is about to go wrong. For instance, in a situation where memory is running very low, the following report was issued when calling glDrawElements:

```
Unknown internal debug message. The NVIDIA
OpenGL driver has encountered an out of memory
error. This application might behave inconsistently and fail.
```

Regarding performance, the implementations may behave very differently. When rendering in debug mode for a scene with small models with a large number of small VAOs, we noticed some performance degradation with NVIDIA, whereas AMD showed no performance difference. However, when testing with a scene containing a single very large VAO, the performance issue with NVIDIA almost vanished. For both drivers, no significant differences were found regarding the synchronicity mode, which suggests that these drivers have not yet implemented, or optimized, the asynchronous mode. When checking the call stacks, considering a large number of events, there was also no evidence that the asynchronous mode has been implemented.

33.10 Further Thoughts on Debugging

While on the theme of OpenGL debugging, there are a few things that could come in handy. For instance, OpenGL has a rich set of functions to query its state regarding buffers, shaders, and other objects, but all these queries operate on numerical names. For anything other than very simple demos, it becomes hard to keep track of all these numbers. Extension EXT_debug_label [Lipchak 11a], available on OpenGL ES 1.1, promotes the mapping of text names to objects.

Another interesting OpenGL ES extension is EXT_debug_marker [Lipchak 11b]. This extension allows developers to annotate, with text markers, the command stream for both discrete events or groups of commands. Unfortunately, it does not provide queries for the current active markers.

OpenGL needs more robust development tools that allow shaders to be debugged and state to be inspected. The above two extensions are a step in the right direction and will improve the productivity of developers when used in this context.

33.11 Conclusion

The ARB_debug_output extension is a highly welcomed addition, as it adds an extra value to the API, making it possible to evaluate its behavior with a more centralized and efficient approach.

Regarding implementations, AMD had a head start, but NVIDIA is catching up. It may be argued that the extension needs some rewriting so that NVIDIA's approach fits more smoothly. The extension was designed for errors and warnings, not the type of information NVIDIA is providing, since even a low-severity setting doesn't apply when reporting that an operation has completed successfully. Adding a `GL_DEBUG_INFO` setting would probably be enough to deal with this issue. Still, it is undeniable that this information can come in very handy when problems emerge.

As with any other functionality in OpenGL, the API has a lot of potential, and it is up to the developers to fully unleashed it.

Bibliography

[Konttinen 10a] Jaakko Konttinen. "AMD_debug_output Extension Spec." http://www. opengl.org/registry/specs/ARB/debug_output.txt, June 10, 2010.

[Konttinen 10b] Jaakko Konttinen. "AMD_debug_output Extension Spec." http://www. opengl.org/registry/specs/AMD/debug_output.txt, May 7, 2010.

[Lipchak 11a] Benj Lipchak. "EXT_debug_label Extension Spec." http://www.opengl.org/ registry/specs/ARB/debug_output.txt, July 22, 2011.

[Lipchak 11b] Benj Lipchak. "EXT_debug_marker Extension Spec." http://www.opengl.org/ registry/specs/ARB/debug_output.txt, July 22, 2011.

The OpenGL Timer Query   34

Christopher Lux

This chapter presents the OpenGL functionality to measure execution times of sequences of OpenGL commands using methods provided through the OpenGL timer query. The special requirement of dedicated OpenGL timing methods for profiling and runtime purposes is highlighted, followed by an introduction of the basic functions and concepts regarding synchronous and asynchronous approaches to OpenGL timing. Different types of applications are demonstrated, while indicating special limitations to this functionality.

34.1   Introduction

How long does it take the graphics hardware (GPU) to execute a certain sequence of OpenGL rendering commands? The answer to this question is essential during the development as well as the runtime of real-time computer graphics applications such as games, simulations, and scientific visualizations.

Profiling a program means measuring and recording, for instance, execution times and memory usage of individual parts of the program. Profiling allows a software engineer to analyze how many resources and how much time is spent in various parts of the program, and thereby identify critical sections in the program source code. These critical sections present the best opportunities for optimizations from which the program performance can benefit the most.

Execution time measurements at program runtime can also be utilized to dynamically adjust the workload of rendering algorithms to achieve or maintain interactive frame times. For instance, a program can use information about rendering times of geometrical models to adapt the used levels-of-detail to decrease or increase the geometry workload of the graphics system. Another application area of runtime timings is resource streaming, where, for instance, information about texture-upload speeds is used to adjust the amount of texture resources transferred to GPU memory.

The timer query functionality, introduced with the **EXT_timer_query** extension [ARB 06] and promoted to core specification with OpenGL Version 3.3 [Segal and Akeley 11], allows us to measure the time it takes to execute a sequence of OpenGL commands and to retrieve the current time stamp of the OpenGL server. This time query mechanism is required because current GPUs are running asynchronous to the CPU. Issuing an OpenGL command ultimately places it in the OpenGL command-queue processed by the GPU at a later point in time, which means, upon calling an OpenGL function, the corresponding command is not necessarily executed directly, nor is it guaranteed to be finished when the call returns control to the CPU. Furthermore, the execution of OpenGL commands stored in the command queue is usually delayed by at least one frame in relation to the current rendering frame on the CPU. This practice minimizes GPU idle times and hides latencies in CPU-GPU interoperation.

Modern immediate-mode GPUs are employing heavily pipelined architectures, which are processing different primitives (e.g., vertices, fragments) in different pipeline stages simultaneously [Ragan-Kelley 10]. This results in the overlapped execution of individually issued draw commands on the GPU. Figure 34.1 illustrates the asynchronous and pipelined execution model of immediate-mode GPUs. This chapter specifically discusses performance measurements for immediate-mode GPUs. The architectural differences of tile-based GPUs and the associated differences in performance profiling are described in Chapter 23.

The basic asynchronous character of the OpenGL server allows the CPU to attend to different tasks while the GPU is executing the issued commands. However, measuring GPU execution times using general CPU timing methods results in cap-

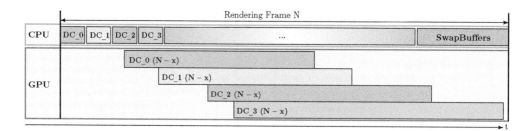

Figure 34.1. Asynchronous and pipelined execution of draw calls (DC_n) on the GPU: four draw calls are issued by the CPU during the rendering frame N. Through the heavily pipelined architecture of modern immediate-mode GPUs, the draw commands are ultimately executed overlapped in parallel.

turing only the time used to submit the OpenGL commands to the command stream and not the actual execution times on the GPU. While it is possible to synchronize the activities of the CPU and the GPU by using `glFinish()` or OpenGL sync objects [Segal and Akeley 11], timing GPU activities this way influences the potentially overlapped program flow and, therefore, affects the general program performance. Hence, such an attempt only allows us to generate meaningful timing results for isolated routines on the GPU, as the measurement adversely affects other program parts. On the other hand, OpenGL timer queries allow us to measure GPU execution times without affecting the established program flow and, when carefully employed, without stalling GPU or CPU execution. This makes them an indispensable tool for every OpenGL software developer looking to understand and optimize the runtime performance of their programs.

34.2   Measuring OpenGL Execution Times

OpenGL offers two approaches for measuring execution times on the GPU: synchronous and asynchronous queries. Before discussing the different types of time queries, it is important to clarify how time is represented in OpenGL.

34.2.1   OpenGL Time

Time in OpenGL is expressed with the granularity of one nanosecond, which is a billionth of a second (10^{-9} s). Because of this very fine granularity, the data types used to store timing results and their representable value ranges have to be considered. The use of 32-bit unsigned integer values (`GLuint`) allows us to represent time intervals of up to approximately four seconds; using 64-bit-wide unsigned integers (`GLuint64`) raises this limit to hundreds of years, plenty for timing rendering routines in real-time applications.

While the OpenGL specification requires implementations to internally offer at least 30 bits of storage, which allows us to represent time intervals of at least one second, modern implementations, however, offer the full 64 bits of internal storage. On the other hand, the programmer is free to choose the data type for storing the timing results retrieved from OpenGL. For most application scenarios in real-time rendering, 32-bit values suffice to measure the duration of relevant program sections without risking arithmetic overflow, but when querying time stamps from OpenGL, 64-bit types are required to avoid overflow issues.

34.2.2   Synchronous Timer Query

The synchronous type of time queries allows us to retrieve the current time stamp of the GPU using a simple `glGetInteger()` query with the `GL_TIMESTAMP` parameter name, as demonstrated in Listing 34.1. This query returns the time stamp

```
// this variable will hold current time on the GPU
GLint64 time_stamp;
// retrieve the current time stamp,
// after all prior OpenGL commands reached the GPU
glGetInteger64v(GL_TIMESTAMP, &time_stamp);
```

Listing 34.1. Synchronous time-stamp query.

of the GPU after all previously issued OpenGL commands have reached the GPU but have not yet necessarily finished execution, causing an implicit command-queue flush similar to a call to `glFlush()`. The query call returns as soon as the result is available, as illustrated in Figure 34.2. Additional synchronization is required to measure GPU execution times similar to the previously described intrusive CPU timing method. This renders the synchronous-timing approach the least useful. Besides, comparisons with CPU timers show only insignificant differences. Note how, in Listing 34.1, a 64-bit signed integer (`GLint64`) is used to store the queried time stamp, as the synchronous time query only allows us to retrieve results into signed integer variables.

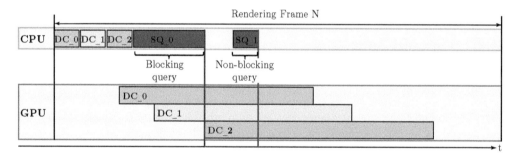

Figure 34.2. Synchronous timer queries: the query SQ_0 blocks the CPU execution until the previous OpenGL commands have reached the GPU, returning the time at the beginning of the execution of draw call DC_2. Query SQ_1 returns an intermediate time stamp without blocking the CPU.

34.2.3 Asynchronous Timer Query

The real strength of OpenGL timing lies with the asynchronous timing approach. Asynchronous timer queries use the same query-object mechanism as occlusion queries. Such timer queries can be used to measure either the amount of time taken to execute a set of OpenGL commands or to record the current time stamp of the GPU without stalling execution on the CPU or GPU.

New query objects are generated using `glGenQueries()`. A timer query can then be prepared and be started and stopped with the `glBeginQuery()` and

```
GLuint timer_query;
// generate query object
glGenQueries(1, &timer_query);
[...]
// start the timer query
glBeginQuery(GL_TIME_ELAPSED , timer_query);
// issue a sequence of OpenGL rendering commands
[...]
// stop the timer query
glEndQuery(GL_TIME_ELAPSED , timer_query);
[...]
// retrieve the query results, potentially stalling GPU execution
GLuint64 timer_result;
glGetQueryObjectui64v(timer_query , GL_QUERY_RESULT , &timer_result);

printf("GPU timing result: %f ms\n", double(timer_result) / 1e06);
```

Listing 34.2. Basic usage of an asynchronous timer query.

glEndQuery() calls using the GL_TIME_ELAPSED target, as demonstrated in Listing 34.2. These calls return immediately without waiting for the measurement results. The timer is actually started and stopped when all OpenGL commands prior
to the begin and end calls are fully executed by the GPU. This enables precise measurements of the GPU execution times required to process the commands enclosed
by the time query.

However, because of the pipelined nature of current GPUs and the consequent
overlapped execution of multiple rendering commands, inaccurate measurements are
possible. The difference in measured to actual execution time is highlighted in Figure 34.3. The actually occurring differences in these times vary with the complexity

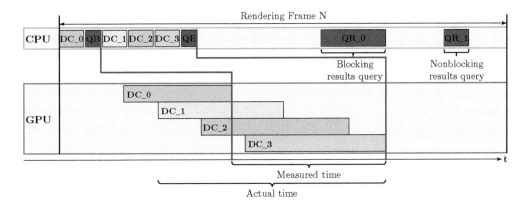

Figure 34.3. Asynchronous timer query: a single query is started (QB) and stopped (QE) to measure the
combined execution time of the enclosed draw calls (DC_n). While the first result request QR_0 blocks CPU
execution until the GPU has finished all commands, the later request QR_1 does not block.

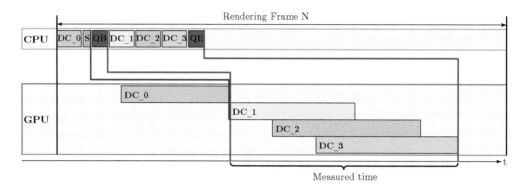

Figure 34.4. Correct timing of overlapped draw calls (DC_n) using an asynchronous timer query and a GPU synchronization point S to defer the execution of the enclosed commands without blocking CPU execution.

of the rendered objects and the surrounding rendering commands. Smaller, less complex objects show smaller divergences, while larger objects offer more opportunities for overlapped execution and therefore show larger divergences between measured and actual rendering times. This issue is resolved without stalling CPU execution by using an OpenGL sync object and a GPU synchronization point (`glWaitSync()`) issued just before the start of the timer query. Through forcing the completion of all commands prior to the synchronization point, the correct timing of the enclosed rendering commands becomes possible at the expense of the overlapped operation. This approach is illustrated in Figure 34.4. It is important to note, that while this intrusive approach allows us to gather very precise measurements of isolated sequences of rendering commands, it is affecting the execution of surrounding operations. On the other hand, the nonintrusive begin/end query mechanism, without additional synchronization points, widely produces results close to the actual execution times.

Once the result of a measurement is available, it is finally stored in the query object. The actual result value of a timer query is acquired from the query object using a `glGetQueryObject()` call requesting the **GL_QUERY_RESULT** object state entry. Since the results may not be directly available after ending the timer query, the acquisition of the result value will be blocked until the necessary information eventually becomes obtainable. Therefore, it is recommended to retrieve the query result at a later point in the program, which is described in closer detail in Section 34.2.5.

A very significant limitation of this timing approach is that pairs of begin/end queries must not be nested or interleaved. Therefore it is not possible to record the overall GPU time of a rendering method while at the same time measuring subroutines of that same method, which might be useful for profiling purposes.

34.2.4 Asynchronous Time Stamp Query

Another way to use asynchronous timer queries that avoids the nesting problem is to record the current time stamp on the GPU to a query object generated by `glGenQueries()`. Calling `glQueryCounter()` with the target `GL_TIMESTAMP` will store the current time stamp into the corresponding query object after all previous OpenGL commands have been fully executed. This call will also return immediately without blocking the application, and the result value is acquired the same way as before using `glGetQueryObject()`.

Through the use of two query objects to record the time stamps at the beginning and end of a sequence of OpenGL commands, the elapsed GPU time can be easily determined. Nevertheless, similar issues to those present with the begin/end mechanism arise when attempting to time commands for which execution is overlapped on the GPU. When requiring very precise measurement results, this can be resolved similarly by using OpenGL sync objects and GPU synchronization points prior to beginning the time stamp query.

The advantage of using asynchronous time stamp queries over the begin/end query mechanism is that calls to `glQueryCounter()` can be used anywhere without interfering with other time queries. It is even completely legal to query a time stamp between `glBeginQuery()` and `glEndQuery()` calls that are using a different query object.

Listing 34.3 demonstrates how to use queried time stamps to determine the times spent on the GPU for multiple rendering routines. By acquiring time stamps at different points, it is possible to calculate the elapsed time duration of the enclosed code segments. Using this approach, each particular query for a time stamp requires

```
GLuint timer_queries[3];
// generate three query objects
glGenQueries(3, &timer_queries);
[...]
// query time stamps around all draw routines
glQueryCounter(timer_queries[0], GL_TIMESTAMP);
draw_world();
glQueryCounter(timer_queries[1], GL_TIMESTAMP);
draw_models();
glQueryCounter(timer_queries[2], GL_TIMESTAMP);
[...]
// later in the program retrieve the query results
GLuint64 time_0, time_1, time_2;
glGetQueryObjectui64v(timer_queries[0], GL_QUERY_RESULT, &time_0);
glGetQueryObjectui64v(timer_queries[1], GL_QUERY_RESULT, &time_1);
glGetQueryObjectui64v(timer_queries[2], GL_QUERY_RESULT, &time_2);

printf("world draw time : %f ms\n", double(time_1 - time_0) / 1e06);
printf("models draw time: %f ms\n", double(time_2 - time_1) / 1e06);
```

Listing 34.3. Using asynchronous time stamp queries.

an individual query object. Otherwise, when reusing a query object, it becomes necessary to retrieve the intermediate results, which can potentially stall the program flow.

While the begin/end paradigm to measure execution times is easier to use and understand, the time stamp query offers certain advantages for more complex application scenarios. When, for instance, implementing a rendering library that internally is depending on time measurements, it is highly recommended to utilize time stamp queries. Consequently, client code is free to use any form of time query without interfering with the internal operation of the library.

34.2.5 Considering Query Retrievals

The main issue when timing OpenGL commands asynchronously is when to retrieve the results without negatively affecting the general program flow. A call to glGetQueryObject() to acquire a query result may stall the program if the result is not available at this point. The most optimal solution would be to know beforehand when a query result is available, as illustrated in Figure 34.3.

The availability of the result of a query object can be explicitly inquired with a nonblocking call to glGetQueryObject(), requesting the GL_QUERY_RESULT_AVAILABLE state. Since the GPU is typically running several frames behind the CPU, this query can be used to decide to skip the retrieval of query results for a series of rendering frames until they are eventually available. However, it is important that existing queries are not reissued and therefore overwritten until their results have been acquired, as illustrated in Listing 34.4.

When trying to avoid explicitly polling query availability, implicitly available synchronization points may be used, such as already-established command-stream synchronization points using OpenGL sync objects and fences. A common misconception is the consideration of the swapping of the front and back buffer of the default framebuffer as an implicit synchronization point. Because the processing of the OpenGL command queue on the GPU is often delayed by multiple frames in relation to the CPU, query results may not be available until a much later point in time. Depending on the frame rate and CPU overhead, the number of rendering frames the GPU is running behind the CPU can be observed to be as high as five frames, depending on the GPUs performance and driver settings. Besides this aspect, all OpenGL commands not influencing the framebuffer are unaffected by the swap operation and are therefore not necessarily synchronized at this point, e.g., texture or buffer transfers. A straightforward way to avoid blocking query retrievals is to use a double-buffered query approach, which allows us to start a new query before acquiring the result from the query issued during the previous rendering frame. If the thereby introduced delay of one frame between issuing the timer query and the retrieval of the result value is insufficient for nonblocking execution, more buffered queries can easily be added to this approach.

```
bool    query_issued = false;
GLuint timer_query;
[...]
// start of rendering frame
[...]
// query time stamps if query is not in use
if (!query_issued) {
    glQueryCounter(timer_query, GL_TIMESTAMP);
    query_issued = true;
}
[...]
// check the availability of the timer query result
GLuint timer_available = GL_FALSE;
glGetQueryObjectuiv(timer_query, GL_QUERY_RESULT_AVAILABLE,
                    &timer_available);

if (timer_available) {
    // retrieve available timer query result without blocking CPU
    glGetQueryObjectui64v(timer_query, GL_QUERY_RESULT, &result_time);
    query_issued = false;
}
[...]
// end of rendering frame
```

Listing 34.4. Nonblocking check for timer query availability.

Finally, it is important to note that execution times of separate sets of OpenGL commands may not combine linearly. Current OpenGL implementations and GPUs expose heavily pipelined architectures that are potentially running multiple tasks in parallel. For example, it is possible that the drawing of a large geometric model or the use of a computational complex shader is actually overlapped with the upload of texture resources. Therefore, the time required to run these tasks combined will probably not be equal to the sum of the individual task execution times (c.f. Figure 34.1). In such cases, the best strategy is to explicitly measure the combined execution time of the overlapped tasks in addition to the individual timings to determine the amount of overlap between the individual tasks. Furthermore, this enables the program to determine the workloads of these tasks relative to each other and to adjust them accordingly for the most optimal utilization of the GPU.

34.3   Conclusion

Modern GPUs are generally running asynchronously to the rendering software executed on the CPU. The addition of the timer query mechanism to the standard OpenGL range of functionality finally allows developers to measure the amount of time required to execute sequences of OpenGL commands on the GPU without affecting the general program performance. This functionality is available in two basic flavors: synchronous and asynchronous timer queries.

The synchronous query only allows us to acquire a GPU time stamp after all prior issued commands have reached the GPU but have not yet necessarily completed execution. Additional efforts are required to generate meaningful results using this approach. The real strength of the timer query interface lies with the asynchronous queries. They allow us to either directly time a sequence of OpenGL commands by employing the begin/end query paradigm or to acquire a GPU time stamp after all commands prior to the query have finished execution. While the first approach only allows for a single active query at a time, the latter can be employed very freely. Therefore, it is generally recommended to employ the asynchronous time stamp query for GPU execution measurements. This enables the use of timer queries for a vast variety of application areas in real-time rendering.

Since current GPUs may execute multiple rendering commands overlapped in parallel, special efforts are required in order to acquire exact measurements for individual rendering commands. There is, however, no approach to handle this issue completely nonintrusively. This presents an area for future improvements to the timer-query functionality: allowing the direct measurements of execution times even for commands executed overlapped on the GPU.

Bibliography

[ARB 06] OpenGL ARB. "OpenGL EXT_timer_query Extension Specification." www.opengl.org/registry/specs/EXT/timer_query.txt, June 2006.

[Ragan-Kelley 10] J. Ragan-Kelley. "Keeping Many Cores Busy: Scheduling the Graphics Pipeline." In *SIGGRAPH 2010: ACM SIGGRAPH 2010 Courses*. New York: ACM, 2010.

[Segal and Akeley 11] M. Segal and K. Akeley. "The OpenGL Graphics System: A Specification (Version 4.2)." www.opengl.org/documentation/specs, August 2011.

A Real-Time Profiling Tool   35

Lionel Fuentes

35.1   Introduction

As time goes on, video games are becoming more complex, presenting rich environments, a high level of interaction with the player, gorgeous graphics, physics simulation, etc. To push the hardware to its limits, developers need to have a precise knowledge of the time taken by the executed tasks, their distribution on the available hardware threads, and the dependencies each task has on the completion of the others. To this end, we focus in this chapter on the use of the time counters present on CPUs and modern GPUs to provide a real-time and easy-to-use profiler that is directly embedded into the application. We discuss the role of such a tool in the context of video game development and how it can benefit both developers and artists.

The proposed tool works by manually marking in the code the beginning and ending of the sections that are to be measured. At runtime, we record time stamps that correspond to the boundaries of the measured sections and display them in a simple and minimal graphical interface. The time interval between two matching time stamps is represented by a colored rectangle whose length represents the amount of time needed for completion of the associated task. We use platform-specific high-precision timers to measure the time spent on the CPU side and the OpenGL extension `ARB_timer_query` on the GPU side. The target is the consumer multicore PC/Mac device featuring one GPU.

35.2   Scope and Requirements

The final goal is to give developers and artists a general look at the time consumption for the different threads of the application, be it on the CPUs or on the GPU. The tool can be used to search for bottlenecks and synchronization problems in the targeted application. We aim at fulfilling the following requirements:

- Accuracy. We want our measurements to be as accurate as possible. We also want to minimize the perturbations due to our measurements and debug display.

- Real time. Coupled with a live update system of in-game assets, this system enables artists to tune the quality of their models, textures, and sound settings in order to fit in the imposed time constraints. Having a real-time profiler also enables us to analyze how the application's performance is impacted during its execution.

- Ease of use. User-friendliness is an important element, as it makes the tool accessible not only to developers but also to artists. We also want the tool to be easy to use on the developer side because making it easy to place markers in the code will result in more markers being inserted and better granularity in the measurements. Finally, we want the data to be displayed in a useful manner, making it easy to spot synchronization problems and performance bottlenecks and identify whether we are CPU-bound or GPU-bound.

- Portability. The proposed tool is embedded inside the game engine itself, and the display is done using the same renderer the game is based on. As a consequence, the time querying functions are the only platform-dependent part. Having a portable profiling tool gives a uniform and coherent feeling across all supported platforms, thus making profiling easy when switching to a new, unknown platform. While it doesn't replace a fine platform-specific external debugger like gDEBugger [Graphic Remedy 10, AMD 11], at the time of switching to a new platform, all previously developed functionality is immediately available and no learning curve is needed.

- Small. We want the profiler to be enabled and displayed throughout the whole development process so that developers can keep track of the evolution of time consumption and detect performance problems as soon as possible. This can only be done if the space taken on the screen is minimal.

35.3   Design of the Tool

35.3.1   User Interface

The profiler is displayed as a set of horizontal rectangles arranged in lines, each line corresponding to a "thread," either a software CPU thread or the GPU (see Figure 35.1). It can be noted that in the ideal case where we create as many threads as the number of available CPU cores and dispatch them accordingly (through thread processor affinity APIs like `SetThreadIdealProcessor` [Microsoft Corporation 11]), we can match each line to a physical CPU core.

Each displayed rectangle corresponds to a measured task, which is surrounded in the code by dedicated macros. We allow nested tasks, which are naturally represented by smaller rectangles. Finally, users can get the name and timing information for a given task if they hover the mouse cursor over it, thus displaying a hierarchy of marker names.

Figure 35.1. Screenshot of our sample implementation, displaying up to three levels of nested markers.

35.3.2   Limitations and Workarounds

Because of the chosen graphical representation, we are limited to a finite number of nested measured tasks. This can be worked around by using thicker rectangles, but the screen space taken by the profiler would degrade the usability of the developed application, so this should be reserved for a possible "expanded" display mode of the profiler.

In certain cases, the positions and sizes of the displayed rectangles will vary a lot from frame to frame. We solve this problem by allowing the user to "freeze" the profiler (in our case through mouse clicking) so that we can take our time to analyze the captured frame. Another solution is to display averages over several frames, which also has the advantage of reducing the chances of missing a particular costly event that happens rarely. The difficulty here would be to match corresponding rectangles from different frames and to order them in time in a meaningful way. Such an improvement is beyond the scope of this chapter.

Finally, the proposed profiler could be completed by displaying information on the current *P-state* of the GPU (see Chapter 37). This information is important to correctly interpret the results of the profiler, particularly when comparing different techniques.

35.3.3 API

The API consists of a few methods to mark the beginning of a frame to mark the beginning and end of the profiled sections and to draw the interface (see Listing 35.1).

```
class Profiler
{
  [...]
  void pushCpuMarker(const char *name, const Color& color);
  void popCpuMarker();
  void pushGpuMarker(const char *name, const Color& color);
  void popGpuMarker();
  void synchronizeFrame();
  void draw();
};
```

Listing 35.1. Exposed API of our profiler.

We can wrap these methods in macros to allow easy removal in a retail version. An example usage of the profiler is shown in Listing 35.2.

```
while(!done)
{
  PROFILER_SYNC_FRAME();
  PROFILER_PUSH_CPU_MARKER("Physics", COLOR_GREEN);
    doPhysics();
  PROFILER_POP_CPU_MARKER();
  PROFILER_PUSH_GPU_MARKER("Render scene", COLOR_RED);
    PROFILER_PUSH_GPU_MARKER("Render shadow maps", COLOR_LIGHT_BLUE);
      renderShadowMaps();
    PROFILER_POP_GPU_MARKER();
    PROFILER_PUSH_GPU_MARKER("Render final scene", COLOR_LIGHT_GREEN);
      renderFinalScene();
    PROFILER_POP_GPU_MARKER();
  PROFILER_POP_GPU_MARKER();
  PROFILER_DRAW();
}
```

Listing 35.2. Example usage.

Profiled code sections are surrounded by the corresponding push and pop macros. When measuring time on the CPU, a high-precision timer is used to record the dates that the push and the pop methods are called. When measuring time on the GPU, asynchronous timer queries are issued. The result is used several frames later at the time the `Profiler::draw()` method is executed.

`Profiler::synchronizeFrame()` has to be called once per frame and pushes a new frame to profile. Finally, `Profiler::draw()` uses the renderer of the application to display an overlay showing a graphical representation of the recorded markers.

35.4   Implementation

35.4.1   Measuring Time on CPUs

The C++ language does not provide any portable high-precision time-querying function. As a consequence, we need to rely on platform-specific APIs. The x86 family of processors provides a high-precision timer that can be read with the RDTSC (ReaD Time Stamp Counter) instruction. However, since multi-CPU systems have become the standard, multiple CPU counters are now in use simultaneously. This leads to synchronization problems between those timers. The problem is even worse when the OS switches the currently running thread from one CPU to another. Those problems are generally addressed by the operating system, which provides APIs to measure time with a high precision [Walbourn 05].

The Windows API exposes the `QueryPerformanceCounter()` and `Query PerformanceFrequency()` functions, which are specifically designed to let the user have access to the highest-precision timers available [Microsoft Corporation 07].

The POSIX API provides nothing better than `gettimeofday()`, which has a maximum precision of one microsecond. Consequently, for Unix-like platforms we prefer to rely on OS-specific APIs. As for MacOS X, the XNU kernel provides `mach_absolute_time()` [Apple, Inc 05], while the Linux kernel provides the `clock_gettime()` function; both represent time at a precision of one nanosecond.

The code provided with this book contains a portable function `uint64_t getTimeNs()` that uses the mentioned APIs to query the highest-precision timer available on the platform and returns the time elapsed since the start of the application in nanoseconds. As discussed in Chapter 34, using 32-bit unsigned integers to hold a value in nanoseconds limits the maximum representable value to $(2^{32} - 1) \times 10^{-9} \approx 4.294$ s so that we need to rely on 64-bit unsigned integers.

35.4.2   Measuring Time on the GPU

The CPU communicates with the GPU through the use of commands that are aggregated in a so-called command buffer. The GPU then asynchronously processes these commands in the order they are submitted. As a consequence, it is impossible to measure the time spent by the GPU executing commands in a synchronous way, as we do for the CPU, without severely affecting the performance. We need to rely on the asynchronous timer query mechanism provided by OpenGL, which is discussed in depth in Chapter 34. In order to support nested markers, we prefer the glQueryCounter mechanism over glBeginQuery/glEndQuery pairs.

A consequence of this is that the profiler cannot display timing information for a given frame until the results of the timer queries issued in this frame become available. Therefore, we record timing information for several frames and display the information related to the most ancient one. We found that a number of NB_RECORDED_FRAMES = 3 recorded frames is sufficient to guarantee that the results of the timer queries are available.

35.4.3 Data Structures

We represent each line, which corresponds to a software or hardware thread, by a C++ structure that contains a fixed-size array of NB_MARKERS_PER_THREAD = NB_RECORDED_FRAMES * MAX_NB_MARKERS_PER_FRAME = 3*100 = 300 markers. We run through this array in a circular fashion while maintaining a read and a write index.

The GPU thread is represented by the structure shown in Listing 35.3. The CPU threads are represented by a very similar structure with an additional identifier for the thread (see Listing 35.4).

The base class Marker encapsulates information that is common to all types of markers. This includes the start and end times of the marker, information on the state at the time the marker was pushed and some identifying information. CPU markers do not need any additional information, while GPU markers also need to store the identifiers for the OpenGL timer queries (see Listing 35.5).

```
struct GpuThreadInfo
{
  GpuMarker markers[NB_GPU_MARKERS];
  int cur_read_id;
  int cur_write_id;
  size_t nb_pushed_markers;

  void init()
  {
    cur_read_id=cur_write_id=0;
    nb_pushed_markers=0;
  }
};
```

Listing 35.3. Data structure for the GPU thread.

```
struct CpuThreadInfo
{
  ThreadId thread_id;
  CpuMarker markers[NB_MARKERS_PER_THREAD];
  int cur_read_id;
  int cur_write_id;
  size_t nb_pushed_markers;

  void init(ThreadId id)
  {
    cur_read_id = cur_write_id = 0;
    nb_pushed_markers = 0;
    thread_id = id;
  }
};
```

Listing 35.4. Data structures for CPU threads.

```
struct Marker
{
  uint64_t start; // Start and end times in nanoseconds
  uint64_t end;   // relative to the start of the application
  size_t layer;   // Number of markers pushed at the time we push this one
  int frame;      // Frame at which the marker was pushed
  char name[MARKER_NAME_MAX_LENGTH];
  Color color;

  Marker() :
    start(INVALID_TIME),
    end(INVALID_TIME),
    frame(-1)
  {} // unused by default
};

typedef Marker CpuMarker;
struct GpuMarker : public Marker
{
  GLuint id_query_start;
  GLuint id_query_end;
};
```

Listing 35.5. Marker structure.

35.4.4 Markers Management

Each thread structure maintains its own circular list of markers. Using circular lists allows us to reuse the same entries several times smoothly while avoiding memory allocations.

When pushing or popping a CPU marker, the profiler needs a way to retrieve the **CpuThreadInfo** corresponding to the calling thread. A possible solution would be to store the **CpuThreadInfo** objects in a hash table, indexed by the thread identifiers. However, this solution imposes the use of a critical section everytime we need to access or modify the hash table, which is unacceptable in our context for performance reasons. Instead, we prefer to rely on a fixed-size array, leaving empty entries at the locations of removed elements (those entries being reused when needed). This way, critical sections can be avoided at the time of searching a **CpuThreadInfo** object by its thread identifier. This comes at a linear cost, which should not be a problem considering the very low number of elements.

Circular list management. Markers are "read" during drawing at the spot indicated by **cur_read_id** and "pushed" at the spot indicated by **cur_write_id**. When pushing, we record the marker's name, color, frame, layer, and start time. Popping is done by starting at the cell **cur_write_id-1**, going backwards while testing for **end != INVALID_TIME**, and updating the value of **end**. This method allows lock-free reading and writing and avoids memory allocations, while maintaining a hierarchy of markers that keeps time coherency.

As shown in Figure 35.2, GPU markers are handled in a similar fashion, the only difference being the use of **glQueryCounter(GL_TIMESTAMP, &id)** and the time of drawing.

Figure 35.2. Circular list of markers.

35.5   Using the Profiler

35.5.1   Levels of Usage

The most basic usage one can make of the profiler is to simply determine the general performance of the application by looking at the length of the total frame. Then, by looking in more detail, we can easily determine the most demanding tasks, as they correspond to the longest rectangles, and identify interesting candidates for optimization. However, such a basic analysis is not enough to determine whether a task is worth the effort of optimizing or not: we need to look at the order in which the tasks are executed, as illustrated in Figure 35.3.

Furthermore, a direct visualization of the task execution enables the programmer to take strategic decisions concerning task ordering. In Figure 35.4, object A is long to update but fast to draw, while object B is long to draw but fast to update. As we can see, different orders of execution yield different performance results.

Such a visualization also makes it easy to determine whether the application is bound by a CPU or by the GPU: the bottleneck corresponds to the thread that ends last. An important point is to avoid surrounding buffer swapping and, generally speaking, thread waiting by profiler push/pop commands, as this results in the synchronization being visualized as a running task.

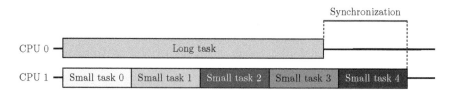

Figure 35.3. Optimizing the longest task is useless as it is not the bottleneck.

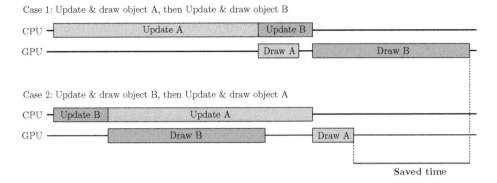

Figure 35.4. Case 1 is longer than case 2, although the execution time for the tasks is the same.

35.5.2   Determining What Should be Measured

As the aim of the profiler is mainly to give a general view of the application's performance state during the development process, the displayed information should be reduced to the minimum most of the time. For example, a GPU could consist of five main markers for shadow maps rendering, G-buffer rendering, lighting calculations, postprocessing, and 2D. However, because of the hierarchical nature of the profiler, it is possible to limit the display to a given layer so that introducing new layers is not a problem and can allow a better granularity when needed.

An interesting alternative would be to give artists the possibility to tune the performances of specific assets, for example, by marking them for profiling during the exporting phase.

35.5.3   Artists

Because they generate the content that is to be treated by the application, artists have a major impact on the final performance. Unfortunately, as they generally have little knowledge of the way the application works, it may be difficult for them to identify their impact on performance. This is why making such a profiling tool accessible to artists is important: by letting them evaluate the implications of their work on general performance, they can tune the parameters of their creations to fit in the imposed timing constraints. Coupled with a live update system of resources, artists can tweak in real time their texture sizes, numbers of vertices, skinning bones numbers, LOD distances, numbers of fur shells, etc., while interacting with the application.

35.5.4   Limitations

The presented profiler can only measure the time spent between markers. Therefore, it is impossible to determine whether the GPU is bound by the texture cache, the vertex shader ALU, the fragment shader ALU, shader-uniform fetching, etc. As a consequence, some testing is needed to determine the correct behavior to adopt to improve GPU performance (e.g., reducing texture size vs. optimizing the number of fragment shader computations).

35.6   Conclusions

We presented a practical method for visualizing in real time the usage of the available processing resources. We use high-precision timers for CPU time measuring and rely on OpenGL timer queries to measure the execution time on the GPU. Compared with external profilers, this approach directly embeds the tool in the application. As a consequence, the information is available on all the supported platforms and can be used throughout the whole development process, making it possible for programmers as well as artists to make strategic decisions regarding performance. Displaying the resources' usage in real time lets us have a general overview of the behavior of the application in real conditions and also allows us to test several use cases for the application without effort.

The code provided with this book (www.openglinsights.com) shows an implementation for the Windows, MacOS X, and Linux platforms that displays an example animation and lets the user visualize in real time the time taken to animate and draw the objects. By hovering the mouse cursor over the markers, the user can display hierarchical timing statistics. Possible improvements include displaying information on the current P-state, which could help in interpreting the results and in multiple-GPUs support. Finally, the system could be ported to other platforms, most notably modern video game consoles.

Bibliography

[AMD 11] AMD. "AMD gDEBugger 6.0." http://developer.amd.com/tools/gdebugger, June 29, 2011.

[Apple, Inc 05] Apple, Inc. "Technical Q&A QA1398 Mach Absolute Time Units." http://developer.apple.com/library/mac/#qa/qa1398/_index.html, January 6, 2005.

[Graphic Remedy 10] Graphic Remedy. "gDEBugger Tutorial." http://www.gremedy.com/tutorial, December 16, 2010.

[Microsoft Corporation 07] Microsoft Corporation. "MSDN." http://support.microsoft.com/kb/172338/en-us, January 20, 2007.

[Microsoft Corporation 11] Microsoft Corporation. "MSDN." http://msdn.microsoft.com/en-us/library/windows/desktop/ms686253%28v=vs.85%29.aspx, September 7, 2011.

[Walbourn 05] Chuck Walbourn. "Game Timing and Multicore Processors." http://msdn.microsoft.com/en-us/library/windows/desktop/ee417693%28v=vs.85%29.aspx, 2005.

Browser Graphics Analysis and Optimizations 36

Chris Dirks and Omar A. Rodriguez

36.1   Introduction

Understanding performance bottlenecks in games helps developers deliver the best gameplay experience. In games, performance bottlenecks are usually grouped in one of two categories: CPU or GPU. Focusing optimization efforts in the appropriate category saves development time and helps get our game running better faster. Optimizing CPU issues when the bottleneck is in the graphics pipeline will result in little to no performance gain and a good amount of frustration. Deploying our game in a web browser complicates the process of isolating bottlenecks. Using the techniques described here, we'll be more successful in identifying the most profitable areas to optimize.

Postprocessing effects have become a standard in AAA games and very often are a performance bottleneck. In this article, we discuss an implementation of the bloom effect in WebGL and its performance characteristics in the browser. Because WebGL runs in a web browser, this poses some special challenges when doing graphics analysis in comparison to a native 3D graphics application. Just as a native application may choose a different code path when detecting a different operating system, the same is true of the browser's implementation of the Canvas or WebGL APIs. Add to this the fact that we'll likely be supporting multiple browsers, and there is the potential for many permutations and a challenge in understanding what happens from "script to pixel." We'll discuss the support for WebGL analysis in common 3D graphics tools and the various implementations of the standard in modern web browsers.

36.2   The Stages of Bloom

The familiarity of the bloom effect in games is one reason it was used for this article. The other major reason is that it is composed of several steps with parameters that can be tweaked to favor quality versus performance. As shown in Figure 36.1, this implementation starts with the original scene rendered to a texture and applies the bloom effect in four major steps:

1. Draw scene to a texture.

2. Identify fragments whose luminance exceeds a threshold.

3. Blur the results of the luminance test.

4. Combine the original rendered scene texture with the blurred highlights.

Each of these steps has parameters that can trade quality for performance. In the luminance step, we can set the luminance threshold to control the number of fragments of the original scene texture that are written to the luminance render target. In the blur step, we can set the number of blur passes and resolution of the render

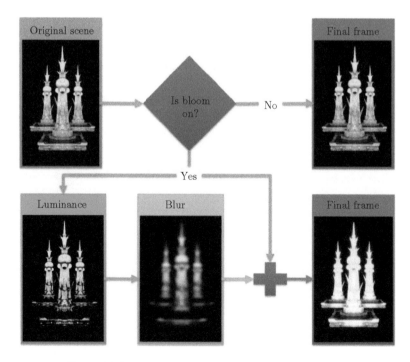

Figure 36.1. Visual representation of the results of each stage.

target to increase/decrease blur quality. In the final step, we can control the weight of the blurred highlights that get combined with the original scene.

Fragments of the original scene that have a luminance value above the luminance threshold are written to the render target. Anything below the luminance threshold is written as black. The number of blur passes determines the number of times the highlights (luminance results) are blurred. The resolution determines the size of the render target used by the blur passes. The weight of the blurred highlights determines how much of the blurred highlights end up in the final frame. We expose some of these parameters as part of the HUD and others are set in code.

The source code that accompanies this chapter is laid out in a simple format to make it easy to follow and understand. The bloom implementation is composed of the following:

- MainLoop (in index.html) takes care of calling update/render loop with the appropriate request-animation frame method for each browser.

- Init (in bloom.js) defines all resources used in the sample, such as shaders, textures, scene objects geometry, and render targets.

- Update (in bloom.js) contains all nonrendering actions such as updating rotations.

- Render (in bloom.js) draws scene geometry, performs luminance test, blurs highlights, and combines results into the final frame.

- bloom-utils.js contains helper functions used to load shaders and textures, parse .obj files, and create geometry.

36.3 Overhead of Bloom

Now that we've described the general implementation of bloom as a postprocessing effect, we'll describe the specifics about our implementation in WebGL. The first thing we measure is the actual overhead of applying bloom to the scene. With the Javascript code in Listing 36.1, we capture a good enough approximation of the frame time to measure overhead and update the scene.

```
var MainLoop = function() {
    nCurrentTime = ( newDate ).getTime();
    fElapsedTime = nCurrentTime - nLastTime;
    nLastTime = nCurrentTime;

    // call Update & Render
    // call requestAnimationFrame( MainLoop );
}
```

Listing 36.1. JavaScript code to approximate frame time.

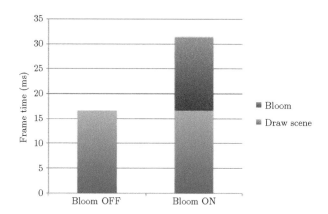

Figure 36.2. Frame time with bloom ON = 1.8 * Frame time with Bloom OFF.

This will measure the time between `requestAnimationFrame` callbacks. Some web browsers may expose performance data at runtime when enabled. For example, running Google Chrome with the `--show-fps-counter` flag displays a frames-per-second counter. With this measurement code in place, introducing bloom approximately doubles our frame time (see Figure 36.2).

The measurements were taken on Google Chrome version 15.0.874.106 running on a prerelease second generation Intel Core processor (Intel microarchitecture code name Sandy Bridge, D1 stepping quad core 2.4 GHz CPU with 4GB DDR3 1333MHz RAM) with Intel HD Graphics 3000 running Windows 7 Ultimate with Service Pack 1. The frame time is composed of the amount of time it takes API calls to set state on the CPU, and the time it takes the GPU to process the draw calls. The JavaScript code above suffices to measure time spent on the CPU. To understand GPU frame time, we'll refer to some offline tools discussed later in this article.

36.4   Analyzing WebGL Applications

Analyzing WebGL applications poses a few interesting challenges because there are many moving parts that have to work together: operating systems, graphics APIs, graphics drivers, browsers, and analysis tools.

36.4.1   Almost Native Graphics Layer (ANGLE)

One of the main challenges when doing analysis on a WebGL application is to understand the difference between running on Windows, Mac OS X, or Linux. On Windows, OpenGL drivers can usually be downloaded from the graphics hardware vendor's website when available. On Mac OS X, OpenGL drivers are part of the system and are updated through the OS update mechanism. On Linux, OpenGL drivers might not be installed by default, but are generally provided through the distribution's package management system or the hardware vendor's website.

For the broadest compatibility on the Windows platform, Chrome and Firefox make use of the Almost Native Graphics Layer Engine [ANGLE 11]. This layer translates OpenGL ES 2.0 calls to DirectX 9 API calls, and translates GLSL shaders to equivalent HLSL shaders. As a user, this translation is completely hidden, but as a developer, this layer is as important as the WebGL application we wrote. ANGLE has a few quirks related to differences in the APIs specifically with buffers and texture fetches. For example, ANGLE does not create/update resources until a draw call is issued, as explained in Chapter 39.

36.4.2 JavaScript profiling

Most modern web browsers have a set of JavaScript developer tools that are prepackaged or can be installed from an extension (see, for example, Figure 36.3). Chrome, Firefox, Internet Explorer, Opera, and Safari have their own JavaScript debuggers

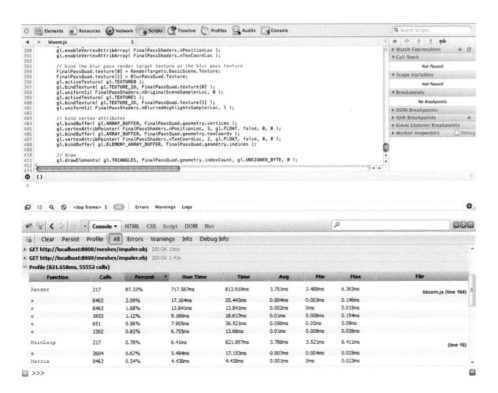

Figure 36.3. Chrome developer tools and Firebug.

and profilers. These help with debugging HTML DOM and network latency issues. JavaScript profilers are helpful in understanding where CPU time is spent. However, these tools don't show contextual information for WebGL beyond the JavaScript API calls.

36.4.3   WebGL Inspector

The other major issue with analyzing a WebGL application is the limited support of tools. WebGL Inspector [Vanik 11] is currently the de facto tool for debugging API calls and understanding bound resources. This tool can capture a frame and show the API calls; state; and bound textures, buffers, and programs. It is available as a Google Chrome extension and as a JavaScript library that can be dropped into our WebGL application—useful when running on browsers other than Chrome. WebGL Inspector, shown in Figure 36.4, is free and available for download from http://benvanik.github.com/WebGL-Inspector/.

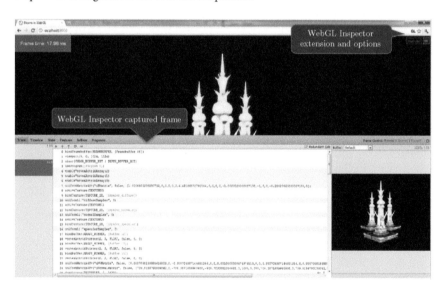

Figure 36.4. WebGL Inspector showing a frame capture of our sample.

36.4.4   Intel Graphics Performance Analyzers (GPA)

A positive side effect of Chrome and Firefox using ANGLE on Windows is that DirectX analysis tools can be used to analyze WebGL applications. In this article, we use Intel GPA Frame Analyzer [Intel 11] to capture frames and analyze the post-translation DirectX draw calls and resources. This article shows frame captures from Intel HD Graphics 3000, but Intel GPA is not restricted to Intel graphics hardware.

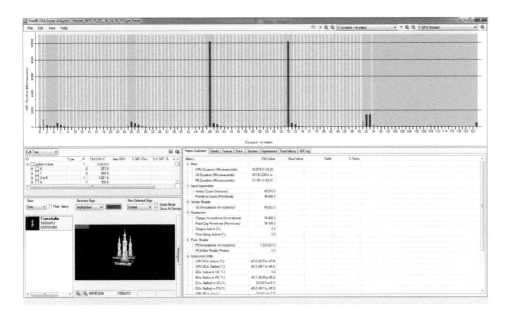

Figure 36.5. Frame Analyzer showing a frame capture of our sample.

Figure 36.5 shows a captured frame of the bloom application described above. You can download Intel GPA for free from http://www.intel.com/software/gpa. Refer to the documentation on the Intel GPA website and the documentation that installs this tool for detailed instructions on capturing frames.

36.5   Analysis Workflow on Windows

In this section, we will learn how to use WebGL Inspector and Intel GPA Frame Analyzer to identify problem areas and/or confirm that our program is doing what we think it is doing. On Windows, WebGL Inspector and Frame Analyzer together show the full graphics pipeline when the browser uses ANGLE. WebGL Inspector shows the WebGL side, and Frame Analyzer shows the post-translation DirectX equivalent. WebGL Inspector works well for tracking down incorrectly bound resources and debugging our graphics code.

Once the WebGL Inspector extension is installed and enabled, or we include the JavaScript library in our project, we should see a "capture" button on the top right. With that said, the first step is to capture a frame with WebGL Inspector and make sure we are binding the correct buffers, shaders, and textures. Figure 36.6 shows the "Programs" tab where all shaders used by the WebGL application are displayed as well as the status, uniform, and attribute information. This tab will also display shader

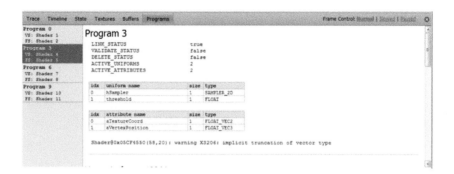

Figure 36.6. Confirming correct shaders are bound with WebGL Inspector.

compilation and link errors. The other tabs in WebGL Inspector show detailed information about the other resources such as buffer contents for bound buffers and texture resolution for all bound textures. WebGL Inspector also shows previews for resources such as vertex buffers and textures. The previews can help as a sanity check to make sure the correct mesh or texture is bound when making a draw call.

Unlike WebGL Inspector, Intel GPA is not integrated into the web browser through an extension or JavaScript library. In addition, capturing a frame gets a bit more interesting because of the multiprocess architecture of some browsers like Google Chrome. Intel GPA can attach to the Chrome process on launch, but the process that handles the rendering calls is a child process of the main Chrome process. Fortunately, starting Chrome with a `--no-sandbox` flag allows GPA to attach to the correct rendering process and trigger frame captures. Note that running Chrome with a `--no-sandbox` flag will not change performance characteristics but will change the security characteristics of the browser. For this reason, this flag should never be used for general browsing.

36.5.1   Tracking Down API Calls

After capturing a frame and opening it with Frame Analyzer, we will see a visualization of all draw calls in the captured frame, as shown in Figure 36.5. Each `Draw`, `Clear`, and `StretchRect` call is shown as a bar whose height is by default set to GPU duration. At first glance, this visualization shows the order in which geometry is drawn as well as which calls are most expensive. `Draw` calls are blue bars, `Clear` calls are light blue bars, and `StretchRect` calls are dark red/magenta bars. The light gray bars are markers for render target changes. `Draw/Clear/StretchRect` calls in between two light gray bars affect the same render target. The labels in Figure 36.7 are not a feature of Frame Analyzer but were added for clarity.

Looking at Figure 36.7, we can see that the tall bars correspond to the blur passes, which is expected since that fragment shader is the bulk of the work in this

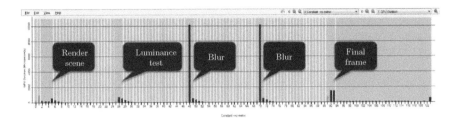

Figure 36.7. Draw call visualization in Frame Analyzer of a frame capture in Google Chrome.

application. Looking closer at the frame, we can see where the scene is drawn, where the luminance test happens, the blur passes, and the final composition of the frame. It is also clear from Figure 36.7 that there are more draw calls in the visualization than what the WebGL Inspector API log shows. If we look at the calls in between the luminance test and the first blur pass, we will notice that they seem to be redrawing the luminance results but using a lower-resolution render target. Comparing this to the API log from WebGL Inspector, we notice that the only thing happening between the `gl.drawArrays` call and the beginning of the blur pass marked by `gl.bindFramebuffer` is this piece of code:

```
gl.bindTexture( gl.TEXTURE_2D, RenderTargets.HighPass.Texture );
gl.generateMipmap( gl.TEXTURE_2D );
```

There aren't any noticeable draw calls in that piece of code. But in Windows, `gl.generateMipmap( gl.TEXTURE_2D )` is translated to multiple draw calls by ANGLE. A quick peek at the ANGLE source code (src/libGLESv2/Texture.cpp) [ANGLE 11] that translates **generateMipmap** to DirectX 9 shows the following:

```
// ...snipsnip
for (unsigned int i = 1; i<= q; i++)
{
    IDirect3DSurface9 *upper = NULL;
    IDirect3DSurface9 *lower = NULL;
    mTexture->GetSurfaceLevel(i-1, &upper);
    mTexture->GetSurfaceLevel(i, &lower);

    if (upper != NULL && lower != NULL)
    {
        getBlitter()->boxFilter(upper, lower);
    }
    if (upper != NULL) upper->Release();
    if (lower != NULL) lower->Release();
    mImageArray[i].dirty = false;
}
// ...snipsnip
```

In short, `getBlitter()->boxFilter( upper, lower )` results in a draw call and because it's in a loop, it's called multiple times, creating all the extra draw calls we see in Figure 36.7 between the different phases. Since it's creating all the mipmaps for the previous draw based on the resolution of the render target used, reducing the initial render target resolution will not only reduce the work that each pass needs to do, but it will also reduce the number of mipmaps created.

Looking at Figure 36.7, we can see that each labeled region begins with a `Clear` (light blue), followed by one or more `Draw` (blue) calls, and ends with a `StretchRect` (dark red). Like the name suggests, `StretchRect` will stretch the results to the bound render target to fit the viewport. In some cases, it might be an undesirable effect, but it mostly works well to fill the viewport with our scene. Unfortunately, this results in another hidden call that is unaccounted for compared to the API log in WebGL Inspector.

36.6   Optimized Bloom

Now that we understand how to analyze the graphics side of our sample with WebGL Inspector and Intel GPA, we can begin using that information to make changes to our code where it will have the most impact. As clearly shown in Figure 36.8, the blur passes are the bottleneck in our bloom implementation. Using Intel GPA Frame Analyzer, we see that these two calls make up approximately 63% of the frame time.

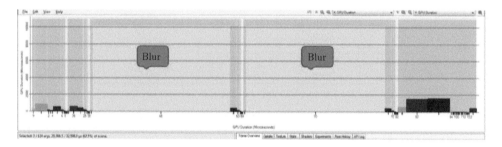

Figure 36.8. The tallest and thickest bars are the blur calls.

36.6.1   Lower Render Target Resolution

In our implementation, we have exposed two parameters we can tweak for the blur: number of passes and render-target resolution. From Figure 36.8, we can see that there are only two blur passes, which is fairly low and gives us good quality. Lowering the resolution of the render target we use for the blur passes will have two effects: reducing the number of fragments processed and the number of extra draw

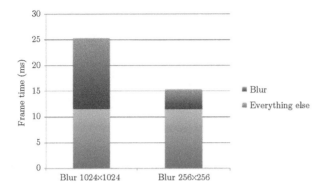

Figure 36.9. Performance impact of lowering resolution of blur render target (frame time in this graph refers to GPU frame time as reported by Intel GPA Frame Analyzer).

calls caused by `gl.generateMipmap`, as discussed above. After lowering the resolution to one quarter of the original resolution, we notice that the two blur passes are now only approximately 11% of rendering. That is a significant performance improvement, as shown in Figure 36.9, with an easy code change.

Looking at Figure 36.10, it's hard to tell the difference by just looking at the final frames, even in WebGL Inspector, since the quality was not noticeably degraded.

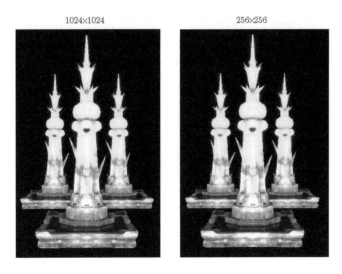

Figure 36.10. Original final frame with 1024 × 1024 blur render target and after lowering the resolution of the blur render target to 256 × 256.

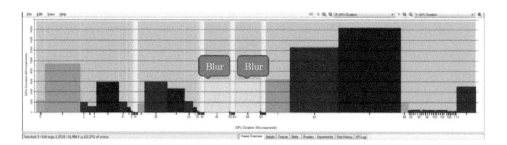

Figure 36.11. Blur calls are no longer the most expensive.

However, we can confirm the improvement in Intel GPA by capturing a new frame, as shown in Figure 36.11.

We could go with an even lower resolution, but there is a point where the quality might be affected. In this case, lowering the resolution works well and produces acceptable results because we are working with a blur. For other applications, lowering the resolution might not be the solution.

36.6.2 Unnecessary Mipmap Generation

As discussed in Section 36.5.1, there was a call to `generateMipmap` after every bloom stage. In Windows, this resulted in several more API calls than we could account for in the WebGL Inspector log and the code. Originally, we were planning to map the render target textures to quads and display them all on screen to show the bloom stages. We discarded that idea and instead we map each bloom stage to a fullscreen quad. The bloom stages' results can be displayed one at a time. This allowed us to remove the call to `generateMipmap` and thus remove all the extra API calls. This can be confirmed by comparing Figures 36.7 and 36.12.

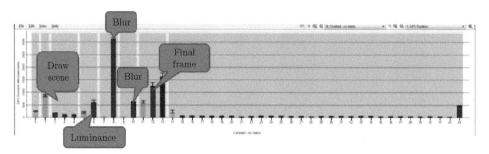

Figure 36.12. Frame capture after removing `generateMipmap`.

36.6.3   Floating-Point Framebuffers

After removing the call to `generateMipmap` in between bloom stages, we looked into the `OES_texture_float` extension to enable floating-point buffers. Originally, we used `gl.UNSIGNED_BYTE` as the format for the framebuffer, which created A8R8G8B8 framebuffers. With the `OES_texture_float` extension enabled, we create floating-point buffers by passing `gl.FLOAT` as the texture format. This creates A32R32G32B32F framebuffers. After lowering the resolution and removing unnecessary mipmap generation, it allows us to create higher-quality blur for approximately the same cost. The code change happened in our `MakeRenderTarget` function (see Listing 36.2).

```
var MakeRenderTarget = function( gl, nWidth, nHeight ) {
    // create the new framebuffer

    // use floating point framebuffers if OES_texture_float extension exists
    var nTexFormat = ( gl.getExtension( "OES_texture_float" ) ) ? gl.FLOAT :
        gl.UNSIGNED_BYTE;

    // create the offscreen texture
    var pTexture = gl.createTexture();
    gl.bindTexture( gl.TEXTURE_2D, pTexture );
    gl.texParameteri( gl.TEXTURE_2D, gl.TEXTURE_MAG_FILTER, gl.NEAREST );
    gl.texParameteri( gl.TEXTURE_2D, gl.TEXTURE_MIN_FILTER, gl.NEAREST );
    gl.texParameteri( gl.TEXTURE_2D, gl.TEXTURE_WRAP_S , gl.CLAMP_TO_EDGE );
    gl.texParameteri( gl.TEXTURE_2D, gl.TEXTURE_WRAP_T , gl.CLAMP_TO_EDGE );
    gl.texImage2D( gl.TEXTURE_2D, 0, gl.RGBA, pFrameBuffer.width,
        pFrameBuffer.height, 0, gl.RGBA, nTexFormat, null );

    // create the offscreen depth buffer
    // attach texture and depth buffer to framebuffer
    // reset bindings to defaults

    return { "FrameBuffer" : pFrameBuffer ,
            "Texture" : pTexture,
            "Depth" : pDepthBuffer ,
            "Width" : nWidth ,
            "Height" : nHeight
        };
}
```

Listing 36.2. Creating floating-point frame buffers with `OES_texture_float`.

According to [Lipchak 05], it requires **NEAREST** magnification filter and **NEAREST** and **NEAREST_MIPMAP_NEAREST** minification filters to be supported. For the bloom sample, we draw these textures in a way that does not need the minification filter, so we set both to `gl.NEAREST`.

36.7   Conclusion

Support for WebGL is progressing at a steady pace and is helping the browser become a viable development and distribution platform for games with higher-quality graphics. Like any other platform, getting the best performance allows our games to shine and improve the gameplay experience. Tools play an important role in helping game and graphics developers deliver these experiences in the browser. In this article, we presented several tools that work well with WebGL applications and explained some of the areas where potential bottlenecks might appear in the current implementations on Windows. In short, developers should understand the differences between hardware platforms and operating systems to get the best performance. The web browser has always been a way to abstract away the hardware and OS, but with WebGL we're getting closer to these layers and can now use that to our advantage.

Bibliography

[ANGLE 11] ANGLE. "ANGLE: Almost Native Graphics Layer Engine." http://code.google. com/p/angleproject/, December 15, 2011.

[Intel 11] Intel. "Intel Graphics Performance Analyzers 4.3." http://www.intel.com/software/ gpa, December 15, 2011.

[Lipchak 05] BenjLipchak.   "OES_texture_float".   http://www.khronos.org/registry/gles/ extensions/OES/OES_texture_float.txt, November 9, 2011.

[Vanik 11] Ben Vanik. "WebGL Inspector: An advanced WebGL debugging toolkit." http:// benvanik.github.com/WebGL-Inspector/, July 29, 2011.

Performance State Tracking 37

Aleksandar Dimitrijević

37.1   Introduction

Reducing power consumption and dissipation is one of the predominant goals of all modern integrated circuit designs. Besides the design-time optimizations, all CPU/GPU vendors implement various real-time methods to reduce power consumption while preserving acceptable performance. One of the consequences of power management is a dynamic change in working frequencies and, hence, the overall performance capabilities of the system. Modern GPUs, for both desktop and mobile platforms, can be very aggressive in changing working frequencies according to the current load.

Consider a simple case of rendering a triangle on a system with an NVIDIA GeForce GTX 470 graphics card. NVIDIA drivers raise the frequencies to the highest level instantly if they detect a 3D application. Even a creation of the OpenGL rendering context is enough to make the GPU enter the highest performance state. The moment the application starts, the GPU frequency is 607.5 MHz, while the memory IO bus frequency is 1674 MHz. A frame rendering time is less than 0.16 ms for the full HD MSAA 8x screen and the GPU utilization is about 0%. After a dozen seconds, since the utilization is extremely low, the GPU enters a lower performance state. The frame rendering time is changed to about 0.24 ms. Since the GPU remains at low utilization, the performance is further reduced. After changing four performance levels, the GPU finally enters the lowest performance state with the GPU frequency at 50.5 MHz, and memory IO bus frequency at 101 MHz. The rendering capabilities are reduced by an order of magnitude, while the frame rendering time rises up to 1.87 ms. If we do not track the performance state, we are not able to interpret measured results correctly. Furthermore, for less demanding applications, it is possible to get shorter execution time on some older and less powerful graphics cards because their lower performance states may involve much higher frequencies.

37.2   Power Consumption Policies

For many years, graphics card vendors have been developing a highly advanced form of dynamic power management (DPM). DPM estimates the relative workload and aggressively conserves power when the workload is low. Power consumption is controlled by changing voltage levels, GPU frequencies, and memory-clock frequencies. A set of values that define the current power consumption and performance capabilities of the graphics card is known as a *performance state* (P-state).

NVIDIA defines sixteen P-states, where P0 is the highest P-state, and P15 is the idle state. Not all P-states are present on a given system. The state P0 is activated whenever a 3D application is detected. If the utilization is below some threshold for a certain period of time, the P-state is changed to a lower level.

AMD defines three P-states, where P0 is the lowest, and P2 is the highest performance state. P0 is the starting state, and it is changed only by demanding applications. The latest AMD technology, known as PowerTune [AMD 10], defines a whole range of working frequencies in the highest P-state. When the GPU reaches the thermal design power (TDP) limits, the GPU frequency is gradually decreased while maintaining the high power state. This enables much better performance for demanding applications, while preserving acceptable power level.

Having in mind such advanced power-management scenarios, a fair comparison of different rendering algorithms cannot be done on a frame-rate basis only. If the same or an even lower frame-rate is achieved in the lower P-state, it certainly qualifies the algorithm as more efficient, or at least less demanding. That is why P-state tracking is an important part of profiling software. So far, OpenGL doesn't have a capability to track P-states; thus, we will take a look at how it can be implemented using vendor-specific APIs: NVAPI for NVIDIA and ADL for AMD hardware.

37.3   P-State Tracking Using NVAPI

NVAPI is NVIDIA's core API that allows direct access to NVIDIA drivers on all Microsoft Windows platforms [NVIDIA 11c], and it is shipped as a DLL with the drivers.[1] NVAPI has to be statically linked to an application; hence, a software development kit (SDK) has been released with appropriate static library and

---

[1] The official documentation states that NVAPI is supported by drivers since Release 81.20 (R81.20), but there are problems in accessing most of its functionality through the SDK in pre-R195 drivers. The first NVAPI SDK was released with R195 in October 2009. Since R256 drivers, all settings have become wide open to change with NVAPI.

header files.[2] It is both forward and backward compatible. Calling a function that is not implemented in the current version of the DLL only returns a NVAPI_NO_ IMPLEMENTATION error and does not result in an application crash [NVIDIA 11a].

When reading or changing some driver parameters, communication with the drivers is session-based [NVIDIA 11a]. An application has to create a session, load system settings into the session, get a profile, and finally read or write some setting to the profile. All driver settings are organized into profiles. Some profiles are shipped with the driver as Predefined Profiles, while others are created by the user as User Profiles. A profile can have an arbitrary number of applications associated to it, while each application can be associated with only a single profile. A profile associated with applications is called an Application Profile. If the application is not associated with a certain Application Profile, or the specific setting is not defined in the associated profile, the Current Global Profile is used. All profiles that are not associated with applications are called Global Profiles. Only one of the Global Profiles can be selected as the Current Global Profile. If the setting is not found in the Current Global Profile, the Base Profile is used. The Base Profile is system wide, and its settings are automatically applied as defaults.

The driver's settings are loaded and applied at the moment when the driver DLL is initialized. If the settings are changed during the application execution, the application has to be restarted in order to take advantage of new settings. Considering OpenGL, NVAPI offers the ability to configure OpenGL Expert Mode, its feedback and reporting mechanism.

P-states tracking does not require reading or changing any driver settings, which eliminates the need for sessions and profile manipulation. The only required step is to initialize NVAPI through **the NvAPI_Initialize** function call.

37.3.1 GPU Utilization

The GPU utilization directly affects the current P-state. High utilization activates a higher P-state if the GPU is not in the highest state already. The function that can be used to retrieve utilization is NvAPI_GPU_GetDynamicPstatesInfoEx. Unlike its name would suggest, the function does not tell which P-state the GPU is currently in, but rather information about the utilization in the current state. The utilization is defined over three GPU domains:

- graphic engine (GPU),

- framebuffer (FB), and

- video engine (VID).

The official documentation [NVIDIA 11c] states that P-state thresholds can also be retrieved, although this functionality is not yet exposed through the SDK.

---

[2]http://developer.nvidia.com/nvapi

```
#define UTIL_DOMAIN_GPU 0
#define UTIL_DOMAIN_FB 1
#define UTIL_DOMAIN_VID 2

NvPhysicalGpuHandle m_hPhysicalGPU[NVAPI_MAX_PHYSICAL_GPUS];
NvU32 m_gpuCount;
NV_GPU_DYNAMIC_PSTATES_INFO_EX m_DynamicPStateInfo;
NvAPI_EnumPhysicalGPUs(m_hPhysicalGPU, &m_gpuCount);
m_DynamicPStateInfo.version = NV_GPU_DYNAMIC_PSTATES_INFO_EX_VER;
NvU32 utilGPU, utilFB, utilVID;

NvAPI_Status status = NvAPI_GPU_GetDynamicPstatesInfoEx(m_hPhysicalGPU[0], &↵
    m_DynamicPStateInfo);

if(status == NVAPI_OK ){
    utilGPU = m_DynamicPStateInfo.utilization[UTIL_DOMAIN_GPU].percentage;
    utilFB  = m_DynamicPStateInfo.utilization[UTIL_DOMAIN_FB].percentage;
    utilVID = m_DynamicPStateInfo.utilization[UTIL_DOMAIN_VID].percentage;
}
```

Listing 37.1. Reading GPU utilization using NVAPI.

Since the system can have multiple GPUs, `NvAPI_GPU_GetDynamicPstates InfoEx` requires a handle to a physical GPU for which utilization should be retrieved. The total number of physical GPUs and the handles to them can be retrieved with `NvAPI_EnumPhysicalGPUs`. Listing 37.1 illustrates reading GPU utilization using NVAPI. The utilization is read for the default graphics adapter (`m_hPhysicalGPU[0]`).

All NVAPI functions require setting a proper value for the `version` field of the structures passed to them as parameters. For the structures defined in the SDK, the proper values of the *version* fields are defined as `<structure_name>_VER`.

The retrieved utilization value is not a single clock-interval sample, but an averaged value over the last second. If the GPU utilization drops below a certain threshold, depending on the mutual relationship of two adjacent P-states, the next lower state is activated. Experimental results show that the lower threshold varies from 5% to 30%. If GPU utilization crosses the upper threshold (usually about 60%), the next higher level is activated. The threshold values may vary depending on the hardware, P-state settings, and the driver's policy. The transition to a lower P-state requires having a low utilization for about 15 s for pre-R280 drivers on Windows, while the transition to a higher P-state is instantaneous. Starting from R280, NVIDIA decreases the amount of time required at low GPU utilization before transitioning to a lower P-state [NVIDIA 11c].

37.3.2 Reading P-States

All available P-states of a physical GPU, with accompanying parameters, can be retrieved using the `NvAPI_GPU_GetPstatesInfoEx` function, which has three parameters:

- a handle to a physical GPU,

- a pointer to an NV_GPU_PERF_PSTATES_INFO structure, and

- input flags.

Input flags are allocated to define various options, but currently, only bit 0 is used to select whether the returned values are the defaults, or the current settings. The current settings might differ from the defaults if the GPU is overclocked.

If a call to NvAPI_GPU_GetPstatesInfoEx succeeds, an NV_GPU_PERF_PSTATES_INFO structure is filled with parameters regarding P-states. In the version of NVAPI shipped with R290 drivers, NV_GPU_PERF_PSTATES_INFO contains the following fields:

- version. Version of NV_GPU_PERF_PSTATES_INFO; it should be set to NV_GPU_PERF_PSTATES_INFO_VER before calling the function.

- flags. Reserved for future use.

- numPstates. Number of available P-states.

- numClocks. Number of domains for which clocks are defined; there are currently three public clock domains: NVAPI_GPU_PUBLIC_CLOCK_GRAPHICS, NVAPI_GPU_PUBLIC_CLOCK_MEMORY, and NVAPI_GPU_PUBLIC_CLOCK_PROCESSOR.

- numVoltages. Number of domains for which voltages are defined; currently, only one domain is presented: NVAPI_GPU_PERF_VOLTAGE_INFO_DOMAIN_CORE.

- pstates[16]. Parameters of each P-state:

    ○ pstateId. ID of the P-state (0...15),

    ○ flags:

        · bit 0. PCI-e limit (version 1 or 2),
        · bit 1. P-state is overclocked,
        · bit 2. P-state can be overclocked,
        · bits 3–31. Reserved for future use.

- clocks[32]:

    ○ domainId. Domain for which the particular clock is defined: NVAPI_GPU_PUBLIC_CLOCK_GRAPHICS, NVAPI_GPU_PUBLIC_CLOCK_MEMORY, or NVAPI_GPU_PUBLIC_CLOCK_PROCESSOR,

    ○ flags:

        · bit 0. Clock domain can be overclocked,
        · bits 1–31. Reserved for future use,

○ `freq`. Clock frequency in kHz.

- `voltages[16]`:

  ○ `domainId`. Domain for which the voltage is defined (`NVAPI_GPU_PERF_VOLTAGE_INFO_DOMAIN_CORE`),

  ○ `flags`. Reserved for future use,

  ○ `mvolt`. Voltage in mV.

The current P-state ID of a physical GPU is retrieved using `NvAPI_GPU_GetCurrentPstate`. Unlike `NvAPI_GPU_GetPstatesInfoEx`, which should be called only once, usually during the application initialization; `NvAPI_GPU_GetCurrentPstate` must be called frequently, at least once per frame.

Unfortunately, the NVAPI SDK does not expose all the functionality of NVAPI. Most of the functionality is available only in the NDA version of the SDK. Furthermore, the official documentation refers to some functions and structures that are not included even in NDA version. We hope that more functions will be published in the future.

37.4   P-State Tracking Using ADL

AMD Display Library (ADL) is an API that allows access to various graphics driver settings. It is a wrapper around a private API for both Windows and Linux. ADL binaries are delivered as a part of the Catalyst display driver package for Windows or Linux, while the SDK (documentation, definitions, and sample code) can be downloaded from the website.[3]

P-state management is exposed openly through the ADL OverDrive Version 5 (OD5) API. OD5 provides access to the engine clock, memory clock, and core voltage level. Each state component can be read and also changed within some predefined range. The range is defined inside the BIOS of the graphics card and prevents hardware malfunctioning.

P-states have to be enumerated in an ascending order, with each component having the same or a greater value compared to the previous state. If the rule is violated, the state will not be set. Custom settings are not preserved after a system restart, and should be maintained by the application. Since the standard P-state settings are determined through a comprehensive qualification process, it is not recommended to change them. We will confine our interaction with OD5 only to P-state tracking. Listing 37.2 illustrates how the current P-state setting can be read.

All relevant parameters of the current P-state can be retrieved using the `ADL_Overdrive5_CurrentActivity_Get` function call. The values are stored in an

---

[3]http://developer.amd.com/sdks/ADLSDK/Pages/default.aspx

```
typedef int (*ADL_OVERDRIVE5_CURRENTACTIVITY_GET) (int, ADLPMActivity *);

HINSTANCE hDLL = LoadLibrary(_T("atiadlxx.dll")); // try to load native DLL
if(hDLL == NULL){        // if fails (32-bit app on 64-bit OS), load 32-bit DLL
    hDLL = LoadLibrary(_T("atiadlxy.dll"));
}

ADL_Overdrive5_CurrentActivity_Get = (ADL_OVERDRIVE5_CURRENTACTIVITY_GET)←
    GetProcAddress( hDLL, "ADL_Overdrive5_CurrentActivity_Get");
ADLPMActivity activity;

activity.iSize = sizeof(ADLPMActivity);
ADL_Overdrive5_CurrentActivity_Get (0, &activity);
```

Listing 37.2. Retrieving the current P-state parameters using ADL OverDrive5.

`ADLPMActivity` structure, which, among others, contains the following P-state members:

- `iCurrentPerformanceLevel`. Current P-state ID,

- `iEngineClock`. GPU engine clock in tens of kHz,

- `iMemoryClock`. Memory clock in tens of kHz,

- `iVddc`. Core voltage level in mV, and

- `iActivityPercent`. GPU utilization in %.

The greatest advantage of the OD5 P-state tracking is its simplicity. All parameters are retrieved with a single function call. Each P-state is uniquely identified by **iCurrentPerformanceLevel**, where a higher value corresponds to a higher P-state. The first parameter of the **ADL_Overdrive5_CurrentActivity_Get** is the adapter index. The previous example assumes the default adapter; hence, the value is 0.

37.5   Conclusion

P-states tracking is essential for all profilers. Each measured value should be stamped with the current state in order to be properly interpreted and filter out unwanted values. Special care must be taken during the interpretation, since the state change might be recorded with one-frame delay. So, not only the current state is important, but also the frame in which a transition occurs. Another problem can arise if the state transition happens during the measured interval that spans multiple frames. If we measure frequent or periodical events, the intervals that enclose state changes could be just ignored. In the case of events that are not periodic, we should subdivide the measured interval in order to catch the frame in which the transition occurs.

The performance state policies differ widely according to graphics hardware, current drivers, and vendors' preferences. NVIDIA aggressively raises the P-state to the highest value as soon as a 3D application is detected. If the application is less demanding, the P-state is gradually decreased. AMD has a different policy and starts with the lowest performance state. In the case of both vendors, the GPU utilization is tracked precisely, and the P-state is changed accordingly.

Thus far, OpenGL does not have the ability to track P-states. In order to reach all relevant parameters, like working frequencies or GPU utilization, we have to use vendor-specific APIs. NVAPI gathers detailed information, but most of its functionality is still hidden, while ADL openly provides an easy-to-use interface to the required information, and, furthermore, enables customization of P-states parameters. Since power consumption becomes more and more important with each new generation of graphics cards, we can expect a further development of P-state-accessing APIs. Perhaps even OpenGL will provide an insight into what is really happening beneath the powerful graphics cards' coolers.

Bibliography

[AMD 10] AMD. "AMD PowerTune Technology." http://www.amd.com/us/Documents/PowerTune_Technology_Whitepaper.pdf, December 2010.

[NVIDIA 11a] NVIDIA. "NVIDIA Driver Settings Programming Guide." PG-5116-001-v02, http://developer.download.nvidia.com/assets/tools/docs/PG-5116-001_v02_public.pdf, January 19, 2011.

[NVIDIA 11b] NVIDIA. "Understanding Dynamic GPU Performance Mode, Release 280 Graphics Drivers for Windows—Version 280.26." RN-W28026-01v02, http://us.download.nvidia.com/Windows/280.26/280.26-Win7-WinVista-Desktop-Release-Notes.pdf, August 9, 2011.

[NVIDIA 11c] NVIDIA. "NVAPI Reference Documentation (Developer)," Release 285, http://developer.nvidia.com/nvapi, September 15, 2011.

Monitoring Graphics Memory Usage 38

Aleksandar Dimitrijević

38.1 Introduction

The struggle to achieve higher levels of realism in computer graphics always leads to high memory demands. Despite the fact that modern graphics accelerators are equipped with more and more onboard memory with each new generation, applications' demands grow even faster. Since memory is a limited and expensive resource, an application needs tools to help it make clever decisions on how this resource can be used more effectively.

Until several years ago, OpenGL implementations hid resource management from applications. The resource shielding was justified by stating that it enabled a hardware abstraction and a higher level of portability. However, the knowledge about the environment in which an application is executing is more than useful. There is a wide variety of graphics cards, each card with different GPU power and an arbitrary amount of onboard memory. Furthermore, nowadays many computers are equipped with more than one graphics card that can be used for scalable rendering (see Chapter 27). Which of them should be used for a specific task depends on their capabilities (see Chapter 9). Even on a single-accelerator system, an application can make wise decisions, like which level of detail or algorithms to apply, according to available resources. Knowledge about the maximum available resources is useful for the initial setup, but the current state must be tracked during the whole application's life. The reasons for varying available resources can be various, from the complexity of the current scene to a competition between different applications for the same resource.

In this chapter, we take a look at graphics memory allocation and how its current status can be retrieved using two vendor-specific OpenGL extensions.

38.2   Graphics Memory Allocation

Graphics memory can be classified into two major categories: dedicated and shared. *Dedicated graphics memory* is memory associated with the graphics subsystem, and it is exclusively accessed by graphics applications. It can be either onboard memory (dedicated video memory) or a portion of system memory (system video memory). Onboard memory is a "privilege" of discrete graphics adapters. It usually uses a wide and high-speed local bus, resulting in much better performance compared to system memory. Integrated graphics adapters can only use portions of system memory as dedicated video memory. The allocation of system video memory can be done by BIOS or by a driver. System BIOS allocation is done at a system startup, effectively hiding a portion of the memory from the operating system, while driver's memory allocation happens during operating system boot. In the second case, the operating system reports dedicated graphics memory as a part of system memory although it is exclusively owned by the graphics driver and cannot be used for other purposes.

Shared system memory is a portion of the system memory that can be used by the graphics subsystem when needed. This memory can be used by nongraphics applications as well; hence, there is no guarantee that it is available. The amount of shared system memory reported by the operating system, like Vista or Windows 7, is the maximum amount. The actual amount depends on the system load. More detailed information about memory classification and reporting through Windows Display Driver Model (WDDM) can be found in [Microsoft 06].

Total available graphics memory is a sum of dedicated graphics memory and shared system memory. The highest performance is achieved if the graphics objects are stored in dedicated graphics memory. However, in some applications, the capacity of dedicated memory is not enough to store all objects. If newly allocated objects, or objects currently being used, cannot be stored in dedicated memory, the driver has to evict some of the objects already stored in order to make space for new ones. An GL_OUT_OF_MEMORY exception should be raised only if the object cannot be allocated in dedicated or in shared system memory.

Querying memory status is not a part of the OpenGL core functionality, but the two major graphics cards' vendors have published some useful extensions for the purpose. The following sections give a closer look at those extensions.

38.3 Querying Memory Status on NVIDIA Cards

Since Release 195 of NVIDIA graphics drivers, the current memory status is accessible through the experimental OpenGL extension: NVX_gpu_memory_info [Stroyan 09]. This extension defines several new enumerations that can be passed to glGet Integerv in order to retrieve specific information. The symbolical names and the corresponding hexadecimal values are the following:

- GL_GPU_MEMORY_INFO_DEDICATED_VIDMEM_NVX (0x9047),

- GL_GPU_MEMORY_INFO_TOTAL_AVAILABLE_MEMORY_NVX (0x9048),

- GL_GPU_MEMORY_INFO_CURRENT_AVAILABLE_VIDMEM_NVX (0x9049),

- GL_GPU_MEMORY_INFO_EVICTION_COUNT_NVX (0x904A), and

- GL_GPU_MEMORY_INFO_EVICTED_MEMORY_NVX (0x904B).

The hexadecimal values are listed because NVX_gpu_memory_info is an experimental extension, and as such, its enumerations are not part of the standard OpenGL extension header file: glext.h.

GL_GPU_MEMORY_INFO_DEDICATED_VIDMEM_NVX retrieves the total size of dedicated graphics memory in kB. This value needs to be read only once since it will not change during the application's life. NVX_gpu_memory_info enables reading only the size of the dedicated graphics memory. The sizes of shared system memory can be retrieved only by using WDDM [Microsoft 06] or NVAPI [NVIDIA 11].

GL_GPU_MEMORY_INFO_TOTAL_AVAILABLE_MEMORY_NVX retrieves the maximum available dedicated graphics memory in kB. This value may differ from the total size of dedicated graphics memory if the certain amount of the memory is allocated for a special purpose. However, in many implementations, the value is identical to a dedicated memory total size. This information also doesn't need to be read by the application more than once.

GL_GPU_MEMORY_INFO_CURRENT_AVAILABLE_VIDMEM_NVX retrieves the currently free dedicated graphics memory in kB. This is one of the most important values that the application should track. If the current amount of free graphics memory is not enough to store new objects, OpenGL starts to swap objects between dedicated and shared system memory, significantly affecting the overall performance. The swapping may start even if the total amount of free memory is enough to store newly created objects because of memory fragmentation.

GL_GPU_MEMORY_INFO_EVICTION_COUNT_NVX retrieves the count of evictions since the operating system or an application start. For Windows XP and Linux, the eviction count is a per-process information. The count is reset with the application start, and as long as it is 0, object swapping has not started yet; therefore, the application runs at full speed. For Windows Vista and Windows 7, the eviction information is system wide, and the eviction count is not 0 on the first query. The eviction count is an important piece of information that should be tracked. The rise of the eviction count signals memory overload and drop of performance.

GL_GPU_MEMORY_INFO_EVICTED_MEMORY_NVX retrieves the amount of evicted memory. It is the total size of all objects removed from the dedicated memory in order to make space for new allocations. In Version 1.2 of NVX_gpu_memory_info, each query resets the eviction count and the size of the evicted memory. In Version 1.3, the values increase with each new eviction.

Although NVX_gpu_memory_info enables efficient memory-allocation tracking on NVIDIA graphics cards, some pieces of information are still missing. One of them is the size of the maximum free memory block. Knowing this, we can predict evictions more precisely and have better insight into the drivers' memory defragmentation algorithm. The other missing piece of information is the shared-system memory-allocation size. We can read a cumulative amount of evicted memory only, but it cannot be used to calculate a shared system memory allocation size.

38.4   Querying Memory Status on AMD Cards

On AMD graphics cards, memory information is retrieved using the ATI_meminfo [Stefanizzi 09] OpenGL extension. It is also based on the glGetIntegerv function, but unlike NVIDIA's counterpart, it retrieves a 4-tuple instead of simple integers. Information on free graphics memory is retrieved by specifying one of the three memory pools:

- GL_VBO_FREE_MEMORY_ATI. Memory status for the pool used for vertex buffer objects,

- GL_TEXTURE_FREE_MEMORY_ATI. Memory status for the pool used for textures, or

- GL_RENDERBUFFER_FREE_MEMORY_ATI. Memory status for the pool used for render buffers.

For each pool, a 4-tuple integer is returned containing the following information:

- param[0]. Total dedicated graphics memory free in kB,

- param[1]. Largest available dedicated graphics memory free block in kB,

- param[2]. Total shared system memory free in kB, and

- param[3]. Largest shared system memory free block in kB.

```
UINT maxCount;
UINT* ID;
size_t memTotal = 0;   // total size of dedicated graphics memory in MB
maxCount = wglGetGPUIDsAMD(0, 0);
ID = new UINT[maxCount];
wglGetGPUIDsAMD(maxCount, ID);
wglGetGPUInfoAMD(ID[0], WGL_GPU_RAM_AMD, GL_UNSIGNED_INT, sizeof(size_t), & ↩
    memTotal);
```

Listing 38.1. Querying dedicated graphics memory size using WGL_AMD_gpu_association.

The pools can be independent or shared, depending on the implementation. Thus far, each of the pools maps the whole graphics memory, and the same values are retrieved for all pools (shared implementation). A returned value does not need to reveal the exact information, but instead, it could return a conservative value of 80% of actual availability. The precise values for the free memory space, for both NVIDIA's and AMD's extensions are not of paramount concern. From the moment when the information is retrieved to the moment of new allocation, even if it is instantaneously issued, the amount of free memory can be significantly changed. The delay can be a consequence of a command queue, or, more severely, of the postponed allocation, imposed by the driver, to a moment of the first usage of the allocated object. Even a glFinish call cannot force the driver to commit the allocation. For example, calls to glTexImage* and glBufferData do not change memory allocation on the graphics card until the objects are used for the first time.

ATI_meminfo gives no clue about the total amount of graphics memory. If we want to calculate memory utilization, we have to make use of another AMD extension: WGL_AMD_gpu_association [Haemel 09]. This extension provides a mechanism for applications to explicitly bind to a specific GPU in a multi-GPU system. Since different GPUs can have different capabilities, this extension enables querying those capabilities, one of which is the total memory size in MB.

The function wglGetGPUInfoAMD serves to retrieve properties of the specified GPU. In order to access the information, we need IDs for GPUs presented in the system. Even if we have just one, querying IDs is a mandatory step. The function wglGetGPUIDsAMD(maxCount, ID) fills the array ID with up to maxCount values and retrieves the total number of GPUs. We could choose an arbitrary value for maxCount, but we can also use the wglGetGPUIDsAMD function just to get the number of GPUs by setting the ID parameter to NULL. Having an ID, we can retrieve the amount of memory dedicated to a specific GPU by calling wglGet GPUInfoAMD with a specified ID and the second parameter set to WGL_GPU_RAM_AMD. Listing 38.1 demonstrates querying dedicated graphics memory size using WGL_AMD_gpu_association.

38.5   Conclusion

The amount of available dedicated graphics memory may affect application execution significantly. Discrete graphics adapters are more sensitive to memory overload since onboard memory has higher throughput and significantly outperforms system memory. When memory utilization reaches full capacity, OpenGL object management is likely to cause a negative impact on the application's performance due to object swapping or access to objects residing in the shared system memory. In order to help applications avoid reaching memory limits, GPU vendors provide extensions for determining the amount of available graphics memory. These extensions do not have to retrieve the exact amount of free memory, but rather provide a hint to the application.

Both extensions provide additional information that gives better insight into the current memory status. A very useful piece of information that `NVX_gpu_memory_info` can retrieve is the eviction count. If the count increases, the memory is overloaded, objects are swapped, and hence, the performance is reduced. `ATI_meminfo` does not report evictions, but enables more precise prediction of such events by retrieving the maximum free memory block.

The full utilization of the retrieved information is impossible; new allocations are not committed at the moment a command is issued, but are postponed to the most convenient moment for the driver, usually on the first use of the object. In any case, an application can benefit from memory usage tracking and clever resource management. By avoiding evictions, we prevent object swapping and, hence, preserve high performance.

Bibliography

[Haemel 09] Nick Haemel. "AMD_gpu_association," Revision 1.0, March 3, 2009.

[Microsoft 06] Microsoft. "Graphics Memory Reporting through WDDM," http://www.microsoft.com/whdc/device/display/graphicsmemory.mspx, January 9, 2006.

[NVIDIA 11] NVIDIA. "NVAPI Reference Documentation (Developer)," Release 285, http://developer.nvidia.com/nvapi, September 15, 2011.

[Stefanizzi 09] Bruno Stefanizzi, Roy Blackmer, Bruno Stefanizzi, Andreas Wolf, and Evan Hart. "ATI_meminfo," Revision 0.2, March 2, 2009.

[Stroyan 09] Howard Stroyan, "GL_NVX_gpu_memory_info," Revision 1.3, December 4, 2009.

VII

Software Design

Developers work with OpenGL at many levels of the software stack. Some developers create OpenGL implementations by writing drivers or, as we will see, using another graphics API; other developers create middleware or engines that simplify the use of OpenGL and raise the level of abstraction; and perhaps the majority of OpenGL developers create actual applications, whether by directly calling OpenGL or by using OpenGL-based engines. In this section, we look at software design at each layer of this stack. We consider implementing OpenGL ES 2.0, engines and applications built on WebGL, making legacy OpenGL code modern, and building cross-platform OpenGL applications.

ANGLE, or the Almost Native Graphics Layer Engine, provides an OpenGL ES 2.0 implementation using Direct3D 9. It is used as the default WebGL backend for Chrome and Firefox on Windows. Implementing ANGLE is not nearly as simple as converting OpenGL calls to Direct3D calls; the differences in capabilities of the APIs need to be taken into account. In Chapter 39, "The ANGLE Project: Implementing OpenGL ES 2.0 on Direct3D," Daniel Koch and Nicolas Capens discuss the implementation challenges in ANGLE, provide performance results, and suggest recommended practices.

Given how low-level WebGL is compared to other web APIs, it was clear from its start that there would be demand for higher-level 3D engines built on WebGL. Here, we look at two such engines. SceneJS is an open-source 3D engine, based on a scene graph optimized for rendering large numbers of individually pickable and articulated objects. In Chapter 40, "SceneJS: A WebGL-Based Scene Graph Engine," Lindsay Kay presents SceneJS' architecture and how it makes efficient use of JavaScript and WebGL.

SpiderGL is another 3D graphics library that uses WebGL. Instead of providing higher-level constructs like a scene graph, SpiderGL provides utilities, data structures, and algorithms to simplify WebGL development but still allows the use of other WebGL code in the same application. In Chapter 41, "Features and Design Choices in SpiderGL," Marco Di Benedetto, Fabio Ganovelli, and Francesco Banterle discuss some design and implementation decisions in SpiderGL including its model representation and allowing seamless interoperability with naive WebGL calls.

WebGL is enabling a whole new class of applications. In Chapter 42, "Multimodal Interactive Simulations on the Web," Tansel Halic, Woojin Ahn, and Suvranu De present a framework for visualization, simulation, and hardware integration for multimodal interactive simulations using WebGL. Think practicing surgical procedures using a web browser!

Maintaining legacy and modern OpenGL code in the same code base can prove challenging. Jesse Barker and Alexandros Frantzis share their experiences in Chapter 43, "A Subset Approach to Using OpenGL and OpenGL ES." They suggest ways to move to a single modern code base written against both OpenGL and OpenGL ES.

In "The Build Syndrome," the final chapter of this section and of the book, Jochem van der Spek and Daniel Dekkers discuss in detail building cross-platform OpenGL applications with C++/Objective-C and CMake.

The ANGLE Project: Implementing OpenGL ES 2.0 on Direct3D

39

Daniel Koch and Nicolas Capens

39.1 Introduction

The Almost Native Graphics Layer Engine (ANGLE) project is an open-source implementation of OpenGL ES 2.0 for Windows. This chapter explores the challenges that we encountered in the design of ANGLE and the solutions we implemented.

We begin the chapter by providing the motivation for ANGLE and some potential uses of it. We then delve into the implementation details and explore the design challenges that were involved in developing ANGLE. We discuss the feature set that ANGLE provides, including the standard OpenGL ES and EGL extensions that ANGLE supports, as well as some ANGLE-specific extensions [ANGLE 11]. We also describe in detail some of the optimizations that were implemented to ensure high performance and low overhead. We provide performance tips and guidance for developers who may wish to use ANGLE directly in their own projects. We end with some performance comparisons of WebGL implementations using ANGLE and native Desktop OpenGL drivers.

39.2 Background

ANGLE is a conformant implementation of the OpenGL ES 2.0 specification [Khronos 11c] that is hardware-accelerated via Direct3D. ANGLE version 1.0.772 was certified as compliant by passing the ES 2.0.3 conformance tests in October

543

2011. ANGLE also provides an implementation of the EGL 1.4 specification [Khronos 11b].

TransGaming did the primary development for ANGLE and provides continued maintenance and feature enhancements. The development of ANGLE was sponsored by Google to enable browsers like Google Chrome to run WebGL content on Windows computers that may not have OpenGL drivers [Bridge 10].

ANGLE is used as the default WebGL backend for both Google Chrome and Mozilla Firefox on Windows platforms. Chrome, in fact, uses ANGLE for all graphics rendering, including for the accelerated Canvas2D implementation and for the Native Client sandbox environment.

In addition to providing an OpenGL ES 2.0 implementation for Windows, portions of the ANGLE shader compiler are used as a shader validator and translator by WebGL implementations across multiple platforms. It is used on Mac OS X (Chrome, Firefox, and Safari), Linux (Chrome and Firefox), and in mobile variants of the browsers. Having one shader validator helps to ensure that a consistent set of GLSL ES (ESSL) shaders are accepted across browsers and platforms. The shader translator is also used to translate shaders to other shading languages and to optionally apply shader modifications to work around bugs or quirks in the native graphics drivers. The translator targets Desktop GLSL, Direct3D HLSL, and even ESSL for native OpenGL ES 2.0 platforms.

Because ANGLE provides OpenGL ES 2.0 and EGL 1.4 libraries for Windows, it can be used as a development tool by developers who want to target applications for mobile, embedded, set-top, and Smart TV–based devices. Prototyping and initial development can be done in the developer's familiar Windows-based development environment before final on-device performance tuning. Portability tools such as the GameTree TV SDK [TransGaming 11] can further help to streamline this process by making it possible to run Win32 and OpenGL ES 2.0-based applications directly on set-top boxes. ANGLE also provides developers with an additional option for deploying production versions of their applications to the desktop, either for content that was initially developed on Windows, or for deploying OpenGL ES 2.0–based content from other platforms such as iOS or Android.

39.3   Implementation

ANGLE is implemented in C++ and uses Direct3D 9 [MSDN 11c] for rendering. This API was chosen to allow us to target our implementation at Windows XP, Vista, and 7, as well as providing access to a broad base of graphics hardware. ANGLE requires a minimum of Shader Model (SM) 2 support, but due to the limited capabilities of SM2, the primary target for our implementation is SM3. There are some implementation variances, and in some cases, completely different approaches used, in order to account for the different set of capabilities between SM2 and SM3. Since

SM3 is our primary target, the focus of this chapter is on the description of our implementation for this feature set.

The main challenge of implementing OpenGL ES on top of another graphics API, such as Direct3D, is accounting for different conventions and capabilities. Some differences can be implemented in a straightforward manner, while others are much more involved.

This section begins with one of the most well-known differences between the APIs: the differences in coordinate conventions. Dealing with these in a mathematically sound manner is critical to achieving correct results. Next, we cover another key aspect of the project: the translation of OpenGL ES shaders into their Direct3D equivalents. Following this, we delve into handling data resources such as vertex buffers and textures. Finally, we cover the finer details of the different API paradigms and interfaces, tying the individual aspects into a complete OpenGL ES implementation on top of Direct3D.

39.3.1 Coordinate Systems

It is often said that OpenGL has a right-handed coordinate system and Direct3D has a left-handed coordinate system, and that this has application-wide implications [MSDN 11a]. However, this is not entirely correct. The differences can be best understood by looking at the coordinate transformation equations. Both OpenGL and Direct3D take the position output from the vertex shader in homogeneous (clip) coordinates, perform the same perspective division to obtain normalized device coordinates (NDC), and then perform a very similar viewport transformation to obtain window coordinates. The transformations as performed by OpenGL are shown in Figure 39.1 and Equation (39.1) [Khronos 11c, Section 2.12]. The parameters p_x and p_y represent the viewport width and height, respectively, and (o_x, o_y) is the center

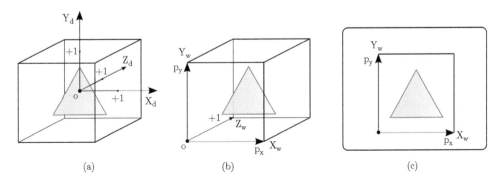

Figure 39.1. GL coordinate spaces: (a) NDC space, (b) window space, and (c) screen space.

of the viewport (all measured in pixels):

$$
\begin{pmatrix} x_c \\ y_c \\ z_c \\ w_c \end{pmatrix} \rightarrow \begin{pmatrix} x_d \\ y_d \\ z_d \end{pmatrix} = \begin{pmatrix} x_c/w_c \\ y_c/w_c \\ z_c/w_c \end{pmatrix} \rightarrow \quad (39.1)
$$

vertex shader
clip coords

perspective division
NDC coords

$$
\begin{pmatrix} x_w \\ y_w \\ z_w \end{pmatrix} = \begin{pmatrix} \frac{p_x}{2}x_d + o_x \\ \frac{p_y}{2}y_d + o_y \\ \frac{f-n}{2}z_d + \frac{n+f}{2} \end{pmatrix} \rightarrow \begin{pmatrix} x_s \\ y_s \end{pmatrix} = \begin{pmatrix} x_w + x_{pos} \\ y_w + y_{pos} \end{pmatrix}.
$$

viewport transform
window coords

present transform
screen coords

The transformations performed by Direct3D are shown in Figure 39.2 and Equation (39.2) [MSDN 11k]:

$$
\begin{pmatrix} x_c \\ y_c \\ z_c \\ w_c \end{pmatrix} \rightarrow \begin{pmatrix} x_d \\ y_d \\ z_d \end{pmatrix} = \begin{pmatrix} x_c/w_c \\ y_c/w_c \\ z_c/w_c \end{pmatrix} \rightarrow \quad (39.2)
$$

vertex shader
clip coordinates

perspective division
NDC coordinates

$$
\begin{pmatrix} x_w \\ y_w \\ z_w \end{pmatrix} = \begin{pmatrix} \frac{p_x}{2}x_d + o_x \\ \frac{p_y}{2}(-y_d) + o_y \\ (f - n)z_d + n \end{pmatrix} \rightarrow \begin{pmatrix} x_s \\ y_s \end{pmatrix} = \begin{pmatrix} x_w + x_{pos} \\ p_y - y_w + y_{pos} \end{pmatrix}.
$$

viewport transform
window coordinates

present transform
screen coordinates

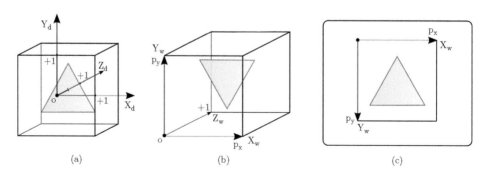

Figure 39.2. Direct3D coordinate spaces: (a) NDC space, (b) window space, and (c) screen space.

Window origin.   One notable difference between Equations (39.1) and (39.2) is that Direct3D inverts the y-axis during the viewport transformation. Direct3D also considers the window origin to be in the top-left corner with the y-axis pointing down, whereas OpenGL considers the window origin to be in the lower-left corner with the y-axis pointing up, as shown in Figure 39.3. These operations cancel each other out. This means that when the homogeneous coordinates output from an OpenGL vertex shader are fed into Direct3D using the same viewport parameters, the resulting image will correctly appear upright on the screen.

The problem is that when rendering to a texture, the image is stored in window coordinates, and hence, there is no vertical flip performed, leaving the image upside down. Furthermore, the window coordinates are also an input to the pixel shader, so things like fragment coordinates and gradients are inverted.

There are several ways to deal with this issue. The first is to append code to the original OpenGL ES vertex shader to negate the y-component. This way, the negation in the viewport transformation is canceled, meaning the window coordinates are the way OpenGL expects them, and when rendering to a texture, the image appears upright. Since Direct3D flips the image when viewed on screen, we also have to counteract that by explicitly flipping it before the **Present** call. Originally, we chose this option; since negating the y-component in the vertex shader is trivial, it easily solves the render-to-texture issue, and no changes are required to pixel shaders or regular texture handling. It only comes at the cost of an extra pass to copy the rendered result into a texture and flip it upside down before presenting it on the screen. Unfortunately, this pass caused a significant performance impact—up to 20% slower—on low-end hardware when rendering simple scenes.

The second way to deal with the inversion of the y-coordinate is to invert the texture sampling coordinate system by rewriting every sampling operation to use modified texture coordinates: $(s', t') = (s, 1 - t)$. This implies that the data for

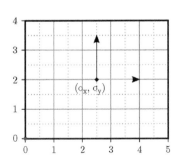 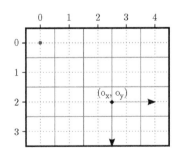

Figure 39.3. Window origin and fragment coordinate differences between OpenGL (left) and Direct3D (right). The red dot represents the location of $(0, 0)$ in window coordinates and (o_x, o_y) is the center of a 5×4 pixel viewport.

regular textures must be stored in an upside down fashion. Cube maps are handled by additionally swapping the top (+Y) and bottom (−Y) faces. It also requires all pixel shader operations that use the window y-coordinate to be adjusted. This is the solution currently implemented and is discussed further in Section 39.3.2. The texture inversions on upload are a potential source of inefficiency, but we already swizzle and convert most texture data on load, so this does not add additional overhead. Another concern is that the modification of the texture coordinates turns them into dependent texture reads. This could prevent prefetching of texture data on some GPU architectures, and the extra instructions add computational overhead. Fortunately, this does not appear to be a problem on most desktop GPUs, and we have not observed negative effects due to these modifications.

The third way of solving this issue is to invert the rendering only when rendering into a texture and using the shader unmodified when rendering to a window. This approach could avoid the drawbacks of the first two methods, but it is not without additional implementation complexity. The shaders would have to be compiled differently depending on the rendering destination and it could also affect the fill convention. This approach is still under evaluation and might be implemented in the future.

Winding order. Another interesting consequence of the difference in viewport transformations between OpenGL and Direct3D is that the winding order of a triangle's vertices is reversed. The winding order determines whether a triangle is considered front facing or back facing and hence which primitives are culled. Since the winding order is computed using window coordinates, the need to invert the culling parameters also depends on whether or not the viewport transformation difference is handled in the vertex shader.

Dithering. No specific dithering algorithm is required in OpenGL ES, only that the dithering algorithm depends solely on the fragment's value and window coordinates. When the viewport is inverted, this has the potential to make the dithering algorithm also depend on the viewport height. However, if the identity function is used, this dithering requirement is trivially fulfilled. Direct3D 9 does have a D3DRS_DITHERENABLE render state, but dithering is typically no longer directly supported on recent hardware.

Fill convention. One last interesting effect of the different viewport transformations is that it also affects the fill convention. The fill convention is the rule that decides whether a pixel whose center is directly on a triangle's edge is considered covered by that triangle or not. This is vital to prevent adjoining triangles from filling the same pixels twice or leaving gaps. Direct3D enforces a top-left fill convention. OpenGL does not require a specific fill convention, only that a well-defined convention is used consistently. Although ANGLE complies with this, it is worth noting that the OpenGL specification does not guarantee exact pixel results. In particular, screen-space rectangles should be aligned to pixel edges instead of pixel centers to avoid unexpected results.

Depth range. In addition to the window-origin differences, there is also a difference in the depth range of the homogeneous coordinates that must be accounted for. OpenGL clips the z-coordinate to the $[-1, 1]$ range and then transforms it to the $[near, far]$ range specified with `glDepthRangef`. Direct3D uses the $[0, 1]$ range instead. Note again that, contrary to popular belief, the z-axis of OpenGL does not point out of the screen. Both OpenGL and Direct3D applications are free to use whichever coordinate system(s) they prefer, as long as the projection takes care of correctly transforming the camera-space coordinates into the intended clip-space coordinates. Since clipping takes place right after the vertex shader stage, we can account for the differences by appending code to the original vertex shader that adjusts the output z-coordinate. We will revisit this in Section 39.3.2.

Fragment coordinates. The numerical coordinates for pixel centers are also different between OpenGL and Direct3D 9. In OpenGL, the pixel centers are located at half-pixel locations, and thus, the (x, y) fragment coordinate of the pixel closest to the origin is $(0.5, 0.5)$. In Direct3D 9, pixel centers are located at integral locations, and the location of the pixel closest to the origin is $(0, 0)$. This also means that viewports are not symmetric around the origin, as shown in Figure 39.3. This oddity has been corrected in Direct3D 10, but for ANGLE on Direct3D 9, a half-pixel offset is required to adjust the fragment coordinates for this difference. This adjustment can also be done at the output of the vertex shader stage, so in homogeneous coordinates, the half-pixel offset becomes $(\frac{1}{p_x}w_c, \frac{1}{p_y}w_c)$.

39.3.2 Shader Compiler and Linker

The initial design of the OpenGL Shading Language was done by 3Dlabs. As part of their work, they developed and released an open-source GLSL compiler front-end and shader validator for the initial version of GLSL [3Dlabs 05]. This GLSL compiler front-end was used as the starting point for ANGLE's shader compiler and translator. The 3Dlabs compiler front-end was designed for Version 1.10 of the GLSL specification and thus needed to be adapted for the GLSL ES Version 1.00 language [Khronos 11e]. The differences between GLSL 1.10 and GLSL ES 1.00 are summed up in a student report from the Norwegian University of Science and Technology [Ek 05].

Architecture. In OpenGL ES 2.0, individual vertex and fragment shaders are compiled using `glCompileShader` and linked into a single program using `glLinkProgram`. With Direct3D 9, however, there is no explicit linking step between the vertex and pixel shaders (the Direct3D equivalent of the ESSL fragment shader). Vertex shader outputs and pixel shader inputs have to be assigned a "semantic" [MSDN 11j], essentially a register identifier, within the HLSL code itself, and they are implicitly linked when the shaders are made active. Since assigning matching semantics can only be done when both the vertex and pixel shaders are known, the actual HLSL compilation has to be deferred until link time. During the compilation call, ANGLE can only translate the ESSL code into HLSL code, leaving the output and input declarations blank. Note that this is not unique to ANGLE, as other OpenGL and OpenGL ES implementations also defer some of the compilation until link time.

The ANGLE shader compiler component functions as either a translator or a validator. It consists of two main components: the compiler front-end and the compiler back-end. The compiler front-end consists of the preprocessor, lexer, parser, and abstract syntax tree (AST) generator. The lexer and parser are generated from the shading language grammar using the flex [Flex 08] and bison [FSF 11] tools. The compiler back-end consists of several output methods that convert the AST to a desired form of 'object' code. The forms of object code that are currently supported are the HLSL, GLSL, or ESSL shader strings. The shader compiler can validate shaders against either the ESSL specification [Khronos 11e] or the WebGL specification [Khronos 11f]. ANGLE uses the former, and the web browsers use the latter.

During program object linking, the translated HLSL shaders from the "compiled" vertex and fragment shaders are compiled into binary shader *blobs*. The shader blobs include both the Direct3D 9 bytecode for the shaders and the semantic information required to map uniforms to constants. The `D3DXGetShaderConstant Table` method is used to obtain the uniform information and define the mappings between the uniform names and the vertex and pixel shader constant locations. Note that ANGLE uses the Direct3D 10 shader compiler instead of the one included with D3DX9 because it comes as a separately updated DLL, produces superior shader assembly/binary code, and can handle complex shaders more successfully without running out of registers or instruction slots. Unfortunately, there are still some shaders that contain complex conditionals or loops with a high number of iterations that fail to compile even with the Direct3D 10 compiler.

Shader translation.   The translation of ESSL into HLSL is achieved by traversing the AST and converting it back into a textual representation while taking the differences between the languages into account. The AST is a tree structure representation of the original source code, so the basic process of turning each node into a string is relatively straightforward. We also extended 3Dlabs' definition of the AST and their traversing framework to preserve additional source information like variable declarations and precisions.

HLSL supports the same binary and unary operators as ESSL, but there are some noteworthy differences in semantics. In ESSL, the first matrix component subscript accesses a column vector while the second subscript (if any) selects the row. With HLSL, this order is reversed. Furthermore, OpenGL constructs matrices from elements specified in column-major order while Direct3D uses row-major order. These differences were addressed by transposing matrix uniforms. This also required (un-)transposing matrices when used in binary operations. Although it may seem in-efficient to transpose matrices within the HLSL shader, at the assembly level it simply results in having multiply-add vector instructions instead of dot-product instructions or vice versa. No noticeable performance impact was observed.

Another significant semantic difference between the two languages is the eval-uation of the ternary select operator (`cond ?  expr1 :  expr2`). With HLSL, both expressions are evaluated, and then the result of one of them is returned based on the condition. ESSL adheres to the C semantics and only evaluates the expression that is selected by the condition. To achieve the ESSL semantics with HLSL, ternary operators are rewritten as if/else statements. Because ternary operators can be nested and statements can contain multiple ternary operators, we implemented a separate AST traverser that hierarchically expands the ternary operators and assigns the re-sults to temporary variables that are then used in the original statement containing the ternary operator. The logical binary Boolean AND (`&&`) and OR (`||`) operators also require short-circuited evaluation and can be handled in a similar manner.

To prevent temporary variables and differences in intrinsic function names from colliding with names used in the ESSL source, we "decorate" user-defined ESSL names with an underscore. Reserved names in the ESSL code use the same `gl_` prefix in HLSL, while variables needed to implement or adjust for Direct3D-specific behavior have a `dx_` prefix.

Shader built-ins. The OpenGL ES shading language provides a number of built-in shader variables, inputs, and functions that are not directly provided by Direct3D's HLSL or that require different semantics between the two languages.

The vertex shading language has no built-in inputs but instead supports application-defined *attribute* variables that provide the values passed into a shader on a per-vertex basis. The attributes are mapped directly to HLSL vertex shader inputs using the `TEXCOORD[#]` semantics.

The *varying* variables form the interface between the vertex and fragment shaders. ESSL has no built-in varying variables and supports only application-defined vary-ings. These varyings are mapped to HLSL vertex shader outputs and pixel shader inputs using the `COLOR[#]` semantics. In most cases, we could alternatively use the `TEXCOORD[#]` semantics, but these are treated differently for point-sprite rendering, so instead, we always use the `COLOR[#]` semantics for user-defined varyings. The exception for this is in SM2, where variables with the `COLOR[#]` semantics have lim-ited range and precision, and thus we must use the `TEXCOORD[#]` semantic. For this reason, we cannot directly support large points when using SM2.

The vertex shading language has two built-in output variables: `gl_PointSize` and `gl_Position`. The `gl_PointSize` output controls the size at which a point is rasterized. This is equivalent to the HLSL vertex shader PSIZE output semantic, but to meet the GL requirements, it must be clamped to the valid point size range. The `gl_Position` output determines the vertex position in homogeneous coordinates. This is similar to the HLSL vertex shader `POSITION0` output semantic; however, we

```
output.gl_PointSize = clamp(gl_PointSize, 1.0, ALIASED_POINT_SIZE_RANGE_MAX_SM3);
output.gl_Position.x = gl_Position.x - dx_HalfPixelSize.x * gl_Position.w;
output.gl_Position.y = gl_Position.y - dx_HalfPixelSize.y * gl_Position.w;
output.gl_Position.z = (gl_Position.z + gl_Position.w) * 0.5;
output.gl_Position.w = gl_Position.w;
output.gl_FragCoord = gl_Position;
```

Listing 39.1. Vertex shader epilogue.

must account for several differences between Direct3D and OpenGL coordinates at this point before we can use it. As described previously in Section 39.3.1, the x- and y-coordinates are adjusted by the half-pixel offset in screen space to account for the fragment coordinate differences, and the z-coordinate is adjusted to account for the depth-range differences. Listing 39.1 shows the vertex shader epilogue that converts the ESSL shader to Direct3D semantics.

The fragment shading language has three built-in read-only variables: `gl_Frag Coord`, `gl_FrontFacing`, and `gl_PointCoord`. The `gl_FragCoord` variable provides the window-relative coordinate values $(x_w, y_w, z_w, 1/w_c)$ for the fragments that are interpolated during rasterization. This is similar to the HLSL VPOS semantic that provides the (x, y)-coordinates. We use the VPOS semantic to provide the base (x, y) screen-space coordinates and then adjust for both the fragment-center and window-origin differences. To compute the z- and w-components of `gl_FragCoord`, we pass the original `gl_Position` from the vertex shader into the pixel shader via a hidden varying. In the pixel shader, the z-value is multiplied by $1/w_c$ to perform perspective correction and is finally corrected by the depth factors calculated from the near and far clipping planes, as shown in Listing 39.2.

The `gl_FrontFacing` variable is a boolean value which is TRUE if the fragment belongs to a front-facing primitive. Under HLSL, similar information is available via the pixel shader VFACE input semantic; however, this is a floating-point value that uses negative values to indicate back-facing primitives and positive values to indicate front-facing ones [MSDN 11h]. This can easily be converted to a boolean value, but we must also account for the different face-winding convention and the fact that point and line primitives are always considered front-facing under OpenGL, whereas the face is undefined for those primitives under Direct3D (see Listing 39.3).

```
rhw = 1.0 / input.gl_FragCoord.w;
gl_FragCoord.x = input.dx_VPos.x + 0.5;
gl_FragCoord.y = dx_Coord.y - input.dx_VPos.y - 0.5;
gl_FragCoord.z = (input.gl_FragCoord.z * rhw)* dx_Depth.x + dx_Depth.y;
gl_FragCoord.w = rhw;
```

Listing 39.2. Calculation of the built-in fragment coordinate for SM3.

```
gl_FrontFacing = dx_PointsOrLines || (dx_FrontCCW ? (input.vFace>= 0.0) : input.↩
    vFace <= 0.0));
```

Listing 39.3. Calculation of front-facing built-in variable.

The gl_PointCoord variable provides a set of 2D coordinates that indicate where in a point primitive the current fragment is located. The values must vary from 0 to 1 horizontally (left to right) and from 0 to 1 vertically (top to bottom). These values can be used as texture coordinates in order to provide textured point sprites. Direct3D also has the ability to synthesize texture coordinates for the generated vertices of the point sprite [MSDN 11f]. When this is enabled via the D3DRS_POINTSPRITEENABLE render state, the TEXCOORD semantic is used to generate texture coordinates that serve as the values for gl_PointCoord. Since all points in OpenGL ES are point sprites, we only need to enable this render state once on the Direct3D device initialization.

The OpenGL ES shading language also provides one built-in uniform: gl_DepthRange. This is defined as a structure that contains the depth range parameters that were specified via the glDepthRangef command in the API. Since HLSL does not provide any built-in uniforms, we pass these parameters in the shaders via a hidden uniform and define and populate the gl_DepthRangeParameters structure explicitly in the shader source when referenced by the ESSL code.

Both ESSL and HLSL have a variety of built-in, or intrinsic, functions. Many of the built-in functions have both the same names and functionality, but there are some cases where either the name or functionality is slightly different. Differences in name, such as frac (HLSL) and fract (ESSL), are easily handled at translation time. In cases where there are functionality differences or simply missing functions, such as modf (HLSL) and mod (ESSL), this is handled by defining our own functions with the required semantics.

The OES_standard_derivatives extension provides the built-in shader functions dFdx, dFdy, and fwidth in the shading language. These gradient computation functions are available in GLSL 1.20 and are commonly used for custom mipmap LOD computations (necessary when using vertex texture fetch) or for extracting screen-space normals. They are translated into the HLSL ddx, ddy, and fwidth intrinsics, respectively, with ddy being negated to account for the window origin difference.

The ANGLE_translated_shader_source extension [ANGLE 11] provides the ability to query the translated HLSL shader source. This is provided as a debugging aid for developers, as some of the error or warning messages that are reported are relative to the translated source and not to the original shader source.

39.3.3   Vertex and Index Buffers

OpenGL ES 2.0 supports buffer objects that can be used both for vertex and index data, while Direct3D only supports vertex buffers and index buffers separately. This means ANGLE has to wait until a draw call is issued to be able to determine which data can go into which type of Direct3D buffer. Furthermore, Direct3D 9 does not support all of the vertex element types that OpenGL does, so some elements may need to be translated to wider data types. Because this translation can be expensive and not all vertex elements are necessarily used during a draw call, we decided that our baseline implementation should stream the used range of vertex elements into Direct3D vertex buffers sequentially instead of in packed structures. Figure 39.4 shows the basic process.

The streaming buffer implementation uses a Direct3D vertex buffer in a circular manner. New data is appended at the point where the previous write operation ended. This allows the use of a single Direct3D vertex buffer instead of requiring a new one to be created for every draw call. Appending new data is very efficient by making use of the D3DLOCK_NOOVERWRITE flag [MSDN 11b] when locking the buffers so that the driver does not need to wait for previous draw calls to complete. When the end of the buffer is reached, the D3DLOCK_DISCARD flag is used to allow the driver to rename the buffer. This does not affect data that is already in use by a previous draw call. The streaming vertex buffer only needs to be reallocated when the buffer is not large enough to fit all of the vertex data for a single draw call.

As previously mentioned, unsupported vertex element types need to be translated. Direct3D 9 always supports elements with one to four floating-point values, which offers a universal fallback for any format; however, ANGLE converts the data into more efficient formats whenever possible. For instance, if the Direct3D driver supports the D3DDECLTYPE_SHORT4N format, three normalized short values get converted into this format, with the fourth element being set to the default value. We make extensive use of C++ templates in the translation in order to make the code as efficient as possible and avoid writing several dozen customized routines.

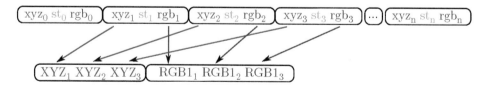

Figure 39.4. Example of streaming buffer translation for a single-triangle draw call. The GL buffer (top) contains position (xyz), texture (st), and color (rgb) vertex data in an interleaved fashion. This is translated into the Direct3D vertex buffer (bottom) that contains the condensed streams of translated position (XYZ) and color (RGB1) values. The texture coordinates and other vertices are not included since they were not referenced by this draw call.

Despite these optimizations, the streaming implementation is not optimal. When drawing the same geometry multiple times, the same data must be resent to the hardware on each draw call. To improve on this, ANGLE also features a static buffer implementation. When the data in a GL buffer is not modified between draw calls, we can reuse the same Direct3D data from the previous draw call that used this buffer. This is achieved by associating a Direct3D vertex buffer with each OpenGL buffer. Instead of streaming data into the global circular vertex buffer, it is streamed into the static buffer on the first use. A cache keeps track of which vertex element formats are stored in the static buffer and at which offset. The static buffer gets invalidated when the OpenGL buffer is subsequently modified or when some formats specified by `glVertexAttribPointer` no longer match those in the cache. ANGLE takes the buffer usage parameter into account when determining whether or not to initially attempt to place data in a static buffer. In our testing, we have also found that some applications set the usage flags incorrectly. Thus, we track whether a nonstatic buffer remains unmodified for a number of uses so it can be heuristically promoted to a static buffer if appropriate. Still, we recommend that applications use the `GL_STATIC_DRAW` hint whenever they are certain a buffer will not be modified after its first use in a draw call.

In addition to vertex array data specified via `glVertexAttribPointer`, OpenGL also supports current attribute values, i.e., attributes that remain constant during a draw call. Direct3D does not have a similar concept. Even though the value stays constant per draw call, using an actual Direct3D vertex shader constant would be complicated because, in one draw call, an attribute can be specified by a vertex array attribute while, in another draw call, it can use the current attribute, and that would require rewriting the Direct3D shader. Instead, we opted to implement current vertex attributes by using vertex buffers with only one element and a stride of zero. When the current attribute value is modified, a whole new Direct3D buffer is created because some drivers do not correctly support updating dynamic buffers that are used with a stride of zero.

ANGLE supports the `OES_element_index_uint` extension, which provides the ability to use 32-bit unsigned integer index buffers with `glDrawElements`. Without this extension, OpenGL ES only supports 8- and 16-bit unsigned indices.

39.3.4 Textures

There are some fundamental texture handling differences between OpenGL and Direct3D. In Direct3D 9, the texture format, usage, and shape (number of mipmaps) must all be declared at texture-object creation time and cannot change over the lifetime of the object. In OpenGL, textures are defined one level at a time and in any level order; the usage is not known in advance, and the shape can change over time as mipmaps are added. Furthermore, any or all levels of a texture can be redefined at any time with the `glTexImage2D` or `glCopyTexImage2D` commands.

In order to handle the differences between Direct3D and OpenGL textures, the application-provided data for each level are stored in a system memory surface. The creation of the Direct3D texture is deferred until draw time when the shape and usage of the texture are known. At Direct3D texture creation time, we must choose whether the texture will be renderable or not. Under OpenGL, any texture can become renderable simply by attaching it to a framebuffer object. Creating all Direct3D textures as render targets can result in degraded performance and can lead to early out-of-memory situations since render target textures are typically pinned to video memory and the driver is unable to page them out to system memory as necessary. Since many textures are never used as render targets, the Direct3D textures are created nonrenderable by default and are loaded with data from the system memory surfaces. This allows the driver to more effectively manage the texture memory. As a consequence of this, whenever a renderable version of a GL texture is required, we create a renderable Direct3D texture and migrate any existing data from either the nonrenderable Direct3D texture or from the system memory surfaces into the renderable texture. We retain the system memory surfaces, which contain the application-provided texture data, as these continue to serve as staging areas for texture updates via `glTexSubImage2D`. The system memory surfaces are also used to avoid reading back texture data from the graphics memory in the cases where the texture is redefined.

Texture redefinition occurs whenever the format or dimensions of level 0 of a texture are changed. When this happens, any existing Direct3D backing texture must be discarded. Ideally, the contents of any existing mip-levels of the texture at that point are preserved in the system memory surfaces. These mip-images should be kept because it is possible for the images to be used again if the texture is later redefined in a way that is consistent with the original data. For example, consider a texture that has four levels with sizes 8×8, 4×4, 2×2, and 1×1. If level 0 is redefined as a 2×2 image, it could be used as a single-level texture with mip-filtering disabled. If level 0 were once again redefined as an 8×8 image with the same format as originally used, this would once again result in a complete texture with four levels, and levels 1 through 3 would have the same data as before. This is the behavior implied by the specification, but not all drivers (including some versions of ANGLE) have correctly implemented image preservation on redefinition. Hence, portable applications should not rely on this behavior; it is recommended that redefining textures be avoided, as this can cause expensive reallocations inside the driver.

OpenGL has recently introduced a new texture creation mechanism that allows the creation of immutable textures: `ARB_texture_storage` [Khronos 11d]. The `glTexStorage` command is used to create a texture with a specific format, size, and number of levels. Once a texture has been defined by `glTexStorage`, the texture cannot be redefined and can only have its data specified by the `gl*SubImage2D` commands or by render-to-texture. This new texture creation API is beneficial for many drivers, as it allows them to allocate the correct amount of memory up front without having to guess how many mip-levels will be provided. ANGLE supports

EXT_texture_storage [ANGLE 11], an OpenGL ES version of this extension, in order to provide a more efficient texture implementation. With the shape and format of the texture known at creation time, we can immediately create a Direct3D texture that corresponds to the GL texture. The system memory surfaces can be omitted because we can load the application-provided texture data directly into the Direct3D9 texture, and we do not have to preserve the system memory copies of the data because TexStorage textures are immutable. The ANGLE_texture_usage extension [ANGLE 11] further provides the ability to let the implementation know the expected usage of a texture. When it is known that a texture will be rendered into, the usage parameter can be specified so that the implementation will know to allocate a renderable texture.

OpenGL also has the notion of *incomplete textures*. This occurs when insufficient levels of a texture are present (based on the filter state), or when the formats or sizes are inconsistent between levels. When sampled in a shader, an incomplete texture always returns the value $(R, G, B, A) = (0, 0, 0, 1)$. Support for incomplete textures is implemented by creating a 1-level 1×1 Direct3D texture of the appropriate type that is bound to the sampler during a draw call.

Another texture difference between OpenGL ES and Direct3D 9 is the set of texture formats that are supported. In addition, OpenGL applications typically supply the texture data in an RGB(A) format, while Direct3D uses a BGR(A) component order for most format types. Because of the difference in component ordering and the limited support for the Direct3D equivalents of some of the packed formats (e.g., the 4444, 5551, and 565 variants), we expand and swizzle texture data into the D3DFMT_A8R8G8B8 format at load time. The main exceptions are the luminance and luminance-alpha unsigned byte texture formats, which are loaded directly as D3DFMT_L8 and D3DFMT_A8L8 textures when natively supported. While we are loading the texture data, we must also flip the texture data vertically to account for the window coordinate differences as described earlier.

To optimize the most common texture loading operations, SSE2 optimized code is used when supported by the CPU. Similarly, glReadPixels requires flipping the image and swizzling the color components, but since it is not expected to be a particularly fast function (because it waits on the GPU to finish rendering), these operations are not yet optimized using SSE2. However, the EXT_read_format_bgra extension is provided in case the application does not require the components to be swizzled.

ANGLE supports a number of extensions that provide a wider range of texture and renderbuffer formats and related capabilities. OES_texture_npot provides support for the full complement of mipmapping, minification filters, and repeat-based wrap modes for nonpower of two textures. 8-bit per component RGB and RGBA renderbuffers (OES_rgb8_rgba8), and BGRA textures (EXT_texture_format_BGRA8888, EXT_read_format_bgra) provide support for 32-bpp rendering as well as exposing formats that do not require conversions for performance reasons. The 16- and 32-bit floating-point texture formats (OES_texture_half_float, OES_ texture_float), including support for linear filtering (OES_texture_half_float_linear, OES_texture_float_linear), are supported in order to provide more precise texture data for algorithms that require it, particularly those that also make use of vertex textures. The DXT1 (EXT_texture_compression_dxt1), DXT3 (ANGLE_texture_compression_dxt3), and DXT5 (ANGLE_texture_compression_dxt5) compressed texture formats [ANGLE 11] are also provided to improve performance by using less texture bandwidth in the GPU and by reducing system and video memory requirements.

39.3.5   Vertex Texture Fetch

OpenGL ES 2 provides the capability to support texture sampling in vertex shaders (also referred to as vertex texture fetch or VTF) although support for this is not mandated. VTF is often used for techniques such as displacement mapping where a heightmap is stored in a texture and then used to adjust the position of the vertex based on the value obtained from a texture lookup. In order to determine whether VTF is supported on a particular implementation and device combination, the application must query the MAX_VERTEX_TEXTURE_IMAGE_UNITS limit. If the value for this limit is zero, VTF is not supported.

The initial implementation of ANGLE did not support vertex textures; however, support was later added as this was a highly sought-after feature. The potential difficulty with implementing VTF in ANGLE is that some SM3 hardware has no support for it, and on other hardware, it is only supported in a very limited form—typically only for 2D textures with 32-bit floating-point formats and only with point filtering. Unlike Direct3D 9, which exposes capabilities like this at a very granular level, OpenGL and OpenGL ES do not provide a way to limit what types of textures or formats can be used with vertex texturing; it is required for all textures types and formats. With OpenGL, using a format or type that is not directly supported by hardware will cause vertex processing to fall back to software. With Direct3D 9, it is possible to get a more complete set of vertex texture capabilities by enabling software vertex processing [MSDN 11g], but that is not without its own drawbacks. First, the Direct3D 9 device must be created with mixed vertex processing and that may not perform as well as a pure hardware device. Next, in order to use a texture with software vertex processing, the texture must be created in the scratch memory pool [MSDN 11b], necessitating additional copies of the texture data and ensuring that they are all kept in sync. Finally, software vertex processing is likely to be significantly slower, and in many cases, developers would rather do without the functionality than have it available but executing in a software fallback.

Unlike SM3 hardware, SM4 (Direct3D 10 capable) hardware does provide full support for vertex textures for all formats, for both 2D and cube textures, and with linear filtering. Furthermore, these capabilities are also exposed via Direct3D 9 on this hardware. As a result, ANGLE only exposes support for vertex texture fetch when it detects that it is running on SM4 hardware and can provide the full complement of vertex texture functionality without falling back to software vertex processing. However, even though SM4 hardware supports 16 vertex texture samplers, the Direct3D 9 API only supports four vertex texture samplers, and thus, this is the maximum supported under ANGLE.

39.3.6   Primitive Types

Both OpenGL and Direct3D provide a number of different types of rendering primitives. They both include primitives for rendering points; line strips and lists; and triangle strips, fans, and lists. OpenGL ES also provides an additional primitive type that is not available under Direct3D 9: the line loop. Line loops are similar to line strips with the addition of a closing line segment that is drawn between the last vertex v_n and the first vertex v_0. Thus, for a render call with n vertices, there are $n - 1$ line segments drawn between vertices $(v_{i-1}, v_i) | 1 \leq i \leq n$ and a final line segment between vertices (v_n, v_0). In ANGLE, this is implemented by drawing two line strips. The first draw call, either arrayed or indexed as specified by the original drawing command, renders the first $n - 1$ line segments via a line strip. The second draw call renders the final line segment using a streaming index buffer that contains the indices of the last and first vertex from the original draw command.

Large points and wide lines are optional capabilities in OpenGL ES 2. Support for these must be queried by checking the maximum available point size range and line width range. Large points are often used for particle systems or other sprite-based rendering techniques, as they have a significant memory and bandwidth saving compared to the fallback method of drawing two triangles forming a screen-aligned quadrilateral. ANGLE supports points with sizes up to a maximum of 64 pixels in order to support point sprite rendering. Wide lines are used less frequently and, as of the time of writing, ANGLE does not support lines with width larger than one.

39.3.7   Masked Clears

Another OpenGL capability not directly supported by Direct3D is masked clear operations. Under Direct3D 9, the color, depth, and stencil masks do not apply to clear operations, whereas they do in OpenGL. Thus, in cases where only some of the color or stencil components are to be cleared, we implement the clear operation by drawing a quad the size of the framebuffer. As with `glClear`, the scissor test limits the area that is affected by the draw command. One of the drawbacks to implementing the clear call via a draw operation is that the current state of the Direct3D device must be modified. Since we do significant caching in order to minimize the state setup that must be done at draw time, this draw command has the potential to interfere with that caching. In order to minimize the individual state changes that must be done, we preserve the current Direct3D rendering state in a stateblock, configure the state for the clearing draw call, perform the draw, and then restore the previous state from the stateblock. In cases where masked clear operations are not required, we directly use the Direct3D 9 `Clear` call for performance.

39.3.8 Separate Depth and Stencil Buffers

Framebuffer configuration in OpenGL ES allows applications to separately specify depth and stencil buffers. Depth and stencil buffers are not separable in Direct3D, and thus, we are not able to support arbitrary mixing of depth and stencil buffers. However, this is not uncommon for OpenGL or other OpenGL ES implementations and can be disallowed by reporting `GL_FRAMEBUFFER_UNSUPPORTED` when separate buffers are simultaneously bound to the depth and stencil binding points. In order to provide support for simultaneous depth and stencil operation, the `OES_packed_depth_stencil` extension is supported in ANGLE. This extension provides a combined depth and stencil surface internal format (`DEPTH24_STENCIL8_OES`) that can be used for renderbuffer storage. In order to use simultaneous depth and stencil operations, the application must attach the same packed depth-stencil surface to both the depth and stencil attachment points of the framebuffer object. The packed depth-stencil format is also used internally for all formats that require only depth or stencil components, and the Direct3D pipeline is configured so that the unused depth or stencil components have no effect. Note that since ANGLE does not yet support depth textures, packed depth-stencil textures are also not supported.

39.3.9 Synchronization

The `glFlush` command is required to flush the GL command stream and cause it to finish execution in finite time. The flush command is implemented in ANGLE via Direct3D 9 event queries [MSDN 11i]. In Direct3D 9, issuing an event query and calling `GetData` with the `D3DGETDATA_FLUSH` parameter causes the command buffer to be flushed in the driver, resulting in the desired effect.

The `glFinish` command is required to block until all previous GL commands have completed. This can also be implemented using Direct3D event queries by issuing an event query and then polling until the query result is available.

ANGLE also supports the `NV_fence` extension in order to provide finer-grained synchronization than is possible with only flush and finish. Fence objects are also implemented via Direct3D 9 event queries as they have very similar semantics.

39.3.10 Multisampling

ANGLE does not currently expose any EGL multisample configurations. This is not due to any inherent technical difficulty, but rather due to lack of demand for it. Support for multisampling is provided with multisampled renderbuffers. The `ANGLE_framebuffer_multisample` extension [ANGLE 11] is a subset of the `EXT_framebuffer_multisample` extension from OpenGL. It provides a mechanism to attach multisampled images to framebuffer objects and resolve the multisampled framebuffer object into a single-sampled framebuffer. The resolve destination can either be another application-created framebuffer object or the window-system provided one.

ANGLE also provides support for copying directly from one framebuffer to another. The `ANGLE_framebuffer_blit` extension [ANGLE 11] is a subset of the `EXT_framebuffer_blit` extension from OpenGL. It adds support for separate draw- and read-framebuffer attachment points and makes it possible to copy directly between images attached to framebuffer objects. `glBlitFramebufferANGLE` is implemented via the Direct3D 9 `StretchRect` function and therefore has some further restrictions compared to the desktop version. In particular, color conversions, resizing, flipping, and filtering are not supported, and only whole depth and stencil buffers can be copied. `glBlitFramebufferANGLE` is also used to resolve multisample framebuffers.

39.3.11   Multiple Contexts and Resource Sharing

ANGLE supports multiple OpenGL ES contexts as well as sharing objects between contexts as described in Appendix C of the OpenGL ES 2.0.25 specification [Khronos 11c]. The object types that can be shared are the resource-type objects: shader objects, program objects, vertex buffer objects, texture objects, and render-buffer objects. Framebuffer objects and fences are not shareable objects. The requirement to share framebuffer objects was removed from the OpenGL ES 2.0.25 specification in order to be more compatible with OpenGL. In general, it is not desirable to share container-type objects, as this makes change propagation and deletion behavior of the shared objects difficult to specify and tricky to implement and use correctly. Furthermore, there is little value to be had from sharing container objects since they are typically quite small and have no data associated with them.

Shared contexts are specified at context creation time via the `share_context` parameter to `eglCreateContext`. As defined in the EGL 1.4 specification, a newly created context will share all shareable objects with the specified `share_context` and, by extension, with any other contexts with which `share_context` already shares. To implement these semantics, we have a resource manager class that is responsible for creating, tracking, and deleting all shared objects. All nonshared objects, framebuffers and fences, are always managed directly by the context. The resource manager can be shared between contexts. When a new, nonshared context is created, a new resource manager is instantiated. When a shared context is created, it acquires the resource manager from the shared context. Since contexts can be destroyed in any order, the resource manager is reference counted and not directly tied to any specific context.

Direct3D 9 does not have the concept of share groups like OpenGL. It is possible to share individual resources between Direct3D 9Ex devices, but this functionality is only supported on Windows Vista and later. Thus, in order to share resources between ANGLE's GL contexts, the ES and EGL implementations only make use of a single Direct3D 9 device object. The device is created by and associated with the EGL default display and made accessible to each of the GL contexts as necessary. In order to provide the required separation of state between GL contexts, we must completely transition the Direct3D state when we switch GL contexts. The `eglMakeCurrent` call provides us with the opportunity to do this when the current context is changed. With our state-caching mechanism, we simply need to mark all our cached state dirty at this point, and the necessary Direct3D state will be set for the next draw command.

The current GL context and corresponding EGL display are tracked using thread-local storage (TLS). The TLS is used to hold a pointer to the GL context that has last been made current on this thread via `eglMakeCurrent`. When a GL function call is made, the current GL context for the thread is obtained from the TLS, and the command is dispatched to the GL context. If no GL context is presently current on the thread, the GL command is silently ignored.

ANGLE supports creation of both window- and pbuffer–based EGL surfaces. Window surfaces are implemented by creating a windowed Direct3D 9 swapchain for the EGL surface using the `HWND` window handle that is passed in to `eglCreate WindowSurface` as the native window. The `eglSwapBuffers` command maps to the swapchain's `Present` method. Window resizing is handled by recreating the swapchain. Resizing can be detected either by registering a window handler for the `WM_SIZE` message or by checking the window size at the swap buffer's call. The preferred method is via the window handler, but this does not work for windows that were created in a different process. Pbuffer surfaces, which are used purely for off-screen rendering and do not need to support swapping or resizing, are implemented using Direct3D 9 render-target textures. The `eglBindTexImage` API can also be used to bind a pbuffer as a texture in order to access the contents of the pbuffer.

ANGLE also supports several EGL extensions that enable more efficient integration with applications that use Direct3D directly, such as a browser that uses it internally for the compositor or video decoding. These extensions provide a mechanism that allows textures to be shared between ANGLE's Direct3D device and other Direct3D devices. This also provides the ability to share images between processes since Direct3D resources can be shared across processes. The Direct3D 9 render-target textures that back the pbuffer surfaces can either be created from, or provide, a sharing handle [MSDN 11d]. In order to make use of this, we need a mechanism to provide or extract the Direct3D share handle via EGL.

The `ANGLE_surface_d3d_texture_2d_share_handle` extension [ANGLE 11] allows an application to obtain the Direct3D share handle from an EGL surface. This handle can then be used in another device to create a shared texture that can be used to display the contents of the pbuffer. Similarly, the `ANGLE_d3d_share_handle_client_buffer` extension [ANGLE 11] creates a pbuffer from a Direct3D share handle that is specified via `eglCreatePbufferFromClientBuffer`. This provides the ability to have ES2 content rendered into a texture that has been created by a different Direct3D device. When sharing a surface between Direct3D devices in different processes, it is necessary to use event queries to ensure that rendering to the surface has completed before using the shared resource in another device. From

the ANGLE side, this can be achieved with appropriate use of a fence or by calling
`glFinish` to ensure that the desired operations have finished.

39.3.12   Context Loss

Direct3D 9 devices can, under various scenarios, become "lost" [MSDN 11e]. On
Windows XP, this can happen when the system has a power management event such
as entering sleep mode, or screen saver activation. On Window Vista and later, when
using Direct3D 9Ex, device loss is much more infrequent but can still happen if the
hardware hangs or when the driver is stopped [MSDN 11d]. When the device is
lost, resources that were located in graphics memory are lost, and rendering related
operations are ignored. To recover from a lost Direct3D device, the application must
release the video memory resources and reset the device.

Unextended OpenGL ES does not provide a mechanism to notify the application of a lost or reset device. EGL does have the `EGL_CONTEXT_LOST` error code that
corresponds to the loss of a hardware device. By default, when a device loss occurs,
ANGLE generates an out-of-memory error on GL calls, and the context-lost error
on EGL calls, to indicate that the context is in an undefined state. In both cases,
the proper response is to destroy all the GL contexts, recreate the contexts, and then
restore any state and objects as necessary. EGL surfaces do not need to be recreated,
but their content is undefined. For details, see Section 2.6 of the EGL 1.4 specification [Khronos 11b]. WebGL applications should additionally follow the advice for
Handling Context Lost [Khronos 11a].

ANGLE supports the `EXT_robustness` extension [ANGLE 11], which is based
on the OpenGL `ARB_robustness` extension [Khronos 11d], in order to provide
a better mechanism for reporting reset notifications. This extension provides an
inexpensive query, `glGetGraphicsResetStatusEXT`, which applications can use
to learn about context resets. After receiving a reset notification, the application
should continue to query the reset status until `GL_NO_ERROR` is returned, at which
point the contexts should be destroyed and recreated.

Applications must opt into receiving reset notifications at context creation time
by specifying the reset notification strategy attribute as defined in the `EXT_create_`
`context_robustness` extension [ANGLE 11]. Note that even if an application
does not opt into receiving reset notifications, or explicitly requests no reset notifications, context loss and resets can still happen at any time. Applications should be
made capable of detecting and recovering from these events.

39.3.13   Resource Limits

The OpenGL ES 2.0 API is quite feature-rich; however, there are still some features that are optional or allow for wide variability between implementations. These
include the number of vertex attributes, varying vectors, vertex uniform vectors,
fragment uniform vectors, vertex texture image units, fragment texture image units,

maximum texture size, maximum renderbuffer size, point size range, and line width range. Applications that need more than the minimum values for any of these limits should always query the capabilities of the GL device and scale their usage based on the device's feature set. Failing to do so and assuming sufficient limits typically results in reduced portability. This is particularly important to keep in mind for WebGL development or when otherwise using a OpenGL ES 2.0 implementation, such as ANGLE, that is provided on desktop hardware. In many cases, the capabilities provided far exceed those available on mobile platforms. The complete listing of minimum requirements for the various implementation-dependent values can be obtained from Tables 6.18–6.20 of the OpenGL ES 2.0.25 specification [Khronos 11c].

Most of the ANGLE limits have been chosen to provide a maximum set of consistent capabilities across a wide range of common hardware. In some cases, the limits are constrained by the Direct3D 9 API even if the hardware has greater capabilities that could be exposed under a different API such as OpenGL or Direct3D 10. In other cases, the limits vary based on the underlying hardware capabilities which are denoted with an asterisk in Table 39.1.

The maximum vertex (254) and fragment (221) uniforms are based on the common capabilities for SM3 vertex (256) and pixel shader (224) constants, but must be lowered to account for the hidden uniforms we may use to implement some of the shader built-ins. The maximum number of varying vectors (10) is the maximum available on SM3 hardware and does not need to be reduced to account for built-in varyings since these are explicitly included in the ESSL varying packing algorithm, as described in Issue 10.16 in the ESSL specification [Khronos 11e]. The maximum texture, cube map, and renderbuffer sizes are directly based on the capabilities of the underlying device, so they range between 2048 and 16384, depending on the hardware.

Capability	ES 2.0 Minimum	ANGLE
MAX_VERTEX_ATTRIBS	8	16
MAX_VERTEX_UNIFORM_VECTORS	128	254
MAX_VERTEX_TEXTURE_IMAGE_UNITS	0	0, 4*
MAX_VARYING_VECTORS	8	10
MAX_FRAGMENT_UNIFORM_VECTORS	16	221
MAX_TEXTURE_IMAGE_UNITS	8	16
MAX_TEXTURE_SIZE	64	2048-16384*
MAX_CUBE_MAP_SIZE	16	2048-16384*
MAX_RENDERBUFFER_SIZE	1	2048-16384*
ALIASED_POINT_SIZE_RANGE (min, max)	(1, 1)	(1, 64)
ALIASED_LINE_WIDTH_RANGE (min, max)	(1, 1)	(1, 1)

Table 39.1. Resource limits. The most commonly used implementation-dependent values showing both the minimum OpenGL ES 2.0 values and the ANGLE-specific limits. The ANGLE limits are for SM3-capable hardware as of ANGLE revision 889.

39.3.14 Optimizations

To ensure that ANGLE performs as closely as possible to a native implementation of OpenGL ES 2.0, we strive to avoid redundant or unnecessary work, both on the CPU side and on the GPU side.

Much of the effective rendering state is only known at the time of a draw call, so ANGLE defers making any Direct3D render-state changes until draw time. For example, Direct3D only supports explicitly setting culling for clockwise or counterclockwise vertex-winding orders while OpenGL indicates which winding order is considered front-facing by using `glFrontFace`. `glCullFace` determines which of these sides should be culled, and `GL_CULL_FACE` enables or disables the actual culling. In theory, changing any of the `glFrontFace`, `glCullFace`, or `GL_CULL_FACE` states would alter the corresponding Direct3D render state, but by deferring this to the draw call, we reduce it to at most one change (per state) per draw call. For each related group of states, ANGLE keeps a "dirty" flag to determine whether the affected Direct3D states should be updated.

OpenGL identifies resources by integer numbers (or "names"), while the implementation requires pointers to the actual objects. This means ANGLE contains several map containers that hold the associations between resource names and object pointers. Since many object lookups are required per frame, this can cause a noticeable CPU hotspot. Fortunately the associations do not typically change very often, and for currently bound objects, the same name would be looked up many times in a row. Thus, for the currently bound objects like programs and framebuffers, the pointer is cached and replaced or invalidated only when an action is performed which modifies the association.

ANGLE also keeps track of the textures, buffers, and shaders that are currently set on the Direct3D device. To avoid issues with cases where an object gets deleted and a new one coincidentally gets created at the same memory location, resources are identified by a unique serial number instead of their pointer.

Another place caching plays a critical role in optimizing performance is in applying the vertex attribute bindings. Direct3D 9 requires all attributes to be described in a vertex declaration. Creating and later disposing of this object takes up valuable time and potentially prevents the graphics driver from minimizing internal state changes, so a cache was implemented to store the most recently used vertex declarations.

We also endeavor to minimize the GPU workload, both in terms of data transfers to/from the GPU and in terms of computational workload. As discussed earlier, we have eliminated the overhead in flipping the rendered image at presentation time, added support for buffers with static usage, implemented mechanisms to minimize texture reallocations, and used direct clear operations when masked clears are not required. We also optimize out the computation of any shader built-in variables that are not used in the shaders.

It is important to note that while all these optimizations have made ANGLE more complex, they have also significantly helped ensure that the underlying hardware, accessed through Direct3D, is used as efficiently as possible. Native driver implementations of OpenGL and OpenGL ES also require many of the same optimizations and inherent complexity in order to achieve high performance in practice.

39.3.15   Recommended Practices

Throughout this chapter, we have touched on a variety of practices that should help improve the performance and portability of applications. While these recommendations are targeted specifically at ANGLE's implementation, we expect that many of these practices will also be applicable to other GL implementations:

- Always check for optional features and validate resource limits.

- Group objects in buffers based on data format (type and layout) and update frequency.

- Ensure that appropriate buffer usage flags are used.

- Use static buffers and fully specify the contents of buffers before draw time.

- Use separate buffers for index and vertex data.

- Use immutable textures when available. If `EXT_texture_storage` is not supported, ensure that a complete texture is created and consistently defined.

- Avoid redefining the format or size of existing textures, and create a new texture instead.

- Use the `BGRA_EXT` / `UNSIGNED_BYTE` texture format to minimize texture conversions on load and for pixel readback.

- Use packed depth-stencil for combined depth and stencil support.

- Opt in to reset notifications, and handle context resets appropriately.

- Avoid masked clear operations.

- Avoid line loops by drawing closed line strips instead.

- Use fences instead of `glFinish` for finer synchronization control.

- Avoid using complex conditional statements and loops with a high maximum number of iterations in shaders.

39.3.16   Performance Results

At the time of this writing, there are no de facto benchmarks for WebGL. To correctly interpret performance results of applications and demos, one should first realize that once a draw call command reaches the GPU driver, there are, in theory, few fundamental differences between OpenGL and Direct3D. For ANGLE, in particular, the ESSL and HLSL shaders are largely equivalent, so the GPU performs essentially the same operations. Therefore applications or demos with high numbers of vertices or high levels of overdraw do not really test the graphics API implementation but rather the hardware performance itself.

Potential differences in performance between ANGLE and native OpenGL implementations would stem mainly from the graphics commands issued between draw calls (texture, buffer, and uniform updates), the setup work performed to translate a GL draw call into a Direct3D draw call, and the vertex-shader epilogue and pixel-shader prologues. Therefore, the applications and demos we chose to use for performance comparisons perform a relatively high number of draw calls, use various textures, and/or use nontrivial animations.

The results, shown in Table 39.2, reveal that ANGLE typically performs on par with desktop OpenGL drivers. This demonstrates that on Windows, it is viable to implement OpenGL ES 2.0 on top of Direct3D, and the translation does not add significant overhead.

	Desktop GL (fps)	ANGLE (fps)
MapsGL, San Francisco street level http://maps.google.com/mapsgl	32	33
WebGL Field, "lots" setting http://webglsamples.googlecode.com/hg/field/field.html	25–48	25–45
Flight of the Navigator http://videos.mozilla.org/serv/mozhacks/flight-of-the-navigator/	20 minimum	40 minimum
Skin rendering http://alteredqualia.com/three/examples/webgl_materials_skin.html	62	53

Table 39.2. Performance comparison between ANGLE and native OpenGL implementations in sample applications. The results were obtained using Google Chrome 15.0.874.106m on a laptop with a Core i7-620M (2.67 GHz dual core), GeForce 330M, running Windows 7 64-bit. Framerates were determined using FRAPS (http://www.fraps.com/), and vsync was forced off.

39.4   Future Work

ANGLE is continuing to evolve, and there is future work to be done implementing new features, improving performance, and resolving defects. Additional features that could be added include depth textures, wide lines, and multisample EGL configs. Areas for improving performance include target-dependent flipping of rendering, optimizations to texture loading and pixel readback, and bottlenecks as shown by profiling applications. Another possible future direction for ANGLE's development could be to implement a Direct3D 11 back-end. This would allow us to support features not available in Direct3D 9, future versions of the OpenGL ES API, and future operating systems where Direct3D 9 is not ubiquitous.

39.5   Conclusion

This chapter explained the motivation behind ANGLE and described how it is currently used in web browsers both as an OpenGL ES 2.0-based renderer and as a shader validator and translator. We discussed many of the challenging aspects of the implementation of this project, primarily in mapping between OpenGL and Direct3D, and explained how they were mastered. We discussed some of the optimizations we have made in our implementation in order to provide a conformant Open GL ES 2.0 driver that is both competitive in performance and fully featured. The development of ANGLE is ongoing, and we welcome contributions.

39.6   Source Code

The source for the ANGLE Project is available from the Google Code repository.[1] This repository includes the full source for the ANGLE libGLESv2 and libEGL libraries as well as some small sample programs. The project can be built on Windows with Visual C++ 2008 Express Edition or newer.

Acknowledgments We would like to acknowledge the contributions of our TransGaming colleagues Shannon Woods and Andrew Lewycky, who were coimplementers of ANGLE. Thanks also to Gavriel State and others at TransGaming for initiating the project, and to Vangelis Kokkevis and the Chrome team at Google for sponsoring and contributing extensions and optimizations to ANGLE. Finally, we thank the Mozilla Firefox team and other community individuals for their contributions to the project.

---

[1]http://code.google.com/p/angleproject/

Bibliography

[3Dlabs 05] 3Dlabs. *GLSL Demos and Source Code from the 3Dlabs OpenGL 2 Website.* http://mew.cx/glsl/, 2005 (accessed November 27, 2011).

[ANGLE 11] ANGLE Project. *ANGLE Project Extension Registry.* https://code.google.com/p/angleproject/source/browse/trunk/extensions, 2011 (accessed November 27, 2011).

[Bridge 10] Henry Bridge. *Chromium Blog: Introducing the ANGLE Project.* http://blog.chromium.org/2010/03/introducing-angle-project.html, March 18, 2010 (accessed November 27, 2011).

[Ek 05] Lars Andreas Ek, Øyvind Evensen, Per Kristian Helland, Tor Gunnar Houeland, and Erik Stiklestad. "OpenGL ES Shading Language Compiler Project Report (TDT4290)." *Department of Computer and Information Science at NTNU.* http://www.idi.ntnu.no/emner/tdt4290/Rapporter/2005/oglesslc.pdf, November 2005, (accessed November 27, 2011).

[FSF 11] Free Software Foundation. "Bison—GNU parser generator." *GNU Operating System.* http://www.gnu.org/s/bison/, May 15, 2011 (accessed November 27, 2011).

[MSDN 11a] Microsoft. *Coordinate Systems (Direct3D 9) (Windows).* http://msdn.microsoft.com/en-us/library/bb204853(VS.85).aspx, September 6, 2011 (accessed November 27, 2011).

[MSDN 11b] Microsoft. *D3DUSAGE (Windows).* http://msdn.microsoft.com/en-us/library/bb172625(VS.85).aspx, September 6, 2011 (accessed November 27, 2011).

[MSDN 11c] Microsoft. *Direct3D 9 Graphics (Windows).* http://msdn.microsoft.com/en-us/library/bb219837(VS.85).aspx, September 6, 2011 (accessed November 27, 2011).

[MSDN 11d] Microsoft. *Feature Summary (Direct3D 9 for Windows Vista).* http://msdn.microsoft.com/en-us/library/bb219800(VS.85).aspx, September 6, 2011 (accessed November 27, 2011).

[MSDN 11e] Microsoft. *Lost Devices (Direct3D 9) (Windows).* http://msdn.microsoft.com/en-us/library/bb174714(VS.85).aspx, September 6, 2011 (accessed November 27, 2011).

[MSDN 11f] Microsoft. *Point Sprites (Direct3D 9) (Windows).* http://msdn.microsoft.com/en-us/library/bb147281(VS.85).aspx, September 6, 2011 (accessed November 27, 2011).

[MSDN 11g] Microsoft. *Processing Vertex Data (Direct3D 9) (Windows).* http://msdn.microsoft.com/en-us/library/bb147296(VS.85).aspx, September 6, 2011 (accessed November 27, 2011).

[MSDN 11h] Microsoft. *ps_3.0 Registers (Windows).* http://msdn.microsoft.com/en-us/library/bb172920(VS.85).aspx, September 6, 2011 (accessed November 27, 2011).

[MSDN 11i] Microsoft. *Queries (DirectD9) (Windows).* http://msdn.microsoft.com/en-us/library/bb147308(VS.85).aspx, September 6, 2011 (accessed November 27, 2011).

[MSDN 11j] Microsoft. *Semantics (DirectX HLSL).* http://msdn.microsoft.com/en-us/library/bb509647(VS.85).aspx, September 6, 2011 (accessed November 27, 2011).

[MSDN 11k] Microsoft. *Viewports and Clipping (Direct3D 9) (Windows).* http://msdn.microsoft.com/en-us/library/bb206341(VS.85).aspx, September 6, 2011 (accessed November 27, 2011).

[Flex 08] The Flex Project. "Flex: The Fast Lexical Analyzer." *Sourceforge.* http://flex. sourceforge.net/, 2008 (accessed November 27, 2011).

[Khronos 11a] The Khronos Group. *Handling Context Lost.* http://www.khronos.org/webgl/ wiki/HandlingContextLost, November 17, 2011 (accessed November 27, 2011).

[Khronos 11b] The Khronos Group. "Khronos Native Platform Graphics Interface (EGL Version 1.4)." *Khronos EGL API Registry.* Edited by Jon Leech. http://www.khronos.org/ registry/egl/specs/eglspec.1.4.20110406.pdf, April 6, 2011 (accessed November 27, 2011).

[Khronos 11c] The Khronos Group. *OpenGL ES 2.0 Common Profile Specification (Version 2.0.25).* Edited by Aaftab Munshi and Jon Leech. http://www.khronos.org/registry/gles/ specs/2.0/es_full_spec_2.0.25.pdf, November 2, 2010 (accessed November 27, 2011).

[Khronos 11d] The Khronos Group. *OpenGL Registry.* http://www.opengl.org/registry/, (accessed November 27, 2011).

[Khronos 11e] The Khronos Group. "The OpenGL ES Shading Language (Version 1.0.17)." *Khronos OpenGL ES API Registry.* Edited by Robert J. Simpson and John Kessenich. http://www.khronos.org/registry/gles/specs/2.0/GLSL_ES_Specification_1.0.17. pdf, May 12, 2009 (accessed November 27, 2011).

[Khronos 11f] The Khronos Group. "WebGL Specification (Version 1.0)." *Khronos WebGL API Registry.* Edited by Chris Marrin. https://www.khronos.org/registry/webgl/specs/1.0/, February 10, 2011 (accessed November 27, 2011).

[TransGaming 11] TransGaming. *GameTree TV: Developers.* http://gametreetv.com/ developers, 2011 (accessed November 27, 2011).

SceneJS: A WebGL-Based Scene Graph Engine   40

Lindsay Kay

40.1   Introduction

The WebGL graphics API specification extends the capabilities of the JavaScript language to enable compatible browsers to generate 3D graphics on the GPU without the need for plugins. With JavaScript execution speed a potential bottleneck, high-performance WebGL applications rely on executing minimal JavaScript while offloading as much work as possible to the GPU in the form of shader programs written in GLSL.

This chapter describes key concepts of SceneJS, an opensource 3D engine for JavaScript that applies some simple scene-graph concepts such as state inheritance on top of WebGL [Kay 10]. The framework focuses on efficient rendering of large numbers of individually pickable and articulated objects as required for high-detail, model-viewing applications such as BIMSurfer and the BioDigital Human shown in Figure 40.1 [Berlo and Lindeque 11, BioDigital 11].

Essentially, SceneJS works by maintaining a state-optimized list of WebGL calls that is updated through a simple scene graph API based on JSON [Crockford 06]. As updates are made to the graph, SceneJS dynamically rebuilds only the affected portions of the call list, while automatically taking care of shader generation.

This chapter describes the general architecture of SceneJS, focusing mainly on the JavaScript strategies it uses to efficiently bridge its abstract scene representation with an efficient use of WebGL and how those strategies can be exploited through its API.

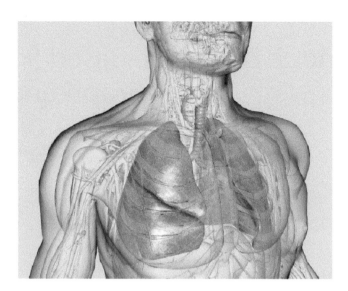

Figure 40.1. SceneJS is the rendering engine within the BioDigital Human, a free Web-based atlas of human anatomies and conditions. When all visible, the 1,886 meshes and 126 textures in the Human's male anatomy view render at around 10–15 FPS in Chrome 14.0.835.202 on a computer with an i7 CPU and an NVIDIA GeForce GTX 260M GPU.

40.2   Efficiently Abstracting WebGL

A scene graph is a data structure that arranges the logical and spatial representation of a graphical scene as a collection of nodes in a graph, typically a tree. A key feature of most scene graphs is *state inheritance*, in which child nodes inherit the states set up by parents (e.g., coordinate spaces, appearance attributes, etc.). Scene graphs typically provide a convenient abstraction on top of low-level graphics APIs, which encapsulates optimizations and API best practices, leaving the developer free to concentrate on scene content.

WebGL is based on OpenGL ES 2.0, which offloads most of the rendering work to the GPU in the form of shaders written by the graphics programmer. Thus, WebGL is geared for the limited execution speed of JavaScript, encouraging JavaScript in the application's graphics layer to be used for little more than directing GPU state: buffer allocation and binding, writing variables, draw calls, and so on.

SceneJS bridges the gap between its scene-graph API and WebGL through a five-stage pipeline:

1. Scene definition. A JSON definition like that of Listing 40.1 is parsed to create a scene graph like Figure 40.2 with resources such as vertex buffer objects (VBOs) and textures stored for its nodes on the GPU. Note the geometry nodes at the leaves.

```
SceneJS.createScene({ // Scene graph root
  type : "scene",
  id : "the-scene",
  canvasId : "my-canvas", // Bind to HTML5 canvas
  nodes: [{ // View transform with node ID
      type: "lookAt",
      id: "the-lookat",
      eye : { x : 0.0, y : 10.0, z : 15 },
      look : { y : 1.0 },
      up : { y : 1.0 },

      nodes: [{ // Projection transform
          type : "camera",
          id : "the-camera",
          optics : {
            type: "perspective",
            fovy : 25.0,
            aspect : 1.47,
            near : 0.10,
            far : 300.0
          },

        nodes: [{ // Light source
            type : "light",
            mode : "dir",
            color : { r : 1.0, g : 1.0, b : 1.0 },
            dir : { x : 1.0, y : -0.5, z : -1.0 }
          },

          { // Teapot geometry
              type : "teapot"
          },

          { // Texture for two cubes
            type : "texture",
            uri : "images/texture.jpg",

            nodes : [{ // Translate first cube
                type : "translate",
                x : 3.0,

                nodes : [{ // Cube geometry
                  type : "cube"
                }]
              },

              { // Translate second cube
                type : "translate",
                x : 6.0,

                nodes : [{ // Cube geometry
                  type : "cube"
                }]
              }]
          }]
        }]
      }]
  }]
});
```

Listing 40.1. Scene-graph definition. The scene graph is a DAG expressed in JSON, in this case defining a scene containing one teapot and two textured cubes, all illuminated by a directional light source and viewed in perspective. Geometry nodes are normally at the leaves, where they inherit the state defined by higher nodes.

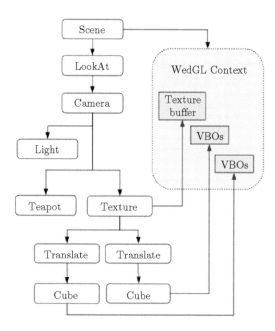

Figure 40.2. Scene graph compiled from the scene definition of Listing 40.1. Note that the geometries at the leaves inherit state from parent nodes and that various nodes hold resources allocated for them on the GPU.

2. **Draw list compilation.** The scene graph is traversed to compile a sequence of WebGL state changes. This is described in more detail in Section 40.2.1.

3. **Call list compilation.** The draw list is compiled into a fast list of WebGL calls with arguments prepared from the draw list states. As shown in Listing 40.2, call list nodes are functions that wrap WebGL calls and are created by higher-order functions that prepare and memorize their arguments in closures.

4. **State sorting.** The call-list nodes are sorted on their corresponding draw list states to minimize the number of state changes that will go down the OpenGL pipeline, as described in Section 40.2.2.

5. **Call list execution.** The call list is executed to render the frame.

Once the scene is created, we start its render loop, which executes these stages to render the first frame. Note that each stage caches its results. Then, with the render loop running, we can receive scene-state updates through the API's scene accessor methods, as shown in Listing 40.3, which we buffer for batch processing at the start of each loop.

```
//..
callList.push(
  (function() {
    // Call arguments prepared and cached in a closure.
    var uEyePosLoc = currentDrawListNode.shader.getUniformLocation("uEyePos");
    var eye = currentDrawListNode.lookAt.eye;

    // The WebGL call. The eye is a state object that is shared
    // by reference with the scene graph's lookAt node and the
    // draw list node.
    return function() {
      glContext.uniform3fv(uEyePosLoc, [eye.x, eye.y, eye.z]);
    }
})());
```

Listing 40.2. Call-list compilation. Each WebGL call is wrapped by a function that is created by a higher-order function that prepares the arguments and caches them in a closure. In this example, for efficiency, the higher-order function finds and caches the location of a shader uniform and gets the lookAt state's eye position in a variable for faster access.

Different types of scene-state updates require re-execution from different stages of the pipeline in order to synchronize the rendered view. As we process the buffered updates, we minimize JavaScript execution by re-executing the pipeline from the latest stage, which will synchronize the view for all updates. Note that the pipeline is not executed when the buffer is empty.

Most types of scene update are written straight through to the draw and call lists without requiring retraversals to rebuild states and without the addition/removal of

```
// Find the scene and start it:
var scene = SceneJS.scene("the-scene");
scene.start();

// Find the lookAt node and get its eye attribute:
var lookAt = scene.findNode("the-lookat");
var eye = lookAt.get("eye");

// Set the lookAt's eye attribute:
lookAt.set({ eye: { x : eye.x + 5.0 } });

// Create another light:
scene.findNode("the-camera").add({
  nodes: [{
    type : "light", dir : { y : -1.0 }
  }]
});
```

Listing 40.3. Scene-graph accessors. The scene graph is encapsulated by API functions that provide read and write access to node states, render loop control, picking, and so forth. Note that write access is not provided for states that would require reallocation of GPU-bound resources.

list nodes. This is supported by sharing state between the lists via common objects, restrictions on what state may be updated, and the simple approach to state inheritance described in Section 40.2.1. Therefore, for most types of update, including camera movements, color changes, and object visibility,[1] we need only re-execute the pipeline from Stage 5.

This approach is tuned to applications in which the scene-graph structure does not change often, where it suffices to hold content in the graph most of the time, toggling its visibility to enable or disable it.

The most expensive type of update involves the addition of nodes to the scene. For this type, we must re-execute the pipeline from Stage 1 to reparse the JSON definitions for the new nodes, then rebuild the draw and call lists. Almost as expensive are node relocations and removals, for which we need to re-execute from Stage 2.

SceneJS is a lean rendering kernel that does not include visibility culling and physics. However, the efficiency with which it processes updates to object visibilities and transforms makes it practical for integrating external libraries for these tasks, such as jsBVH for culling [Rivera 10] and ammo.js for physics [Zakai 11].

40.2.1   Draw-List Compilation

We construct the draw list by traversing the scene graph in depth-first order while maintaining a stack for each scene-node type, pushing each node's state to the appropriate stack on pre-visit, then popping it again on post-visit. At each geometry, we create a draw-list node that references the state at the top of each stack. We also generate a GLSL shader for the draw-list node, tailored to render the configuration of states that the node references. For reuse by other nodes with similar states, we hash the shader on those states and store it in a pool.

Each draw-list node has everything needed for a draw call to render a scene object. Figure 40.3 shows the state-sorted draw list compiled from the scene graph of Figure 40.2.

For most node types, the state at the top of the stack completely overrides the states lower in the stack, resulting in geometries inheriting state only from the closest parent of that type. As mentioned in Section 40.2, this means that updates to inherited states of these types will write straight through to the draw and call lists via shared state objects, requiring neither scene retraversal nor addition/removal of draw- or call-list nodes.

Two node types are special cases, however:

1. For modeling transform nodes, we maintain a stack of matrices; at each of these nodes, we multiply that node's matrix by the top of the stack before pushing it. The top matrix at each leaf geometry is then referenced by a draw-list node. An update to any transform node (e.g., changing a rotation angle),

---

[1]The call list nodes are actually indexed by their draw-list nodes: as we execute the calls, we can therefore efficiently skip the calls associated with invisible draw-list nodes.

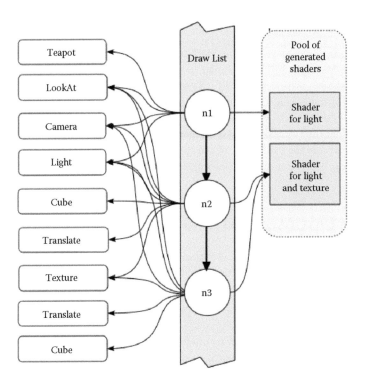

Figure 40.3. State-sorted draw list compiled from the scene graph of Figure 40.2. Nodes n1, n2, and n3 reference the states needing to be set on WebGL to draw the teapot and cubes at the leaves of the scene graph. Nodes n2 and n3 reference a similar state configuration and therefore reference the same shader.

therefore, requires us to re-execute the SceneJS pipeline from Stage 2 to retraverse the branch to recalculate stale draw-list matrices.

2. Geometry nodes may be nested to support VBO sharing, as described in Section 40.3.2, which is where a parent geometry node defines vertex arrays that are inherited by child geometries. For this case, draw-list nodes are created for leaf geometries as usual, except that as we stack geometry states, we accumulate on those the arrays belonging to any state already on the top of the stack. Updates to the vertex arrays on the geometry nodes are still efficient, however, since the arrays themselves are shared by reference amongst the scene, draw- and call-list nodes.

40.2.2   State Sorting

State sorting involves minimizing the number of state changes that go down the OpenGL pipeline by grouping similar states within the call list. We sort the call-list nodes by shader, texture, then VBO. Shader is our primary order because switching shaders causes widespread disruption of the OpenGL pipeline, necessitating the re-bind of all other states. We order on textures next because during development, we observed that they were slower to bind than VBOs.[2] A further state sort is performed when we execute the call list, in which we track the ID of the last state change that we made on WebGL so that we don't make the same change twice.

40.3   Optimizing the Scene

The API supports several scene-definition techniques that improve scene performance by exploiting the state sorting order and the pipeline described in Section 40.2.

40.3.1   Texture Atlases

A texture atlas is a large image that contains many subimages, each of which is used as a texture for a different geometry, or different parts of the same geometry. The subtextures are applied by mapping the geometries' texture coordinates to different regions of the atlas. As mentioned earlier, SceneJS sorts the draw list by shader, then by texture. As long as each of the geometry nodes inherits the same configuration of parent-node states and can therefore share the same shader, the draw list will bind the texture once for all the geometries. Another important benefit of texture atlases is that they reduce the number of HTTP requests for texture images [NVIDIA 04].

40.3.2   VBO Sharing

VBO sharing is a technique in which a parent geometry node defines vertices (consisting of arrays of positions, normal vectors, and UV coordinates) that are inherited by child geometry nodes, which supply their own index arrays pointing into different portions of the vertices. The parent VBOs are then bound once across the draw calls for all the children. Each child is a separate object, around which, as shown in Listing 40.4, each child geometry can be wrapped by a different texture or material, etc. This is efficient to render as long as each child geometry inherits a similar combination of states and thus avoids needing to switch generated shaders, as described in Section 40.2.1.

---

[2] In Chrome 14.0.835.202, running on Ubuntu 10.0.4 with NVIDIA GeForce GTX 260M GPU.

```
{
  type : "geometry",
  positions : [...], // All positions
  normals : [...], // All normals
  uv : [...], // All UVs

  nodes: [{
      type : "texture",
      uri :  "someTexture.jpg",
      nodes : [{
        type : "geometry",
        primitive : "triangles",
        indices : [...] // Faces for this geometry
      }]
    },
    {
      type : "texture",
      uri : "anotherTexture.jpg",
      nodes : [{
        type : "geometry",
        primitive : "triangles",
        indices : [...] // Faces for this geometry
      }]
    },
    {
      type : "texture",
      uri :  "oneMoreTexture.jpg",
      nodes : [{
        type : "geometry",
        primitive : "triangles",
        indices : [...] // Faces for this geometry
      }]
    }
  ]
}
```

Listing 40.4. VBO sharing to reduce binding calls, as described in Section 40.3.2. In this example, a parent defines VBOs of positions, UVs, and normals that are inherited by the children, which define their primitives through index arrays pointing into different portions of the VBOs. Each child also applies a different texture to its portion.

40.3.3   Sharable Node Cores

Traditionally, reuse within a scene graph is done by attaching nodes to multiple parents. For dynamically updated scenes, this can have a performance impact when the engine must traverse multiple parent paths in the scene graph, so SceneJS takes an alternative approach with *node cores*, a concept borrowed from OpenSG [OpenSG 10].

A node core is the node's state. Having multiple nodes share a core means that they share the same state. This can have two performance benefits:

1. An update to a shared node can write through to multiple draw- and call-list nodes simultaneously.

```
// Define a couple of nodes, in a library
// to prevent them rendering by themselves:
{
  type : "library",
  nodes : [
    {
      type : "geometry",
      coreId  : "my-geometry-core",
      positions : [..],
      indices : [..],
      primitive : "triangles"
    },
    {
      type : "material",
      coreId : "my-material-core",
      baseColor : { r: 1.0 }
    }
  ]
},

// Share their cores:
{
  type : "material",
  id : "my-material",
  coreId : "my-material-core",
  nodes : [
    {
      type : "geometry",
      coreId : "my-geometry-core"
    }
  ]
}
```

Listing 40.5. State reuse through shared node cores, described in Section 40.3.3. We define `geometry` and `material` nodes within a `library` node, which prevents them from being rendered. The `geometry` and `material` each have a `coreId` which allows their state (VBOs, color etc.) to be shared by other nodes of the same type later in the scene.

2. There is increased chance of identical repeated states having matching IDs when executing the call list, which, as described in Section 40.2.2, tracks the state IDs to avoid redundantly reapplying them.

Listing 40.5 shows an example of node-core sharing through the scene-definition API.

40.4   Picking

We use a variation of the pipeline described in Section 40.2 for mouse picking. When a pick is made, we compile the scene graph to special *pick-mode* draw and call lists, which render each pickable object in a different color to an offscreen pickbuffer. We then read the pixel at the pick coordinates and map its color back to the picked object.

Frameworks using this technique typically reduce the viewport to a 1×1 region at the pick coordinates for efficiency while rendering the pickbuffer. SceneJS uses the entire original viewport so that it can retain the pick buffer to support fast repicking at different coordinates for the case when nothing has changed in the image since the last pick. This supports fast mouseover effects such as tool-tips.

40.5   Conclusion

When aiming for high-performance 3D graphics in the browser, the greatest performance bottleneck is JavaScript overhead. To overcome this bottleneck, WebGL applications can greatly benefit from clever caching strategies and the use of optimizations like compilation to closures. The retained mode API of SceneJS benefits from this kind of preprocess optimization where complex dynamic code can be compiled to a fast static form. That said, classical techniques such as vertex sharing and texture mapping still have the same impact as in any other OpenGL application and should still be applied.

SceneJS is opensource software with many more features than were described here. Moving forward, its road map will continue to focus on high-detail, model-viewing applications; extend its optimizations for scenes in which nodes are frequently added, relocated, and removed; and leverage emerging technologies such as Web Workers and Google Native Client for additional performance.

Bibliography

[Berlo and Lindeque 11] Leon Van Berlo and Rehno Lindeque. "BIMSurfer." http://bimsurfer.org, September 8, 2011.

[BioDigital 11] BioDigital. "BioDigital Human." http://biodigitalhuman.com, August 31, 2011.

[Crockford 06] Douglas Crockford. "RFC 4627." http://tools.ietf.org/html/rfc4627, July 2006.

[Kay 10] Lindsay Kay. "SceneJS." http://scenejs.org, January 22, 2010.

[NVIDIA 04] NVIDIA. "Improve Batching Using Texture Atlases." ftp://download.nvidia.com/developer/NVTextureSuite/Atlas_Tools/Texture_Atlas_Whitepaper.pdf, September 7, 2004.

[OpenSG 10] OpenSG. "OpenSG: Node Cores." http://www.opensg.org/htdocs/doc-1.8/NodeCores.html, February 8, 2010.

[Rivera 10] Jon-Carlos Rivera. "jsBVH." https://github.com/imbcmdth/jsBVH, April 4, 2010.

[Zakai 11] Alon Zakai. "ammo.js." https://github.com/kripken/ammo.js, May 29, 2011.

Features and Design Choices 41
in SpiderGL

Marco Di Benedetto, Fabio Ganovelli, and
Francesco Banterle

41.1   Introduction

Technologies related to computer graphics (CG) are constantly growing. This is
mostly due to the widespread availability of 3D acceleration hardware with an un-
precedented ratio of performance to cost. In the past, access to such accelerators was
confined to workstations; nowadays, even handheld devices such as smartphones are
equipped with powerful graphics hardware. On a parallel timeline, with the introduction of OpenGL, CG software has moved to proprietary solutions from royalty-
free specifications. In addition, widespread access to broadband Internet connections
have led to a tremendous increase in content availability, as well as a great enrichment
of web technologies, such as HTML5.

In this mature scenario, the WebGL specification was introduced to allow CG
and web programmers to leverage the power of GPUs directly within web pages.
WebGL is a powerful technology based on the OpenGL ES 2.0 specification, and
it thus adheres to the philosophy of a barebones low-level API. As it happens in
similar contexts, a series of higher-level libraries have been developed to ease usage
and implement more complex constructs.

SpiderGL [Di Benedetto et al. 10] is a JavaScript CG library that uses WebGL
for real-time rendering. The library exposes a series of utilities, data structures, and
algorithms to serve typical graphics tasks. When developing SpiderGL, we wanted
to create a library able to simplify the most common usage pattern of WebGL, and
that could guarantee a seamless integration into complex software packages. Its role
of *middleware* imposed on us a need to enforce consistency whenever users wanted

to access the underlying WebGL layer, and to provide a solid foundation for the development of higher-level components. The library can be downloaded from the SpiderGL website, http://spidergl.org.

In this chapter, we discuss the most important choices that we made while designing and developing SpiderGL. In Section 41.2, we will briefly discuss the library architecture. The definition of 3D objects is detailed in Section 41.3. Section 41.4 discusses the problems arising from the object-binding paradigm imposed by the API and how we deal with it. In Section 41.5, we describe how SpiderGL wraps native WebGL objects and how we guarantee a robust interoperability with low-level calls. Section 41.6 draws conclusions from our work.

41.2   Library Architecture

The global philosophy of the SpiderGL library is to provide a procedural interface to typical CG algorithms and data structures. With the procedural approach, it is possible to create higher-level interfaces, i.e., scene graphs, that use SpiderGL as a lower-level library. In designing this software, we imposed on ourselves a series of requirements, the most important of which was to never prevent the user from directly accessing WebGL native functionality. Guaranteeing this property means that a seamless cooperation of high-level SpiderGL code and low-level WebGL calls can be achieved, giving more freedom to users.

The library is composed of several modules, implemented as JavaScript namespace objects. The top-level object, `SpiderGL`, serves as the main library namespace and avoids polluting the JavaScript global object. The encapsulation of symbols within modules create a clean structure but results in more verbose code. For this reason, we provide a function that opens each module namespace, making contained symbols properties of the global object and thus accessible without qualifying them. For example, after opening namespaces, the generic object `SpiderGL.Some`
`Module.SomeClass` is aliased by `SglSomeClass`; this means that when adding new symbols, we have to avoid name clashes across modules.

There are top-level modules intended to provide most of the interfaces needed by users, and transversal modules, e.g., components whose functionalities are used by other modules. The following is a brief description of what SpiderGL modules contain:

- Core. Basic constant definitions and the `SglObject` class, the base prototype used by every object of the library.

- Type. Symbolic constants that represents scalar types, i.e., `SGL_UINT16` and `SGL_FLOAT32`, as well as functions to convert from and to WebGL-type symbolic constants. Utility functions to identify JavaScript types, i.e., `isArray()`, and implement prototypal inheritance are also provided.

- Utility. Functions for object merging, retrieving of default values, and other common functionalities.

- DOM. Access function to DOM elements such as text retrieval.

- Math. Definition of the most common mathematical objects used in computer graphics, such as vectors, matrices, and quaternions.

- Space. Geometric entities and transformation-related utilities such as the `SglTransformationStack`, which provides an easy-to-use interface resembling the fixed-functionality OpenGL matrix stack.

- IO. Classes and functions to access remote content. The `SglRequest` class serves as the base type for text, JSON, and binary requests.

- WebGL. Functions and wrappers that simplify the usage of the corresponding WebGL objects and expose an expressive interface for object editing.

- Model. Classes and functions for defining and rendering of 3D objects. These allow us to use the same structure both for JavaScript-based algorithms, e.g., relying on system memory storage, and WebGL rendering.

- UI. Interfaces inspired by the GLUT library to handle rendering canvas events.

To ease the use of the library, all functions and object methods have default values. Object methods also have the possibility of restoring state default values by using the special SGL_DEFAULT symbolic constant, i.e.,

```
texture.minFilter = gl.NEAREST;
// ...
texture.minFilter = SGL_DEFAULT; // Restore default value
```

Default values can be changed by simply redefining them after the library script has been processed. In this way, it is possible to configure the default behavior of the library on a per-application, e.g., per-page, basis.

41.3 Representing 3D Objects

One of the features that most characterizes a CG library is how 3D models are represented. Approaches like *scene graphs* generally organize the model as a set of nodes (see SceneJS in Chapter 40), possibly resembling an identifiable, rooted subtree in a more complex graph that comprehends all the elements of a scene. Each node serves as a basic building block, like data sources, i.e., vertex buffers, rendering states, submodel partitions, and hierarchical and spatial relationships through transformation chains. SpiderGL is mostly a *procedural library* that exposes several fundamental

components, intended to be combined in a procedural way to form more complex
entities. Even if a scene graph layer can be built on top of the library, it is indeed clear
that a flexible way of representing 3D models is needed, both for creating content-
rich scenes and for offering a flexible and performancewise data structure that can be
effectively used in applied research or algorithm prototyping.

In SpiderGL, the 3D model went through an upgrading design process, during
which we tried to keep the flexibility of a raw structure while adding expressiveness.

In the first versions, we used a *mesh* to represent a 3D object: the structure was
simply a set of *vertex* and *primitive streams*. Each vertex stream was composed of a
data container, implemented as a vertex buffer, and a data-layout descriptor, which
encapsulated all the information needed to describe the stream, and the parameters
to pass to a call to `vertexAttribPointer()`. *Constant vertex streams*, i.e., a single attribute shared by all vertices, were represented as a four-component array of
floats, to be used as the input of a `vertexAttrib4fv()` call. Similarly, a primitive stream was composed of an index buffer and the associated parameters to call
`drawElements()`. In the case of nonindexed primitives, the stream was just composed of the parameter set needed by `drawArrays()`. This structure was raw, direct,
and simple to use, but it lacked the possibility of organizing vertex attributes in an interleaved layout. Due to memory-controller architecture and prefetching strategies,
tightly packed attributes together can improve performance, especially on low-end
devices.

In the second implementation of the mesh structure, we relaxed the constraint
that a data source could serve only one stream. A vertex or indexed primitive stream
could refer by name to the source buffer, thus allowing interleaved layouts.

An important feature that we believed to be a powerful point in exploiting the
generality of the WebGL API was the lack of *semantic* information associated with
vertex streams. They were only identified by arbitrary names, and it was up to
the programmer to establish a correspondence between them and vertex-shader attributes. For example, by reusing a standard flat-color shader program, it was possible
to use the per-vertex texture coordinates as vertex positions to perform a color rendering in texture space. However, even if this made it possible to decouple vertex
streams from vertex shader attributes, not having semantic information implied that
common algorithms, i.e., bounding box and surface normal calculation, did not have
a way to identify the vertex attributes they needed.

Finally, we decided to add semantic information and redesign the mesh as a more
complete structure. The result was a more expressive representation, namely, the
model. Contrary to a mesh, a model is a complex structure made of logic *parts*. Each
part represents a structural piece of geometry that should be considered indivisible.
However, to cope with the WebGL limitation that sets to $2^{16} - 1$ the maximum representable vertex index in an indexed primitive stream, each model part is composed
of a set of chunks.

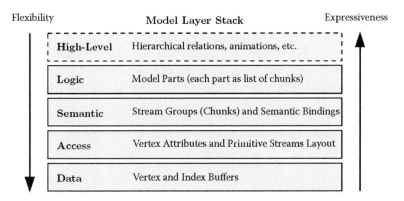

Figure 41.1. The stack of layers composing the model structure.

41.3.1 The Model Layer Stack

As shown in Figure 41.1, the model is a *stack of layers*. Each layer represents information at a different level-of-detail and depends only on the previous one in a bottom-up fashion. As the stack is walked bottom to top, information becomes higher level, adding expressiveness to data. Conversely, in descending layers from top to bottom, fewer restrictions are imposed, incrementing flexibility. In the following, we see what each layer represents and how it is encoded.

Data layer. This is where raw data are stored; it is partitioned into a vertex and an index data source. Each source can be stored in three ways: regular JavaScript arrays, typed arrays [Group 11b], and WebGL buffers. The storage alternatives are

```
model.data = {
  vertexBuffers : {
    "vbufferA" : {
      type : SGL_FLOAT32 ,
      untypedArray : // [ ... ],
      typedArray : new Float32Array(...),
      glBuffer : new SglVertexBuffer(gl, ...)
    },
    "vbufferB" : {
      // Similar to "vbufferA"
    },
    // ...
  },
  indexBuffers : {
    "ibufferA" : { /* similar to a vertex buffer */ },
    // ...
  }
};
```

Listing 41.1. An example of the model Data layer.

not mutually exclusive, meaning that model data can be kept in system and graphics memory at the same time. This is particularly useful because it avoids the definition of two different model structures. For example, algorithms that perform calculations on the geometry can access the regular or typed array, while rendering algorithms will use wrapped `WebGLBuffer` objects. Listing 41.1 shows the data-layer structure.

Access layer. The access layer provides the needed information to generate vertex attribute and primitive streams that will be fed into the rendering pipeline.

A vertex attribute stream can refer *by name* to a vertex buffer in the data layer along with layout and accessing parameters (i.e., the needed information to perform a `vertexAttribPointer()` call), or it can store a single 4-dimensional value that will be used by every vertex (i.e., as in `vertexAttrib4fv()`).

Similarly, a primitive stream can define an indexed primitive flow by referencing an index buffer in the data layer and its layout parameters (i.e., to be used in `drawElements()`) or a nonindexed primitive array range (i.e., translated in a `drawElements()` call) (see Listing 41.2).

```
model.access = {
  vertexStreams : {
    "vstreamA" : {
      buffer : "vbufferA",
      size : 3,
      type : SGL_FLOAT32,
      normalized : false,
      stride : 0,
      offset : 0
    },
    "vstreamB" : { /* similar to "vstreamA" */ },
    "vstreamC" : { value: [1, 0.5, 0, 1] }, // Constant stream
    // ...
  },
  primitiveStreams : {
    "pstreamA" : { // indexed primitives
      buffer : "ibufferA",
      mode : SGL_TRIANGLES,
      count : triCount * 3,
      type : SGL_UINT16,
      offset : 0
    },
    "pstreamB" : { // non-indexed primitives
      mode : SGL_POINTS,
      first : 0,
      count : verticesCount
    },
    // ...
  }
};
```

Listing 41.2. An example of the model Access layer.

Semantic layer. The general idea of the semantic layer is to define, for each way a model is intended to be rendered, e.g., a shader program or rendering pass, a group

```
model.semantic = {
  bindings : {
    "bindingA" : {
      vertexStreams : {
        "POSITION" : [ "vstreamA" ],
        "TEXCOORD" : [ "vstreamB" /*, "vstreamB2", ... */ ],
        "COLOR" : [ "vstreamC" ]
      },
      primitiveStreams : {
        "FILL" : [ "pstreamA" ],
        "POINT" : [ "pstreamB" ]
      }}},
  chunks : {
    "chunkA" : {
      techniques : {
        "common" : { binding : "bindingA" }
  }}}
};
```

Listing 41.3. An example of the model Semantic layer.

of vertex streams with associated semantics. This information can then be used by computational geometry or rendering algorithms, e.g., bounding-box calculation, or to bind model vertex streams to the corresponding input attributes of a vertex shader.

The semantic layer is also used to define indivisible model subparts. This necessity comes from the WebGL specification that limits the number of indexable vertices in a buffer to 2^{16}. Once subparts, or *chunks*, have been defined, the logic layer can assemble them to form whole model parts. Inspired by the COLLADA [Group 11a] schema, each chunk can specify several semantic bindings, depending on the access or *rendering technique* that will operate on it, as shown in Listing 41.3.

For each semantic value, e.g., `"TEXCOORD"`, it is possible to specify an array of streams, each one referring to a semantic *set*, i.e., two sets of texture coordinates. As in COLLADA, the `common` technique refers to a reasonable, general-purpose semantic binding.

Logic layer. Each model can be composed of parts that have a logical or structural meaning, i.e., the wheel, windshield, and body parts of a car model. The purpose of the logic layer is just to group chunks to form a named model part (see Listing 41.4).

```
model.logic = {
  parts : {
    "whole" : {
      chunks : [ "chunkA" /*, "chunkB", ... */ ]
    }
  }
};
```

Listing 41.4. An example of the model Logic layer.

High-level layers.   The layer stack of the model is kept open to future additions. The high-level category is intended to host layers that progressively add more expressive information. Such layers can be used to define hierarchical relations among model parts, animation paths, or even annotations.

The layered structure of the model allows flexibility and expressiveness during algorithm development. As features are added to SpiderGL, we exploit the extendability of this structure to give users a thorough object that can be used at the level of abstraction required by the application being developed.

To give the the library a good usability level, however, the flexible model structure must be coupled with a series of manageable WebGL support utilities. The next section discusses the most important design choices we adopted in the WebGL module to ease the development of a real-time rendering application.

41.4   Direct Access to WebGL Object State

WebGL exposes a powerful API that allows its users to leverage the performance of graphics accelerators. The API deals with low-level objects and operations and follows the philosophy of providing everything that is necessary, but nothing more. In this situation, it is often necessary to develop higher-level libraries that add expressiveness and, at the same time, simplify the most common usage patterns. Such libraries are classified as *middleware*, to underline their placement between low-level access and higher-level systems, such as thorough engines.

With SpiderGL, we wanted to develop a library that allowed a seamless interoperability with native WebGL calls. To achieve this, we had to tackle a usage pattern that is imposed by the WebGL specification. This pattern comes from the context-centric state machine nature of the API, which requires the adoption of a particular binding paradigm to operate on resources or objects in general.

In general, WebGL objects have an internal state, like attributes or *parameters*, and encapsulate some sort of data, like raw memory chunks in buffers or images in textures. Objects can be *edited* to make changes to their internal state or data, or they can be *bound* to particular *binding sites* or *targets* of the rendering context to be used by some stages of the rendering pipeline. As an example, consider Listing 41.5.

Function **update** modifies the **paintTex** texture object, i.e., sets the color of one of its texels, while function **draw** uses it to perform rendering. Here, we are witnessing a twofold or overloaded usage of the **bindTexture()** method: at line 3 **paintTex** is bound so that the following *editing* command, **texSubImage2D()**, operates on it; at line 9, the same **paintTex** is bound to the rendering context so that it can be accessed by some pipeline stages, e.g., by vertex and fragment shaders, when a drawing command is issued. These syntactically equal but semantically different ways in which the bind function is used are collectively known to OpenGL developers as the *bind-to-edit/bind-to-use* paradigm.

```
1  function update(x, y) {
2    // Update a single texel of the texture image
3    gl.bindTexture(gl.TEXTURE_2D, paintTex);
4    gl.texSubImage2D(gl.TEXTURE_2D, 0, x, y, 1, 1,
5      gl.RGBA, gl.UNSIGNED_BYTE, selectedColor);
6  }
7  function draw() {
8    // Clear framebuffer, setup matrices, program etc.
9    gl.bindTexture(gl.TEXTURE2D, paintTex);
10   doSomething();
11   gl.drawElements(...);
12 }
```

Listing 41.5. Example of bind-to-edit/bind-to-use paradigm.

41.4.1 The Problem

It is important to understand the side effects of this paradigm in the editing phase: the previous binding is *broken*, that is, the object T previously bound to the involved target (**TEXTURE_2D** in the above example) is unbound in favor of the object to be edited. This may not be a problem if whoever has bound T is aware that the binding has been or is going to be broken. In the above example, whoever wrote the **draw** function probably wanted **paintTex** to be bound at the time **drawElements()** is called (line 11). To this end, the developer must be sure that the function call **doSomething()** at line 10 does not break the binding. Of course, in this simple example, the code could be probably rearranged to ensure this precondition (i.e., swap lines 9 and 10), but in real and more complex scenarios, this is not easily feasible. This is particularly true whenever third-party middleware, layered libraries, are used.

OpenGL developers are aware of this, so they changed their coding habits to avoid such situations. But this comes at some cost, especially for the ones who write layered libraries. In fact, the advocated solution to this issue is that, whenever a function acts on a binding, it must recover the existing one, as shown in Listing 41.6.

At line 2, the context is queried to retrieve the object currently bound to the target of interest; at line 3 the object that must be edited or used is bound, and operations occurs on it (line 4); at line 5 the previously bound object is restored. This *query/bind/set/restore* strategy causes of course a burden both in code writing and at runtime.

```
1  function doSomething() {
2    var boundTex = gl.getParameter(gl.TEXTURE_BINDING_2D);
3    gl.bindTexture(gl.TEXTURE_2D, someTex);
4    gl.texParameteri(gl.TEXTURE_2D, gl.TEXTURE_WRAP_S, gl.REPEAT);
5    gl.bindTexture(gl.TEXTURE_2D, boundTex);
6  }
```

Listing 41.6. A possible solution to the layered library problem.

41.4.2   A Solution

A simpler and cleaner implementation of `doSomething()` could be made if we have
the opportunity to directly specify the object we want to operate on:

```
function doSomething() {
  gl.texParameteri(someTex, gl.TEXTURE_2D, gl.TEXTURE_WRAP_S, gl.↵
    REPEAT);
}
```

Other than making development easier, this way of operating on objects is also closer
to an object-oriented paradigm. To overcome the issues of the bind-to-edit/bind-
to-use paradigm, the **EXT_direct_state_access** (DSA) extension [Kilgard 10]
was developed and made official in desktop OpenGL. For each editing function in
the specification that relies on the current binding (or other context state, in which
case, it is referred to as *selector state*), the DSA extension exposes a corresponding
function that takes, usually as first argument, the object to operate on. Even if
DSA does not completely solve all the problems, it is a great step toward a cleaner
API.

Unfortunately, WebGL does not have DSA, so current bindings and state selec-
tors are the only way to manipulate object state. SpiderGL can be used as a middleware library, meaning that we have to cope with the above problems. Since the
first version of the library, wrappers for WebGL objects (e.g., buffers, framebuffers,
programs, renderbuffers, shaders, and textures) were developed and exposed to simplify their usage, with expressive constructor options, methods, and parameter setters
and getters (see Section 41.5); in the initial releases, wrappers were required to be explicitly bound before any editing on them occurred. The usage pattern was of the
form:

```
var tex = new SglTexture2D(...); // Encapsulates a WebGLTexture
tex.bind();
tex.wrapS = gl.REPEAT; // Hidden call to gl.texParameteri()
tex.unbind();
```

We did not want to impose this requirement and did not feel comfortable with it
while we were coding.

An important design choice had to be taken. The first option was to secretly apply the *query/bind/set/restore* strategy, but this would have made the library code full
of replicated and tedious code, not to mention the redundant or avoidable object-
binding penalties that arise when setting several parameters on the same object. Another option was to add special methods to set a whole bunch of parameters at once,
but this would not have prevented the user set from tiny parameters individually.
Similarly bad, removing single-parameter settings could have caused the wrapper usage to be more verbose than necessary.

```
gl._spidergl = { };   // private SpiderGL injections container.

gl._spidergl.setupXYZ = setupXYZ;
gl._spidergl.xyz = null;
// ... other extensions ...

// A reference to native getExtension is saved ...
gl._spidergl.getExtension = gl.getExtension;

// ... and replaced to expose new extensions
gl.getExtension = function (name) {
  var sgl = this._spidergl;
  switch (name) {
    case "SGL_XYZ":
      if (!sgl.xyz) {
        sgl.setupXYZ(this); // setup extension on first call
      }
      return sgl.xyz;
    // ... other extensions ...
    default: // call to native getExtension
      return sgl.getExtension.apply(this, arguments);
  }
};
```

Listing 41.7. The modified `getExtension()` method for extension injection.

A drastic design choice had to be taken, even if it meant hijacking the `WebGL RenderingContext` object. This decision breaks our initial policy that we not modify the context object in any way. However, after realistic tests showed us that the replacement of some methods of the context object does not sensibly impact performance, we decided to inject the direct state access functionality through custom extensions. We defined two extensions, `SGL_current_binding` and `SGL_direct_state_access`, accessible using the standard WebGL extension mechanism, that is, the `getExtension()` method of the context object. The `SGL_current_binding` extension is used to track the current binding of each target and avoid querying the WebGL context via `getParameter()`, while `SGL_direct_state_access` is based on the query/bind/set/restore strategy. To make extensions available, the `get Extension()` method was replaced with the code in Listing 41.7.

The property `_spidergl` is added to the context as a container for all SpiderGL-related injections. For each installed extension, a setup function and the extension object itself are stored in the container property. The purpose of having a setup function is to comply with the WebGL specification: in fact, an extension is enabled and exposed when it is requested for the first time; later calls will just return the already created extension object, if any. In Listing 41.7, considering a hypothetical XYZ extension, placeholders `"SGL_XYZ"`, `setupXYZ`, and `xyz` refer, respectively, to the extension name string, the function that initializes and installs the extension, and the name of the property of the `_spidergl` injections container that will refer to the extension object. For example, placeholders for the `SGL_current_binding`

```
 1  function setupXYZ(gl) {
 2    var ext = { };  // the object returned by getExtension()
 3
 4    // store extension in SpiderGL container:
 5    //   "cb"  -> SGL_current_binding
 6    //   "dsa" -> SGL_direct_state_access
 7    //   ...
 8    gl._spidergl.xyz = ext;
 9
10    // extension private data with reference to context
11    ext._ = { gl : gl };
12
13    setupPrivateXYZ(gl);
14    hijackContextXYZ(gl);
15    setupPublicXYZ(gl);
16  }
```

Listing 41.8. Extension setup skeleton.

extension will be replaced by "SGL_current_binding", setupCurrentBinding, and cb.

We will show how our extensions work and are implemented for a single type of WebGL object, namely, the WebGLBuffer. Other object types are handled in the same way, and the relative implementation simply follows the code that handles buffer objects. A slightly different solution has been used: for WebGLTexture objects, even if using the same concepts, a further level of tracking and handling is introduced to take into account the different state of each texture unit.

To show how extensions are implemented, we use the code in Listing 41.8 as a general setup skeleton, where XYZ is a placeholder for the extension being discussed. If needed, the function setupPrivateXYZ() sets up the extension internal state and functions, hijackContextXYZ() replaces public methods of the WebGLRenderingContext object with extension-specific modified versions, and setupPublicXYZ() defines public extension-specific constants and functions.

41.4.3   Bind Tracking and Binding Stack with SGL_current_binding

The purpose of the *current binding* (CB) extension is to have a fast way for retrieving the object currently bound to a specific target. After benchmarking, we found that a naive implementation is much faster than querying the context with getParameter(). The extension also provides a utility *stack* for every binding target, with typical *push* and *pop* functions. Referring to line 8 in Listing 41.8, the extension object is accessed by the cb property of the _spidergl container object installed in the rendering context.

For each target, extension private data consist of a reference to the currently bound object and an array of object references, initially empty, to implement stack

```
function setupPrivateCB(gl) {
  var _ = gl._spidergl.cb._; // Extension private data

  _.currentBuffer = { }; // Store per-target binding state
  _.currentBuffer[gl.ARRAY_BUFFER] =
    gl.getParameter(gl.ARRAY_BUFFER_BINDING);
  _.currentBuffer[gl.ELEMENT_ARRAY_BUFFER] =
    gl.getParameter(gl.ELEMENT_ARRAY_BUFFER_BINDING);

  _.bufferStack = { }; // Per-target object stack
  _.bufferStack[gl.ARRAY_BUFFER] = [ ];
  _.bufferStack[gl.ELEMENT_ARRAY_BUFFER] = [ ];

  _.bindBuffer = gl.bindBuffer; // Save native bindBuffer

  // ... other types of WebGLObject ...
}
```

Listing 41.9. Private data setup function for the SGL_current_binding extension.

operations. Additionally, native binding functions are saved to be used internally by hijacked ones. The private data setup, referred to by the underscore variable (_), is implemented as shown in Listing 41.9.

To track the current binding state, we need to hijack every native object binding method. In our implementation, we avoid redundant bindings if the object to be made current is already bound:

```
function hijackContextCB(gl) {
  gl.bindBuffer = function (target, buffer) {
    var _ = this._spidergl.cb._;
    if (_.currentBuffer[target] == buffer) {
      return;
    }
    _.currentBuffer[target] = buffer;
    _.bindBuffer.call(this, target, buffer);
  };
  // ... other bind calls ...
}
```

Public extension functions must be exposed as methods of the object returned by getExtension(). Thus, they are installed as functions of the ext object (created at line 2 in Listing 41.8). The implementation of the get, push, and pop is straightforward:

```
function setupPublicCB(gl) {
  var ext = gl._spidergl.cb;
  ext.getCurrentBuffer = function (target) {
    return this._.currentBuffer[target];
  };
  ext.pushBuffer = function (target) {
    var _ = this._;
    _.bufferStack[target].push(_.currentBuffer[target]);
  };
```

```
ext.popBuffer = function (target) {
  var _ = this._;
  if (_.bufferStack[target].length == 0) {
    return;
  }
  _.gl.bindBuffer(target, _.bufferStack[target].pop());
};
// ... other types of WebGLObject ...
}
```

We executed a series of benchmarks to evaluate the performance of object binding and query. On average, results show that the hijacked binding functions run 30% slower than the native binding, while accessing the currently bound object is five times faster than querying the context in the standard way. Other than to expose functions to programmers, this extension has been introduced as a utility for the more important direct state access functionality, so we accept the loss of some performance during binding operations in favor of a consistent gain in accessing the current object.

41.4.4   Direct Object Access with SGL_direct_state_access

The DSA extension is intended to provide functions to directly access WebGL object state and data without the need for binding them to a specific target. The WebGL API already provides functions that follow this philosophy, such as all the ones related to shaders and programs (with the exception of uniform setting). However, several methods have to be implemented for other objects. Our implementation of DSA functionalities uses a query/bind/set/restore strategy. In general, extension functions take a WebGLObject as first argument, followed by all the remaining arguments required by the original, non-DSA function. Listing 41.10 shows how the DSA version of a generic function editObject(target, arg1, ..., argN) is implemented.

```
1   ext.editObject(object, target, arg1, ..., argN) {
2     var _ = this._; var gl = _.gl;
3     var current = _.cb.getCurrentObject(target); // Query
4     if (current != object) {
5       gl.bindObject(target, object);                 // Bind
6     }
7     gl.editObject(target, arg1, ..., argN);          // Set
8     if (current != object) {
9       gl.bindObject(target, current);                // Restore
10    }
11  }
```

Listing 41.10. Implementation of an edit function in the SGL_direct_state_access extension.

Using the skeleton in Listing 41.10, it is straightforward to define the DSA counterparts of native functions. The **SGL_current_binding** extension is used to query the current object (line 3).

Similar to the `cb` property used to access the CB extension, the rendering context will use the `dsa` property of the `_spidergl` container to access the DSA extension object. The private state of the extension object just consists of a reference to the CB extension, which is thus enabled (if it is the first access) and retrieved in the private setup function:

```
function setupPrivateDSA(gl) {
  var _ = gl._spidergl.dsa._; // Extension private data
  _.cb = gl.getExtension("SGL_current_binding"); // Activate CB
}
```

Contrary to CB, the DSA extension does not need to hijack native context functions, meaning that the `hijackContextDSA()` function (line 14 of the extension skeleton code in Listing 41.8) is not needed. Public extension functions are exposed as shown in Listing 41.11. We have also chosen to add direct versions for functions that do not explicitly refer to the current binding state and for functions that rely on the state *latched* by other commands. To the first class belong functions like `clear()`, `readPixels()`, and `copyTexImage2D()`, for which the direct versions accept a WebGLFramebuffer object as first argument. The second class encapsulates functions that use the buffer binding state to configure a pipeline run. Those functions are `vertexAttribPointer()` and `drawElements()`, which rely,

```
function setupPublicDSA(gl) {
  var ext = gl._spidergl.dsa;
  ext.getBufferParameter = function (buffer, target, pname) {
    var _ = this._; var gl = _.gl;
    var current = _.cb.getCurrentBuffer(target);
    if (current != buffer) {
      gl.bindBuffer(target, buffer);
    }
    var result = gl.getBufferParameter(target, pname);
    if (current != buffer) {
      gl.bindBuffer(target, current);
    }
    return result;
  };
  ext.bufferData = function (buffer, target, dataOrSize, usage) {
    var _ = this._; var gl = _.gl;
    var current = _.cb.getCurrentBuffer(target);
    if (current != buffer) {
      gl.bindBuffer(target, buffer);
    }
    gl.bufferData(target, dataOrSize, usage);
    if (current != buffer) {
      gl.bindBuffer(target, current);
    }
  }
  // ... other buffer-related functions and WebGLObject types ...
}
```

Listing 41.11. Implementing the public interface of the `SGL_direct_state_access` extension.

respectively, on the current `ARRAY_BUFFER` and `ELEMENT_ARRAY_BUFFER` binding. In a similar way, the `bindTexture()` function operates in the currently active texture unit; an overridden version of it is exposed by the extension, allowing the programmer to directly specify the target texture unit.

Before committing ourselves to the discussed implementation, we have also tried a different strategy: binding the object involved in the DSA call, executing the edit function, and recording in a *fix table* that the user-bound object must be restored. All native functions that rely on current binding have been hijacked to execute the needed fixes before forwarding the call to the native function. Even if optimizations are done to avoid redundant bindings and unneeded fixes, this solution has lower performance, is less maintainable, and is more error-prone than the simpler query/bind/set/restore strategy.

41.4.5   Drawbacks

With a terminology borrowed from the operating systems field, implementing the extensions the way we did in *user space* (i.e., above the API layer) has the drawback of potentially violating the WebGL specification from the user's point of view. These issues are a consequence of the query/bind/set/restore strategy used in the DSA extension: in some situations, the hidden binding and unbinding of objects could change the context error state, resulting in misleading error diagnostics when using the `getError()` function. Worse, it can cause some objects to be deleted prematurely according to user's expectation. In fact, when `delete*()` is called on certain types of `WebGLObject`, e.g. `WebGLProgram` or `WebGLShader`, that are currently bound to some target or container, the object is *flagged* as deleted, but it will continue to serve its purpose, and the actual destruction will only be performed when all the bindings are broken. When making a DSA call, the currently bound object is unbound (if it is not the target object of the call) in favor of the object on which the call operates, causing its actual destruction if it is flagged as deleted. The binding changes hidden in a DSA call may thus result in an apparent discrepancy of a conformant API implementation. However, to our experience, relying on this behavior is not common. Due to the benefits such an extension brings, in SpiderGL, we have nonetheless chosen to implement and rely on it. We must be effective in making users aware of these issues, as we do in the documentation.

When a future official extension or API version with the same goal becomes available, we will just need to fix some internal calls, with the effect of removing the above issues while keeping the same interface.

41.5   WebGLObject Wrappers

The rendering pipeline that OpenGL-family APIs specify is a compute machine composed of several processing stages. Each stage operates accordingly to a global state (i.e., the *rendering context* state) and uses specific objects both as sources of operational parameters and generic data, as well as targets for storing the computed stage output.

Working with OpenGL objects using the functions provided by the API is not complex. The major source of difficulty comes from the bind-to-edit paradigm, which can cause misleading interpretations about what is actually happening, especially in the API learning phase. A step toward a easier and cleaner object handling can be taken by using the DSA extension, but for most programmers a class-based, object-oriented approach is almost always preferred. For this reason, many OpenGL libraries provide object *wrappers* that simplify typical usage patterns and offer a friendly interface. In designing SpiderGL, we were aware that WebGL object wrappers would play a fundamental role both in the overall library usability and during the development of higher-level constructs. We implemented a wrapper for every WebGL object, that is, `WebGLBuffer`, `WebGLFramebuffer`, `WebGLProgram`, `WebGLRenderbufer`, `WebGLShader`, and `WebGLTexture`. In the actual implementation, all wrappers inherit from the base `SglObjectGL` class. An example of how wrappers are used is shown in Listing 41.12.

In general, constructors and methods of a GL wrapper take a JavaScript object with optional properties, whose default values are defined on a per-object basis and are publicly exposed, such that library users can change them at any time. To edit the object, there is no need to bind the object before setting any of its parameters or data, as was mandated in the first versions of the library before the introduction of the DSA extension.

Wrapper constructor functions internally create an instance of the corresponding WebGL object and set the passed optional parameters or default values. To fulfill one of our most important requirements, e.g., to allow a seamless interoperability of native WebGL calls with SpiderGL, every constructor also accepts a `WebGLObject`

```
var texture = new SglTexture2D(gl, {
  url : "url-to-image.png",
  onLoad : function () { /* ... */},
  minFilter : gl.LINEAR,
  wrapS : gl.CLAMP_TO_EDGE ,
  autoMipmap : true
});

// single parameter setter...
texture.magFilter = gl.NEAREST;

// ... or modify a set of sampling parameters
texture.setSampler({
  minFilter : SGL_DEFAULT , // reset to default value
  wrapT : gl.REPEAT
});
```

Listing 41.12. Usage example of a `WebGLObject` wrapper.

```
1   // Constructs a renderbuffer wrapper.
2   // the actual implementation uses SglObjectGL as base class.
3   function SglRenderbuffer(gl, options) {
4     var isImported = (options instanceof WebGLRenderbuffer);
5
6     if (isImported && options._spidergl) {
7       return options._spidergl; // Already wrapped
8     }
9
10    this._gl  = gl;
11    this._dsa = gl.getExtension("SGL_direct_state_access");
12
13    if (isImported) {
14      this._handle = handle; // Store handle
15      // query object state
16      this._width  = this._dsa.getRenderbufferParameter(
17        this._handle, gl.RENDERBUFFER, gl.RENDERBUFFER_WIDTH);
18      // ... query other properties ...
19    }
20    else {
21      this._handle = gl.createRenderbuffer(); // Create handle
22    }
23    // install a reference to the wrapper
24    this._handle._spidergl = this;
25    // ...
26  }
27  SglRenderbuffer.prototype = {
28    get handle() { return this._handle; },
29    // ...
30  };
```

Listing 41.13. The constructor function of a `WebGLObject` wrapper.

in input, in which case, no internal object is created. This is particularly useful whenever SpiderGL is used in conjunction with other libraries that may want to directly operate on native `WebGLObject` handles. The wrapped object, regardless of whether it was internally created or passed at construction, can be retrieved by using the `handle` getter of the wrapper object. As shown in Listing 41.13, to ensure that no conflicts will be created by wrapping a native handle more than once, the wrapped object is augmented with the pseudoprivate `_spidergl` property that references the first wrapper that used the native handle. In case such a property is found, it is immediately returned as the constructed object (line 7). This means that multiple wrapper objects on the same native object actually point to the same instance. Moreover, if a native handle is provided, the DSA extension is used to query the object state and store it in private properties (line 16).

Wrapping existing WebGL objects and exposing the native handle have the major consequence of potentially causing a discrepancy between the actual object state and the internal state maintained by the wrapper object. This divergence occurs whenever native APIs are called directly on a wrapped native handle. For example, the `SglProgram` wrapper maintains the set of shaders attached to it, that are, in turn, wrapped by `SglShader`-derived objects, as well as some post-link states. Calling attachShader(), detachShader() or linkProgram() on the wrapped object must cause the wrapper to update its internal state. In the first versions of SpiderGL, the library user had to explicitly call the synchronize() method of the wrapper to keep the wrapper state consistent. It worked but also implied that the programmer must be aware that a synchronization was needed, or they had to act conservatively and synchronize whenever they suspected that some external event or call could have modified the object state. Again, we had to make an important design choice. Our goal was to keep the wrapper state up-to-date without user intervention. This was the reason that led us to the definition of another extension: SGL_wrapper_notify.

41.5.1   Keep Wrappers Updated with SGL_wrapper_notify

The SGL_wrapper_notify (WN) extension is intended to notify wrapper objects whenever native API calls are executed on native handles that have been wrapped. The implementation is straightforward and consists of replacing each method of the rendering context that operates on WebGL objects, whether directly (i.e., all shader-related functions that take a WebGLShader as argument) or indirectly (i.e., buffer-related functions that operate on the currently bound WebGLBuffer) with a *notify* function. The purpose of the new method is to execute the original native call, retrieve the object on which it operates on and, if the object has been wrapped, forward the call arguments to the corresponding callback method of the wrapper. In the case of indirect calls, the current object is retrieved by using the CB extension.

Referring to the extension injection skeleton in Listing 41.8, we install the wn property on the _spidergl container and proceed to setup. The private data setup function is aimed at saving a reference to all the context methods that will be hijacked:

```
1   function setupPrivateWN(gl) {
2     var _ = gl._spidergl.wn._; // Extension private data
3     // Access the CB extension
4     _.cb = gl.getExtension("SGL_current_binding");
5     // Save native functions
6     _.bufferData = gl.bufferData;
7     // ...
8     _.shaderSource = gl.shaderSource;
9     // ...
10  }
```

Native functions are then replaced with notifying ones. If the target object has the _spidergl property, it means that it has been wrapped by a SpiderGL wrapper object, which thus need to be notified. Note that the installed _spidergl property refers to a single wrapper object and not to a list of them, as has been guaranteed by avoiding the wrap of an already wrapped handle (see Listing 41.13). The hijacking setup functions is shown in Listing 41.14. As can be deduced from lines 8 and 18, every wrapper contains methods of the form _gl_* that act as native function

```
1   function hijackContextWN(gl) {
2     gl.bufferData = function (target /* ... */) {
3       var _ = this._spidergl.wn._;
4       _.bufferData.apply(this, arguments);   // native call
5       var h = _.cb.getCurrentBuffer(target); // get bound object
6       if (h && h._spidergl) {
7         // if wrapped, forward call
8         h._spidergl._gl_bufferData.apply(h._spidergl, arguments);
9       }
10    }
11    // ...
12    gl.shaderSource = function (shader, source) {
13      var _ = this._spidergl.wn._;
14      _.shaderSource.apply(this, arguments);
15      // the target object is explicitly passed as arguments:
16      // no need to use the SGL_current_binding extension
17      if (shader && shader._spidergl) {
18        shader._spidergl._gl_bufferData.apply(shader._spidergl, ↩
             arguments);
19      }
20    };
21    // ...
22  }
```

Listing 41.14. Native methods are hijacked to allow the SGL_wrapper_notify extension to track changes to WebGL objects.

callbacks. This extension does not expose any additional API, meaning that the function setupPublicWN() is not needed.

With this scheme, it is also possible to give wrappers the possibility of preventing object usage via direct API calls on the native handle. For example, we could add a *seal* state to each wrapper, accessible by methods like seal() and unseal() and the isSealed property getter. The WN extension could then be easily modified such that native calls are not performed on wrapped handles whose isSealed property is true.

41.6   Conclusion

In designing SpiderGL we imposed on ourselves a series of requirements that would lead to an easy-to-use library that could work seamlessly and robustly in the presence of native WebGL calls. We found the extension mechanism to be a perfect and elegant ally that we could exploit to inject new functionalities. We defined the SGL_current_binding extension to have a fast access to the objects currently bound to a particular target. The SGL_direct_state_access extension allowed us to edit WebGL objects, states, and resources in a clean way, and SGL_wrapper_notify helped GL wrappers synchronize with native handles.

The structure of the 3D model has undergone various iterations. We started with a raw mesh that was easy to construct and handle, and we kept upgrading it to allow more flexibility. However, the first solutions lacked in expressiveness, so we switched to a layered structure that could be used at various levels of detail. As layers are walked bottom to top, the raw information acquires semantic attributes, and flexibility is traded off with expressiveness.

SpiderGL was born as a middleware library, and we feel that its structure can serve as a solid foundation for developing higher-level constructs, such as whole-scene management. We will be adding new functionalities with the hope of providing a robust and usable library to CG and web developers.

Acknowledgments. We would like to thank everyone at the Visual Computing Lab, especially Roberto Scopigno for believing in this project and Federico Ponchio for introducing us to JavaScript. A special thanks goes to Gianni Cossu for setting up the SpiderGL website.

Bibliography

[Di Benedetto et al. 10] Marco Di Benedetto, Federico Ponchio, Fabio Ganovelli, and Roberto Scopigno. "SpiderGL: A JavaScript 3D Graphics Library for Next-Generation WWW." In *Web3D 2010, 15th Conference on 3D Web Technology*, 2010.

[Group 11a] Khronos Group. "COLLADA 1.5.0 Specification." http://www.khronos.org/collada/, 2011.

[Group 11b] Khronos Group. "TypedArray Specification." http://www.khronos.org/registry/typedarray/specs/latest/, 2011.

[Kilgard 10] Mark J. Kilgard. "EXT_direct_state_access." http://www.opengl.org/registry/specs/EXT/direct_state_access.txt, 2010.

Multimodal Interactive Simulations on the Web 42

Tansel Halic, Woojin Ahn, Suvranu De

42.1   Introduction

Multimodal interactive simulations (MIS), also known as virtual environments, represent synthetic computer-generated environments that allow interactions by one or more users using multiple sensory modalities, e.g., vision, hearing, touch, and smell. The interaction may be accomplished using specialized interface devices such as the mouse, space balls, robot arms, etc. Such simulations may be used in a variety of applications spanning video games, virtual malls, and psychomotor skill training. One application we are interested in is using MIS to develop interactive medical simulations.

Conventional MIS systems are restricted and highly dependent on the underlying software and hardware systems. The web, unlike traditional software platforms, provides the simplest solution. Web-based simulation systems may be run independent of the client systems and with a very negligible code footprint on a browser that complies with open standards. This creates ubiquitous simulation environments independent of hardware and software.

Web browsers have an essential role to play in this paradigm [Murugesan et al., 11, Rodrigues, Oliveira, and Vaidya 10]. With the web browsers, the hardware systems and software platforms, device drivers, and runtime libraries become transparent to the user. Highly realistic 3D interactive scenes can now be generated using the recently introduced standard plugin free visualization API: WebGL [Khronos 11].

To enable highly realistic MIS on the web, we have introduced a platform-independent software framework for multimodal interactive simulations: Π-SoFMIS [Halic, Ahn, and De 12]. This allows efficient generation of 3D interactive applications using WebGL, including visualization, simulation, and hardware-integration modules. We present our framework, some performance tests to demonstrate the capabilities of WebGL and some implementation details along with a case study in medical simulation.

42.2 Π-SoFMIS Design and Definitions of Modules

Π-SoFMIS is designed for modularity and extensibility [Halic et al., 11]. The functional components can be easily replaced or extended through custom implementations independent of any prerequisite configuration. Π-SoFMIS is a module-oriented framework since the modular structure isolates the components and eliminates inter-dependencies. This also allows the flexibility to be used for multiple applications, which is one of the most common uses. Another benefit of modularity in the context of web-based simulations is that the users may use only the parts of the framework that they need. This increases cacheability of the web application and decreases the download time of the framework to the client devices which is often critical in mobile environments or client devices that have limited network capabilities.

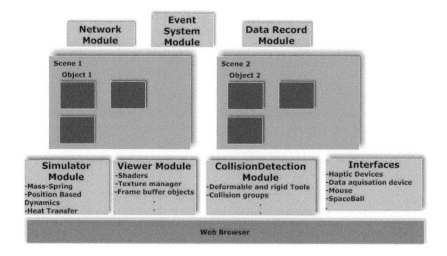

Figure 42.1. Π-SoFMIS overall architecture.

There are three major entities in *Π*-SoFMIS (Figure 42.1): *objects*, *modules*, and *interfaces*. Modules are an abstraction of the major functionalities of the framework, which are pluggable and removable components (which are generally in separated JavaScript files), e.g., visualization (rendering) is a module that renders shapes of framework objects. This module may be removed from the execution pipeline if needed, e.g., when only the simulation or the hardware module is used in the application.

Interfaces are the components that manage the integrated hardware devices. For instance, a mouse, a force feedback device, and Microsoft Kinect may be integrated into the *Π*-SoFMIS environment with interfaces. The analogy to interface in computer terminology is very similar to the device drivers for a specific hardware installed on an operating system. Therefore, for each custom or special device, the framework communicates with the interfaces. At present, haptic devices such as Sensable [Sensable 12] and Novint Falcon [Novint 12] devices are supported in *Π*-SoFMIS.

Objects in *Π*-SoFMIS are simulation or visualization entities. For instance, in a virtual surgery scene, organs and surgical tools are all objects. The objects in the framework are fundamental concepts in its design. The simulation part of the framework operates on the objects. Therefore, the physical simulation of the object is correlated with its type. For example, the objects that are simulated with Position Based Dynamics [Müller et al., 07] may be denoted as PBD objects, thus encapsulating every detail that PBD requires, including spring connectivity, geometry, discretization, and boundary/initial conditions, constraints, etc. The scene is an abstraction that includes the objects in the environment. Apart from the scene-graph context, the PBD defines physical relations such that the objects can have physical interactions with other objects in the same scene.

42.3 Framework Implementation

This section provides details on some key aspects of the *Π*-SoFMIS implementation.

42.3.1 Modularity

Apart from classical object-oriented languages where the functionality is embedded in the class definition, JavaScript functionalities reside in the object. Therefore, an object is not tied to a strict class definition as in strongly-typed languages. However, the initial definitions of the object are stored in prototype definitions, which can be used to implement object-oriented hierarchies. With prototyping, the object definitions and methods of one object can be augmented to another object. This supports multiple augmentations that resemble multiple inheritance in conventional object-oriented languages.

In *Π*-SoFMIS, we used the prototype features to create modularity. For instance, the basic object definition in *Π*-SoFMIS is `smSceneObject`. `smSceneSurface`

`Object` inherits all the prototype definitions and adds 3D mesh representation of the model and mesh routines specific to the surface mesh. It also has basic WebGL rendering routines that are called by the rendering module. This can be overridden by the prototype assignment by the child implementations. For instance, a thin deformable object (`smClothObject`) and a 2D heat transfer object (`smSceneHeat2D`) simply augment all the `smSceneSurfaceObject` definitions. In Π-SoFMIS, one can simply augment both deformable and heat transfer objects to create new objects that simultaneously support both physics-based heat transfer and deformation.

42.3.2   Shaders

In Π-SoFMIS, the rendering module has a default shader that supports decal texturing, bump mapping, specular mapping, ambient occlusion, and displacement mapping. These mappings have default bindings in the shaders to simplify creating or extending a new shader. However, each object can override the default shading by simply attaching the custom shader. Therefore, prior to rendering, custom shaders are enabled for each object which is switched back to the default shader after the object rendering is completed. Custom and built-in shaders are initialized after HTML canvas, which is initialized by the rendering module. During initialization, shaders extract all the uniform and attribute declarations and bind them in uniform variables that are performed by parsing the shader source code. This eases the development of additional shaders and eliminates the need to write additional code.

42.3.3   File Format

Π-SoFMIS uses JSON (JavaScript Object Notation) to import 3D geometry. JSON is a standard language-independent data interchange format. Since it is derived from a subset of JavaScript, its use, especially parsing and execution, is simple. Moreover, the files are in a human-readable format, and extending the definitions is straightforward. In Π-SoFMIS, any 3D model, such as .obj or .3ds, is converted to JSON on the server. The generated JSON file is downloaded and imported into the Π-SoFMIS mesh file structures. The defined file format is in Listing 42.1.

```
{
    "vertexPositions" : [...],
    "vertexNormals" : [...],
    "vertexTextureCoords":[...],
    "vertextangents" :[...],
    "indices" :[...],
    "tetras":[...],
    "type": ,
    "version":
}
```

Listing 42.1. JSON file format for 3D surface and volumetric topology.

We use versioning in the file format to provide compatibility and extension. The file format has the type of file definition to differentiate a surface from a volumetric structure. In the file format, we also compute tangent vectors to render the geometry for bump mapping. The vertex normals are also computed for the objects that are not deformable in the scene to eliminate initial computation time. For the deformable objects, the vertex and triangle neighborhood information (which is located in `smSceneSurfaceObject` definition) is computed after the initial loading of the objects and normals are updated at the end of simulation execution.

42.4   Rendering Module

The rendering module is based on WebGL, so the visualization is accelerated using the GPU. WebGL is a low-level, cross platform, plugin-free 3D graphics API for the web. It is an open standard managed by the Khronos group and supported by the majority of web browsers. Apart from other 3D plugin rendering solutions, WebGL provides JavaScript APIs to directly access the GPU hardware for shading capabilities. WebGL, unlike OpenGL, doesn't support the fixed-pipeline functionality. All the rendering routines and lighting computations need to be implemented in shaders. The supported shading language is based on GLSL ES, and at present, only the vertex- and fragment-level programmability are supported. Since WebGL is based on OpenGL ES 2.0, the capabilities provided by the API can be used on the majority of existing devices and also on upcoming low-end CPU and GPU capabilities as in smart TVs.

WebGL provides its low-level graphics API through the canvas element of HTML5. Our rendering module is based on WebGL, which incorporates all routines

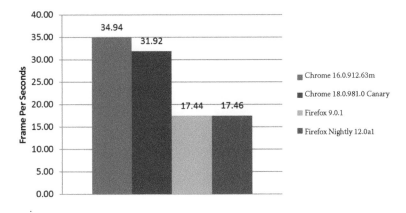

Figure 42.2. Average rendering performance.

for loading the JSON format of 3D objects and texturing and specifying material properties and lighting effects in the shaders. The module includes various shaders to render different objects such as plastic, metal, water, etc.

Our rendering module also creates the context for manipulating 2D content. The 2D context is mainly utilized by our texture manager within the rendering module, which encapsulates and works as middleware used for all the texture operations including resizing, filtering, and raw data processing. The texture operations also consist of a texture image loading and initialization, resizing, raw data access, creating the arbitrary texture, framebuffer textures or video textures, and an arbitrary texture

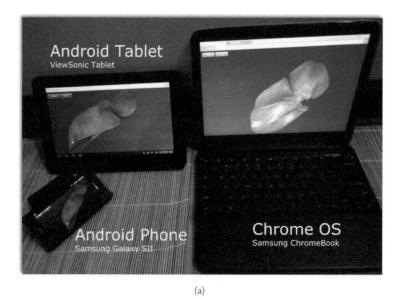

(a)

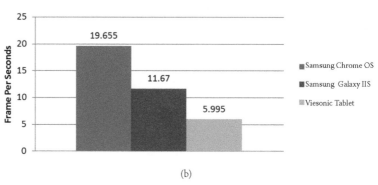

(b)

Figure 42.3. (a) Screenshot of the scene. (b) Average rendering performance for tablet, phone, and ChromeBook.

update. Apart from basic operations, our module also supports display manipulation and interactive camera manipulation with device interfaces.

We perform rendering tests to show the WebGL capabilities and also present the minimum rendering rates that are attainable with the existing WebGL implementation in the browsers. In fact, the presented rates can be regarded as a reference that gives intuition about minimum approximate rendering frame rates in a realistic surgery scene. We expect better frame rates as the implementation of WebGL in the browsers become more mature.

We obtained results on a Windows XP machine with an Intel Quad core 2.83 GHz CPU with 2.5GB Memory and an Nvidia GeForce 9800 GX GPU. In this virtual scene, only rendering and haptic device interface modules are allowed. The total number of vertices and triangles rendered per frame corresponds to 18,587 and 24,176, respectively. The high-resolution textures (2048 × 2048) are used for rendering the virtual organs in the scene. Total texture size of the scene approximately amounts to 151MB. There are three different shaders enabled in rendering. During rendering, the screen is set to 1900 × 1200 pixel resolution. Our results, shown in Figure 42.2, indicate that the rendering performance of Chrome is superior to Firefox.

In addition to browser performance tests, we carried out rendering tests for different devices such as Chrome OS, Android ViewSonic Tablet, and Android Samsung Galaxy SII Phone using Firefox Android browser version 9.0. The rendering is performed with a full screen canvas for all devices. Our wet shading of the framework is used during the rendering with the bump map enabled. The texture image resolution is 2048 × 2048. The total vertices and triangles are 2526 and 4139, respectively. The measured performance of each device is given in Figure 42.3. The slow speed is reported as an implementation problem of the mobile version of the browser that arises due to lack of the texture-sharing mechanism between the web page compositing process and the final rendering process (See WebGL developer email list).

42.5 Simulation Module

The simulator module orchestrates the "object simulators," where the actual physics simulation algorithms reside. The simulator module does not have any information regarding the content of the object simulators. It is primarily responsible for triggering the object simulators, e.g., thermal simulator or deformable object simulator, and synchronizing all the simulators when the job is done. This is needed for prospective design where multithreaded execution in the browser is crucial. This design provides a straightforward way of supporting both task and data parallelism. We carried out simulations to test the performance benefit of the web workers in our framework. Our simulation is based on an explicit heat-transfer simulation for a regular mesh having 12,228 (64 × 192) nodes. Results are presented in Figure 42.4(a). Based on our results, the best performance is 42.6 fps with the three threads. The decreasing

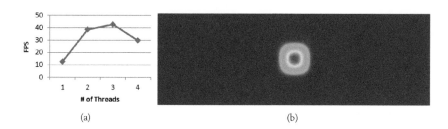

(a)   (b)

Figure 42.4. (a) Performance of parallel heat transfer. (b) Example: parallel finite difference-based heat transfer.

performance is due to message copy overhead between the main thread and the web worker threads in each simulation frame.

We tested the simulation module performance using the Chrome and Firefox browsers. During the simulation test, the rendering and the hardware interface were also allowed. Similar to rendering tests, our aim is to present the competency of JavaScript and WebGL combination for real-time interactivity and minimum frame rates rather than a comparison of performance of browsers. During the simulation, the frame rates are written to HTML5 local storage through our data module at the end of the performance test. Our simulation module executes the deformable thin structure with cutting enabled. The total number of nodes used in the simulation is 900. The results are shown in Figure 42.5.

In addition to simulation and rendering tests, we executed tests to determine the overhead of JavaScript language for our simulations. This simulation is executed entirely on the CPU side with a varying number of nodes. The simulation is based on a PBD simulation with length constraints. We compared Firefox, the Chrome version, and the C++ version of the simulation; the comparison is given in Figure 42.6.

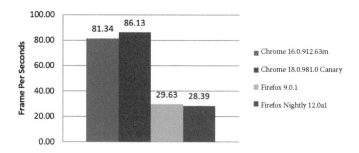

Figure 42.5. Average simulation performance.

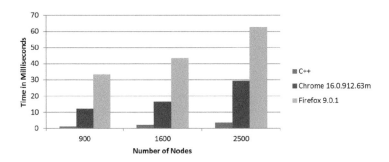

Figure 42.6. Performance comparison of computational performance.

42.6 Hardware Module

Since web browsers do not allow access to the hardware using JavaScript and HTML, interfacing the hardware input devices is not straightforward. Hardware access is only allowed through browser plugins where native code can execute. We have therefore created a plugin to access hardware interfaces for haptic devices and other custom data-reading devices. The overall architecture is in Figure 42.7. Our plugin code is based on the Netscape Plugin Application Programming Interface (NPAPI) [O'Malley and Hughes 03], which is a cross-platform plugin architecture.

The plugin is simply interfaced by the object definition within the HTML page. When the web page is loaded, the DLL of our plugin is initialized by an `NP_Initialize` procedure, which is the first function called by the browser for

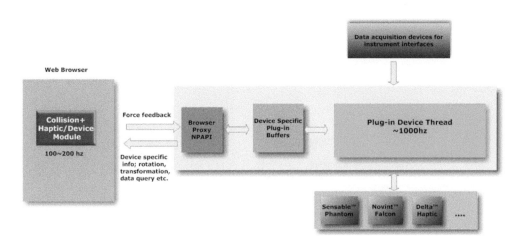

Figure 42.7. Plugin architecture.

the plugin. This is our entry point for global initialization of our plugin where we directly call each device-specific initialization routine in order. Once the initialization is complete, the entry points of the plugin and the properties of the plugin are registered.

Once the plugin is initialized, the functions and plugin properties can be accessed through a JavaScript plugin object. For simplicity, we define several properties to obtain the position in world coordinates in the environment and rotational data, which is defined as a quaternion.

During the simulation execution, the hardware information may be directly accessed by the simulation module, or it can be separated as a simulator that runs independently to achieve high update rates. In our plugin, the device runs at its own frequency of 1 KHz. In force-feedback enabled simulations, the hardware module achieves between 100 and 200 Hz depending on the browser [Halic et al., 11].

42.7   Case Study: LAGB Simulator

This section describes a virtual laparoscopic adjustable gastric banding (LAGB) simulator that we developed based on the Π-SoFMIS. LAGB is a minimally invasive surgical procedure that is performed on morbidly obese patients. In the procedure, an adjustable band is placed around the stomach to avoid excessive food intake by providing early satiation leading to weight loss. In order to place the band, the lesser omentum must be divided to create a pathway for the band to slide behind the stomach. This dissection is performed using a monopolar electrosurgical tool.

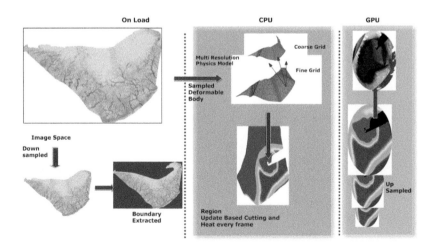

Figure 42.8. Initialization, CPU, and GPU execution of heat transfer, deformable body and electrosurgical simulation of the lesser omentum.

In our scene, the lesser omentum is simulated as a deformable object which also allows heat transfer. A mass-spring model is used for tissue deformation. Two different grids, coarse and fine, are generated (Figure 42.8). Each mass point (i,j) is connected to its eight neighbors $(i \pm 2, j)$, $(i \pm 1, j)$, $(i, j \pm 1)$, and $(i, j \pm 2)$ with springs and dampers.

The 2D boundary of the heat transfer object is extracted from the texture image for node sampling. This helps in creating independent resolutions at initialization regardless of the rendering-mesh resolution. In addition, since this works in texture space, it is independent of the discretization used for the deformation simulation. The projection of the results to high resolution can be easily performed on the GPU without additional burden. When the simulation loads, the texture image is downsampled to create a low-resolution domain, as seen in Figure 42.8, for thermal simulation to improve computational efficiency.

The boundary of the image is then extracted by simple image alpha-channel thresholding. Different values of the heat conduction coefficient are assumed over the domain. For instance, the thinner and more transparent layers are assigned higher heat conduction coefficients compared to the thicker, less transparent regions. This is simply taken into consideration when the boundary extraction is done.

During simulation execution, interaction of the electrosurgical tool with the tissue results in tissue cutting. When the tissue is cut, the cut region is successively updated using the texture coordinates of the fine mesh. Therefore, the cut region is tracked at the texture domain as seen in Figure 42.9. The updated texture domain is reflected in the thermal domain and upsampled in the GPU for higher resolution in the thermal simulation. Tissue vaporization is assumed to occur when the temperature exceeds a prescribed value. This is, of course, an oversimplified version of the actual physics. When this condition is reached for a particular node, the temperature value is written in the texture image permanently. On the GPU, this upsampled temperature texture value is multiplied with the fragment color to render a finer burnt region. A screenshot of the simulation of tissue vaporization can be seen in Figure 42.10.

Tissue vaporization is associated with the generation of smoke. For smoke generation, Π-SoFMIS provides an efficient solution based on our previous work [Halic, Sankaranarayanan, and De 10]. A smoke video is placed in an HTML page, which is loaded by our rendering module as a video texture image. In the main WebGL thread, the video texture is initialized with our renderer *create texture* function call, which simply creates WebGL texture context and prepares the structure for later usage in Listing 42.2.

In the simulation, each frame needs to be fetched when the cautery contacts the fatty tissue. Therefore, video frame is processed before it is updated. To manipulate the video frames, we have used HTMLVideoElement `currentTime` attribute, which is defined as double, which indicates and also sets the current playback position as a unit of seconds.

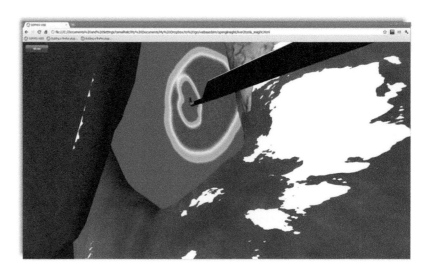

Figure 42.9. Region update in heat transfer during electrosurgery.

We update the video frames as texture images in the each rendering frame with the framework function in Listing 42.3.

Screenshots of tool-tissue interaction and smoke rendered in the laparoscopic scene can be seen in Figure 42.11. On the CPU, we can control the rate of smoke

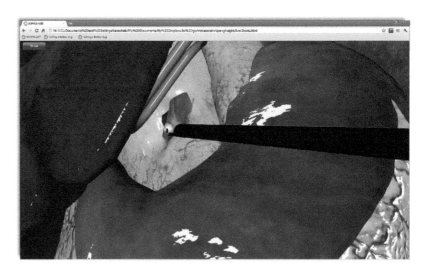

Figure 42.10. Tissue vaporization during electrosurgery.

```
smRenderer.prototype.createTexture=function (p_textureName){
    this.smTextures[p_textureName].texture=gl.createTexture(); //WebGL texture ←
        creation
    this.smTextures[p_textureName].textureName=p_textureName; //texture name
    this.smTextures[p_textureName]=this.texture; //reference by name
    this.smTextures[p_textureName].width=0; //empty texture
    this.smTextures[p_textureName].height=0; //empty texture
    this.smTextures[this.smTextures.lastIndex++]=this.smTextures[p_textureName];
    return this.smTextures.lastIndex-1; //reference by index
}
smRenderer.prototype.bindTexture=function (p_shader,p_textureName,p_textureType){
    if(p_textureType=="decal"){
        gl.activeTexture(gl.TEXTURE0); //zero texture channel for decal texture
        gl.bindTexture(gl.TEXTURE_2D, this.smTextures[p_textureName]);
        gl.uniform1i(p_shader.decalSamplerUniform, 0); //pre defined decal sampler ←
            in the shader
    }
//...
}
//main thread at the initialization part
smRenderer.createTexture("myVideoTexture");

//update of video texture
//videoElement is the HTML video element
smRenderer.updateTextureWithVideo("myVideoTexture",videoElement);
smRenderer.bindTexture(smokeShader.shaderProgram,"myVideoTexture","decal");//update ←
    to decal
```

Listing 42.2. Video texture creation and update in each frame for smoke videos.

generation as well as the origin of the smoke when the electrosurgical tool is applied. The whole scene is rendered, and then the smoke is overlaid on it. We enabled the WebGL blending to achieve simple transparency. Rendering of smoke at the tip of the electrosurgical tool is performed by drawing small quads with mapped smoke video textures. The video frames are sent to the WebGL shader, which carries out the extraction of the background from the smoke. We convert the RGB texture sample

```
smRenderer.prototype.updateTextureWithVideo=function (p_textureName,p_videoElement){
    gl.bindTexture(gl.TEXTURE_2D, this.smTextures[p_textureName]); //bind WebGL ←
        texture
    gl.texImage2D(gl.TEXTURE_2D, 0, gl.RGBA, gl.RGBA,gl.UNSIGNED_BYTE, ←
        p_videoElement);
//video element id in page DOM
    gl.texParameteri(gl.TEXTURE_2D, gl.TEXTURE_MAG_FILTER, gl.LINEAR);
    gl.texParameteri(gl.TEXTURE_2D, gl.TEXTURE_MIN_FILTER, gl.LINEAR);
    if(this.smTextures[p_textureName].nonPower2Tex){
        gl.texParameteri(gl.TEXTURE_2D, gl.TEXTURE_WRAP_S, gl.CLAMP_TO_EDGE);
        gl.texParameteri(gl.TEXTURE_2D, gl.TEXTURE_WRAP_T, gl.CLAMP_TO_EDGE);
    }

    gl.generateMipmap(gl.TEXTURE_2D);
    gl.bindTexture(gl.TEXTURE_2D, null);
}
```

Listing 42.3. Video texture update in each frame.

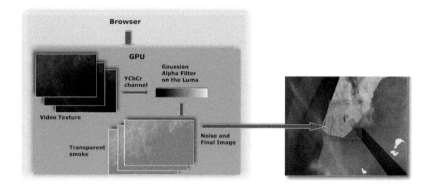

Figure 42.11. Smoke generation in the framework.

```
#ifdef GL_ES
precision highp float;
#endif
varying vec2 vTextureCoord;
uniform sampler2D uSampler;
vec4 sum=vec4(0.0);
vec3 yuv;
vec2 texCoord;
uniform float fadeControl;
uniform float xOffset;
uniform float yOffset;
uniform float leftCutOff;
uniform float rightCutOff;

vec3 RGBTOYUV(vec3 rgb){
    vec3 yuv;
    yuv.r=0.299*rgb.r+0.587*rgb.g +0.114*rgb.b;
    yuv.g=-0.14713*rgb.r-0.28886*rgb.g +0.436*rgb.b;
    yuv.b=0.615*rgb.r-0.51499*rgb.g -0.10001*rgb.b;
    return  yuv;
}
void main(void){
    texCoord=vTextureCoord; //if manipulation needed, varying texture coord cannot ←
        be changed. Place in texCoord and then change.
    sum= vec4(texture2D(uSampler, texCoord).xyz ,1); //fetch video texture
    yuv=RGBTOYUV(sum.rgb); //convert to YUV
    float xDist=abs(texCoord.x-xOffset); //offset in s
    float yDist=abs(texCoord.y-yOffset); //offset in t
    sum.a=smoothstep(leftCutOff,rightCutOff,yuv.r); //basic filter for alpha
    gl_FragColor.rgb=vec3(1.0,1.0,1.0); //smoke color
    gl_FragColor.a=smoothstep(leftCutOff,rightCutOff,sum.a*exp(-xDist)*exp(-yDist));
//based on the actual video, it eliminates the edge artifacts
    gl_FragColor.a=gl_FragColor.a*fadeControl; //fade is used for control
}
```

Listing 42.4. WebGL shader code for filtering the video images for each frame.

to a YUV color space to separate luma from chrominance. A simple filter for the alpha channel such as the *smoothstep* function with user-defined cutoff thresholds in the WebGL fragment shader provides satisfying results to obtain seamless synthesis with the scene. The additional thresholding improves the edge effect in the final smoke image. An example shader code is given in the Listing 42.4 for one video texture image.

42.8 Conclusion

In this chapter, we present a platform-independent software framework for web-based interactive simulations. Our case study runs on WebGL-supported browsers and demonstrates the various aspects of this framework. Unlike most existing web applications, *Π*-SoFMIS supports full interactivity and multiphysics simulation with realistic rendering. In *Π*-SoFMIS, realistic simulation scenes with large amounts of data are handled with sufficient refresh rates on desktop PCs [Halic, Ahn, and De 12, Halic, Ahn, and De 11], and the results are promising on tablet devices as well. Although we achieved appealing results for simulation performance and sufficient interactive rates, the overhead of JavaScript and WebGL execution need to be reduced to achieve more realistic physics-based simulations for more complex scenarios.

The proposed framework is expected to encourage development, distribution, and use of MIS, especially in applications where accessibility is critical. This will also be invaluable for assessment and eventually telementoring applications.

Bibliography

[Halic, Ahn, and De 11] Tansel Halic, W. Ahn, and S. De. (2011). "A Framework for 3D Interactive Applications on the Web." Poster presented at SIGGRAPH ASIA, 2011.

[Halic, Ahn, and De 12] Tansel Halic, W. Ahn, and S. De. "A Framework for Web Browser-Based Medical Simulation Using WebGL." *19th Medicine Meets Virtual Reality* 173 (2012): 149–155.

[Halic, Sankaranarayanan, and De 10] Tansel Halic, G. Sankaranarayanan, and S. De. "GPU-Based Efficient Realistic Techniques for Bleeding and Smoke Generation in Surgical Simulators." *The International Journal of Medical Robotics and Computer Assisted Surgery: IJMRCAS* 6:4 (2010): 431–443.

[Halic et al., 11] Tansel Halic, S. A. Venkata, G. Sankaranarayanan, Z. Lu, W. Ahn, and S. De. "A Software Framework for Multimodal Interactive Simulations (SoFMIS)." *Studies in Health Technology and Informatics* 163 (2011):213–217.

[Khronos 11] Khronos. "WebGL—OpenGL ES 2.0 for the Web." http://www.khronos.org/webgl/, 2011.

[Müller et al., 07]   M. Müller, B. Heidelberger, M. Hennix, and J. Ratcliff. "Position Based Dynamics." *Journal of Visual Communication and Image Representation* 18:2 (2007):109–118.

[Murugesan et al., 11]   S. Murugesan, G. Rossi, L. Wilbanks, and R. Djavanshir. "The Future of Web Apps." *IT Professional* 13:5 (2011):12–14.

[Novint 12]   Novint. "Novint Falcon: The Most Immersive Way to Play Video Games." http://www.novint.com/index.php/novintfalcon, 2012.

[O'Malley and Hughes 03]   M. O'Malley and S. Hughes. "Simplified Authoring of 3D Haptic Content for the World Wide Web." *Proceedings of the 11th Symposium on Haptic Interfaces for Virtual Environment and Teleoperator Systems*, pp. 428–429, Washington, DC: IEEE, 2003.

[Rodrigues, Oliveira, and Vaidya 10]   J. J. P. C. Rodrigues, M. Oliveira, and B. Vaidya. "New Trends on Ubiquitous Mobile Multimedia Applications." *EURASIP Journal of Wireless Communication Networks* 10 (2010):1–13.

[Sensable 12]   "Sensable." http://www.sensable.com/, 2012.

A Subset Approach to Using OpenGL and OpenGL ES   43

Jesse Barker and Alexandros Frantzis

43.1   Introduction

The modern GPU is no longer a specialized processor with discrete bits of fixed functionality, many of which are mutually exclusive. It is a powerful, fully programmable compute engine, in most cases on par with or even surpassing the computational power of the CPU.

The modern versions of the OpenGL and OpenGL ES APIs reflect this evolution, though much of the code written against them does not, which limits use on many platforms. Many of the features that were removed from the core profile of OpenGL or omitted from OpenGL ES, while not directly supported by the GPU, must now be implemented by the developer. This represents significant effort, both in terms of understanding and implementation, on the part of developers, which impedes their ability to keep their code current.

In our work with opensource software projects at Linaro, we have encountered a wealth of existing OpenGL code in a variety of applications and toolkit libraries. For us, this presents a couple of problems. First, we required OpenGL ES 2.0, and second, the upstream maintainers of the code required that their code continue to work with desktop OpenGL. We needed compatibility with both API variants. One option (and one that we have encountered on a number of projects) is to have multiple code paths, governed by `#ifdef` constructs. This satisfies the conditions but makes the code ugly, hard to maintain, and prone to lots of bugs that occur in one path and not the other. Our team is not large, and this approach is not scalable to the number of projects in which we participate. We found another solution.

The solution is to take advantage of the similarity between the modern desktop OpenGL and OpenGL ES 2.0 APIs in order to produce a single code base that can be compiled with minimal compile-time code-path selections against both versions. We call this approach the *subset approach*, and in our experience, it has proved an excellent way to simplify supporting code across multiple API versions. We have successfully applied it to a number of production code bases, making them easier to maintain and make available across a variety of platforms.

43.2   Making Legacy Code Modern

Since our work has tended to include a fair amount of porting along the way to a clean Subset code base, we cover porting topics first. The amount of work needed to update a legacy OpenGL or OpenGL ES code base to a more modern profile, i.e., at least version 2.x of either specification, is largely proportional to the complexity of the application. However, we have found that there is a coarse subset of common topics that applies to all such efforts. This partial list largely applies whether targeting OpenGL ES 2.0, OpenGL 2.1, or later. The programmer

- Converts immediate-mode draw-call sequences to vertex- and index-array call sequences, preferably stored in buffer objects.

- Reduces the set of rendering primitives.

- Needs to handle fixed-function vertex processing—matrix stacks, transformation APIs, per-vertex lighting, material properties, etc.—either directly in the application or in vertex shaders.

- Needs to handle fixed-function fragment processing—per-fragment lighting, fog, texenv, related texture, and fog enables, etc.—in fragment shaders.

- Does not use bitmaps or polygon stipples anymore.

- Does not use `glCopyPixels` anymore.

- Needs to provide config, context, and surface management using the EGL API.

Executing the API conversion in the order presented in the above list helps prevent breakage and regression of existing OpenGL functionality independently of any OpenGL ES–specific work.

43.2.1 Immediate Mode vs. Vertex Attribute Arrays

In the early days of OpenGL, the input to the pipeline took the form of commands and attributes. For example, we could tell the pipeline that we wanted it to draw some triangles, after which it would expect a multiple of three vertex coordinates followed by the command terminator. It looked something like Listing 43.1.

This was called immediate mode, and even though vertex arrays were added as an extension to Version 1.1, it was largely how the pipeline was fed for the first decade of the existence of OpenGL. The best way to optimize vertex feeding with immediate mode was to put groups of commonly issued commands into display lists; this was basically a record/playback mechanism for OpenGL commands. Such a technique had its own set of drawbacks. Display lists had to be compiled before execution, which could affect performance when the data were dynamic. Additionally, there were a number of useful commands that could not be put into display lists, and the developer bore the burden of understanding which calls were deferred and which were executed immediately. Today, display lists suffer the drawback that they are not available in OpenGL ES 2.0 or in the OpenGL core profile. There is still a lot of code out there that is written this way.

Immediate mode was great for getting something up quickly, e.g., drawing very simple objects, and it used to be a good teaching tool, though it is now eschewed even for that purpose. For large data sets, it is not very efficient, and the code gets ugly fast. The concept of vertex arrays was introduced for efficient processing of larger data sets. The basic idea was to set up all of our vertex data, e.g., positions, normals, etc., in a single memory buffer and tell OpenGL how to traverse that data in order to yield primitive descriptions. This is done when passing the buffer pointer to OpenGL, e.g., there are 136 3D floating-point vertices in this buffer. The draw call simply tells OpenGL what kind of primitive to draw, at what offset into the buffer to begin, and how many vertices to use.

Listing 43.2 is a trivial example of vertex arrays but still illustrates the point. The data can be separate from the code, which makes for cleaner code and fewer API calls, and the implementation can be more efficient at traversing the data. For more detail on geometry submission, there is an excellent section in the *OpenGL Programming Guide* [Shreiner and Group 09].

Now that we've gotten all of our draw calls converted from immediate mode to vertex and element arrays, we can put all of our vertex arrays into a vertex array

```
glBegin(GL_TRIANGLES);
  glVertex3f(1.0, 0.0, 0.0);
  glVertex3f(1.0, 1.0, 0.0);
  glVertex3f(0.0, 0.0, 0.0);
glEnd();
```

Listing 43.1. Immediate mode.

```
GLfloat my_data[] =
{
  1.0, 0.0, 0.0,
  1.0, 1.0, 0.0,
  0.0, 0.0, 0.0
};
glVertexAttribPointer(0, 3, GL_FLOAT, GL_FALSE, 0, my_data);
glDrawArrays(GL_TRIANGLES, 0, 3);
```

Listing 43.2. Using a vertex array.

buffer object (VBO). Essentially, VBOs give us a server-side container for all of our
vertex attribute data, i.e., positions, normals, texture coordinates, and related data
like indices. Access to our data is even more efficient than with basic vertex arrays
because the data for buffer objects can reside in memory that is local to the GPU at
the time the draw call is made; the implementation avoids a draw-call-time copy and
a synchronization point [NVIDIA 03]. All data are placed into the bound buffer
object ahead of time, as presented in Listing 43.3.

The critical difference between Listing 43.2 and Listing 43.3 is that the final
argument in the call to **glVertexAttribPointer** is no longer a pointer to the
application memory containing the vertex array. Because there is a bound buffer
object, the final argument is treated as a byte offset into the buffer data. In this case,
it indicates that the implementation should start at the first vertex coordinate when
processing the draw call.

```
// This is the setup code, only done once at initialization time.

// Create the buffer object
unsigned int bufferObject;
glGenBuffers(1, &bufferObject);
// Set up the vertex data by binding the buffer object,
// allocating its data store, and filling it in with our vertex data.
GLfloat my_data[] =
{
  1.0, 0.0, 0.0,
  1.0, 1.0, 0.0,
  0.0, 0.0, 0.0
};
glBindBuffer(GL_ARRAY_BUFFER, bufferObject);
glBufferData(GL_ARRAY_BUFFER, sizeof(my_data), my_data, GL_STATIC_DRAW);
// Unbind the buffer object to preserve the state.
glBindBuffer(GL_ARRAY_BUFFER, 0);

//
// This sequence is executed each time the object gets drawn.
//
glBindBuffer(GL_ARRAY_BUFFER, bufferObject);
glVertexAttribPointer(0, 3, GL_FLOAT, GL_FALSE, 0, 0);
glDrawArrays(GL_TRIANGLES, 0, 3);
```

Listing 43.3. Using a vertex buffer object.

43.2.2   Primitive Choices

Now that we understand how drawing requests must be described in modern OpenGL and OpenGL ES, it is worth a brief mention of what primitives may actually be drawn. Most noticeably, the quad, quad strip, and polygon primitives are no longer available for draw commands in the core profile of OpenGL and have never been part of OpenGL ES 2.0. The conversion of these to triangle strips or triangle fans was reasonably straightforward for the projects we have engaged.

43.2.3   Bitmaps and Polygon Stipples

In OpenGL, bitmaps and polygon stipples are rectangular masks of 1-bit color index data, where a value of 0 yields transparency, or rather, leaves the buffer contents unchanged, and a value of 1 yields the current raster color, or possibly a texture sample. These are no longer available in OpenGL and have never been part of OpenGL ES 2.0. Where legacy code uses these, a simple substitution is to use a 1-byte alpha texture and handle any special sampling logic in the shader. Listings 43.4 and 43.5 represent a replacement for a piece of polygon-stipple-enabled rendering from an old OpenGL demo.

The example in Listing 43.5 is for a recent version of GLSL. For GLSL ES, remove the declaration of **fragColor** and replace it with the built-in **gl_FragColor**

```
// Initialize the stipple pattern
GLubyte textureImage[32][32];
const unsigned int textureResolution(32);
static const unsigned int patterns[] = { 0xaaaaaaaa , 0x55555555 };
for (unsigned int i = 0; i < textureResolution; i++)
{
  for (unsigned int j = 0; j < textureResolution; j++)
  {
    // Alternate the pattern every other line.
    unsigned int curMask(1 << j);
    unsigned int curPattern(patterns[i % 2]);
    textureImage[i][j] = ((curPattern & curMask) >> j) * 255;
  }
}

// Set up the texture that the shadow program will use...
GLuint textureName;
glGenTextures(1, &textureName);
glBindTexture(GL_TEXTURE_2D , textureName);
glTexParameteri(GL_TEXTURE_2D , GL_TEXTURE_WRAP_S, GL_REPEAT);
glTexParameteri(GL_TEXTURE_2D , GL_TEXTURE_WRAP_T, GL_REPEAT);
glTexParameteri(GL_TEXTURE_2D , GL_TEXTURE_MAG_FILTER, GL_NEAREST);
glTexParameteri(GL_TEXTURE_2D , GL_TEXTURE_MIN_FILTER, GL_NEAREST);
glTexImage2D(GL_TEXTURE_2D , 0, GL_ALPHA8 ,
  textureResolution, textureResolution,
  0, GL_ALPHA , GL_UNSIGNED_BYTE , textureImage);
```

Listing 43.4. Polygon stipple texture image setup.

```
uniform sampler2D tex;
out vec4 fragColor;

void main()
{
  vec2 curPos;
  curPos.x = float(int(gl_FragCoord.x) % 32) / 32.0;
  curPos.y = float(int(gl_FragCoord.y) % 32) / 32.0;
  vec4 color = texture(tex, curPos);
  if (color.w < 0.5)
  {
    discard;
  }
  fragColor = color;
}
```

Listing 43.5. Polygon stipple fragment shader.

in the shader main. The remainder operator (%) is illegal in GLSL ES, so the texture coordinate computation would also need to be adjusted accordingly.

43.3   Keeping Code Maintainable across API Variants

After a code base is ported to a modern core profile of OpenGL, there is still some work needed to ensure compatibility with both the desktop and embedded variants. The goal is to ensure that only functions and definitions common to both variants are used. To this end, we have found the *OpenGL ES 2.0 Difference Specification* document [Khronos 10] to be extremely helpful.

The GL_ARB_ES2_compatibility extension adds supports for some OpenGL ES 2.0 features that are missing from modern OpenGL versions. However, the details of the supplied features may differ slightly, and not all points of divergence are addressed, so we recommend that interested readers study the issues section of the extension specification carefully.

During this step, it is common to come across functionality that is seemingly missing from OpenGL ES 2.0. However, there is often an alternative way to achieve or simulate this functionality, using constructs that are present in both variants. In the following sections, we discuss a selection of cases that fall into this category and that we have found to be common, but not straightforward, to handle.

43.3.1   Vertex and Fragment Processing

Replacing the fixed-function vertex processing in a legacy project can be a daunting task. Because we were faced with having to do this for several projects, we developed the libmatrix project. A version is available on the OpenGL Insights website, www.openglinsights.com, as well as from the project page at http://launchpad.net/

libmatrix. The core of libmatrix is a simple set of C++ template classes. These provide GLSL-like data-types for vectors and matrices along with most of the useful vector and componentwise arithmetic operations appropriate to those objects. Most of the standard transformations previously supported by the OpenGL API itself are included. `glOrtho`, `glFrustum`, `glRotate`, `glTranslate`, and even `gluLookAt` and `gluPerspective` all have analogs in libmatrix. The matrix stack template class supports the entire OpenGL matrix API without any of the previous restrictions on stack depth. Additionally, libmatrix also has a reasonable GLSL program object abstraction, along with a handy function to load the shader source from a file, which is nice for development so the entire application does not have to be rebuilt in order to test new shaders. The glmark2 project is a good example of the usage of these objects to provide programmable vertex and fragment processing. The code for glmark2 is available from www.openglinsights.com, as well as from the project page at http://launchpad.net/glmark2. Additionally, there are good sections implementing the fixed-function pipeline in GLSL in both the *OpenGL ES 2.0 Programming Guide* [Munshi et al. 08] and the *OpenGL Shading Language* [Rost 05].

43.3.2 GLX vs. EGL

Some implementations offer access to both OpenGL and OpenGL ES contexts through EGL, but it is far from a common practice at this time. For the time being, applications that want to support both flavors of the rendering API will also have to support both flavors of the context and surface management API.

The good news is that, due to the inherent similarity between GLX and EGL, it is usually straightforward to create a common abstraction layer around their functionalities. The abstraction layer doesn't change the fact that we need to make a decision—probably at compile time—of which API to use. It does, however, provide a clean and effective way to hide the details and noise of context and surface handling from the main application code.

We have successfully used such an abstraction layer in both glmark2 and even in the glcompbench project, available from http://launchpad.net/glcompbench, which uses the additional texture-from-pixmap functionality provided by GLX and EGL. We have implemented a basic canvas object from which we derive more specific class instances to handle some of the subtle, and not so subtle, differences between window system interfaces. In the glmark2 project, this has allowed us to support desktop OpenGL through GLX, both OpenGL ES and desktop OpenGL through EGL, as well as OpenGL ES on Android.

43.3.3 Vertex Array Objects

Conceptually, vertex array objects (VAOs) are simply a container object that gives the programmer and the implementation an easy handle for the array buffer, element array buffer, and vertex format that go along with a mesh or meshes to be rendered.

Rather than keeping track of all of the vertex attributes and element array buffer, the VAO allows all of this metainformation to be associated with a single object that can then simply be bound and unbound. Sounds great, right? Here's the catch: while they have been available in a platform-independent fashion since OpenGL 3.0 with some availability on older implementations via the GL_ARB_vertex_array_object extension, as of this writing, VAOs have only recently been available in OpenGL ES via the GL_OES_vertex_array_object extension with very limited vendor support. As of OpenGL 3.1, VAOs actually become mandatory while remaining optional for later versions of the compatibility profile. This makes necessary some slightly subtle handling in code bases that provide common OpenGL and OpenGL ES support.

43.3.4   Wireframe Mode

The wireframe mode feature is used extensively in CAD applications and is also popular as a debugging aid. When using desktop OpenGL, it is easy to achieve this effect: just set the polygon rasterization mode to GL_LINE.

When using OpenGL ES 2.0, however, this approach is not an option since the ability to set the polygon rasterization mode has been removed. Nevertheless, we can still achieve this effect in various ways.

One solution is to draw the mesh using the GL_LINES or GL_LINE_STRIP primitives. One drawback of this method is that, in the general case, the developer has to prepare a dedicated element array to perform the wireframe rendering. Furthermore, if the polygon content is also required, this method requires two rendering passes, which, like in the fixed-function case, are expensive and suffer from z-fighting artifacts.

Another solution is to handle wireframe drawing in the shaders. Although the shaders become more complex, this solution has the advantage that it can handle both wireframe and polygon content rendering in a single pass. One method, described in [Bærentzen et al. 08], is to use the minimum distance from each fragment to the edges of the primitive to decide how to mix the primitive content with the wireframe color. This method produces smooth wireframe lines and doesn't suffer from z-fighting artifacts, but requires that additional attributes be attached to each vertex. These attributes can be added either in geometry shaders or by explicitly setting them in the application and using a special vertex shader to handle them. In the buffer glmark2 benchmark, we have used the second approach in order to remain compatible with OpenGL ES 2.0, which lacks geometry shader support.

43.3.5   Texture Wrap Modes

Support for texture borders and the related GL_CLAMP_TO_BORDER wrap mode was removed in OpenGL ES 2.0. Fortunately, it is not difficult to provide a good simulation of this mode using the fragment shader.

```
uniform vec4 border_color;
uniform sampler2D sampler;

varying vec2 texcoords;

float clamp_to_border_factor(vec2 coords)
{
  bvec2 out1 = greaterThanEqual(coords, vec2(1.0));
  bvec2 out2 = lessThan(coords, vec2(0.0));
  bool do_clamp = (any(out1) || any(out2));
  return float(!do_clamp);
}

void main()
{
  vec4 texel = texture2D(sampler, texcoords);
  float f = clamp_to_border_factor(texcoords);
  gl_FragColor = mix(border_color, texel, f);
}
```

Listing 43.6. Simulating GL_CLAMP_TO_BORDER with GL_NEAREST.

For nearest-neighbor filtering, i.e., **GL_NEAREST**, it is enough to use the border color instead of the texel color when the normalized texture coordinates are outside [0.0, 1.0]; see the shader example in Listing 43.6.

When using **GL_LINEAR** filtering, the texture sampler returns bilinearly filtered values, taking into account nearby texels. For texture coordinates near the edges, the returned value is affected by whatever texels the current wrapping method dictates, which is usually not what we want.

To simulate **GL_CLAMP_TO_BORDER** with **GL_LINEAR** correctly, we need to use **GL_NEAREST** instead and perform the bilinear filtering plus clamp to border tweaks

```
uniform sampler2D sampler;
uniform vec4 border_color;
uniform vec2 dims; // texture dimensions (in texels)

varying vec2 texcoords;

float clamp_to_border_factor(vec2 coords, vec2 dims)
{
  vec2 f = clamp(-abs(dims * (coords - 0.5)) + (dims + vec2(1.0)) * 0.5, 0.0, 1.0);
  return f.x * f.y; // Good enough in most cases
}

void main()
{
  vec4 texel = texture2D(sampler, texcoords);
  float f = clamp_to_border_factor(texcoords, texdims);
  gl_FragColor = mix(border_color, texel, f);
}
```

Listing 43.7. Simulating GL_CLAMP_TO_BORDER with GL_LINEAR.

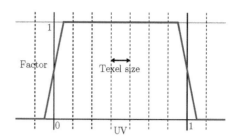

Figure 43.1. Mixing factor for linear border interpolation as a function of UV coordinates.

in the fragment shader. Unfortunately, in contrast with GL_LINEAR, which takes advantage of optimized GPU support for bilinear sampling, this method requires four explicit texture accesses and the interpolation logic to be performed in the fragment shader, incurring a significant performance penalty.[1] Another approach, when 100% correctness is not needed, is to provide just the effect of the linear interpolation of the texture to the border color near the edges using the already filtered values; see the shader example in Listing 43.7. The result of the used formula for each dimension is presented in Figure 43.1. For the 2D case, we have found that by multiplying the calculated factors for each dimension we get a satisfactory visual result.

43.3.6   Non-Power-of-Two Textures

The support for non-power-of-two (NPOT) textures in the core OpenGL ES 2.0 specification is quite limited. In particular, NPOT textures are only allowed to use the GL_CLAMP_TO_EDGE wrap mode and the GL_NEAREST and GL_LINEAR filtering modes; otherwise, they are marked as incomplete. This restriction has been the source of many seemingly inexplicable texturing problems.

Although NPOT textures are not widely used in typical OpenGL applications, they play an important role in modern compositing desktops. Modern compositing is built on accelerated texture-from-pixmap functionality and needs to support surfaces, and therefore textures, of arbitrary dimensions.

The GL_OES_texture_npot extension adds support for the two repeat wrap modes and all the minification filters, including filters involving mipmaps, to NPOT textures. Unfortunately, our experience is that this extension is not universally supported. Developers that want maximum platform support should simulate the repeat and mirrored repeat wrap modes in the fragment shader (Listing 43.8).

---

[1]Our experiments showed a 20% performance decrease in a simple case of texturing the faces of a cube, on both desktop and embedded GPUs.

```
vec2 wrap_repeat(vec2 coords)
{
  return fract(coords);
}

vec2 wrap_mirrored_repeat(vec2 coords)
{
  return mix(fract(coords), 1.0 - fract(coords), floor(mod(coords, 2.0)));
}
```

Listing 43.8. Simulating GL_REPEAT and GL_MIRRORED_REPEAT.

43.3.7 Image Formats and Types

OpenGL ES 2.0 provides a small selection of image formats and types. There is no support for packed INT formats or for mechanisms to automatically reverse the color components. The only Truecolor image format that is available by default is RGB(A), with the components in R,G,B,(A) order in memory. The GL_EXT_texture_format_BGRA8888 extension adds limited support for the BGRA format. Finally, in OpenGL ES 2.0, the internal image format and the format of the client data must match; there is no support for automatic format conversions.

Compressed image formats are supported by the API but only for unpack operations. The core OpenGL ES 2.0 specification doesn't require any particular format to be available; all such formats are optional and specified in extensions. However, the ETC1 format, provided by the GL_OES_compressed_ETC1_RGB8_texture extension, is widely available in modern devices.

The limited selection of image formats can become a problem when interfacing with external graphics libraries. Popular libraries like cairo, pixman, and skia express the component order of their image formats in terms of the order of the bits in an integer type, making the memory order of the components dependent on the endianness of the architecture. For 4-byte formats, this layout corresponds to an INT packed format, which OpenGL ES 2.0 lacks. Therefore, when using such libraries, and in order to avoid manual pixel conversions, care should be taken to use a format that can be understood natively by OpenGL ES 2.0.

An effective way to handle this situation, is to check the system endianness at runtime and use an integer pixel format that matches the memory order used by the GL format. We have successfully applied this method in our work to add OpenGL ES 2.0 support to the cairo graphics library.

43.3.8 Image Layouts

In addition to image-format limitations, OpenGL ES 2.0 restricts the supported layouts for pixel transfers. In particular, the only options accepted by glPixelStore are GL_PACK_ALIGNMENT and GL_UNPACK_ALIGNMENT.

The lack of GL_PACK_ROW_LENGTH and GL_UNPACK_ROW_LENGTH makes it impossible to pack or unpack pixel rectangles with a length different from the source image length without additional processing. To handle such rectangles, the contained pixels need to be extracted manually and saved as a smaller image with the correct layout.

43.3.9 Shading Language

GLSL ES 1.0 is based on version 1.20 of desktop GLSL and is therefore lacking features that were added in subsequent desktop GLSL versions. It does, however, have some properties that were later adopted by the core profile of OpenGL. The most important one is that neither GLSL ES nor GLSL under the core profile of OpenGL supports built-in attributes and built-in uniforms, with the exception of gl_DepthRange. The ftransform() function is also missing, so all transformations must be handled manually using custom attributes and uniforms.

GLSL ES adds support for precision qualifier keywords, both globally per-type and per-variable. The accepted types are int, float, sampler2D, and sampler Cube, and the accepted qualifiers are lowp, mediump, and highp. Two important points to remember for the fragment shader are that there is no default precision for floating-point types and that support for high precision is optional. In order to deal with this situation in a manner compatible with both GLSL and GLSL ES, it is common to use a preamble in the fragment shader like the one in Listing 43.9.

GLSL 1.30 accepts the GLSL ES 1.0 precision keywords but without any semantic meaning and only for the int and float types. Therefore, even when the target GLSL version is 1.30 or higher, it is recommended to guard the default precision statements with the GL_ES preprocessor definition.

Integers are supported in GLSL ES 1.0, but there is no guarantee that they will be implemented with real integer types at the hardware level. One side effect of this is that the integer remainder operator (%), which in GLSL is only defined for nonnegative operands, is unsupported in GLSL ES 1.0. This operation can be implemented using the mod() function, with the caveat that mod() is less restricted than %, i.e., it can handle negative numbers.

```
#ifdef GL_ES
// For high precision use:
#ifdef GL_FRAGMENT_PRECISION_HIGH
precision highp float;
#else
precision mediump float;
#endif // GL_FRAGMENT_PRECISION_HIGH
// For medium precision use:
precision mediump float;
#endif // GL_ES
```

Listing 43.9. Fragment-shader preamble for default float precision statements.

43.4 What if I Need a Specific Piece of Functionality?

The subset approach promotes the use of functionality that is common to both desktop OpenGL and OpenGL ES 2.0. However, there are inevitably going to be cases when using the common functionality is not enough, either for functional or performance reasons. What is the best way to handle such situations while still keeping the code base elegant and maintainable?

An additional question arises when considering the variations on GLSL. Not only do OpenGL and OpenGL ES have different variants of GLSL, but there are multiple versions of GLSL, just as there are multiple versions of the core specification. Even there, one might attempt to use a subset approach as we suggest for the core API; however, this is not always possible. Take the case of the polygon stipple example above. For recent versions, the built-in shader variables used for input and output are simply not there. It is possible to declare a GLSL version in the shader to address this, and that may well solve your particular problem.

We have found that an abstraction layer, even a very thin and simple one, can help here. For GLSL, we have implemented an object to manage shader source for us. This object has methods to fetch the source from a file on disk, append the shader source with additional strings, inject constant and other variable definitions at both the local and global scope, and even a primitive version of macro instantiation. So, ultimately, the shader string we pass to the API is a processed version of what we read in from disk. For more detail on our shader-management abstractions, see the definition and usage of the **ShaderSource** object in the glmark2 source, available from the OpenGL Insights website, www.openglinsights.com, as well as from the project page at http://launchpad.net/glmark2. In glmark2 we also wanted to be able to show any performance difference between client-side vertex arrays and those stored in buffer objects; the solution is a simple abstraction. It is possible to find a pathological case where conditionally compiling code is the only option. Our goal is to minimize this.

43.5 Conclusion

We have seen how to take an old piece of OpenGL code or even new code written in an old way, and make it compatible with not just one, but multiple modern OpenGL API variants. The way is largely common sense:

- Stick to APIs and constructs that work for both OpenGL and OpenGL ES.

- Solve the problems at hand, not the ones that might eventually occur.

- Pick the right tool for the job.

We believe that the example of glmark2 represents exactly this philosophy. We have made it very easy to add new scenarios to the test framework, which increases the likelihood that it will continue to perform its job moving forward.

Bibliography

[Bærentzen et al. 08]   J. Andreas Bærentzen, Steen Lund Nielsen, Mikkel Gjøl, and Bent D. Larsen. "Two Methods for Antialiased Wireframe Drawing with Hidden Line Removal." In *Proceedings of the 24th Spring Conference on Computer Graphics, SCCG '08*. New York: ACM, 2008.

[Khronos 10]   Khronos. "OpenGL ES Common Profile Specification 2.0.25 (Difference Specification)." http://www.khronos.org/registry/gles/specs/2.0/es_cm_spec_2.0.25.pdf, 2010.

[Munshi et al. 08]   Aaftab Munshi, Dan Ginsburg, and Dave Shreiner. *OpenGL ES 2.0 Programming Guide*, First edition. Reading, MA: Addison-Wesley, 2008.

[NVIDIA 03]   NVIDIA. "Using Vertex Buffer Objects (VBOs)." http://developer.download.nvidia.com/assets/gamedev/docs/Using-VBOs.pdf, 2003.

[Rost 05]   Randi J. Rost. *OpenGL Shading Language*, Second edition. Reading, MA: Addison-Wesley, 2005.

[Shreiner and Group 09]   Dave Shreiner and The Khronos OpenGL ARB Working Group. *OpenGL Programming Guide: The Official Guide to Learning OpenGL, Versions 3.0 and 3.1*, 7th edition. Reading, MA: Addison-Wesley, 2009.

The Build Syndrome 44

Jochem van der Spek and Daniel Dekkers

44.1   Introduction

In the current age of desktop, mobile, and console computing, the number of platforms, operating systems, and OpenGL versions that are in active use has become so large that developing and deploying our application for all those different configurations has become a trying and time-consuming part of development. When a game studio wants to release its latest title on as many platforms as possible, it needs to manage a combinatoric explosion of all the different configuration parameters.

We recognize two steps in the process to reduce the complexity of this task. The first is to write OpenGL agnostic code, meaning that the code encapsulates the platform- and OpenGL version–specific details into classes that are fully transparent to any combination of platform and OpenGL version. The second method is to use a metabuild system that wraps all that code into a usable project for many different IDEs on many different platforms. Each platform comes with its own set of APIs for creating a window to draw. Some of these APIs support OpenGL ES for embedded systems, even on nonembedded desktop platforms such as the iPad simulator on OS X, while some only support the OpenGL version that is enabled by the OpenGL drivers on that platform. Different OpenGL implementations on various platforms can be seen in Table 44.1. A complete list can be found on the OpenGL.org website [Khronos 97]. A completely different way of achieving the same goal is to use JavaScript with WebGL and is described in detail in Chapter 3. In this article we will focus on C++/Objective-C.

	OpenGL(1.0–4.2)	OpenGL ES(1.0/2.0)
OS X desktop	GLUT, QT, wxWidgets, X11	QT
iOS embedded	N/A	CoreAnimation (iOS 2.0/3.0)
SGI desktop	GLUT, QT, X11	EGL
Windows desktop	GLUT, QT, wxWidgets, EGL	EGL
Windows embedded	N/A	EGL, QT
Unix desktop	GLUT, QT, wxWidgets, EGL	EGL
Linux desktop	GLUT, QT, wxWidgets, X11, EGL	EGL
Linux embedded	N/A	EGL/QT
Android embedded	N/A	Android (1.0/2.2), EGL
Symbian embedded	N/A	EGL, QT
Blackberry embedded	N/A	BlackberryOS (5.0/7.0)
Web browsers	N/A	WebGL (ES2.0 only)

Table 44.1. Overview of the main OpenGL implementations on the various platforms.

As a demonstration, we show how to implement a very minimalistic OpenGL program on a subset of all the possible platforms, as can be seen in Table 44.2. For the sake of simplicity, we further limit ourselves to considering only APIs that interface the creation of the so-called OpenGL drawing context, which specifies to the operating system how a pixel is to be drawn to the screen. See [OpenGL 11] for a more extensive discussion of this topic.

In describing the use of our selection of APIs on the subset of platforms, we draw from the experience of writing the RenderTools [RenderTools 11] software library. The library was created over the course of the past three years (2008–2011) to serve as a code base to create any conceivable OpenGL application on many different platforms. We tried to keep the classes lightweight: the library, in its simplest form, depends as little as possible on external libraries. We used the whimsically named Extension Wrangler Library, or GLEW [Sourceforge 11], to manage the various OpenGL extensions on each platform. Many deprecated math func-

	OpenGL1.0–4.2	OpenGL ES 1.0–2.0
iOS	N/A	CoreAnimation(iOS 2.0/3.0)
Windows	GLUT, QT, EGL	EGL
OS X	GLUT, QT	N/A

Table 44.2. The selection of APIs and subset of platforms used in this article.

tions such as `glRotate`, `glOrtho`, and `glPerspective`, were implemented in OpenGL-compliant `Matrix` classes. Currently only `GLfloat` types are supported, though abstraction of the type-to-a-compilersetting is on the wish list. There are many such open issues, but we believe that the design of the library is sound and can be built upon and extended by the community; hence, we release it under the GNU public license (GPL), which ensures open-source distribution, but we also allow binary distribution under licenses that are free for artists, charities, contributors, and educators.

44.2   Using Utility Libraries

Where the predecessor to OpenGL, Silicon Graphics' IrisGL, had functions to create a window to draw in, OpenGL does not. This makes OpenGL portable to different operating systems and Windows APIs but also makes it difficult to set up without intimate knowledge of the underlying Windows API of the platform at hand. Each platform has its own platform-specific implementation for creating an OpenGL Context and a window, such as WGL [Wikipedia 12b] on Windows, GLX [Wikipedia 12a] on XWindows systems and Cocoa on OS X. Fortunately, there are many cross-platform software libraries that unify those platform-specific APIs, one of the most prominent being the OpenGL Utility Toolkit, or GLUT [Kilgard 97] for short. GLUT was originally written by Mark J. Kilgard to accompany the first OpenGL programming guide in 1994, the so called red book, and even though it is no longer supported, it has been in use ever since. Because of licensing issues GLUT is no longer maintained, but a reimplementation that is more-or-less actively maintained called FreeGlut [Olszta 03] is also available. GLUT is standard with OS X/XCode, and can be easily downloaded and installed for Windows and Linux. An extensive list of the various toolkits for different platforms can be found on the OpenGL website [OpenGL 12].

44.2.1   "Hello World" with GLUT

In the example in Listing 44.1, the main routine initializes the GLUT library and then tells the windowing system to create an OpenGL window that is double buffered and has an RGBA pixel format. Then it registers a display callback that is called the first time the window is displayed on the screen and when a previously obscured part of the window is shown again. Finally, it calls `glutMainloop`, which is a bit atypical, because GLUT never returns from this function. GLUT's work is now done, and it gives control to the window it has created. This example can be built and run provided that the compiler or development IDE knows the include and linker paths in order to find glut.h and link to the correct library (Glut.a on Linux, GLUT.framework on OS X, glut32.lib on Windows and so on). The rather amazing thing is that this code runs exactly as it is printed here on all the desktop systems

```
#include <glut.h>
void displayFunc(void)
{
  glClearColor(0.0, 0.0, 0.0, 1.0);
  glClear(GL_COLOR_BUFFER_BIT);
  glViewport(0, 0, 400, 400);

  glColor4f(1.0, 0.0, 0.0, 1.0);
  GLfloat vertices[8] = { -0.1, -0.1, 0.1, -0.1, 0.1, 0.1, -0.1, 0.1 };
  glEnableClientState(GL_VERTEX_ARRAY);
  glVertexPointer(2, GL_FLOAT, 0, vertices);
  glDrawArrays(GL_QUADS, 0, 4);

  glutSwapBuffers();
}

void main(int argc, char **argv)
{
  glutInit(&argc, argv);
  glutInitWindowSize(400, 400);
  glutInitDisplayMode(GLUT_DOUBLE | GLUT_RGBA);
  glutCreateWindow("GLut");
  glutDisplayFunc(displayFunc);
  glutMainLoop();
}
```

Listing 44.1. A minimal OpenGL example using GLUT.

listed in Table 44.1, and has done so since its inception for the systems that were available at that time.

44.2.2   "Hello World" with Qt

The same example can be written for Qt [Nokia 08], which can hardly be categorized as a utility library as it is a complete graphical user interface framework including a GUI designer, audio facilities, etc. In the context of drawing OpenGL content we can regard the **QtOpenGL** component of the Qt suite as similar to GLUT in that it facilitates the creation of an OpenGL context and window for us. Qt originated from Quasar Technologies, later TrollTech, in 1992 and was bought by Nokia in 2008. The library is now available under the LGPL Open Source license, and also under a commercial license from Nokia.

Compiling and linking the Qt example in Listing 44.2 is not quite as simple as building the GLUT example, because it requires the installation of the entire Qt suite, but the developers have made it as easy as possible by providing a configuration utility that lets us select which options we want to include and then generates the build scripts for us.

44.2.3   "Hello World" with EGL

Finally, the same example written in EGL [Khronos 12] can be seen in Listing 44.3. EGL interfaces OpenGL ES with the native Windows API on a wide variety of plat-

```
#include <QtCore/QtCore>
#include <QtGui/QtGui>
#include <QtOpenGL/QtOpenGL>

class MyView : public QGLWidget
{
Q_OBJECT
public:
  MyView(QWidget *parent = 0)
    : QGLWidget(QGLFormat(QGL::DoubleBuffer | QGL::Rgba), parent)
  {
    resize( 400, 400 );
  }
  ~MyView(){}

protected:
  void paintGL(QGLPainter *painter)
  {
    makeCurrent();

    glClearColor(0.0, 0.0, 0.0, 1.0);
    glClear(GL_COLOR_BUFFER_BIT);
    glViewport(0, 0, 400, 400);

    glColor4f(1.0, 0.0, 0.0, 1.0);
    GLfloat vertices[8] = { -0.1, -0.1, 0.1, -0.1, 0.1, 0.1, -0.1, 0.1 };
    glEnableClientState(GL_VERTEX_ARRAY);
    glVertexPointer(2, GL_FLOAT, 0, vertices);
    glDrawArrays(GL_QUADS, 0, 4);
  }
};

int main(int argc, char **argv)
{
  QApplication app(argc, argv);
  MyView view;
  return app.exec();
}
```

Listing 44.2. A minimal OpenGL example using Qt.

forms, including mobile and desktop. However, using EGL is a bit more involved because unlike Qt and GLUT, EGL does not provide a mechanism for creating a window in a platform-independent way. EGL allows us to create the rendering context and a drawing surface, and connect it to an existing window or display but no more. We can create a native display ourselves, or we can use the EGL_DEFAULT_DISPLAY flag to obtain the default display for the current system. Either way, we need to create a native window on that display.

Since we are now building for OpenGL ES, the convenient glOrtho, glMatrix Mode, etc. functions are not in the API, and we need to reimplement them in our own library.

```
void main(void)
{
  EGLint attribList [] =
  {
    EGL_BUFFER_SIZE , 32,
    EGL_DEPTH_SIZE , 16,
    EGL_NONE
  };

  // Even though we may obtain the EGL_DEFAULT_DISPLAY, we need
  // to create a handle to a window in which we create the drawing
  // surface, a HDC on windows, a Display on X11, etc.
  EGLNativeDisplayType nativeDisplay = EGL_DEFAULT_DISPLAY;
  EGLNativeWindowType nativeWindow = platformSpecificCreateWindow();
  EGLDisplay iEglDisplay = eglGetDisplay(nativeDisplay);
  eglInitialize(iEglDisplay, 0, 0);

  EGLConfig iEglConfig;
  EGLint numConfigs;
  eglChooseConfig(iEglDisplay, attribList, &iEglConfig, 1, &numConfigs );
  EGLContext iEglContext = eglCreateContext(iEglDisplay,
    iEglConfig, EGL_NO_CONTEXT, 0);
  EGLSurface iEglSurface = eglCreateWindowSurface(iEglDisplay,
    iEglConfig, &nativeWindow, 0);

  // For brevity, we omit a display function similar to
  // the one in the GLUT and Qt examples
}
```

Listing 44.3. A minimal OpenGL example using EGL.

44.3   OpenGL Agnosticism

In order to transparently differentiate the request from the programmer to draw a red square to the different GL APIs, we can abstract the request completely away from any OpenGL specifics but would like to offer the ease and flow of the immediate-mode, fixed-function API. We also want to stay close to the OpenGL naming conventions so that when we think about the objects that we use, we hear the same names as those that are used in the OpenGL registry. Thus, we want a **Vertexbuffer** class that is completely transparent to the underlying implementation.

```
Vertexbuffer quad;
quad.color(1.0, 0.0, 0.0);
quad.begin(GL_QUADS);
quad.vertex(-10.0,  -10.0);
quad.vertex( 10.0,  -10.0);
quad.vertex( 10.0,   10.0);
quad.vertex(-10.0,   10.0);
quad.end();
```

Listing 44.4.   Using a RenderTools::Vertexbuffer to emulate the immediate-mode API.

The code in Listing 44.4 can be used for all the different dialects of the GL but internally, this seemingly simple piece of code fragments into at least three different code paths:

1. Using a VBO (available in all versions).

2. Using a VBO with a VAO (from OpenGL 3.0).

3. Use programs (available from OpenGL 2.0 and ES 2.0).

Implementation of the simple example becomes far from trivial (see Listing 44.5). To accommodate the various versions of OpenGL within the same code base and to allow different implementations of the code base for different platforms, we make extensive use of *selective compilation* by defining compiler flags that specify the platform and OpenGL version that we compile for. A typical example of such conditional compilation is the `RenderTools::ViewController` class, which encapsulates the OpenGL Versions 1.1 through 4.x, OpenGL ES 1.x and 2.x; the different APIs, Qt, GLUT, EGL, Cocoa, EAGL; and even the different languages C++ and Objective-C. To accommodate for communication between the different APIs and languages that are used simultaneously at runtime on different platforms, we implemented the `ViewController` as a global static singleton that can be accessed from anywhere in the system. This is the way that events from the Objective-C–based iOS are passed along to the C++ hierarchy of `RenderTools`. When a `ViewController` is instantiated, it starts life as a platform-specific class such as the `IOSViewController` on iOS but is exposed to the developer simply as a `ViewController` class by means of conditional compilation. If the Render-Tools library is compiled for iOS, `RT_IOS` is defined and the `ViewController` class will be a typedef of `IOSViewController`. For GLUT on windows, OSX or Linux, `RT_GLUT` will be defined and `ViewController` will be a typedef of `GLUTViewController`, etc. The different implementations of the `View Controller` class are wrapped in `#ifdef/#endif` blocks so as to include or exclude the code from the compilation. Combining these techniques results in the "HelloWorld" example that can be found in the RenderTools/examples directory. It can be compiled and run on all the platforms and OpenGL versions supported by RenderTools without changing a single letter of code and in fact, with just one single configuration action, as we shall see in the next section.

All of this together leads to a massive number of possible configuration states. We have the various libraries that we need to include, conditional compilation flags, different OpenGL libraries, possibly third-party libraries depending on the platform, and finally different IDE's on different platforms for which we need to create and maintain project files in order to build all the various combinations.

```
#include <RenderTools.h>

using namespace RenderTools;
using namespace RenderTools::Matrix;

class HelloWorldView : public RendergroupGLView
{
public:
  static PropertyPtr create(const XMLNodePtr& xml)
  {
    boost::shared_ptr<HelloWorldView> p(new HelloWorldView());
    return boost::dynamic_pointer_cast<AbstractProperty, HelloWorldView>(p);
  }

  virtual const std::string getTypeName(bool ofComponent) const
  {
    return "HelloWorldView";
  }

  virtual void onInitialize(void)
  {
    m_buffer = Vertexbuffer::create()->getSharedPtr< Vertexbuffer >();
    m_buffer->begin(GL_TRIANGLES);
    m_buffer->color(Vec3( 0.0, 1.0, 0.0));
    m_buffer->vertex(Vec2( -10.0, -10.0));
    m_buffer->vertex(Vec2(  10.0, -10.0));
    m_buffer->vertex(Vec2(  10.0,  10.0));
    m_buffer->vertex(Vec2(  10.0,  10.0));
    m_buffer->vertex(Vec2( -10.0,  10.0));
    m_buffer->vertex(Vec2( -10.0, -10.0));
    m_buffer->end();
  }

  virtual void onRender(const ComponentFilterPtr& components)
  {
    m_buffer->render(GEOMETRIES);
  }

  VertexbufferPtr m_buffer;
};

int main(int argc, char **argv)
{
  initialize(argc, argv);
  Factory::registerContainerType("HelloWorldView", HelloWorldView(), HelloWorldView::↩
      create);
  run("<app type=\"Application\" ><viewcontroller type=\"HelloWorldView\" /></app>");
}
```

Listing 44.5. The platform-independent and OpenGL-version agnostic minimal example.

44.4   Configuration Spaces

Now that we have defined an abstraction layer over the different OpenGL versions, a next logical step is to further investigate platform-independence. In order to build the agnostic OpenGL example, we have to introduce different platforms and a coupling between OpenGL versions and platform specifics. To start administrating this increasing complexity, we introduce the concept of a *configuration space*. A configuration space is an exhaustive enumeration of all the possible configuration flags, where a configuration flag may involve the current platform, OpenGL version, and/or external library, either related to OpenGL like GLUT or EGL or independent of the rendering like Boost [Dawes and Abrahams 04] or Bullet physics [Coumans 10]. We create names for these configuration flags within the namespace of RenderTools by prefixing the flag with RT_, such as RT_APPLE, RT_WIN32, RT_GLUT, RT_IOS, RT_ES1, etc.; these are treated as standard C preprocessor defines. Some RT_[VALUE] definitions depend on context and are implied by the platform the build is performed on (RT_APPLE, RT_WIN32), some are dictated by the OpenGL version that is targeted (RT_ES1 or RT_ES2) and some are required for including the third-party external libraries (RT_GLUT, RT_BULLET). Any one combination of flags out of the entire configuration space is called a configuration state.

Examples of configuration states are

- RT_WIN32, RT_GLUT, RT_DEBUG, RT_BULLET. A Windows build, using GLUT as the windowing interface, in debug mode, using Bullet as an external library.

- RT_APPLE, RT_GLUT. A Mac OS X release build, using GLUT as the windowing interface.

- RT_WIN32, RT_EGL, RT_ES2. A Windows release build, using EGL as the interface between OpenGL ES 2.0 and Windows.

- RT_APPLE, RT_IOS, RT_ES1, RT_DEBUG. An iOS build for iPhone and iPad, using OpenGL ES1 fixed-function pipeline to support earlier devices, in debug mode.

Not all configuration states are valid. We cannot simultaneously build for RT_ES1 and RT_ES2 and some third-party libraries are mutually exclusive like RT_BULLET and RT_BOX2D.

44.5   Metabuilds and CMake

One of the most time consuming aspects of platform-independent programming is the cumbersome task of defining all the individual settings for the different IDE's: Visual Studio on Windows, Xcode on Apple, or makefiles on Unix-based systems. Recently, several so-called *metabuild* or *build automation* systems have been gaining popularity to aid in this task. Examples of metabuild systems are premake [Perkins 07] or waf [WAF 11].

The sheer quantity of settings in IDE's can be overwhelming. The metabuild system creates sensible defaults for all of them, and if we want to adjust, we adjust locally via the configuration files. In this way, the exceptions are clearly visible in isolation instead of hidden in a long enumerations of settings in the IDE.

An advantage of a metabuild system is that it provides the opportunity to migrate back and forth between different versions of an IDE. In almost every IDE, it is a very painful process to go back to a previous version when all the project files have been converted to a newer version. Another advantage of a metabuild system is the relative ease in which projects can be shared between different developers. Every developer has a slightly different path to his sources or has adjusted a few settings in the IDE to achieve a local successful build. This makes exporting project files directly to other developers undesirable. With metabuild systems, developers generate fresh project files themselves out of the source tree after having adjusted a few absolute paths clearly stated in configuration files in the build system. A rather unexpected advantage we found while developing was that the latest version of Xcode at the time, Version 4.0.2 on Mac OS X Snow Leopard, proved to be quite unstable, and we were a lot more productive developing in Visual Studio even though the final target was going to be an iOS application. Metabuilds let developers choose their favorite development IDE.

One of the more popular and well established tools is CMake [CMa 11], a free, platform-independent, open-source build system. CMake works with human readable configuration files—always named "CMakeLists.txt"—that contain CMake scripts and exist in directories of the source tree. These CMake configuration files link to each other via the CMake ADD_SUBDIRECTORY() command. A tree traversal is performed starting from a top-level CMake configuration file, passing through the sources, creating project setups for libraries and executables as it goes. After this so-called *configure* process, CMake *generates* IDE project files (Visual Studio, Xcode), or makefiles on Unix based systems. In daily practice, we typically lose our fixed, static, platform-dependent project files and generate them dynamically every time a change is made in the build configuration. The CMake structure and especially the syntax takes some time getting used to, but the advantage is that we only have to learn a single language. Traditional makefiles are not much easier to read and only give platform/compiler-specific results.

44.6   CMake and the Configuration Space

We can fit our concept of the configuration state in a top-level CMake configuration file. The RT_[VALUE] elements of the configuration state can be mapped directly onto so-called *options* in CMake. These options are communicated to the developer and can be adjusted in the CMake GUI (Figure 44.1).

We define the configuration state in a CMake includable file "configuration space.cmake." In this file, we not only set the various RT_[VALUE] options, but also, based on these settings, set include directories and add definitions. A boolean RT_[VALUE] that is either ON or OFF in CMake will be passed on to the compiler as a preprocessor definition with the CMake commands:

```
IF(RT_[VALUE]) ADD_DEFINITION(-DRT_[VALUE])
```

Furthermore, we have to locate third-party libraries such as GLUT, Bullet, Boost, etc., that are needed for this particular configuration state. These paths are developer dependent, so they cannot be known in advance. CMake provides a `find_package()` mechanism to find the packages after a root path is set. It also searches in platform-specific standard locations in case the libraries are installed systemwide. If the package finding is omitted in this phase, the individual CMake configuration files of RenderTools will invoke `find_package()` calls themselves for the needed libraries. As a whole, configurationspace.cmake creates a "context" from which the library as well as the application(s) can be built.

A typical main-development source tree with CMake configuration files is shown in Listing 44.6. In this directory structure, `/rendertools` is the directory that holds the "suite" containing the library and the examples. It contains a CMake-Lists.txt that is a logical start of a build (see the "Where is the source code" entry in the screenshot of the CMake GUI, Figure 44.1). With the project that is generated from this CMakeLists.txt, we can build the library based on the `RT_[VALUE]` settings we choose and build the examples that are dependant on this library.

Figure 44.1. The CMake (2.8.6) GUI.

```
+ development
  (CmakeLists.txt)
  + ARenderToolsApp
    CMakeLists.txt
    + src
    + rsrc
    + config
  + rendertools
    CMakeLists.txt
    + src
    + examples
      CMakeLists.txt
      + HelloWorld
        CMakeLists.txt
        + src
        + rsrc
        + config
      + CameraTest
        CMakeLists.txt
        + src
        + rsrc
        + config
      + ...
    + config
      configurationspace.cmake
  + bullet (external)
    CMakeLists.txt
    + src
  + boost (external)
  + glut (external)
  + ...
```

Listing 44.6. A typical main-development source tree with CMake configuration files.

The general structure of a top-level CMakeLists.txt in a RenderTools context looks like this:

1. Include "configurationspace.cmake" to define the configuration state RT_APPLE, RT_DEBUG, RT_IOS, ..., set the paths to the (external) third-party libraries, add include directories and pass on definitions that are needed for this particular configuration state.

2. Recurse into the actual source-code directory of the RenderTools library by invoking ADD_SUBDIRECTORY (rendertools/src). If we don't want to build RenderTools from source, we can omit this step and link to a binary prebuilt RenderTools from the applications directly.

3. Recurse source-code directory of a RenderTools–dependent application, or an intermediate directory representing a set of applications as is the case with the examples.

The CMakeLists.txt of the RenderTools library itself, located in rendertools/src, has a simple structure:

1. Create a new project for the library: `PROJECT(RenderTools)`.

2. Gather the RenderTools sources: `FILE(RT_SOURCES ... )`.

3. Combine these sources with sources from third-party libraries, depending on the ones defined for inclusion by the `RT_[VALUE]` options if `RT_SOURCE` is defined. Or, if `RT_SOURCE` is not defined, link third-party libraries directly.

4. Create a library with these sources: `ADD_LIBRARY(RenderTools $RT_SOURCES)`.

One could imagine RenderTools being distributed as a set of prebuilt binaries, which would actually be a large collection for all the different configuration states on all the different platforms. Instead, we chose to let developers build RenderTools from source. We feel we can do so because we supply the sources, assist in the build process via the CMake configuration files, and provide sensible defaults for common configurations.

The CMakeLists.txt of an intermediate directory that contains various applications simply recurses into these source-code directories. As an example, the CMakeLists in /examples looks like this:

1. Create a new project for this application suite: `PROJECT(Examples)`

2. Recurse into lower-level source directories:

```
ADD_SUBDIRECTORY(HelloWorld)
ADD_SUBDIRECTORY(CameraTest)
...
```

Finally, the CMakeLists.txt in the directories of individual applications have the following structure:

1. Create a new project for the application:

```
PROJECT(HelloWorld)
```

2. Gather application-specific sources and resources:

```
FILE(APP_SOURCES ...)
FILE(APP_RESOURCES ...)
```

3. Create an executable with these sources and resources:

```
ADD_EXECUTABLE(HelloWorld
  ${APP_SOURCES} ${APP_RESOURCES})
```

4. Link in the RenderTools library:

```
TARGET_LINK_LIBRARY(HelloWorld RenderTools)
```

5. Set the dependency:

```
ADD_DEPENDENCY(HelloWorld RenderTools)
```

For applications residing outside the /rendertools directory, e.g., ARenderToolsApp, we can write a CMakeLists.txt in /development that includes ARenderToolsApp and the RenderTools library. Such a top-level CMakeLists.txt file looks like this:

```
PROJECT(MyDailyWork)
INCLUDE(rendertools/config/configurationspace.cmake)
ADD_SUBDIRECTORY(ARenderToolsApp)
# Recurse directly into the library, avoiding double
inclusion of configurationspace.cmake and the examples:
ADD_SUBDIRECTORY(rendertools/src)
```

Note that this is a volatile file and changes regularly, depending on the projects you are working on at that particular moment.

44.7   CMake and Platform Specifics

The CMake structure mentioned above is the general structure that most CMake-based builds follow. There are of course a lot of platform-specific peculiarities that have to be dealt with. Some of the nontrivial ones we encountered are listed below.

44.7.1   Windows

Windows is fairly straightforward. GLUT or EGL handles the windowing interface. OpenGL as binary library is available with the operating system or via a dynamic link library (DLL) provided by the hardware manufacturer of the video card. The OpenGL header and library file are shipped with Visual Studio.

- Resources. On Windows, we simply copy all the resources the application needs to the build directory, avoiding a more involved search mechanism. Unlike Apple, Windows doesn't use application bundles, so some of the work of placing resources in the final distribution will have to be done in the installer. CMake has a postbuild command mechanism in which tasks can be specified that have to be performed after the build. The following CMake script fragment copies the resources to the directory where the executable resides:

```
FOREACH(NAME ${APP_RESOURCES})
  GET_FILENAME_COMPONENT(NAMEWITHOUTPATH ${NAME} NAME)
  ADD_CUSTOM_COMMAND(
    TARGET ${APP_NAME}
      POST_BUILD
      COMMAND ${CMAKE_COMMAND} -E copy
              ${NAME}
              ${PROJECT_BINARY_DIR}/
                ${CMAKE_CFG_INTDIR}/
                ${NAMEWITHOUTPATH})
ENDFOREACH()
```

The CMake variable `PROJECT_BINARY_DIR` is the build directory of the project; `CMAKE_CFG_INTDIR` is the current configuration, e.g., Debug, Release, etc., so together, they form the actual path to the executable. The `${CMAKE_COMMAND}` `-E copy` is the CMake platform-independent copy command.

44.7.2   Mac OS X

The procedure for Mac OS X is similar to Windows. Again, GLUT handles the windowing interface. We have no OpenGL ES build for Mac OS X at the moment of writing.

- Resources. Our Mac OS X application bundles have the standard hierarchy where the application itself is represented by a bundle (e.g., HelloWorld.app) containing a /Contents directory, which, in turn, contains a /MacOS directory with the actual executable, e.g., HelloWorld, and a /Resources directory containing the resources. Using a similar CMake postbuild construct to the one we used in Windows leads to conflicts with the copying that Xcode performs internally. We chose to just let Xcode do its job. In CMake, we present sources and resources to `ADD_EXECUTABLE()`:

```
ADD_EXECUTABLE(${APP_NAME} MACOSX_BUNDLE
  ${APP_SOURCES}
  ${APP_RESOURCES})
```

We make sure the resources are "labeled" as resources so Xcode will treat them correctly during the build. That is, we make them visible in the /Resources folder in the Xcode IDE and copy them to the correct location in the application bundle:

```
SET_TARGET_PROPERTIES(${APP_NAME} PROPERTIES
  RESOURCE "${APP_RESOURCES}")
```

- Information property list files. Mac OS X application bundles need an information property list file that enumerates various aspects of the application in the application bundle, which is located directly in the root of the bundle. CMake lets you identify a template file with wildcards, which we name Info.plist.in.

```
SET(APP_PLIST_FILE
  ${APP_ROOT}/config/apple/osx/Info.plist.in)
SET_TARGET_PROPERTIES(${APP_NAME} PROPERTIES
  MACOSX_BUNDLE_INFO_PLIST ${APP_PLIST_FILE})
```

CMake will read the Info.plist.in, substitute the wildcards, and generate a Info.plist in a private section of its build directory, e.g., path/to/build/CMakeFiles/HelloWorld.dir/Info.plist. This file is linked and added to the Xcode project files automatically, after which Xcode will copy it to the root of the application bundle as a prebuild step.

- Objective-C(++). In order to use C++ code in Objective-C, we need to compile all sources as Objective-C++, which we can do with

```
SET(CMAKE_CXX_FLAGS "-x objective-c++")
```

We need to add the .mm files to the sources in order for them to be built, so we include those with:

```
FILE(GLOB APP_SOURCES ${APP_ROOT}/src/[^.]*.[mmcpph]*)
```

44.7.3   iOS

iOS is a lot more involved. Only OpenGL ES is supported on the devices. OpenGL ES 2.0 is supported only on newer models (iPhone 3GS and up, iPad 2). OpenGL ES 1.1 is supported on all models. Furthermore, a distinction is made between applications that run on the simulator on the Intel architecture or on the device itself with the ARM architecture. The signing and provisioning of applications needs special attention, and resource management is a bit more involved than on Mac OS X.

- Configurating targets. CMake presents a method of cross compiling when the build platform is different from the target platform, which was our first approach to creating iOS applications, resulting in different so-called *toolchain* files for device and simulator. This turned out to be an unnecessary in-between step. The compiler can be the default compiler (Apple LLVM compiler 3.0 for Xcode 4.2) also used for Mac OS X builds. The base SDK is selected via the CMAKE_OSX_SYSROOT variable. The CMake script fragment for iOS 5.0 follows:

```
SET(IOS_BASE_SDK_VER "5.0"
  CACHE PATH "iOS Base SDK version")
SET(IOS_DEVROOT
  "/Developer/Platforms/iPhoneOS.platform/Developer")
SET(IOS_SDKROOT "${IOS_DEVROOT}/SDKs/
  iPhoneOS${IOS_BASE_SDK_VER}.sdk")
SET(CMAKE_OSX_SYSROOT "${SDKROOT}")
```

The architecture has to be set:

```
SET (CMAKE_OSX_ARCHITECTURES
  "$(ARCHS_STANDARD_32_BIT)")
```

This will result in the standard armv7 setting. We set the target to create universal applications for both iPad and iPhone. The representation "1,2" will be translated correctly to "iPhone/iPad" in Xcode:

```
SET_TARGET_PROPERTIES(${APP_NAME} PROPERTIES
  XCODE_ATTRIBUTE_TARGETED_DEVICE_FAMILY "1,2")
SET_TARGET_PROPERTIES(${APP_NAME} PROPERTIES
  XCODE_ATTRIBUTE_DEVICES "Universal")
```

We can set the minimal iOS deployment version, iOS 4.3 in this case:

```
SET_TARGET_PROPERTIES(${APP_NAME} PROPERTIES
  XCODE_ATTRIBUTE_IPHONEOS_DEPLOYMENT_TARGET 4.3'')
```

- Frameworks. The different frameworks needed for linking can be added via linker flags. They will not be clearly visible in the Xcode IDE, but the applications link correctly:

```
# Enumerate frameworks to be linked to on iOS...
SET(IOS_FRAMEWORKS ${IOS_FRAMEWORKS} OpenGLES)
SET(IOS_FRAMEWORKS ${IOS_FRAMEWORKS} UIKit)
SET(IOS_FRAMEWORKS ${IOS_FRAMEWORKS} Foundation)
SET(IOS_FRAMEWORKS ${IOS_FRAMEWORKS} CoreGraphics)
SET(IOS_FRAMEWORKS ${IOS_FRAMEWORKS} QuartzCore)
...
FOREACH(NAME ${IOS_FRAMEWORKS})
  SET(CMAKE_EXE_LINKER_FLAGS
    "${CMAKE_EXE_LINKER_FLAGS} -framework ${NAME}")
ENDFOREACH()
```

- Effective platforms. New in the latest version of CMake, Version 2.8.6, is the concept of effective platforms. Setting this parameter makes sure that if we switch between device or simulator schemes in the Xcode IDE, the correct build path to the corresponding library is automatically selected by Xcode. This will be either path/to/build/[config]-iphoneos or path/to/build/[config]-

iphonesimulator, where config represents your current configuration, Debug, Release, etc.:

```
SET(CMAKE_XCODE_EFFECTIVE_PLATFORMS
  -iphoneos;-iphonesimulator)
```

- **Information property list files.** As in Mac OS X builds, an Info.plist property list file is needed in the bundle. In CMake, they are treated similar to the Mac OS X builds, only we provide a different template because iOS has some additional properties like orientations of the device and minimal device requirements, e.g., gyroscope, GPS:

```
SET(PLIST_FILE
  ${APP_ROOT}/config/apple/ios/Info.plist.in)
```

- **Interface builder.** Xib files are interface builder user interface files. As a prebuild step, Xcode compiles them into binary nib files and adds them to the bundle, but only if they are properly identified as resource. The CMake script fragment follows:

```
FILE(GLOB XIB_FILES
  ${APP_ROOT}/config/apple/ios/*.xib) # Gather xib files
SET_TARGET_PROPERTIES(${APP_NAME} PROPERTIES
  RESOURCE "${XIB_FILES}")
```

- **Provisioning and code signing.** Provisioning and code signing is one of the more error-prone new aspects of iOS development. After subscribing to the Apple Developer Program, a developer will have to spend quite some time in the "iOS Provisioning Portal" on the Apple Developer website. First, developer and distribution certificates have to be generated that can be added to the personal keychain. For each application, we generate an application identifier called the AppID and generate developer, AdHoc and AppStore distribution provisioning profiles called *.mobile-provisioning files that need to be linked with our bundle. Without those, we can only run applications in the simulator. With a developer provisioning profile, we can run and debug our application on the device that is tethered to our development machine directly from Xcode. With the AdHoc distribution, we can create a so-called archive that can be sent around and installed locally on a limited set of trusted devices via iTunes. We need to know and enumerate the unique UID keys of these devices in advance. The AppStore distribution allows us to distribute our application via the AppStore after it is approved by Apple. The AppID in reversed domain notation is set through the CMake MACOS_BUNDLE_GUI_IDENTIFIER variable. This entry will also be substituted in the Info.plist file via a wildcard as value for the **CFBundleIdentifier** key:

```
SET(IOS_APP_IDENTIFIER nl.cthrough.helloworld)
# this has to match to your App ID (case sensitive)
SET(MACOSX_BUNDLE_GUI_IDENTIFIER ${IOS_APP_IDENTIFIER})
```

The provision profile is a separate setting:

```
SET(IOS_CODESIGN_ENTITLEMENTS
  ${APP_ROOT}/config/apple/ios/
  entitlements/EntitlementsDebug.plist)
  # replace with EntitlementsDistributionAdHoc.plist or
  # EntitlementsDistributionAppStore.plist
SET_TARGET_PROPERTIES(${APP_NAME} PROPERTIES
  XCODE_ATTRIBUTE_CODE_SIGN_ENTITLEMENTS
  ${IOS_CODESIGN_ENTITLEMENTS})
```

- **Archiving.** Archiving consists of creating an archive for distribution, either AdHoc or AppStore. To create a successful archive, we have to make sure that, in Xcode, the skip install property is not set for the application but set for static libraries, which is the CMake default. Furthermore, we make sure that the path to an installation directory is not empty:

```
SET_TARGET_PROPERTIES(${APP_NAME} PROPERTIES
  XCODE_ATTRIBUTE_SKIP_INSTALL NO)
SET_TARGET_PROPERTIES(${APP_NAME} PROPERTIES
  XCODE_ATTRIBUTE_INSTALL_PATH "/Applications")
```

We also have to make sure that in the code-signing field, a valid iPhone Distribution as opposed to an iPhone developer profile is set. Unfortunately, with the latest version of CMake, it is not yet possible to set different values for different configurations in Xcode, but this feature is on the road map for the next version (2.8.7). We hope to be able to do the following:

```
SET( IOS_CODE_SIGN_IDENTITY_DEVELOPER
  "iPhone Developer"
  CACHE STRING "code signing identity" )
  # For developing
SET( IOS_CODE_SIGN_IDENTITY_DISTRIBUTION
  "iPhone Distribution"
  CACHE STRING "code signing identity" )
  # AdHoc or AppStore distribution
SET_TARGET_PROPERTIES( ${APP_NAME} PROPERTIES
  XCODE_ATTRIBUTE_CODE_SIGN_IDENTITY[variant=''Debug'']
  ${IOS_CODE_SIGN_IDENTITY_DEVELOPER} )
SET_TARGET_PROPERTIES( ${APP_NAME} PROPERTIES
  XCODE_ATTRIBUTE_CODE_SIGN_IDENTITY[variant=''Release'']
  ${IOS_CODE_SIGN_IDENTITY_DISTRIBUTION} )
```

Instead of manually changing the value of the code-sign identity as we have to do now, the following with work:

```
SET( IOS_CODE_SIGN_IDENTITY "iPhone Developer"
  CACHE STRING "code signing identity" )
  # Change to iPhone Distribution'' for archiving
SET_TARGET_PROPERTIES( ${APP_NAME} PROPERTIES
  XCODE_ATTRIBUTE_CODE_SIGN_IDENTITY
  ${RT_CODE_SIGN_IDENTITY} )
```

44.8 Conclusion

Fortunately, the last decade has shown an incredible increase in the number of community-driven software projects aiming to help deal with the complexities of cross-platform development (Boost, CMake) and to help avoid overly complex code bases when targeting different OpenGL versions (GLEW, GLUT). Unfortunately, the task of selecting the best set of these projects is a difficult one. There are many alternatives to the selection we made, but we believe that we have made the most sensible choice at this time.

We would like to thank contributors from the very active CMake community, especially David Cole and Michael Hertling. And George van Venrooij, for pointing out CMake in the first place.

Bibliography

[CMa 11] "CMake: A Cross-Platform, Open-Source, Build System." http://www.cmake.org, 2011.

[Coumans 10] Erwin Coumans. "Bullet Physics Library." http://bulletphysics.org, 2010.

[Dawes and Abrahams 04] Beman Dawes and David Abrahams. "Boost C++ Libaries." http://www.boost.org, 2004.

[Khronos 97] Khronos. "OpenGL Platform and OS Implementations." http://www.opengl.org/documentation/implementations, 1997.

[Khronos 12] Khronos. "EGL: Native Platform Interface." http://www.khronos.org/egl, 2012.

[Kilgard 97] Mark Kilgard. "GLUT: The OpenGL Utility Toolkit." http://www.opengl.org/resources/libraries/glut/, 1997.

[Nokia 08] Nokia. "Qt: A Cross-Platform Application and UIFramework." http://qt.nokia.com/products, 2008.

[Olszta 03] Pawel W. Olszta. "FreeGLUT: The OpenSourced alternative to GLUT." http://freeglut.sourceforge.net/, 2003.

[OpenGL 11] OpenGL. "Creating an OpenGL Context." http://www.opengl.org/wiki/Creating_an_OpenGL_Context, 2011.

[OpenGL 12] OpenGL. "OpenGL Toolkits and APIs." http://www.opengl.org/wiki/Related_toolkits_and_APIs#Context.2FWindow/Toolkits, 2012.

[Perkins 07] Jason Perkins. "Premake: Build Script Generation." http://premake.sourceforge.net/, 2007.

[RenderTools 11] RenderTools. "RenderTools: A (Lightweight) OpenGL–Based Scenegraph Library by J. van der Spek." http://rendertools.dynamica.org, 2011.

[Sourceforge 11] Sourceforge. "GLEW: The OpenGL Extension Wrangler Library." http://glew.sourceforge.net, 2011.

[WAF 11] WAF. "WAF: The Meta Build System—Google Project Hosting." http://code.google.com/p/waf/, 2011.

[Wikipedia 12a] Wikipedia. "GLX." http://en.wikipedia.org/wiki/GLX, 2012.

[Wikipedia 12b] Wikipedia. "WGL (software)." http://en.wikipedia.org/wiki/WGL_(software), 2012.

About the Contributors

Woojin Ahn
ahnw@rpi.edu

Woojin is a postdoctoral research associate at the Center for Modeling, Simulation and Imaging in Medicine at Rensselaer Polytechnic Institute. He received his PhD in Mechanical Engineering from Korea Advanced Institute of Science and Technology in 2010. His current research interests include surgery simulation, physics-based animation, and web-based multimodal interactive 3D applications.

Alina Alt
aalt@nvidia.com

Alina is an applied engineer at NVIDIA where her responsibilities include helping users incorporate NVIDIA's GPUs, video products, and video-related driver features into their solutions and applications. She specializes in combining technologies in video-processing applications and optimizing application performance in systems with multiple GPUs. Her past experience includes developing augmented reality applications for live sports telecasts and developing a scalable, CPU-based compute cluster graphics driver.

Edward Angel
angel@cs.unm.edu

Ed is Professor Emeritus of Computer Science at the University of New Mexico (UNM) and was the first UNM Presidential Teaching Fellow. At UNM, he held joint appointments in Computer Science, Electrical and Computer Engineering, and Cinematic Arts. He has held academic positions at the University of California at

Berkeley, the University of Southern California, and the University of Rochester, and has held visiting positions in Sweden, the U.K., India, Venezuela, and Ecuador. His research interests have focused on computer graphics and scientific visualization. Ed's textbook *Interactive Computer Graphics* is now in its sixth edition. The third edition of the companion book, *The OpenGL Primer*, was published in 2006. He has taught over 100 professional short courses, including OpenGL courses at both SIGGRAPH and SIGGRAPH Asia. He received a BS from the California Institute of Technology and a PhD from the University of Southern California.

Nakhoon Baek

oceancru@gmail.com

Nakhoon is currently an associate professor in the School of Computer Science and Engineering at Kyungpook National University, Korea. He received his BA, MS, and PhD in computer science from Korea Advanced Institute of Science and Technology (KAIST) in 1990, 1992, and 1997, respectively. His research interests include graphics standards, graphics algorithms, and real-time rendering. He implemented an in-house version of CGM/CGI graphics standards in the late 1990s, for a telephone company in Korea. Since 2005, he has been coworking with the graphics team in HUONE Inc. to commercially implement a set of graphics standards for embedded systems including OpenVG, OpenGL ES, OpenGL SC, and Collada.

Mike Bailey

mjb@cs.oregonstate.edu

Mike is a professor in computer science at Oregon State University. Mike holds a PhD from Purdue University, and has worked at Sandia National Labs, Purdue University, Megatek Corporation, and the San Diego Supercomputer Center at UC San Diego. Mike has taught numerous classes at the college level (a combined 4000+ students), and at conferences (SIGGRAPH, SIGGRAPH Asia, SIGCSE, IEEE Visualization, and Supercomputing). Mike was five times voted Computer Science Teacher of the Year by the UCSD CS seniors. He was also voted Most Enthusiastic Professor by the OSU students in 2005 and received the Austin Paul teaching award from OSU's College of Engineering in 2008. Mike's research areas include a variety of topics in the field of scientific computer graphics, with a specific interest in GPU programming, visualizing volume data sets, solid freeform fabrication for visualization hardcopy, and stereographics.

Francesco Banterle

francesco.banterle@isti.cnr.it

Francesco is a post-doc researcher at the Visual Computing Laboratory at ISTI-CNR Italy. He received a PhD in Engineering from Warwick University in 2009. During his PhD, he developed inverse tone mapping, which bridges the gap between low dynamic range imaging and high dynamic range (HDR) imaging. He holds a BSc and an MSc in computer science from Verona University. He is the first coauthor of the book *Advanced High Dynamic Range*, published by A K Peters in 2011. His main research fields are HDR Imaging, Rendering, and Parallel Processing (GPUs and shared-memory systems).

Jesse Barker

jesse.barker@linaro.org

Jesse is a principal software engineer at ARM Ltd., where he is currently seconded as technical lead of the graphics working group to Linaro, a not-for-profit open-source engineering company aimed at making Linux development for the ARM ecosystem easier and faster. Prior to his arrival at ARM in 2010, he enjoyed stints at ATI/AMD, Silicon Graphics, Digital, and a few smaller companies. Efforts for those enterprises have ranged from development to design to leadership of technology as well as process and policy. He has touched just about every layer of the graphics stack on a number of platforms, and is excited to see how Linaro can help shape the direction of the graphics stack on Linux moving forward.

Venceslas Biri

biri@univ-mlv.fr

Venceslas is an associate professor in the LIGM laboratory of Université Paris-Est. He specializes in real-time rendering and global illumination, and has good knowledge in virtual reality. He also served as headmaster of the higher school of engineering, IMAC (Image, Multimedia, Audiovisual and Communication), from 2006 to 2011. A former engineering student of ENSIMAG, he also teaches mathematics and computer graphics.

Nicolas Capens
nicolas@transgaming.com

Nicolas received his MSciEng degree in computer science from Ghent University in 2007. Even at a young age, he was fascinated by computer graphics, and he developed a passion for bringing 3D graphics to a wider audience. He wrote the fastest software renderer with shading capabilities known to date and is deeply involved in projects to provide efficient translations between graphics APIs. Fueled by the ongoing convergence between CPU and GPU technology, he strives to further blur the line between software and hardware rendering and make incompatibilities and limitations a thing of the past.

Won Chun
wonchun@gmail.com

Won is one of the tech leads for Google's websearch infrastructure efforts in NYC. In his 20% time, he also helped build and maintain Google Body, including designing a high-performance mesh-compression format. Prior to Google, he dabbled in virtualization and user-interface design at moka5 and developed holographic and volumetric rendering algorithms at Actuality Systems. Won has an SB in Electrical Engineering and Computer Science from MIT.

Patrick Cozzi
pjcozzi@siggraph.org

At Analytical Graphics, Inc. (AGI), Patrick leads the graphics development for Cesium, an open-source WebGL virtual globe. He teaches GPU Programming and Architecture at the University of Pennsylvania. Patrick is coeditor of *OpenGL Insights* and coauthor of *3D Engine Design for Virtual Globes*. Before joining AGI in 2004, he worked for IBM and Intel. He has an MS in computer and information science from the University of Pennsylvania and a BA in computer science from Penn State.

Cyril Crassin
ccrassin@nvidia.com

Cyril received his PhD in computer graphics from Grenoble university at INRIA in 2011. He is now a postdoctoral fellow at NVIDIA research. His PhD work focused on using prefiltered voxel representations for real-time rendering of large detailed scenes and complex objects, as well as global illumination effects.

In this context, he developed the GigaVoxels rendering pipeline. Cyril has been supporting OpenGL development for many years through his icare3d website.

Suvranu De
des@rpi.edu

Suvranu is the Director of the Center for Modeling, Simulation and Imaging in Medicine, and Professor in the department of Mechanical, Aerospace and Nuclear Engineering at Rensselaer Polytechnic Institute with joint appointments in the Departments of Biomedical Engineering and Information Technology and Web Science. He received his ScD in Mechanical Engineering from MIT in 2001. He is the recipient of the 2005 ONR Young Investigator Award and serves on the editorial board of *Computers and Structures* and scientific committees of numerous national and international conferences. He is also the founding chair of the Committee on Computational Bioengineering of the US Association for Computational Mechanics. His research interests include the development of novel, robust, and reliable computational technology to solve challenging and high-impact problems in engineering, medicine, and biology.

Charles de Rousiers
charles.derousiers@gmail.com

Charles is currently a PhD candidate at INRIA Grenoble Rhone-Alpes in the ARTIS research team. He studies complex materials representation for realistic rendering under the supervision of Nicolas Holzschuch. He was a visiting scholar at UC Berkeley under the supervision of Ravi Ramamoorthi for six months.

Daniel Dekkers
d.dekkers@cthrough.nl

After graduating from Eindhoven University of Technology, Department of Mathematics and Computing Science with honorable mention, Daniel Dekkers (1971) formed the company cThrough, which focuses on collaborations between computer graphics–related computing science and various (artistic) fields, mainly contemporary art, modern dance, architecture, and education. Various projects include "Prometheus, poem of fire," a 25-minute animation by artist P. Struycken, for Dutch national television; "SpaceJart," an interactive zero-gravity biljart simulation for an exhibition at Eindhoven University of Technology; "Dynamix," a sensor-based stage projection for a ballet by Khrisztina de Châtel; "OptiMixer," a multicriteria optimization tool in collaboration with architectural firm MVRDV and Climatizer; a climate-simulation game that was shown at the Cité de sciences et l'Industry, Paris.

At the moment, Dekkers is working on GPU programming (OpenCL, CUDA), cross-platform development, and iOS applications.

Marco Di Benedetto
marco.dibenedetto@isti.cnr.it

Marco is a researcher at the Istituto di Scienza e Tecnologie dell'Informazione (ISTI) of the National Research Council (CNR) in Pisa, Italy. He received his PhD in computer science from the University of Pisa in 2011 with a thesis on real-time rendering of large multiresolution data sets. These topics are part of his research and publishing work in Computer Graphics, along with photorealistic rendering, out-of-core processing and rendering, and parallel GPU techniques. He is the creator of the SpiderGL library (http://spidergl.org) for the development of CG applications on the web platform.

Aleksandar Dimitrijević
adimitrijevic73@gmail.com

Aleksandar is a teaching assistant, researcher, senior programmer, team leader, and a Cisco Networking Academy instructor in the Faculty of Electronic Engineering, University of Niš. Since the completion of his undergraduate studies in 1997, he has been involved in teaching several courses at the University, such as data structures, programming, computer networks, computer graphics, and human-computer interaction. Aleksandar received an MSc degree in electrical engineering in 2003 in the Faculty of Electronic Engineering, University of Niš. As a member of the Computer Graphics and Geographic Information Systems Laboratory, he has been involved in designing and implementing various information systems. Currently, his main research topic is the development of a large terrain-rendering algorithm, which is a part of his PhD thesis.

Chris Dirks
ChrisDirks1@gmail.com

Chris is a JavaScript software engineer specializing in game and simulation development. His professional work includes content surrounding HTML5 and WebGL technologies. He is also an avid gamer, with his favorite genre being RPGs.

Benjamin Encz
benjamin.encz@googlemail.com

Benjamin started with WebGL in January 2011 at IBM, developing a UI framework for his bachelor thesis. Currently, he lives and works in Stuttgart, Germany. He has a bachelor's degree in Applied Computer Science from the Baden-Wuerttemberg Cooperative State University. Benjamin is a software engineer at Excelsis Business Technology AG, where he focuses on the conception and development of iOS applications. Next to his job, he enjoys tracing WebGL's development, and video game programming.

Lin Feng
asflin@ntu.edu.sg

Dr. Lin Feng is currently an Associate Professor and the Program Director, MSc (Digital Media Technology), at the School of Computer Engineering, Nanyang Technological University, Singapore. His research interests include computer graphics, biomedical imaging and visualization, as well as high-performance computing. He has published more than 150 technical papers, and he has been serving on the editorial board and as a guest editor / reviewer for many journals and books. Dr. Lin is a senior member of IEEE.

Alexandros Frantzis
alexandros.frantzis@linaro.org

Alexandros is an electrical and software engineer and a long-time free (as in speech) software supporter. He has worked on many aspects of graphics and multimedia technology on GNU/Linux–based embedded systems, including protocol and data handling of video streaming, user-interface creation, DirectFB driver development, and OpenGL ES 2.0 application development. He is currently a member of the Linaro Graphics Working Group, developing benchmarking tools for OpenGL ES 2.0, and enhancing graphics-related free and open source software libraries and applications to take advantage of the powerful 3D GPUs available on modern ARM-based hardware.

Lionel Fuentes
lfuentes@asobostudio.com

Lionel started programming at the age of 15 out of curiosity to understand how computers work and for the fun of making programs and video games. He graduated from INSA

Toulouse Engineering School, specialized in computer science, and studied one year in Tohoku University, Japan, researching the field of real-time global illumination. He now works for video games editor Asobo Studio as an engine programmer. His tasks include audio engine development, graphics programming, memory management, optimization, and tools development. He enjoys spending his free time playing the guitar, participating in amateur video games development, and playing Wii with his girlfriend.

Fabio Ganovelli
fabio.ganovelli@isti.cnr.it

Fabio received his PhD from the University of Pisa in 2001. Since then, he has published in the fields of deformable objects, geometry processing, out-of-core rendering and manipulation of massive models, photorealistic rendering, image-to-geometry registration, and education. He is a core developer of the Visualization and Computer Graphics Library and has served as reviewer and/or chair for all the main journals and conferences in computer graphics. He is currently a research scientist at the Istituto di Scienza e Tecnologie dell'Informazione (ISTI) of the National Research Council (CNR) in Pisa, Italy.

Simon Green

Simon is a senior member of the Developer Technology group at NVIDIA. He started graphics programming on the Sinclair ZX-81, which had 1 KB of RAM and a screen resolution of 64 by 48 pixels, and has been trying to improve the quality of real-time graphics ever since. He received a BS in computer science from the University of Reading in 1994. Simon has been at NVIDIA since 1999, where he has worked on numerous projects including the early Geforce graphics demos, games such as Doom 3, and NVIDIA's OpenGL and CUDA SDKs. He is a frequent presenter at the GDC and SIGGRAPH conferences, and was a section editor for the original *GPU Gems* book. His research interests include cellular automata, physically based simulation on GPUs, and analogue synthesizers.

Stefan Gustavson
stefan.gustavson@liu.se

Stefan, born in 1965, received his PhD in image processing in 1997. His interest in computer graphics has had him fiddling with raytracers since the 1980s, and he has been hacking in OpenGL since Version 1.0. Apart from the procedural noise and texture-related work presented in this book, he is involved in research in next-generation image-based lighting by higher-dimensional light fields, an area where computer graphics meets image processing.

Tansel Halic
halict@rpi.edu

Tansel received his BSc and MSci in computer science from Marmara University, Istanbul, in 2001 and 2004, respectively. He later continued his research at the University of Arkansas at Little Rock. His research focused on surgical simulation in virtual and augmented environments. He obtained an MS in applied science and specialized in applied computing. He later moved to Rensselaer Polytechnic Institute, Troy, New York, and has been pursuing his PhD degree in the Department of Mechanical, Aerospace and Nuclear Engineering. His research interests include framework design, surgical simulations in virtual reality environments, and real-time algorithms for interactive multimodal simulations.

Ashraf Samy Hegab
ashraf.hegab@orange.com

After working in the games industry for seven years as a Rendering engineer for console titles such as F1 2010, 50 Cent Blood on the Sand, and Brian Lara International Cricket, Ashraf moved to the Service Evolution and Games division of Orange R&D, where he focuses on the intersection between mobile, desktop, and web to improve software development strategies and the utilization of emerging technologies into Orange's products and services.

Adrien Herubel
herubel@gmail.com

Adrien is an R&D engineer in the motion picture department of Ubisoft. He is part of the team developing a proprietary real-time previsualization engine and an offline renderer. He also worked in a VFX studio called DuranDuboi, where he developed the low-level layers of the geometry pipeline. He is currently in the process of finishing his thesis on real-time massive model rendering.

Sébastien Hillaire
sebastien.hillaire@gmail.com

Sébastien obtained his PhD in computer science from the French National Institute of Applied Science in 2010. After one year at Dynamixyz, he became a graphics programmer at Criterion—Electronic Arts. He fell in love with OpenGL many years ago, and cannot stop using it for high quality graphics and appealing visual effects.

Ladislav Hrabcak
hrabcak@outerra.com

Ladislav has been interested in computer graphics since 1997 and cofounded Outerra where he currently works, mainly on Outerra Engine's OpenGL-based renderer.

Scott Hunter
scott.k.hunter@gmail.com

Scott is a software developer at Analytical Graphics, Inc. (AGI), where he builds analysis libraries in C# and Java, and client-side visualization in HTML, JavaScript, and WebGL. Prior to joining AGI, he wrote software as a consultant for a wide range of clients in the pharmaceutical, legal, retail, and game industries, using a mix of nearly every modern platform and language. Scott has a bachelor's degree in Computer Science from Rensselaer Polytechnic Institute.

Lindsay Kay
lindsay.kay@xeolabs.com

Lindsay is the author of SceneJS, an open-source, WebGL-based 3D scene graph engine geared towards rendering detailed scenes for visualization applications. By day, he works as a software developer at BioDigital Systems, where he is responsible for the 3D engine within the BioDigital Human. With a background in agile development, his interests include the design of APIs that make access to high-performance graphics easier for Web developers.

Brano Kemen
cameni@outerra.com

Brano is the cofounder of Outerra. His main interests include procedural techniques for the generation of terrain and other natural and artificial phenomena as well as large-scale world rendering.

Pyarelal Knowles
pyar.knowles@rmit.edu.au

Pyarelal is a PhD student at RMIT University, Melbourne, with research interests in real-time computer graphics and physics simulations. He completed his BS of IT (games and graphics programming) in 2008, before a Comp. Sci. (Honors) year in 2009 at RMIT.

Daniel Koch

dgkoch@gmail.com

Daniel received his M.Math degree in computer science from the University of Waterloo in 2002. He has a strong background in 3D graphics, specializing in OpenGL. He is an active member of the Khronos OpenGL and OpenGL ES working groups. Daniel is currently the Senior Graphics Architect at TransGaming. He has been with TransGaming since 2002, where he has been instrumental in advancing the graphics technology used for Cedega, Cider, and GameTree TV which provide an implementation of Direct3D using OpenGL/OpenGL ES. He is the project lead for ANGLE, which provides an implementation of OpenGL ES 2 using Direct3D.

Geoff Leach

gl@rmit.edu.au www.cs.rmit.edu.au/ gl/

Geoff is a lecturer at RMIT University, Melbourne, where he has been using OpenGL for teaching computer graphics since the 1.0 days. He has won a number of teaching awards and finds a rewarding challenge in guiding and enthusing students about learning an area which many find technically difficult. His research interests are fairly broad, and include computer graphics, computational geometry, GPU computing and computational nanotechnology. Geoff received a BAppSc with distinction from Swinburne University in 1984 and MAppSc from RMIT University in 1990.

Hwanyong Lee

hylee@hu1.com

Hwanyong is currently Chief Technical Officer of HUONE Inc., Korea. He received his BA in computer science from Korea Advanced Institute of Science and Technology (KAIST) in 1990, MS in computer engineering from Pohang University of Science and Technology (POSTECH) in 1992, and PhD in computer engineering from Kyungpook National University in 2011. His research interests include computer graphics; embedded-system software; and game design and development. Since 2004, he has been developing graphics software for mobile devices as Chief Technical Officer of HUONE Inc.

Christopher Lux

christopherlux@gmail.com

Christopher Lux currently is a predoctoral research associate with the Virtual Reality Systems department at Bauhaus-Universität Weimar, Germany. In 2004 he graduated from the Ilmenau University of Technology in computer science with a major in computer graphics. His research interests include real-time rendering, scientific visualization, and visual computing.

Dzmitry Malyshau

kvarkus@gmail.com

Dzmitry is an enthusiast in computer science. He was born in Belarus and there received his professional degree in mathematics and programming. He moved to Canada in order to work on a real-time 3D engine and computer games development for touchscreen devices. Besides experimenting with 3D rendering ideas, Dzmitry also researches data compression and artificial intelligence.

Arnaud Masserann

Arnaud1602@gmail.com

Arnaud graduated from the INSA of Rennes, France in 2010. He works as an R&D engineer at Virtualys, which has been making serious games for more than ten years. He spends most of his time playing with Unity, Ogre, and bare OpenGL. He is the main author of opengl-tutorial.org and makes triangles for a living.

Jon McCaffrey

mccaffrey.jonathan@gmail.com

Jon works at NVIDIA on the Tegra Graphics Performance team, working to improve performance and user experience. He graduated in 2011 from the University of Pennsylvania with an MSE in computer science and a BSE in digital media design. At Penn, he was a teaching assistant for two years for CIS 565, GPU Programming, and Architecture. Before coming to NVIDIA, he interned at LucasArts in 2010 working on in-engine animation tools and worked as a research assistant at the SIG Center for Computer Graphics.

Bruce Merry

bmerry@gmail.com

Bruce did his PhD at the University of Cape Town, specializing in character animation. In 2008, he joined ARM as a software engineer working on Mali graphics products. He has now returned to the University of Cape Town to do a postdoc. He is funded by the Centre for High Performance Computing to do research in GPU acceleration of computer graphics algorithms. When not doing computer graphics, Bruce is a regular participant in programming contests.

Muhammad Mobeen Movania

mova0002@e.ntu.edu.sg

Muhammad Mobeen received his Bachelor of Computer Sciences from Iqra University Karachi in 2005. After his graduation, he joined the Data Communication and Control (Pvt.) Ltd as a software engineer, working on DirectX and OpenGL APIs to produce real-time interactive tactical simulators and dynamic integrated training simulators. His research interests include volumetric rendering, GPU technologies, and real-time volumetric lighting, shading, and shadows. He is currently pursuing his PhD from NTU, and his proposed area of research is GPU-accelerated advanced volumetric deformation and rendering under the advice of Associate Professor Lin Feng. He is the author of the open-source project OpenCloth, http://code.google. com/p/opencloth, which details all of the existing cloth and soft-body simulation algorithms in a simple OpenGL-based C++ library.

Bruno Oliveira

bruno.oliveira@dcc.fc.up.pt

Bruno was born on Christmas day in 1978 in Porto, the place where he still lives today. He studied computer science and later on got his MSc in computer graphics. In between, he had several jobs, from network administrator, to software development, to trainee, to researcher on different University projects. Today he is a researcher at the Porto Interactive Center, a research group dedicated to innovation in computer graphics and human-computer interaction and is completing his PhD dissertation in the same area.

Matt Pettineo
mpettineo@gmail.com

Matt first began studying graphics programming during college while developing an interactive 3D simulation program for an autonomous vehicle. Today he works as a full-time graphics programmer in the games industry, and regularly contributes graphical samples and research to his blog, "The Danger Zone." His interests include image processing, physically based lighting and material models, and GPU optimizations. Matt is currently a graphics/engine programmer for Ready At Dawn Studios, and has been a DirectX/XNA MVP since 2009.

Daniel Rákos
daniel.rakos@rastergrid.com

Daniel is a Hungarian software designer and developer, computer graphics enthusiast, and has been hobbyist OpenGL developer for ten years. His primary field of research is GPU-based scene management, batching, and culling algorithms. He's currently working for AMD as an OpenGL driver developer. In his spare time he writes articles about OpenGL, computer graphics, and other programming-related topics at the RasterGrid Blogosphere (http://www.rastergrid.com/blog/).

António Ramires Fernandes
arf@di.uminho.pt

António is an assistant professor at the University of Minho, where for the past 15 years, he has been teaching and researching computer graphics, focusing on real-time graphics. He is also the maintainer of www.lighthouse3d.com, a site devoted to teaching OpenGL and 3D graphics.

Christophe Riccio
christophe.riccio@g-truc.net

Christophe is a graphics programmer with a background in digital content creation tools, game programming, and GPU design research. He is also a keen supporter of real-time rendering as a new media for art. An enthusiast since high school, he has an MSc degree in computer game programming from the University of Teesside. He joined e-on software to study terrain editing and to design a multi-threaded graphics renderer. He worked for Imagination Technologies on the PowerVR series 6 architecture. He is currently working for AMD doing some OpenGL gardening. For the past ten years, Christophe has been an active OpenGL community contributor, including contributions to the OpenGL specifications. Through G-Truc Creation, he writes articles to promote modern OpenGL programming. He develops tools, GLM and the OpenGL Samples Pack, which are part of the official OpenGL SDK.

Philip Rideout

Philip works on shading tools at an animation studio. In his previous lives he worked on surgery simulators, GPU developer tools, and GLSL compilers. Philip has written a book on 3D programming for iOS devices and he has a blog at http://prideout. net. In his spare time, he can be found walking his dog at the Berkeley Marina.

Omar A. Rodriguez

omar.a.rodriguez@intel.com

Omar is a software engineer with Intel's Software and Service Group. He focuses on real-time 3D graphics and game development. Omar holds a BS in computer science from Arizona State University. Omar is not the lead guitarist for The Mars Volta.

Jochem van der Spek

j@jvanderspek.com

Jochem (1973) studied Media Design at the High School of the Arts in Utrecht, The Netherlands. Following a short career as CGI artist and operator of motion capture systems, he created the indy-game "Loefje," which is about artificial biological evolution and various artwork that focuses on the origin of "alive" motion versus "mechanical" motion. This work was exhibited in numerous shows and acquired by several museums worldwide. Recently, he has created the game "StyleClash: The Painting Machine Construction Kit" and is currently working on a version of Loefje for the iPad.

Dirk Van Gelder

Dirk has worked on tools for rigging, animating, and simulating characters in the feature film industry since 1997. Most recently, this includes leveraging the GPU for visual detail in animator interaction.

Shalini Venkataraman
shaliniv@nvidia.com

Shalini is a senior applied engineer at NVIDIA where she works on using GPUs to solve imaging and visualization problems in medical, oil and gas, and scientific computing domains. Prior to that she was a research staff at various high-performance computing centers in the US and Singapore. Her interests are in parallel and large-data visualization. She earned her MS from the University of Illinois at Chicago and BS from the National University of Singapore.

Fabio Zambetta
fabio.zambetta@rmit.edu.au

Fabio Zambetta received his MS and PhD in computer science from the University of Bari (Italy) investigating the use of 3D personas as adaptive intelligent interfaces. He is now a senior lecturer with the School of Computer Science and IT, RMIT University (Australia). His current research focus is on procedural generation of game play, player modeling, and GPU computing for video games.

Index